Street by Street

CARDIFF
NEWPORT

BARRY, CAERPHILLY, CHEPSTOW, CWMBRAN, PONTYPOOL, PONTYPRIDD

Abersychan, Caerleon, Caldicot, Church Village, Cowbridge, Crosskeys, Llantrisant, Llantwit Major, Magor, Penarth, Radyr, Risca, Rogerstone

GAZETTEER SYMBOL KEY

☎ - telephone number

🕿 - telephone booking service

@ - email address

🖰 - web address

🗎 - fax number

✆ - map page number & grid reference

1st edition published May 2009
© Automobile Association Developments Limited 2009

  This product includes map data licensed from Ordnance Survey® with the permission of the Controller of Her Majesty's Stationery Office.
© Crown copyright 2009.
All rights reserved. Licence number 100021153.

Published by AA Publishing (a trading name of AA Media Limited, whose registered office is Fanum House, Basing View, Basingstoke, Hampshire RG21 4EA. Registered number 06112600).

Cartography produced by the Mapping Services Department of The Automobile Association. (A03843)

A CIP Catalogue record for this book is available from the British Library.

Design and management for listings section by ey communications Ltd. (www.eysite.com). Editorial services by Pam Stagg

Listings data provided by Global DataPoint Limited, London

Printed by Oriental Press in Dubai

The Automobile Association would like to thank the following photographers, companies and picture libraries for their assistance in the preparation of this book.

Abbreviations for the pictures credits are as follows – (t) top; (b) bottom; (c) centre; (l) left; (r) right; (AA) AA World Travel Library.
Cover AA/N Jenkins
3t AA/N Jenkins; 3cr(l) Colin Palmer Photography/Alamy; 3cr (II) AA/N Jenkins; 3bl AA/I Burgum; 4 AA; 5 AA/I Burgum; 6 AA/H Williams; 8 AA/I Burgum; 9 AA/N Jenkins; 12 James Hughes/Alamy; 16 AA/N Jenkins.

Ref: ML064x

Opposite page
Top: Mermaid Quay, Cardiff Bay
Centre top: Wales Millennium Centre, Cardiff Bay
Centre bottom: Pierhead Building, Cardiff Bay
Bottom: Castell Coch

Cardiff

Cardiff is in every sense the capital of Wales. It has a rich industrial, commercial and cultural heritage, but has evolved into a modern, vibrant and cosmopolitan city. The city's revamped Cardiff Bay waterfront area offers plenty of shops, bars, restaurants and visitor attractions including the Wales Millennium Centre, a showpiece for Welsh culture, hosting opera, ballet and musicals. Major festivals and events in Cardiff include the International Festival of Musical Theatre, the Harbour and Bay Festival and the Cardiff Screen Festival.

The city centre buildings are a mix of modern, Victorian and Edwardian with shopping arcades criss-crossing the main streets, while the open spaces of Bute Park behind Cardiff Castle take you to the banks of the River Taff. Here you can catch a waterbus past Cardiff Arms Park and the much larger Millennium Stadium (a state-of-the-art sports stadium hosting major sports and music events), to thriving Cardiff Bay.

To help you make the most of your leisure time in and around Cardiff we have provided a useful gazetteer covering a range of attractions from outstanding art galleries and museums to cinemas and grand theatres featuring everything from opera and ballet to musicals. Lively St Mary Street, busy with bars and clubs at weekends, is situated near the bus and train stations. Mill Lane and the Brewery

Quarter, other popular areas in the city centre, both have lively bars, cafés and restaurants, while Greyfriars Road is home to smart cocktail and wine bars. Student-friendly pubs, bars and clubs are mostly situated in the Cathays area of the city.

Entries are listed alphabetically (ignoring The) under each category heading. The map reference denotes the map page number in the

mapping section and the grid square(s) in which the street/road is to be found, not the individual establishments. We have given the street name and post code, telephone and fax numbers and, where possible, email and website details.

Please note: the entries in the this listings section were provided by a third party and are not in any way recommended or endorsed by the AA.

TOURIST ATTRACTIONS

Barry Island Pleasure Park

Friars Road, Barry Island,
Vale of Glamorgan CF62 5TR
☎ 01446 732844,
01446 732332
@ info@barryisland.com
🖰 www.pleasureparkonline.co.uk
🖷 01446 721888
✆ page 3-F7

Caerleon Roman Baths

Caerleon was an important Roman military base, with accommodation for thousands of men. The foundations of barrack lines and parts of the ramparts can be seen, with remains of the cookhouse, latrines and baths. The amphitheatre nearby is one of the best examples in Britain.

Caerleon NP6 1AE
☎ 01663 422518
🖰 www.cadw.wales.gov.uk
✆ page 42-B4

Caerphilly Castle

The concentrically planned castle was begun in 1268 by Gilbert de Clare and completed in 1326. It is the largest in Wales, and has extensive land and water defences. A unique feature is the ruined tower – the victim of subsidence – which manages to out-lean even Pisa! The south dam platform, once a tournament-field, now displays replica medieval siege engines.

Caerphilly Castle, Caerphilly CF83 1JD
☎ 029 2088 3143
🖰 www.caerphilly.gov.uk
✆ page 69-E1

Caldicot Castle & Country Park

Caldicot Castle's well-preserved fortifications were founded by the Normans and fully developed by the late 14th century. Restored as a family home by a wealthy Victorian, the castle offers the chance to explore medieval walls and towers in a setting of tranquil gardens and wooded country parkland. Visitors also have the opportunity to play giant chess or draughts.

Church Road, Caldicot, Monmouthshire NP26 4HU
☎ 01291 420241
@ caldicotcastle@monmouthshire.gov.uk
🖰 www.caldicotcastle.co.uk
🖷 01291 435094
✆ page 63-F2

Cardiff Bay Ice Rink

Empire Way, Grangetown, Cardiff Bay, Cardiff CF11 0SP
☎ 029 2038 2001
🖰 www.planet-ice.co.uk/
✆ page 128-C4

Cardiff Castle

Cardiff Castle is situated in the heart of the city. Contained within its mighty walls is a history spanning nearly 2,000 years, dating from the coming of the Romans to the Norman Conquest and beyond. Discover spectacular interiors on your guided tour, and enjoy magnificent views of the city from the top of the 12th-century Norman keep. Regular events throughout the year include a teddy bears' picnic, open-air theatre and medieval and Roman re-enactments.

Castle Street, Cardiff CF10 3RB
☎ 029 2087 8100
@ cardiffcastle@cardiff.gov.uk
🖰 www.cardiffcastle.com
🖷 029 2023 1417
✆ page 4-C4

Cardiff Bay Visitor Centre

Harbour Drive, Britannia Quay, Cardiff Bay, Cardiff CF10 4PA
☎ 029 2046 3833
🖰 www.visitcardiff.com
✆ page 7-H6

Detail of the gilded ceiling in Cardiff Castle's Arab Room

The squat towers of 13th-century Caerphilly Castle

Cardiff Visitor Centre

The Old Library, The Hayes,
Cardiff CF10 1AH
☎ 0870 1211 258
🖰 www.visitcardiff.com
🖉 page 4-D6

Castell Coch

Castell Coch is Welsh for red
castle, an appropriate name
for this fairy-tale building with
its red sandstone walls and
conical towers. The castle
was originally built in the 13th
century but fell into ruins, and
the present castle is a late
19th-century creation. Inside,
the castle is decorated in
fantasy style.

Tongwynlais, Cardiff CF15 7JS
☎ 029 2081 0101
🖰 www.cadw.wales.gov.uk
🖉 page 83-H5

Cefn Mably Farm Park

The Cefn Mably Farm Park
offers picnic areas, pony rides
and a network of paths to
explore.

Began Road, Cefn Mably,
Cardiff CF3 6XL
☎ 01633 680312,
   07970 593666
@ mail@cefnmablyfarmpark.
   com
🖰 www.cefnmablyfarmpark.
   com
🖉 page 88-D2

Chepstow Castle

Built by William FitzOsbern,
Chepstow is the first recorded
Norman stone castle. It
stands in a strategic spot
above the Wye. The castle
was strengthened in the
following centuries, but was
not besieged (as far as is
known) until the Civil War,
when it was twice lost to the
Parliamentarians. The remains
of the domestic rooms and the
massive gatehouse with its
portcullis grooves and ancient
gates are still impressive, as
are the walls and towers.

Chepstow NP6 5EZ
☎ 01291 624065
🖰 www.cadw.wales.gov.uk
🖉 page 28-C3

Cosmeston Lakes Country Park & Medieval Village

Deserted during the plagues
and famines of the 14th
century, the original village
was rediscovered through
archaeological excavations.
The buildings have been
faithfully reconstructed on the
excavated remains, creating
a living museum of medieval
village life. Special events
throughout the year include
re-enactments, archery, crafts
and festivals.

Lavernock Road, Penarth, Vale
of Glamorgan CF64 5UY
☎ 029 2070 1678
@ cosmestonlakes@
   valeofglamorgan.gov.uk
🖰 www.valeofglamorgan.
   gov.uk
🖺 029 2070 8686
🖉 page 142-B2

Cowbridge Physic Garden

Old Hall, Cowbridge, Vale
of Glamorgan CF71 7AD
☎ 029 2059 6742,
   01446 774534
🖰 www.cowbridgephysic
   garden.org.uk
🖉 page 122-D3

Chepstow's splendid Norman castle occupies a commanding position above the River Wye

Dyffryn Gardens

Set in the heart of the Vale of Glamorgan, this exceptional example of Edwardian garden design is the result of a unique collaboration between landscape architect Thomas Mawson and plant collector Reginald Cory. The 55 acres of gardens boast splendid lawns, an arboretum of rare and unusual trees, and a beautiful selection of intimate garden 'rooms'.

St Nicholas, Cardiff CF5 6SU
☎ 029 2059 3328
@ dyffryn@valeofglamorgan.
   gov.uk
🖰 www.dyffryngardens.org.uk

🖹 029 2059 1966
⦿ page 130-B1

Flat Holm Island

Flat Holm Island, a haven for wildlife, is home to shelducks, slow worms and wild tortoises. It has been a retreat for monks and also acted as sanctuary for Vikings, Anglo-Saxons, silver miners, smugglers and cholera victims. A short day visit, by boat, gives visitors 3 hours on the island, see website for details.

Flat Holm Booking Office, c/o Channel View Lesiure Centre, Jim Driscol Way, Grangetown, Cardiff CF11 7HB

☎ 029 2035 3917
🖹 029 2038 7107
@ flatholmproject@cardiff.
   gov.uk
🖰 www.flatholmisland.com
⦿ page C-C6

Greenmeadow Community Farm

The farm is home to cattle, sheep, goats, lambs, calves and tortoises.

Greenforge Way, Cwmbran
NP44 5AJ
☎ 01633 647662
@ greenmeadowcommunity
   farm@torfaen.gov.uk
🖰 www.greenmeadow
   communityfarm.org.uk

🖹 01633 647671
⦿ page 19-F5

Howard Gardens Gallery

Cardiff School of Art and Design, Howard Gardens, Cardiff
CF24 0SP
☎ 029 2041 6608,
   029 2041 6678
🖰 www.uwic.ac.uk
⦿ page 5-G4

Llandaff Cathedral

A medieval cathedral begun in the 12th century on the site of an early Christian place of worship. The cathedral was severely damaged during the bombing raids on Cardiff

during World War II. The interior is dominated by a modernistic post-war Christ in Majesty sculpture by Epstein. Visit the website for details of events running throughout the year.

Cathedral Close, Llandaff CF5 2LA
☎ 029 2056 4554
@ office@llandaffcathedral. org.uk
🖥 www.llandaffcathedral. org.uk
🔗 page 111-F4

Newport Leisure Centre
The Newport Leisure Centre has a leisure pool with flume and wave machine. The multipurpose sports hall has facilities for badminton, netball, tennis, basketball, volleyball and squash.

1 Kingsway, Newport NP20 1UH
☎ 01633 656757
@ newportcentre.enquiries@ newport.gov.uk
🖥 www.newport.gov.uk
🔗 page 9-F4

Newport Wetlands
This wildlife reserve, situated on part of the tranquil Gwent Levels, at the edge of the city of Newport, was created as mitigation for the loss of mudflats of Cardiff Bay. Covering over 1,100 acres from Uskmouth to Goldcliff, the reedbeds, saline lagoons, wet grassland and scrub, have attracted a wealth of wetland birds. The reserve is also an excellent place to see other wildlife, such as orchids, butterflies, dragonflies and otters. Many footpaths criss-cross the reverse and there is a cycle track from Uskmouth.

West Nash Road, Nash Village, Newport NP18 2BZ
☎ 0845 130 6229
🖥 www.rspb.org.uk/ reserves/
🔗 page 93-G3

Porthkerry Country Park
Porthkerry Country Park is situated a mile west of the town of Barry on the Bristol Channel coast. The park has extensive woodlands, access to the beach, open spaces, a varied wildlife and a rich history.

Park Road, Barry, Vale of Glamorgan CF62 3BY
☎ 01446 733589
🖥 www.valeofglamorgan. gov.uk/
🔗 page 138-B5

Red Dragon Centre
This lively leisure and entertainment complex is in the heart of Cardiff Bay.

Cardiff Bay, Cardiff CF10 4DJ
☎ 029 2025 6261
🖥 www.thereddragoncentre. co.uk
🔗 page 7-G4

Taff Valley Quad Bike and Activity Centre
Multi-activity centre near Cardiff offering quad-biking treks through the countryside, archery, clay shooting and gorge walking in the Brecon Beacons National Park. Other activities which can be arranged include paintball, horse-riding, speedboats, climbing and golf.

Cwrt-y-Celyn Farm, Upperboat, Pontypridd CF37 5BJ
☎ 029 2083 1658
@ hopkinsmith@btconnect. com
🖥 www.adventurewales. co.uk/
🔗 page 46-C4

Techniquest
Located in the heart of the Cardiff Bay, there's always something new to explore at this exciting science discovery centre. Journey into space in the planetarium, enjoy an interactive Science Theatre Show or experience one of the 150 hands-on exhibits. Please

visit the website for details of events running throughout the year.

Stuart Street, Cardiff Bay, Cardiff CF10 5BW
☎ 029 2047 5475
@ catherine@techniquest.org
🖥 www.techniquest.org
📄 029 2048 2517
🔗 page 7-F6

Tredegar House & Park
Tredegar House is set in a 90-acre park and offers an insight into the history of the house through guided tours of the state rooms and the servants' quarters. The park also features a lake, a children's playground and a woodland trail, and also hosts family events, concerts, exhibitions, halloween and Christmas celebrations.

Tredegar House, Newport NP10 8YW
☎ 01633 815880
@ tredegar.house@newport. gov.uk
🖥 www.newport.gov.uk/
📄 01633 815895
🔗 page 75-G5

Vale of Glamorgan Railway
The Vale of Glamorgan Railway operates steam locomotives on two 2-mile branch lines from Barry Island to Hood Road or Woodham Halt stations. The railway organises a range of events including ghost trains, Santa Specials and festivals with activities for children.

Barry Island Station, Romanswell Road, Barry Island, Vale of Glamorgan CF62 5TH
☎ 01446 748816
@ valeofglamrail@hotmail. com
🖥 www.valeofglamorgan railway.co.uk
📄 01466 749018
🔗 page 3-F7

MUSEUMS

1st The Queen's Dragoon Guards Regimental Museum
The museum, located in the grounds of Cardiff Castle, is currently closed for refurbishment. It is expected to open in autumn 2009.

Cardiff Castle, Cardiff CF10 2RB
☎ 029 2078 1213
@ adminofficer@qdg.org.uk
🖥 www.qdg.org.uk
🔗 page 4-C4

Chepstow Museum
The museum's exhibits reflect the development of Chepstow. The wine trade, shipbuilding and salmon fishing are among Chepstow's many industries featured in displays with atmospheric settings. Photographs, programmes and posters recall the pastimes of local people, while 18th- and 19th-century paintings and prints illustrate the everlasting appeal of Chepstow and the Wye Valley to artists and tourists alike.

Bridge Street, Chepstow NP16 5EZ
☎ 01291 625981
@ chepstowmuseum@ monmouthshire.gov.uk
🖥 www.monmouthshire. gov.uk
📄 01291 635005
🔗 page 28-C3

Craft in the Bay
A unique Victorian dockside building houses Craft in the Bay, the home of the Makers Guild in Wales. Showcasing and selling fine contemporary craft, the Gallery, in the centre of Cardiff Bay, includes a retail area, exhibition space, workshops, café and conference room.

The Flourish, Lloyd George Avenue, Cardiff CF10 4QH
☎ 029 2048 4611
@ admin@ makersguildinwales.org.uk

⌂ www.makersguildinwales.
   org.uk
▤ 029 2049 1136
◈ page 7-G4

Nantgarw China Works Museum

Nantgarw China Works Museum displays archaeology, decorative and applied art, science and technology. Visitors can see where the world-famous porcelain was made and see a bottle kiln.

Nantgarw House, Tyla Gwyn, Nantgawr, Rhondda Cynon Taff CF15 7TB
☎ 01443 841703
@ enquiries@friendsofncwm.
   org
⌂ www.nantgarwchinaworks.
   org
◈ page 67-E5

National Museum Cardiff

This establishment, in Cathays Park, is unique among British museums and galleries in its range of art and science displays. 'The Evolution of Wales' exhibition takes visitors on a spectacular journey, tracing the world from the beginning of time and the development of Wales. There are displays of Bronze Age gold, early Christian monuments, Celtic treasures, silver coins and medals, ceramics, fossils and minerals. A significant collection of French Impressionist paintings sits alongside the work of Welsh artists, past and present, in the elegant art galleries.

Cathays Park, Cardiff CF10 3NP
☎ 029 2039 7951
@ post@nmgw.ac.uk
⌂ www.museumwales.ac.uk
▤ 029 2057 3321
◈ page 4-D2

Newport Museum & Art Gallery

Since 1888 Newport Museum and Art Gallery has been collecting and displaying

Traditional Welsh buildings have been reconstructed at the National History Museum, St Fagans

evidence of Newport's history, culture and environment.

John Frost Square, Newport NP20 1PA
☎ 01633 414701,
   01633 656656
@ museum@newport.gov.uk
⌂ www.newport.gov.uk
◈ page 8-E4

The Old Library (Cardiff Museum)

The museum is due to open in 2010 in the historic Old Library in the city centre. It will be rich in stories, objects, photographs and film telling the history of Cardiff through the eyes of those who created the city – its people. Until then various exhibitions and events will be held in the Old Library.

Trinity Street, Cardiff CF10 1BH
☎ 029 2035 3266
@ museum@cardiff.gov.uk
⌂ www.cardiffmuseum.com
◈ page 4-D5

Pontypool Museum

The museum houses a collection of local artefacts with an outstanding display of Japanware, which was made

in the town from the middle of the 18th century. Learn more about Pontypool Park and ponder on the interesting collection depicting Victorian domestic life. The refurbished and very imposing Glantorfaen Room Dining Furniture Display has audio facilities, lighting, projections and tactile imagery.

Park Buildings, Pontypool NP4 6JH
☎ 01495 752036
@ pontypoolmuseum@
   hotmail.com
⌂ www.pontypoolmuseum.
   org.uk
◈ page 14-C4

Pontypridd Museum

An old Welsh Baptist Chapel has been converted into a museum which tells the story of the town and its industrious people.

Bridge Street, Pontypridd, Rhondda Cynon Taff CF37 4PE
☎ 01443 490748
⌂ http://pontypridd-museum.
   wales.info
▤ 01443 490746
◈ page 44-D3

Roman Legionary Museum

The museum illustrates the history of Roman Caerleon and the daily life of its garrison. On display are arms, armour and equipment, with a collection of engraved gemstones, a labyrinth mosaic and finds from the legionary base at Usk. Please telephone for details of children's holiday activities.

High Street, Caerleon, Newport NP18 1AE
☎ 01633 423134
@ roman@museumwales.
   ac.uk
⌂ www.museumwales.ac.uk
◈ page 42-A5

St Fagans: National History Museum

A stroll around the indoor galleries and 100 acres of beautiful grounds will give you a fascinating insight into how people in Wales have lived, worked and spent their leisure hours since Celtic times. You can see people practising the traditional means of earning a living,

the animals they kept and, at certain times of year, the ways in which they celebrated the seasons.

St Fagans, Cardiff CF5 6XB
☎ 029 2057 3500
🖰 www.museumwales.ac.uk
✆ page 116-C1

Welsh Regiment Museum

Located in the grounds of Cardiff Castle, the museum commemorates the services of the infantry in South Wales, namely the Welch Regiment (1719–1969) and more recently the Royal Regiment of Wales.

Cardiff Castle, Cardiff CF10 3RB
☎ 029 2022 9367
@ welch@rrw.org.uk
🖰 www.rrw.org.uk
✆ page 4-C4

ART GALLERIES AND VISUAL ARTS

Albany Gallery

The Albany Gallery was established in 1965 and is recognised as one of Wales' most successful and long-established privately owned commercial art galleries. The monthly exhibition programme of leading Welsh and British artists provides a showcase for one man and mixed exhibitions in a variety of media. Exhibitors include Royal Academicians, members of the New English Art Club and The Institute of Painters.

74b Albany Road, Cardiff CF24 3RS
☎ 029 2048 7158
@ info@albanygallery.com
🖰 www.albanygallery.com
📄 029 2048 9158
✆ page 113-E5

BayArt

BayArt is a new addition to the expanding arts scene in Cardiff, the capital city of Wales. It is situated in the heart of the Bay area, an increasingly important recreational, tourist and cultural area. The gallery promotes major exhibitions by Welsh and international artists in an environment and climate that is conducive to accessibility and inclusivity. It aims to develop and promote up to six exhibitions per year with educational activities.

54B/C Bute Street, Cardiff CF10 5AF
☎ 029 2065 0016
@ bayart@tiscali.co.uk
🖰 www.bayart.org.uk
📄 029 2065 0016
✆ page 7-G4

Cardiff g39

Contemporary Temporary Artspace is an artist-run initiative providing exhibiting opportunities for unestablished artists and recent graduates. Operating from its base gallery g39, it was set up in 1998 with a cash kick-start from the Arts Council of Wales, the support of local businesses and the hard labour and determination of Cardiff-based artists. The CTA profiles the best of British contemporary visual art, with an emphasis on installation, photography, video and sculpture.

Wyndham Arcade, Mill Lane, Cardiff CF10 1FH
☎ 029 2025 5541
@ post@g39.org
🖰 www.g39.org
✆ page 4-D6

Cardiff Bay's thriving waterfront development

Castle Galleries: Cardiff Bay

Unit 21, Mermaid Quay, Cardiff
CF10 5BZ
☎ 02920 495 240
⌂ www.castlegalleries.com
⌖ page 7-G6

Chepstow Workshop Gallery

The Gallery mounts six
exhibitions each year, showing
the work of three potters,
sometimes complemented by
a fabric artist or print maker.

13, Lower Church Street,
Chepstow NP6 5HJ
☎ 01291 624836
@ nedheywood@aol.com
⌂ members.aol.com/
nedheywood/gallery.html
⌖ page 28-D3

Ffotogallery

Ffotogallery is the national
development agency for
photography in Wales
and the premier arts
organisation dedicated to the
promotion and presentation
of photographic art in the
country. The gallery looks at
photographic practice in the
broadest sense, and initiates
exhibitions which focus on
documentary as well as more
expansive uses of photography
which may involve the use of
projection, digital and other
lens-based forms.

Turner House Gallery,
Plymouth Road, Cardiff
CF64 3DM
☎ 029 2070 8870
@ turnerhouse@ffotogallery.
org
⌂ www.ffotogallery.org
⌖ page 134-D2

GPF Gallery

18 George Street, Newport
NP20 1EN
☎ 01633 264581
@ gpfgallery@hotmail.com
⌂ www.gpf.co.uk
⌖ page 9-G5

Kooywood Gallery

The gallery opened in 2004,
in the cultural centre of
Cardiff, to provide a forum for
established and new artists
to show and sell their work.
The gallery has a collection
of contemporary visual art
including painting, sculpture,
ceramics, glass, photography
as well as prints.

8 Museum Place, Cardiff
CF10 3BG
☎ 029 2023 5093
@ enquiries@
kooywoodgallery.com
⌂ www.kooywoodgallery.com
⌖ page 4-D2

La Mostra Gallery

La Mostra Gallery is Cardiff's
first commercial art gallery to
exhibit international paintings,
sculpture and objects d'art
exclusively.

Mermaid Quay, Cardiff Bay,
Cardiff CF10 5BZ
☎ 029 2049 2225
@ enquiries@
lamostragallery.com
⌂ www.lamostragallery.com
▤ 029 2049 2226
⌖ page 7-G6

The Magpie Gallery

Gallery with an eclectic mix
of contemporary, graphic and
street art with a specific focus
on illustration and graphic
design.

11a–12 Church Street, Cardiff
CF10 1BG
☎ 029 2022 8883
@ contact@wearemagpie
gallery.com
⌂ www.wearemagpiegallery.
com/
⌖ page 4-C5

Martin Tinney Gallery

The gallery was established in
1989 and specialises in past
and present Welsh and Wales-
based artists. It exhibits
work by living Welsh artists
including Harry Holland, Sally
Moore, Peter Prendergast,
Gwilym Prichard, Shani Rhys
James, Kevin Sinnott and
Sir Kyffin Williams as well
as those of the younger
generation. There are monthly
solo exhibitions in the main
gallery, while there is a
constantly changing exhibition
of paintings, prints, sculpture
and ceramics by gallery artists
on the other two gallery floors.

18 St Andrew's Crescent,
Cardiff CF10 3DD
☎ 029 2064 1411
@ mtg@artwales.com
⌂ www.artwales.com
⌖ page 4-E3

Model House Craft and Design Centre

Model House craft gallery
has gained a reputation for
providing high quality craft
work since it opened in 1989.
It quickly became established
as one of Wales' leading
centres for contemporary craft
and design. Later Model House
was selected for quality by the
Crafts Council of Britain.

Bull Ring, Llantrisant
CF72 8EB
☎ 01443 237758
@ marketing@
modelhousecraft.co.uk
⌂ www.modelhousecraft.
co.uk
▤ 01443 224718
⌖ page 95-E2

Oriel Canfas Gallery

Canfas provides a broad
and diverse platform for
contemporary visual art in
Wales. The gallery hosts
exhibitions in painting,
sculpture, photography, photo-
visual works as well as fine
art prints and more.

44a Glamorgan Street,
Canton, Cardiff CF5 1QS
☎ 029 2066 6455
@ oriel@olacanfas.co.uk
⌂ www.olacanfas.co.uk
⌖ page 118-D2

Oriel Washington Gallery

1–3 Washington Buildings,
Stanwell Road, Penarth, Vale
Of Glamorgan CF64 2AD
☎ 029 2071 2100
@ info@washingtongallery.
co.uk
⌂ www.washingtongallery.
co.uk
▤ 029 2070 8047
⌖ page 134-D2

Sculpture Studio

Sculpture Studio was created
by Cardiff-based artist Cecile
Johnson Soliz to host a
series of residencies, events,
workshops and discussion
forums that focus on the
sculptural object. Soliz has
developed a flexible working
space with custom-made
furniture plus equipment
and tools that give artist-
sculptors an open, practical
and contemplative space
in which to think about and
make sculpture. As part of
the programme she has
invited a number of artists to
undertake short residencies
and to host public seminars,
dialogue and film screenings
that all broadly focus on the
notion of the sculptural form.

Market Road, Canton, Cardiff
CF5 1QE
☎ 029 2031 1050
℡ 029 2030 4400
@ gallery@chapter.org
⌂ www.chapter.org
⌖ page 118-D2

Trace Installation Artspace

Trace exists in order to
promote time-based art
and work emerging from
performance, installation,
sonic and interactive arts.
The gallery produces regular
events and exhibitions,
inviting artists to produce
time-based work that has
an installation exhibition
component, promoting work
at a local, national and
international level, and works
with artists and arts agencies.

26 Moira Place, Cardiff
CF24 0ET
☎ 029 2040 7338
@ Tracegallery@aol.com
⌂ www.tracegallery.org
⌖ page 5-G4

ART CENTRES

Chapter Arts Centre

Chapter is one of Europe's largest and most dynamic arts centres with cinemas, theatres, exhibition spaces, studios, a café, award-winning bars, over 60 cultural workspaces and more. Chapter has an international reputation for excellence, innovation and collaboration. It offers an everchanging programme of the best performance, films and exhibitions from Wales and from around the world. Chapter is the flagship for the contemporary arts in Wales and is one of the largest complexes of its kind in Europe.

Market Road, Canton, Cardiff CF5 1QE
☏ 029 2030 4400
@ enquiry@chapter.org
🖰 www.chapter.org
🕭 page 118-D2

The Gate

The Gate, with a 350-seat performance theatre space, dance studio and art gallery, offers an enticing and intimate setting for audiences and performers alike. It holds workshops in dance, music and theatre and presents quality performances by leading artistic groups.

Keppoch Street, Roath, Cardiff CF24 3JW
☏ 029 2048 3344
@ boxoffice@thegate.org.uk
🖰 www.thegate.org.uk
🕭 page 113-E5

Llanover Hall Arts Centre

Llanover Hall Arts Centre offers an exciting specialist programme of hands-on arts activities for people of all ages and abilities.

Romilly Road, Llanover, Cardiff CF5 1FH
☏ 029 2063 1144
@ SBawler@cardiff.gov.uk
🖰 www.cardiff.gov.uk
🕭 page 118-D2

Llantarnam Grange Arts Centre

St David's Road, Cwmbran, Torfaen NP44 1PD
☏ 01633 483321
@ llantarnamgrange@bt.collect.com;
art@llantarnamgrange.fnset.co.uk
🖰 www.torfaen.gov.uk
🕭 page 20-A4

Muni Arts Centre

The Muni Arts Centre is set in a beautiful converted church, in the centre of Pontypridd. Its programme of events and arts includes band nights, music, events for children and young adults, exhibitions, dance, educational events, puppetry, mime, comedy and productions by community groups. The venue also has the Footlights Café Bar and Gallery Shop.

Gelliwastad Road, Pontypridd CF37 2DP
☏ 01443 485934
🖰 www.rct-arts.co.uk
🖺 01443 401832
🕭 page 44-D3

Norwegian Church Arts Centre

The Norwegian Church Arts Centre is a charitable organisation which provides exhibition space and a beautiful setting for concerts. It also provides lecture facilities and a special ambiance for conferences. The church itself was closed in 1974. A decade later, in 1987, it was dismantled and stored to be rebuilt at a later time in its present location. It became an Arts Centre and was not reconsecrated. However, the present day uses of the building recreate the tranquil, relaxed and welcoming chararcter of the former church.

Harbour Drive, Cardiff Bay, Cardiff CF10 4PA
☏ 029 2045 4899

@ norwegianchurch@cardiff.gov.uk
🖰 www.norwegianchurchcardiff.com
🖺 029 2049 5122
🕭 page 7-H6

The Riverfront

The Riverfront is a thriving arts centre, full of activities for participation, enjoyment and education, with a diverse range of live entertainment, workshops and free exhibitions.

Bristol Packet Wharf, Newport NP20 1HG
☏ 01633 656757
@ the.riverfront@newport.gov.uk
🖰 www.newport.gov.uk/riverfront
🕭 page 9-F3

LIVE MUSIC VENUES

10 Feet Tall

Trendy, live entertainment venue in Cardiff where the street level Deli and Café Bar serves a colourful array of dishes inspired by the varied flavours of North Africa and the Mediterranean. Local and touring bands/DJs.

11a–12 Church Street, Cardiff CF10 1BG
☏ 02920 228883
🖰 www.thisis10feettall.co.uk
🕭 page 4-C5

Barfly, Cardiff

Along with its sister venues around the country, the Cardiff Barfly provides a stage for up-and-coming indie and rock bands.

Kingsway, Cardiff CF10 3FD
☏ 029 2039 6589
@ cardiff.info@barflyclub.com
🖰 www.barflyclub.com
🕭 page 4-C4

Burleigh Academy

Burleigh Hall, Llanthewy Road, Newport NP20 4LD
☏ 01633 262002
@ info@burleighacademy.co.uk

🖰 www.burleighacademy.co.uk
🖺 01633 211817
🕭 page 8-A5

Café Bar Europa

Café Bar Europa is a licensed venue that serves light meals as well as a selection of sandwiches, snacks and beverages. They also have live acoustic music every Wednesday and Thursday.

25 Castle Street, Cardiff CF10 1BT
☏ 029 2066 7776
🕭 page 4-B5

Café Jazz

Café Jazz is a jazz, blues and food venue. As its name suggests, it is an establishment founded on a desire to host jazz sounds new and old, local and international.

21 St Mary Street, Cardiff CF10 1PL
☏ 029 2038 7026
@ mm@cafejazzcardiff.com
🖰 www.cafejazzcardiff.com
🖺 029 3038 3998
🕭 page 4-D6

Cardiff International Arena (CIA)

Cardiff's largest purpose-built exhibition facility hosts exhibitions, conferences, concerts and cultural and sporting events.

Mary Ann Street, Cardiff CF10 2EQ
☏ 029 2022 4488
🖰 www.livenation.co.uk
🕭 page 4-E6

Cardiff University Students Union

Park Place, Cardiff CF10 3QN
☏ 029 2078 1400
@ StudentsUnion@Cardiff.ac.uk
🖰 www.cardiffstudents.com
🕭 page 4-C1

Chilli's

Churchill Way, Cardiff CF10 2HD
☏ 02920 641 010
🕭 page 4-E5

Clwb Ifor Bach

This cult bilingual music venue in Cardiff, named after the 12th-century Welsh rebel Ifor Bach, hosts regular live music, as well as popular rock, indie, punk and electro club nights.

11 Womanby Street,
Cardiff CF10 1BR
☎ 029 2023 2199
@ post@clwb.net
🖰 www.clwb.net
🖺 029 2030 1113
✐ page 4-C5

The Coal Exchange

The Coal Exchange was built between 1883 and 1886 to the designs of James, Seward and Thomas. It was here that Cardiff's leading businessmen of shipping firms, coal mines and allied businesses met to fix their deals, some with far distant countries. At present it is an arts and entertainment centre playing host to live music, theatre and other events.

The Exchange Buildings, Mount Stuart Square, Cardiff Bay, Cardiff CF10 5EB
☎ 029 2049 4917
@ admin@coalexchange.co.uk
🖰 www.coalexchange.co.uk
🖺 029 2049 4927
✐ page 7-F5

Coopers Field

Castle Street, Cardiff
CF10 3RB
✐ page 4-B5

Dempsey's

Popular Irish jazz pub in Cardiff city cenre.

Castle Street, Cardiff CF10 1BS
☎ 029 2025 2024
🖰 www.myspace.com/
dempseysjazz
✐ page 4-B5

District Club

Music venue open on Friday nights, hosting both local and national bands.

Pencerrig Street, Pontypridd
CF37 2HS
☎ 01443 402550
@ mikedavies40@hotmail.com
🖰 uk.geocities.com/
districtmike
✐ page 44-C3

The Globe

With live music seven nights a week from local, national and international bands, the Globe brings you blues, jazz, rock, ska, funk, Americana, soul and much, much more in a beautifully decorated, two-tiered venue with standing and seated areas. The Globe offers the ultimate live music experience.

125 Albany Road, Roath,
Cardiff CF24 3NS
☎ 07738 983947
@ info@theglobecardiff.com
🖰 www.theglobecardiff.com
✐ page 113-E5

The Gower

Pub with live music.

Gwennyth Street, Cathays,
Cardiff CF24 4PH
☎ 029 2066 7243,
029 2019 1713
@ colin@bluesdragon.co.uk
🖰 www.bluesdragon.org.uk
✐ page 112-C4

Le Pub

Venue for up-and-coming alternative bands.

1 Caxton Place, Newport
NP20 4BN
☎ 01633 221477
🖰 www.myspace.com/le_pub
✐ page 8-D3

Llantrisant Folk Club

The Windsor Hotel, Llantrisant Road, Llantrisant, Rhondda Cynon Taff CF72 9DQ
☎ 01443 226892
@ folkclub@folkwales.org.uk
🖰 www.folkwales.org.uk
✐ page 107-F1

Meze Lounge

Live venue hosting a variety of bands.

6 Market Street, Newport
NP20 1FU
☎ 01633 211432
© 01633 213161
@ mezelounge@hotmail.com
🖰 www.myspace.com/
mezenewport
🖺 01633 213161
✐ page 8-E2

Millennium Stadium

This massive stadium hosts major music events, exhibitions, international rugby and soccer matches and other major sporting events. Its capacity of around 75,000 and its retractable roof make it unique in Europe. It is the home of Welsh Rugby and Welsh Football.

Golate House, St Mary Street,
Cardiff CF10 1GE
☎ 0870 013 8600
@ info@cardiff-stadium.co.uk
🖰 www.millenniumstadium.com
🖺 029 2023 2678
✐ page 4-B6

Wales Millennium Centre presents the performing arts

O'Neill's

85–87, St Mary Street,
Cardiff CF10 1FA
℡ 029 2066 4103
www.oneills.co.uk
page 4-D6

Oz Bar

Venue hosting regular rock,
stoner and punk gigs in the
basement with occasional and
indie and rock gigs on the
upper floor.

112 Mary Street, Cardiff
CF10 1DX
☎ 029 2066 8008
page 4-C6

The Point

The Point, formerly the
Church of St Stephen in the
Cardiff Bay area, is a popular
live music venue with rare
stained-glass windows, a fully
operational permanent stage,
lighting fixtures, in-house
PA and projection systems.
The Point has played host
to some of the UK's best
local and international bands
including The Stereophonics,
Manic Street Preachers,
Steve Winwood and Cerys
Matthews.

Mount Stuart Square, Cardiff
Bay, Cardiff CF10 6EB
☎ 029 2046 0873
@ info@thepointcardiffbay.
com
www.thepointcardiffbay.com
029 2048 8538
page 7-F5

Tommy's Bar

Live music venue playing up-
and-coming bands from inside
and outside Wales.

UWIC Howard Gardens
(off Newport Road), Cardiff
CF24 0SP
☎ 029 2041 6192
www.myspace.com/
thefamily_hg
page 5-F3

Tom's Rock Bar

Live music venue.

71 Wood Road, Treforest,
Pontypridd CF37 1RJ

℡ 01443 406666
www.tomspub.co.uk
page 45-E5

COMEDY CLUBS AND VENUES

Jongleurs Cardiff

Opened in November 2001,
next to the Millennium
Stadium, the Jongleurs Cardiff
has three floors featuring
relaxing, uncluttered modern
interiors and state-of-the-art
audio-visual equipment with
Bar Risa on the ground floor
and Club Risa underneath
Bar Risa.

Millennium Plaza, Wood
Street, Cardiff CF10 1LA
☎ 084 4499 4065
@ enquiries@jongleurs.com
www.jongleurs.com
page 4-C7

The Glee Club Cardiff

Mermaid Quay, Cardiff Bay,
Cardiff CF10 5BZ
☎ 0870 241 5093
℡ 0871 472 0400
@ duncan@glee.co.uk
www.glee.co.uk
page 7-G6

CLASSICAL MUSIC VENUES

Cardiff University Concert Hall

Cardiff University, 31 Corbett
Road, Cardiff CF10 3EB
☎ 029 2087 4816
℡ 0870 013 1812
@ music-enq@cardiff.ac.uk
www.cardiff.ac.uk/music
029 2087 4379
page 4-B1

Royal Welsh College of Music and Drama

Castle Grounds, Cathays Park,
Cardiff CF10 3ER
☎ 029 2034 2854
www.rwcmd.ac.uk
page 4-C2

St David's Hall

Situated in the heart of Cardiff,
St David's Hall is the National
Concert Hall and Conference
Centre of Wales, providing
entertainment events,
exhibitions, conferences,
workshops and bars.

The Hayes, Cardiff CF10 1SH
☎ 029 2087 8500
℡ 029 2087 8444
@ st.davidshallreception@
cardiff.gov.uk
www.stdavidshallcardiff.
co.uk
029 2087 8599
page 4-D5

CINEMA

Cineworld Cardiff

Mary Ann Street,
Cardiff CF10 2EN
☎ 0870 777 2775
℡ 08712 002000
@ customer.services@
cineworld.co.uk
www.cineworld.co.uk
page 4-E6

Cineworld Newport

Newport Retail Park, Spytty
Road, Newport NP19 4QQ
☎ 0870 777 2775
℡ 08712 002000
www.cineworld.co.uk
page 78-C2

Odeon Cardiff

Multiscreen cinema situated
in the Red Dragon Centre near
the city centre.

Red Dragon Centre,
Hemingway Road, Cardiff
CF10 4JY
☎ 0870 010 2030
℡ 08712 244007
www.odeon.co.uk
page 7-H4

Scene

Scene Cinemas is situated in
the Cwmbran shopping centre.
There are 3 screens within
the cinema: Screen 1 has 100
seats, Screen 2 has 80 seats
and Screen 3 has 130 seats.

1–3 The Mall, Cwmbran
NP44 1PX
☎ 016 3386 6621
www.southwalescinemas.
co.uk
page 19-H5

Showcase Cinemas Nantgarw

Heol-yr-Odyn, Parc Nantgarw,
Pontypridd CF15 7QX
☎ 08712 201000
www.showcasecinemas.
co.uk
page 67-E4

Vue Cardiff

Millennium Plaza, Wood
Street, Cardiff CF10 1LA
☎ 08712 240240
@ customerservices@
vuemail.com
www.myvue.com
page 4-B7

Vue Cwmbran

Cwmbran Leisure Park,
Glyndwr Road, Cwmbran
NP44 1QS
☎ 08712 240240
www.myvue.com
page 20-A4

THEATRES

Bute Theatre

Castle Grounds, Cathays Park,
Cardiff CF10 3ER
☎ 029 2039 1391,
029 2034 2854
@ boxoffice@rwcmd.ac.uk
www.rwcmd.ac.uk
029 2039 1301
page 4-C2

Congress Theatre

50 Gwent Square, Cwmbran
NP44 1PL
☎ 01633 868239
@ info@congresstheatre.net
www.congresstheatre
cwmbran.co.uk
01633 867809
page 19-H4

Dolman Theatre

The theatre was purpose
built for Newport Playgoers
Society in 1967, following a
redevelopment of Newport
town centre. With a 400-seat
auditorium, 38-ft (11.5m)
proscenium arch stage,
three large rehearsal rooms,
orchestra pit, bar, box office,
cafeteria, council room,

extensive dressing rooms, and a 60-seat studio, the Dolman Theatre offers facilities for all theatrical styles, and is a hub of amateur theatre and performing arts in south Wales.

Kingsway Centre, Newport NP20 1HY
☎ 01633 263670
✆ 01633 251358
@ dolmantheatre@tiscali.co.uk
⌂ www.dolmantheatre.co.uk
✆ page 9-F5

Memorial Hall Theatre

Gladstone Road, Barry, Vale of Glamorgan CF62 8NA
☎ 01446 400111
✆ 01446 738622
@ enquiries@barrymemo.co.uk
⌂ www.memorialhalltheatre.co.uk
✆ page 3-F2

New Theatre

Park Place, Cardiff CF10 3LN
☎ 029 2087 8787,
029 2087 8900
✆ 029 2087 8889
⌂ www.newtheatrecardiff.co.uk
✆ page 4-D4

The Paget Rooms

Victoria Park, Penarth, Vale of Glamorgan CF64 3EG
☎ 02920 713546
⌂ www.pagetrooms.com/
✆ page 134-C3

Sherman Theatre

The Sherman Theatre is many things to many people – a producing theatre, a touring company, a youth theatre and a receiving venue. There is a restaurant and bar, a costume-hire facility, conference facilities, rehearsal spaces and much more.

Senghennydd Road, Cardiff CF24 4YE
☎ 029 2064 6900
@ boxoffice@shermantheatre.demon.co.uk
⌂ www.shermantheatre.co.uk

☎ 029 2064 6901
✆ page 4-D2

Wales Millennium Centre

Wales Millennium Centre is a leading arts venue. With two theatres, five function rooms, galleries, shops, restaurants and foyer spaces, Wales Millennium Centre offers entertainment from big-name West End shows in the 1,900-seat Donald Gordon Theatre, to more intimate shows in the 250-seat Weston Studio, to a free daily foyer.

Bute Place, Cardiff CF10 5AL
☎ 029 2063 6400
@ info@wmc.org.uk
⌂ www.wmc.org.uk
🖹 029 2063 6401
✆ page 7-H5

BARS AND PUBS

Amigos

11 Windsor Place, Cardiff CF10 3BY
☎ 029 2023 8228
✆ page 4-E4

Ba Orient

Sophisticated cocktail bar in the heart of the Cardiff Bay entertainment area.

Unit 27, Mermaid Quay, Cardiff Bay, Cardiff CF10 5BZ
☎ 029 2046 3939
@ info@baorient.com
⌂ www.baorient.com
🖹 029 2046 3339
✆ page 7-G6

Bar Cwtch

Bute Crescent, Cardiff CF10 5AN
☎ 029 2048 8775
@ info@jolyons.co.uk
⌂ www.jolyons.co.uk
✆ page 7-G5

Cafe Floyd

An intimate, chilled-out bar hidden away from the chaos of the city centre.

23, High Street, Cardiff CF10 1PT
☎ 029 2039 8757
⌂ www.cafefloyd.co.uk
✆ page 4-C5

Fat Cat Café Bar

A stylish bar on the Greyfriars strip.

Grosvenor House, Greyfriars, Cardiff CF10 3AD
☎ 029 2022 8378
@ cardiff@fatcatcafebars.co.uk
⌂ www.fatcatcafebars.co.uk/cardiff
✆ page 4-D4

Hard Rock Cafe, Cardiff

The Old Brewery Quarter, 49 St Mary Street, Cardiff CF10 1AD
☎ 029 2037 3403
@ Cardiff_Sales@hardrock.com
⌂ www.hardrock.com
🖹 029 2037 5680
✆ page 4-D6

Inncognito

An up-market bar situated opposite the National Museum.

Park Place, Cardiff CF10 3BA
☎ 029 2041 2190
✆ page 4-D2

Iota

7 Mill Lane, Cardiff CF10 1FL
☎ 029 2022 5592
✆ page 4-D7

Koko Gorillaz

7–9 Miskin Street, Salisbury Square, Cathays, Cardiff CF24 4AP
☎ 029 2034 1767
⌂ www.kokogorillaz.com
✆ page 4-D1

O'Neill's

20–21 Trinity Street, Cardiff CF10 1BH
☎ 029 2023 6981
⌂ www.oneills.co.uk
✆ page 4-D5

Owain Glyndwr

Pub hosting live DJs.

St John Street, St John Square, Cardiff CF10 2DL
☎ 029 2022 1980
⌂ www.laurelpubco.com
✆ page 4-C5

Q Bar

Pool bar by day and nightclub by night, Q Bar boasts 30 pool tables and regular DJ nights.

2 Greyfriars Road, Cardiff CF10 3AD
☎ 029 2022 9311
⌂ www.myspace.com/qbarcardiff
✆ page 4-D4

Reflex, Cardiff

89 St Mary Street, Cardiff CF10 1DW
☎ 029 2064 9831
⌂ www.reflex-bars.co.uk
✆ page 4-D6

Reflex, Newport

42 High Street, Newport NP20 1GF
☎ 01633 254273
⌂ www.reflex-bars.co.uk
✆ page 8-E2

Revolution Bar, Cardiff

Offering premium drinks, fresh food, hand-picked music, tailor-made parties and of course, lashings of premium world and home-made vodka.

9–11 Castle Street, Cardiff CF10 1BS
☎ 029 2023 6689
⌂ www.revolution-bars.co.uk/bars/
✆ page 4-B5

Revolution Bar, Newport

Revolution Bar is a short walk from the main High Street shops, opposite the indoor market on Griffin Street.

8–11 Griffin Street, Newport NP20 1GL
☎ 016 3321 4071
⌂ www.revolution-bars.co.uk
🖹 01633 214 065
✆ page 8-E3

Riverside Tavern

63 Clarence Place, Newport NP19 7AB
☎ 01633 666699
⌂ www.myspace.com/riversidetavern
✆ page 9-F2

Sodabar

7–10 Mill Lane, Cardiff
CF10 1AD
🖰 www.thesodabar.com
📍 page 4-D7

Varsity, Cardiff

Popular bar with regular quiz
nights and competitions.

Greyfriars Road, Cardiff
CF10 3AD
☎ 029 2023 2562
@ cardiff@varsitybars.com
🖰 www.varsitybars.com
📍 page 4-D4

Walkabout Cardiff

65–74 St Marys Street,
Cardiff CF10 1FA
☎ 02920 727 930
@ wbi.cardiff@walkabout.
    eu.com
🖰 www.walkabout.eu.com
🖷 02920 727 931
📍 page 4-D6

The Wharf

121 Schooner Way, Atlantic
Wharf, Cardiff CF10 4ET
📞 029 2040 5092
📍 page 7-G1

Zync Bar

63 St Mary Street, Cardiff
CF10 1FE
☎ 029 2034 5189
🖰 www.myspace/zyncbar.com
📍 page 4-D6

NIGHTCLUBS

Aqua

3–6 St Mary Street, Cardiff
CF10 1AD
☎ 0870 350 1099
📍 page 4-D6

Berlins

5–9 Church Street, Cardiff
CF10 2BG
☎ 029 2034 4468
🖷 029 2034 4468
📍 page 4-C5

Buffalo

Bar and music venue in
a converted townhouse,
with two floors, two sound
systems, a beer garden,
barbecue, big screen
projectors, retro computer
gaming, full menu and free
Wi-Fi.

11 Windsor Place, Cardiff
CF10 3BY
☎ 029 2031 0312
🖰 www.myspace.com/
    wearebuffalobar
🖷 029 2031 0313
📍 page 4-E4

Callaghan's

Castle Street, Cardiff
CF10 1XD
☎ 029 2034 7247
🖰 www.myspace.com/
    callaghansbar
📍 page 4-B5

Club Seven

Unit 5, Millenium Plaza,
Cardiff CF10 1LA
@ cardiff@seven-bars.co.uk
🖰 www.myspace.com/
    clubsevencardiff
📍 page 7-F3

Club X

Popular Cardiff gay venue.

35–39 Charles Street, Cardiff
CF10 2GB
☎ 029 2040 0876
@ info@club-x-cardiff.co.uk
🖰 www.club-x-cardiff.co.uk
📍 page 4-E5

Conti's Lounge Bar & Night Club

Stylish café, bar and nightclub
in Cardiff city centre.

11 Mill Lane, Cardiff CF10 1FL
☎ 029 2066 5500
🖰 www.gios.co.uk
📍 page 4-D7

The Cotton Club

This nightclub, on three floors,
hosts regular events during
the day as well as frequent
club nights.

54 Cambrian Road, Newport
NP20 4AB
☎ 01633 843344,
    07970 141898
🖰 www.cottonclubnewport.
    co.uk
📍 page 8-D2

Elements

3 Churchill Way, Cardiff
CF10 2HD
☎ 029 2064 1010
@ info@pulsecardiff.com
🖰 www.pulsecardiff.com
📍 page 4-E5

Emporium Night Club

8–10 High Street, Cardiff
CF10 1AW
☎ 029 2066 4577
📍 page 4-C5

Escapade, Newport

Nightclub with two floors
consisting of a number of
themed rooms and bars.

40 Stow Hill, Newport
NP20 1JG
☎ 01633 250978
@ newport@zanzibar.co.uk
🖰 newport.clubescapade.
    co.uk/
🖷 01633 259510
📍 page 8-E3

Exit

48 Charles Street, Cardiff
CF10 2GF
☎ 029 2064 0102
@ info@exitclubcardiff.co.uk
🖰 www.exitclubcardiff.com
📍 page 4-E5

Flares, Cardiff

96–97 St Mary's Street,
Cardiff CF10 1DX
☎ 029 2023 5825
📍 page 4-D6

Glo Bar

A very exclusive venue,
formerly known as Bar Ice.

4 Churchill Way, Cardiff
CF10 2DW
📞 029 2023 7177
🖰 www.myspace.com/
    globarcardiff
📍 page 4-E5

Jumpin Jaks Cardiff

1st Floor Millennium Plaza,
Wood Street, Cardiff CF10 1GE
☎ 029 2034 0737
@ cardiff@jumpinjaks.com
🖰 www.jumpinjaks.co.uk
🖷 029 2034 0886
📍 page 4-C7

Lava Lounge

A popular nightclub situated in
Cardiff's Old Brewery Quarter.

Unit 15 The Old Brewery
Quarter, Cardiff CF10 1FG
☎ 029 2038 2313
🖰 www.lavalounge.co.uk/
    cardiff
📍 page 4-D6

Liquid-Life

Consisting of nightclub Liquid
and bar Life, Liquid-Life holds
various funky house, electro
and R'n'B club nights.

Imperial Gate, St Mary's
Street, Cardiff CF10 1FA
☎ 029 2064 5464
🖰 www.liquidclubs.com/cardiff
📍 page 4-D6

Mbargo

A trendy club amid the busy
chain bars of St Mary Street.
Plays the best in all genres
of music.

60–62 St Mary Street, Cardiff
CF10 1FE
☎ 029 2039 8036
@ cardiff@mbargo.net
📍 page 4-D6

Metros

Metros is a stronghold of
the alternative scene in
Cardiff, growing up with the
progression of alternative
music trends from the early
'90s indie, grunge and
industrial scenes, to the nu-
metal, punk and emo offerings
of today.

10 Bakers Row, Cardiff
CF10 1AL
☎ 029 2037 1549,
    029 2039 9939
🖰 www.myspace.com/
    metroscardiff
📍 page 4-D5

OTT Nightclub

OTT is the place to be for
groove-based tunes with
melody. This independent
nightclub plays funk, disco,
R'n'B, drum and bass, hip-hop,
reggae, soul and afrobeat.

7 Market Street, Newport
NP20 1FU

☎ 01633 215000, 01633 258884
@ info@ottnightclub.com
⌐ www.ottnightclub.com
✆ page 8-E2

Pulse
3 Churchill Way, Cardiff CF10 2HD
☎ 029 20 641010
⌐ www.pulsecardiff.com
✆ page 4-E5

Strads
7–8 Market Street, Pontypridd CF37 2ST
☎ 01443 485331
@ bookings@markettavern hotel.ssbusiness.co.uk
✆ page 44-D3

TJ's Rock Club and Disco
The place for live music, drink and dance.
16–18 Clarence Place, Newport NP19 0AE
☎ 01633 216608
@ gigs@tjsnewport.com
⌐ www.tjs-newport.demon. co.uk
✆ page 9-F2

Tabu
31 Westgate Street, Cardiff CF10 1EH
☎ 02920 399400
⌐ www.tabucardiff.co.uk
✆ page 4-B5

Yellow Kangaroo
Home to regular live music, karaoke, comedy nights, great beer, friendly bar staff and probably the largest beer garden in Cardiff.
1 Elm Street, Roath, Cardiff CF24 3QR
☎ 029 2045 5056, 029 2025 8127
✆ page 5-H2

SPECIAL EVENTS' VENUES

Cardiff Bay
An exciting calendar of local, national and international water and land-based events

is held in Cardiff Bay.
Cardiff Bay, Cardiff CF10 5AN
⌐ www.cardiffbay.co.uk
✆ page 7-H6

Cardiff International Arena (CIA)
Cardiff's largest purpose-built exhibition facility hosts a range of exhibitions, conferences, concerts and cultural and sporting events.
Mary Ann Street, Cardiff CF10 2EQ
☎ 029 2022 4488
⌐ www.livenation.co.uk
✆ page 4-E6

Chepstow Racecourse
Chepstow, NP16 6BE
☎ 01291 622 260
@ hannah.rickards@

chepstow-racecourse.co.uk
⌐ www.chepstow-racecourse. co.uk
📄 01291 622 260
✆ page 28-A1

Millennium Stadium
This massive stadium hosts major music events, exhibitions, international rugby and soccer matches and other major sporting events. Its capacity of around 75,000 and its retractable roof make it unique in Europe. It is the home of Welsh Rugby and Welsh Football.
Golate House, St Mary Street, Cardiff CF10 1GE
☎ 0870 013 8600
@ info@cardiff-stadium.co.uk
⌐ www.millenniumstadium. com

📄 029 2023 2678
✆ page 4-B6

Wales Millennium Centre
Wales Millennium Centre is a leading arts venue. With two theatres, five function rooms, galleries, shops, restaurants and foyer spaces, Wales Millennium Centre offers entertainment, from big-name West End shows in the 1,900-seat Donald Gordon Theatre, to more intimate shows in the 250-seat Weston Studio, to a free daily foyer.
Bute Place, Cardiff CF10 5AL
☎ 029 2063 6400
@ info@wmc.org.uk
⌐ www.wmc.org.uk
📄 029 2063 6401
✆ page 7-H5

The Millennium Stadium, Cardiff

Street by Street

CARDIFF NEWPORT

BARRY, CAERPHILLY, CHEPSTOW, CWMBRAN, PONTYPOOL, PONTYPRIDD

Abersychan, Caerleon, Caldicot, Church Village, Cowbridge, Crosskeys, Llantrisant, Llantwit Major, Magor, Penarth, Radyr, Risca, Rogerstone

Key to map pages	ii–iii
Key to map symbols	iv–1
Enlarged map pages	2–9
Main map pages	10–147
Index - towns & villages	148
Index - streets	149–167
Index - featured places	168–171
Acknowledgements	171

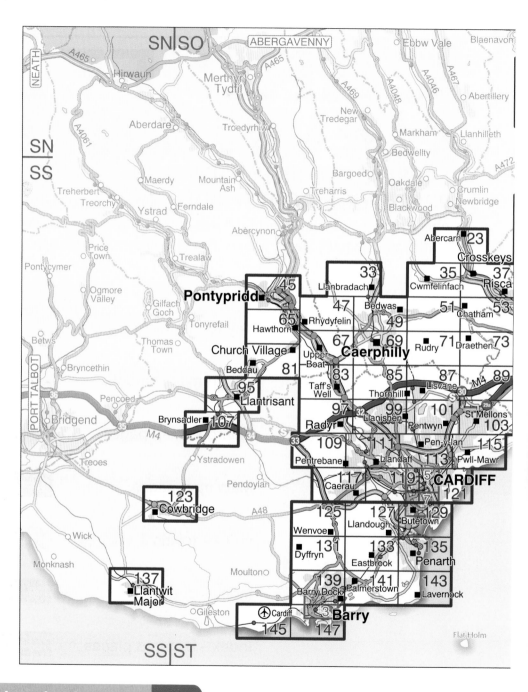

Enlarged scale pages 1:10,000 6.3 inches to 1 mile

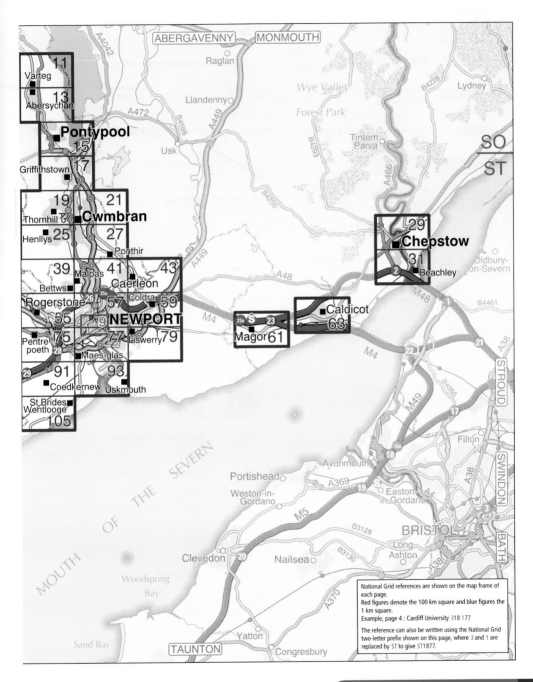

ABERGAVENNY   MONMOUTH

Raglan

Wye Valley

Forest Park

Lydney

11
Varteg

13
Abersychan

Pontypool

15

17

Griffithstown

19   21

Cwmbran

Thornhill

25   27

Henllys

Ponthir

39   41   43

Malpas

Caerleon

Bettws

Rogerstone

26   57   Coldra   59

55

NEWPORT

75   77   79

Pentre-
poeth   28

Maes-glas

Liswerry

29   91   93

Coedkernew   Uskmouth

St Brides
Wentlooge

105

Llandenny

Usk

Tintern
Parva

SO

ST

29

Chepstow

31

Beachley

Oldbury-
on-Severn

Magor   61

23a   S   23

Caldicot

63

Stroud

Portishead

Avonmouth

Weston-in-
Gordano

Easton-
in-Gordano

Filton

SWINDON

BRISTOL

BATH

Long
Ashton

Clevedon   Nailsea

Woodspring
Bay

MOUTH OF THE SEVERN

Sand Bay

Yatton

TAUNTON   Congresbury

National Grid references are shown on the map frame of
each page.
Red figures denote the 100 km square and blue figures the
1 km square.
Example, page 4 : Cardiff University 318 177

The reference can also be written using the National Grid
two-letter prefix shown on this page, where 3 and 1 are
replaced by ST to give ST1877.

4.2 inches to 1 mile   **Scale of main map pages** 1:15,000

0   1/4   miles   1/2   3/4   1

0   1/4   1/2   kilometres   3/4   1   1 1/4   1 1/2

Junction 9 Motorway & junction	Railway & minor railway station
Services Motorway service area	Underground station
Primary road single/dual carriageway	Light railway & station
Services Primary road service area	Preserved private railway
A road single/dual carriageway	*LC* Level crossing
B road single/dual carriageway	Tramway
Other road single/dual carriageway	Ferry route
Minor/private road, access may be restricted	Airport runway
One-way street	County, administrative boundary
Pedestrian area	Mounds
Track or footpath	**17** Page continuation 1:15,000
Road under construction	**3** Page continuation to enlarged scale 1:10,000
Road tunnel	River/canal, lake, pier
30 Speed camera site (fixed location) with speed limit in mph	Aqueduct, lock, weir
V Speed camera site (fixed location) with variable speed limit	465 ▲ Winter Hill Peak (with height in metres)
40 Section of road with two or more fixed camera sites; speed limit in mph or variable	Beach
50→ ←50 Average speed (SPECS™) camera system with speed limit in mph	Woodland
P Parking	Park
P+ Park & Ride	Cemetery
Bus/coach station	Built-up area
Railway & main railway station	

	Industrial/business building		Abbey, cathedral or priory
	Leisure building		Castle
	Retail building		Historic house or building
	Other building	Wakehurst Place (NT)	National Trust property
	City wall		Museum or art gallery
A&E	Hospital with 24-hour A&E department		Roman antiquity
PO	Post Office		Ancient site, battlefield or monument
	Public library		Industrial interest
i	Tourist Information Centre		Garden
i	Seasonal Tourist Information Centre		Garden Centre Garden Centre Association Member
	Petrol station, 24 hour Major suppliers only		Garden Centre Wyevale Garden Centre
†	Church/chapel		Arboretum
	Public toilet, with facilities for the less able		Farm or animal centre
PH	Public house AA recommended		Zoological or wildlife collection
	Restaurant AA inspected		Bird collection
Madeira Hotel	Hotel AA inspected		Nature reserve
	Theatre or performing arts centre		Aquarium
	Cinema	V	Visitor or heritage centre
	Golf course		Country park
▲	Camping AA inspected		Cave
	Caravan site AA inspected		Windmill
	Camping & caravan site AA inspected		Distillery, brewery or vineyard
	Theme park	•	Other place of interest

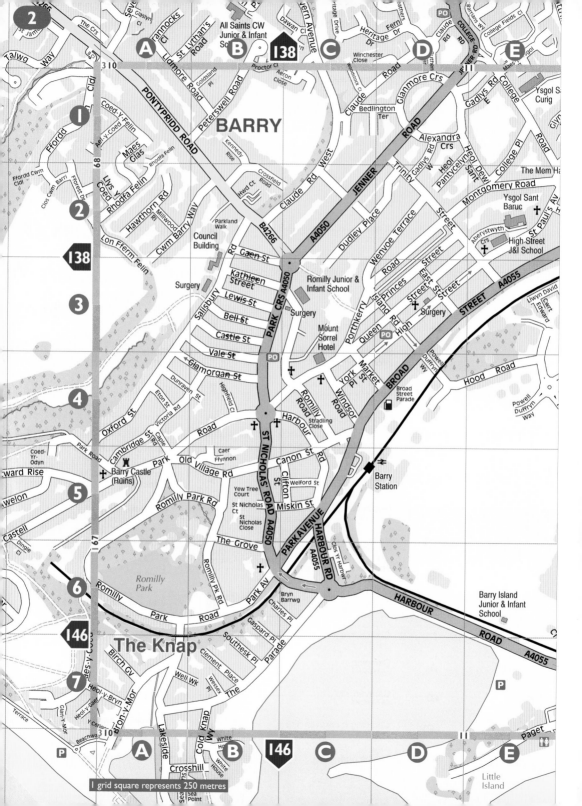

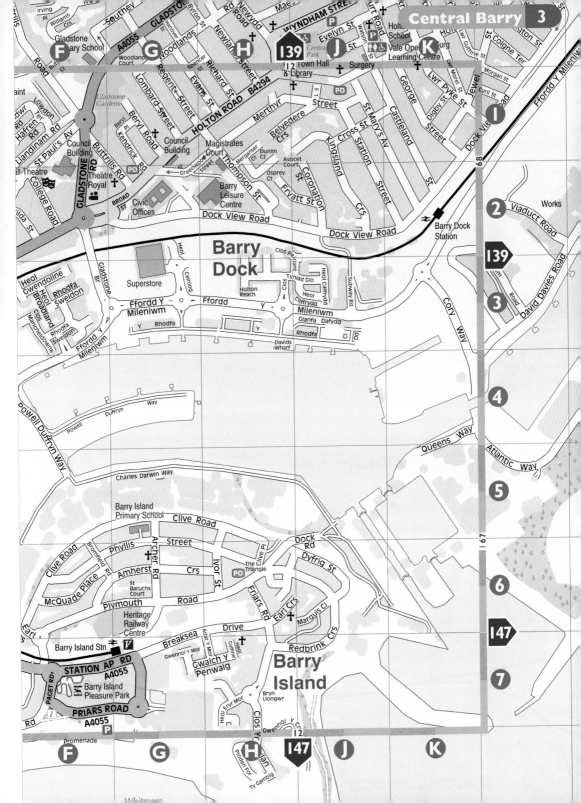

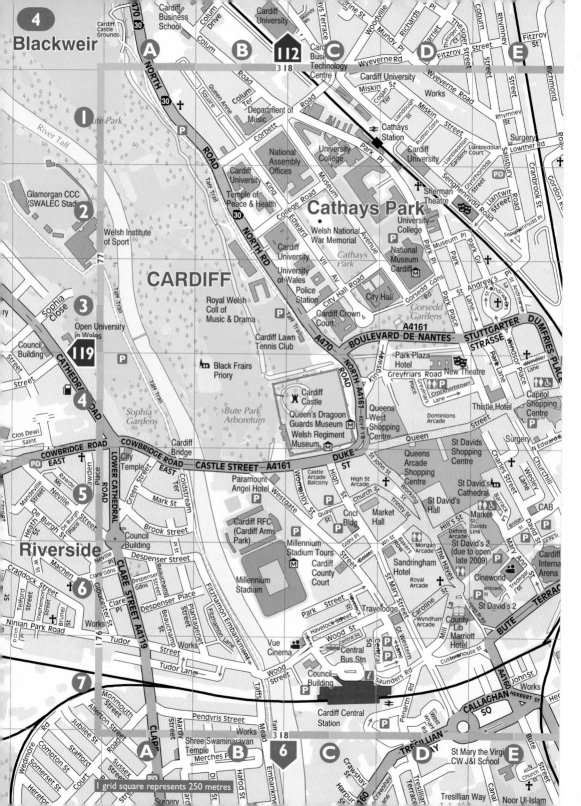

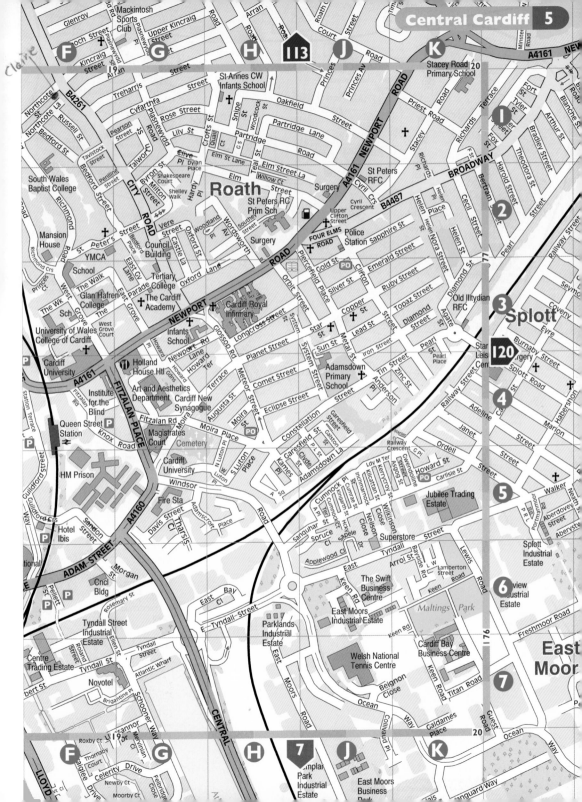

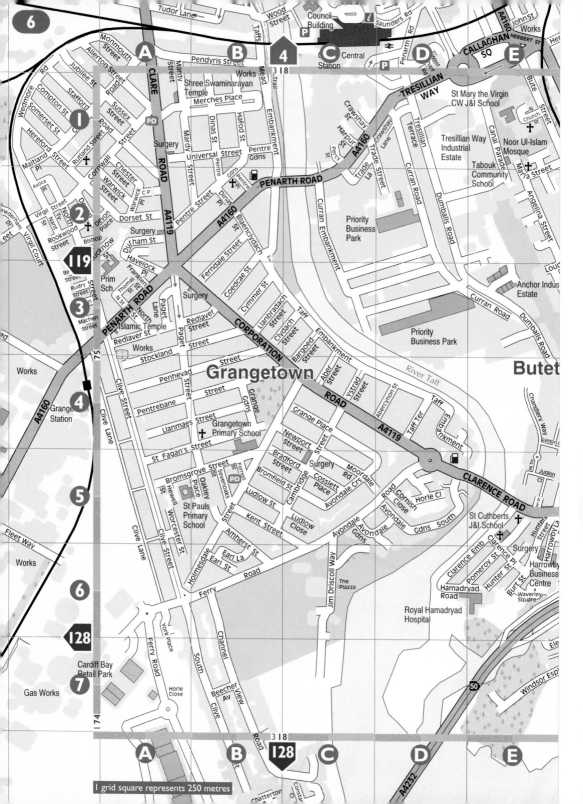

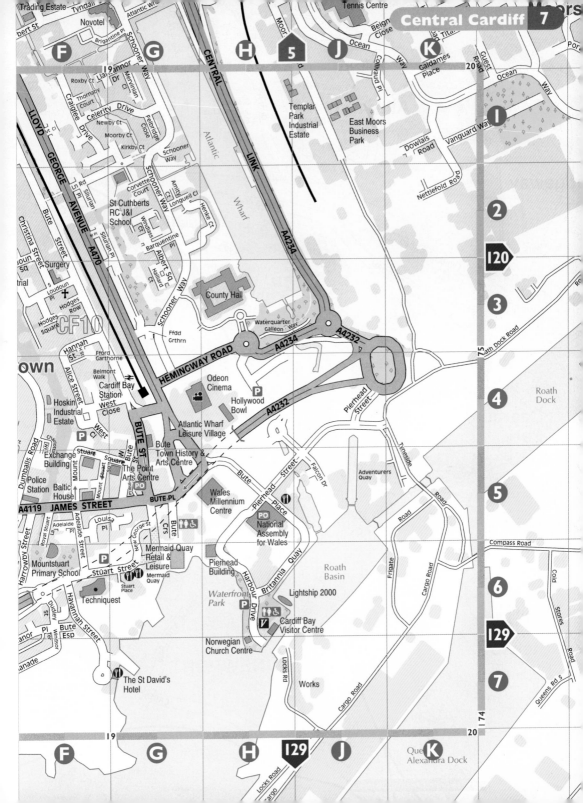

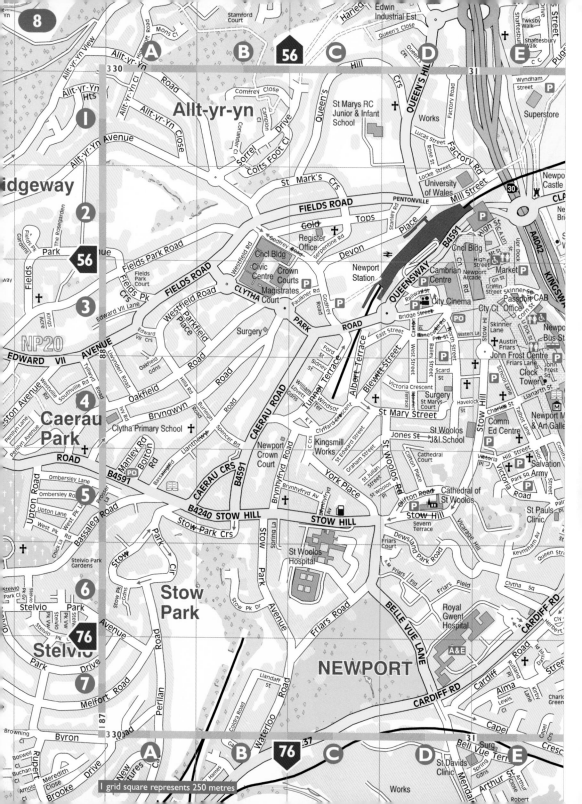

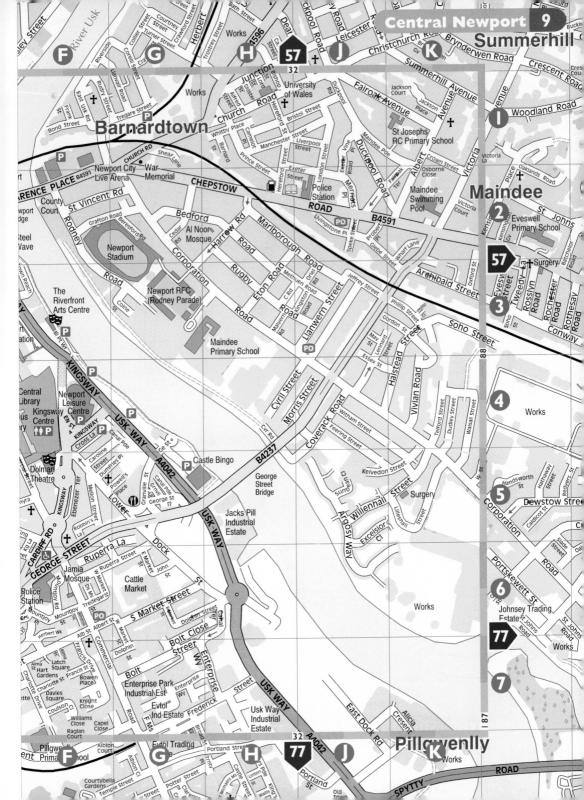

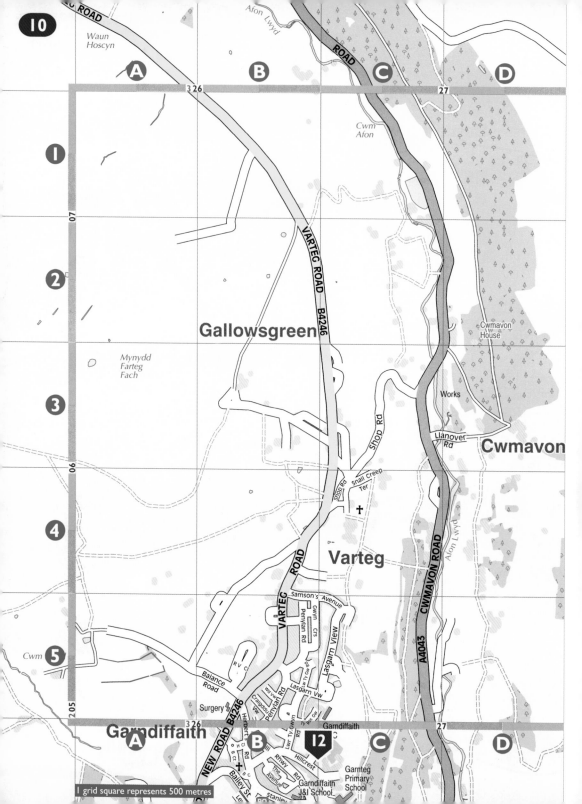

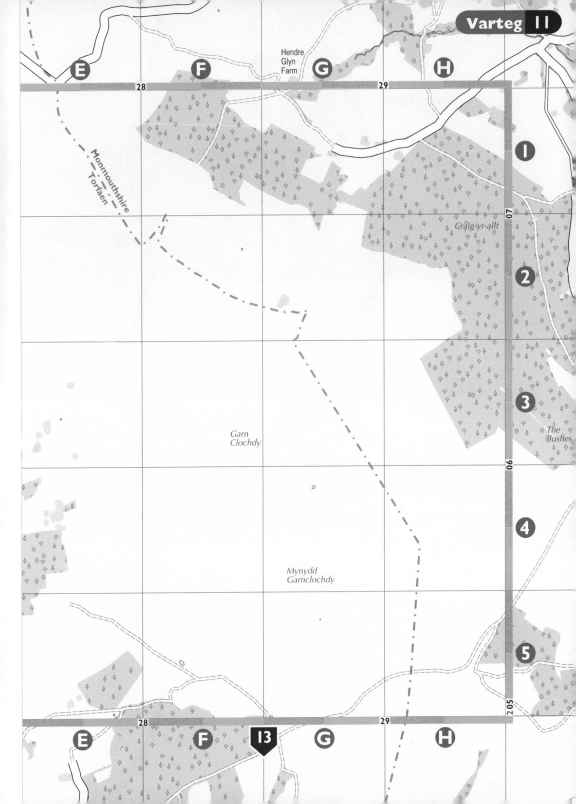

E

F

Hendre
Glyn
Farm

G

H

28

29

Monmouthshire
Torfaen

I

07

Craig-yr-allt

2

3

The
Bushes

06

4

Garn
Clochdy

Mynydd
Garnclochdy

5

205

28

E

F

13

G

29

H

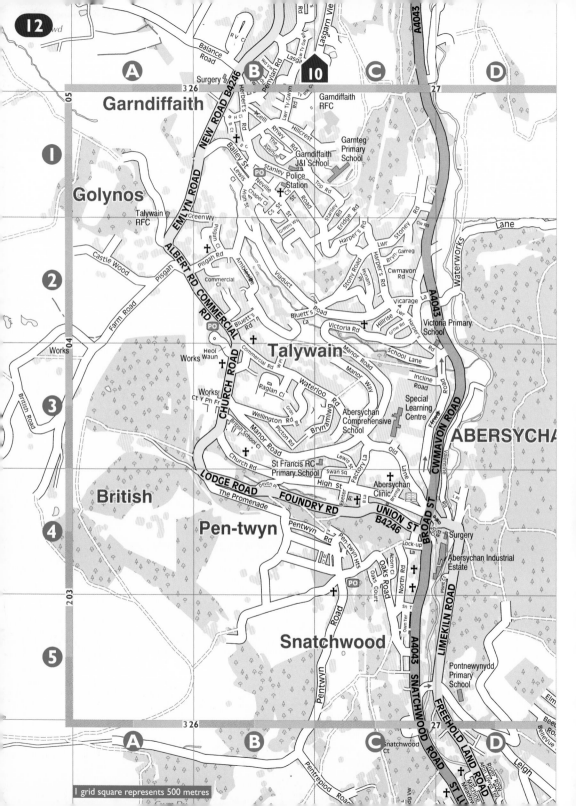

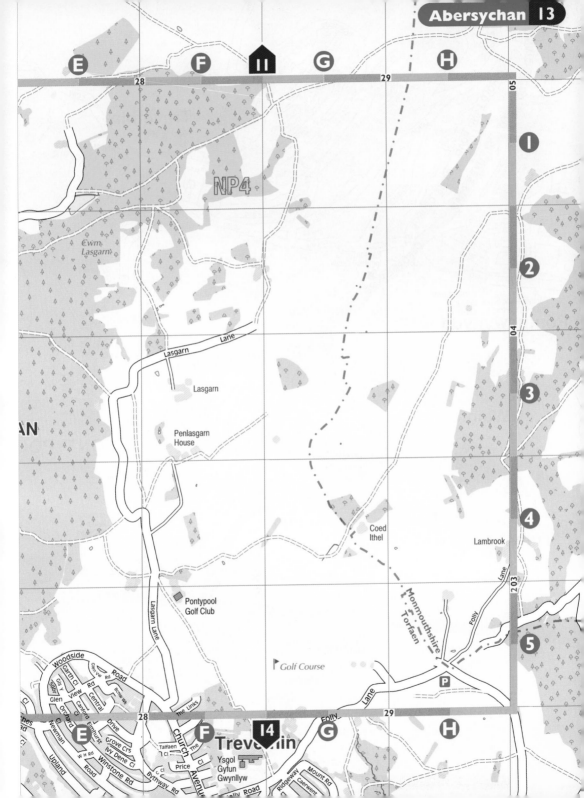

E   F   G   H

28   29   05

NP4

I

2

Cwm
Lasgarn

3

Lasgarn Lane

Lasgarn

04

Penlasgarn
House

Coed
Ithel

4

Lambrook

AN

203

Pontypool
Golf Club

Monmouthshire
Torfaen

Folly Lane

5

Lasgarn Lane

Woodside

Road

Golf Course

P

Garth Cl
Cus y
sgar
Glen Rd
Bryn Wk
Central

Glen
Orchard
Camd a
Cl
Elmhurst

Drive

The Links

Church

Folly

28   29

E   F   14   G   H

Newman
Grove Crs
Ivy Dene Cl

Upland
Road
W H Rd
Winstone Rd
Brynway Rd
Price Cl
Cl
The Cl
Talfaen
Cl

Avenue

Trevethin

Ysgol
Gyfun
Gwynllyw

Ridgeway
Caerwent
Mount Rd

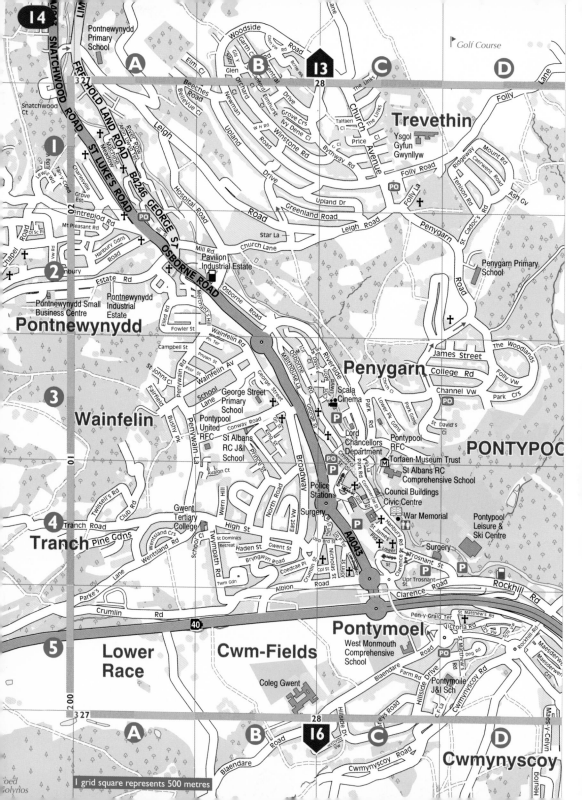

E F G H

29 30 31

Works

Eastway

Central Avenue

Works

Southway

I

Monmouthshire & Brecon Canal

USK ROAD

02

Wern Farm

2

Works

Pen-y-Llan Lane

Ty-mawr

Twyn-gwyn

Ty-poeth Farm

3

Llanvihangel Pontymoel

Usk Road

10

4

Sunlea Crescent

Usk V Ct

Usk Rd

A4042

Panteg Cemetery

Hand Farm Rd

Lodge Wd

Hillcrest Rd

Coed-y-Cando Rd

The Highway

Fountain Road

Pontypool & New Inn Station

A4042

Heol Deiniol

Heol Isaf

Heol Derwen

Poplar Avenue

Laburnum Drive

Chester Cl

Jerusalem Lane

5

The Moors Rd

The

Coed Camlas

The Av

Ruth Rd

South Rd

Heol Madoc

Caroline Rd

Heol Tello

Palm Cl

Alder Cl

Chestnut Close

Hazel Cl

Golf Rd

200

29 30 31

E F G H

South Pont Industrial P

17

A4042

Pnt WV

Council Building

Way

New

Pine Tree Cl

Larch Cl

Golf

The

Road

New Inn Primary School

Green Lawn Junior School

Hillcrest

Ambryn Rd

Medical C

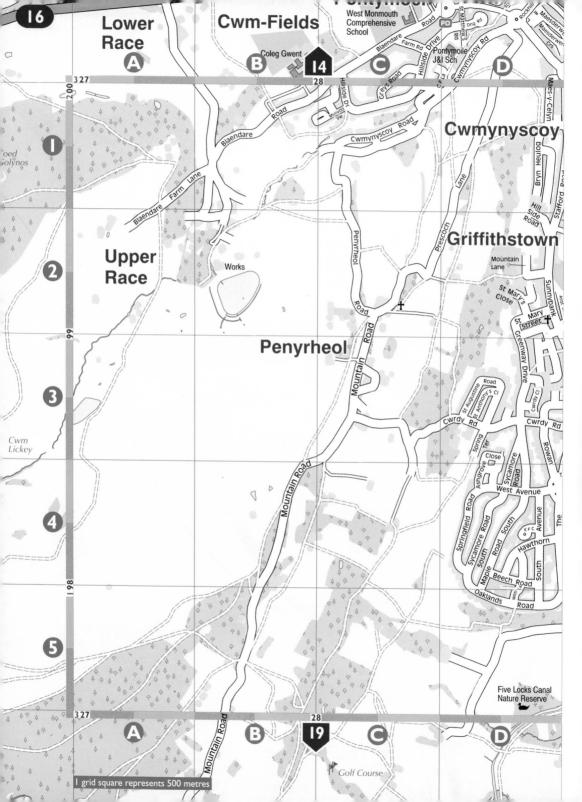

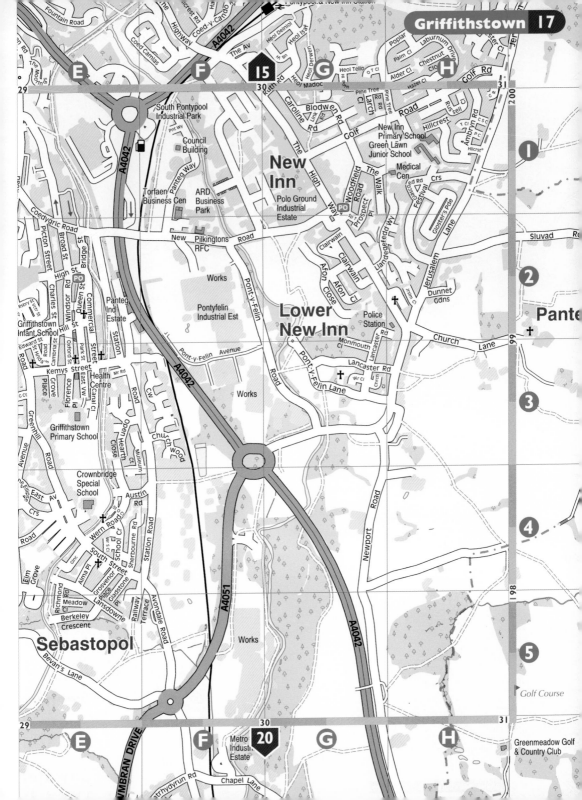

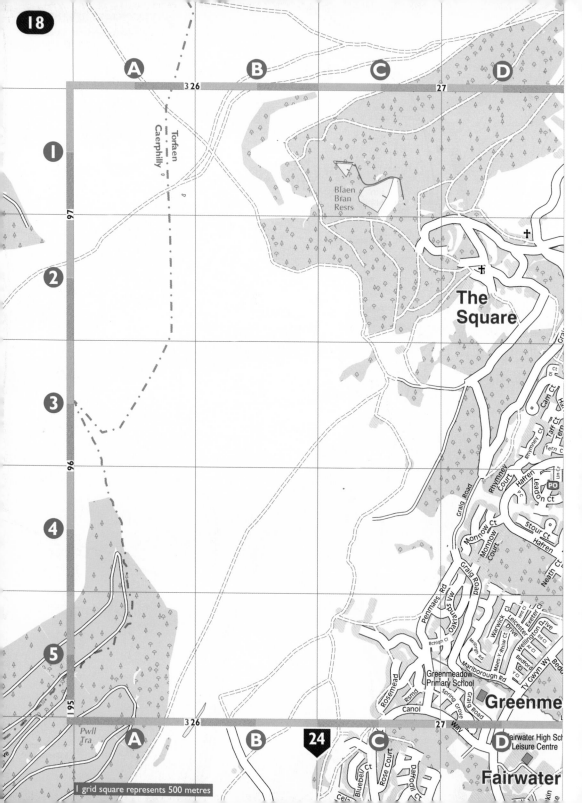

18

A 326 B C 27 D

97

1

Torfaen Caerphilly

Blaen Bran Resrs

2

The Square

3

96

4

Cam Ct

Taff Ct

Tern Ct

Rhymney Ct

Tefn Ct

Rhymney Court

Hafren

Lead

On Ct

PO

Monnow Ct

Stour Ct

Monnow Court

Hafren

Neath Ct

5

195

Penmaes Rd

Oakleys Vw

Graig Road

Bchlgn Ct

Warwick Cl

Maes-Y-Rhiw Ct

Mfdo Rd

Leicester Cl

Exeter Ct

Wellington Drive

Bedford

Marlborough Rd

Ty Gwyn Wy

Rosemead

Rsmd

Canol

Spring Grove

Greenmeadow Primary School

Graig Road

Way

Greenme

326 27

A B **24** C D Fairwater High Sch Leisure Centre

Pwll Tra

Rose Court

Bluebell Ct

Daffodil Ct

Fairwater

1 grid square represents 500 metres

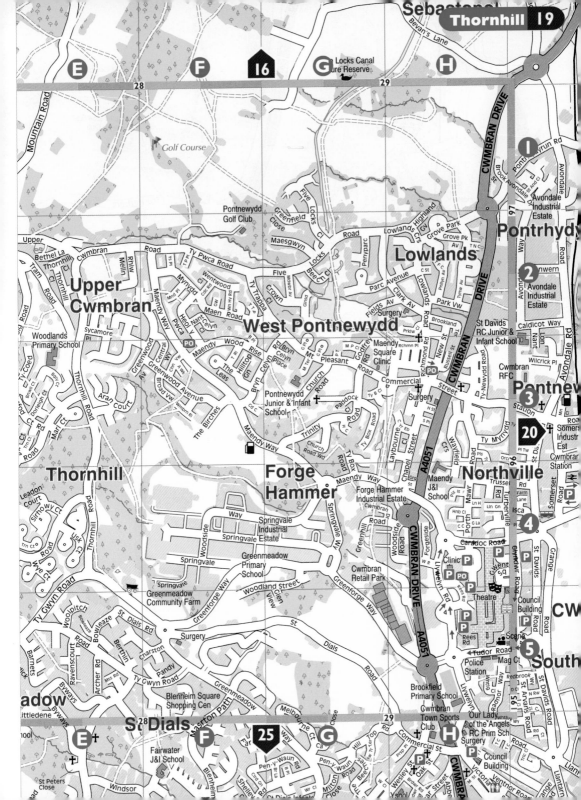

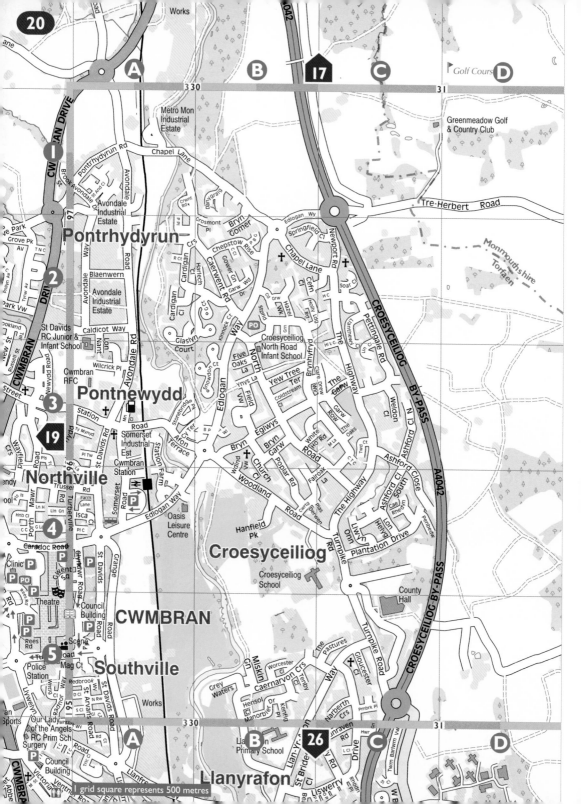

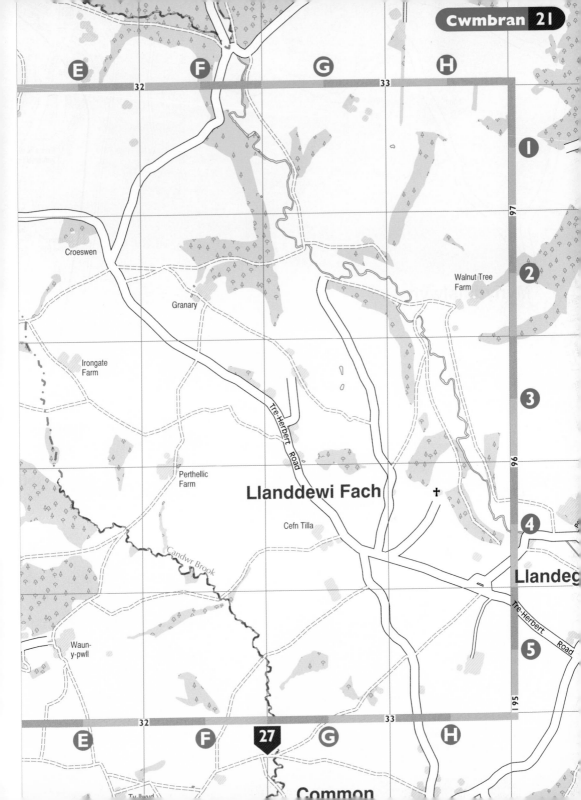

E   F   G   H

32   33

I

Croeswen

Walnut Tree
Farm

2

Granary

Irongate
Farm

3

96

Tre-Herbert Road

Perthellic
Farm

Llanddewi Fach

4

Cefn Tilla

Llandeg

Candwr Brook

Tre-Herbert Road

Waun-
y-pwll

5

195

32   33

E   F   27   G   H

Common

Ty-llwyd

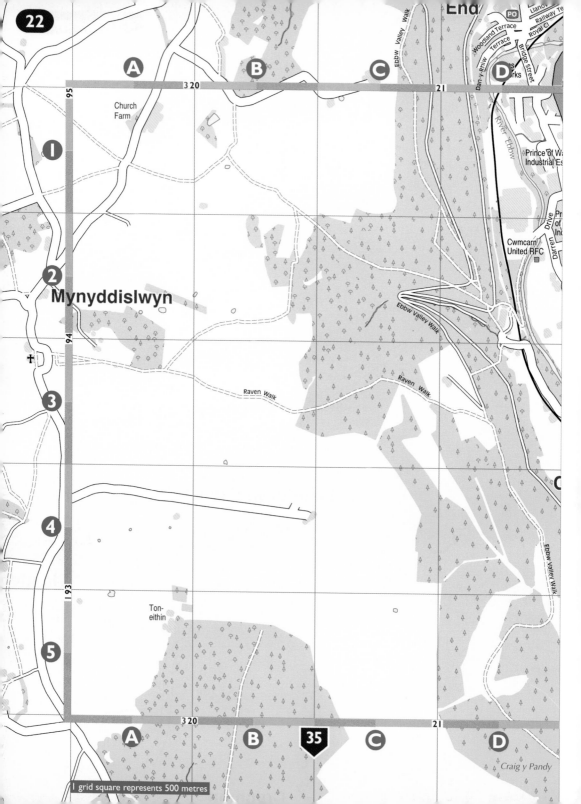

A 3 20 **B** **C** 95 21 **D** End

PO

Woodland Terrace
Railway Cl
Llanot
Royal Cl
Terrace

Bridge Street

Dan-y-Rhiw

Church Farm

I

River Ebbw

Prince of Wa
Industrial Es

Drive

Pr

Darren

Cwmcarn
United RFC

2 94 **Mynyddislwyn**

Ebbw Valley Walk

✝

3

Raven Walk

Raven Walk

C

4

Ebbw Valley Walk

193

5

Ton-eithin

A 3 20 **B** **35** **C** 21 **D**

Craig y Pandy

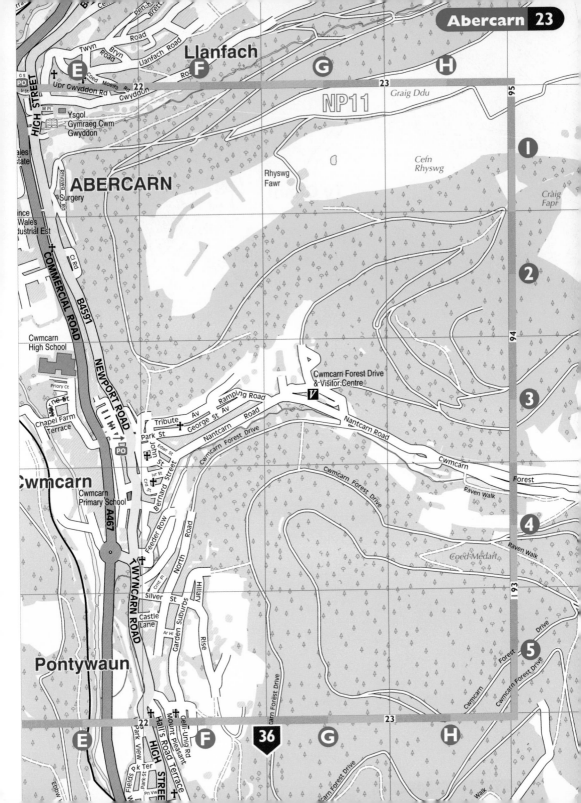

NP11

Graig Ddu

Cefn Rhyswg

Craig Fapr

I

2

3

4

5

E

F

Llanfach

G

H

Twyn Bryn Road

Llanfach Road

Pen-tr

Bret

Road

Upr Gwyddon Rd

Coed Moelfa Rd

Gwyddon

Gwyddon

22

23

Ysgol Gymraeg Cwm Gwyddon

ABERCARN

Surgery

Rhyswg Rd

Rhyswg Fawr

ales Estate

nce Wales Industrial Est

HIGH STREET

M Pl

PO

GS PO

Cwmcarn High School

COMMERCIAL ROAD

B4591

Cl Rd

NEWPORT ROAD

Priory Ct

ne St

Chapel Farm Terrace

PO

Tribute Av

Rampling Road

George St Av

Nantcarn Road

Park St

Cwmcarn Forest Drive

Cwmcarn Forest Drive & Visitor Centre

Nantcarn Road

Cwmcarn

Forest

Raven Walk

Cwmcarn

Cwmcarn Primary School

A467

Eqwr St

Jo

Ivr St

Crd St

Bernard Street

Feeder Row

North Road

WYNCARN ROAD

Silver St

Castle Lane

Garden Suburbs

Ar Hl

Hillary St

Rise

Coed Medart

Raven Walk

Cwmcarn Forest Drive

Pontywaun

Cwmcarn Forest Drive

Cwmcarn

Forest

Drive

Cwmcarn Forest Drive

E

F

36

G

H

22

23

Hall's Road

Park View

Gell-fung Rd

Mount Pleasant Terrace

HIGH STREET

Ter

Pl St

St

Fields

Ebbw

Pn Vw

Walk

95

94

93

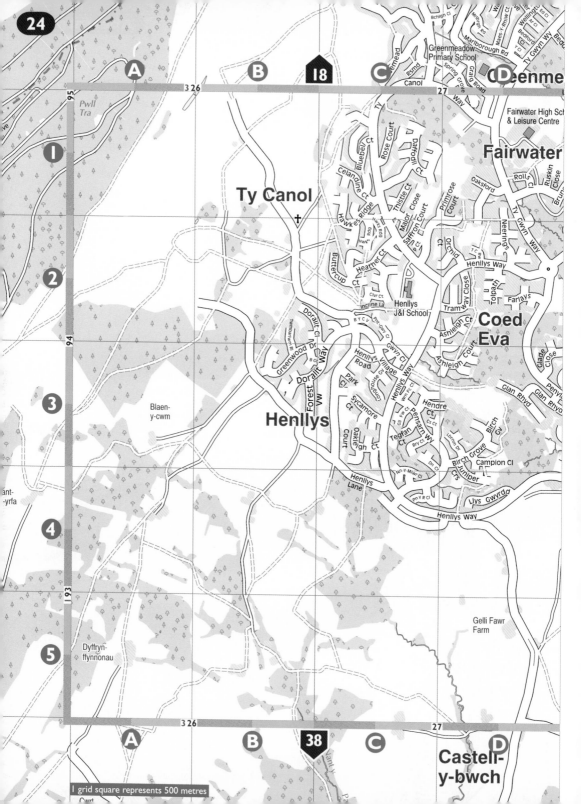

24

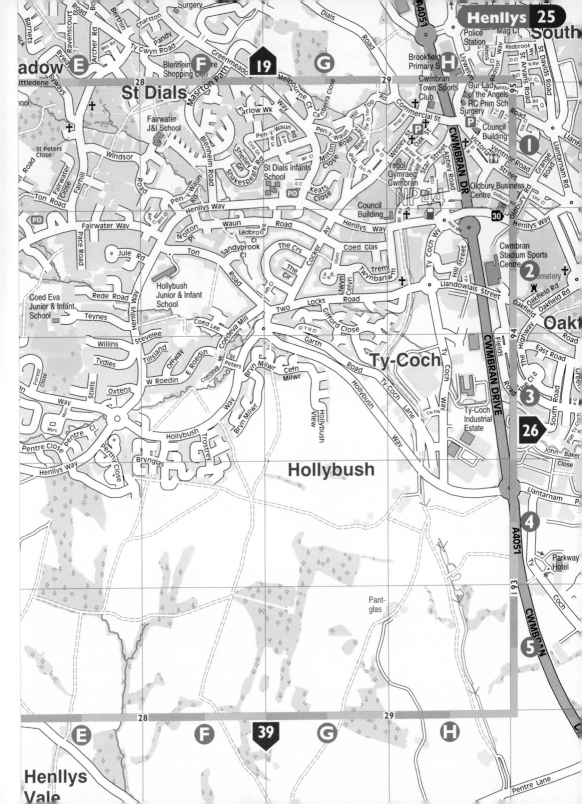

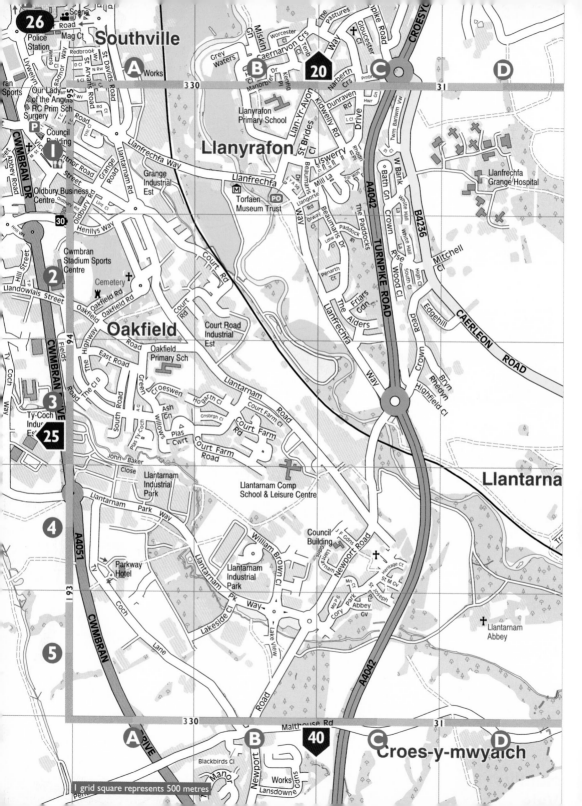

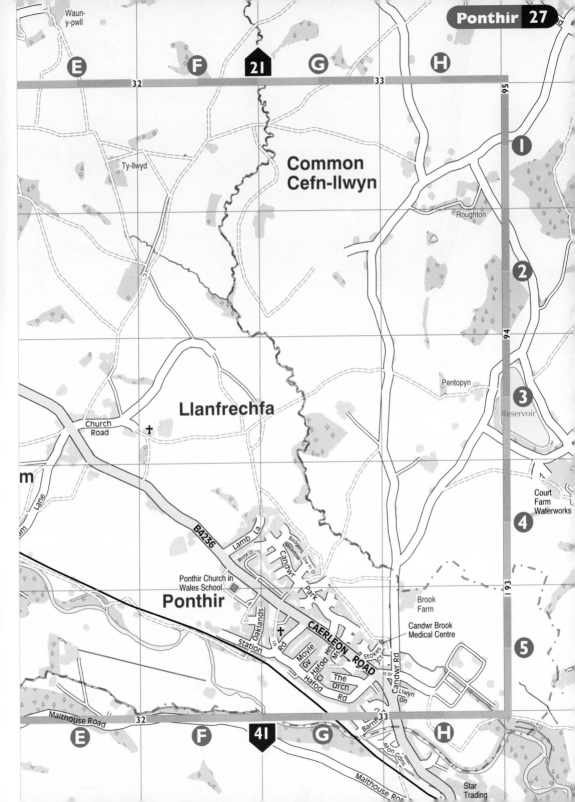

E F **21** G H

32 33 95

I

Waun-y-pwll

Ty-llwyd

Common Cefn-llwyn

Roughton

2

94

Pentopyn

3

Reservoir

Llanfrechfa

Church Road

✝

Court Farm Waterworks

4

Lane

m

193

B4236

Lamb La

Brcnfr Cl

Candwr

Park

Badgers Meadow

Cnwr Fr Cl

Ponthir Church in Wales School

Ponthir

Brook Farm

Candwr Brook Medical Centre

Station

Oaklands

✝

Hafod Ct

Rd

Moyle Gv

Hafod Rd

CAERLEON ROAD

The Orch Rd

Stokes

Candwr Rd

St Dr

Llwyn On

Barn

5

Malthouse Road

32

E F **41** G 33 H

Afon Cans

Malthouse Rd

Star Trading

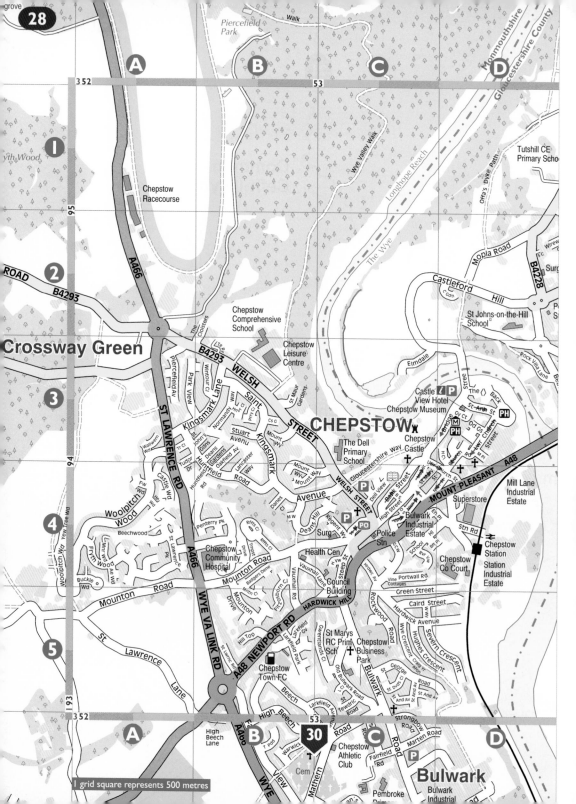

28

Piercefield Park

Walk

Monmouthshire
Gloucestershire County

352

53

A   **B**   **C**   **D**

Tutshill CE
Primary School

1

yth Wood

Wye Valley Walk

Chepstow
Racecourse

Longhope Reach

MOpla Road

B4228

Castleford Hill

Surg

The Wye

St Johns-on-the-Hill
School

Rock Vill Lane

Wirew

2

ROAD
B4293

A466

Chepstow
Comprehensive
School

Elmdale

Castle
View Hotel
Chepstow Museum

The

St Ann St

PH

P

Crossway Green

The Cloisters

B4293

Chepstow
Leisure
Centre

CHEPSTOW

Chepstow
Castle

Church
Street

PH

3

Kingsmark Lane

Piercefield Av

Park View

Wintour Cl

WELSH

Saint

St Maur
Gardens

CS G

Gloucestershire Way

MPH

Back

ST LAWRENCE RD

Normanby Cl

STREET

Kingsmark

Mount

The Dell
Primary School

Dell View

High Street

A48

9 4

Tudor
Dr

Huntfield
Rd

Deans
Gardens

Oakfield Av

Lancaster
Way

Mount
Way

WELSH STREET

Gloucestershire Way

P

Mill Lane
Industrial
Estate

MOUNT PLEASANT

Superstore

4

Woolpitch
Wood

Beechwood

St Lawrence
PK

Penterry Pk

Danes

M W

Avenue

Deans Hill

Regent W

P   PO

Surg

X

Police
Stn

Bulwark
Industrial
Estate

Stn Rd

Chepstow
Station

Station
Industrial
Estate

A466

Woolpitch Wa

Yew Tree Wa

Frith Wood Ae Wd

LMnr Wd

Buckle
Wd

Chepstow
Community
Hospital

Badgers Dene

Mounton Road

Health Cen

Vauxhall Lane

Steep Hill

Vine Portwall Rd

Portwall
Cottages

Green Street

Chepstow
Co Court.

5

St
Lawrence

Mounton   Road

Mounton
Drive

Hill Top

WYE VA LINK RD

A466

A48 NEWPORT RD

HARDWICK HILL

Council
Building

St Marys
RC Prim
Sch

Gwentlands Cl

Chepstow
Business
Park

BULWARK

Rockwood Road

Caird Street

Hardwick Avenue

Hughes Crescent

Wye Crescent

Severn Crescent

193

352

A   **B**   **30**   **C**   **D**

High Beech
Lane

High Beech

WYE VIEW

A466

Chepstow
Town FC

Larkfield Gv

Larkfield Park

Larkfield Avenue

Tewdric
Road

Old Bulwark Road

St Dog's
Cl

St And Av

St George
Road

Strongbow Road

Marten Road

P

Bulwark

Bulwark
Industrial

Beech

Warwick

53

Road

Chepstow
Athletic
Club

Fairfield
Rd

Cem

Mathern

Pembroke
Drive

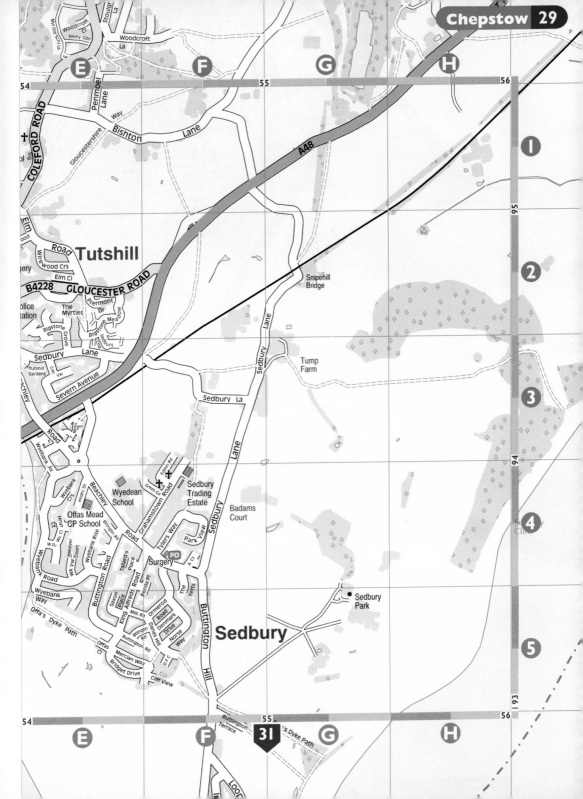

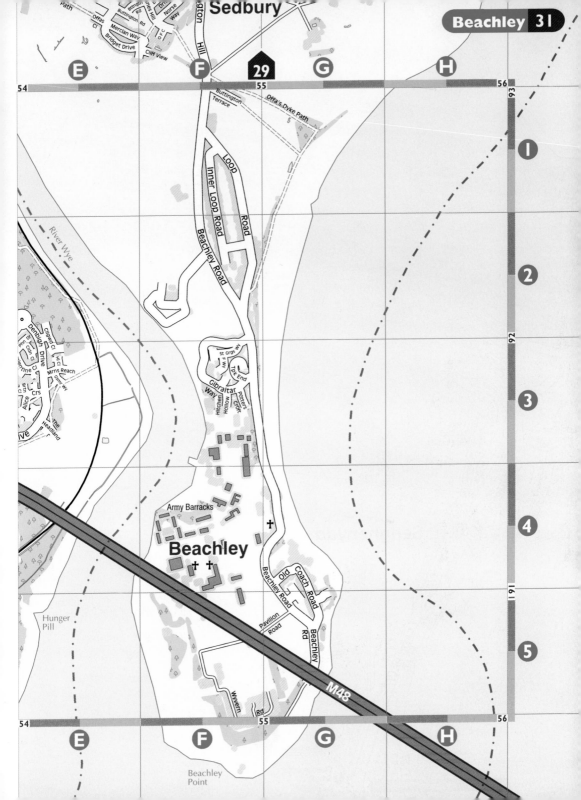

Superstore

Llanbradach Fawr

E **F** **G** **H**

Mill Lane

14

15

Colliery Road

Coed-y-Pia

Brynw

Graddfa

Telor-y-Coed

Craig Ysgolhan

Dan-y-Darren

Wingfield

Crescent

Rhymny River

I

92

2

Glyn Beaw

Glyn Collen

Glyn Llwyfen

Glyn Eiddew

Cwm Glas Infant School

Pant Glas

Glyn Derwen

Victoria St

Heol Ty-Gwyn

Oakfield St

A469

91

3

Llanbradach Isaf

Colliery Road

Lon-yr-Afon

The Bryn

Llanbradach

4

Graddfa Industrial Estate

Glenview Ter

Garden Cl

Garden St

Surgery

Ffrwd Ter

Monmouth Vw

The Av

A469

5

Mynyd Dimla

Chrch St

Mrgn St

Pencerrig St

Tyn-y-Craig Rd

Gry St

Jm St

High St

Colliery Road

Station Rd

Thomas St

De Winton Ter

Llwyd

PO

Llanbradach Station

Chrch Sch

Tre

Bedybrain Court

Coed-y-brain J&I School

Cwrt Ty-Fferm

Beulah

A469

190

E **F** **G** **H**

14

15

48

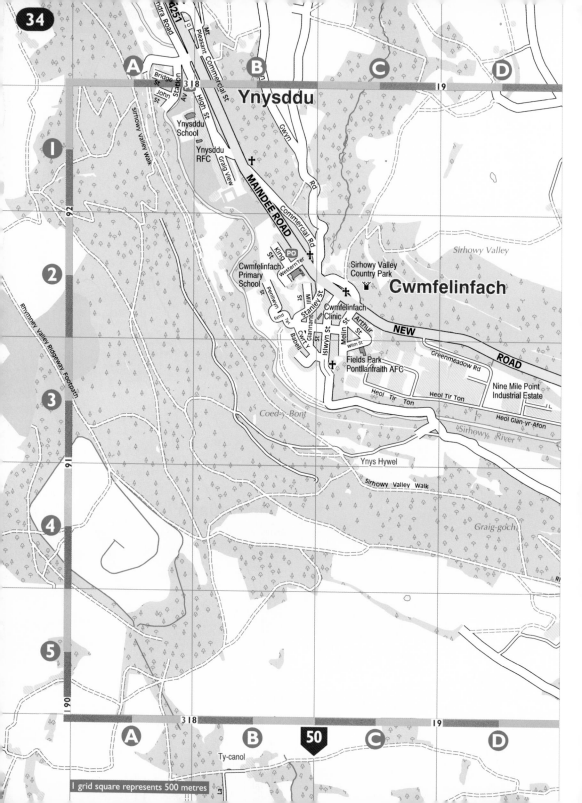

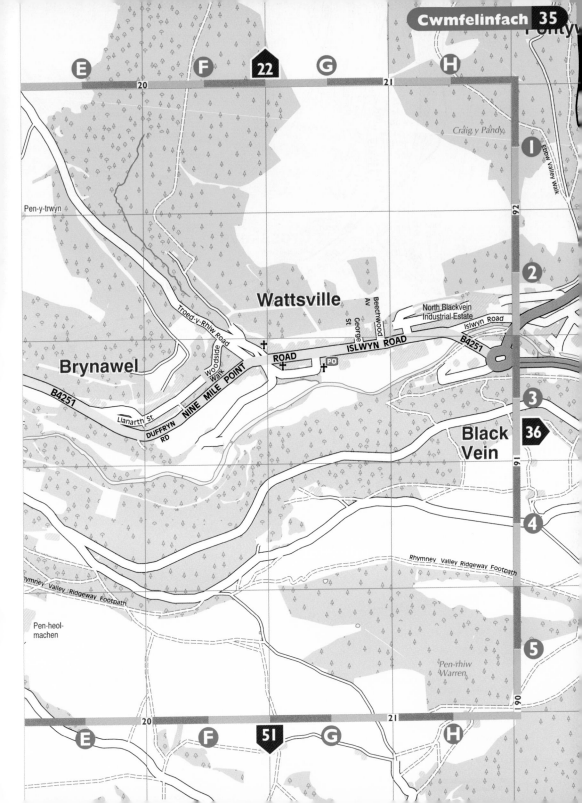

Pontyw

E F **22** G H

20 21

Cràig y Pandy

Ebbw Valley Walk

Pen-y-trwyn

92

2

Wattsville

Beechwood Av

George St

North Blackvein
Industrial Estate

Islwyn Road

Troed-y-Rhiw Road

ISLWYN ROAD

B4251

Brynawel

Woodside Walk

ROAD

PO

3

36

B4251

Llanarth St

NINE MILE POINT

DUFFRYN RD

**Black
Vein**

16

4

Rhymney Valley Ridgeway Footpath

Rhymney Valley Ridgeway Footpath

Pen-heol-machen

Pen-rhiw
Warren

90

5

E F **51** G H

20 21

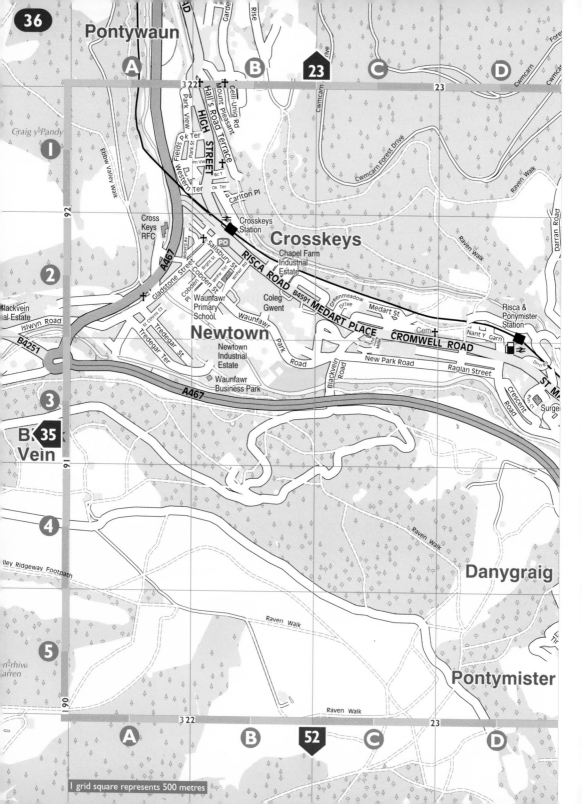

Pontywaun

A   B   23   C   D

Craig y Pandy

1

2

Blackvein ... Estate

B4251

3

B 35 Vein

4

lley Ridgeway Footpath

5

n rhiw ... arren

Ebbw Valley Walk

Cross Keys RFC

A467

Islwyn Road

Gladstone Street

Cobden Street

St Cttrms Ct

Tredegar St

Tredegar Ter

HIGH STREET

Park View

Fields

Pk Ter

Jb Park

Pn Vw

Western Ter

Mount Pleasant

Gelli-Unig Rd

Hall's Road Terrace

BC T

Ok Ter

Carlton Pl

Crosskeys Station

Crosskeys

Salisbury St

PO

Bright's ...

Wnfw Ter

Cobden Pl

Wntwr Ter

RISCA ROAD

Chapel Farm Industrial Estate

Waunfawr Primary School

Newtown

Newtown Industrial Estate

Waunfawr Business Park

Coleg Gwent

B4591 MEDART PLACE

Greenmeadow Drive

Medart St

Park Road

New Park Road

Blackvein Road

Cem

CROMWELL ROAD

The Mdw

Nant Y Garn

Raglan Street

Cwmcarn

Cwmcarn Forest Drive

23

Raven Walk

Darran Road

Cwmcar...

Forest...

Risca & Ponymister Station

Risca & Ponymister Station

ST M...

Crescent Road

Drn R...

Surger...

Danygraig

Raven Walk

Raven Walk

Pontymister

Raven Walk

A   B   52   C   D

3 22   23

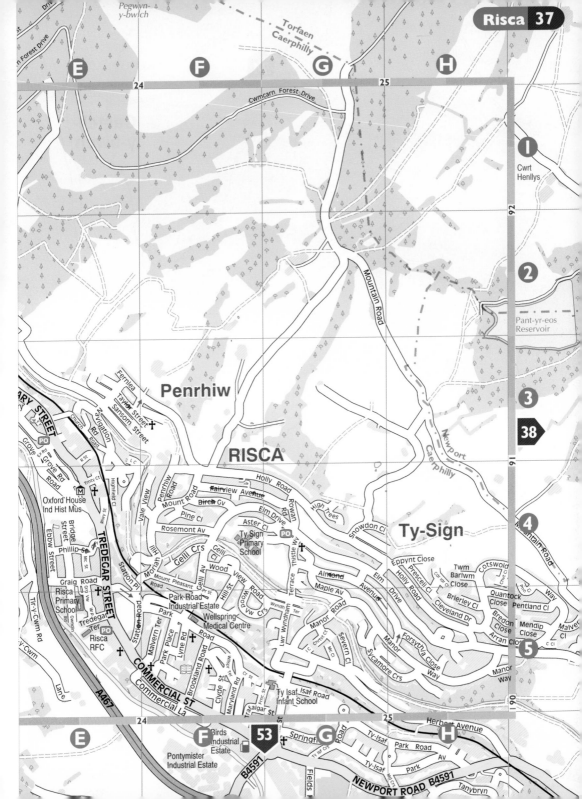

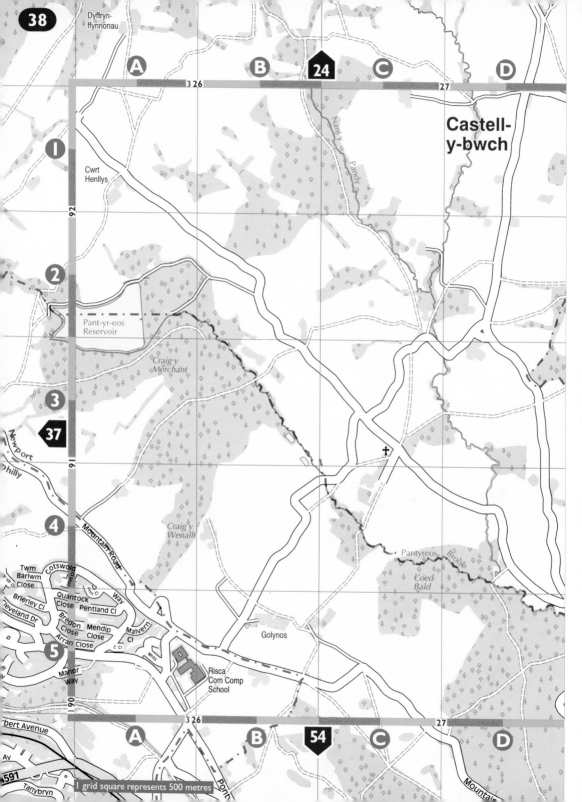

A   3 26   B   24   C   27   D

Castell-y-bwch

Dyffryn-ffynnonau

1

Cwrt Henllys

92

Nant y Pandy

2

Pant-yr-eos Reservoir

Craig y Merchant

3

37

Newport

Philly

6

4

Mountain Road

Craig y Wenallt

Pantyreos Brook

Coed Bald

Twm Barlwm Close

Cotswold Way

Brierley Cl

Cleveland Dr

Quantock Close

Pentland Cl

Bredon Close

Mendip Close

Malvern Cl

Arran Close

5

Manor Way

Risca Com Comp School

Golynos

bert Avenue

Av

591

Tanybryn

A   3 26   B   54   C   27   D

Porth

Mountain

1 grid square represents 500 metres

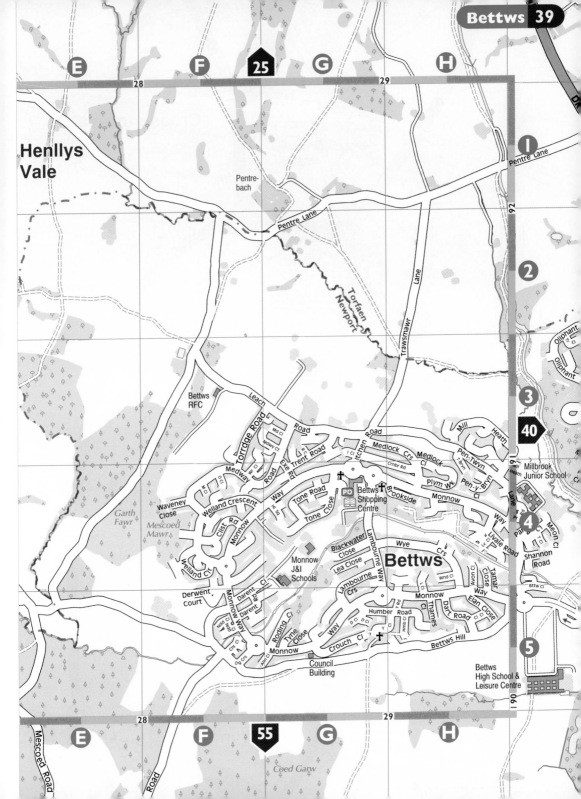

E **F** **25** **G** **H**

28 29

Henllys Vale

Pentre-bach

Pentre Lane

I

Pentre Lane

92

2

Torfaen Newport

Trawsmawr Lane

Bettws RFC

Leach Road

3

40

Oliphant

Oliphant

Torrage Road

Md Cl
Mdwy Ct

Medlock Crs

Medlock Cl

Mill

Heath

Pen-Twyn

Pen-y-Bryn

Heath

Exe Rd

Trent Road

Itchen Road

Crmbr Rd

Plym Wk

Pen-y Cl

Millbrook Junior School

Medway

Road

Way

Tone Road

PO

Bettws Shopping Centre

Brookside

Monnow

Lane

Garth Fawr

Waveney Close

Welland Crescent

Clst Rd

Monnow

Tone Close

Way

4

Livale Road

Meon Cl

Mescoed Mawr

Blackwater Close

Lambourne Way

Bettws

Wye

Crs

Tamar Close

Shannon Road

Welland Ct

Monnow J&I Schools

Lea Close

Lambourne Crs

Way

Wnd Cl

Avon Cl

Way

Elan Close

Bttw Cl

Derwent Court

Darent Cl
Darent Rd

Monnow Way

Humber Road

Monnow

Thames

Dart Road

5

Rodring Cl

Tyne Close

Way

Crouch Cl

Hmbr Cl

Bettws Hill

Monnow

Council Building

Bettws High School & Leisure Centre

90

E **F** **55** **G** **H**

28 29

Mescoed Road

Road

Coed Garw

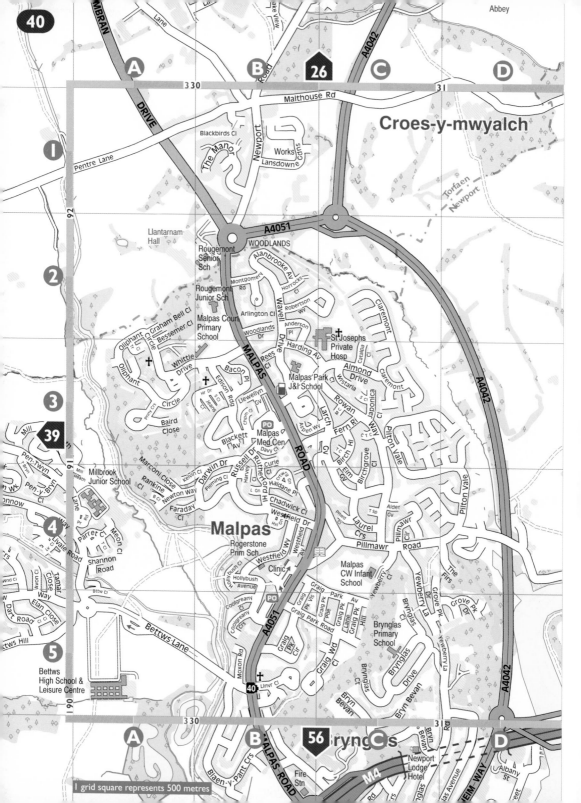

40

A   330   B   **26**   C   31   D

Croes-y-mwyalch

Abbey

I

Pentre Lane

CWMBRAN DRIVE

Lane

Lake View

Blackbirds Cl

The Manor

Newport Road

Works

Lansdowne Gdns

Malthouse Rd

Torfaen
Newport

A4042

92

2

Llantarnam
Hall

Rougemont
Senior
Sch

Rougemont
Junior Sch

Montgomery
Rd

Alanbrooke Av

Horrocks
Cl

Robertson Wy

A4051

WOODLANDS

Arlington Cl

Woodlands Dr

Anderson
Pl

Harding Av

St Josephs
Private
Hosp

Claremont

Waveli

Rees

Catalpa

Almond
Drive

Claremont

3

Oliphant

Graham Bell Cl

Bessemer Cl

Malpas Court
Primary
School

Whittle
Drive

Oliphant

Circle

Baird
Close

Bacon Pl

Edison Rdg

Llewellyn

Malpas
MALPAS
ROAD

Wistaria

Japonica

Rowan
Way

Larch

Fern Rd

Pilton Vale

39

Mill Heath

Pen-Twyn

Pen-y-Bryn

Millbrook
Junior School

Marconi Close

Rankine
Cl

Newton Way

Darwin Dr

Russell Dr

Rutherford

Harvey

Fleming

Curie

Haldane Pl

Birch
Cl

Elm
Gv

Birchgrove

Alder
Gv

Pilton Vale

4

Way

Dart Road

Uvale Road

Parret Cl

Meon Cl

Shannon
Road

Faraday
Cl

Kelvin

Malpas

Rogerstone
Prim Sch

Chadwick Pl

Westfield Dr

Westfield Av

Westfield WY

Laurel
Crs

Pillmawr
Cir

Pillmawr Road

The
Firs

Grove Pk

Yewberry La

5

Tamar
Close

Elan Close

Way

Bettws Hill

Bettws
High School &
Leisure Centre

Bettws Lane

A4051

Clinic

Hollybush
Avenue

Coolgreany
Crs

Malpas
CW Infant
School

Craig Park Road

Craig Pk
Cir

Moxon Rd

Craig Pk

Brynglas
Primary
School

Brynglas
Drive

Bryn Bevan

A4042

330

A   B   **56**   Bryngl C s   D

40

Newport
Lodge
Hotel

Albany
St

M4

Fire
Stn

Blaen-y-Pant Crs

MALPAS ROAD

Bryn Bevan

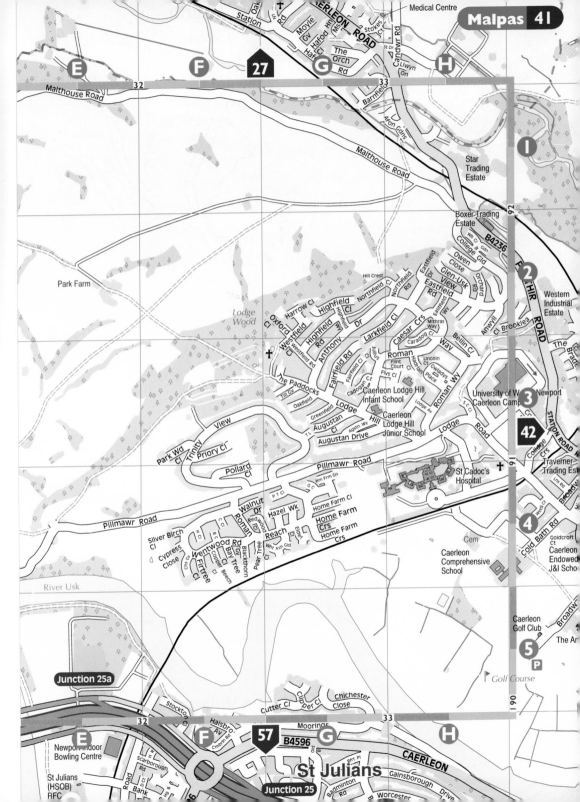

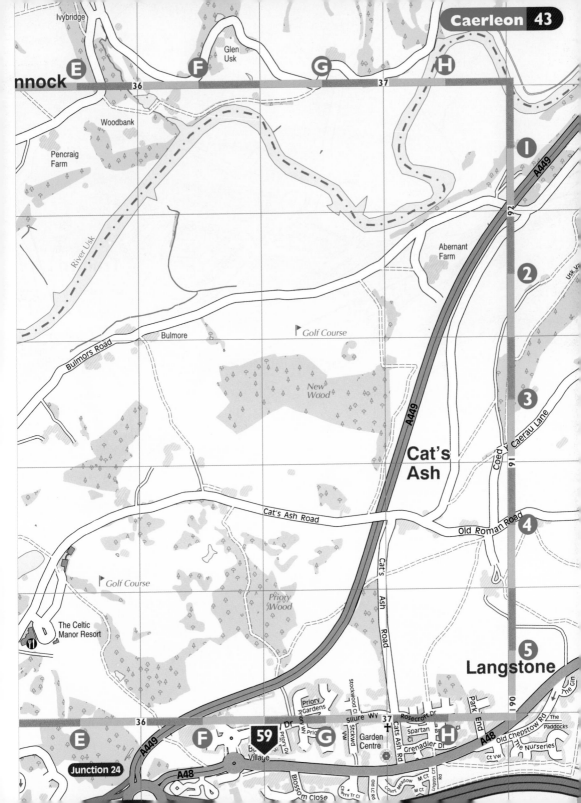

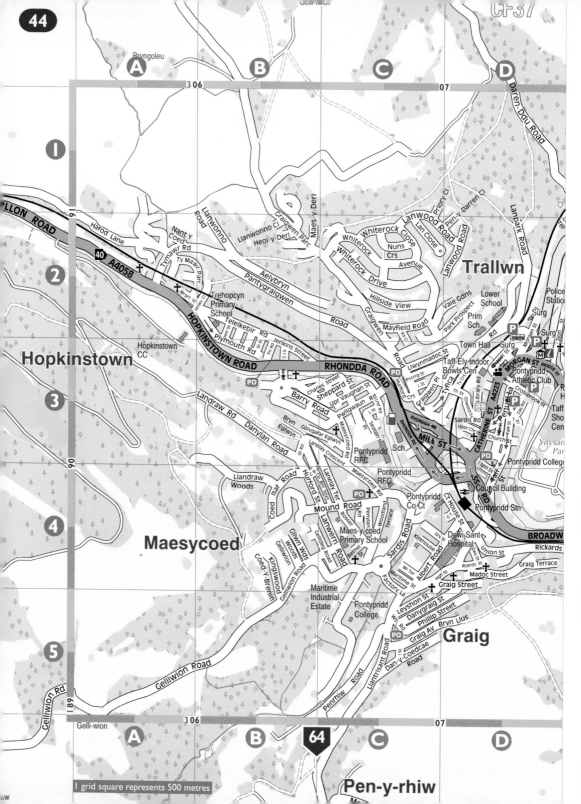

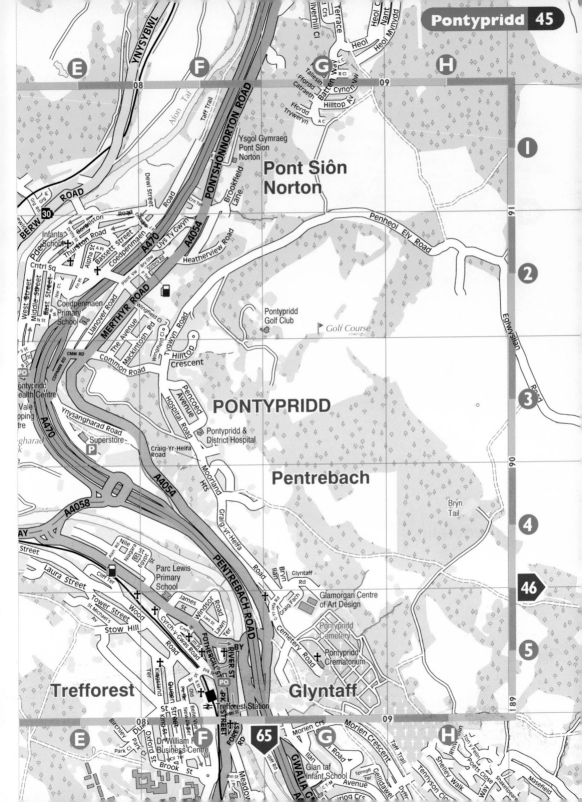

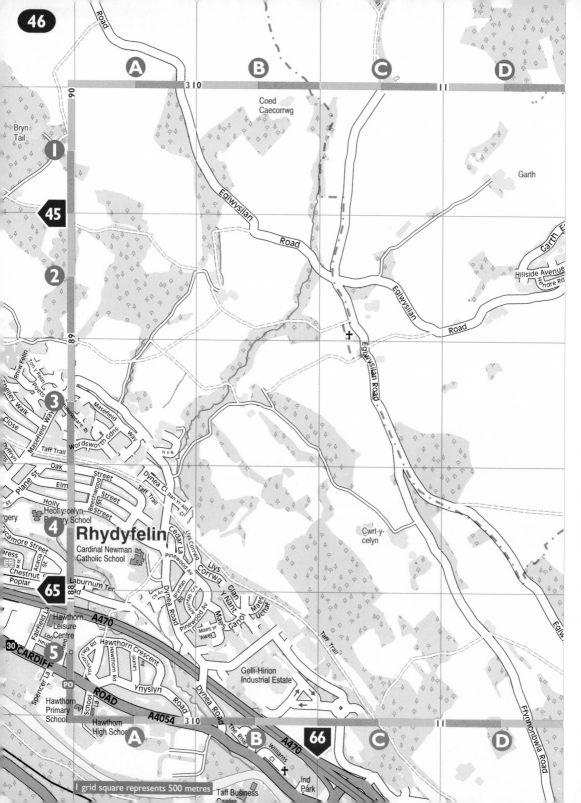

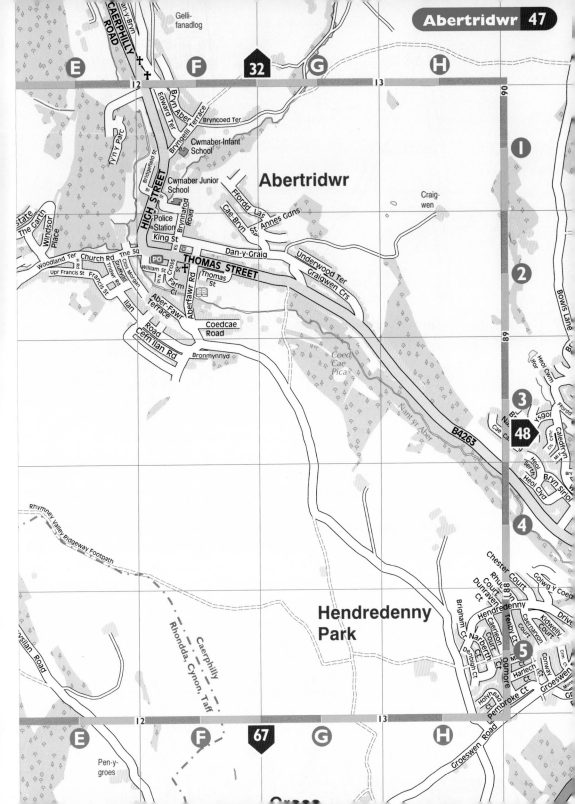

Gelli-fanadlog

CAERPHILLY ROAD

an-y-Bryn

E F **32** G H

Bryn Aber Terrace

Bryncoed Ter

Edward Ter

Bryngelli Terrace

Ty'n y Parc

Cwmaber Infant School

Abertridwr

Bridgefield St

Craig-wen

HIGH STREET

Cwmaber Junior School

Fflordd Las

Cae-Bryn

Annes Gdns

Brynmafod Road

I

Estate

The Garth

Windsor Place

Police Station

Dan-y-Graig

Underwood Ter

Woodland Ter

Church Rd

King St

KS

Graigwen Crs

2

Upr Francis St

Cros Morgan

William St

Cross St

THOMAS STREET

The Sq

Gruffydd

Tudur Rd

PO

Farm Cl

Thomas St

Francis St

Ilan

Aber-Fawr Terrace

Aberfawr Rd

Coedcae Road

Cefn Ilan Rd

Bronmynnyd

Coed 'Cae Pica'

3

Nant yr Aber

B4263

48

Na

Cae Ca

Heol Cwn

Ysgol

Caledfryn

Heol Serth

Bryn Siriol

Heol Clyd

4

Rhymney Valley Ridgeway Footpath

Chester Court

Colwg y Coed

Rhu-881n Court

Dunraven Ct

Hendredenny

Drive

Brigham Ct

Caerleon Court

Caernarvon Court

Kidwelly Court

Hendredenny Park

Narberth Court

Tenby Ct

Conway

wysian Road

Caerphilly Rhondda, Cynon, Taff

Denbigh Ct

Ogmore Ct

Harlech Ct

5

Groeswen

Holyhead Ct

Pembroke Ct

E F **67** G H

Pen-y-groes

Groeswen Road

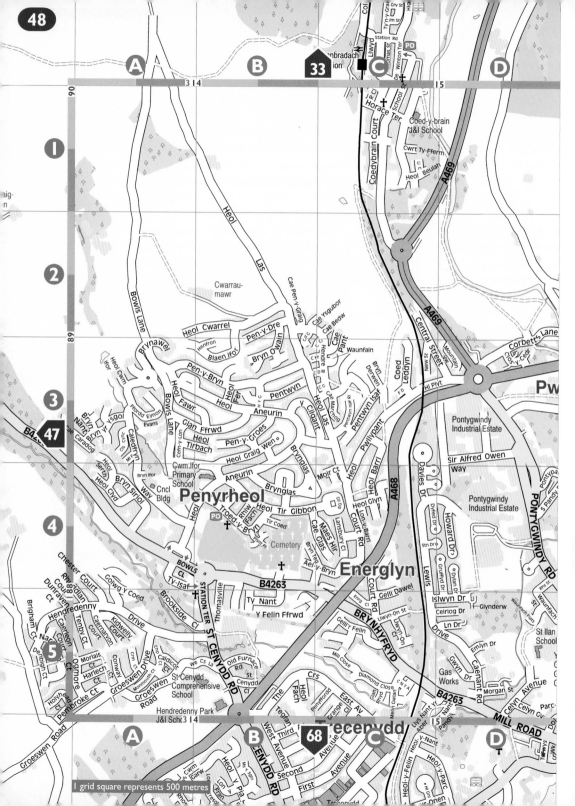

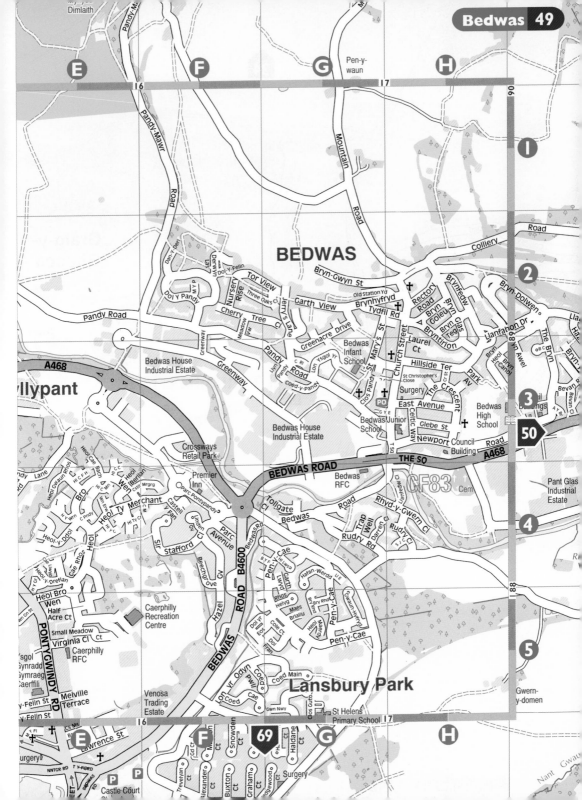

BEDWAS

Pen-y-waun

Mountain Road

Dimlaith

Pandy-Mawr Road

Colliery Road

Bryn-Gwyn St

Tor View

Nursery Rise

Jerry's Lane

Three Oaks

Garth View

Old Station Yd

Brynhyfryd

Brynfedw

Rectory Road

Bryn Coleu

Bryn Clas

Bryntirion

Bryn-Dolwen

Llanfabon Dr

The Bryn

Cherry Tree Cl

Meadow

Greenacre Drive

Tydfil Rd

St Mary's St

Church Street

Laurel Ct

Llwyn Pandy

Hillside Ter

Nwl Awel

Heol Bryn Canol

Pandy Road

Dol Y Pandy

Derwen Las

Dol-y-Felin

Pandy Road

Pandy Road

Greenway

Greenway

Bedwas House Industrial Estate

Bedwas House Industrial Estate

Coed-y-Pandy

Clos Pandy

Lon Ysgol

Bedwas Infant School

St Christopher's Close

Surgery

East Avenue

The Crescent

Park Av

Bedwas High School

Newport Road

Bedwas Junior School

Celtic Way

Glebe St

Council Building

A468

A468

Pontypandy

A468

Llanfabon

CF83 Cem

50

3

Buildings

Bevan Cl

Pant Glas Industrial Estate

2

I

H

G

F

E

3

4

5

Llypant

Pandy Lane

Heol Gwaun

Heol Cae

Heol Ty Merchant

Bro

Heol-y-Ddol

Cae Rhos

Castell Par

Linden Cl

Sir Stafford

Crossways Retail Park

Premier Inn

Parc Pontypandy

Tollgate Cl

Bedwas Cl

BEDWAS ROAD

Bedwas RFC

THE SQ

Rhyd-y-Gwern Cl

Trap Well

Rudry Rd

Daren Cl

Rudry Cl

Parc Avenue

Beechey Gv

Hazel Gv

BEDWAS ROAD B4600

Pen-y-Cae

Garth

Llwyd

Rhos

Helyg

Maes Brialiu

Pen-y-Cae

Gwaun-Hyfryd

Pen-y-Cae

Caerphilly Recreation Centre

Heol Bro Wen

Half Acre Ct

Small Meadow Ct

Virginia Cl

Caerphilly RFC

Ysgol Gynradd Gymraeg Caerffili

PONTYGWINDY RD

Melville Terrace

Y-Felin St

Y-Felin St

Venosa Trading Estate

BEDWAS ROAD

Dol yr Eos

Cole Ct

Dol Fran

Odyn yr

Clos Coed

Coed Cae

Pwll

Coed Main

Gwn Nwy

Clos Guto

St Helens Primary School

Lansbury Park

Gwern-y-domen

69

Lawrence St

Trevelyan Ct

Alexander Ct

Snowden Ct

Buxton Ct

Graham Ct

Edgewood Ct

Haldane Ct

Surgery

Castle Court

NNTGR RD

T Y FFRWD

Nant Gwatwr

16

17

06

88

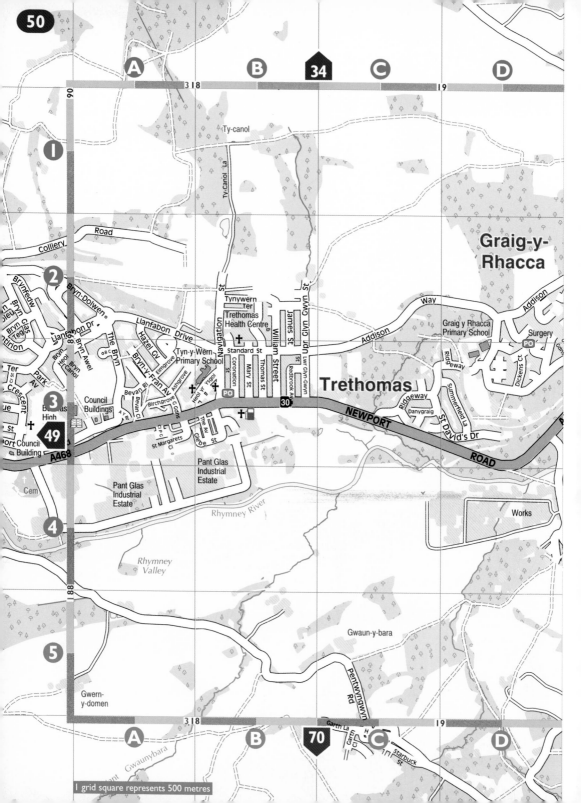

A **318** B **34** C **19** D

90

1

Ty-canol

Ty-Canol La

2

Colliery Road

Graig-y-Rhacca

Bryn Dolwen

Llanfabon Dr

Bryn Awel

Llanfabon Drive

The Bryn

Hazel Cv

Elmgrove

Ashgrove

Birchgrove

Bryn-y-Fran Av

Bevan Rd

Bevan Cl

Navigation St

Tynywern Ter

Trethomas Health Centre

Coronation St

Standard St

Mary St

Thomas St

William Street

James St

St Gwyn Llyn

Lwr Glyn-Gwyn

Redbrook Av

Addison Way

Graig y Rhacca Primary School

Addison

Surgery

PO

Dickens Ct

Ridgeway

3

Ysgol Hinh

49

A468

Cem

Tyn-y-Wern Primary School

Heol yr Ysgol

PO

30

Trethomas

Summerfield La

Ridgeway

Danygraig

St David's Dr

NEWPORT ROAD

Council Buildings

St Margarets Cl

The Av

Glebe St

Pant Glas Industrial Estate

Pant Glas Industrial Estate

4

88

Rhymney River

Rhymney Valley

Works

5

Gwaun-y-bara

Gwern-y-domen

Pentwyngwyn Rd

A **318** B **70** C **19** D

Garth La

Garth Cl

Starbuck St

Gwaunybara

I grid square represents 500 metres

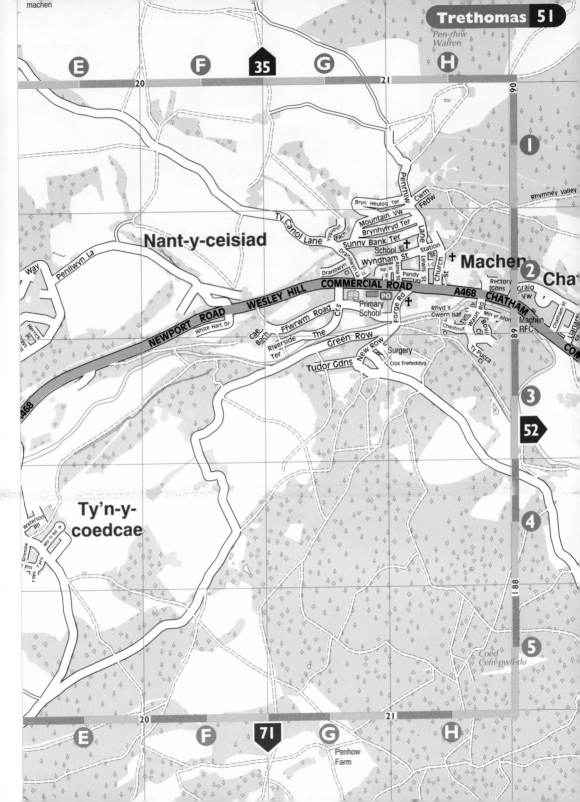

Pen-rhiw
Warren

machen

E F **35** G H

20 21 90

I

Rhymney Valley

Pen-rhiw

Cwm
Fedw

Bryn Heulog Ter

Mountain Vw

Ysgubor
Fach

Brynhyfryd Ter

Ty Canol Lane

Nant-y-ceisiad

Sunny Bank Ter

Penllwyn La

Way

Draniiwyn
Cl

Draniiwyn La

School

Wyndham St

Alma St

Np St

Pandy
Lane

Station

Lewis St

St
Cl

Church St

Machen Cha

Rectory
Gdns

Graig
Vw

2

Herrick
Pl
Grays

White Hart Dr

NEWPORT ROAD **WESLEY HILL** **COMMERCIAL ROAD** **A468** **CHATHAM**

PO

Primary
School

Forge Rd

Rhyd Y
Gwern Isaf

Chestnut
Cl

Min yr Afon

Waun St

Beovil

Machen
RFC

Chatham St

Llanarth

CO

Cae
Bach

Ffwrwm Road

Crs

Riverside
Ter

The

Green Row

New Row

Surgery

Clos Trefeddyg

Ty Pucca
Cl

A468

Tudor Gdns

3

52

**Ty'n-y-
coedcae**

Waterloo
Pl

Grimow
T Pns Pns

Witt Rd o

4

I 88

5

Coed
Cefn-pwll-du

20 21

E F **71** G H

Penhow
Farm

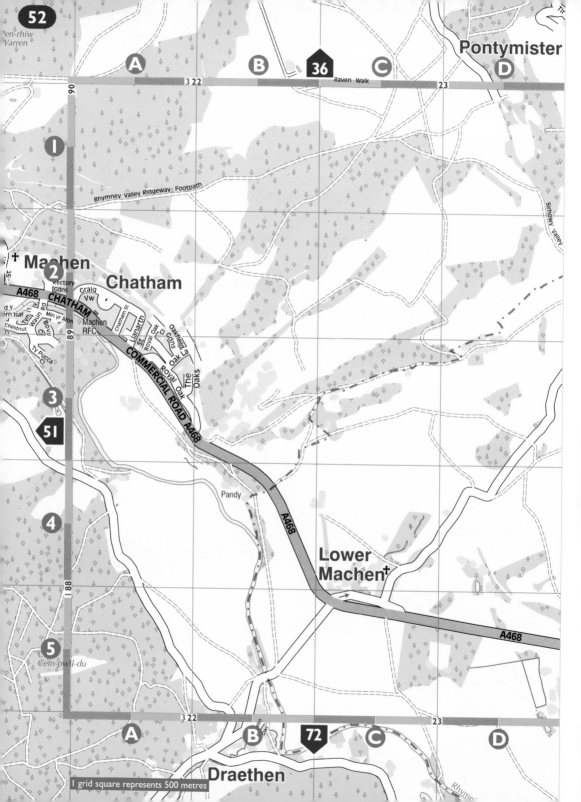

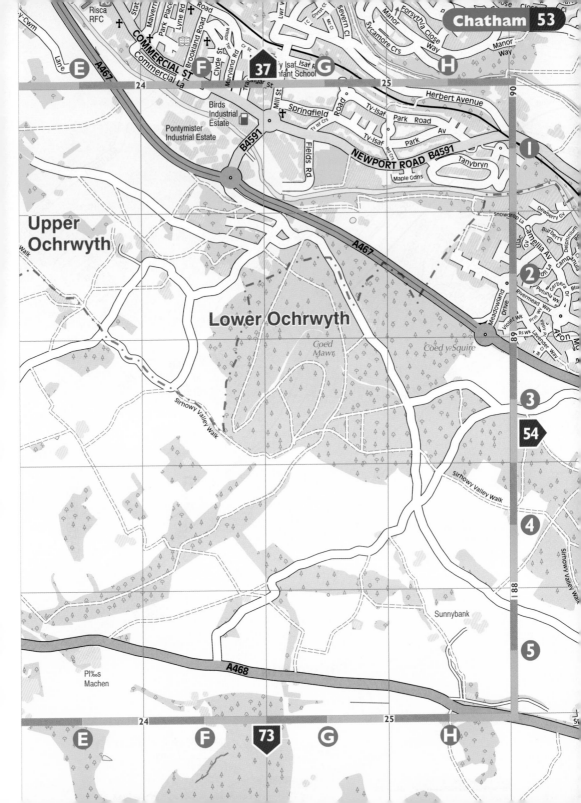

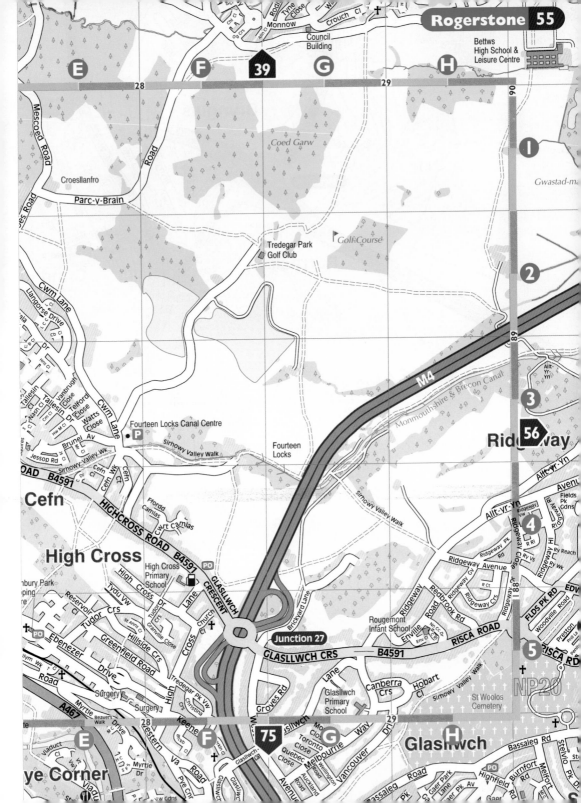

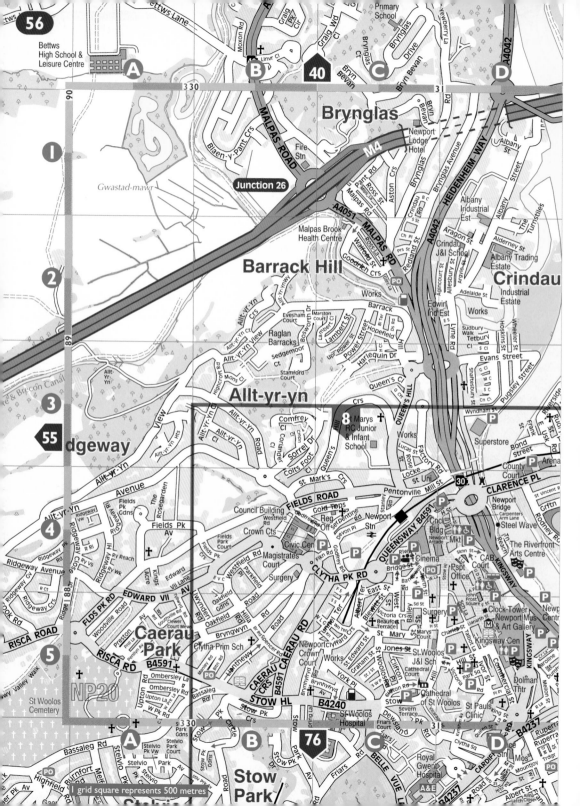

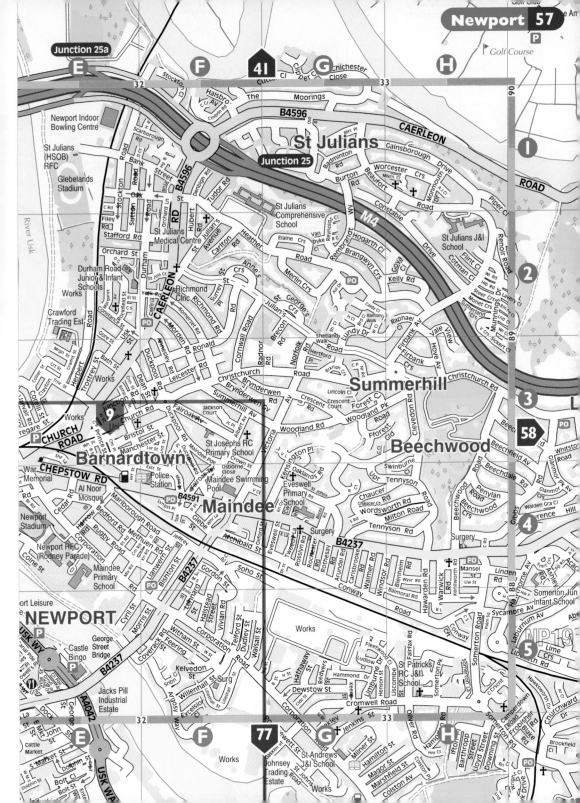

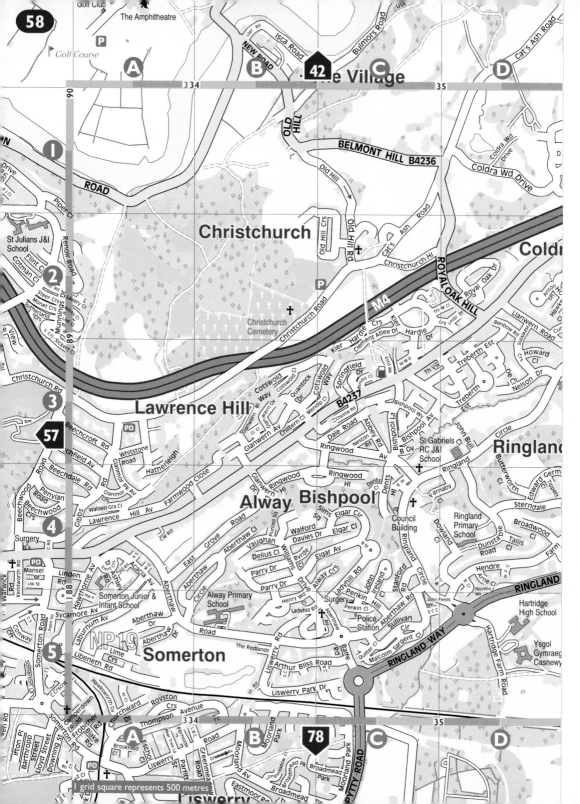

Golf Club
The Amphitheatre

Golf Course

P

A   334   90   **B**   NEW ROAD   Isca Road   LWr Rd   Bulmors Road   Usk   **42** he Village   **C**   35   Cat's Ash Road   **D**

I

Drive   ROAD   OLD HILL   BELMONT HILL B4236   Coldra Wd   Coldra Wd Drive

Piper Cl   Renoir Road   Old Hill   Old Hill Crs   Coldr

St Julians J&I School   Flint Cl   Cotman Cl   **Christchurch**   Old Hill Rd   Christchurch Hl   Cat's Ash Road   ROYAL OAK HILL   Cold

2   Turner Rd   Lavery Cl   Christchurch Cemetery   Royal Oak Dr   Anson Cl   Hawke

Steer Crs   Constable Cl   Monet Crs   Sutherland Crs   V Crs   Sickert Cl   Christchurch Road   M4   Kier Hardie Crs   Clement Atlee Dr   Hardie Dr   Crg Unbor   Benbow Rd   Llanwern Road   Cumr

Christchurch Rd   Springfield Dr   Kier Vw   Tm W D   Treberth Est   Howard Cl   De Cl   Nelson Dr

3   **Lawrence Hill**   Cotswold Way   B4237   Chpstw Rd   Bishpool Wy   Treberth Est   Circle   **Ringland**

Beechcroft Rd   PO   Cotswold Cl   Cotswold Gv   Quantock Dr   Mendip Cl   Chiltern Cl   Dale Road   Abbey Rd   Neston Cl   Bishpool La   B Gv   John Bull   Butterworth Cl   Edward Germ

57   itchfield Av   Whitstone Road   Hatherleigh   Glanwern Way   Glanwern Av   Ringwood   Ringwood Av   St Gabriels RC J&I School   Ringland   sterndale   Tippett

Beechdale Rd   Glanmor Rd   Glanmor Pk Av   Farmwood Close   Ringwood Hl   Ringwood Hl   Dents   Dents Cl   Farnaby   Broadwood

Beechwood Road   Penylan Road   Beechwood Crs   Gibbs   Walden Gra Cl   Lawrence Hill Av   Clanwern Rd   **Alway**   **Bishpool**   R Pl   Ringland Primary School   Tallis Cl   Farm

4   Surgery   C Rd   CW Rd   East Grove Road   Aberthaw Cl   Sims Sq   Elgar Clr   Elgar Cl   Council Building   Dunstable Road   Broadwood

Mansel St   Linden Rd   Hawthorne Av   Aberthaw Circle   Vaughan   Walford   Davies Dr   Elgar Cl   Dowland   Ringland Circle   Hendre   Arne Cl   Novello Wk   RINGLAND   Hartridge High School

Kenilworth Rd   Somerton Junior & Infant School   Delius Cl   Byrde   Elgar Av   Ladyhill Rd   Stanford   John Fields Wk   RINGLAND WAY   Ysgol Gymraeg Casneway

Warwick   PO   Ashley   Acacia Av   Parry Dr   Wilams Drive   Alway Crs   Ireland   Penkin Hill   Aberthaw Cl   Sullivan   Hartridge Farm Road

Conway   Laburnum Av   Aberthaw Dr   Alway Primary School   Parry Dr   Henry W d   Surgery   Penkin Hill   Cir   Malcolm Sargent Cl

5   Sycamore Av   Lime Crs   **Somerton**   Road   The Redlands   Ladyhill Rd   Police Station   Quilter Cl   RINGLAND WAY

Somerton Road   Libeneth Rd   NP19   Lisworry Rd   Arthur Bliss Road   Balfe Rd   Broadmead Park

Hawksworth Rd   Camperdown   Royston Crs   Thompson Avenue   Lisworry Park Dr

Ifton Pl   Barthropp Street   Lloyd Street   Downing St   Somerton Rd   Frobisher Rd   Churchward Dr   Blake Rd   **A**   Brookfield   Escholl   Lisworry St   Parfitt   Greenmead   Road   **B**   Moorland Av   Moorland Park   **78**   Broadmead Park   **C**   35   **D**

PO   Camperdown   Fernside   Tree Ln   Greenmead Pk   Ongmoreat Pk   Broadmead Park   SPYTTY ROAD

grid square represents 500 metres   isworry   Eastmoor R

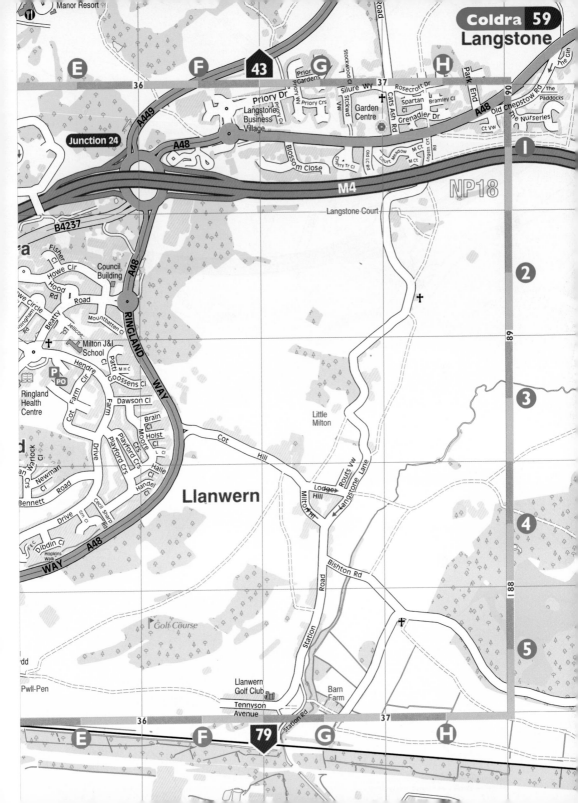

E F **43** G H

Manor Resort

The Gin

Prior Gardens

Priory Dr

Stockwood Cl

Silure Wy 37

Rosecroft Dr

Park End

The Paddocks

Priory W

Priory Crs

Langstone Business Village

Stckwd Vw

Spartan

Cats Ash Rd

Grenadier Dr

Bramley Cl

Old Chepstow Rd

The Nurseries

Garden Centre

Ct VW

A449

Junction 24

A48

A48

A90

I

Blossom Close

Old LC Rd

Cherry Tr Cl

court meadow

M Cl

M Cl

Lngstn Ct Rd

M4

NP18

Langstone Court

B4237

2

89

Fisher Cl

Howe Clr

Hood Rd

Council Building

Road

Mountbatten Cl

RINGLAND

A48

†

3

Beatty

Jellicoe

Milton J&I School

Hendre

Patti

MHC

Goossens Cl

Little Milton

Cot Farm Cir

Dawson Cl

Farm

Brain Cl

WAY

Routs Vw

Langstone Lane

P

PO

Ringland Health Centre

Drive

Playford Crs

Playford Crs

Moore Cl

Holst Cl

Cot Hill

Halle

Cecil Sharp Rd

Handel Cl

Warlock Cl

Newman Cl

Bennett

Road

Llanwern

Lodge Hill

Milton Hill

4

Dibdin Cl

Hopkins Walk

A48

WAY

Bishton Rd

Station Road

†

5

88

Golf Course

Pwll-Pen

Llanwern Golf Club

Tennyson Avenue

Barn Farm

Station Rd

E F **79** G H

36 37

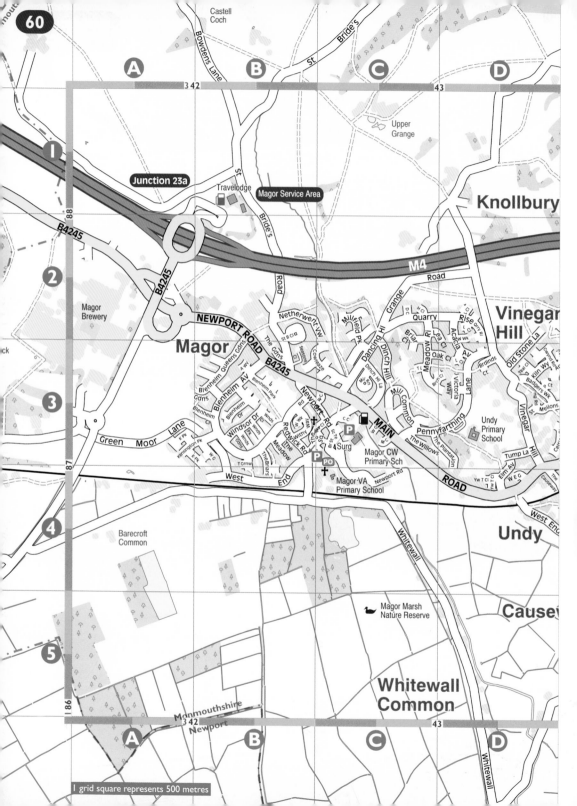

A   3 42   B   C   43   D

Castell Coch

Bowdens Lane

St Bride's

Upper Grange

1

Junction 23a

88

B4245

Travelodge

Magor Service Area

Knollbury

M4

2

Magor Brewery

B4245

NEWPORT ROAD

Netherwent Vw

St Bride's Road

The Gdns

Millfield Pk

Dancing Hl

Grange Road

Quarry

Rise

Vinegar Hill

Magor

B4245

87

Blenheim Av

Queens Gdns

Blenheim Park

Blenheim Dr

Blenheim Cl

Windsor Dr

Newport Rd

The Gdns

Cowbeese

Dinch Hl La

Dinch Hill

Mill Common

Oak Cl

Meadow Rd

Acacia Av

Victoria Way

Briar

Old Stone La

Badgers Wk

Mellons

3

Green Moor Lane

Kensington Pk

The Meadow

Redwick Rd

The Briars

Surg

P

P PO

Magor CW Primary Sch

Pennyfarthing

The Willows

The Plantation

Undy Primary School

Vinegar Hill

Elm Av

Tump La

West End

Magor VA Primary School

Newport Rd

MAIN ROAD

4

Barecroft Common

Whitewall

Undy

West End

86

Magor Marsh Nature Reserve

Causey

5

Monmouthshire
3 42
Newport

Whitewall Common

Whitewall

A   B   C   43   D

I grid square represents 500 metres

Thicket Wood

E   F   G   H   **I**

44   45

Bencroft Lane

Minnetts Lane

Windmill La

Minnett's

Lane

Minnett'

M48

CALDICOT ROAD

88

Junction 23

The Elms

Rockfield Vw
Rockfield Wy
Rockfield

Grove

B4245

M4

Llanfihangel Rogiet

Siskin
Merlin Cl
Widok Cl
Buzzard
Crescent
Station

Barn Owl Rd
Martin Cl

2

Church

†

Rockdale
The Paddocks
Pembroke
Ct

Manor Cha

ELMS HILL

St Ames Crescent
St Joseph's Cl
Arlington
Cl

Church Road

Great House

3

Toll

87

B4245
Tudor Ct

Rectory Gdns

Church Rise

Church Lane

Church Road

†

Church

The Ramp
Whitehall Gdns

4

The Causeway

way

5

86

44   45

E   F   G   H

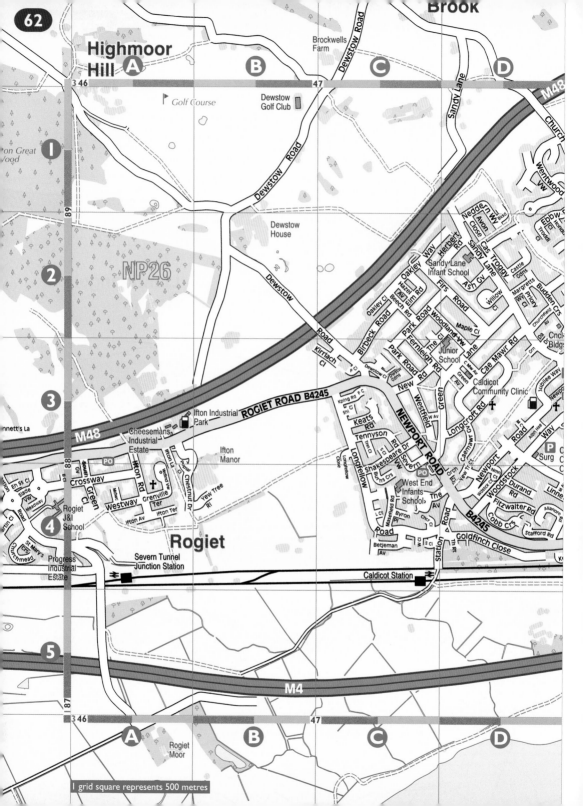

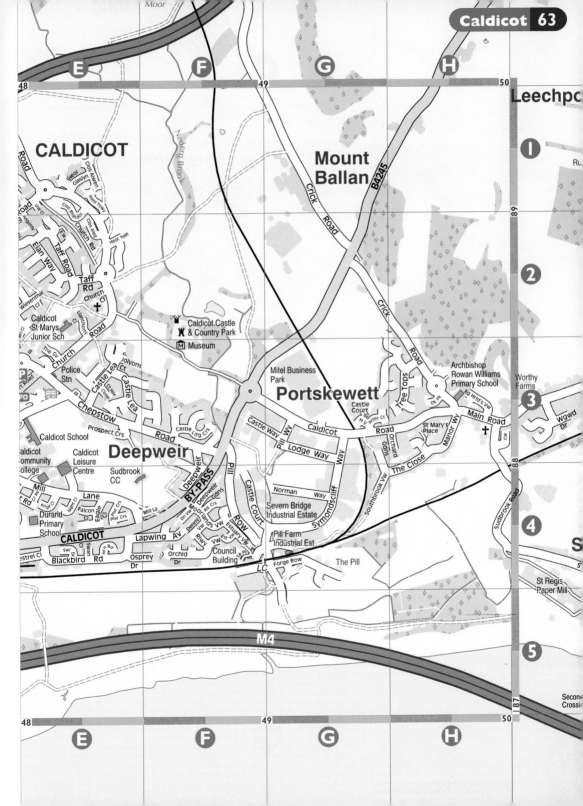

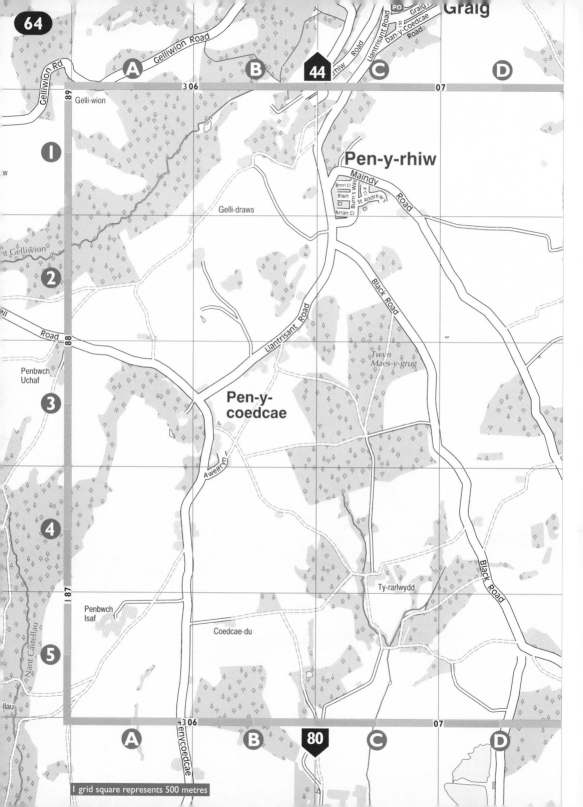

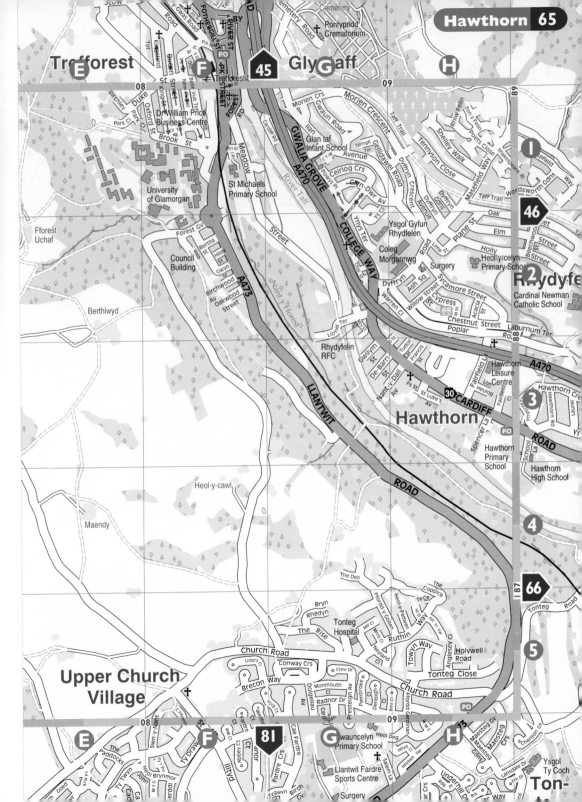

Trefforest

Dr William Price Business Centre

University of Glamorgan

St Michaels Primary School

Fforest Uchaf

Berthlwyd

Council Building

Maendy

Heol-y-cawl

Upper Church Village

The Paddocks

Pontypridd Crematorium

Glyn-Taff

Trefforest

Morien Crs
Cwaun Road
Morien Crescent
Taff Trail
Glan taf Infant School
Caradoc Avenue
Cellidawe Road
Ceiriog Crs
Gwyn Dwr
Dyffryn Crescent
Dyffryn Gdns
Dyffryn Avenue

Shelley Walk
Poets Close
Shakespeare Rd
Rhiw Felin
Ty'n y Felin
Temyson Close
Tennyson Close
Oak
Plane St
Elm
Masefield Way
Taff Trail
Wordsworth Gdns

Ysgol Gyfun Rhydfelen
Coleg Morgannwg
Surgery
Heol-y-celyn Primary School
Holly
Beechwood
St

Rhydyfelin

Cardinal Newman Catholic School

Rhydyfelin RFC

Ash Sq
Willow Street
Warren Cl
Sycamore Street
Cypress
Acacia
Chestnut Street
Poplar
Laburnum Ter

Gwilym St
De Barri St
Nant-y-Dall
St Luke's
Tudor
Francis
Fairfield La
Hawthorn Leisure Centre

Hawthorn

Spencer La
CARDIFF
ROAD
Hawthorn Primary School
Hawthorn High School

LLANTWIT ROAD

Tonteg

Tonteg Hospital
Bryn Rhedyn
The Rise
The Dell
Ruthin
The Coppice
Church Road

Church Road

Gwauncelyn Primary School
Llantwit Fardre Sports Centre
Surgery

Ysgol Ty Coch

Ton-

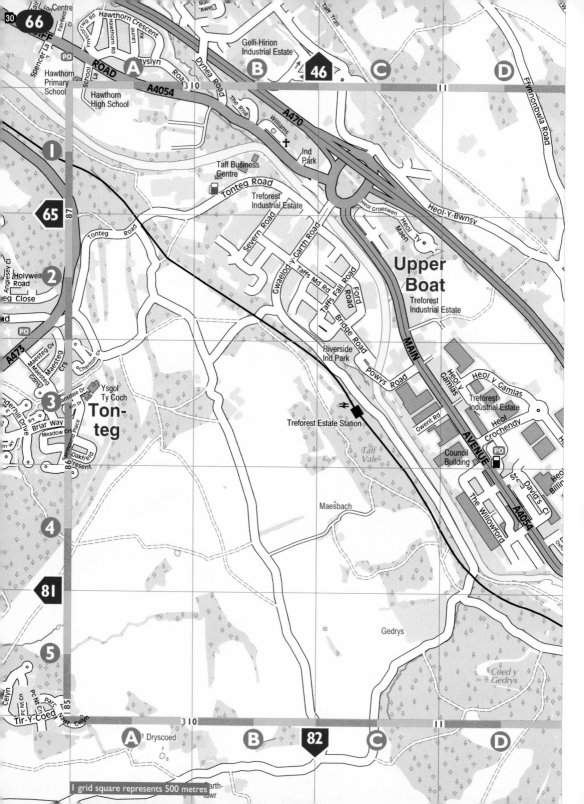

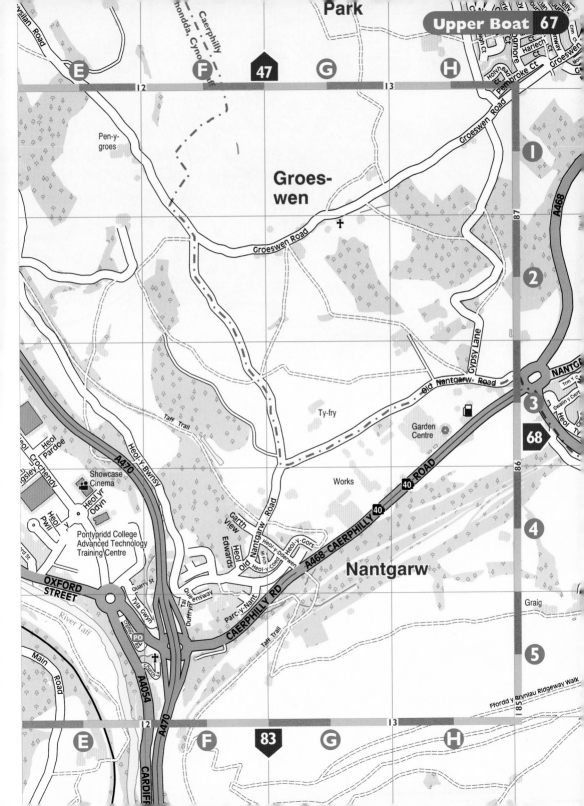

E F 47 G H

Park

I

A468

Groes-
wen

2

Pen-y-
groes

Groeswen Road

Groeswen Road

87

Gypsy Lane

NANTG

Old Nantgarw Road

3

Heol Ty

68

Ty-fry

Garden
Centre

Taff Trail

Heol Pardoe

Showcase
Cinema

Heol-y-bwnsy

A470

Works

40

86

ROAD

40

4

Heol Crochendy

Heol yr Odyn

Heol Y Pwll

Pontypridd College
Advanced Technology
Training Centre

Garth
View

Heol
Edwards

Old Nantgarw Road

Hi Fch

Heol-y-Gors

Heol-y-odenwen

Heol-y-coed

A468 CAERPHILLY

Nantgarw

Graig

Quarry st

Queensway

Tal Duffryn

Parc-y-Nant

CAERPHILLY RD

5

185

OXFORD
STREET

River Taff

Tyla cwrt

PO

Church

Main Road

A4054

A470

Taff Trail

Ffordd y Bryniau Ridgeway Walk

E F 83 G H

CARDIFF

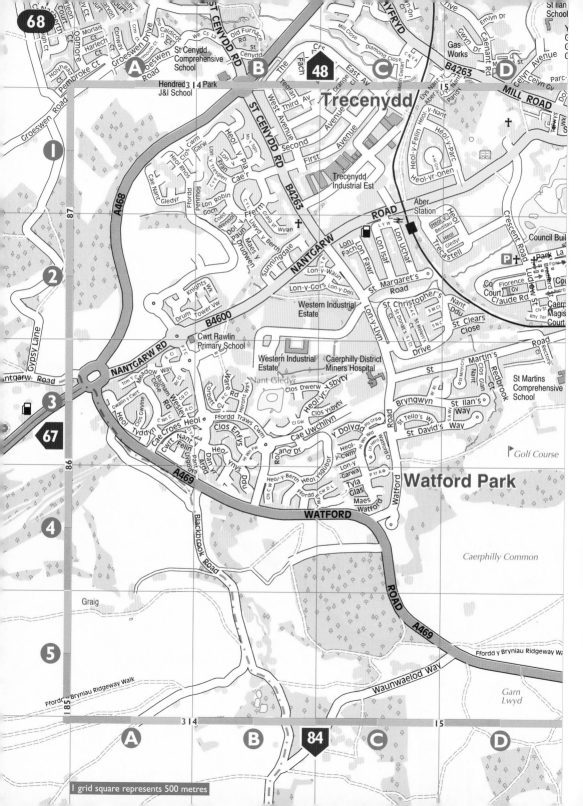

ST CENYDD RD

48

Trecenydd

B4263

MILL ROAD

Gas Works

St Cenydd Comprehensive School

Hendred 3|4 Park J&I School

West Avenue

St Martin's Comprehensive School

Council Buildings

Aber Station

NANTGARW

ROAD

B4263

ST CENYDD RD

A468

Groeswen Road

Groesy Road

Gypsy Lane

Nantgarw Road

67

NANTGARW RD

Cwrt Rawlin Primary School

B4600

Western Industrial Estate

Western Industrial Estate

Caerphilly District Miners Hospital

Nant Gledyr

Golf Course

Watford Park

A469

Blackbrook Road

Graig

WATFORD

WATFORD

ROAD

A469

Caerphilly Common

Garn Lwyd

84

Fforddy Bryniau Ridgeway Walk

Fforddy Bryniau Ridgeway Wa

Waunwaelod Way

185

3|4

15

A

B

C

D

I grid square represents 500 metres

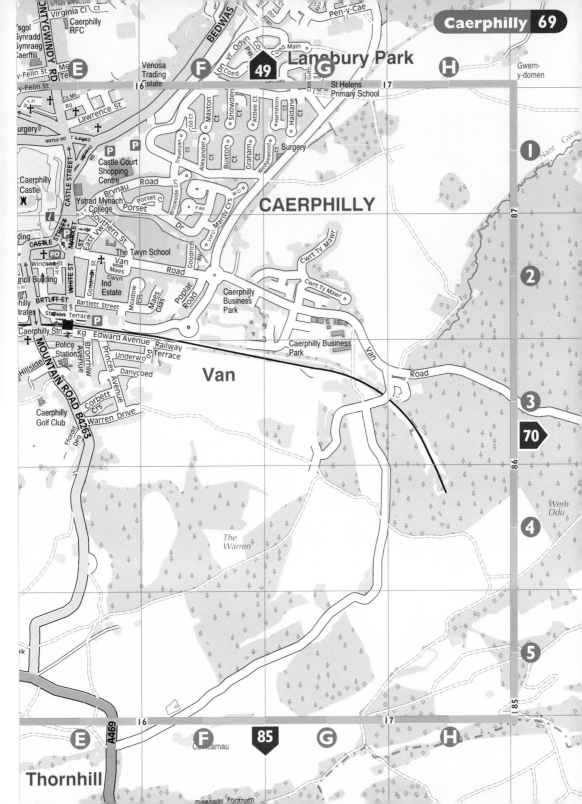

Lansbury Park

CAERPHILLY

Van

Thornhill

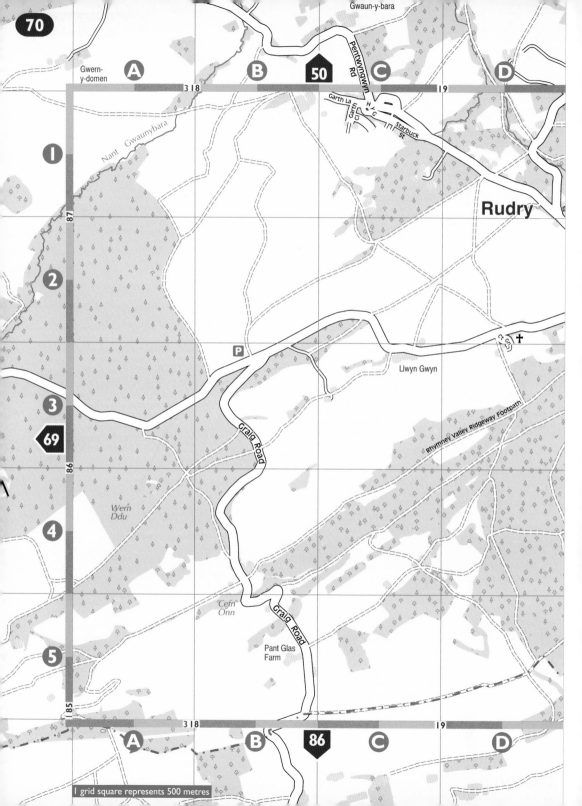

70

Gwaun-y-bara

A   **B**   **50**   **C**   **D**

Gwern-
y-domen

Pentwyngwyn Rd

Garth La

Garth Cl

H Y C

Starbuck St

Rudry

318   19

87

Nant Gwaunybara

1

2

P

Llwyn Gwyn

†

Rhymney Valley Ridgeway Footpath

3

69

Craig Road

86

4

*Wern
Ddu*

5

*Cefn
Onn*

Craig Road

Pant Glas
Farm

85

318   19

A   **B**   **86**   **C**   **D**

1 grid square represents 500 metres

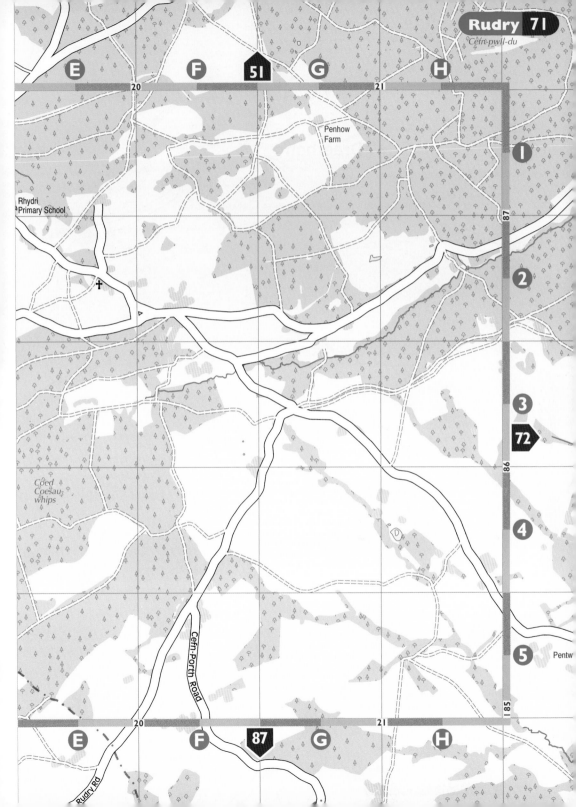

E F **51** G H

20 21

Penhow
Farm

Rhydri
Primary School

I

87

2

Coed
Coesau
whips

3

72

86

4

Pentw

5

Côed
Coesau
whips

Cefn-Porth Road

185

20 21

E F **87** G H

Rudry Rd

72

A

B

52

C

D

3 22

23

Melin Dwr

Draethen

Rhymni River

1

87

Coed Craig
Ruperra

2

Ruperra
Castle

3

71

86

Ruperra
Home Farm

4

5

Pentwyn

1 85

3 22

23

A

B

88

C

D

Cefn-
llwyd

1 grid square represents 500 metres

A468

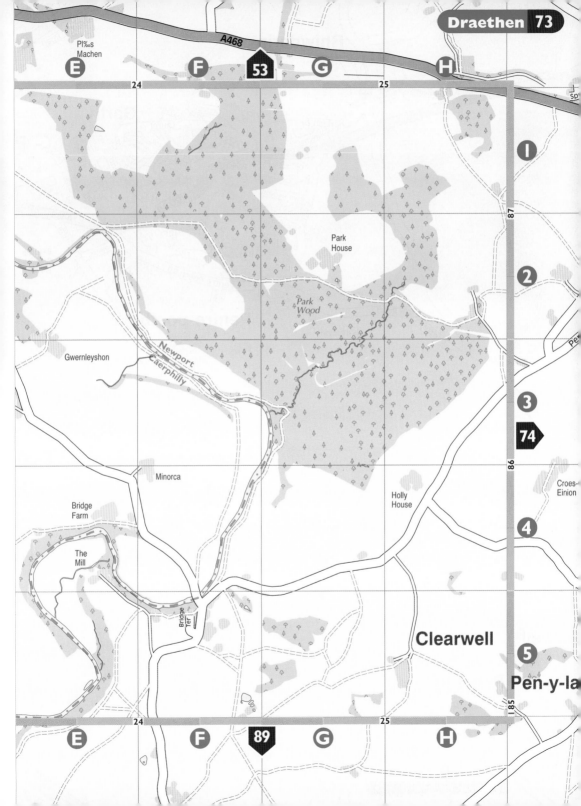

A468

Pl‰s
Machen

E

F

53

G

H

24

25

I

87

Park
House

2

Park
Wood

Newport
Caerphilly

Gwernleyshon

Pew

3

74

86

Minorca

Holly
House

Croes-
Einion

Bridge
Farm

4

The
Mill

Clearwell

5

Bridge
Ter

Pen-y-la

185

E

F

89

G

H

24

25

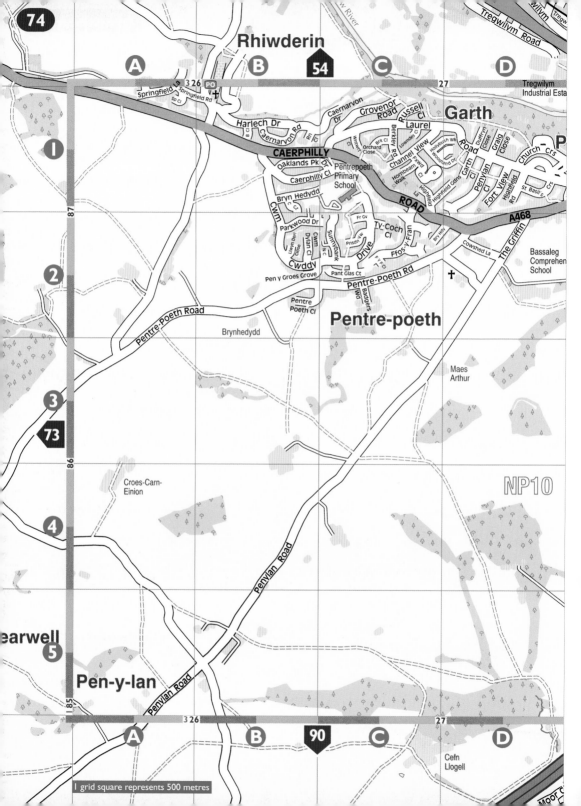

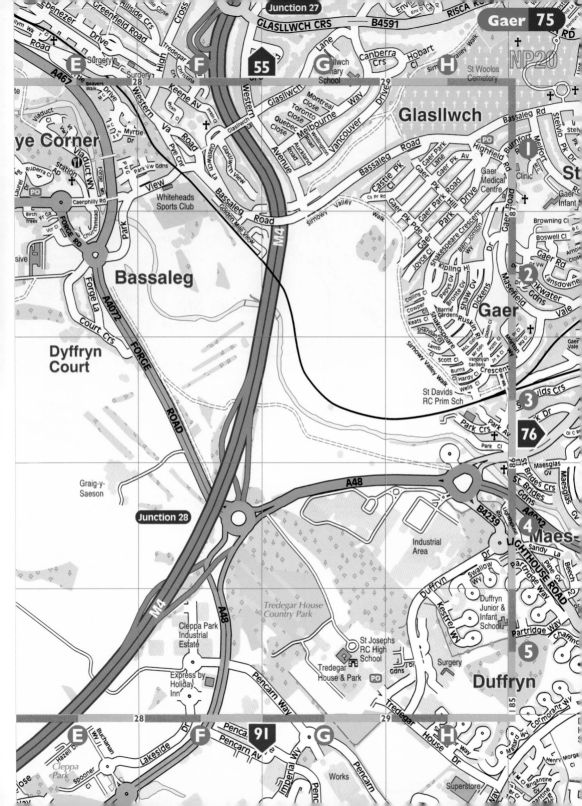

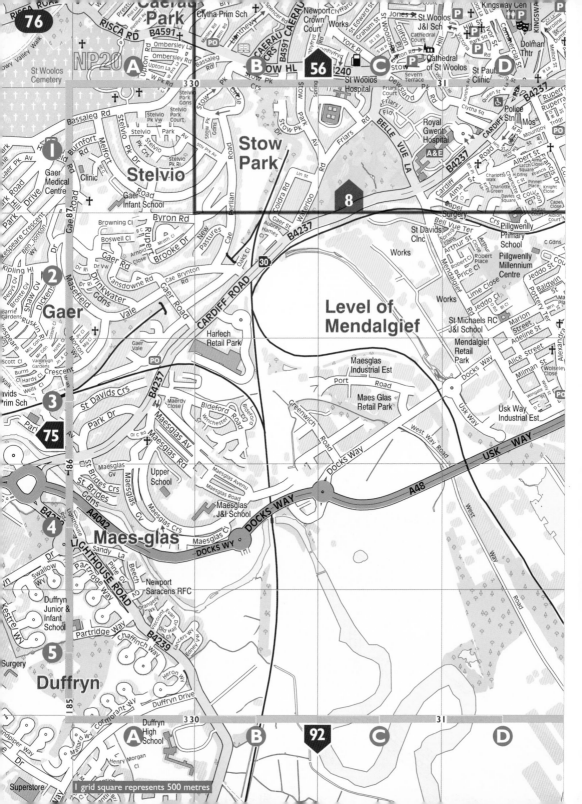

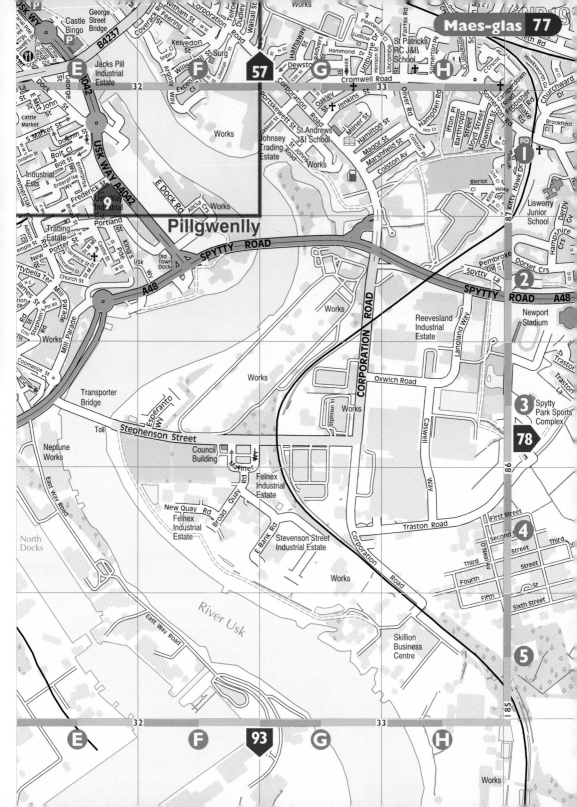

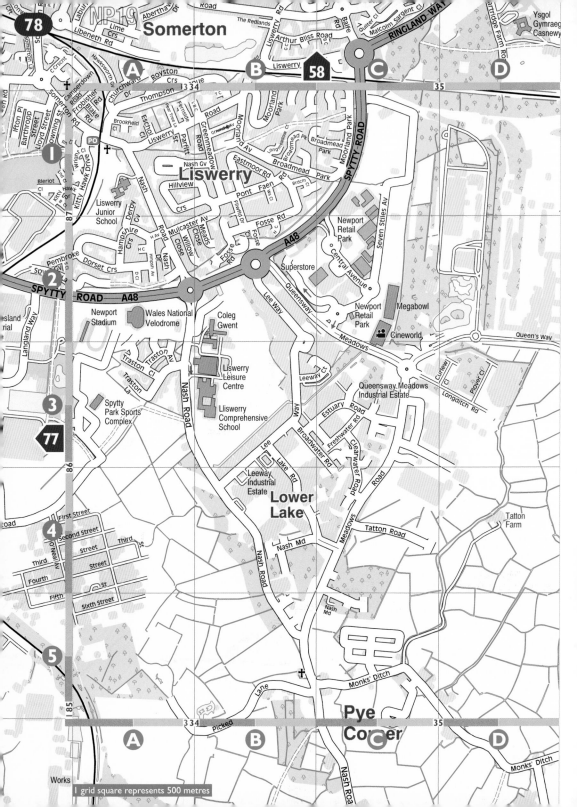

E F 59 G H

Pwll-Pen

Llanwe
Golf
Ten
Avenue

Station Rd

arn
arm

I

87

2

Spencer
Steelworks

Queen's Way

3

86

4

Broad Street

Common

Moor
Barn

Monks' Ditch

5

185

E F G H

Chapel Road

**Broadstreet
Common**

Whitson
Court

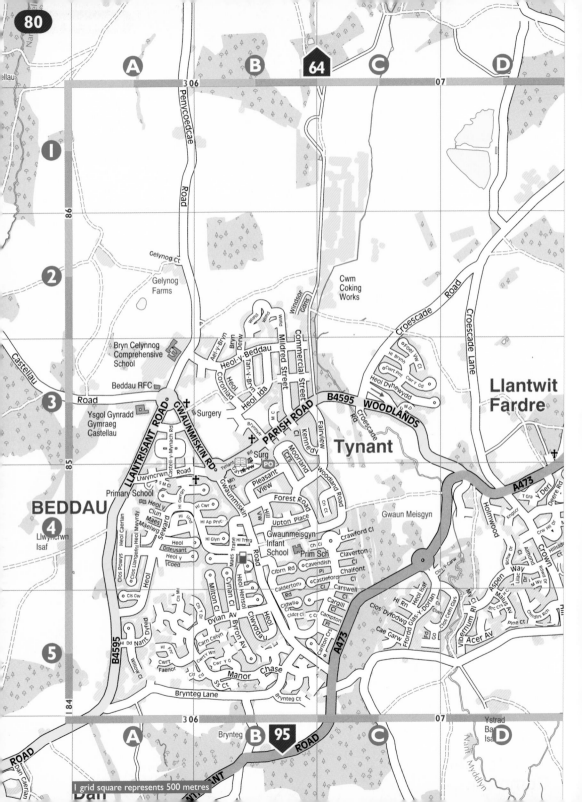

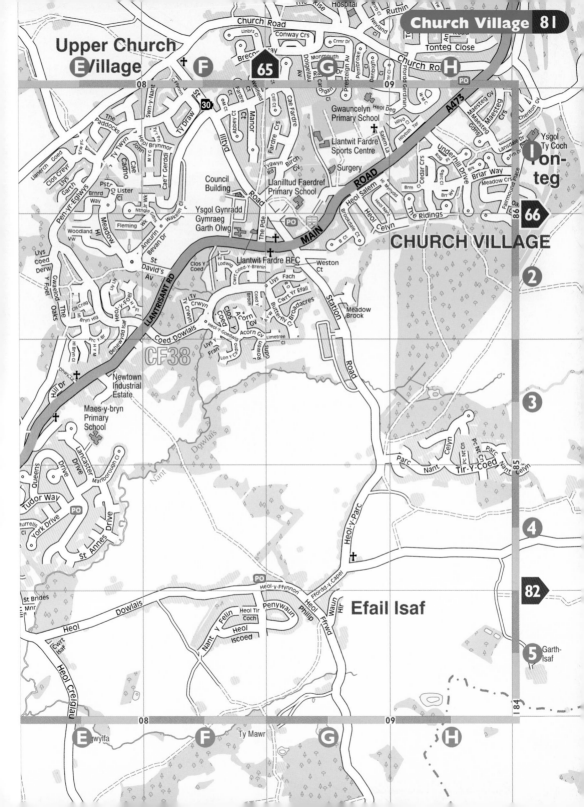

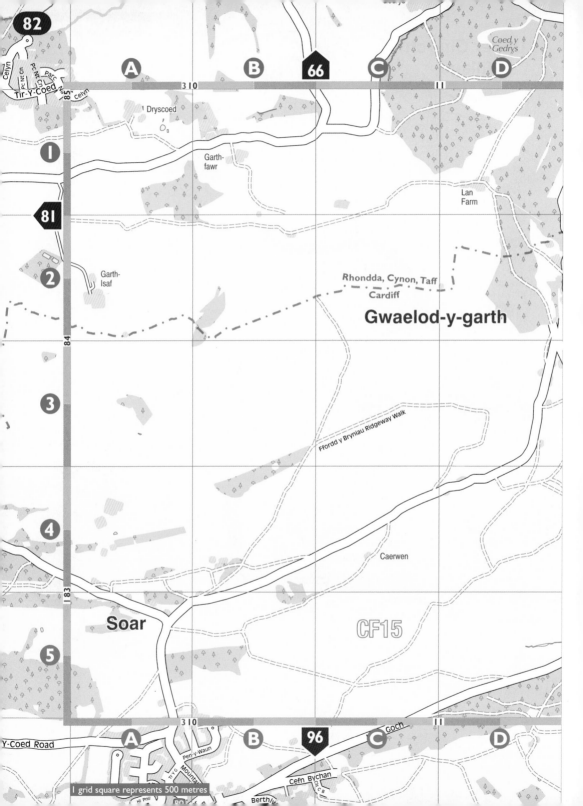

82

Tir-Y-Coed

A 310 **B** **66** **C** 11 **D**

Dryscoed

1

Garth-fawr

Lan Farm

81

2

Garth-Isaf

Rhondda, Cynon, Taff
Cardiff

Gwaelod-y-garth

3

Ffordd y Bryniau Ridgeway Walk

4

Caerwen

CF15

Soar

5

A 310 **B** **96** **C** Goch 11 **D**

Y-Coed Road

Pen-y-Waun

Cefn Bychan

Berthl

Coed y Gedrys

1 grid square represents 500 metres

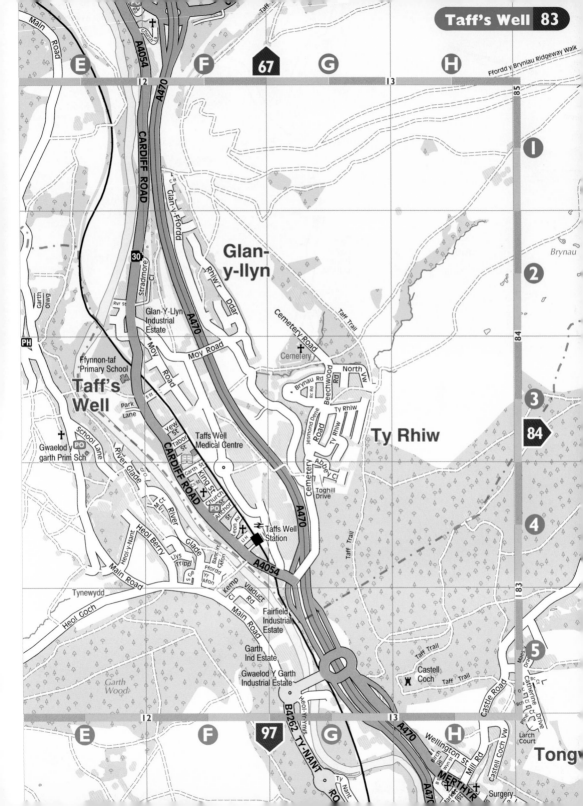

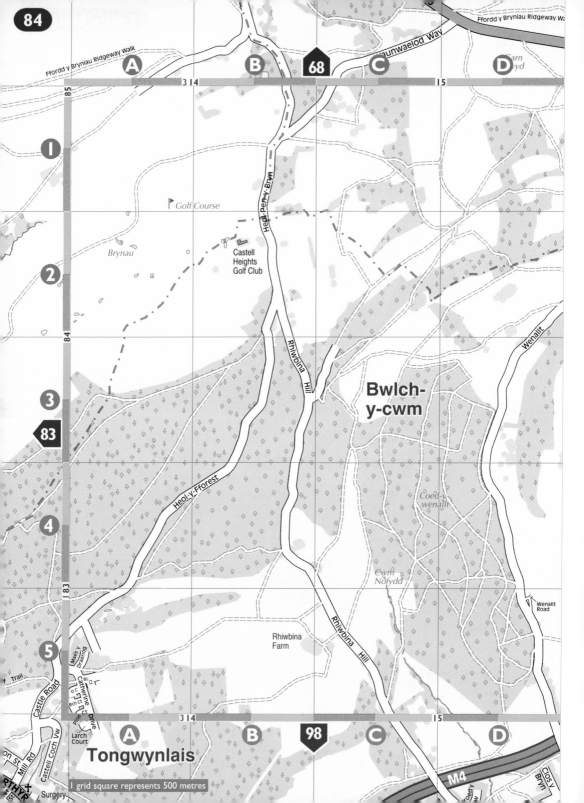

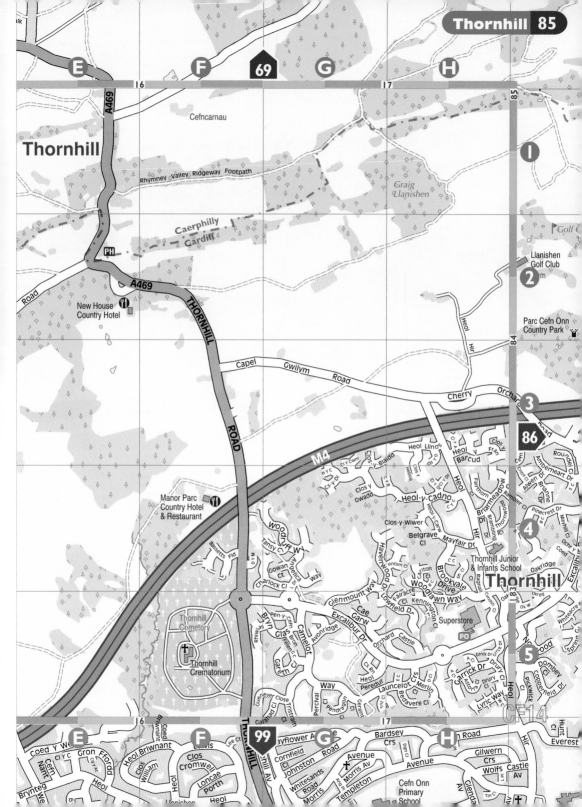

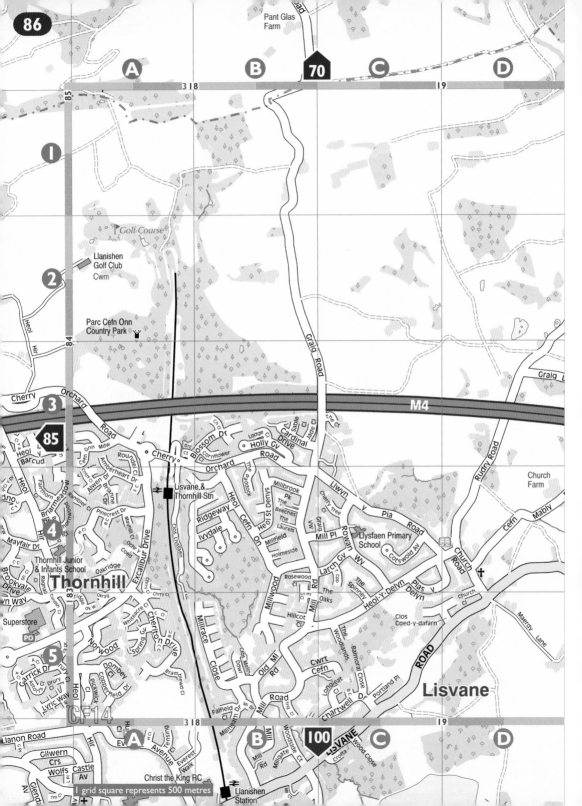

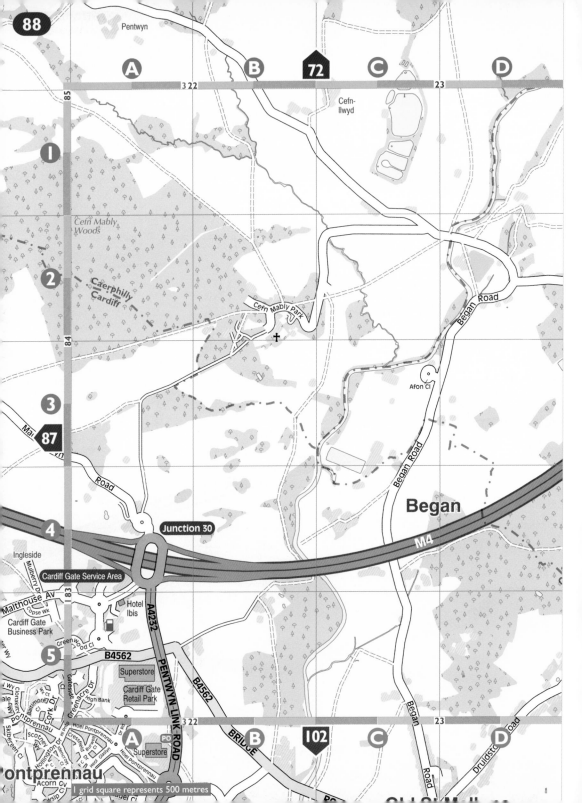

A 3 22 **B** 72 **C** 23 **D**

Pentwyn

Cefn-llwyd

1

Cefn Mably Woods

2

Caerphilly
Cardiff

Cefn Mably Park

Began Road

84

†

Afon Cl

3

87

Mai

Road

Began Road

Began

4 Junction 30

Ingleside

Cardiff Gate Service Area

M4

Mulberry Dr
Malthouse Av
Copse Wk

Hotel Ibis

Cardiff Gate Business Park

A4232

5 B4562

Greenwood Cl

Superstore

High Bank

Cardiff Gate Retail Park

Gateside Dr

Greenacre Dr

PENTWYN LINK ROAD

B4562

Began Road

Druidstone Road

ontprennau

Mulberry Wy
Clonakilty Wy
Baltimore Way
Cork Dr

Hoel Pontprennau
Hollington Dr
Cressfield Cl
Bucknell Cl
Hoel Glaslyn
Hoel Pontprennau

A 3 22 **B** BRIDGE 102 **C** 23 **D**

Superstore PO

Old St Mellons

Acorn Gv

1 grid square represents 500 metres

8

Skillion
Business
Centre

E

F

77

G

H

32

33

85

Works

I

South
Docks

Works

2

Newport
(Uskmouth)
Sailing Club

River Usk

West

Nash

84

Works

3

Works

Road

West Nash Road

P

Uskmout

4

83

5

E

F

G

H

32

33

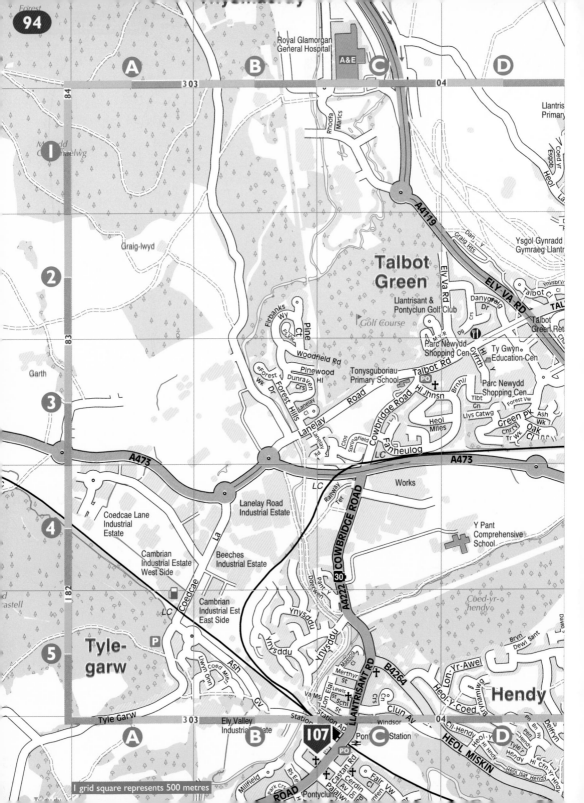

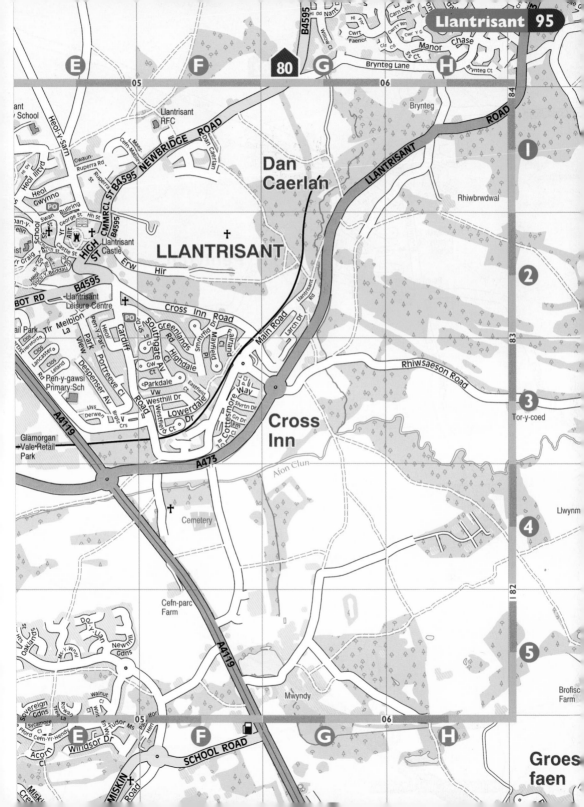

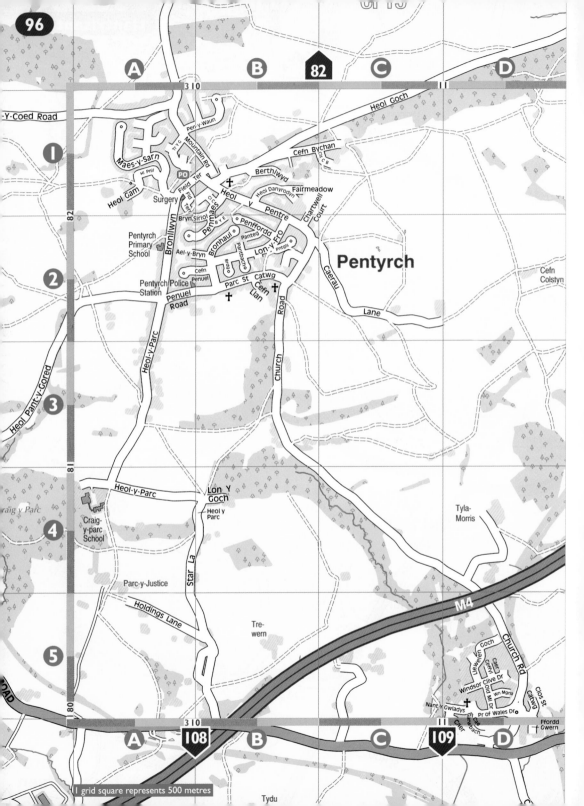

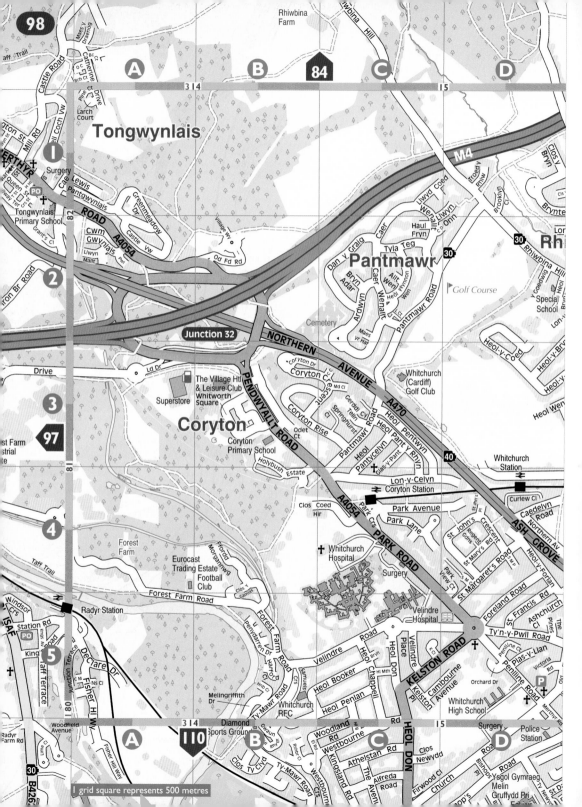

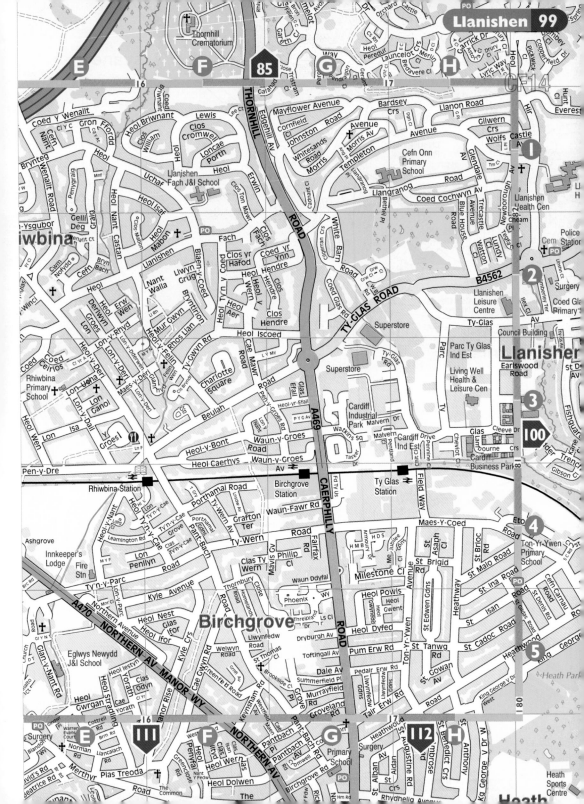

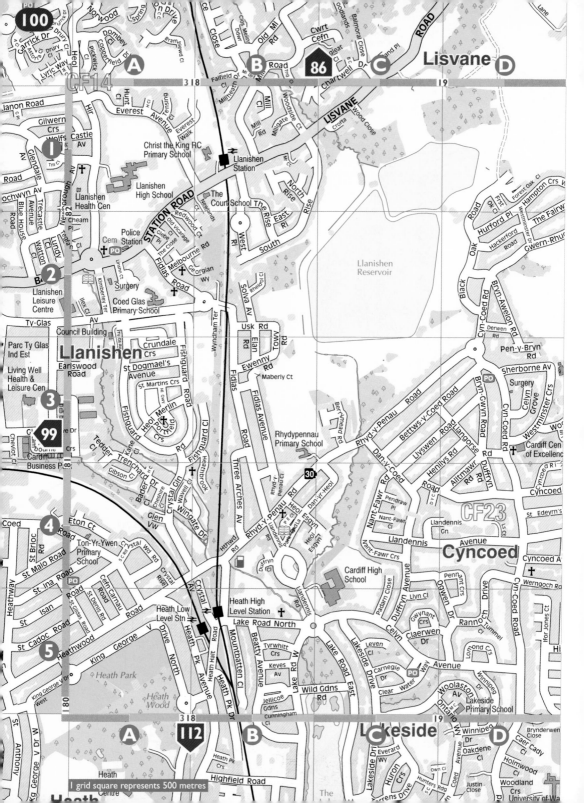

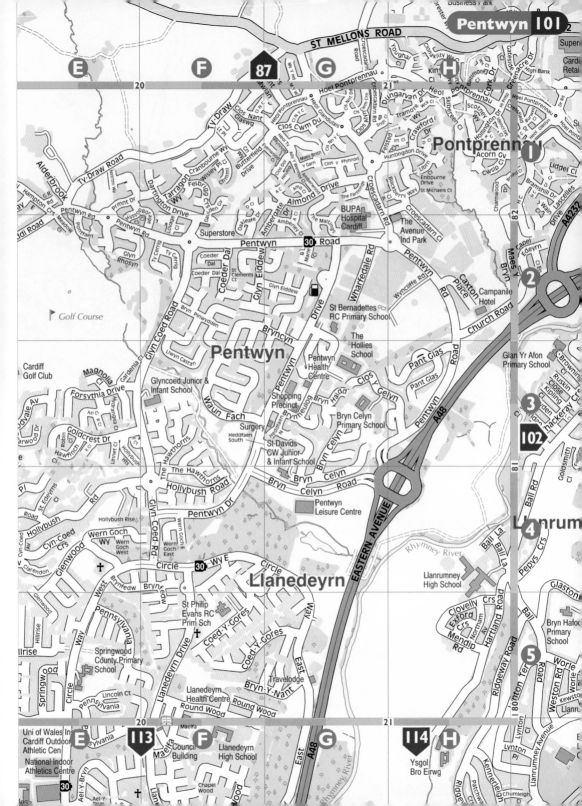

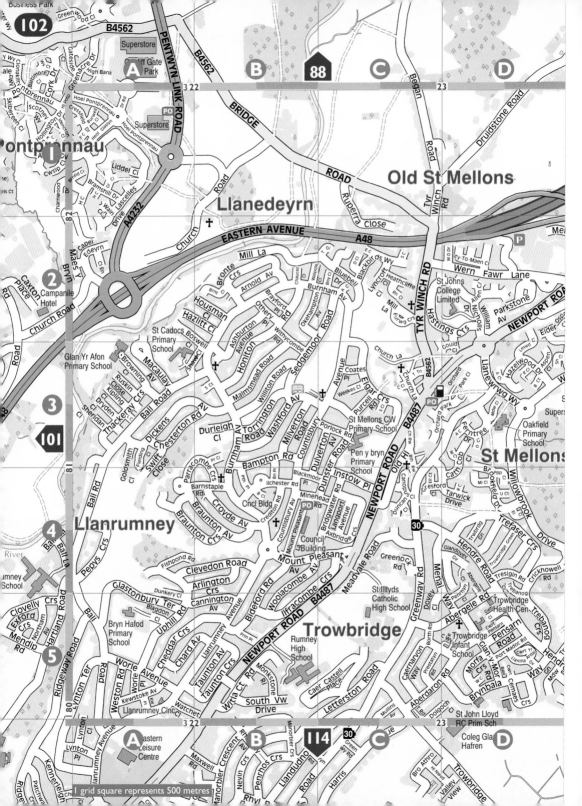

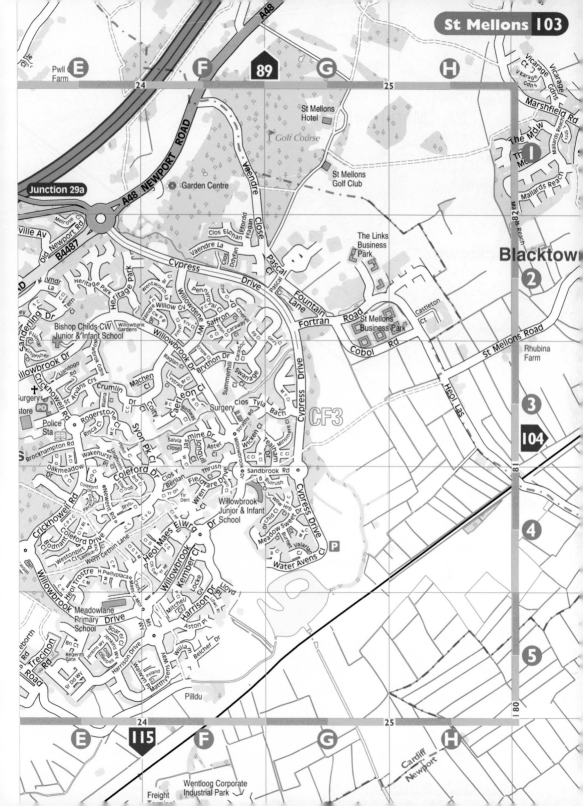

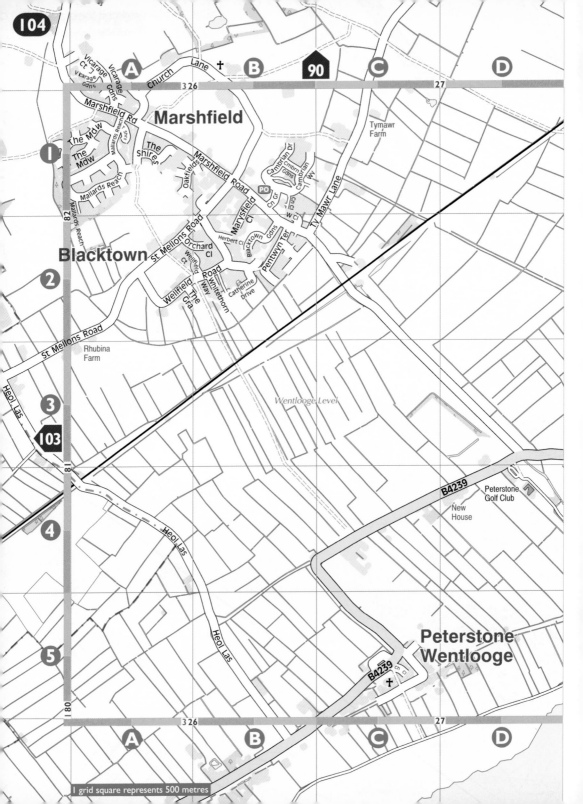

A B 90 C D

1

Marshfield

Tymawr
Farm

Vicarage
Ct
Vicarage
Gdns

Church   Lane
3 26   27

Marshfield Rd

The Mdw

The
Mdw

The
shires

Mallards Reach

Oakfields

Marshfield   Road

Cambrian Dr

Cmbrn
Gdns

PO

Cambrian
Wy

Ty Mawr Lane

Mallards Reach

82

Blacktown

St Mellons Road

Orchard
Cl

Herbert Cl

Blacktown Gdns

Pentwyn Ter

Marysfield
Cl

2

Wellfield
Road

Wellfield Way

Whitethorn

The Gra.

Catherine
Drive

St Mellons Road

Rhubina
Farm

3

103

81

Wentlooge Level

4

Heol Las

B4239

Peterstone
Golf Club

New
House

5

Heol Las

Peterstone
Wentlooge

B4239

Heol Las

180

3 26   27

A B C D

E F **91** G H

28 29

Hawse Lane

Hawse Farm

St Brides Wentlooge

✝

Church Rd

Neville Pk

B4239

I

82

Sealand Reen

2

Hawse Lane

B4239

Outfall Lane

Orchard Farm

3

81

B4239

Ty-côch Farm

4

Golf Course

Peterstone Gout

80

5

28 29

E F G H

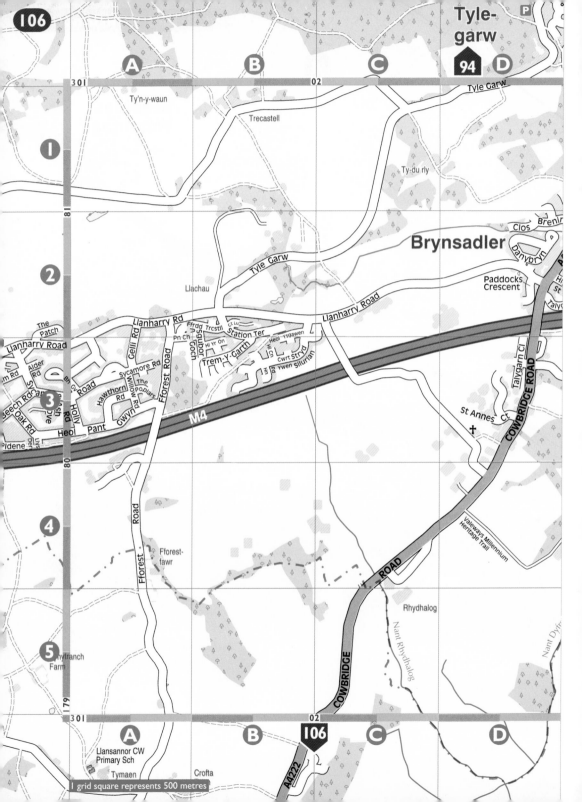

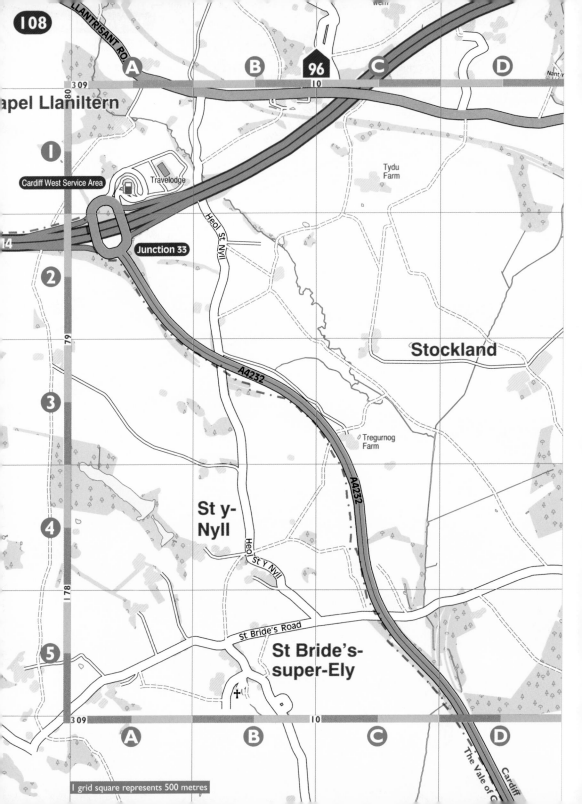

108

LLANTRISANT RO...

A B **96** C D
10

apel Llaniltern

3 09
80

I

Cardiff West Service Area Travelodge

Tydu Farm

14

Junction 33

Heol St Nyll

79

Stockland

2

A4232

3

Tregurnog Farm

St y-
Nyll

A4232

4

Heol St y Nyll

178

St Bride's Road

5

St Bride's-
super-Ely

3 09
A B C D
10

The Vale of...

Cardiff...

I grid square represents 500 metres

Golf Course

Church Rd

Goch

Verwey

Clos St
Catwg

Windsor Clive Dr

Gwladys

Cae'r
Cefn

Pr of Wales Dr

Caer
 Errai

Gwenbach

Fford
Gwern

Rhydlafr
Farm

A4119

LLANTRISANT ROAD

Drover's Way

Green

Stella
Maes Cl

Llantarnam
Dr

Llantarnam dr

Plas-Y-Mynach

Radyr
Farm

Radyr
Farm Rd

Clos Parc Radyr

LLANTRISANT RD

Maes-y-
llech

Crofft-y-Genau Road

Crofft-y-Genau Road

Ashcroft Crs

Lilac Cl

Cherry
Cl

Cedar
Grove

Pentrebane Road

Elderberry Road

Orange

Clover
Gv

Beechley

Maple Road

Lime Gv

Pentrebane
Primary School

Treetops
Cl

Honeysuckle Cl

Drive

Pentrebane

Holy Family
RC Primary
School

Beechley

Beech Rd

Willowdale

Road

Lynar

Yewtr

Firs Avenue

Shamrock
Rd

Briar

Avenue

Rosedale

Tynewydd

Firs

Clos T Bronna

St Fagans Driv

Greenwood Lane

St Fagans Road

Forest

Oaky

Tatem Dr

St Fagans
Road

Chorley
Close

Monkton
Close

St Fagans

St Fagans: National
History Museum

The Old
Post Office
Hotel

Cardiff

Road

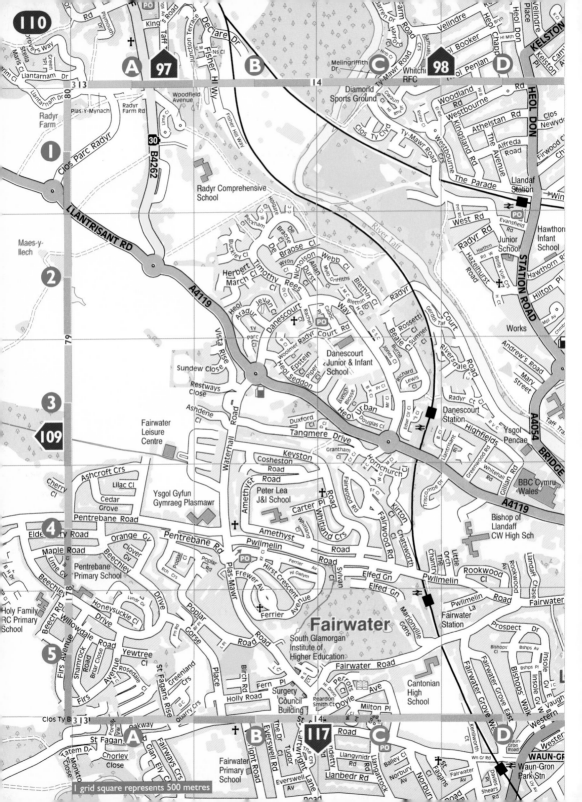

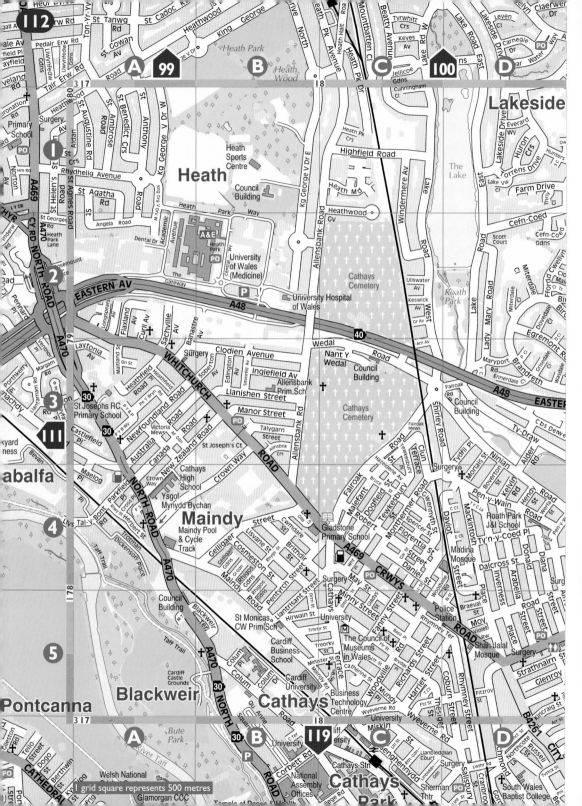

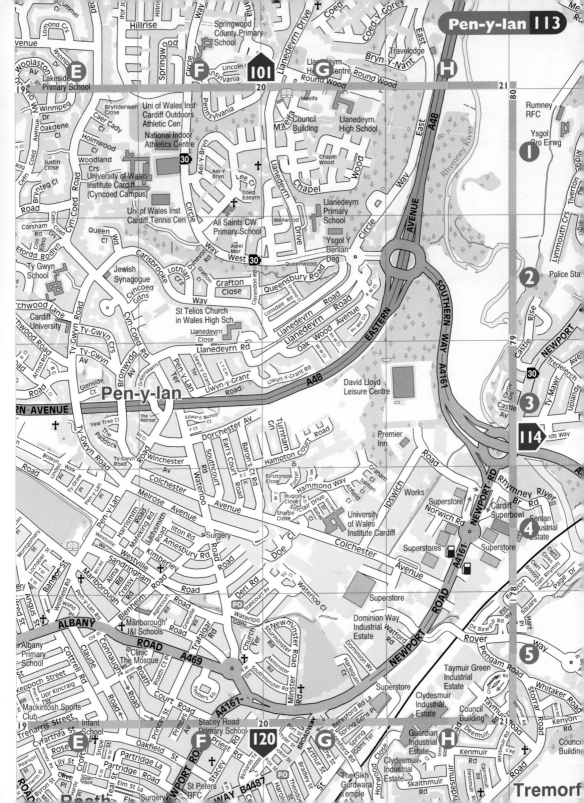

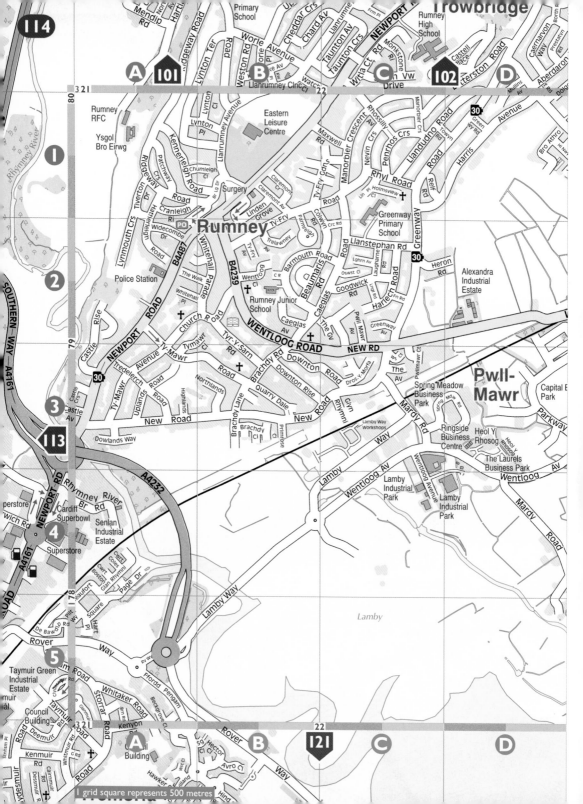

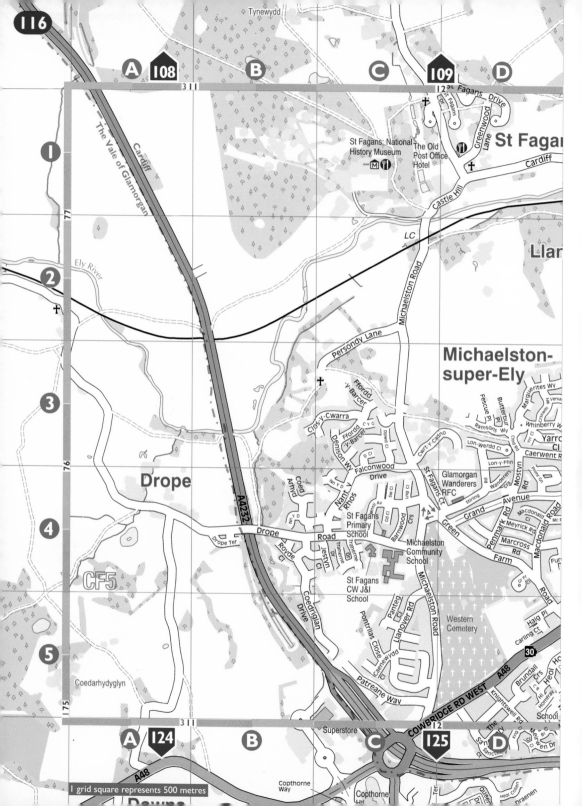

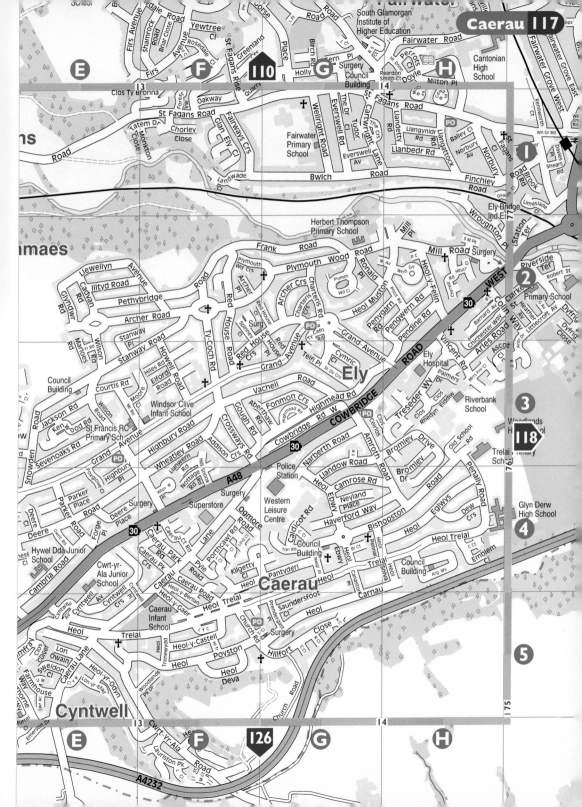

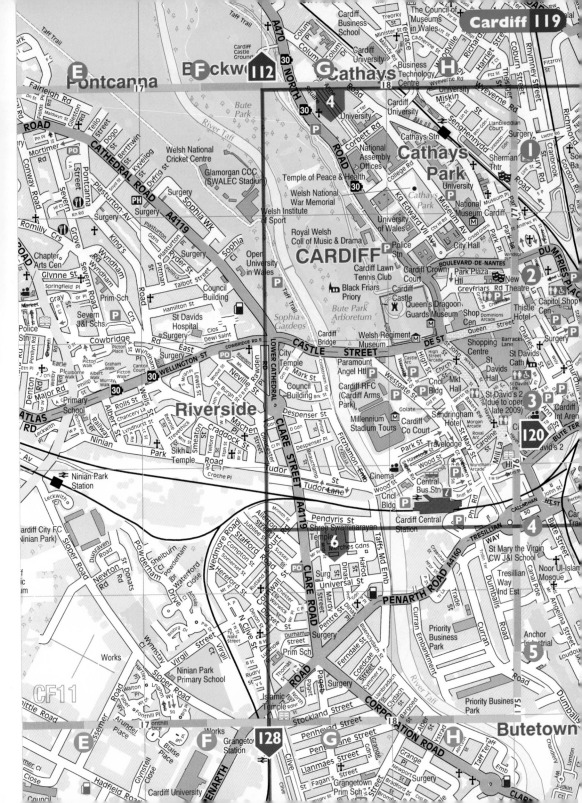

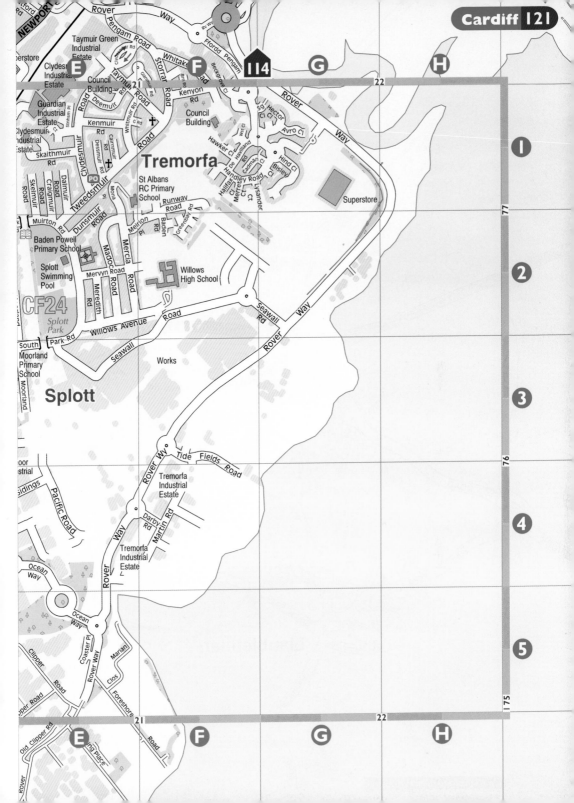

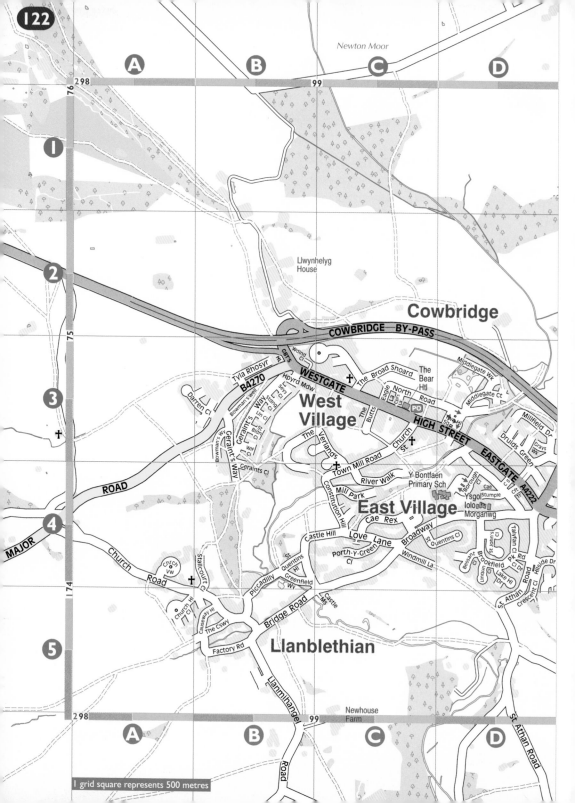

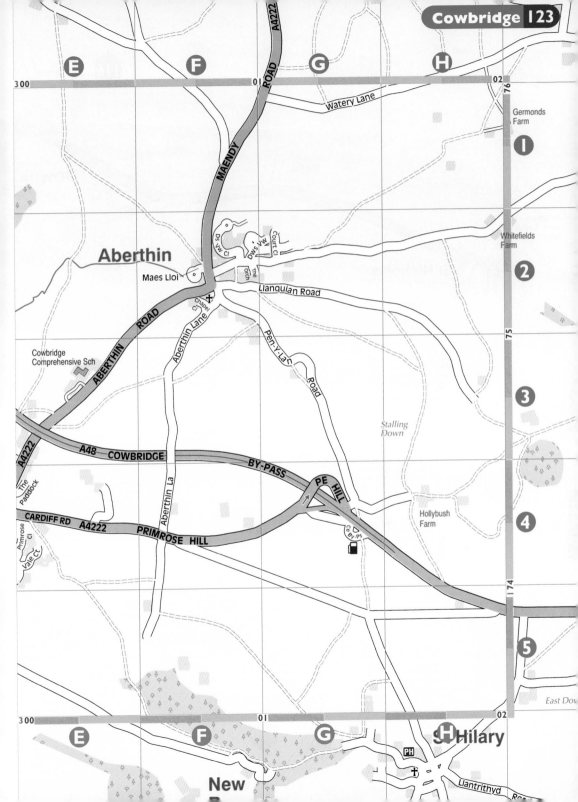

E   F   G   H

300

76

Watery Lane

Germonds Farm

I

MAENDY ROAD

A4222

Whitefields Farm

Court Cl

Dws Vw

Maes Lw Cl

Aberthin

Maes Lloi

The Orch

2

75

Llanquian Road

Chapel Cl

Aberthin Lane

ABERTHIN ROAD

Pen-y-Lan Road

Cowbridge Comprehensive Sch

Stalling Down

3

A4222

A48   COWBRIDGE

BY-PASS

PE HILL

Hollybush Farm

4

The Paddock

Aberthin La

Pe By-ps

174

CARDIFF RD   A4222

PRIMROSE HILL

Primrose Vale Ct

5

E   F   G   H

300

01   02

S HILARY

PH

New

East Dow

Llantrithyd Rd

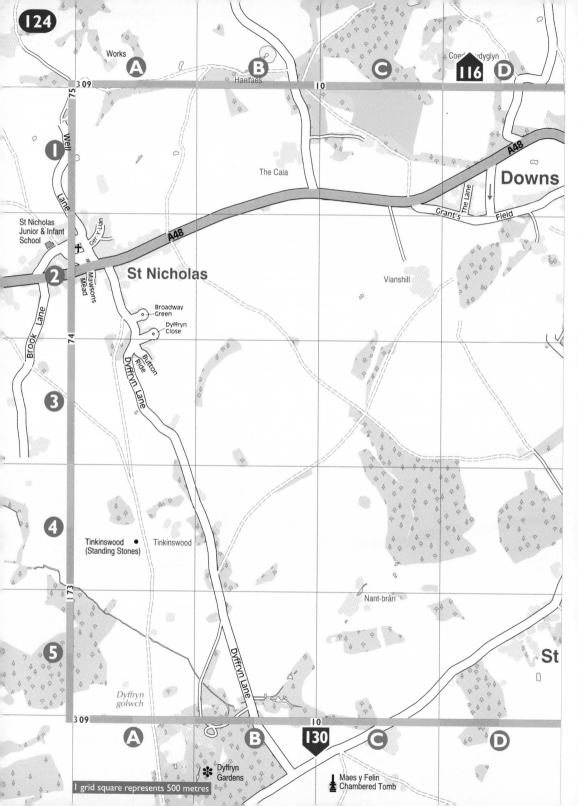

124

Works

A

B

Haelfaes

C

Coed-y-cyrdyglyn

116 **D**

Well

1

The Caia

A48

Downs

St Nicholas
Junior & Infant
School

Cae-y-lan

Grant's

The Lane

Field

Mawsons Mead

2

St Nicholas

A48

Vianshill

Brook Lane

Broadway
Green

Dyffryn
Close

Button Ride

74

Dyffryn Lane

3

4

Tinkinswood
(Standing Stones)

Tinkinswood

73

5

Nant-brân

Dyffryn Lane

St

Dyffryn
golwch

3 09

A

B

130 **C**

D

Dyffryn
Gardens

Maes y Felin
Chambered Tomb

I grid square represents 500 metres

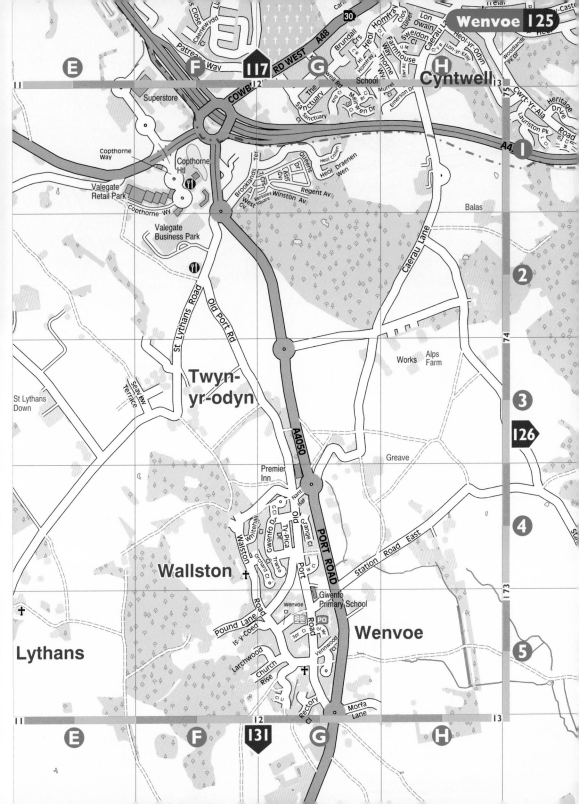

126

yntwell

Trelai

Heol-y-Castell

Poyston
Heol

Heol-Yr-Odyn

Lon-yr-Efail

Heol Deva

Woodlands PK DF

Church Road

Surgery

Hillfort

A

B

117

14

C

D

Heritage Drive

Cwrt-Yr-Ala

Lauriston Pk

Road

I

A4232

Balas

Brynwell

2

74

ips arm

3

73

125

4

Station Road East

Cwrt-yr-ala

Cwrt-Yr-Ala

Rd

5

Michaelston-l

Wrinstone Farm

313

A

B

14

132

C

D

Beauville Farm

Beauville

1 grid square represents 500 metres

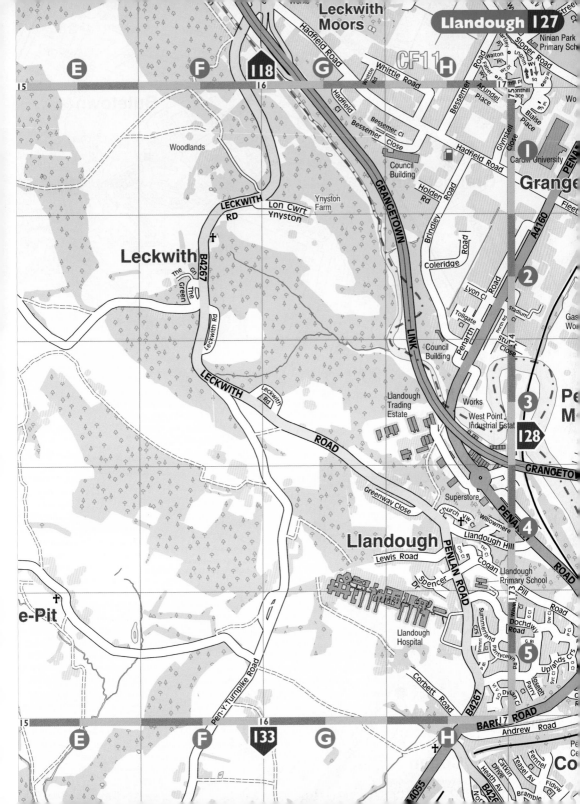

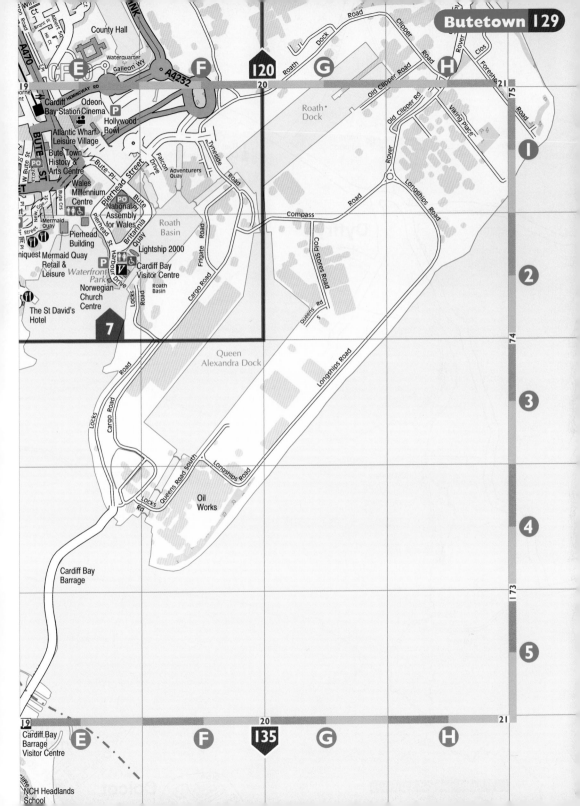

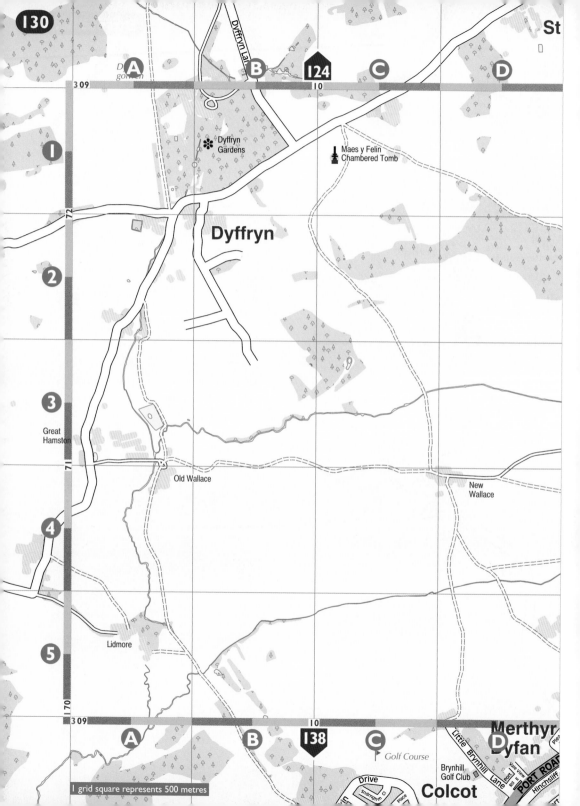

St

A D gorsen

B

124

C

D

3 09   10

1

72

Dyffryn Gardens

Maes y Felin Chambered Tomb

Dyffryn

2

3

Great Hamston

71

Old Wallace

New Wallace

4

5

170

3 09   10

A

B

138

C

Golf Course

Merthyr Dyfan

Little Brynhill Lane

PORT ROAD

Hinchsliff

Brynhill Golf Club

Drive

Colcot

Lidmore

I grid square represents 500 metres

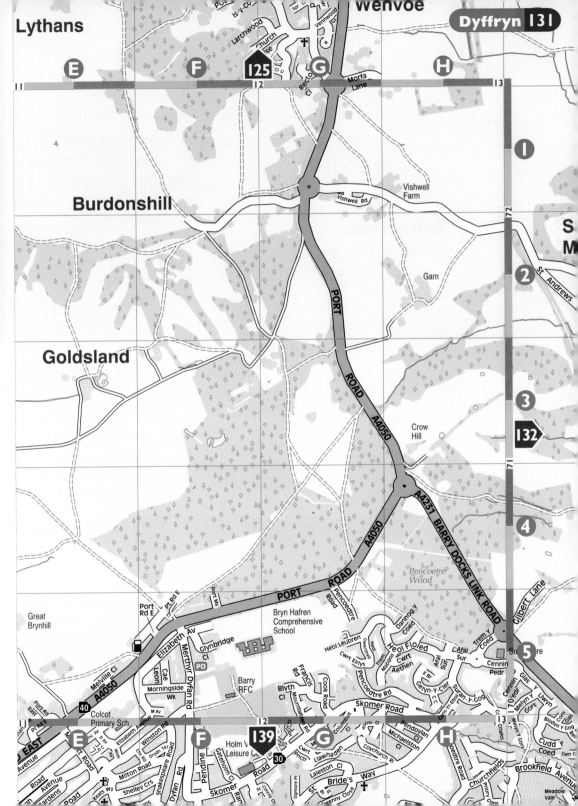

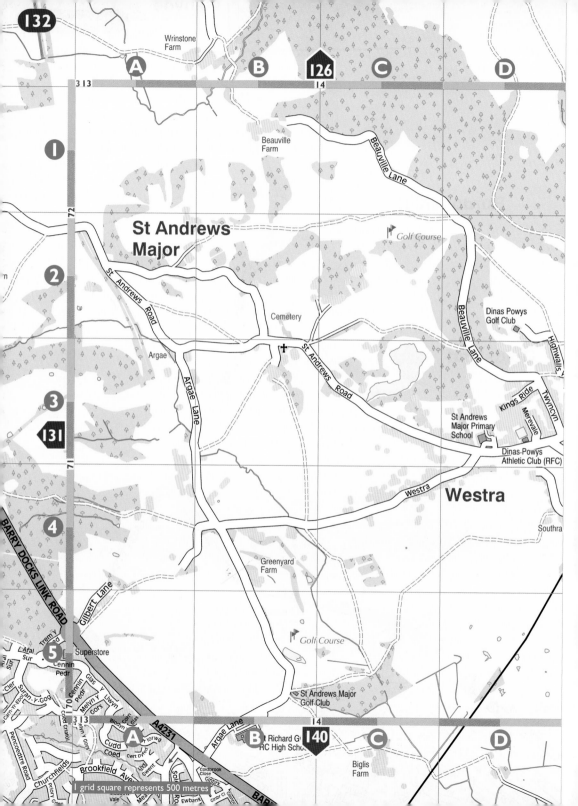

132

Wrinstone Farm

A   **B**   **126**   **C**   **D**

313   14

I

72

Beauville Farm

Beauville Lane

St Andrews Major

Golf Course

2

Cemetery

Dinas Powys Golf Club

Argae

St Andrews Road

Beauville Lane

Highwalls

3

131

Argae Lane

†

St Andrews Road

St Andrews Major Primary School

Kings Ride

Merevale

Twyncyn

71

Dinas-Powys Athletic Club (RFC)

4

Westra

Westra

Southra

Greenyard Farm

Gilbert Lane

BARRY DOCKS LINK ROAD

Golf Course

5

Tremy Yd

Afal Sur

Superstore

Cennin Pedr

70   313

Melyn Y Gors

Llwyn Glas

St Andrews Major Golf Club

A   A4231   **B** St Richard G RC High Schoo   **140**   **C**   **D**

Coldbrook Close

Biglis Farm

Brookfield Ave

Churchfields

Pencoedtre Road

Priory Green

I grid square represents 500 metres

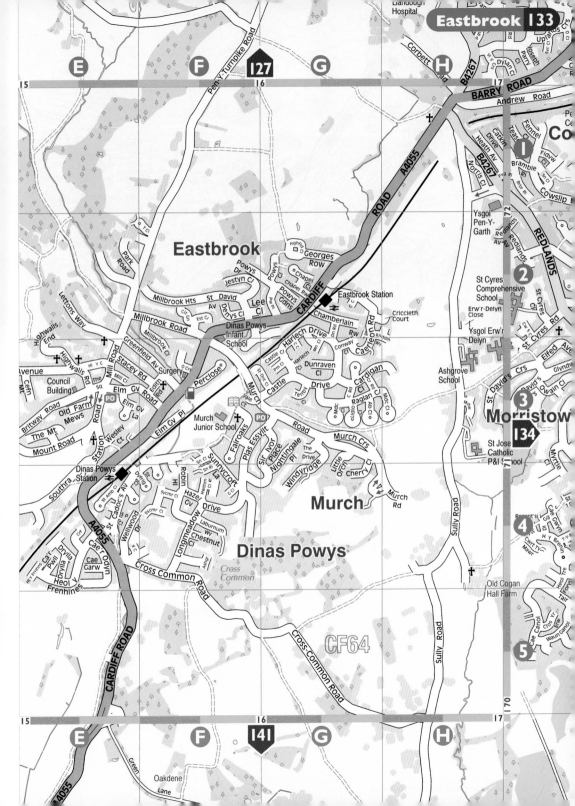

Llandough Hospital

Corbett Road

E **F** **127** **G** **H**

Pen-Y-Turnpike Road

BARRY ROAD

Andrew Road

B4267

Upcratus Crs
Joseph Parry
Dylan Cl

I

Co

Heath Av
Catkin Dr
Tease
Fennel

Norris Cl
B4267
Flavw
Bramble Pl
Cowslip

A4055

Ysgol Pen-Y-Garth

Redlands Av

REDLANDS

Park Road

Eastbrook

Highfld
Georges Row

Chapel
chapel Row
Powys Cl
Powys Cl
Powys Gdns
Powys Dr
Jestyn Cl

Millbrook Hts
St David Av
Denys Cl
Lee Cl
Est Cl
Denys Cl

2

St Cyres Comprehensive School
Erw'r-Delyn Close

Eastbrook Station

Criccieth Court

Ysgol Erw'r Delyn

St Cyres Rd

3

Letrons Way

Millbrook Road

CARDIFF ROAD

Chamberlain

Conway
Rw
Caerleon Rd

Rhdin

Ashgrove School

St David's Crs
David's Cl
Owain
Elfed Ave
Glyndw

Morristow

134

Highwalls End

Millbrook Cl

Greenfield Av
Dinas Powys Infant School
Surgery
Perclose

Harlech Drive
Castle Cl
Harlech
Dunraven Cl
Tenby
Drive
Cardigan Cl
Raglan Cl

Mdc Cl

St Joseph Catholic P&I School

Myrtle

Highwalls Rd
HI Y C
Stacey Rd
Mill Road
Elm Gv Road
Elm Gv La

Council Building
PO

Cefn Mt
Avenue
Britway Road
Old Farm Mews
The Mt
Mount Road

Murch Junior School
PO

Wesley Ct
Station Road
St

Dinas Powys Station

St Cadoc's Av
Wellwood Dr
Robin Cl
Hazel Gv
Sunnycroft
Fairoaks
Plas Essyllt
Sir Ivor Place
Nightingale Pl
The Drive
Murch Crs
Windyridge
Little Orchard
cherry Cl

Murch

Murch Road

Regent's Cl
Cwrt Y Mawr

4

Southra
A4055
Caer Odyn
Cae Carw
Heol y Frenhines
Sycmr Cl
Longmeadow
Laburnum
Chestnut
Sycamore Cl

Dinas Powys

Cross Common Road

Cross Common

Old Cogan Hall Farm

5

CARDIFF ROAD
A4055

Cross Common Road

CF64

Sully Road

E **F** **141** **G** **H**

Green

Oakdene Lane

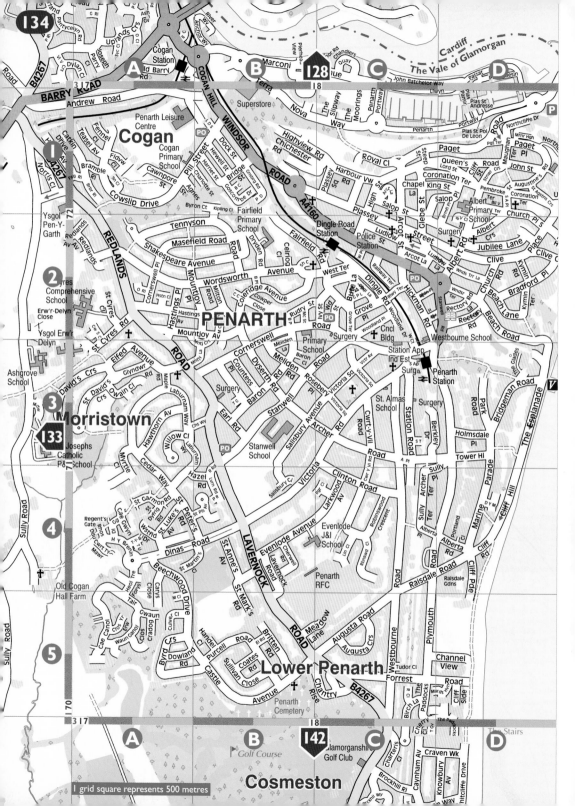

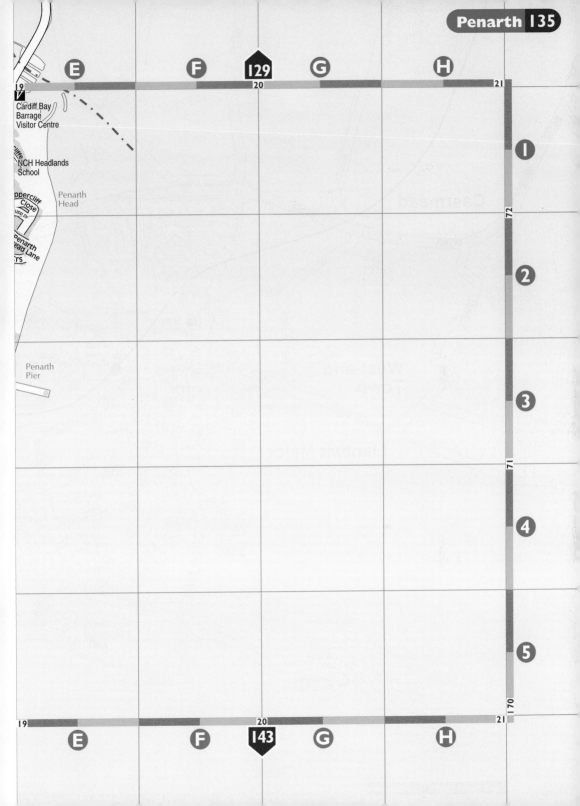

E

F

129

G

H

20

21

19

Cardiff Bay
Barrage
Visitor Centre

NCH Headlands
School

Penarth
Head

Penarth
Pier

ppercliff
Close

enarth
ead Lane
rs

1

72

2

3

71

4

5

170

19

20

143

21

E

F

G

H

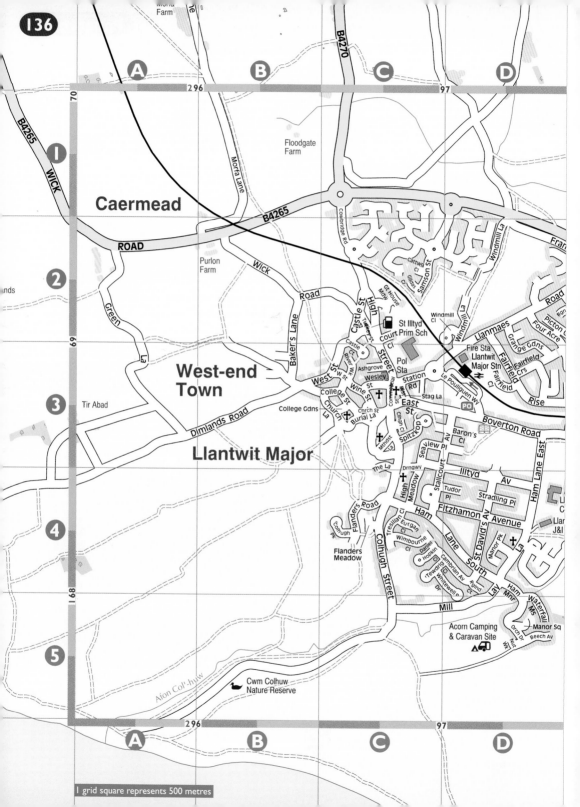

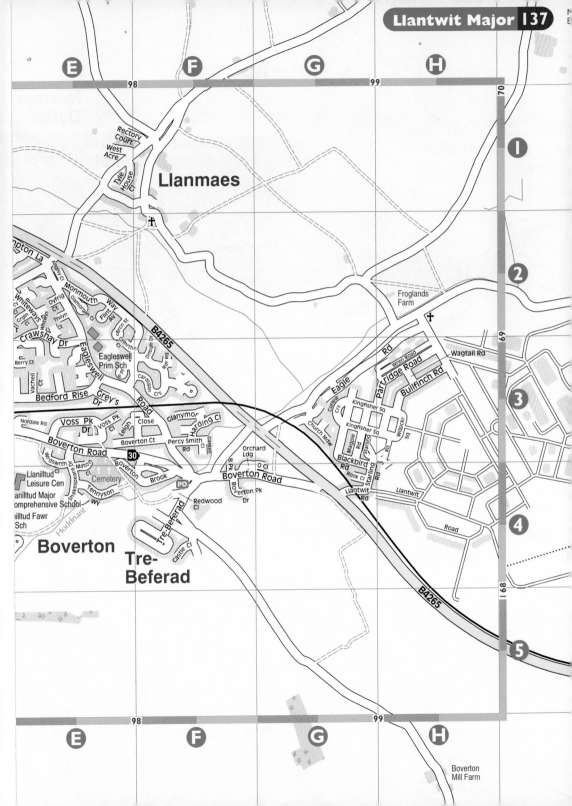

E   F   G   H

98   99   70

I

2

Rectory Court
West Acre
Tyle House
Llanmaes

Froglands Farm

69

rampton La
Angus C
Monmouth
Way
Whiteways
Keys
Dyfrig
Glamorgan Cl
Flint Av
Crawshay Dr
Orgin
eBrcn St
Grmrthn
Eagleswell Prim Sch
Berry Ct
Vachell Ct
Eagleswell Ct
Bedford Rise
Grey's Dr
Cardigan
Crs
Rdr Rd
Dngh
B4265

Eagle Rd
Wren Road
Partridge Road
Wagtail Rd
Bullfinch Rd
Culver Crs
Kingfisher Sq
Church Mdw
Kingfisher Sq
Magpie
Starling
Wdpckr Sq
Rd
Rd

3

Nordale Rd
Voss Pk Dr
Voss Pk
Leigh
Close
Glanymor
Harding Cl
Boverton Road
Wrdswrth Cl
Mltn Ct
Boverton
Shakespeare
Tennyson
Wy
Boverton Ct
Percy Smith Rd
Gaskell
Cl
Orchard Ldg
O Cl
Blackbird Rd
Rook Cl
Starling Rd
Llantwit Rd
Llantwit Road
30
Llanilltud Leisure Cen
Cemetery
Brook
B Pk
Boverton Rd
Boverton Road
Boverton Pk Dr
PO
Redwood Cl

4

Llanilltud Major Comprehensive School
illtud Fawr Sch
Hoddnant
Boverton
Tre-Beferad
Castle Cl
Tre-Beferad

I 68

B4265

5

E   F   G   H

98   99

Boverton Mill Farm

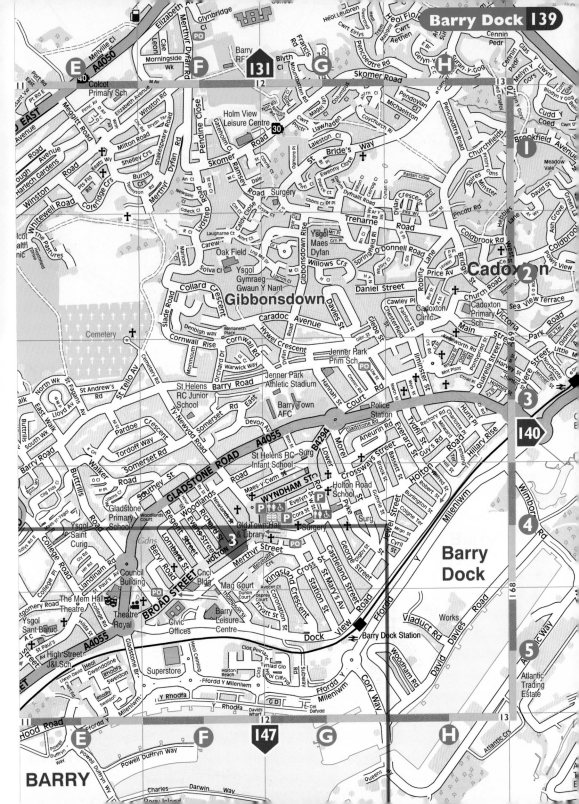

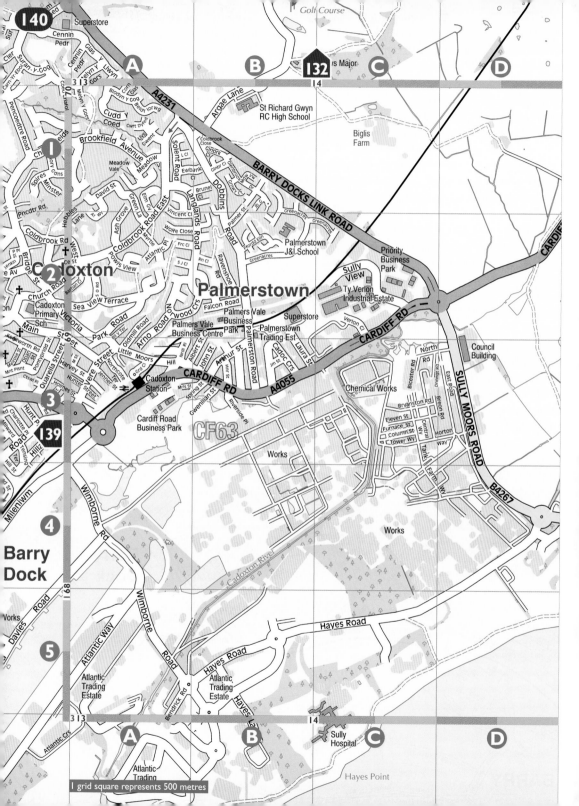

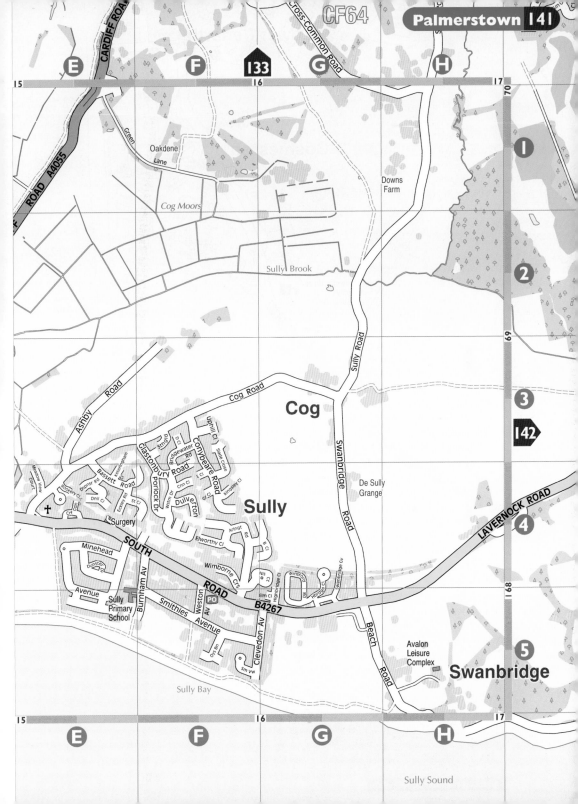

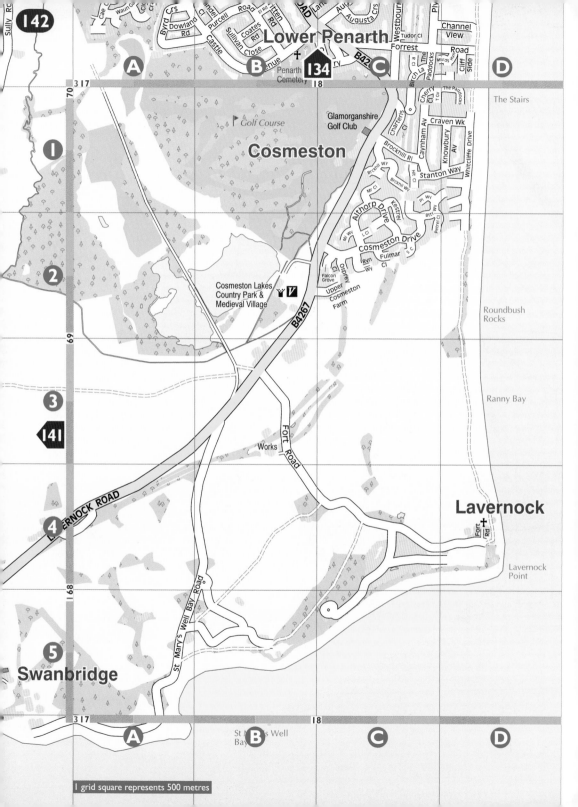

E   F   135   G   H

19   20   21

70

1

2

69

3

4

168

5

19   20   21

E   F   G   H

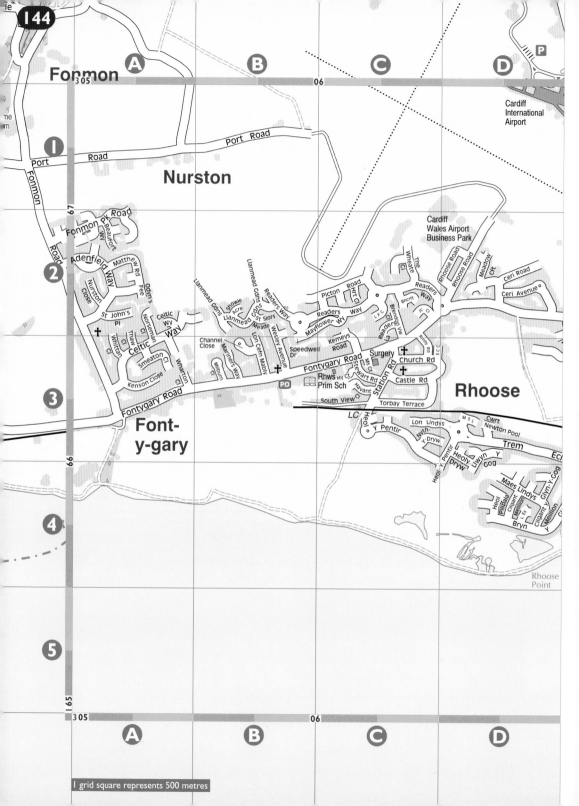

Fonmon

3 05

A · **B** · 06 · **C** · **D**

Cardiff
International
Airport

Port Road

Nurston

Port Road

Port

Road

Fonmon

Cardiff
Wales Airport
Business Park

67

Fonmon Pk Road

Beaufort Wy

Adenfield Way

Matthew Rd Fee

Odyn's

Nurston Close

St John's Pl

Norseman

Whittan Ct

Celtic Wy Way

Thaw Ct

Smeaton Ct

Celtic Way

Wharton

Kenson Close

Fontygary Road

Llanmead Gdns

Snowle Acre

Llanmead

Meade

Llanmead Gdns

St Siors

Readers Way

Channel Close

Marines Way

Milburn

Lon Cefn Mably

Wesley Avenue

Speedwell Dr

Picton Road

Hrt Ct

Readers Way

Mayflower Wy

Readers Way

Way

Kemeys Road

Fontygary Road

Rhws Prim Sch

South View

Stewart Rd

Mx Ct

Havant

Torbay Terrace

The Wheate Cl

Rhoose Road

Rhoose Road

Meadow Cft

L

Ceri Road

Ceri Avenue

Bncrft

Brentcog Vw

L F C

Readers Ln

Bmllg Rd

Jc Ct

S C C

Surgery

Church Rd

Station Rd

Castle Rd

Rhoose

LC

Heol Y Pentir

Lon Lindys

Lnth y dryw

Heol Y Pentir

Heol Y Dryw

Llwyn Y Gog

M s L

Cwrt Newton Pool

Trem

Ech

PO

**Font-
y-gary**

Maes Lindys

Heol Pll Bld

Cllugont

Llllton E g

Bryn

Cllgant Y Meillon

Glyn-Y-Cog

Rhoose
Point

99

A · **B** · **C** · **D**

3 05 · 06

165

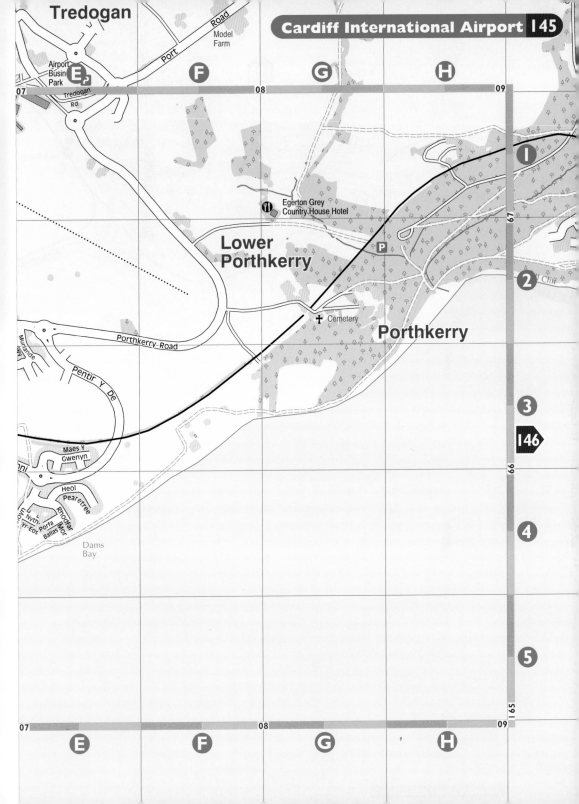

Port Road

Model Farm

Airport Busin Park **E**

Tredogan Rd

F

G

H

07 08 09

I

67

Egerton Grey Country House Hotel

Lower Porthkerry

P

2

Cliff

† Cemetery

Porthkerry

Porthkerry Road

Pentir Y De

3

146

Maes Y Gwenyn

99

4

Heol Pearetree

Muriande

Rhodfa'r Môr

Yr Eos Porfa

Ballas

Dams Bay

5

165

07 08 09

E

F

G

H

St.Baruc
AC
St Paul's
High Street
J&I.Sch

A4055

Gladstone Br.

Offices

Centre

Dock Vie

Barry Dock Station

David Rd

Davie

Heol

Rhodra

Sweldon

Gwendoline

Llwyn David

Superstore

Heol
Cernyg

Clos Peirion

Closel

Tyniad Glo

Holton
Reach

Ffordd Y Mileniwm

Cel
Dafydd

Woodham Rd

Atlantic
Trading
Estate

Y Rhodfa

Ffordd Y Rhodfa

Milenium

David Whart

Cel

Cory Way

139

E

F

139

G

H

11

12

13

Hood Road

Powell
Duffryn
Way

Ffordd Y

Powell Duffryn Way

Powell Duffryn Wy

BARRY

Charles   Darwin   Way

Queens

Atlantic Crs

At
Tr
Es

I

67

Barry Island
PRIMARY
School

Road

Clive

Street

Clive P.

Dock Rd

Archer

Birmit Rd

Clive

Phyllis

The
Triangle

St
Baruchs
Court

Amherst Crs

Dyfrig Street

PO

2

Barry Island
Junior & Infant
School

McQuade P.

Erl Crs

Plymouth

Heritage
Railway
Centre

Barry Island
Station

Friars

Earl Crs

Road

Marquis Close

Redbrink Crs

66

ROAD A4055

PAGET
RD

STATION AP RD

Breaksea

Gwennol Y Mor

Dr

Gwalch
Y Penwaig

Redbrink

Gwennol Y Craig

P

P

FRIARS ROAD

Barry Island
Pleasure Park

3

Heol Eryr Mor

Clos Y Wylan

Ploden For

G.Y.G

A.Y.M

Paget Road

P

Promenade

Barry Island

Whitmore Bay

Nell's Point

3

66

Friars
Point

4

5

165

11

12

13

E

F

G

H

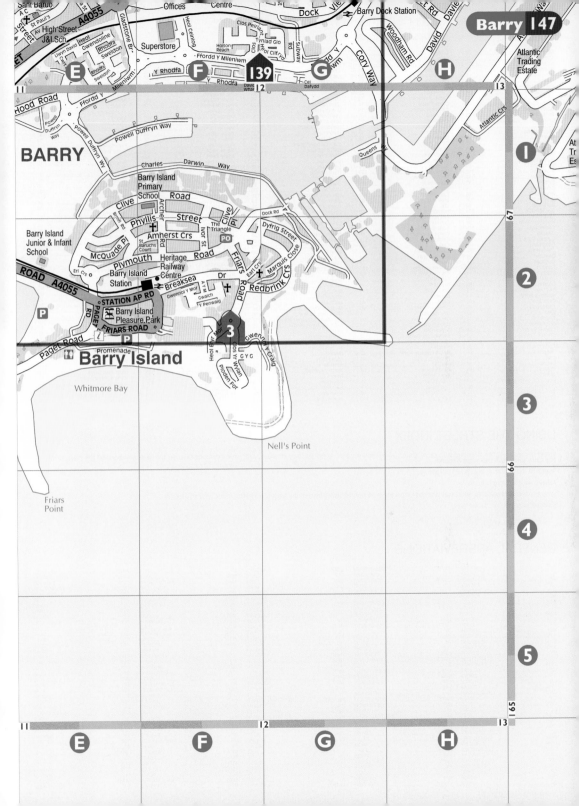

Abercarn ... 23 E1	Crindau ... 56 D2	Langstone ... 43 H5	Nurston ... 144 A1	St Nicholas ... 124 A2
Abersychan ... 12 D3	Croesyceiliog ... 20 B4	Lansbury Park ... 49 G5	Oakfield ... 26 A2	St y-Nyll ... 108 B4
Aberthin ... 125 E2	Croes-y-Mwyalch ... 40 C1	Lavernock ... 142 D4	Palmerstown ... 140 B2	Sebastopol ... 17 E5
Abertridwr ... 47 C1	Cross Inn ... 95 G5	Lawrence Hill ... 58 A3	Pantmawr ... 98 C2	Sedbury ... 29 F5
Allt-yr-yn ... 8 A1	Crosskeys ... 36 B2	Leckwith ... 127 E2	Pantmawr ... 134 B2	Senghenydd ... 32 A4
Alway ... 58 B4	Cwmavon ... 10 D3	Leckwith Moors ... 118 D5	Penarth ... 134 B2	Snatchwood ... 12 B5
Barnardtown ... 9 F1	Cwmbran ... 20 A5	Level of Mendalgief ... 76 C2	Penarth Moors ... 128 A3	Soar ... 82 A5
Barrack Hill ... 56 B2	Cwmcarn ... 22 D4	Lisvane ... 86 C5	Penrhiw ... 37 F3	Somerton ... 58 A5
Barry ... 2 B1	Cwmfelinfach ... 34 C2	Liswerry ... 72 B5	Pentrebach ... 45 G4	Southville ... 20 A5
Barry Dock ... 3 H2	Cwm-Fields ... 14 B5	Llanbethian ... 122 B5	Pentrebane ... 109 G5	Splott ... 121 E3
Barry Island ... 3 H7	Cwmynyscoy ... 16 D1	Llanbradach ... 33 G4	Pentre-Poeth ... 74 C2	The Square ... 18 D2
Bassaleg ... 75 E2	Cyncoed ... 100 D4	Llandaff ... 110 D5	Pen-y-fan ... 72 B4	Stelvio ... 76 A1
Beachley ... 31 F4	Cyntwell ... 117 E5	Llandaff North ... 111 E2	Pentwyn ... 101 F3	Stockland ... 108 C3
Bedwas ... 49 G2	Dan Caerlan ... 95 G1	Llanddewi Fach ... 21 F4	Pentyrch ... 96 C2	Stow Park ... 8 A6
Beechwood ... 57 H3	Danygraig ... 36 D4	Llandough ... 127 G4	Pen-y-Coedcae ... 64 B3	Sully ... 141 F4
Began ... 88 C4	Deepweir ... 63 E3	Llandough ... 101 F4	Penygarn ... 14 C3	Summerhill ... 57 G3
Bettws ... 39 G4	Dinas Powys ... 133 F4	Llanedeyrn ... 101 F4	Pen-y-Lan ... 74 A5	Swanbridge ... 141 H5
Birchgrove ... 99 F5	Downs ... 124 D1	Llanfihangel Rogiet ... 61 H2	Pen-y-Lan ... 113 E3	Taff's Well ... 83 E3
Bishpool ... 58 B4	Draethen ... 72 B1	Llanfrechfa ... 27 F3	Penyrheol ... 16 B3	Talbot Green ... 94 C2
Blacktown ... 103 H2	Drope ... 115 H5	Llanishen ... 99 H3	Penyrheol ... 48 A4	Talywain ... 12 B5
Black Vein ... 35 H3	Dyffryn ... 75 H5	Llanmaes ... 116 D1	Pen-y-rhiw ... 64 C1	Thornhill ... 19 E4
Blackweir ... 112 A5	Dyffryn ... 130 B2	Llanmaes ... 137 F1	Peterstone Wentlooge ... 104 C5	Thornhill ... 85 E4
Boverton ... 137 E4	Dyffryn Court ... 75 E3	Llanrumney ... 102 A4	Pilgwenlly ... 77 F2	Tongwynlais ... 98 A1
British ... 12 A4	Eastbrook ... 133 F2	Llantarnam ... 26 D4	Pontcanna ... 111 H5	Ton-Teg ... 66 A3
Brynawel ... 35 E5	East Moors ... 120 D5	Llantrisant ... 95 F2	Ponthir ... 27 F5	Trallwn ... 44 D2
Brynglas ... 56 C1	East Village ... 122 C4	Llantwit Fardre ... 80 D3	Pontnewydd ... 20 A3	Tre-Beferad ... 137 E4
Brynsadler ... 106 C2	Efail Isaf ... 81 G5	Llantwit Major ... 136 A3	Pontprennau ... 101 H1	Trecenydd ... 68 C1
Bulwark ... 30 C1	Ely ... 117 G3	Llanwern ... 59 F4	Pontrhydyrun ... 19 H2	Trefforest ... 45 E5
Burdonshill ... 131 E1	Energlyn ... 48 C4	Llanyrafon ... 26 B1	Pont Siôn Norton ... 45 G1	Tremorfa ... 121 F1
Butetown ... 4 A4	Fairwater ... 24 D1	Lower Lake ... 78 B4	Pontyclun ... 107 F2	Trethomas ... 50 C3
Bwlch-y-Cwm ... 84 C3	Fairwater ... 110 B5	Lower Machen ... 52 C4	Pontymister ... 36 D5	Trevethin ... 14 C1
Cadoxton ... 139 H2	Font-y-Gary ... 144 A3	Lower New Inn ... 17 G2	Pontymoel ... 14 C5	Trowbridge ... 102 B5
Caerau ... 117 F4	Forge Hammer ... 19 C4	Lower Ochrwyth ... 53 F2	Pontypool ... 14 D5	Tutshill ... 29 E2
Caerau Park ... 56 A5	Gabalfa ... 111 H4	Lower Penarth ... 134 B5	Pontypridd ... 45 F3	Twyn-yr-Odyn ... 125 F3
Caerleon ... 42 B4	Gaer ... 75 H2	Lower Porthkerry ... 145 F2	Pontywaun ... 23 E5	Ty Canol ... 24 B1
Caermead ... 136 A1	Gallowsgreen ... 19 H2	Lower Race ... 14 A5	Porthkerry ... 145 G2	Ty-Coch ... 25 G3
Caerphilly ... 69 F1	Garndiffaith ... 12 A1	Lowlands ... 19 H2	Portskewett ... 63 G5	Tyle-Garw ... 94 A5
Caldicot ... 63 E1	Garth ... 74 D1	Machen ... 51 H2	Pwll-Mawr ... 114 D5	Tynant ... 80 C5
Canton ... 118 D2	Gibbonsdown ... 139 F2	Maes-Glas ... 76 A4	Pwllypant ... 48 D3	Ty'n-y-Coedcae ... 51 E4
Cardiff ... 4 A3	Glan-y-Llyn ... 83 F2	Maesycoed ... 44 A4	Pye Corner ... 74 D1	Ty Rhiw ... 83 C3
Castell-y-Bwch ... 38 D1	Glasllwch ... 75 H1	Magor ... 60 A3	Pye Corner ... 78 C5	Ty-Sign ... 37 H4
Castleton ... 89 H4	Glyntaff ... 45 G5	Maindee ... 9 G2	Radyr ... 97 G5	Undy ... 60 D4
Cathays ... 112 B5	Goldsland ... 131 E3	Mandy ... 112 A4	Rhiwbina ... 112 A4	Upper Boat ... 66 C2
Cathays Park ... 4 C2	Golynos ... 12 A1	Malpas ... 40 B4	Rhiwderin ... 54 B5	Upper Church Village ... 65 E5
Cat's Ash ... 43 H3	Graig ... 44 D5	Marshfield ... 104 A1	Rhoose ... 144 D3	Upper Cwmbran ... 19 E2
Causeway ... 60 D5	Graig-y-Rhacca ... 50 D2	Mathern ... 30 B4	Rhydyfelin ... 46 A4	Upper Ochrwyth ... 53 E2
Cefn ... 55 E4	Grangetown ... 6 B4	Merthyr Dyfan ... 138 D1	Ridgeway ... 55 H3	Upper Race ... 16 A2
Chatham ... 52 A2	Greenmeadow ... 18 D5	Michaelston-le-Pit ... 126 D5	Ringland ... 58 D3	Van ... 69 F3
Chepstow ... 28 B3	Griffithstown ... 16 D2	Michaelston-super-Ely ... 116 D3	Risca ... 37 F3	Varteg ... 10 C4
Christchurch ... 58 B2	Groes-Wen ... 67 G1	Michaelston-y-Fedw ... 89 F2	Riverside ... 119 F3	The Village ... 42 B5
Church Village ... 81 H2	Gwaelod-y-Garth ... 82 C2	Miskin ... 107 H2	Roath ... 5 H2	Vinegar Hill ... 60 D2
Clearwell ... 73 H5	Hawthorn ... 65 H5	Morganstown ... 97 E2	Rogerstone ... 54 C4	Wainfelin ... 14 A3
Coed Eva ... 24 D2	Heath ... 112 A1	Morristown ... 133 H3	Rookwood ... 62 A4	Wallston ... 125 F4
Coedkernew ... 91 E4	Hendredenny Park ... 47 G5	Mount Ballan ... 63 G1	Rudry ... 70 D1	Watford Park ... 35 F2
Cog ... 141 G3	Hendy ... 94 D5	Murch ... 133 G4	Rumney ... 114 A2	Wattsville ... 35 F2
Cogan ... 138 C1	Henllys ... 24 B3	Mynachdy ... 111 H3	St Andrews' Major ... 132 A2	Wenvoe ... 125 G5
Colcot ... 58 D2	Henllys Vale ... 39 E1	Nantgarw ... 67 G4	St Bride's-super-Ely ... 108 B5	West-end Town ... 136 A3
Coldra ... 58 D2	High Cross ... 55 E4	Nant-y-ceisiad ... 51 F2	St Brides Wentlooge ... 105 H1	West Pontnewydd ... 19 F2
Common Cefn-Llwyn ... 27 C1	Hollybush ... 25 G4	New Inn ... 17 G1	St Dials ... 25 E1	Westra ... 132 D4
Coryton ... 98 A3	The Knap ... 2 A7	Newport ... 8 C7	St Fagans ... 116 D1	West Village ... 122 B3
Cosmeston ... 142 B1	Knollbury ... 60 D1	Newton ... 115 F4	St Julians ... 57 G1	Whitewall Common ... 60 C5
Cowbridge ... 122 C2	Lakeside ... 112 D1	Newtown ... 36 A2	St Lythans ... 124 D5	Ynysddu ... 34 B1
		Northville ... 19 H4	St Mellons ... 102 C1	

USING THE STREET INDEX

Street names are listed alphabetically. Each street name is followed by its postal town or area locality, the Postcode District, the page number, and the reference to the square in which the name is found.

Standard index entries are shown as follows:

Abbey Cl *PENT/RAD/TFW* CF15....**83** G4

Street names and selected addresses not shown on the map due to scale restrictions are shown in the index with an asterisk:

Academic Av *CDFN* CF14 *........**112** A2

GENERAL ABBREVIATIONS

ACC .... ACCESS	CREM ...... CREMATORIUM	GDNS .... GARDENS	LTL .... LITTLE	PREC .... PRECINCT
ALY .... ALLEY	CRS .... CRESCENT	GLD .... GLADE	LWR .... LOWER	PREP ...... PREPARATORY
AP .... APPROACH	CSWY ...... CAUSEWAY	GLN .... GLEN	MAG ...... MAGISTRATES'	PRIM .... PRIMARY
AR .... ARCADE	CT .... COURT	GN .... GREEN	MAN ...... MANSIONS	PROM ...... PROMENADE
ASS .... ASSOCIATION	CTRL .... CENTRAL	GND .... GROUND	MD .... MEAD	PRS .... PRINCESS
AV .... AVENUE	CTS .... COURTS	GRA .... GRANGE	MDW ...... MEADOWS	PRT .... PORT
BCH .... BEACH	CTYD ...... COURTYARD	GRG .... GARAGE	MEM ...... MEMORIAL	PT .... POINT
BLDS .... BUILDINGS	CUTT ...... CUTTINGS	GT .... GREAT	MT .... MILL	PTH .... PATH
BND .... BEND	CV .... COVE	GTWY .... GATEWAY	MKT ...... MARKET	PZ .... PIAZZA
BNK .... BANK	CYN .... CANYON	GV .... GROVE	MKTS ...... MARKETS	QD .... QUADRANT
BR .... BRIDGE	DEPT ...... DEPARTMENT	HGR .... HIGHER	ML .... MALL	QU .... QUEEN
BRK .... BROOK	DL .... DALE	HL .... HILL	MNR ...... MANOR	QY .... QUAY
BTM .... BOTTOM	DM .... DAM	HLS .... HILLS	MS .... MEWS	R .... RIVER
BUS .... BUSINESS	DR .... DRIVE	HO .... HOUSE	MSN ...... MISSION	RBT .... ROUNDABOUT
BVD .... BOULEVARD	DRO .... DROVE	HOL .... HOLLOW	MT .... MOUNT	RD .... ROAD
BY .... BYPASS	DRY .... DRIVEWAY	HOSP .... HOSPITAL	MTN ...... MOUNTAIN	RDG .... RIDGE
CATH .... CATHEDRAL	DWGS ...... DWELLINGS	HRB .... HARBOUR	MTS ...... MOUNTAINS	REP .... REPUBLIC
CEM .... CEMETERY	E .... EAST	HTH .... HEATH	MUS ...... MUSEUM	RES .... RESERVOIR
CEN .... CENTRE	EMB .... EMBANKMENT	HTS .... HEIGHTS	MWY ...... MOTORWAY	RFC ...... RUGBY FOOTBALL CLUB
CFT .... CROFT	EMBY ...... EMBASSY	HVN .... HAVEN	N .... NORTH	RI .... RISE
CH .... CHURCH	ESP .... ESPLANADE	HWY .... HIGHWAY	NE .... NORTH EAST	RP .... RAMP
CHA .... CHASE	EST .... ESTATE	IMP .... IMPERIAL	NW .... NORTH WEST	RW .... ROW
CHYD .... CHURCHYARD	EX .... EXCHANGE	IN .... INLET	O/P .... OVERPASS	S .... SOUTH
CIR .... CIRCLE	EXPY ...... EXPRESSWAY	IND EST .... INDUSTRIAL ESTATE	OFF .... OFFICE	SCH .... SCHOOL
CIRC .... CIRCUS	EXT .... EXTENSION	INF .... INFIRMARY	ORCH ...... ORCHARD	SE .... SOUTH EAST
CL .... CLOSE	F/O .... FLYOVER	INFO .... INFORMATION	OV .... OVAL	SER .... SERVICE AREA
CLFS .... CLIFFS	FC .... FOOTBALL CLUB	INT .... INTERCHANGE	PAL ...... PALACE	SH .... SHORE
CMP .... CAMP	FK .... FORK	IS .... ISLAND	PAS ...... PASSAGE	SHOP .... SHOPPING
CNR .... CORNER	FLD .... FIELD	JCT .... JUNCTION	PAV ...... PAVILION	SKWY .... SKYWAY
CO .... COUNTY	FLDS .... FIELDS	JTY .... JETTY	PDE ...... PARADE	SMT .... SUMMIT
COLL .... COLLEGE	FLS .... FALLS	KG .... KING	PH ...... PUBLIC HOUSE	SOC .... SOCIETY
COM .... COMMON	FM .... FARM	KNL .... KNOLL	PK .... PARK	SP .... SPUR
COMM .... COMMISSION	FT .... FORT	L .... LAKE	PKWY ...... PARKWAY	SPR .... SPRING
CON .... CONVENT	FTS .... FLATS	LA .... LANE	PL .... PLACE	SQ .... SQUARE
COT .... COTTAGE	FWY .... FREEWAY	LDG .... LODGE	PLN ...... PLAIN	ST .... STREET
COTS .... COTTAGES	FY .... FERRY	LGT .... LIGHT	PLNS ...... PLAINS	STN .... STATION
CP .... CAPE	GA .... GATE	LK .... LOCK	PLZ ...... PLAZA	STR .... STREAM
CPS .... COPSE	GAL .... GALLERY	LKS .... LAKES	POL ...... POLICE STATION	STRD .... STRAND
CR .... CREEK	GDN .... GARDEN	LNDG .... LANDING	PR .... PRINCE	SW .... SOUTH WEST

TDG............TRADING	TR............TRACK	V............VALE	VLS............VILLAS	WKS............WALKS
TER............TERRACE	TRL............TRAIL	VA............VALLEY	VW............VIEW	WLS............WELLS
THWY............THROUGHWAY	TWR............TOWER	VIAD............VIADUCT	W............WEST	WY............WAY
TNL............TUNNEL	U/P............UNDERPASS	VIL............VILLA	WD............WOOD	YD............YARD
TOLL............TOLLWAY	UNI............UNIVERSITY	VIS............VISTA	WHF............WHARF	YHA............YOUTH HOSTEL
TPK............TURNPIKE	UPR............UPPER	VLG............VILLAGE	WK............WALK	

POSTCODE TOWNS AND AREA ABBREVIATIONS

ABRC/NBR/RIS ....Abercarn/ Newbridge/Risca	BLKWD/PLFR............Blackwood/ Pontllanfraith	CATH/RTH/SPL............Cathays/ Roath/Splott	CHV/BDAU............Church Village/ Beddau	CYN/LLD/PWYN............Cyncoed/ Llanedeyrn/Pentwyn
ABRG............Abergavenny	CAE/CAN/FWR............Caerau/Canton/ Fairwater	CCDF............Central Cardiff	CLN/RNWPTE............Caerleon/Rural Newport east	GTN/RVSD............Grangetown /Riverside
BARRYE............Barry east	CAER............Caerphilly	CDFN............Cardiff north	COWBR............Cowbridge	LLMJ............Llantwit Major
BARRYI/W......Barry island/Barry west	CALD/MAG............Caldicot/Magor	CDFNE............Cardiff northeast	CWM............Cwmbran	LLTR/LLH............Llantrisant/Llanharan
		CHEP............Chepstow		NWPT............Newport

Index - streets

Abb - Bal

A

Abbey Cl PENT/RAD/TFW CF15... 83 G4	
Abbey Ct CHV/BDAU CF38........ 81 F1	
Abbey Gn CWM NP44................ 26 A3	
Abbey Gn NWPT NP20.............. 26 C5	
Abbey Rd CWM NP44................ 25 H1	
NWPT NP19........................... 58 C3	
Abbots Ms NWPT NP20............ 8 D6	
Aberaeron Cl BARRY/W CF62... 139 G1	
Aberbran Rd CDFN CF14.......... 111 F3	
Abercynon St GTN/RVSD CF11.. 6 D4	
Aberdaron Rd CDFNE CF3........ 102 C5	
Aberdore Rd CDFN CF14.......... 111 F3	
Aberdovey Cl PNRTH/DP CF64.. 133 G5	
Aberdovey St	
CATH/RTH/SPL CF24............. 120 D3	
Aberdulais Crs CDFN CF14....... 111 F3	
Aberdulais Rd CDFN CF14........ 111 F3	
Aberfawr Rd CALD/MAG NP26.. 47 F2	
Aber-Fawr Ter CAER CF83........ 47 F2	
Abergele Cl CDFNE CF3............ 102 D4	
Abergele Rd CDFNE CF3........... 102 D5	
Abernethy Cl CDFNE CF3.......... 103 F3	
Aberporth Rd CDFN CF14........ 111 F2	
Aber St GTN/RVSD CF11........... 6 C4	
Aberteifi Cl CDFN CF14........... 111 F3	
Aberteifi Crs CDFN CF14.......... 111 G3	
Aberthaw Av NWPTE NP19...... 58 C5	
Aberthaw Cir NWPTE NP19..... 58 A4	
Aberthaw Cl NWPTE NP19....... 58 B4	
Aberthaw Rd	
CAE/CAN/FWR CF5............... 117 F3	
NWPTE NP19........................ 58 A4	
Aberthin La COWBR CF71......... 123 F4	
Aberthin Rd COWBR CF71........ 123 E3	
Aberystwith St	
CATH/RTH/SPL CF24............. 120 D3	
Aberystwyth Crs	
BARRYI/W CF62..................... 2 E2	
Abingdon St BARRYE CF63........ 139 H2	
Acacia Av CALD/MAG NP26...... 60 D2	
NWPTE NP19........................ 58 A4	
Acacia Sq NWPTE NP19........... 58 A4	
Acacia St PPRD CF37............... 65 H2	
Academic Av CDFN CF14 *....... 112 A2	
Acer Av CHV/BDAU CF38......... 80 B5	
Acer Wy RSTN NP10................ 54 B3	
Acorn Cl LLTR/LLH CF72.......... 107 H1	
PPOOL/BLNAV NP4................. 12 C4	
RSTN NP10............................ 54 C2	
Acorn Gv CHV/BDAU CF38........ 81 F2	
CYN/LLD/PWYN CF23.............. 101 H1	
Adamscroft Pl CCDF CF10........ 5 C5	
Adamsdown La	
CATH/RTH/SPL CF24............. 5 J5	
Adamsdown Pl	
CATH/RTH/SPL CF24............. 5 J5	
Adamsdown Sq	
CATH/RTH/SPL CF24............. 5 H5	
Adam St CATH/RTH/SPL CF24... 5 F6	
Adar y Mor BARRYI/W CF62..... 3 G6	
Addison Crs	
CAE/CAN/FWR CF5................ 117 F3	
Addison Wy CAER CF83............ 50 C3	
Adelaide Pl CCDF CF10............ 7 F5	
Adelaide St CCDF CF10............ 7 F5	
NWPT NP20.......................... 56 D2	
Adeline St	
CATH/RTH/SPL CF24............. 5 K4	
NWPT NP20.......................... 76 D3	
Adit Wk CWM NP44................. 19 F3	
Adventurers Qy CCDF CF10...... 7 G5	
Ael-y-Bryn CAER CF83............. 50 A3	
CAER CF83............................ 80 B3	
CYN/LLD/PWYN CF23.............. 113 F1	
PENT/RAD/TFW CF15............ 96 A2	
Aelybryn PPRD CF37................ 44 B2	
Ael-y-Coed BARRYI/W CF62..... 138 B4	
Aeron Cl BARRYI/W CF62......... 2 B1	
Afal Sur BARRYE CF63.............. 131 H5	
Afan Cl BARRYI/W CF62........... 138 D4	
Afon Cl CDFNE CF3.................. 88 C3	
PPOOL/BLNAV NP4................. 17 G2	
Afon Llwyd Ter	
PPOOL/BLNAV NP4................. 14 A1	
Afon Lwyd Cl	
CLN/RNWPTE NP18................ 42 B3	
Afon Md RSTN NP10................ 54 A2	
Afon Ter CWM NP44................ 20 A3	
Africa Gdns CDFN CF14........... 112 A3	

Agate St CATH/RTH/SPL CF24... 5 K3	
Agincourt Rd	
CYN/LLD/PWYN CF23.............. 113 F5	
Agincourt St NWPT NP20......... 56 D2	
Agnes St PNRTH/DP CF64......... 134 A1	
Ailesbury St NWPT NP20.......... 56 D2	
Aintree Dr CAE/CAN/FWR CF5.. 118 A3	
Alanbrooke Av NWPT NP20 *.... 37 G5	
Albany Rd	
CATH/RTH/SPL CF24............. 113 E5	
Albany St NWPT NP20.............. 56 D1	
Alberta Pl PNRTH/DP CF64....... 134 C4	
Alberta Rd PNRTH/DP CF64...... 134 D4	
Albert Av NWPTE NP19............ 9 K2	
Albert Crs PNRTH/DP CF64....... 134 D2	
Albert Rd PPOOL/BLNAV NP4 *.. 14 B5	
PPOOL/BLNAV NP4................. 12 A2	
Albert Sq CCDF CF10............... 7 G2	
Albert St BARRYE CF63............ 140 A3	
RSTN/RVSD CF11.................... 119 E3	
NWPT NP20.......................... 9 F6	
Albert Ter NWPT NP20............ 45 G1	
Albert Wk GTN/RVSD CF11...... 119 E3	
Albion Cl NWPT NP20.............. 77 E2	
Albion St NWPT NP20.............. 76 D2	
PPRD CF37........................... 45 G1	
Albion Ho CALD/MAG NP26...... 62 D3	
Alder Cl PPOOL/BLNAV NP4...... 15 H5	
Alder Gv NWPT NP20............... 40 C4	
Alderney St NWPT NP20.......... 56 D2	
Alder Rd CYN/LLD/PWYN CF23.. 112 D4	
The Alders CWM NP44............ 26 C2	
Alderwood Cl CDFNE CF3......... 102 D3	
Aldsworth Rd	
CAE/CAN/FWR CF5................ 118 A1	
Aldwych Cl CDFN CF14............ 85 H5	
Alexander Cl CAER CF83.......... 69 F1	
Alexander St	
CATH/RTH/SPL CF24 *........... 112 C5	
Alexandra Crs BARRYI/W CF62.. 2 E2	
Alexandra Rd	
CAE/CAN/FWR CF5................ 118 D3	
CHEP NP16........................... 30 D1	
NWPT NP20.......................... 76 D3	
PPRD CF37........................... 45 E4	
Alexandra Ter CAER CF83......... 32 A3	
Alfreda Rd CDFN CF14............ 110 D1	
Alfred St CATH/RTH/SPL CF24.. 112 D4	
NWPTE NP19......................... 9 H1	
Alianore Rd CALD/MAG NP26... 62 D4	
Alice Crs CHEP NP16................ 31 E3	
Alice St CCDF CF10.................. 7 F4	
NWPT NP20.......................... 76 D3	
Alicia Crs NWPT NP20.............. 9 H2	
Allan Durst Cl	
CAE/CAN/FWR CF5................ 110 B2	
Allen Cl CDFNE CF3................. 102 D2	
NWPT NP20.......................... 39 H5	
Allensbank Crs CDFN CF14...... 112 B3	
Allensbank Rd CDFN CF14....... 112 B3	
Allerton St GTN/RVSD CF11..... 119 F4	
Alltmawr Rd	
CYN/LLD/PWYN CF23.............. 100 D4	
Allt Wen CDFN CF14................ 98 C2	
Allt-yr-Yn Av NWPT NP20........ 56 A3	
Allt-yr-Yn Av NWPT NP20........ 55 H4	
Allt-yr-Yn Cl NWPT NP20......... 8 A1	
Allt-yr-Yn Ct NWPT NP20......... 56 B2	
Allt-yr-Yn Rd NWPT NP20........ 56 A3	
Allt-yr-Yn Vw NWPT NP20....... 56 A4	
Allt-yr-Yn Vw NWPT NP20....... 56 B2	
Allt y Wiwer CHV/BDAU CF38... 81 G2	
Ally y Wennol	
CYN/LLD/PWYN CF23.............. 101 G1	
Alma Pl PPOOL/BLNAV NP4 *.... 12 C2	
Alma Pl PPOOL/BLNAV NP4...... 17 E4	
Alma Rd CYN/LLD/PWYN CF23.. 113 E4	
Alma St CAER CF83................. 51 H2	
CHV/BDAU CF38.................... 8 E7	
Almond Av	
ABRC/NBR/RIS NP11.............. 37 G4	
Almond Cl CHV/BDAU CF38...... 80 D4	
Almond Dr	
CYN/LLD/PWYN CF23.............. 101 G1	
NWPT NP20.......................... 40 C3	
Alpha Pl PPRD CF37................ 45 E2	
Alpha Rd CHEP NP16............... 30 D1	
Alpha St PPRD CF37................ 45 E2	

Althorp Dr PNRTH/DP CF64...... 142 C2	
Alton Ter PPOOL/BLNAV NP4 *.. 14 B5	
Alway Crs NWPTE NP19........... 58 B4	
Alwen Dr BARRYI/W CF62........ 138 C4	
CDFN CF14............................ 86 A4	
Alwyn Cl RSTN NP10................ 54 D2	
Amber Cl	
CYN/LLD/PWYN CF23.............. 101 G2	
Ambergate Dr	
CYN/LLD/PWYN CF23.............. 101 G2	
Amberheart Dr CDFN CF14....... 86 A3	
Amberley Cl	
CYN/LLD/PWYN CF23.............. 101 G1	
Amberley Pl	
PPOOL/BLNAV NP4 *.............. 14 B3	
Amberwood Cl	
CYN/LLD/PWYN CF23.............. 101 G1	
Amblecote Cl	
CYN/LLD/PWYN CF23.............. 101 G1	
Ambleside PPOOL/BLNAV NP4... 12 B2	
Ambleside Av	
CYN/LLD/PWYN CF23.............. 112 C3	
Ambrooke Cl	
CYN/LLD/PWYN CF23.............. 101 G1	
Ambryn Rd	
PPOOL/BLNAV NP4................. 17 H1	
Amesbury Rd	
CYN/LLD/PWYN CF23.............. 113 F4	
Amethyst Rd	
CAE/CAN/FWR CF5................ 110 B4	
Amherst Crs BARRYI/W CF62.... 3 C6	
Amherst St GTN/RVSD CF11..... 6 B5	
Amity Ct CCDF CF10................ 7 G2	
Amroth Ct BARRYI/W CF62....... 139 F2	
Amroth Rd CAE/CAN/FWR CF5.. 117 G3	
Amvas Ct GTN/RVSD CF11....... 119 F4	
Amy Johnson Cl	
NWPTE NP19......................... 78 A1	
Anchor Rd PNRTH/DP CF64...... 128 C5	
Anchor St	
PENT/RAD/TFW CF15............ 83 F4	
Anchor Wy PNRTH/DP CF64...... 128 B5	
Anderson Pl	
CATH/RTH/SPL CF24............. 5 J4	
NWPT NP20.......................... 40 B2	
Andover Cl BARRYI/W CF62...... 138 C4	
Andrew Rd PNRTH/DP CF64...... 133 H1	
Andrews Ar CCDF CF10 *.......... 4 D4	
Andrew's Cl CDFN CF14........... 110 D3	
Aneurin Bevan Dr	
CHV/BDAU CF38.................... 81 F2	
Aneurin Rd BARRYE CF63......... 139 E5	
Angelica Wy CDFN CF14.......... 85 G4	
Angelina St CCDF CF10............ 6 E5	
Angle Cl CWM NP44................ 10 B5	
Angle Cl BARRYI/W CF62.......... 139 F1	
Angle Pl CDFN CF14................ 99 G1	
Anglesey Cl CHV/BDAU CF38.... 65 H5	
LLMJ CF61............................ 137 E2	
Anglesey St	
CAE/CAN/FWR CF5................ 118 D2	
Angus St CATH/RTH/SPL CF24.. 113 E4	
Annesley Rd NWPTE NP19........ 57 F2	
Ann St GTN/RVSD CF11........... 119 E3	
Anson Gn NWPTE NP19............ 78 A1	
Anstee Ct GTN/RVSD CF11....... 119 E3	
Anthony Dr	
CLN/RNWPTE NP18................ 41 G3	
Anwyll Cl CLN/RNWPTE NP18... 41 H5	
Apollo Cl CDFN CF14............... 85 H5	
Apple Av CALD/MAG NP26....... 60 D3	
Appledore Rd CDFN CF14......... 111 G2	
Applewood Cl	
CATH/RTH/SPL CF24............. 5 J6	
Arabella St	
CATH/RTH/SPL CF24............. 112 D4	
Aragon St NWPT NP20............. 56 D2	
Aran Ct CWM NP44................. 19 E3	
Archer Crs CAE/CAN/FWR CF5.. 117 G2	
Archer Pl CAE/CAN/FWR CF5.... 117 G2	
PNRTH/DP CF64.................... 134 C3	
Archer Rd BARRYI/W CF62....... 3 C5	
CAE/CAN/FWR CF5................ 117 G2	
CWM NP44............................ 19 E5	
PNRTH/DP CF64.................... 134 B3	
Archer Ter PNRTH/DP CF64...... 134 C4	
Arch Hl ABRC/NBR/RIS NP11.... 23 F5	
Archibald St NWPTE NP19....... 9 K3	
Arcot Ct (North)	
PNRTH/DP CF64.................... 134 C1	
Arcot St PNRTH/DP CF64......... 134 C2	
Arden Wy BARRYE CF63............ 140 A2	
Ardwyn CDFN CF14................. 98 C2	
Arfonfab Crs PPRD CF37.......... 46 B5	
Argae La BARRYE CF63............ 140 B1	
Argae St PPRD CF37................ 132 A3	

Argosy Wy NWPTE NP19.......... 9 J5	
Argyle St NWPT NP20.............. 56 D2	
Argyle Wy CAE/CAN/FWR CF5... 117 H4	
Aries Rd CALD/MAG NP26........ 117 H3	
Arlington Cl CALD/MAG NP26... 61 E3	
NWPT NP20.......................... 40 B2	
Arlington Ct CHEP NP16.......... 29 F4	
Arlington Crs CDFNE CF3......... 102 A4	
Arlington Rd PNRTH/DP CF64... 141 F4	
Armoury Dr CDFN CF14........... 99 G4	
Armstrong Cl NWPTE NP19...... 58 A5	
Arne Cl NWPTE NP19............... 58 D4	
Arnold Av CDFNE CF3.............. 102 D2	
Arnold Cl NWPT NP20.............. 76 A2	
Arno Rd BARRYE CF63.............. 140 A3	
Arnside Rd	
CYN/LLD/PWYN CF23.............. 113 G5	
Arran Cl ABRC/NBR/RIS NP11... 37 H5	
PPRD CF37........................... 64 C1	
Arran Cl CATH/RTH/SPL CF24.. 113 E5	
Arran St CATH/RTH/SPL CF24... 5 J6	
Arrol St CATH/RTH/SPL CF24... 5 J6	
Arthur Bliss Rd NWPTE NP19.... 58 B5	
Ar y Nant BARRYE CF63........... 139 G2	
Arthur Cl NWPT NP20.............. 76 D2	
Arthurs Ct CALD/MAG NP26..... 63 G3	
Arthur St ABRC/NBR/RIS NP11.. 34 C2	
BARRYE CF63........................ 140 B3	
CATH/RTH/SPL CF24............. 120 D1	
CLN/RNWPTE NP18................ 42 B4	
NWPT NP20.......................... 76 D2	
Arundel Cl CWM NP44............. 18 D5	
Arundel Pl GTN/RVSD CF11...... 119 E5	
Arundel Rd NWPTE NP19......... 58 C5	
Ascot Cl CAE/CAN/FWR CF5..... 117 H5	
Asgog St CATH/RTH/SPL CF24.. 5 K5	
Ashbourne Cl	
CYN/LLD/PWYN CF23.............. 101 H1	
Ashburton Av CDFNE CF3........ 102 D3	
Ashby Rd PNRTH/DP CF64....... 141 E3	
Ashchurch Cl CDFN CF14......... 42 B4	
Ashchurch Rw CDFN CF14....... 98 D5	
Ashcombe Cl NWPT NP20........ 99 E4	
Ashcroft Crs	
CATH/RTH/SPL CF24 *........... 121 E1	
Ashdene Cl CAE/CAN/FWR CF5.. 110 A3	
Ashdown Cl CDFNE CF3........... 103 E5	
Ashfield Cl CDFNE CF3............ 102 D3	
Ashford Cl CWM NP44............. 20 C5	
Ashford Cl North CWM NP44.... 20 C5	
Ashford Cl South CWM NP44.... 20 C5	
Ash Gn CWM NP44.................. 26 A3	
Ash Gv BARRYE CF63............... 140 A2	
CAE/CAN/FWR CF5................ 125 C1	
Ashgrove CAER CF83............... 50 A3	
Ash Gv CALD/MAG NP26.......... 62 D2	
Ashgrove CDFN CF14............... 99 E4	
Ash Gv CDFN CF14.................. 136 C5	
Ashgrove PNRTH/DP CF64....... 133 H4	
Ashgrove Cl	
PPOOL/BLNAV NP4................. 14 D1	
Ashgrove Ct	
PPOOL/BLNAV NP4................. 16 D4	
Ashleigh Ct CWM NP44........... 24 C2	
Ashley Rd NWPTE NP19........... 58 A4	
Aston Cl CAER CF83................. 68 A3	
Ash Sq PPRD CF37.................. 65 H2	
Ash Tree Cl	
PENT/RAD/TFW CF15............ 97 F4	
Ash Wk LLTR/LLH CF72............ 94 D3	
Aspen Cl CDFNE CF3............... 102 D3	
Aspen Wy CHV/BDAU CF38...... 80 D5	
NWPT NP20.......................... 40 B3	
Asquith St PPOOL/BLNAV NP4.. 16 D4	
Aster Cl ABRC/NBR/RIS NP11... 37 H4	
Aston Crs CDFNE CF3.............. 103 E3	
Aston Pl CDFNE CF3................ 85 H5	
Atfield Cl	
CYN/LLD/PWYN CF23.............. 113 G4	
Athelstan Rd CDFN CF14......... 110 D1	
Atlantic Crs BARRYE CF63........ 147 H1	
Atlantic Pl BARRYE CF63......... 140 A2	
Atlantic Wy BARRYE CF63........ 140 A5	
Atlantic Whf CCDF CF10........... 7 G2	
Atlas Pl CAE/CAN/FWR CF5...... 119 E3	
Atlas Rd CAE/CAN/FWR CF5..... 118 D3	
Attlee Ct CAER CF83................ 69 F1	
Aubrey Av CAE/CAN/FWR CF5.. 118 B1	
Aubrey Hames Cl	
NWPT NP20.......................... 76 B2	
Auckland Rd NWPTE NP19....... 75 C1	
Augusta Crs PNRTH/DP CF64.... 134 C5	
Augustan Cl	
CLN/RNWPTE NP18................ 41 G3	
Augustan Dr	
CLN/RNWPTE NP18................ 41 G3	

Augustan Wy	
CLN/RNWPTE NP18................ 41 G3	
Augusta Rd PNRTH/DP CF64.... 134 C5	
Augusta St	
CATH/RTH/SPL CF24............. 5 H4	
Augustus John Cl	
NWPTE NP19......................... 57 H1	
Augustus Pl NWPTE NP19 *..... 58 D2	
Aust Crs CHEP NP16............... 30 C2	
Austen Cl CDFNE CF3.............. 102 C2	
Austin Friars NWPT NP20......... 8 E5	
Austin Rd PPOOL/BLNAV NP4... 12 A3	
Australia Rd CDFN CF14........... 112 A3	
Avalon Ct PPOOL/BLNAV NP4... 14 B4	
Avalon Dr NWPTE NP19........... 57 G2	
The Avenue	
CAE/CAN/FWR CF5................ 111 E4	
CAER CF83............................ 33 G5	
CAER CF83............................ 50 B3	
CALD/MAG NP26................... 62 C4	
CDFNE CF3........................... 110 D1	
CDFNE CF3........................... 114 C3	
NWPT NP20.......................... 8 E6	
PPOOL/BLNAV NP4................. 12 B1	
PPOOL/BLNAV NP4................. 15 F5	
PPRD CF37........................... 45 E3	
RSTN NP10............................ 75 F5	
Avoca Pl GTN/RVSD CF11 *...... 119 F4	
Avocet Ct BARRYE CF63........... 3 H1	
Avon Cl CALD/MAG NP26......... 62 D2	
NWPT NP20.......................... 39 H4	
Avondale Cr CWM NP44........... 20 A4	
Avondale Dr CWM NP44........... 19 H1	
Avondale Gdns	
GTN/RVSD CF11.................... 6 C5	
Avondale Gdns South	
GTN/RVSD CF11.................... 6 D5	
Avondale Rd CWM NP44.......... 20 A3	
GTN/RVSD CF11.................... 6 C5	
PPOOL/BLNAV NP4................. 17 F5	
Avondale Wy CWM NP44......... 20 A2	
Avonmuir Rd	
CATH/RTH/SPL CF24 *........... 121 E1	
Avonridge CDFN CF14............. 85 G5	
Avro Cl CATH/RTH/SPL CF24.... 121 G1	
Awelfryn PPRD CF37................ 64 B4	
Awel Mor	
CYN/LLD/PWYN CF23.............. 113 F2	
Axbridge Crs CDFNE CF3.......... 102 C4	
Axminster Rd	
CYN/LLD/PWYN CF23.............. 113 G5	

B

Baber Cl CYN/LLD/PWYN CF23.. 113 G4	
Backhall St	
CLN/RNWPTE NP18................ 42 B4	
The Back CHEP NP16............... 28 D3	
Bacon Pl NWPT NP20.............. 40 B3	
Bacton Rd CDFN CF14............. 111 F3	
Baden Rd CATH/RTH/SPL CF24.. 121 F2	
Bader Cl CDFN CF14............... 100 A4	
Badgers Dene CHEP NP16........ 28 B4	
Badgers Mdw	
CLN/RNWPTE NP18................ 27 G4	
Badgers Wk CALD/MAG NP26... 60 D5	
Badgers Wy NWPT NP10.......... 74 B2	
Badham Cl CAER CF83............. 68 A3	
Badminton Rd NWPTE NP19..... 57 G1	
Bagley Ct CWM NP44.............. 19 E3	
Bailey St CAE/CAN/FWR CF5.... 117 H1	
Bailey St NWPT NP20.............. 8 D5	
PPOOL/BLNAV NP4................. 12 B1	
Baird Cl NWPT NP20............... 40 A3	
Baker's La LLMJ CF61.............. 136 B3	
Bakers Rw CCDF CF10............. 4 D5	
Bakers Whf PPRD CF37............ 45 E3	
Bakery La CDFNE CF3.............. 90 A5	
Balaclava Rd	
CYN/LLD/PWYN CF23.............. 113 E4	
Bala Dr RSTN NP10................. 54 D2	
Balance Rd PPOOL/BLNAV NP4.. 16 D4	
Bala Rd CDFN CF14................. 111 E3	
Baldwin Cl CAE/CAN/FWR CF5.. 110 B2	
NWPT NP20.......................... 76 D2	
Baldwin St NWPT NP20........... 76 D2	
Balfe Rd NWPTE NP19............. 58 D5	
Ball La CDFNE CF3.................. 103 H4	
Ball Rd CDFNE CF3................. 102 A5	
Balmoral Cl CAE/CAN/FWR CF5.. 86 C5	
PPRD CF37........................... 64 C1	
Balmoral Ct BARRYI/W CF62.... 138 C1	
Balmoral La NWPTE NP19........ 57 H5	
Balmoral Rd NWPTE NP19....... 57 H5	

Baltimore Cl
  CYN/LLD/PWYN CF23 .... 87 H5
Bampton Rd *CDFNE* CF3 ..... 102 B4
Banastre Av *CDFNE* CF14 ..... 112 A5
Banc yr Afon
  PENT/RAD/TFW CF15 .... 83 F4
Baneswell Rd *NWPT* NP20 ..... 8 D3
Bangor Ct
  CATH/RTH/SPL CF24 * 113 E4
Bangor St
  CATH/RTH/SPL CF24 .... 113 E4
Bank La *NWPTE* NP19 .... 57 F1
Bankside Cl *CDFN* CF14 ...... 86 A4
Bank Sq *CHEP* NP16 .... 28 C4
Bank St *CHEP* NP16 .... 28 C4
  NWPTE NP19 .... 57 E1
Bantock Cl *NWPTE* NP19 ...... 58 D4
Banwell Cl *CWM* NP44 .... 19 E3
Banwell Pl *CDFNE* CF3 .... 102 B4
Barberry Rl *PNTRTH/DP* CF64 .. 134 A1
Bardsey Crs *CDFN* CF14 ...... 99 G1
Bardsy Cl *NWPTE* NP19 .... 57 G2
Bargoed St *GTN/RVSD* CF11 ... 6 C4
Barmouth Rd *CDFNE* CF3 ...... 114 B2
Barnard Av *CAE/CAN/FWR* CF5 . 117 H2
Barnard St *NWPTE* NP19 ...... 9 H1
Barnard Wy *CHV/BDAU* CF38 ... 81 E1
Barnets *CWM* NP44 .... 19 E5
Barnett Cl *CLN/RNWPTE* NP18 . 42 A1
Barnfield Cl
  CYN/LLD/PWYN CF23 .... 101 H1
Barnfield Dr
  PENT/RAD/TFW CF15 .... 97 F2
Barnfield Pl *CWM* NP44 ...... 19 E2
Barnstaple Rd *CDFNE* CF3 .... 102 A4
Barnwood Crs
  CAE/CAN/FWR CF5 .... 116 C4
Baroness Pl *PNTRTH/DP* CF64 * 134 B3
Baron Rd *PNTRTH/DP* CF64 .... 134 B3
Baron's Cl *LLAU* CF31 .... 136 D3
Barons Ct *CALD/MAG* CF62 .... 61 E3
Baron's Court Rd
  CYN/LLD/PWYN CF23 .... 113 F3
Barrack Hl *NWPT* NP20 .... 56 C2
Barrack La *CCDF* CF10 .... 4 E5
Barrians Wy *BARRY/W* CF62 ... 139 E4
Barrie Gdns *NWPT* NP20 ...... 75 H2
Barrington Rd *CDFN* CF14 .... 111 F1
Barry Docks Link Rd
  BARRYE CF63 .... 140 B1
Barry Rd *BARRY/W* CF62 ...... 131 H4
  PNTRTH/DP CF64 .... 139 E4
  PPRD CF37 .... 44 B3
Barry Wk *RSTN* NP10 .... 54 D3
Barthropp St *NWPTE* NP19 .... 77 H1
Bartlett St *CAER* CF83 ...... 69 E2
Basil Pl *CATH/RTH/SPL* CF24 . 112 C5
Bassaleg Cl *CDFN* CF14 ...... 103 F5
Bassaleg Rd *NWPT* NP20 ...... 8 A5
Bassett Rd *PNTRTH/DP* CF64 .. 141 E4
Bassetts Fld *CDFN* CF14 ..... 85 F4
Bassett St *BARRYE* CF63 ..... 139 H3
  CAE/CAN/FWR CF5 .... 118 D5
  PPRD CF37 .... 44 B3
Bastian Cl *BARRYE* CF63 ..... 139 H2
Batchelor Rd *CDFN* CF14 ..... 111 H1
  NWPTE NP19 .... 57 G4
Bath Gn *CWM* NP44 .... 26 C1
Bath St *NWPTE* NP19 .... 57 E3
Batten Wy *PPRD* CF37 .... 45 C1
Baylis Cl *CAE/CAN/FWR* CF5 .. 117 H2
Baynton Cl *CAE/CAN/FWR* CF5 . 110 C3
Bayside Rd
  CLN/RNWPTE NP18 .... 41 H4
Bay Tree Cl
  CLN/RNWPTE NP18 .... 41 F4
Beach La *PNTRTH/DP* CF64 .... 134 D2
Beachley Rd *CHEP* NP16 ...... 28 D3
Beach Wy *PNTRTH/DP* CF64 .... 134 D2
  PNTRTH/DP CF64 .... 141 G5
Beacons Cl *RSTN* NP10 .... 54 D2
Beacon St *GTN/RVSD* CF11 .... 118 D1
Beale Cl *CAE/CAN/FWR* CF5 ... 116 D2
Beatrice Rd *CDFN* CF14 ...... 111 F1
Beatty Av
  CYN/LLD/PWYN CF23 .... 100 B5
Beatty Rd *NWPTE* NP19 .... 59 E2
Beauchamp St
  GTN/RVSD CF11 .... 4 A6
Beaufort Cl *CWM* NP44 .... 25 F2
Beaufort Rl *LLTR/LLH* CF72 .. 95 F4
Beaufort Pl *CHEP* NP16 ...... 28 C4
Beaufort Rd *NWPTE* NP19 ..... 57 G1
Beaufort Sq
  CATH/RTH/SPL CF24 .... 113 H6
Beaufort Ter *NWPT* NP20 ..... 8 D4
Beaufort Wy *BARRY/W* CF62 ... 144 A2
Beaumaris Cl *CHV/BDAU* CF38 . 81 H1
Beaumaris Dr *CWM* NP44 ...... 11 H4
Beaumaris Rd *CDFNE* CF3 ..... 114 B2
Beaumont Cl *BARRY/W* CF62 ... 144 B2
Beaumont Ct
  PNTRTH/DP CF64 * 134 B3
Beauville La *PNTRTH/DP* CF64 . 134 D2
Beavers Wk *RSTN* NP10 .... 75 E1
Beckgrove Cl
  CATH/RTH/SPL CF24 .... 114 A5
Bedda Rd *CAE/CAN/FWR* CF5 ... 116 C4
Bedavere Cl *CDFN* CF14 ...... 85 H5
Beddick Rd *CWM* NP44 .... 18 D5
Bedford Cl *CWM* NP44 .... 18 D5
Bedford Pl
  CATH/RTH/SPL CF24 .... 5 G2
Bedford Rl *CDFN* CF14 .... 137 E3
Bedford Rd *NWPTE* NP19 ...... 57 H4
Bedford St
  CATH/RTH/SPL CF24 .... 5 F1
Bedlington Ter
  BARRY/W CF62 .... 2 C1
Bedwas Cl *CDFNE* CF3 .... 103 F3
Bedwas Pl *PNTRTH/DP* CF64 ... 134 A2
Bedwas St *GTN/RVSD* CF11 .... 119 F5
Beecham St *NWPTE* NP19 ...... 58 C4
Beech Cl *CAER* CF83 .... 68 A3
CWM NP44 .... 19 G2
Beech Ct *PENT/RAD/TFW* CF15 . 84 A5
Beechcroft Rd *NWPTE* NP19 ... 57 H3
Beechdale Rd *NWPTE* NP19 .... 57 H3
Beecher Av *GTN/RVSD* CF11 ... 6 B7
Beeches Rd
  ABRC/NBR/RIS NP11 .... 36 B1
The Beeches Cl
  PPOOL/BLNAV NP4 .... 12 D5
The Beeches *CDFN* CF14 ...... 86 B4
Beechfield Av *NWPTE* NP19 ... 57 H3
Beechgrove *CAER* CF83 .... 49 F4
Beech Gv *CHEP* NP16 .... 28 D5
  RSTN NP10 .... 76 A4
Beechlea Cl *LLTR/LLH* CF72 .. 107 H2
Beechleigh Cl *CWM* NP44 ..... 18 C5
Beechley Dr
  CAE/CAN/FWR CF5 .... 109 H4
Beech Rd *CAE/CAN/FWR* CF5 ... 109 H5
  CALD/MAG NP26 .... 62 C2
  PPOOL/BLNAV NP4 .... 16 D4
Beech Tree Cl
  PENT/RAD/TFW CF15 .... 97 F4
Beechwood *CHEP* NP16 .... 28 A4
Beechwood Av
  ABRC/NBR/RIS NP11 .... 35 G2
Beechwood Crs *NWPTE* NP19 ... 57 G4
Beechwood Dr
  CHV/BDAU CF38 .... 80 D4
  PNTRTH/DP CF64 .... 134 A4
Beechwood Rd *NWPTE* NP19 .... 57 H4
  PENT/RAD/TFW CF15 .... 83 G3
Beechwood St *PPRD* CF37 ..... 46 A4
Beechwood Wk
  PPOOL/BLNAV NP4 .... 13 E5
Began Rd *CDFNE* CF3 .... 88 C4
Beidr Iorwg *BARRYE* CF63 .... 140 A1
Beignon Cl
  CATH/RTH/SPL CF24 .... 5 J7
Belle Vue Cl *PNTRTH/DP* CF64 . 85 H4
Bellevue St *NWPTE* NP19 ..... 110 D2
Belle Vue La *NWPT* NP20 ..... 25 H2
Belle Vue Rd *CWM* NP44 ...... 25 H2
Belle Vue Ter *BARRYE* CF63 .. 140 A3
  PNRTH/DP CF64 .... 134 D1
Bellin Cl *CLN/RNWPTE* NP18 .. 41 H2
Bell La *PPOOL/BLNAV* NP4 .... 12 C4
Bellslade Cl *CWM* NP44 ...... 25 H1
Bellvue Cl *CWM* NP44 .... 25 H1
Bell Vue Ter *NWPT* NP20 ..... 76 C2
Belmont Hl
  CYN/LLD/PWYN CF23 .... 58 C1
Belmont St *BARRYE* CF63 ..... 139 G3
Belmont Wk *CCDF* CF10 .... 7 F4
Belvedere Crs *BARRYE* CF63 .. 139 H4
Belvedere Ter *NWPT* NP20 .... 56 C2
Benbow Rd *NWPTE* NP19 .... 58 C2
Bencroft La *CALD/MAG* NP26 .. 61 E1
Benecrofte *BARRY/W* CF62 .... 144 C2
Ben Jonson Wy *NWPT* NP20 .... 75 H2
Benson Rd *RSTN* NP10 .... 54 D2
Beresford Ct
  CATH/RTH/SPL CF24 * 120 D1
Beresford Rd
  CATH/RTH/SPL CF24 .... 120 D1
  NWPTE NP19 .... 9 G2
Beresford Road La
  CATH/RTH/SPL CF24 .... 120 D1
Berkeley Crs
  PPOOL/BLNAV NP4 .... 17 E5
Berkeley Sq
  CAE/CAN/FWR CF5 .... 125 F1
Berkley Cl *RSTN* NP10 .... 74 C1
Berkley Dr *PNRTH/DP* CF64 ... 134 C5
Berkley Rd *RSTN* NP10 .... 74 C1
Bernard Av *CAE/CAN/FWR* CF5 . 118 B2
Bernard St
  ABRC/NBR/RIS NP11 .... 23 F4
Berry Ct *LLAU* CF31 .... 137 E3
Berrymead Rd
  CYN/LLD/PWYN CF23 .... 100 D3
Bertha St *PPRD* CF37 .... 67 F2
Berthin St *CWM* NP44 .... 19 E5
Berthwyd
  PENT/RAD/TFW CF15 .... 96 B1
Berthwin St *GTN/RVSD* CF11 .. 119 E1
Bertram St
  CATH/RTH/SPL CF24 .... 5 K2
Berw Rd *PPRD* CF37 .... 45 E2
Beryl Pl *BARRY/W* CF62 ...... 3 G1
Beryl Rd *BARRY/W* CF62 ...... 3 G1
Bessant Cl *COWBR* CF71 ...... 122 D4
Bessborough Dr
  CAE/CAN/FWR CF5 .... 119 F5
Bessemer Cl *PNRTH/DP* CF64 .. 127 G1
  NWPT NP20 .... 40 A3
Bessemer Rd *GTN/RVSD* CF11 .. 127 H1
Bethania Rw *CDFNE* CF3 ...... 102 C5
Bethania Wy *CDFNE* CF3 ...... 111 F1
Blenheim Av *CALD/MAG* NP26 .. 60 B3
Bethel La *CWM* NP44 .... 19 E2
Bethel Pl *CDFN* CF14 .... 99 G1
Bethel St *PPRD* CF37 .... 44 C4
Bethesda Pl *RSTN* NP10 ...... 54 D3
Bethesda Rl *RSTN* NP10 ...... 54 D3
Betjeman Av *CALD/MAG* NP26 .. 62 C4
Bettws Cl *NWPT* NP20 .... 40 A5
Bettws Hl *NWPT* NP20 .... 39 H5
Bettws La *NWPT* NP20 .... 40 A5
Bettws-y-Coed Rd
  CYN/LLD/PWYN CF23 .... 100 C3
Beulah Rd *CDFN* CF14 .... 99 F3
Bevan Cl *CAER* CF83 .... 50 A3
Bevan Pl *CDFN* CF14 .... 111 H3
Bevan's La *PPOOL/BLNAV* NP4 . 17 E5
Beverley St *BARRYE* CF63 .... 139 H2
Bicester Rd *PNRTH/DP* CF64 .. 140 C3
Bideford Rd *CDFNE* CF3 ...... 102 B5
Bigstone Cl *CHEP* NP16 ...... 29 E2
Bigstone Gv *CHEP* NP16 ...... 29 E2
Bigstone Mdw *CHEP* NP16 ..... 29 E2
Bilston St *NWPTE* NP19 ...... 57 G5
Birbeck Rd *CALD/MAG* NP26 ... 60 C3
Birch Ct *PENT/RAD/TFW* CF15 . 84 A5
Birch Crs *CHV/BDAU* CF38 .... 80 D5
The Birches *CWM* NP44 .... 19 F3
Birchfield Cl *CHV/BDAU* CF38 . 81 H1
Birchfield Crs
  CAE/CAN/FWR CF5 .... 118 A1
Birch Gv *ABRC/NBR/RIS* NP11 . 37 F4
  BARRY/W CF62 .... 2 A7
Birchgrove *CAER* CF83 .... 50 A3
Birch Gv *CHV/BDAU* CF38 ..... 81 C1
Birchgrove Rd *NWPTE* NP19 ... 54 C3
Birchgrove Cl *NWPT* NP20 .... 40 C4
Birchgrove Rd *CDFN* CF14 .... 111 H1
Birch Hl *NWPT* NP20 .... 40 C3
  PENT/RAD/TFW CF15 .... 134 C5
Birch La *PNRTH/DP* CF64 ..... 134 C5
Birchley *PPRD* CF37 .... 65 E1
Birch Pl *CDFN* CF14 .... 110 B5
Birch Trees *RSTN* NP10 ...... 75 E2
Birchwood Av *PPRD* CF37 ..... 65 F2
Birchwood Gdns *CDFN* CF14 ... 100 A2
Birchwood La
  CYN/LLD/PWYN CF23 .... 112 D2
Birchwood Rd
  CYN/LLD/PWYN CF23 .... 112 D2
Birdwood Gdns *CHEP* NP16 .... 30 A3
Birgantine Wy *RSTN* NP10 .... 92 A1
Birkdale Cl *CDFNE* CF3 ...... 103 F2
Bishop Hannon Dr
  CAE/CAN/FWR CF5 .... 109 H4
Bishops' Av
  CAE/CAN/FWR CF5 .... 110 D5
Bishops Cl *CAE/CAN/FWR* CF5 . 110 D5
Bishops Cl *CDFN* CF14 .... 111 E1
  CHEP NP16 .... 30 D3
Bishops Mdl *CHEP* NP16 ...... 30 D3
Bishops Pl *CAE/CAN/FWR* CF5 . 110 D5
Bishop's Rd *CDFN* CF14 ...... 111 E1
Bishopston Rd
  CAE/CAN/FWR CF5 .... 117 G4
Bishop St *GTN/RVSD* CF11 .... 119 F5
  NWPTE NP19 .... 57 E3
Bishops' Wk
  CAE/CAN/FWR CF5 .... 110 D5
Bishpool Av *NWPTE* NP19 ..... 58 C3
Bishpool Cl *NWPTE* NP19 ..... 58 C3
Bishpool Gdns *NWPTE* NP19 ... 58 C3
Bishpool La *NWPTE* NP19 ..... 58 C3
Bishpool Wy *NWPTE* NP19 ..... 58 C3
Bishton La *CHEP* NP16 .... 29 E1
Bishton Rd
  CLN/RNWPTE NP18 .... 59 C4
Bisley Cl *CATH/RTH/SPL* CF24 . 121 C1
Bittern Wy *PNTRTH/DP* CF64 .. 142 C2
Blackberry Dr *BARRY/W* CF62 . 138 C5
Blackberry Wy
  CYN/LLD/PWYN CF23 .... 101 H1
Blackbird Cl *RSTN* NP10 ..... 75 F1
Blackbird Rd *BARRY/W* CF62 .. 137 G3
  CALD/MAG NP26 .... 63 E4
Blackbirds Cl *CWM* NP44 ..... 40 B1
Blackbirds Wy *CDFNE* CF3 .... 103 G3
Blackbrook Rd *CAER* CF83 .... 68 B4
Blackett Av *NWPT* NP20 ...... 40 B3
Black Horse La *NWPTE* NP19 * . 77 H1
Blackmoor Pl *CDFNE* CF3 ..... 102 B4
Black Oak Rd
  CYN/LLD/PWYN CF23 .... 100 D3
Black Rd *PPRD* CF37 .... 64 C2
Blacksmiths Wy *RSTN* NP10 ... 90 D1
Blackstone St
  GTN/RVSD CF11 * 119 F3
Blackthorn Gv
  CLN/RNWPTE NP18 .... 41 H4
Blacktown Gdns *CDFNE* CF3 ... 104 B2
Blackvein Rd
  ABRC/NBR/RIS NP11 .... 36 C3
Blackwater Cl *NWPT* NP20 .... 39 G4
Blackweir Ter *CCDF* CF10 .... 112 A5
Blackwell Cl *BARRYE* CF63 * . 139 H3
Blaenavon Cl *CDFNE* CF3 ..... 103 F3
Blaenclydach Pl
  GTN/RVSD CF11 * 6 B2
Blaenclydach St
  GTN/RVSD CF11 .... 6 B2
Blaendare Farm La
  PPOOL/BLNAV NP4 .... 16 A2
Blaendare Rd
  PPOOL/BLNAV NP4 .... 16 B1
Blaen Ifor *CAER* CF83 .... 48 B3
Blaenwern *CWM* NP44 .... 20 A2
Blaen-y-Coed *CDFN* CF14 ..... 99 F2
  PENT/RAD/TFW CF15 .... 83 H2
Blaen-y-Cwm Vw *CWM* NP44 .... 11 H4
Blaen-y-Pant Av *NWPT* NP20 .. 24 C2
Blaen-y-Pant Crs *NWPT* NP20 . 56 B1
Blagdon Cl *CDFNE* CF3 .... 102 A5
Blaina Cl *CDFNE* CF3 .... 103 F3
Blaise Pl *GTN/RVSD* CF11 .... 128 A1
Blake Rd *NWPTE* NP19 .... 78 A1
Blanche Cl *RSTN* NP10 .... 92 A1
Blanche St
  CATH/RTH/SPL CF24 .... 120 D1
Blandon Wy *CDFN* CF14 .... 111 F1
Blenheim Av *CALD/MAG* NP26 .. 60 B3
Blenheim Cl *CALD/MAG* NP26 .. 60 A3
Blenheim Dr *BARRY/W* CF62 ... 60 A3
Blenheim Gdns
  CALD/MAG NP26 .... 60 B3
Blenheim Pk *CALD/MAG* NP26 .. 60 B3
Blenheim Rd
  CATH/RTH/SPL CF24 .... 113 E5
  CDFNE CF3 .... 25 F1
  NWPTE NP19 .... 57 H1
Bleriot Cl *NWPTE* NP19 ...... 77 H1
Blethin Cl *CAE/CAN/FWR* CF5 . 110 C2
Blewitt St *NWPT* NP20 .... 8 C4
Blodwen Rd
  PPOOL/BLNAV NP4 .... 17 G1
Blodyn y Gog *BARRYE* CF63 ... 140 A1
Bloomfield Cl *NWPTE* NP19 ... 58 D1
Bloom St *GTN/RVSD* CF11 ..... 118 D1
Blosse Rd *CDFN* CF14 .... 99 G1
Blossom Cl
  CLN/RNWPTE NP18 .... 59 G1
Blossom Dr *CDFN* CF14 .... 86 A3
Bluebell Cl *CWM* NP44 .... 24 C1
Bluebell Dr *CDFNE* CF3 ...... 88 D2
  CHEP NP16 .... 30 D2
Bluebell Wy *RSTN* NP10 ...... 54 A2
Blue House Rd *CDFN* CF14 .... 99 H1
Bluett's La *PPOOL/BLNAV* NP4 . 12 B2
Bluett's Rd *PPOOL/BLNAV* NP4 . 12 B2
Blyth Cl *BARRY/W* CF62 ...... 131 G5
Bodnant Cl *CDFNE* CF3 .... 103 E4
Bolwyn Wk
  CYN/LLD/PWYN CF23 .... 113 E3
Bolt Cl *NWPTE* NP20 .... 9 G7
Bolton Rd *NWPT* NP20 .... 8 A5
Bolt St *NWPT* NP20 .... 9 G7
Boncath Rd *CDFN* CF14 .... 111 E3
Bond St *NWPTE* NP19 .... 58 B4
Bonvilston Rd *CDFN* CF14 .... 111 H1
Bonvilston Ter *PPRD* CF37 * . 45 E2
Booker St *CATH/RTH/SPL* CF24 . 120 D1
Boon Cl *BARRYE* CF63 .... 139 G2
Borage Cl
  CYN/LLD/PWYN CF23 .... 101 F1
Borough Av *BARRY/W* CF62 .... 17 B2
Borough Cl *COWBR* CF71 ...... 122 D4
Borrowdale Cl
  CYN/LLD/PWYN CF23 .... 113 E3
Borth Rd *CDFNE* CF3 .... 102 C5
Boswell Cl *CDFNE* CF3 .... 102 A2
  NWPT NP20 .... 76 A2
Bosworth Dr *NWPT* NP20 ...... 56 B2
Boulevard De Nantes
  CCDF CF10 .... 4 C3
Boverton Brook *LLMJ* CF61 ... 137 E4
Boverton Cl *LLMJ* CF61 ...... 137 E3
Boverton Pk *LLMJ* CF61 ...... 137 F3
Boverton Park Dr *LLMJ* CF61 . 137 E4
Boverton Rd *LLMJ* CF61 ...... 136 D3
Boverton St
  CYN/LLD/PWYN CF23 .... 112 D4
Bowen Pl *NWPT* NP20 .... 51 H2
Bowleaze *CWM* NP44 .... 19 E5
Bowls Cl *CAER* CF83 .... 48 A3
Bowls La *CAER* CF83 .... 48 A3
Bowman's Wy *COWBR* CF71 ..... 122 B1
Bowman's Well *COWBR* CF71 ... 122 B3
Boxtree Cl *CLN/RNWPTE* NP18 . 41 F4
Boyle Cl *NWPT* NP20 .... 40 B3
Brachdy Cl *CDFNE* CF3 .... 114 B3
Brachdy La *CDFNE* CF3 .... 114 B3
Brachdy Rd *CDFNE* CF3 .... 114 B3
Bradenham Pl
  PNTRTH/DP CF64 .... 134 C2
The Brades
  CLN/RNWPTE NP18 .... 42 A3
Bradford Pl *PNRTH/DP* CF64 .. 134 C2
Bradford St *CAER* CF83 ...... 68 D2
  GTN/RVSD CF11 .... 6 B5
Bradley St
  CATH/RTH/SPL CF24 .... 120 D1
Braeval St
  CYN/LLD/PWYN CF23 .... 59 F3
Brain Cl *NWPTE* NP19 .... 58 C3
Bramble Av *BARRY/W* CF62 .... 138 C3
Bramble Cl *CAE/CAN/FWR* CF5 . 109 H4
Bramble Rl *PNRTH/DP* CF64 ... 134 C4
Bramblewood Cl *CDFN* CF14 ... 86 A5
Brambling Dr *CDFN* CF14 ..... 85 E5
Bramley Cl *CLN/RNWPTE* NP18 . 59 H1
Bramshill Dr
  CYN/LLD/PWYN CF23 .... 102 A1
Brandreth Gdns
  CYN/LLD/PWYN CF23 .... 113 E3
Brandreth Rd
  CYN/LLD/PWYN CF23 .... 113 E3
Brangwyn Cl *PNRTH/DP* CF64 .. 134 B1
Brangwyn Rd *PNRTH/DP* CF64 .. 134 B1
Branwen Cl
  CAE/CAN/FWR CF5 .... 125 C1
Brassknocker St
  CALD/MAG NP26 .... 60 C3
Braunton Av *CDFNE* CF3 ...... 102 B4
Braunton Crs *CDFNE* CF3 ..... 102 A4
Brayford Pl *CDFNE* CF3 ...... 102 B2
Breaksea Dr *BARRY/W* CF62 ... 144 D1
Brean Cl *PNRTH/DP* CF64 ..... 141 G4
Brechfa Cl *CLN/RNWPTE* NP18 . 27 F4
Brecon Rd *NWPTE* NP19 .... 57 E3
Brecon St *CAE/CAN/FWR* CF5 .. 118 D2
Bredon Cl
  ABRC/NBR/RIS NP11 .... 37 F5
Brendon Ct *CDFNE* CF3 .... 102 B4
Brendon View Cl
  BARRY/W CF62 .... 144 C2
Brenig Cl *BARRY/W* CF62 ..... 138 C3
  CDFN CF14 * 86 A4
Brent Rd *PNRTH/DP* CF64 ..... 140 C3
Brianne Dr *CDFN* CF14 .... 86 A4
Briar Cl *CAE/CAN/FWR* CF5 ... 110 A5
Briardene *CDFNE* CF3 .... 102 B4
Briarmeadow Dr *CDFN* CF14 ... 86 B5
The Briars *CALD/MAG* NP26 ... 60 B3
Briar Wy *CHV/BDAU* CF38 ..... 81 H1
Briarwood Dr
  CYN/LLD/PWYN CF23 .... 100 D3
Bridel La *NWPT* NP20 .... 55 C5
Bridewell Gdns
  CALD/MAG NP26 .... 61 E4
Bridgeman Ct
  PNRTH/DP CF64 * 134 C2
Bridgeman Rd
  PNRTH/DP CF64 .... 134 C2
Bridge Rd *CAE/CAN/FWR* CF5 .. 110 D3
  CDFNE CF3 .... 114 B3
  COWBR CF71 .... 122 B3
  PPRD CF37 .... 45 G2
Bridge St
  ABRC/NBR/RIS NP11 .... 23 E1
  BARRYE CF63 .... 139 G2
  CAE/CAN/FWR CF5 .... 111 E4
  CCDF CF10 .... 5 F4
  CHEP NP16 .... 28 D3
  NWPT NP20 .... 8 C5
  PNRTH/DP CF64 .... 134 B1
  PPRD CF37 .... 45 F2
Bridget Dr *CHEP* NP16 .... 29 F5
Bridge Ter *GTN/RVSD* CF11 ... 73 F5
Bridgewater Rd
  PNRTH/DP CF64 .... 141 F4
Bridgwater Rd *CDFNE* CF3 .... 102 C4
Brierley Cl
  ABRC/NBR/RIS NP11 .... 37 H5
Briers Ga *CWM* NP44 .... 24 B3
Brigante Dr *RSTN* NP10 ...... 92 A1
Brigantine Gv *RSTN* NP10 .... 92 A1
Brigantine Pl *CCDF* CF10 .... 5 J2
Brigham Ct *CDFN* CF14 .... 47 H5
Bright St *ABRC/NBR/RIS* NP11 . 36 B2
Brindley Rd *GTN/RVSD* CF11 .. 127 H2
Bristol Packet Whf
  NWPT NP20 .... 9 F5
Bristol St *NWPTE* NP19 ...... 9 H1
Bristol View Cl *CWM* NP44 * . 18 D4
Britannia Qy *CCDF* CF10 ..... 7 H6
Brithdir St
  CATH/RTH/SPL CF24 .... 112 B4
British Legion Dr *CDFNE* CF3 . 114 B1
British School Cl
  PPOOL/BLNAV NP4 .... 12 B3
Briton Cl *CHEP* NP16 .... 30 D3
Britten Cl *NWPTE* NP19 ...... 58 C5
Britten Rd *CDFNE* CF3 .... 134 B5
Britway Rd *PNRTH/DP* CF64 ... 138 B2
Broadacres *BNE* NP18 .... 81 G2
  GTN/RVSD CF11 .... 118 D4
Broad Cl *BARRY/W* CF62 * 138 B4
Broadcommon Cl
  NWPTE NP19 .... 78 B1
Broadfield Ct
  CAE/CAN/FWR CF5 .... 117 C4
Broadhaven *GTN/RVSD* CF11 ... 118 C4
Broadlands Ct
  CALD/MAG NP26 .... 60 D3
  CDFNE CF3 .... 102 D3
Broadmead Rd *NWPTE* NP19 .... 78 B1
Broadmead *GTN/RVSD* CF11 * .. 118 D3
Broad Quay Rd *NWPTE* NP19 ... 77 F4
The Broad Shoard
  COWBR CF71 .... 122 C3
Broadstairs Rd
  GTN/RVSD CF11 .... 118 D3
Broad St *BARRY/W* CF62 ...... 2 D4
  GTN/RVSD CF11 .... 118 D3
  PPOOL/BLNAV NP4 .... 12 C4
  PPRD CF37 .... 17 E2
Broad Street Comn
  CLN/RNWPTE NP18 .... 79 C5
Broad Street Pde
  BARRY/W CF62 .... 2 D4
Broad Vw *CWM* NP44 .... 19 F3
Broadwalk
  CLN/RNWPTE NP18 .... 42 A4
Broadwater Rd *NWPTE* NP19 ... 78 B3
Broadway
  CATH/RTH/SPL CF24 .... 5 K2
  NWPTE NP19 .... 42 A5
  COWBR CF71 .... 122 C4
  PPOOL/BLNAV NP4 .... 14 B3
  PPRD CF37 .... 44 D4
Broadway Gn
  CAE/CAN/FWR CF5 .... 124 A2
Broadweir Rd *CWM* NP44 ...... 25 H1
Broadwell Cl *CDFNE* CF3 ..... 103 E4
Broadwell Ct
  CLN/RNWPTE NP18 .... 42 A4
Bro Athro *CDFNE* CF3 .... 114 D1
Brocastle Rd *CDFN* CF14 ..... 99 E4
Brockhampton Rd *CDFNE* CF3 .. 103 E3
Brockhill Wy *PNRTH/DP* CF64 . 142 C1
Brodeg *PENT/RAD/TFW* CF15 ... 96 B2
Bromfield Pl *PNRTH/DP* CF64 . 134 D2
Bromfield Rd *BARRY/W* CF62 .. 3 F5
Bromfield St *GTN/RVSD* CF11 . 6 A5
Bromley Dr
  GTN/RVSD CF11 .... 6 A5
Bron Awelon *BARRY/W* CF62 ... 146 B1
Bron Felen *CDFN* CF14 .... 85 G5
Bronhall *LLTR/LLH* CF72 ..... 94 D3
Bronhaul
  PENT/RAD/TFW CF15 .... 96 B2
Bronllwyn
  PENT/RAD/TFW CF15 .... 96 A2
Bronllys Gv *RSTN* NP10 ...... 91 G2
Bronllys Pl *CWM* NP44 .... 20 B3
Bronmynydd *CAER* CF83 .... 47 F3
Bronrhiw Av *CAER* CF83 ...... 69 E3
Bronte Cl *CDFNE* CF3 .... 102 B2
Bronte Gv *NWPT* NP20 .... 75 H2
Bronwydd Av
  CYN/LLD/PWYN CF23 .... 113 E3
Bronwydd Cl
  CYN/LLD/PWYN CF23 .... 113 E3
Bronwydd Rd
  CATH/RTH/SPL CF24 .... 114 A5
Bron-y-Mor *BARRY/W* CF62 .... 146 C3
Brookdale Ct *CHV/BDAU* CF38 . 81 F1
Brookfield Av *BARRYE* CF63 .. 140 A1
Brookfield Cl *NWPTE* NP19 ... 58 C1
Brookfield Dr *CDFNE* CF3 .... 102 D4
Brookfield La *PPRD* CF37 .... 45 F1
Brookfield Park Rd
  COWBR CF71 .... 122 D4
Brooklands Ter
  CAE/CAN/FWR CF5 .... 125 F1
Brookland Ter *CWM* NP44 ..... 19 H2
Brooklea *CALD/MAG* NP26 ..... 60 B3
Brooklyn Cl *CWM* NP44 .... 98 D1
Brook Rd *CAE/CAN/FWR* CF5 ... 118 A1
  CDFN CF14 .... 111 F1
Brookside *BARRYE* CF63 ...... 139 H2
  CAER CF83 .... 62 D2
  CHV/BDAU CF38 .... 81 H1
  NWPT NP20 .... 133 F3
Brookside Cl *CAER* CF83 ..... 48 A5
  CWM NP44 .... 99 F5
Brookside Crs *CAER* CF83 .... 48 A5
Brook St *BARRYE* CF63 .... 139 C3
  CAER CF83 .... 47 F1
  CWM NP44 .... 19 H1
  GTN/RVSD CF11 .... 4 A5

PPRD CF37 .... 65 F1
Brookvale Dr CDFN CF14 .... 85 H4
Brookview Cl CDFN CF14 .... 86 A5
Brookway CHV/BDAU CF38 .... 81 H1
Broom Cl RSTN NP10 .... 54 B3
Broomfield Cl
    PENT/RAD/TFW CF15 .... 81 H1
    NWPTE NP19 * 58 C3
Broomfield St CAER CF83 * 69 E2
Broom Pl
    CAE/CAN/FWR CF5 .... 110 B5
Broughton Pl BARRYE CF63 .... 139 G1
Brown Cl NWPTE NP19 .... 77 H1
Brown Ct CDFNE CF3 .... 105 E5
Browning Cl CDFNE CF3 .... 102 A3
    NWPT NP20 .... 76 A2
Bro-y-Fan CAER CF83 .... 49 F4
Bruce Knight Cl
    CAE/CAN/FWR CF5 .... 110 C3
Bruce St CATH/RTH/SPL CF24 .... 112 C4
Brundall Crs
    CAE/CAN/FWR CF5 .... 116 D5
Brunel Av RSTN NP10 .... 55 E3
Brunel Cl BARRYE CF63 .... 140 B1
Brunel Rd CHEP NP16 .... 30 C1
    NWPT NP20 .... 24 D1
Brunel St CR/RVSD CF11 .... 119 F3
    NWPT NP20 .... 77 E3
Brunswick St
    CAE/CAN/FWR CF5 .... 118 D2
Bruton Pl CAE/CAN/FWR CF5 ..... 111 E4
Bryanston Rd
    PNRTH/DP CF64 .... 140 C3
Brydges Pl
    CATH/RTH/SPL CF24 .... 112 C5
Bryn Aber CAER CF83 .... 47 F1
Bryn Adar CDFN CF14 .... 98 C2
Brynamlwg LLTR/LLH CF72 .... 94 D5
    PPOOL/BLNAV NP4 .... 12 B5
Brynau Rd CAER CF83 .... 69 E1
Bryn Canol CAER CF83 .... 49 H3
Bryn Carreg
    PPOOL/BLNAV NP4 * 12 C2
Bryn Castell
    PENT/RAD/TFW CF15 .... 97 G3
Bryn Celyn
    CYN/LLD/PWYN CF23 .... 101 G4
Bryn Celyn Pl CWM NP44 .... 19 G5
Bryn Celyn Rd CWM NP44 .... 19 F5
    CYN/LLD/PWYN CF23 .... 101 G4
Bryn Cl CAER CF83 .... 50 A3
Bryncoed
    PENT/RAD/TFW CF15 .... 97 F4
Bryncoed Ter CAER CF83 .... 47 F1
Bryncyn
    CYN/LLD/PWYN CF23 .... 101 F2
Bryn Derw CHV/BDAU CF38 .... 80 B3
Bryn Derwen CAER CF83 .... 48 C3
    PENT/RAD/TFW CF15 .... 97 F3
Brynderwen Cl
    CYN/LLD/PWYN CF23 .... 113 E1
Brynderwen Gv
    NWPTE NP19 .... 57 F3
Brynderwen Rd
    NWPTE NP19 .... 57 F3
Bryn Dewi Sant
    LLTR/LLH CF72 .... 94 D5
Bryn-Dolwen CAER CF83 .... 49 H2
Bryn Eglwys CWM NP44 .... 20 B3
    PPRD CF37 .... 44 B3
Brynfab Rd PPRD CF37 .... 46 A5
Brynfedw CAER CF83 .... 49 H2
    CYN/LLD/PWYN CF23 .... 101 E4
Bryn-Garreg
    PPOOL/BLNAV NP4 .... 12 C2
Bryn Garw CWM NP44 .... 20 B3
Bryngelli Ter CAER CF83 .... 47 F1
Bryn Glas CAER CF83 .... 49 H2
    CDFN CF14 .... 85 F5
Brynglas CWM NP44 .... 25 E3
Brynglas Av NWPT NP20 .... 20 B3
Brynglas Ct NWPT NP20 .... 40 C5
Brynglas Dr NWPT NP20 .... 56 C1
Brynglas Crs NWPTE NP20 .... 56 C1
Brynglas Rd NWPT NP20 .... 56 C1
Bryn Goleu CAER CF83 .... 49 H2
Bryn Golwg
    PENT/RAD/TFW CF15 .... 97 G3
Bryn Gomer CWM NP44 .... 20 B2
Bryngwennol CAER CF83 .... 33 H1
Bryngwyn CAER CF83 .... 68 C3
Bryn-Gwyn Rd
    CYN/LLD/PWYN CF23 .... 100 D3
Bryngwyn Rd NWPT NP20 .... 8 A4
    PPOOL/BLNAV NP4 .... 14 B4
Bryn-Gwyn St CAER CF83 .... 49 G2
Brynhafod Rd CAER CF83 .... 47 F2
Bryn Haidd
    CYN/LLD/PWYN CF23 .... 101 G3
Bryn Hedydd RSTN NP10 .... 74 B1
Bryn Heol CAER CF83 .... 48 C3
Brynheulog CDFN CF14 .... 98 C5
    CYN/LLD/PWYN CF23 .... 101 G3
Bryn Heulog
    PPOOL/BLNAV NP4 .... 16 D1
Bryn Heulog Ter CAER CF83 .... 51 G1
Brynhill Cl BARRYI/W CF62 .... 138 D1
Brynhyfryd CAER CF83 .... 48 C5
    CHV/BDAU CF38 .... 80 B3
    CWM NP44 .... 20 B3
    PENT/RAD/TFW CF15 .... 97 F5
Brynhyfryd Av NWPT NP20 .... 36 C5
Brynhyfryd Rd NWPT NP20 .... 8 B5
Brynhyfryd Ter CAER CF83 .... 48 A4
Bryn Ifor CAER CF83 .... 48 A4
Bryn Ilan PPRD CF37 .... 45 G4

Bryn Llus PPRD CF37 .... 44 C5
Brynmawr Cl CDFNE CF3 .... 103 F3
Bryn Milwr CWM NP44 .... 25 F3
Bryn Nant CAER CF83 .... 48 A3
Bryn Olwg PPRD CF37 .... 45 F2
Brynonnen Ct CWM NP44 .... 24 C3
Bryn Owain CAER CF83 .... 48 B3
Bryn Pinwydden
    CYN/LLD/PWYN CF23 .... 101 F2
Bryn-Rhedyn CAER CF83 .... 49 G5
    CHV/BDAU CF38 .... 80 B5
    CWM NP44 .... 26 C3
Bryn Rhosyn
    PENT/RAD/TFW CF15 .... 97 F3
Bryn Siriol CAER CF83 .... 48 A4
    PENT/RAD/TFW CF15 .... 96 A2
Bryn Teg CAER CF83 .... 48 B3
Brynteg CDFN CF14 .... 98 D1
    PPOOL/BLNAV NP4 .... 12 C4
Brynteg Cl
    CYN/LLD/PWYN CF23 .... 113 E1
Brynteg Ct CHV/BDAU CF38 .... 80 B5
Brynteg La LLTR/LLH CF72 .... 80 A5
The Bryn CAER CF83 .... 47 F1
    NWPT NP20 .... 39 H5
Bryntirion CAER CF83 * 48 B4
    CAER CF83 .... 94 D5
    CDFN CF14 .... 99 F2
Bryn-y-Fran Av CAER CF83 .... 50 A2
Bryn y Glown BARRYI/W CF62 ... 144 D4
Bryn-Nant
    CYN/LLD/PWYN CF23 .... 101 F5
Bryn-yr-Eglwys
    PENT/RAD/TFW CF15 .... 96 B2
Bryn yr Ysgol CAER CF83 .... 48 A3
Brython Dr CDFNE CF3 .... 103 F3
Buccaneer Cl RSTN NP10 .... 91 H1
Buccaneer Gv RSTN NP10 .... 91 H1
Buccaneer Wy RSTN NP10 .... 92 A1
Buchanan Wy RSTN NP10 .... 74 A2
Buchan Cl NWPT NP20 .... 76 A2
Buckingham Cl CWM NP44 .... 86 C5
Buckingham Crs NWPTE NP19 .... 57 G3
Buckingham Pl
    BARRYI/W CF62 .... 138 C1
Buckle Wd CHEP NP16 .... 28 A4
Buckley Cl CAE/CAN/FWR CF5 .. 110 B2
Budden Crs CALD/MAC NP26 ..... 62 D2
Builth Cl RSTN NP10 .... 91 G2
Bull Cliff Wk BARRYI/W CF62 .... 146 A2
Bullfinch Rd BARRYI/W CF62 ..... 137 H3
Bulmark Cl LLTR/LLH CF72 .... 95 E2
Bulmors Rd
    CLN/RNWPTE NP18 .... 42 C5
Bulrush Cl CDFNE CF3 .... 103 F4
Bulwark Av CHEP NP16 .... 30 C5
Bulwark Rd CHEP NP16 .... 28 C5
Bunyan Cl CDFNE CF3 .... 102 C2
Burberry Cl RSTN NP10 .... 54 A2
Burges Pl GTN/RVSD CF11 .... 119 F5
Burgesse Crs LLTR/LLH CF72 ..... 95 E1
Burial La LLM/ CF61 .... 136 C3
Burleigh Rd NWPT NP20 .... 8 B4
Burlington St BARRYE CF63 ...... 139 H4
Burlington Ter
    CATH/RTH/SPL CF24 .... 118 C1
Burnaby St
    CATH/RTH/SPL CF24 .... 120 D2
Burne Jones Cl
    CAE/CAN/FWR CF5 .... 110 C3
Burnfort Rd NWPT NP20 .... 75 H1
Burnham Av CDFNE CF3 .... 102 B4
    PNRTH/DP CF64 .... 141 F5
Burns Cl NWPT NP20 .... 75 H3
Burns Crs BARRYI/W CF62 .... 139 E1
    CALD/MAC NP26 .... 62 C4
Burns La CWM NP44 .... 25 C1
Burn's Wy PPRD CF37 .... 64 C1
Burnt Barn Rd CHEP NP16 .... 30 C2
Burreed Cl CDFNE CF3 .... 103 G4
Burton Rd NWPT NP20 .... 57 G1
Burt Pl CCDF CF10 * 6 E5
Burt St CCDF CF10 .... 6 E5
Burwell Cl
    CYN/LLD/PWYN CF23 .... 102 A1
Bushy Pk PPOOL/BLNAV NP4 ... 14 A3
Bute Crs CCDF CF10 .... 4 C5
Bute Esp CCDF CF10 .... 7 G5
Bute La PNRTH/DP CF64 .... 134 C2
Bute Pl CCDF CF10 .... 6 E1
Bute St CCDF CF10 .... 6 E1
    PENT/RAD/TFW CF15 .... 97 H1
Bute Ter CCDF CF10 .... 4 E6
Butleigh Av
    CAE/CAN/FWR CF5 .... 118 B1
Butler's Ct
    PPOOL/BLNAV NP4 .... 12 B1
Butterbur Pl
    CAE/CAN/FWR CF5 .... 116 D3
Buttercup Ct CWM NP44 .... 24 C2
Butterfield Dr
    CYN/LLD/PWYN CF23 .... 101 F1
Butterfly Cl CHV/BDAU CF38 ...... 81 G2
Buttermere Wy
    NWPTE NP19 .... 57 F1
Butterworth Cl NWPTE NP19 ...... 58 D3
Buttington Hl CHEP NP16 .... 29 F5
Buttington Rd CHEP NP16 .... 29 E5
Buttington Ter CHEP NP16 .... 31 F1
Button Ride
    CAE/CAN/FWR CF5 .... 124 A3
Buttrills Rd BARRYE CF63 .... 3 F1
Buttrills Wk BARRYE CF63 .... 139 F1
The Butts COWBR CF71 .... 122 C5
Buxton Ct CAER CF83 .... 69 F1
Bwlch Rd CAE/CAN/FWR CF5 .. 117 G1
Byrd Crs PNRTH/DP CF64 .... 134 A5
Byrde Cl NWPTE NP19 .... 58 B4
Byrn Llongwr
    BARRYI/W CF62 .... 3 H7
Byron Av CHV/BDAU CF38 .... 80 B5
Byron Ct PNRTH/DP CF64 .... 134 A1
Byron Pl CALD/MAC NP26 .... 62 C4
    CWM NP44 .... 25 C3
    PNRTH/DP CF64 .... 134 B2
Byron Rd NWPT NP20 .... 76 A2
Byron St BARRYI/W CF62 .... 139 F4
    CATH/RTH/SPL CF24 .... 5 G2
Bythway Rd
    PPOOL/BLNAV NP4 .... 14 C1

Byways CWM NP44 .... 19 E5

C

Caban Cl RSTN NP10 .... 55 E2
Cader Idris Cl
    ABRC/NBR/RIS NP11 .... 37 H4
Cadman Cl
    CATH/RTH/SPL CF24 .... 121 F1
Cadnant Cl CDFN CF14 .... 99 G1
Cadoc Crs BARRYE CF63 .... 140 D3
Cadoc Pl CAER CF83 .... 110 C2
Cadoc Rd CWM NP44 .... 19 F2
Cadogan Ct
    CLN/RNWPTE NP18 .... 41 G3
Cadvan Rd CAE/CAN/FWR CF5 . 117 E2
Cadwgan Pl
    CAE/CAN/FWR CF5 .... 117 H1
Cadwgan Rd CWM NP44 .... 20 A2
Caeaglas Av CDFNE CF3 .... 114 B2
Caeglas Rd CDFNE CF3 .... 114 B2
Cae Bach CAER CF83 .... 51 F3
Cae Bedw CAER CF83 .... 48 C5
Cae-Brynton Rd NWPT NP20 ...... 76 C2
Cae Cadno CHV/BDAU CF38 ..... 81 G1
Cae Calch CAER CF83 .... 48 B4
Cae Canol PNRTH/DP CF64 ..... 134 A5
Cae Caradog CAER CF83 .... 47 H3
Cae Croes Heol CAER CF83 .... 48 D4
Caedelyn Rd CDFN CF14 .... 98 A4
Cae Du Mawr CAER CF83 .... 48 B2
Cae Fardre CHV/BDAU CF38 ..... 81 G1
Cae Ffynnon CAER CF83 .... 6 C5
Cae Garw CDFN CF14 .... 85 G5
    CHV/BDAU CF38 .... 80 C5
    PNRTH/DP CF64 .... 133 E4
Cae Garwed
    PENT/RAD/TFW CF15 .... 97 H1
Cae Gethin CAER CF83 .... 48 C3
Cae Glas BARRYE CF63 .... 139 H2
    CAER CF83 .... 48 B4
Cae Nant Coch CAER CF83 .... 68 A3
Cae Nant Gledyr CAER CF83 ...... 68 A1
Caenant Rd CAER CF83 .... 68 A1
Caenewydd Cl
    CAE/CAN/FWR CF5 .... 116 C2
Cae Pandy CAER CF83 .... 49 E4
Cae Pen-Y-Graig CAER CF83 ..... 48 B2
Cae Perllan Rd NWPT NP20 .... 75 F5
Caerau Court Rd
    CAE/CAN/FWR CF5 .... 117 H4
Caerau Crs NWPT NP20 .... 8 D5
Caerau La CAE/CAN/FWR CF5 .. 125 H2
    PENT/RAD/TFW CF15 .... 96 C2
Caerau Park Crs
    CAE/CAN/FWR CF5 .... 117 G4
Caerau Park Pl
    CAE/CAN/FWR CF5 * 117 H4
Caerau Park Rd
    CAE/CAN/FWR CF5 .... 117 H4
Cae Rex COWBR CF71 .... 122 C4
Cae'r Fferm CAER CF83 .... 68 B1
Cae'r Ffynnon BARRYI/W CF62 ... 3 G1
Cae'r Graig
    PENT/RAD/TFW CF15 .... 97 F3
Cae Rhedyn CWM NP44 .... 20 C4
Cae Rhos CAER CF83 .... 49 E4
Caerleon Cl CDFNE CF3 .... 103 F3
Caerleon Ct CAER CF83 .... 47 H5
Caerleon Rd CDFN CF14 .... 111 H3
    CWM NP44 .... 26 D2
    NWPTE NP19 .... 57 F2
    PPOOL/BLNAV NP4 .... 133 G3
Caernarvon Cl
    PNRTH/DP CF64 .... 133 G3
Caernarvon Crs CWM NP44 .... 25 H5
Caernarvon Dr RSTN NP10 .... 74 C1
Caernarvon Rd NWPT NP20 .... 74 B1
Caernarvon Wy CDFNE CF3 ..... 102 C5
Cae'r Odyn PNRTH/DP CF64 .... 133 E4
Caerphilly Rd CDFN CF14 .... 85 H3
    RSTN NP10 .... 91 G5
Caerphilly Rd CAER CF83 .... 32 A4
    CDFN CF14 .... 99 G4
    PENT/RAD/TFW CF15 .... 83 E1
    PNRTH/DP CF64 .... 140 D2
    PPRD CF37 .... 65 F1
Caer Wenallt CDFN CF14 .... 85 G5
Caerwent La CHEP NP16 .... 30 D3
Caerwent Rd
    CAE/CAN/FWR CF5 .... 116 D3
    CWM NP44 .... 20 A1
    PPOOL/BLNAV NP4 .... 14 D1
Caesar Crs CLN/RNWPTE NP18 . 41 H3
Cae Stumpie COWBR CF71 .... 122 B5
Cae Syr Dafydd
    GTN/RVSD CF11 .... 118 D1
Cae Yorath CDFN CF14 .... 99 E5
Cae-yr-Ebol CWM NP44 .... 19 H3
Cae Ysgubor CAER CF83 .... 48 C2
Caird St CHEP NP16 .... 28 C5
Cairnmuir Rd
    CATH/RTH/SPL CF24 .... 121 E1

Calaghan Sq CCDF CF10 .... 3 E7
Calderton Rd CHV/BDAU CF38 ... 80 B5
Caldicot Cl CAE/CAN/FWR CF5 . 63 E4
Caldicot Ct CAER CF83 .... 48 A5
Caldicot St NWPTE NP19 .... 57 G5
Caldicott Cl CHV/BDAU CF38 ..... 80 B5
Caldicot Wy CWM NP44 .... 20 A2
Caldwell Cl CHV/BDAU CF62 ... 139 F2
Caldy Cl CDFN CF14 .... 99 G1
Caldy Ct CDFN CF14 .... 111 E2
Caldy Rd CDFN CF14 .... 111 E2
Caledfryn Wy CAER CF83 .... 48 D4
Cambourne Av CDFNE CF3 .... 98 C5
Cambourne Cl BARRYI/W CF62 . 138 C2
Cambria Cl CLN/RNWPTE NP18 . 42 B4
Cambrian Av LLM/ CF61 .... 136 C4
Cambrian Cl CDFNE CF3 .... 104 B1
Cambrian Dr CDFNE CF3 .... 104 B1
Cambrian Gv CDFNE CF3 .... 104 B1
Cambrian Pl PPRD CF37 .... 45 F5
Cambrian Rd NWPT NP20 .... 8 D2
Cambrian Wy CDFNE CF3 .... 104 B1
Cambria Rd
    CAE/CAN/FWR CF5 .... 117 E5
Cambridge Rd BARRYI/W CF62 .. 17 E2
    NWPTE NP19 .... 9 H3
Cambridge St
    GTN/RVSD CF11 .... 118 C1
Cam Ct CVM NP44 .... 18 D3
Camellia Av RSTN NP10 .... 54 A2
Camelot Pl NWPTE NP19 .... 9 H1
Camelot Wy CDFNE CF3 .... 85 G5
Cameron St
    CATH/RTH/SPL CF24 .... 120 D1
Campanula Dr RSTN NP10 .... 54 A2
Campbell Dr CR/RVSD CF11 .... 128 B3
Campbell St
    PPOOL/BLNAV NP4 .... 14 A3
Camperdown Rd
    NWPTE NP19 .... 77 H1
Camperly Cl CHV/BDAU CF38 .... 80 B5
Campion Cl CWM NP44 .... 24 D3
    NWPTE NP20 .... 9 B1
Campton Cl NWPT NP20 .... 30 D1
Campton Pl CHV/BDAU CF38 ..... 80 B5
Camrose Ct BARRYI/W CF62 .... 139 F1
Camrose Rd
    CAE/CAN/FWR CF5 .... 117 G4
Canada Rd CDFN CF14 .... 112 A4
Canal Bnk
    PPOOL/BLNAV NP4 * 14 B2
Canal Cl PPOOL/BLNAV NP4 .... 17 E3
Canal Pde CCDF CF10 .... 6 E1
Canal St NWPT NP20 * 9 F4
Canal Ter NWPT NP20 .... 9 H6
Canaston Pl
    CAE/CAN/FWR CF5 .... 117 C4
Canberra Cl NWPT NP20 .... 25 G1
Canberra Crs NWPT NP20 .... 55 G5
Candwr Pk
    CLN/RNWPTE NP18 .... 27 G4
Candwr Rd
    CLN/RNWPTE NP18 .... 27 H5
Canford Cl PPOOL/BLNAV NP4 .. 14 D1
Cannington Av CDFNE CF3 .... 102 A5
Cannington Cl
    PNRTH/DP CF64 .... 141 F4
Canon St BARRYI/W CF62 .... 2 B5
Canopus Cl CDFNE CF3 .... 102 C4
Canterbury Cl NWPT NP20 .... 56 D3
Canterbury Wy
    CALD/MAC NP26 .... 63 H5
Canton Ct GTN/RVSD CF11 ...... 119 E3
Cantref Cl CDFN CF14 .... 98 A4
    RSTN NP10 .... 54 D2
Capel Cl NWPT NP20 .... 9 F7
Capel Crs NWPT NP20 .... 8 E7
Capel Edeyrn
    CYN/LLD/PWYN CF23 .... 102 A2
Capel Gwilym Rd CDFN CF14 ..... 85 F3
Capel St PPOOL/BLNAV NP4 ..... 14 C4
Caple Rd BARRYI/W CF62 .... 2 A4
Caradoc Av BARRYE CF63 .... 139 F2
Caradoc Cl CDFNE CF3 .... 103 F3
Caradoc Rd CWM NP44 .... 19 H4
Caradoc St
    ABRC/NBR/RIS NP11 .... 23 F4
    PPOOL/BLNAV NP4 .... 12 C4
Caradog Ct
    CLN/RNWPTE NP18 .... 41 H3
Caraway Cl CDFNE CF3 .... 103 F2
Cardiff Br GTN/RVSD CF11 .... 4 A4
Cardiff Castle Gnd CCDF CF10 .. 112 A5
Cardiff Rd BARRYE CF63 .... 139 H4
    CAE/CAN/FWR CF5 .... 116 D1
    CAE/CAN/FWR CF5 .... 116 D1
    COWBR CF71 .... 123 E4
    LLTR/LLH CF72 .... 95 E2
    PENT/RAD/TFW CF15 .... 83 E1
    PNRTH/DP CF64 .... 140 D2
    PPRD CF37 .... 65 F1
Cardigan Cl PNRTH/DP CF64 .... 133 G3
    NWPT NP20 .... 20 A2
Cardigan Crs CWM NP44 .... 137 F3
    LLM/ CF61 .... 137 F3
Cardigan Pl NWPTE NP19 .... 57 F4
Cardigan Rd PNRTH/DP CF64 .. 133 G3
Cardigan St
    CAE/CAN/FWR CF5 .... 118 D2
Cardinal Dr CDFN CF14 .... 86 B3
Carew Cl BARRYI/W CF62 .... 139 F2
Carey Rd NWPTE NP19 .... 57 H4
Carisbrook Rd CAER CF83 .... 68 B3
Cargo Rd CCDF CF10 .... 7 F5
Carisbrooke Rd NWPTE NP19 .... 57 G4
Carisbrooke Wy
    CYN/LLD/PWYN CF23 .... 113 C2
Carling Ct CAE/CAN/FWR CF5 . 116 D2
Carlisle St CATH/RTH/SPL CF24 .. 5 K5
    NWPT NP20 .... 77 E2

Carlton Cl CDFN CF14 .... 85 H4
Carlton Crs CHV/BDAU CF38 ..... 80 B5
Carlton Pl
    ABRC/NBR/RIS NP11 .... 36 B1
Carlton Rd NWPTE NP19 .... 57 F2
Carmarthen Cl LLMJ CF61 .... 137 G2
Carmarthen Ct CAER CF83 .... 48 A5
Carmarthen Dr
    PNRTH/DP CF64 .... 133 G3
Carmarthen St
    CAE/CAN/FWR CF5 .... 118 D2
Carmel Cl CHV/BDAU CF38 .... 80 B5
Carnegie Dr
    CYN/LLD/PWYN CF23 .... 100 C5
Carn-yr-Ebol BARRYE CF63 ..... 139 H1
Caroline Rd
    PPOOL/BLNAV NP4 .... 17 G1
Caroline St CCDF CF10 .... 4 D6
    NWPTE NP19 .... 9 F5
Carpenters Arm La
    NWPT NP20 .... 8 E2
Car'r Pwll PNRTH/DP CF64 ...... 133 E4
Carshalton Rd
    CHV/BDAU CF38 * 80 B5
Carswell Cl CHV/BDAU CF38 ..... 80 B4
Carter Pl CAE/CAN/FWR CF5 ... 110 B4
Cartwright Cl
    CAE/CAN/FWR CF5 .... 112 D4
Cartwright Gn NWPT NP20 .... 30 B4
Cartwright La
    CAE/CAN/FWR CF5 .... 115 G1
Carys Cl CAE/CAN/FWR CF5 ... 125 G1
    PNRTH/DP CF64 .... 134 A4
Caspian Cl CDFNE CF3 * 103 G3
Castan Rd LLTR/LLH CF72 .... 107 F1
Castell Coch Dr RSTN NP10 .... 91 H2
Castell Coch Vw
    CAE/CAN/FWR CF5 .... 97 H1
Castell Meredith CAER CF83 ...... 49 E4
Castell Morgraig CAER CF83 ...... 49 E4
Castell y Fan CAER CF83 .... 49 F4
Castell-y-Mynach Rd
    PPOOL/BLNAV NP4 .... 80 A4
Castle Arcade Balcony
    CCDF CF10 .... 4 C5
Castle Av CDFNE CF3 .... 113 H3
    PNRTH/DP CF64 .... 134 B5
Castle Cl LLMJ CF61 .... 137 H4
    PNRTH/DP CF64 .... 133 C3
Castle Ct CALD/MAC NP26 .... 63 F4
    CWM NP44 .... 24 C5
Castle Crs CDFNE CF3 .... 113 H3
Castle Dr PNRTH/DP CF64 .... 133 H3
Castlefield Pl CDFN CF14 .... 111 H3
Castleford Cl CHV/BDAU CF38 .. 80 B4
Castleford Gdns CHEP NP16 ..... 28 B2
Castleford Hl CHEP NP16 .... 28 B2
Castle Gdns CALD/MAC NP26 ... 62 D2
    CHEP NP16 .... 28 B3
Castle Hl CAE/CAN/FWR CF5 .. 116 C1
    COWBR CF71 .... 122 B4
Castle Ivor St PPRD CF37 .... 44 B3
Castleland St BARRYE CF63 .... 3 K1
    CATH/RTH/SPL CF24 .... 5 G2
    CLN/RNWPTE NP18 .... 42 B4
Castle Lea CALD/MAC NP26 ...... 63 F3
Castle Lodge Crs
    CALD/MAC NP26 .... 63 F3
Castle Ms CLN/RNWPTE NP18 .. 42 B3
    COWBR CF71 .... 122 C5
    PPOOL/BLNAV NP4 .... 14 C5
Castle Park Rd CAE/CAN/FWR CF5 75 G1
Castle Park Rd NWPT NP20 .... 75 G1
Castle Ri CDFNE CF3 .... 114 A3
Castle Rd BARRYI/W CF62 .... 144 C3
    PENT/RAD/TFW CF15 .... 97 H1
Castle St BARRYI/W CF62 .... 69 E1
    CAER CF83 .... 69 E1
    CLN/RNWPTE NP18 .... 42 B4
    GTN/RVSD CF11 .... 4 B5
    LLM/ CF61 .... 136 C2
    LLTR/LLH CF72 .... 95 E2
    NWPT NP20 .... 77 E2
    PENT/RAD/TFW CF15 .... 83 F5
    PPRD CF37 .... 45 F5
Castleton Ct CDFNE CF3 .... 103 H2
Castleton Rl CDFNE CF3 .... 89 H4
Castle Vw CHEP NP16 .... 29 E3
Castle Vw CHEP NP16 .... 29 E3
    CAER CF83 .... 98 A2
    PPOOL/BLNAV NP4 .... 16 A5
Castle Wd CHEP NP16 .... 29 E3
Cas Troggy CALD/MAC NP26 .... 62 D2
Caswell Rd CDFNE CF3 .... 114 B2
Caswell Wy NWPTE NP19 .... 77 H5
Catalpa Cl NWPT NP20 .... 58 C3
Cathays Ter
    CATH/RTH/SPL CF24 .... 112 C4
Cath Cob Cl CDFNE CF3 .... 102 D4
Cathedral Cl
    CAE/CAN/FWR CF5 .... 111 F4
Cathedral Ct NWPT NP20 .... 8 D5
The Cathedral Gn
    CAE/CAN/FWR CF5 .... 111 E4
Cathedral Rd GTN/RVSD CF11 . 111 G5
Cathedral Vw CDFN CF14 .... 85 F3
Catherine Cir RSTN NP10 * 92 A2
Catherine Dr CDFNE CF3 .... 104 B2
    PENT/RAD/TFW CF15 .... 84 A5
Catherine St
    CATH/RTH/SPL CF24 .... 112 C3
    NWPT NP20 .... 44 D3
Catkin Dr PNRTH/DP CF64 .... 133 E5
Cat's Ash Rd
    CLN/RNWPTE NP18 .... 59 H1
Cat's Ash Rd
    CLN/RNWPTE NP18 .... 59 H1
Causeway Cl CWM NP44 .... 136 C2
Causeway Hl COWBR CF71 .... 122 B5
The Causeway
    CALD/MAC NP26 .... 60 D4
    COWBR CF71 .... 122 D5
Cavendish Cl CDFN CF14 .... 85 H5
Cavendish Pl CHV/BDAU CF38 .. 80 B4
Cawley Pl BARRYE CF63 .... 139 H2

Cawnpore St *PNRTH/DP* CF64 .... 134 A1
Caxton Pl
  CYN/LLD/PWYN CF23 .... 101 H2
  NWPT NP20 .... 8 D3
Caynham Av *PNRTH/DP* CF64 .. 142 C1
Cecil Sharp Rd *NWPTE* NP19 .. 59 E4
Cecil St *CATH/RTH/SPL* CF24 .. 5 K2
Cedar Cl *CHEP* NP16 .... 30 C2
Cedar Ct *CHV/BDAU* CF38 .... 8 H1
Cedar Gv *CAE/CAN/FWR* CF5 .. 110 A4
Cedar La *PPRD* CF37 .... 46 A4
Cedar Rd *NWPTE* NP19 .... 9 G2
Cedar Wood Cl *RSTN* NP10 .... 54 A2
Cedar Wood Dr *RSTN* NP10 .... 54 A2
Cefn Bychan
  PENT/RAD/TFW CF15 .... 96 B1
Cefn Carnau Rd *CDFN* CF14 .. 100 A4
Cefn Coch
  RSTN NP10 .... 55 E4
  PENT/RAD/TFW CF15 .... 97 F3
Cefn Coed Av
  CYN/LLD/PWYN CF23 .... 113 E1
Cefn-Coed Crs
  CYN/LLD/PWYN CF23 .... 113 E1
Cefn-Coed Gdns
  CYN/LLD/PWYN CF23 .... 112 D2
Cefn-Coed Rd
  CYN/LLD/PWYN CF23 .... 112 D2
Cefn Ct *NWPT* NP20 * 8 A6
Cefn Dr *RSTN* NP10 .... 55 E3
Cefn Graig *CDFN* CF14 .... 55 E4
Cefn Ilan Rd *CAER* CF83 .... 47 E2
Cefn Llan
  PENT/RAD/TFW CF15 .... 96 B1
Cefn Mably Pk *CDFNE* CF3 .... 88 B2
Cefn Mably Rd *CDFN* CF14 .. 86 B2
Cefn Milwr *CWM* NP44 .... 25 C3
Cefn Mt *PNRTH/DP* CF64 .. 133 E3
Cefn Nant *CDFN* CF14 .... 99 E1
Cefn Onn Mdw *CDFN* CF14 .. 86 A3
Cefn Penuel
  CAE/CAN/FWR CF5 .... 96 A2
Cefn-Porth Rd *CDFN* CF14 .. 71 F5
Cefn Ri *RSTN* NP10 .... 54 D3
Cefn Rd *CDFN* CF14 .... 111 G2
Cefn Wk *RSTN* NP10 .... 55 E4
Cefn-y-Lon *CAER* CF83 .... 48 A3
Cei Dafydd *BARRYE* CF63 .. 3 J3
Ceiriog Cl *BARRYE* CF63 .. 139 C1
  PNRTH/DP CF64 .... 134 B2
Ceiriog Crs *PPRD* CF37 .... 65 C1
Ceiriog Dr *CAER* CF83 .... 48 C5
  CDFN CF14 .... 98 C2
Celandine Ct *CHEP* NP16 .. 30 D2
  CWM NP44 .... 11 H1
Celandine Rd
  CAE/CAN/FWR CF5 .... 116 D3
Celerity Dr *CCDF* CF10 .... 7 F1
Celtic Cl *CALD/MAG* NP26 .. 60 D3
Celtic Gn *PNRTH/DP* CF64 .. 133 H2
Celtic Rd *CDFN* CF14 .... 111 H2
Celyn Av *BARRY/W* CF62 .. 144 A2
  CAER CF83 .... 49 H5
  RSTN NP10 .... 91 F1
Celyn Av *CAER* CF83 .... 48 D5
Celyn Gv *CAER* CF83 .... 48 D5
  CYN/LLD/PWYN CF23 .. 100 C5
Cemaes Crs *CDFNE* CF3 .. 102 D5
Cemetery Rd
  BARRY/W CF62 .... 139 F3
  PENT/RAD/TFW CF15 .. 83 C4
  PPRD CF37 .... 45 C5
Cenfedd St *NWPTE* NP19 .. 57 E2
Cennin Pedr *BARRYE* CF63 .. 131 H5
Centenary Ct
  CHV/BDAU CF38 .... 80 C4
Central Av *NWPTE* NP19 .. 78 C2
  PPOOL/BLNAV NP4 .... 15 H1
Central Link *CF* CF10 .... 5 H7
Central Sq *CCDF* CF10 .... 4 E3
  PPRD CF37 .... 45 E2
Central St *CAER* CF83 .... 48 C2
Central Wy *CDFN* CF14 .. 112 B2
  CWM NP44 .... 19 F3
  PNRTH/DP CF64 .... 140 C3
Centurion Ct
  CAE/CAN/FWR CF5 .... 117 G5
Centurion Ga
  CLN/RNWPTE NP18 .... 42 B4
Cerdin Av *LLTR/LLH* CF72 .. 107 F3
Ceredig Ct *CWM* NP44 * .. 26 C1
Ceri Av *BARRY/W* CF62 .. 144 D2
Ceri Rd *BARRY/W* CF62 .. 144 D2
Chadwick Cl *NWPT* NP20 .. 40 B4
Chaffinch Wy *RSTN* NP10 .. 76 A5
Chaffron Cl *CHV/BDAU* CF38 .. 80 A4
Chalvington Dr
  CHV/BDAU CF38 .... 80 B4
Chamberlain Rd *CDFN* CF14 .. 110 D2
Chamberlain Rw
  PNRTH/DP CF64 .... 133 C2
Chamomile Cl
  CYN/LLD/PWYN CF23 .. 101 F1
Chancery La *GTN/RVSD* CF11 .. 119 E3
Chandlers Qy
  PNRTH/DP CF64 .... 128 C5
Chandlers Reach
  CHV/BDAU CF38 .... 80 D5
Chandlery Wy *CCDF* CF10 .. 6 E4
Channel Cl *BARRY/W* CF62 .. 145 E3
Channel Vw *BARRY/W* CF62 .. 89 G4
  CHEP NP16 .... 30 C1
  CWM NP44 .... 19 F3
  PNRTH/DP CF64 .... 134 D5
  PPOOL/BLNAV NP4 .... 8 C2
  RSTN NP10 .... 74 C1
Channel View Rd
  GTN/RVSD CF11 .... 6 B6
Chantry Ri *PNRTH/DP* CF64 .. 134 C5
The Chantry
  CAE/CAN/FWR CF5 .... 110 C4
Chapel Cl *COWBR* CF71 .... 123 F2
  PNRTH/DP CF64 .... 133 G2
  PPOOL/BLNAV NP4 .... 12 B1

Chapel Farm Ter
  ABRC/NBR/RIS NP11 .... 23 E3
Chapel La *CWM* NP44 .... 20 A1
Chapel Rd *CDFNE* CF3 .... 134 C1
Chapel Rd
  PENT/RAD/TFW CF15 .. 97 G2
Chapel Rw *CDFNE* CF3 .. 102 C3
  PNRTH/DP CF64 .... 133 G2
Chapel St *CAE/CAN/FWR* CF5 .. 111 E5
  CWM NP44 .... 19 H4
  PPRD CF37 .... 37 F5
Chapel Ter
  PPOOL/BLNAV NP4 * .. 14 A2
Chapel Wd
  CYN/LLD/PWYN CF23 .. 113 G1
Chapman Cl *NWPT* NP20 .. 40 B3
Chard Av *GTN/RVSD* CF11 .. 102 A5
Chargot Rd
  CAE/CAN/FWR CF5 .... 118 C1
Charles Darwin Wy
  BARRY/W CF62 .... 3 G5
Charles Pl *BARRY/W* CF62 .. 2 C4
Charles St *CCDF* CF10 .... 4 E5
  CWM NP44 .... 19 H2
  NWPT NP20 .... 8 D3
  PPOOL/BLNAV NP4 .... 17 E2
  PPRD CF37 .... 44 B3
Charlock Cl *CDFN* CF14 .. 85 F4
Charlotta Wy *CCDF* CF10 .. 7 F4
Charlotte Dr *NWPT* NP20 .. 9 F7
Charlotte Gv *CDFNE* CF3 .. 105 E4
Charlotte Pl *BARRYE* CF63 .. 139 H3
Charlotte Sq *CDFN* CF14 .. 99 F3
Charlotte St *CDFN* CF14 .. 99 F3
  PNRTH/DP CF64 .... 134 A1
Charlotte Wk *NWPT* NP20 * .. 9 F7
Charnwood Dr
  CYN/LLD/PWYN CF23 .. 101 H1
Charnwood Rd *NWPTE* NP19 .. 57 E1
Charston *CWM* NP44 .... 19 F5
Charteris Av *BARRY/W* CF62 .. 138 D1
Charteris Cl *PNRTH/DP* CF64 .. 142 C1
Charteris Crs
  CAE/CAN/FWR CF5 .... 117 G2
Charteris Rd
  CAE/CAN/FWR CF5 .... 117 G2
Chartist Ct
  ABRC/NBR/RIS NP11 .. 37 G5
Chartist Dr *RSTN* NP10 .. 54 D4
Chartist Rd *LLTR/LLH* CF72 .. 94 D2
Chartwell Cl *CHEP* NP16 .. 30 C2
Chartwey Cl *CDFN* CF14 .. 103 F3
Chartwell Ct
  PENT/RAD/TFW CF15 .. 96 B2
Chartwell Dr *CDFN* CF14 .. 100 C1
Chatham *CAER* CF83 .. 51 H2
Chatham St *CAER* CF83 .. 52 A2
Chatsworth Cl
  CAE/CAN/FWR CF5 .... 110 C4
Chatterton Sq
  CYN/LLD/PWYN CF23 .. 128 B3
Chaucer Cl *CALD/MAG* NP26 .. 62 C4
  CDFNE CF3 .... 102 B2
  PNRTH/DP CF64 .... 134 B2
Chaucer Gv *NWPTE* NP19 .. 57 G4
Chaucer Rd *NWPTE* NP19 .. 57 G4
Cheam Pl *CDFN* CF14 .. 99 H2
Cheddar Crs *CDFNE* CF3 .. 102 A5
Chelmer Cl *NWPT* NP20 .. 39 F5
Chelston Pl *NWPT* NP20 .. 56 C2
Chepstow Cl
  CAE/CAN/FWR CF5 .... 117 G4
  NWPT NP20 .... 20 B2
Chepstow Ct *CAER* CF83 .. 48 A5
Chepstow Ri *CWM* NP44 .. 21 E2
Chepstow Rd *CALD/MAG* NP26 .. 63 E3
  NWPTE NP19 .... 57 H3
Cheriton Dr *CDFN* CF14 .. 99 H2
Cheriton Gv *CHV/BDAU* CF38 .. 66 A3
Cherry Cl *CALD/MAG* NP26 .. 61 H5
  PNRTH/DP CF64 .... 133 G4
Cherrydale Rd
  CAE/CAN/FWR CF5 .... 117 H2
Cherrydown Cl *CDFN* CF14 .. 86 A5
Cherry Orchard Rd *CDFN* CF14 .. 85 H5
Cherry Tree Cl *CAER* CF83 .. 49 F2
  CDFN CF14 .... 86 C4
  CLN/RNWPTE NP18 .. 42 A5
  CWM NP44 .... 20 C3
  NWPT NP20 .... 40 C3
Cherry Tree Wk
  LLTR/LLH CF72 .... 94 D3
Chervil Cl *CDFNE* CF3 .. 86 A4
Chervil Cl *CDFNE* CF3 .. 103 F2
Cheshire Cl *PNRTH/DP* CF64 .. 134 B4
Chesnut Cl *CAE/CAN/FWR* CF5 .. 100 A4
Chesnut Gv
  CLN/RNWPTE NP18 .. 41 F4
  PPOOL/BLNAV NP4 .. 15 H5
Chester Cl *CDFNE* CF3 .. 103 E4
  PPOOL/BLNAV NP4 .. 15 H5
Chester Ct *CAER* CF83 .. 47 H4
Chesterfield St *BARRYE* CF63 .. 139 G2
Chester Pl *GTN/RVSD* CF11 .. 6 A2
Chester St *GTN/RVSD* CF11 .. 6 A1
Chesterton Rd *CDFNE* CF3 .. 102 A3
Chestnut Cl *CALD/MAG* NP26 .. 61 H2
  CDFN CF14 .... 51 H2
  PNRTH/DP CF64 .... 133 F4
  PPOOL/BLNAV NP4 .. 15 H5
Chestnut Gv
  CAE/CAN/FWR CF5 * .. 110 B5
The Chestnuts *LLTR/LLH* CF72 .. 107 H2
Chestnut St *PPRD* CF37 .. 65 H2
Chestnut Tree Cl
  PENT/RAD/TFW CF15 .. 97 F4
Cheviot Cl
  ABRC/NBR/RIS NP11 .. 37 H4
  CDFN CF14 .... 99 H3
Chichester Cl *NWPTE* NP19 .. 41 G5
Chichester Rd
  PNRTH/DP CF64 .... 134 B1
Chichester Wy
  CAE/CAN/FWR CF5 .... 117 H3
Chick La *NWPT* NP20 .. 76 A1
Chiltern Cl
  ABRC/NBR/RIS NP11 .. 38 A5
  CDFN CF14 .... 99 H4

NWPTE NP19 .... 58 B3
Chirk Cl *NWPT* NP20 .. 91 G2
Chorley Cl *CAE/CAN/FWR* CF5 .. 117 F1
Christchurch Hl
  CLN/RNWPTE NP18 .. 58 C2
Christchurch Rd *NWPTE* NP19 .. 57 F3
Christina Crs *RSTN* NP10 .. 55 F5
Christina St *CCDF* CF10 .. 7 F2
Chumleigh Cl *CDFNE* CF3 .. 114 A1
Church Av *PPOOL/BLNAV* NP4 .. 14 C3
Church Cl *CALD/MAG* NP26 .. 63 E2
  CDFN CF14 .... 86 D5
  CHV/BDAU CF38 .. 81 E4
  NWPT NP20 .... 20 B3
  PPOOL/BLNAV NP4 .. 17 G3
  RSTN NP10 .... 55 F5
Church Ct *NWPTE* NP19 * .. 57 H1
Church Crs *RSTN* NP10 .. 90 D2
Church La *CAE/CAN/FWR* CF5 .. 125 F5
  CALD/MAG NP26 .. 61 F4
  CDFNE CF3 .... 90 A5
  CDFN CF14 .... 86 D5
  LLMJ CF61 .... 136 C3
  PENT/RAD/TFW CF15 .. 67 E5
  PPOOL/BLNAV NP4 .. 14 B2
  PPOOL/BLNAV NP4 .. 17 H2
  RSTN NP10 .... 90 D4
Church Mdw *RSTN* NP10 .. 75 E2
Church Mdw *LLMJ* CF61 * .. 137 E2
Church Ms
  NWPT NP20 * 14 C4
Church Pl South
  PNRTH/DP CF64 .... 134 D1
Church Rd *ABRC/NBR/RIS* NP11 .. 37 E3
  BARRYE CF63 .... 139 H2
  CAE/CAN/FWR CF5 .. 114 C3
  CAE/CAN/FWR CF5 .. 96 D5
  CAE/CAN/FWR CF5 .. 117 F5
  CAE/CAN/FWR CF5 .. 119 E3
  CAER CF83 .... 47 E2
  CALD/MAG NP26 .. 61 H3
  CDFNE CF3 .... 86 D4
  CDFNE CF3 .... 110 D1
  CDFNE CF3 .... 102 A2
  CHV/BDAU CF38 .. 68 C5
  COWBR CF71 .... 122 A4
  CWM NP44 .... 19 C3
  CWM NP44 .... 27 E3
  CYN/LLD/PWYN CF23 .. 101 H2
  NWPT NP20 .... 14 C4
  PENT/RAD/TFW CF15 .. 96 B3
  PNRTH/DP CF64 .... 134 D2
  PPOOL/BLNAV NP4 .. 12 B3
  PPRD CF37 .... 45 E1
  RSTN NP10 .... 54 B3
Church Ter
  CYN/LLD/PWYN CF23 .. 113 F5
Church Vw *COWBR* CF71 .. 122 A4
Church View Cl
  PNRTH/DP CF64 .... 127 H4
Churchward Dr *NWPTE* NP19 .. 78 A1
Churchwood
  PPOOL/BLNAV NP4 .. 17 F5
Church Wood Cl *CWM* NP44 .. 19 C3
Cidermill Cl *CHEP* NP16 .. 30 D3
Cilfedw *PENT/RAD/TFW* CF15 .. 97 G3
Cilgant y Meillion
  BARRY/W CF62 .... 144 D4
Cilgerran Crs *CDFNE* CF3 .. 99 G2
Cil-Hendy *LLTR/LLH* CF72 .. 107 G1
The Circle *CWM* NP44 .. 25 G2
Circle Wy East
  CYN/LLD/PWYN CF23 .. 113 G2
Circle Wy West
  CYN/LLD/PWYN CF23 .. 113 F1
City Hall Rd *CCDF* CF10 .. 4 C3
City Rd *CATH/RTH/SPL* CF24 .. 5 F1
Claerwen Dr
  CYN/LLD/PWYN CF23 .. 100 C5
Clairwain *PPOOL/BLNAV* NP4 .. 17 G2
Clan-yr-Afon *LLTR/LLH* CF72 .. 107 F1
Carbeston Rd *CDFN* CF14 .. 111 E3
Clare Drew Wy *CWM* NP44 .. 20 B5
Clare Dr *COWBR* CF71 .. 122 D4
Clare Gdns *CDFN* CF14 .. 99 H3
Claremont *NWPT* NP20 .. 40 C2
Claremont Av *CDFNE* CF3 .. 114 A1
Claremont Crs *CDFNE* CF3 .. 114 B1
Clarence Emb *CCDF* CF10 .. 6 E5
Clarence Pl
  ABRC/NBR/RIS NP11 .. 37 G4
  CCDF CF10 .... 6 E5
Clarence Rd *GTN/RVSD* CF11 .. 6 D5
  PPOOL/BLNAV NP4 .. 14 C4
Clarence St *NWPT* NP20 .. 77 E2
Clarendon
  CYN/LLD/PWYN CF23 .. 101 E4
Clarendon Cl *CHEP* NP16 .. 31 E3
Clarendon Rd
  CYN/LLD/PWYN CF23 .. 113 F5
Clare Pl *GTN/RVSD* CF11 .. 4 A6
Clare Rd *GTN/RVSD* CF11 .. 4 A7

Clare St *GTN/RVSD* CF11 .. 4 A6
Clark Av *NWPT* NP20 .. 19 H2
Clarke St *CAE/CAN/FWR* CF5 .. 118 A3
Clas Dyfrig *CDFN* CF14 .. 99 F1
Clas Gabriel *CDFN* CF14 * .. 111 F1
Clas Heulog *CDFN* CF14 .. 111 F1
Clas Illtyd *CDFN* CF14 .. 99 E5
Clas Isan *CDFN* CF14 .. 111 G1
Clas Odyn *CDFN* CF14 .. 99 E5
Clas Teilo *CDFN* CF14 .. 111 G1
Clas Tynewydd *CDFN* CF14 .. 111 F1
Clas Ty'n-y-Cae *CDFN* CF14 .. 99 F4
Clas Ty Wern *CDFN* CF14 .. 99 F4
Clas Yorath *CDFN* CF14 .. 99 E4
Claude Pl *CATH/RTH/SPL* CF24 .. 115 E5
Claude Rd *CATH/RTH/SPL* CF24 .. 2 C1
  CAER CF83 .... 68 D2
  CATH/RTH/SPL CF24 .. 115 E5
Claude Rd West
  CYN/LLD/PWYN CF23 .. 2 B2
Claverton Ct *CHV/BDAU* CF38 .. 80 A5
Claymore Pl *CATH/RTH/SPL* CF11 .. 128 C3
Clayton Cl *NWPTE* NP19 .. 57 E3
Clayton St *NWPTE* NP19 .. 57 E3
Clearwater Rd *NWPTE* NP19 .. 78 A1
Clear Water Wy
  CYN/LLD/PWYN CF23 .. 100 C5
Clearwell Ct *RSTN* NP10 .. 55 F3
Cleaves Ter
  PPOOL/BLNAV NP4 * .. 12 C4
Cleddau Cl *CDFNE* CF3 .. 102 B4
Cledwen Cl *BARRY/W* CF62 .. 138 B4
Cleeve Dr *CDFN* CF14 .. 99 H3
Clement Atlee Dr
  NWPTE NP19 .... 58 C3
Clement Pl *BARRY/W* CF62 .. 2 B7
Clevedon Av *PNRTH/DP* CF64 .. 141 F5
Clevedon Cl *RSTN* NP10 .. 54 D3
Clevedon Rd *CDFNE* CF3 .. 102 A4
  NWPTE NP19 .... 57 G3
Cleveland Dr
  ABRC/NBR/RIS NP11 .. 37 H5
Clewer Court Ms *NWPT* NP20 .. 56 A5
Cliff Hl *PNRTH/DP* CF64 .. 134 D4
Cliff Pde *PNRTH/DP* CF64 .. 134 D4
Cliff Pl *CAE/CAN/FWR* CF5 .. 118 C2
Cliff Rd *PNRTH/DP* CF64 .. 134 D4
Cliff Side *PNRTH/DP* CF64 .. 134 D4
Cliff St *PNRTH/DP* CF64 .. 134 D1
  CAER CF83 .... 47 E2
Cliff Ter *PPRD* CF37 .. 29 F5
Clifton Pl *NWPT* NP20 .. 8 D5
Clifton Rd *NWPT* NP20 .. 8 D5
Clifton St *BARRY/W* CF62 .. 2 C5
  CATH/RTH/SPL CF24 .. 5 J3
Clinton Rd *PNRTH/DP* CF64 .. 144 A4
Clipper Cl *NWPTE* NP19 .. 41 G5
Clipper Rd *CCDF* CF10 .. 7 H1
Clive Cres *PNRTH/DP* CF64 .. 134 D2
Clive Pl *BARRY/W* CF62 .. 3 H6
  CATH/RTH/SPL CF24 .. 5 G1
  PNRTH/DP CF64 .... 134 D2
Clive Rd *BARRY/W* CF62 .. 2 C5
  CAE/CAN/FWR CF5 .. 118 C1
Clive St *CAER* CF83 .. 32 A4
  CAER CF83 .... 68 D3
  GTN/RVSD CF11 .. 6 A4
Clodien Av *CDFN* CF14 .. 112 B3
Cloister Ct *CAE/CAN/FWR* CF5 .. 117 H4
The Cloisters *CHEP* NP16 .. 28 A1
Clomendy Rd *CWM* NP44 .. 25 C1
Clonakilty Wy
  CYN/LLD/PWYN CF23 .. 87 H5
Clos Afon Llwyd
  PPOOL/BLNAV NP4 .. 15 C5
Clos Aled *CALD/MAG* NP26 .. 63 E2
Clos Alwen *CALD/MAG* NP26 .. 63 E2
Clos Alyn
  CYN/LLD/PWYN CF23 .. 101 C1
Clos Aneurin *PPRD* CF37 .. 46 A5
Clos Brenin *LLTR/LLH* CF72 .. 106 D2
Clos Bron Iestyn *PPRD* CF37 .. 44 A5
Clos Brynderi *CDFN* CF14 .. 99 F3
Clos Brynmelyn
  PENT/RAD/TFW CF15 .. 97 G4
Clos Cadwgan
  CHV/BDAU CF38 .. 80 A5
Clos Cae'r Wern *CAER* CF83 .. 68 B4
Clos Cae Wal
  PENT/RAD/TFW CF15 * .. 97 H1
Clos Caradog *CHV/BDAU* CF38 .. 81 E2
Clos Cefn Bychan
  PENT/RAD/TFW CF15 .. 96 B3
Clos Cefn Glas
  CHV/BDAU CF38 .. 80 C5
Clos Cefni *BARRY/W* CF62 .. 138 C3
Clos Ceirios
  CDFN CF14 .... 117 C3
Clos Cemmaes *CDFN* CF14 .. 111 F2
Clos Coed Hir *CDFN* CF14 .. 98 B4
Clos Coed-y-Dafarn
  CDFN CF14 .... 86 C5
Clos Collwyn *CHV/BDAU* CF38 .. 80 A5
Clos Cornel *CDFN* CF14 .. 111 F2
Clos Corris *CDFN* CF14 .. 111 F2
Clos Cradog *PNRTH/DP* CF64 .. 133 G4
Clos Creyr *CHV/BDAU* CF38 .. 80 A5
Clos Cromwell *CDFN* CF14 .. 85 H4
Clos Culver
  CAE/CAN/FWR CF5 .. 117 C5
Clos Cwm Barri
  BARRY/W CF62 .... 138 C3
Clos Cwm Creunant
  CYN/LLD/PWYN CF23 .. 101 C1
Clos Cwm Du
  CYN/LLD/PWYN CF23 .. 101 C1
Clos Cwm Garw *CAER* CF83 .. 68 A1
Clos Cyncoed *CAER* CF83 .. 48 A3
Clos Dyfan *CDFNE* CF3 .. 105 C2
Clos Derwen
  CYN/LLD/PWYN CF23 .. 112 D3
Clos Dewi Saint
  GTN/RVSD CF11 .. 119 F2

Clos Dol Heulog
  CYN/LLD/PWYN CF23 .. 101 G1
Clos Dwerw *CAER* CF83 .. 68 B3
Clos Dyfnant *CDFNE* CF3 .. 103 F4
Clos Dyfodwg
  CHV/BDAU CF38 .. 80 C5
Clos Edno
  CYN/LLD/PWYN CF23 .. 113 E2
Clos Eiddiw
  CAE/CAN/FWR CF5 .. 117 H3
Clos Elphan *CDFNE* CF3 .. 103 F2
Clos Enfys *CAER* CF83 .. 68 B3
The Close *CALD/MAG* NP26 .. 62 C3
  CDFN CF14 .... 100 A2
  CWM NP44 .... 26 A3
Clos Fach *CDFN* CF14 .. 99 F2
Clos Hafodyrynys *CDFNE* CF3 .. 103 F4
Clos Hafren *CDFNE* CF3 .. 103 F4
Clos Halkett *GTN/RVSD* CF11 .. 119 F4
Clos Hendre *CDFN* CF14 .. 99 E3
Clos Hereford *LLTR/LLH* CF72 .. 95 E3
Clos Heulwen
  PENT/RAD/TFW CF15 .. 83 F1
Clos Lancaster *LLTR/LLH* CF72 .. 95 E3
Clos Leland *LLTR/LLH* CF72 .. 95 E3
Clos Lindsay
  CAE/CAN/FWR CF5 .. 116 D5
Clos Llanfair
  CAE/CAN/FWR CF5 .. 125 C3
Clos Llangefni
  CHV/BDAU CF38 .. 80 A4
Clos Llawhaden
  BARRY/W CF62 .... 139 C1
Clos Llysfaen *CDFN* CF14 .. 86 A4
Clos-Mabon *CDFN* CF14 .. 99 E2
Clos Maedref
  PENT/RAD/TFW CF15 .. 98 A5
Clos Maerun *CDFNE* CF3 .. 103 E4
Clos Maes Brag *CAER* CF83 .. 69 E1
Clos Maes-y-Mor *CDFNE* CF3 .. 103 E4
Clos Mair
  CYN/LLD/PWYN CF23 .. 112 D2
Clos Manchdlowe
  BARRY/W CF62 .... 3 F3
Clos Mannoel *CDFNE* CF3 .. 103 E4
Clos Marian *CCDF* CF10 .. 121 E5
Clos Meifod *CDFN* CF14 .. 111 F2
Clos Melin Ddwr *CDFN* CF14 .. 86 B5
Clos Menter *CDFN* CF14 .. 111 G3
Clos Morgan Gruffydd
  CAER CF83 .... 47 E2
Clos Myddlyn *CHV/BDAU* CF38 .. 80 A5
Clos Nant Coslech
  CYN/LLD/PWYN CF23 .. 101 F1
Clos Nant Ddu
  CYN/LLD/PWYN CF23 .. 101 G1
Clos Nant Glaswg
  CYN/LLD/PWYN CF23 .. 101 F1
Clos Nant Mwlan
  CYN/LLD/PWYN CF23 .. 87 G5
Clos Nant y Cor
  CYN/LLD/PWYN CF23 .. 101 G1
Clos Nant y Cwm
  CYN/LLD/PWYN CF23 .. 101 G1
Clos Nant yr Aber *CAER* CF83 .. 48 C5
Clos Newydd *CDFN* CF14 .. 110 D1
Clos Pandy *CAER* CF83 .. 49 G3
Clos Pant Glas *CAER* CF83 .. 50 A3
Clos Pantycosyn *CDFNE* CF3 .. 103 E4
Clos Parc Radyr
  PENT/RAD/TFW CF15 .. 109 H3
Clos Peiriant *BARRYE* CF63 .. 3 H2
Clos Pen y Clawdd *CDFNE* CF3 .. 103 E4
Clos Powys *CHV/BDAU* CF38 .. 80 A4
Clos Rhedyn
  CAE/CAN/FWR CF5 .. 117 H3
Clos Rheidol *CALD/MAG* NP26 .. 63 E2
Clos Rhiannon *CDFN* CF14 .. 85 G5
Clos St Catwg
  CAE/CAN/FWR CF5 .. 96 D5
Clos Springfield
  LLTR/LLH CF72 .. 94 C3
Clos Taf *CAE/CAN/FWR* CF5 .. 110 D3
Clos Tawe *BARRY/W* CF62 .. 138 C3
Clos Tecwyn
  CYN/LLD/PWYN CF23 .. 112 D2
Clos Ton Mawr *CDFN* CF14 .. 99 F1
Clos Trefeddyg *CAER* CF83 .. 51 H3
Clos Tregare *CDFNE* CF3 .. 103 E4
Clos y Bronna
  CAE/CAN/FWR CF5 .. 117 H3
Clos Ty Clyd *CDFN* CF14 .. 110 C1
Clos Ty Bach *CDFNE* CF3 .. 103 F3
Clos Ty-Melin *PPRD* CF37 .. 65 C1
Clos Tynlal Glo *BARRYE* CF63 .. 3 H3
Clos William *CDFN* CF14 .. 99 F1
Clos y Berllan *CDFNE* CF3 .. 103 F4
Clos-y-Betws *CDFNE* CF3 .. 103 E4
Clos-y-Blaidd *CDFN* CF14 .. 85 G5
Clos-y-Broch *CDFN* CF14 .. 85 G4
Clos y Bryn *CDFN* CF14 .. 85 H4
Clos-y-Carw *CHV/BDAU* CF38 .. 80 C4
Clos-y-Cedr *CAER* CF83 .. 48 D3
Clos y Ceinach *CDFN* CF14 .. 85 H4
Clos y Coed *CHV/BDAU* CF38 .. 81 E2
Clos Coed *CHV/BDAU* CF38 .. 99 E1
Clos-y-Cwarra
  CAE/CAN/FWR CF5 .. 116 D3
Clos y Dolydd *CHV/BDAU* CF38 .. 80 B5
Clos-y-Draenog *CDFN* CF14 .. 85 H4
Clos y Dryw *CDFN* CF14 .. 85 H3
Clos-y-Dyfrisi *CDFN* CF14 .. 85 H3
Clos y Ffynnon
  CYN/LLD/PWYN CF23 .. 101 G1
Clos y Fran *CDFN* CF14 .. 85 H3

Clos y Gamlas CDFN CF14 ... 98 B4
Clos y Gelyn CYN/LLD/PWYN CF23 * ... 101 G3
Clos-y-Gof CAE/CAN/FWR CF5 ... 116 C3
Clos y Gwadd CDFN CF14 ... 85 G4
Clos y Gwaich CDFN CF14 * ... 85 H3
Clos y Gwyddfid PENT/RAD/TFW CF15 ... 97 F2
Clos y Hebog CDFN CF14 ... 85 H3
Clos y Nant CAE/CAN/FWR CF5 * ... 110 B5
Clos yr Alarch CDFN CF14 ... 85 H3
Clos yr Arad CAER CF83 ... 68 A3
Clos yr Ardd CDFN CF14 ... 99 E3
Clos yr Erw PNRTH/DP CF64 ... 134 A5
Clos-yr-Cornant CDFNE CF3 ... 103 F4
Clos yr Harbwr BARRY/C CF62 ... 2 C5
Clos-y-Rhiw CATH/RTH/SPL CF24 ... 113 H5
Clos-yr-Onnen CDFNE CF3 ... 103 F4
Clos yr Wenallt CDFN CF14 ... 98 D1
Clos y Wylan BARRY/W CF62 ... 3 H7
Clos Ysbyty CAER CF83 ... 68 B5
Clos-y-Wiwer CDFN CF14 ... 98 D1
Clovelly Crs CDFNE CF3 ... 101 H5
Clover Ct CWM NP44 ... 10 B4
Clover Gv CAE/CAN/FWR CF5 ... 110 A4
Club Rd PPOOL/BLNAV NP4 ... 14 A4
Club Rw PPOOL/BLNAV NP4 * ... 12 C5
Clun Av CDFN CF14 ... 99 E3
Clun Crs LLTR/LLH CF72 ... 94 C5
Clun Ter CATH/RTH/SPL CF24 ... 112 C3
Clydach CI NWPT NP20 ... 39 H5
Clydach St GTN/RVSD CF11 ... 6 B5
Clydesmuir Rd CATH/RTH/SPL CF24 ... 113 H5
Clyde St ABRC/NBR/RIS NP11 ... 37 F5
  CATH/RTH/SPL CF24 ... 5 H5
Clyffard Crs NWPT NP20 ... 8 C4
Clyro PI CDFN CF14 ... 110 D2
Clytha Crs NWPT NP20 ... 8 E5
Clytha Park Rd NWPT NP20 ... 8 B3
Clytha Sq NWPT NP20 ... 8 E6
Coal Pit La CDFN CF14 ... 89 F3
Coaster PI CCDF CF10 ... 135 H5
Coates PI CDFN CF14 ... 102 C5
Coates Rd PNRTH/DP CF64 ... 134 B5
Cobb Crs CALD/MAG NP26 ... 62 D4
Cobden PI ABRC/NBR/RIS NP11 ... 36 A2
Cobden St ABRC/NBR/RIS NP11 ... 36 A2
Cobner CI PPOOL/BLNAV NP4 ... 14 C1
Cobol Rd CDFNE CF3 ... 105 G3
Cocker Av CWM NP44 ... 25 G2
Coed Arhyd CAE/CAN/FWR CF5 ... 116 B4
Coed Arian CDFN CF14 ... 111 F2
Coed Briwnant CDFN CF14 ... 99 F1
Coed Cae CAER CF83 ... 48 B3
  CWM NP44 ... 19 F3
Coedcae La LLTR/LLH CF72 ... 94 A5
Coedcae PI PPOOL/BLNAV NP4 ... 14 B3
Coedcae St GTN/RVSD CF11 ... 5 F3
Coed Camlas PPOOL/BLNAV NP4 ... 15 E5
Coed Ceirios CDFN CF14 ... 99 G3
Coed Cochwyn Av CDFN CF14 ... 99 F1
Coed Criafol BARRY/C CF63 ... 131 H5
Coed Dowlais CHV/BDAU CF38 ... 81 F2
Coed Edeyrn CYN/LLD/PWYN CF23 ... 113 F1
Coeder Dal CYN/LLD/PWYN CF23 ... 101 F2
Coedeva Mi CWM NP44 ... 25 F3
Coed Garw CWM NP44 ... 20 B2
Coed Gethin CAER CF83 ... 48 B3
Coed Glas CWM NP44 ... 20 C2
Coed Glas Rd CDFN CF14 ... 99 G2
Coed Isaf Rd PPRD CF37 ... 44 B4
Coed Leddyn CAER CF83 ... 48 C3
Coed Lee CWM NP44 ... 25 F2
Coed Main CAER CF83 ... 49 G5
Coed Mawr BARRY/W CF62 ... 144 D5
Coed Mieri LLTR/LLH CF72 ... 71 F5
Coedpenmaen Rd PPRD CF37 ... 45 E3
Coed Pwll CAER CF83 ... 49 F5
Coedriglan Dr CAE/CAN/FWR CF5 ... 116 B4
Coedybrain Ct CAER CF83 ... 48 B3
Coed y Broch CHV/BDAU CF38 ... 81 F2
Coed y Caerau La CLN/RNWPTE NP18 ... 43 H4
Coed-y-Cando Rd PPOOL/BLNAV NP4 ... 15 F5
Coed-y-Gores CYN/LLD/PWYN CF23 ... 101 F5
Coedgygric Rd PPOOL/BLNAV NP4 ... 17 E1
Coed y Llinos CAER CF83 ... 68 B1
Coed-y-Llyn CYN/LLD/PWYN CF23 ... 112 D1
  PENT/RAD/TFW CF15 * ... 97 F3
Coed-y-Pandy CAER CF83 ... 49 G3
Coed-y-Pia CAER CF83 ... 33 H1
Coed yr Eos CAER CF83 ... 68 B1
Coed yr Esgob LLTR/LLH CF72 ... 71 F4
Coed y Ynn CDFN CF14 ... 99 F2
Coed y Wenallt CDFN CF14 ... 98 D4
Coed y Wennol CAER CF83 ... 68 B2
Cogan Hl PPOOL/BLNAV NP4 ... 128 B5
Cogan Pill Rd PNRTH/DP CF64 ... 127 H4
Cogan Ter CATH/RTH/SPL CF24 ... 4 C1
Coggins CI CAER CF83 ... 68 A3
Cog Rd PNRTH/DP CF64 ... 141 F3
Coigne Ter BARRYE CF63 ... 139 H4
Coity CI CDFNE CF3 ... 103 F3
Colborne Wk CAE/CAN/FWR CF5 ... 119 E3
Colbourne Rd CHV/BDAU CF38 ... 80 B4
Colchester Av CYN/LLD/PWYN CF23 ... 113 G4

Colchester Est CYN/LLD/PWYN CF23 * ... 113 G4
Colcot Rd BARRY/W CF62 ... 138 D2
Cold Bath Rd CLN/RNWPTE NP18 ... 42 A4
Coldbrook Rd East BARRYE CF63 ... 140 A2
Coldbrook Rd West BARRYE CF63 ... 139 H2
Coldra Rd NWPT NP20 ... 76 B2
Coldra Wd CLN/RNWPTE NP18 * ... 59 E1
Coldra Wood Dr CLN/RNWPTE NP18 ... 58 D1
Cold Stores Rd CCDF CF10 ... 129 G2
Coldstream Ct CWM NP44 ... 20 B3
Coldstream Ter GTN/RVSD CF11 ... 4 A5
Cole Ct CAER CF83 ... 49 G5
Coleford Dr CDFNE CF3 ... 105 E4
Coleford Rd CHEP NP16 ... 29 E1
Coleridge Av PNRTH/DP CF64 ... 134 B2
Coleridge Crs BARRY/W CF62 ... 139 E1
Coleridge Gn CWM NP44 ... 25 F1
Coleridge Rd GTN/RVSD CF11 ... 127 H2
  NWPT NP19 * ... 57 H4
Colhugh CI LLMJ CF61 ... 136 C4
Colhugh Pk LLMJ CF61 ... 136 C4
Colhugh St LLMJ CF61 ... 136 C4
Colin Wy CAE/CAN/FWR CF5 ... 116 D2
Collard Crs BARRY/W CF62 ... 139 F2
College CI CDFN CF14 ... 111 F1
College Crs CLN/RNWPTE NP18 ... 42 A3
College Fields CI CLN/RNWPTE NP18 ... 42 A3
College Gdns LLMJ CF61 ... 136 B3
College Gld CLN/RNWPTE NP18 ... 41 H2
College PI BARRY/W CF62 ... 2 E1
College Rd BARRY/W CF62 ... 2 E1
  CCDF CF10 ... 4 B2
  CDFN CF14 ... 111 E3
  CLN/RNWPTE NP18 ... 42 A3
College St CLLMJ CF61 ... 136 C3
College Wy PPRD CF37 ... 65 G2
Collier St NWPT NP19 ... 57 E5
Colliery Rd CAER CF83 ... 33 F1
Collingwood CI CDFNE CF3 ... 105 E4
Collingwood Crs NWPT NP19 ... 57 H1
Collins CI NWPT NP19 ... 75 H2
Collins Ter PPRD CF37 ... 65 F1
Collivaud PI CATH/RTH/SPL CF24 ... 5 J7
Coine St NWPT NP19 ... 9 G3
Colston Av NWPT NP19 * ... 77 G1
Colston Av NWPT NP19 ... 77 H1
Colston PI NWPT NP19 ... 77 H1
Colts Foot CI NWPT NP19 ... 8 B2
Columbus CI BARRY/W CF62 ... 144 C5
Columbus Wk CCDF CF10 * ... 5 F7
Colum Dr CCDF CF10 ... 112 B5
Column St PNRTH/DP CF64 ... 140 C3
Column Rd CCDF CF10 ... 112 B5
Colum Ter CCDF CF10 ... 4 B1
Colwill Rd CDFN CF14 ... 111 F3
Colwinstone CI CDFN CF14 ... 111 E2
Colwinstone St CDFN CF14 ... 111 E2
Colwyn Rd CDFNE CF3 ... 105 E4
Comet St CATH/RTH/SPL CF24 ... 5 H4
Comfrey CI CDFNE CF3 ... 103 F2
  NWPT NP20 ... 8 B1
Commercial CI ABRC/NBR/RIS NP11 ... 12 B2
Commercial La ABRC/NBR/RIS NP11 ... 37 E5
Commercial Rd ABRC/NBR/RIS NP11 ... 23 E2
  ABRC/NBR/RIS NP11 ... 34 D1
  BARRYE CF63 ... 139 G5
  CAER CF83 ... 51 G2
  NWPT NP20 ... 9 F6
  PPOOL/BLNAV NP4 ... 12 B2
Commercial St ABRC/NBR/RIS NP11 ... 37 E5
  CAER CF83 ... 38 D2
  CWM NP44 ... 25 H1
  LLMJ CF61 ... 136 C1
  LLTR/LLH CF72 ... 95 E2
  NWPT NP20 ... 9 F4
Common Rd PPRD CF37 ... 45 E5
The Common CDFN CF14 ... 111 H1
Compass Rd CCDF CF10 ... 129 G1
Compton CI RSTN NP10 ... 55 E5
Compton St GTN/RVSD CF11 ... 119 H4
Conifer CI CLN/RNWPTE NP18 ... 41 F4
Coniston CI NWPT NP19 * ... 57 G1
Connaught Rd CATH/RTH/SPL CF24 ... 113 G5
Constable Dr NWPT NP19 ... 57 G1
Constables CI NWPT NP19 ... 77 E2
Constance St NWPTE NP19 ... 57 E2
Constant CI GTN/RVSD CF11 ... 128 C3
Constellation St CATH/RTH/SPL CF24 ... 5 H4
Constitution Hl COWBR CF71 ... 122 C4
Conway CI CWM NP44 ... 19 H4
Conway Ct CCDF CF10 ... 133 G3
Conway Ct CWM/BDAU CF38 ... 65 G5
Conway Crt NWPTE NP19 ... 57 H5
Conway Dr BARRY/W CF62 ... 138 C3
Conway Gv RSTN NP10 ... 91 G2
Conway Rd GTN/RVSD CF11 ... 119 E1
  NWPTE NP19 ... 57 H5
  PPOOL/BLNAV NP4 ... 14 B3
Conway Sac NWPTE NP19 ... 57 H5
Conway Ter CWM NP44 ... 20 A3
Conybeare Rd CAE/CAN/FWR CF5 ... 118 C1
  PNRTH/DP CF64 ... 141 F4
Cook Rd BARRY/W CF62 ... 131 C5
Coolgreany CI NWPT NP20 ... 40 B5
Coolgreany Crs NWPT NP20 ... 40 B5
Coomassie St NWPT NP20 ... 77 E3

Co-operative Ter PPOOL/BLNAV NP4 * ... 12 B1
Coopers La COWBR CF71 ... 122 C5
Copleston Rd CDFN CF14 ... 111 E3
Copper Beech CI CLN/RNWPTE NP18 ... 41 F4
Copperfield Dr CDFN CF14 ... 86 A5
Copper St CATH/RTH/SPL CF24 ... 5 J5
The Coppice CHV/BDAU CF38 ... 65 H4
The Coppins CDFN CF14 ... 86 C4
Copse Wk NWPT NP20 ... 40 C3
Copse Wk CYN/LLD/PWYN CF23 ... 87 H5
Copthorne Wy CATH/RTH/SPL CF24 ... 125 E1
Cora St BARRYE CF63 ... 139 G4
Corbett Crs CAER CF83 ... 69 E3
Corbett Gv CAER CF83 ... 68 B3
Corbett Rd CCDF CF10 ... 4 B1
Corbetts La CAER CF83 ... 48 D3
Corelli St NWPT NP19 ... 57 E3
Coriander CI NWPT NP20 ... 8 B1
Corinthian CI PNRTH/DP CF64 ... 127 H4
Cork Dr CYN/LLD/PWYN CF23 ... 100 B3
Cormorant CI CDFNE CF3 ... 103 E2
Cormorant Wy RSTN NP10 ... 92 A1
Cornbrook Rd NWPT NP20 ... 39 H4
Cornelly CI CDFN CF14 ... 111 E2
Cornelly St CDFN CF14 ... 111 E2
Cornerswell PI PNRTH/DP CF64 ... 134 A2
Cornerswell Rd PNRTH/DP CF64 ... 134 B3
Cornfield CI CDFN CF14 ... 99 G1
Cornfield Ri CAER CF83 ... 49 G3
Cornflower CI CDFN CF14 ... 86 B3
Corn Glas BARRY/W CF62 ... 140 A1
Cornish CI GTN/RVSD CF11 ... 119 H3
Corn St NWPT NP20 ... 9 F5
Cornwall Ri BARRY/W CF62 ... 139 F2
Cornwall Rd BARRY/W CF62 ... 139 F3
  NWPTE NP19 ... 57 F3
Cornwall St GTN/RVSD CF11 ... 119 F5
Cornwood CI CAE/CAN/FWR CF5 ... 109 G4
Coronation PI ABRC/NBR/RIS NP11 ... 23 F4
Coronation Rd CDFN CF14 ... 111 H1
Coronation St ABRC/NBR/RIS NP11 ... 37 F5
  CAER CF83 ... 3 J2
  CAER CF83 ... 50 B3
Coronation Ter CAER CF83 ... 32 A3
  PNRTH/DP CF64 ... 134 C1
  PPRD CF37 ... 45 F1
Corporation Rd GTN/RVSD CF11 ... 6 B3
  NWPTE NP19 ... 9 G2
Corsham St CYN/LLD/PWYN CF23 ... 113 E2
Corvette Ct CCDF CF10 ... 5 G7
Corwen Crs CDFN CF14 ... 111 E2
Cory Pk CWM NP44 ... 26 C5
Cory Rd GTN/RVSD CF11 * ... 119 H2
Coryton Cl CDFN CF14 ... 98 C3
Coryton Crs CDFN CF14 ... 98 C3
Coryton Dr CDFN CF14 ... 98 B3
Coryton Ri CDFN CF14 ... 98 B3
Cory Wy BARRYE CF63 ... 3 K3
Coshston Rd CAE/CAN/FWR CF5 ... 110 B3
Cosmeston Dr PNRTH/DP CF64 ... 142 C2
Cosmeston St CATH/RTH/SPL CF24 ... 112 B4
Cosslett PI GTN/RVSD CF11 ... 6 C5
Cot Farm CI NWPT NP19 ... 59 E3
Cot Hil CLN/RNWPTE NP18 ... 58 C3
Cotman CI NWPT NP19 ... 57 H2
Cotswold Av CDFN CF14 ... 86 C2
Cotswold CI NWPT NP19 ... 58 B3
Cotswold Ri BARRYE CF63 ... 139 H3
Cotswold Wy ABRC/NBR/RIS NP11 ... 37 H4
  NWPTE NP19 ... 58 B3
Cottage CI CDFN CF14 ... 86 A5
Cottesmore Wy LLTR/LLH CF72 ... 95 F3
Cottrell Av CDFN CF14 ... 98 D4
Cottrell Rd CATH/RTH/SPL CF24 ... 113 C5
  CDFN CF14 ... 111 F1
Cottrell Sq BARRYE CF63 ... 139 G2
Coulson CI NWPT NP20 ... 9 F7
Countess PI PNRTH/DP CF64 ... 134 A3
Countisbury Av CDFNE CF3 ... 102 B3
Court CI CDFN CF14 ... 111 G2
  COWBR CF71 ... 122 C2
Court Crs RSTN NP10 ... 75 E2
Courtenay CI CDFNE CF3 ... 102 C3
Courtenay Rd BARRYE CF63 ... 139 H3
  CATH/RTH/SPL CF24 ... 5 K4
Court Farm CI CWM NP44 ... 26 B5
Court Farm Rd CWM NP44 ... 26 B5
Courtfield CI RSTN NP10 ... 54 D4
Court Gdns RSTN NP10 ... 54 D4
Court House CI CALD/MAG NP26 ... 63 C4
Court House St PPRD CF37 ... 44 D4
Courtis Rd CAE/CAN/FWR CF5 ... 117 E3
Court Meadow CLN/RNWPTE NP18 ... 59 C1
Courtney St NWPTE NP19 ... 57 E5
Court Rd BARRYE CF63 ... 138 C3
  CAER CF83 ... 48 C4
  CDFN CF14 ... 26 A2
  CWM NP44 ... 26 A2
Court St BARRYE CF63 ... 3 J1
  CDFN CF14 ... 111 F1
  PPRD CF37 * ... 45 G5
The Court CATH/RTH/SPL CF24 * ... 113 F5
  CDFN CF14 ... 111 G2
  PPRD CF37 * ... 45 G5
Court Vw CLN/RNWPTE NP18 ... 59 H1
The Courtyard RSTN NP10 ... 91 C1
Courtybella Gdns NWPT NP20 ... 76 C2
Courtybella Ter NWPT NP20 ... 76 D2
Coveny St CATH/RTH/SPL CF24 ... 120 D2
Coverack Rd NWPT NP19 ... 9 H4

Cowbridge By COWBR CF71 ... 122 C2
Cowbridge Rd LLMJ CF61 ... 136 C1
  LLTR/LLH CF72 ... 94 C4
  LLTR/LLH CF72 ... 106 C5
Cowbridge Rd East CAE/CAN/FWR CF5 ... 118 B2
Cowbridge Rd West CAE/CAN/FWR CF5 ... 125 F1
Cowbridge St BARRYE CF63 ... 139 H2
Cowleaze CALD/MAG NP26 ... 60 B5
Cowper CI NWPT NP20 ... 75 H2
Cowper PI CATH/RTH/SPL CF24 * ... 5 H2
Cowshed La RSTN NP10 ... 74 D2
Cowslip CI CYN/LLD/PWYN CF23 ... 101 H1
Cowslip Dr PNRTH/DP CF64 ... 134 A1
Coychurch Ri BARRYE CF63 ... 139 G1
Craddock St GTN/RVSD CF11 ... 4 B4
Cragside CI CDFNE CF3 ... 103 E4
Craig Castell PENT/RAD/TFW CF15 ... 97 G3
Craigddu Vw PPOOL/BLNAV NP4 ... 10 B5
Craigie Dr CCDF CF10 ... 7 F1
Craigmuir Rd CATH/RTH/SPL CF24 ... 121 E1
Craig-y-Haul Dr CDFNE CF3 ... 89 H4
Craig yr Afron CHEP NP16 ... 28 C5
Craig yr Allt CDFN CF14 ... 99 E1
Craig-yr-Helfa Rd PPRD CF37 ... 45 F3
Cranbourne Wy CYN/LLD/PWYN CF23 ... 101 F1
Cranbrook St CATH/RTH/SPL CF24 ... 4 E1
Crane St PPOOL/BLNAV NP4 ... 14 C4
Cranleigh Ri CDFNE CF3 ... 114 A1
Cranwell CI CAE/CAN/FWR CF5 ... 110 C5
Crawen Wk PNRTH/DP CF64 ... 142 C1
Crawford CI CDFNE CF3 ... 103 F4
Crawford Dr CYN/LLD/PWYN CF23 ... 101 H1
Crawford St NWPTE NP19 ... 57 E3
Crawley CI CDFN CF14 ... 85 H4
Crawshay Dr LLMJ CF61 ... 137 E5
Crawshay La CCDF CF10 ... 6 C1
Crawshay St CCDF CF10 ... 5 G7
Crediton Rd CDFNE CF3 ... 102 B4
Crescent CAE/CAN/FWR CF5 ... 125 C1
Crescent CI COWBR CF71 ... 122 D5
Crescent CAE/CAN/FWR CF5 ... 57 G3
Crescent Rd ABRC/NBR/RIS NP11 ... 36 D3
  CAER CF83 ... 68 D1
  NWPT NP19 ... 57 H4
The Crescent BARRY/W CF62 ... 138 B4
  CAE/CAN/FWR CF5 ... 117 C1
  CAER CF83 ... 48 B5
  CAER CF83 ... 51 G3
  CWM NP44 ... 25 G2
Cressfield Dr CYN/LLD/PWYN CF23 ... 101 H1
Cresswell CI CDFNE CF3 ... 103 F3
Cresswell Ct BARRY/W CF62 ... 139 F1
Cressy Rd CYN/LLD/PWYN CF23 ... 113 G5
Criccieth CI RSTN NP10 ... 91 H2
Criccieth Ct PNRTH/DP CF64 ... 133 H2
Criccieth Rd CDFNE CF3 ... 114 C2
Crickhowell Rd CDFNE CF3 ... 102 D4
Crick Rd CALD/MAG NP26 ... 61 H5
Crindau Rd NWPT NP20 ... 56 C1
Crockherbtown La CCDF CF10 ... 4 D4
Crocus CI RSTN NP10 ... 54 B3
Croescadarn CI CYN/LLD/PWYN CF23 ... 101 G1
Croescadarn Rd CYN/LLD/PWYN CF23 ... 101 G1
Croescade La CHV/BDAU CF38 ... 80 C2
Croescade Rd CHV/BDAU CF38 ... 80 C2
Croesllanfro Gdns RSTN NP10 ... 54 D1
Croeswen CWM NP44 ... 26 A3
Croesyceiliog By-Pass CWM NP44 ... 20 C5
Croffta PNRTH/DP CF64 ... 133 E4
Crofft-y-Genau Rd CAE/CAN/FWR CF5 ... 109 E2
Crofta CDFN CF14 ... 100 C1
Croft Gdns PNRTH/DP CF64 ... 141 E4
Crofts St CATH/RTH/SPL CF24 ... 112 D4
Croft Ter COWBR CF71 ... 122 D4
Cromwell Rd ABRC/NBR/RIS NP11 ... 36 C2
  CDFN CF14 ... 99 H2
  CHEP NP16 ... 30 C2
  NWPTE NP19 ... 57 G5
Crosbrook St PPRD CF37 ... 44 B4
Cross-Common Rd PNRTH/DP CF64 ... 133 E4
Crossfield Rd BARRY/W CF62 ... 139 E1
Crosslink BARRY/W CF62 ... 146 C3
Cross Inn Rd LLTR/LLH CF72 ... 95 F2
Cross La NWPT NP20 ... 9 F4
Cross St NWPT NP19 ... 112 A4
Cross St BARRYE CF63 ... 3 J1
  CAER CF83 ... 49 H5
  CLN/RNWPTE NP18 ... 42 B4
  PENT/RAD/TFW CF15 ... 97 H1
  PPOOL/BLNAV NP4 ... 14 B2
  PPRD CF37 ... 45 G5
The Cross CALD/MAG NP26 * ... 63 E3
Crossways CI CALD/MAG NP26 ... 61 E4
Crossways Rd CYN/LLD/PWYN CF23 ... 117 F3
Crossways St BARRYE CF63 ... 139 G4
  PPRD CF37 * ... 45 E2
Crosswells Wy CAE/CAN/FWR CF5 ... 116 D3
Crouch CI NWPT NP20 ... 59 H1
Crown CI CLN/RNWPTE NP18 ... 58 C3
  CWM NP44 ... 19 G2
Crown Hill CHV/BDAU CF38 ... 80 D4
Crown Hill Dr CHV/BDAU CF38 ... 80 C4
Crown Ri CWM NP44 ... 19 G2
Crown Rd CWM NP44 ... 26 C5

Crown St NWPTE NP19 ... 9 K1
Crown Wy CDFN CF14 ... 112 A4
Croyde Av CDFNE CF3 ... 102 B4
Crumlin Dr CDFNE CF3 ... 103 E5
Crumlin Rd PPOOL/BLNAV NP4 ... 14 A5
Crumlin St PPOOL/BLNAV NP4 ... 14 B4
Crundale Crs CDFNE CF3 ... 101 H5
Crwys PI CATH/RTH/SPL CF24 * ... 112 D5
Crwys Rd CATH/RTH/SPL CF24 ... 112 C4
Crystal Av CYN/LLD/PWYN CF23 ... 100 A4
Crystal Gln CDFN CF14 ... 100 A4
Crystal Ri CDFN CF14 ... 100 A4
Crystal Wood Rd CDFN CF14 ... 100 A4
Cuckoofield CI PENT/RAD/TFW CF15 ... 97 F2
Cudd y Coed BARRYE CF63 ... 140 A3
Culver CI PNRTH/DP CF64 ... 134 A5
Cumberland Rd NWPTE NP19 ... 57 F1
Cumberland St CAE/CAN/FWR CF5 ... 118 D3
Cumnock PI CATH/RTH/SPL CF24 ... 5 J5
Cumnock Ter CATH/RTH/SPL CF24 ... 5 J5
Cumrae St CATH/RTH/SPL CF24 ... 5 J5
Cunningham CI CYN/LLD/PWYN CF23 ... 112 C1
Cunningham Rd NWPTE NP19 ... 58 D2
Curie CI NWPT NP20 ... 40 B4
Curlew Av CALD/MAG NP26 ... 63 E4
Curlew CI CDFNE CF3 ... 103 E2
  NWPT NP19 ... 98 C3
Curlew Crs BARRY/W CF62 ... 137 G3
Curll Av CDFN CF14 ... 112 A3
Curran Emb CCDF CF10 ... 6 C2
Curran Rd CCDF CF10 ... 6 D1
Custom House PI PNRTH/DP CF64 * ... 134 D1
Customhouse St CCDF CF10 ... 4 D7
Cutter CI NWPTE NP19 ... 41 F5
Cwlwm Cariad BARRYE CF63 ... 131 H5
Cwmavon Rd PPOOL/BLNAV NP4 ... 10 C5
Cwm Barry Wy BARRY/W CF62 ... 2 A2
Cwmbran Dr CWM NP44 ... 19 G4
Cwmcarn CI CDFNE CF3 ... 103 E3
Cwmcarn Forest Dr ABRC/NBR/RIS NP11 ... 23 H5
Cwm-Cidy La BARRY/W CF62 ... 138 A3
Cwm Cwddy Dr RSTN NP10 ... 74 B1
Cwmdare St CATH/RTH/SPL CF24 ... 112 B4
Cwm Dylan CI RSTN NP10 ... 74 B2
Cwm Farm La PPOOL/BLNAV NP4 ... 16 C1
Cwm Fedw CAER CF83 ... 51 H1
Cwm Gwynlais PENT/RAD/TFW CF15 ... 98 A2
Cwm La RSTN NP10 ... 55 E3
Cwm Nofydd CDFN CF14 ... 99 E2
Cwm Parc BARRY/W CF62 ... 138 C4
Cwm Ser PPOOL/BLNAV NP4 ... 17 H1
Cwmynyscoy Rd PPOOL/BLNAV NP4 ... 16 C5
Cwrdy CI PPOOL/BLNAV NP4 ... 16 D3
Cwrt Aethen BARRYE CF63 ... 131 H5
Cwrt Bala CDFNE CF3 ... 102 D5
Cwrt Bleddyn CWM NP44 ... 20 D4
Cwrt Boston CYN/LLD/PWYN CF23 ... 114 A4
Cwrt Camlas RSTN NP10 ... 55 F4
Cwrt Cefn CDFN CF14 ... 86 B5
Cwrt Coed-y-Brenin CHV/BDAU CF38 ... 81 F2
Cwrt Coles CYN/LLD/PWYN CF23 ... 114 A4
Cwrt Dowlais CWM NP44 ... 25 H3
Cwrt Draw Llyn CAER CF83 ... 68 C4
Cwrt Dyfed BARRYE CF63 ... 140 A1
Cwrt Edward BARRY/W CF62 ... 2 E5
Cwrt Eirlys BARRYE CF63 ... 131 C5
Cwrt Faenor CHV/BDAU CF38 ... 80 A5
Cwrtglas CWM NP44 ... 20 B4
Cwrt Griffin CAER CF83 ... 70 D2
Cwrt Isaf CHV/BDAU CF38 ... 80 B5
Cwrt Llechau LLTR/LLH CF72 ... 106 B2
Cwrt Newton BARRYE CF63 ... 68 A3
Cwrt Newton Pool BARRY/W CF62 ... 144 D3
Cwrt Pencoedtre BARRYE CF63 ... 139 G1
Cwrt Pensarn CDFNE CF3 ... 102 D5
Cwrt Pentre Bach CDFNE CF3 ... 103 F2
Cwrt Pentwyn CHV/BDAU CF38 ... 80 C3
Cwrt Roberts CAE/CAN/FWR CF5 ... 116 D5
Cwrt St Cyres PNRTH/DP CF64 ... 134 A2
Cwrt Ty-Fferm CAER CF83 ... 48 C1
Cwrt Ty Mawr CAER CF83 ... 69 G2
Cwrt Ty-Newydd CAER CF83 ... 134 A4
Cwrt-Ty-Mynydd PENT/RAD/TFW CF15 * ... 97 G4
  PENT/RAD/TFW CF15 * ... 97 G4
Cwrt y Babell ABRC/NBR/RIS NP11 ... 34 B2
Cwrt-y-Cadno CAE/CAN/FWR CF5 ... 116 C3
Cwrt y Garth CHV/BDAU CF38 ... 80 B5
Cwrt-y-Goedwig CHV/BDAU CF38 ... 80 C3
Cwrt y Parc CDFN CF14 ... 99 H3
Cwrt y Porth Fawr PPOOL/BLNAV NP4 ... 12 A3
Cwrt-yr-Ala Rd CAE/CAN/FWR CF5 ... 126 A1
Cwrt yr Ardal CDFNE CF3 ... 102 D5
Cwrt yr Efail CHV/BDAU CF38 ... 81 G2
Cwrt y r Ysgol ABRC/NBR/RIS NP11 ... 37 E3
Cwrt-y-Vil Rd PNRTH/DP CF64 ... 134 C4
Cwrt-y-Vil Rd (Lower) PNRTH/DP CF64 ... 134 C3

Cwrt y Waun CHV/BDAU CF38 .... 80 B5
Cwrt Ywen LLTR/LLH CF72 ..... 106 B3
Cyfarthfa St
  CATH/RTH/SPL CF24 ...... 5 C1
Cymmer St GTN/RVSD CF11 ..... 6 B5
Cymric Cl CAE/CAN/FWR CF5 .. 117 G3
Cynan Cl BARRYE CF63 .... 139 H1
  CHV/BDAU CF38 .... 80 B4
Cyncoed Av
  CYN/LLD/PWYN CF23 .... 100 D4
Cyn-Coed Av
  CYN/LLD/PWYN CF23 .... 101 G4
Cyncoed Crs
  CYN/LLD/PWYN CF23 .... 101 G4
Cyncoed Gdns
  CYN/LLD/PWYN CF23 .... 113 E2
Cyncoed Pl
  CYN/LLD/PWYN CF23 .... 100 D4
Cyncoed Ri
  CYN/LLD/PWYN CF23 .... 100 D4
Cyn-Coed Rd
  CYN/LLD/PWYN CF23 .... 100 D4
Cynon Vw PPRD CF37 .... 45 G1
Cyntwell Av
  CAE/CAN/FWR CF5 ...... 117 E5
Cyntwell Crs
  CAE/CAN/FWR CF5 ...... 117 E5
Cyntwell Pl CAE/CAN/FWR CF5 117 E4
Cypress Cl CLN/RNWPTE NP18.. 41 F4
Cypress Dr CDFNE CF3 .... 103 F2
Cypress St PPRD CF37 .... 65 H2
Cyrch-y-Gwas Rd PPRD CF37 .. 97 F4
Cyril Crs CATH/RTH/SPL CF24.. 5 J2
Cyril St BARRYE CF63 .... 139 H4
  NWPTE NP19 .... 9 H4

D

Daffodil Ct CWM NP44 .... 24 C1
Daffodil La RSTN NP10 .... 54 A2
Dafydd Pl BARRYE CF63 .... 139 C1
Daisy St CAE/CAN/FWR CF5 .... 118 C2
Daisy Vw PPOOL/BLNAV NP4 ... 14 D5
Dalcross St
  CATH/RTH/SPL CF24 .... 112 D4
Dale Av CDFN CF14 .... 99 C5
Dale Cl BARRYE/W CF62 .... 139 F1
Dale Rd NWPTE NP19 .... 58 C1
Dalmuir Rd
  CATH/RTH/SPL CF24 .... 121 E1
Dalton St CATH/RTH/SPL CF24.. 112 C5
Dan Caerlan LLTR/LLH CF72 ... 95 F1
Dancarga Dr CALD/MAG NP26 .. 62 D2
Dancing Cl CALD/MAG NP26 ... 60 C3
Dancing Hl CALD/MAG NP26 ... 60 C3
Danes Cl CHEP NP16 .... 28 B4
Danescourt Wy
  CAE/CAN/FWR CF5 ...... 110 B2
Danes Hl CHEP NP16 .... 28 B4
Daniel Hopkin Cl LLMJ CF61 .. 136 C4
Daniell Cl PNRTH/DP CF64 .... 141 E4
Daniel Pl NWPT NP20 .... 8 E7
Daniel St BARRYE CF63 .... 139 G2
  CATH/RTH/SPL CF24 .... 112 C4
Dannog y Coed BARRYE CF63 . 131 H5
Danybryn LLTR/LLH CF72 ...... 94 D2
Dan-y-Bryn Av
  PENT/RAD/TFW CF15 .... 97 F4
Dan-y-Bryn Cl
  PENT/RAD/TFW CF15 .... 97 F4
Danycoed CAER CF83 .... 69 E3
Dan-y-Coedcae Rd PPRD CF37.. 44 C5
Dan-y-Coed Cl
  CYN/LLD/PWYN CF23 * .. 100 C4
Dan-y-Coed Ri
  CYN/LLD/PWYN CF23 * .. 100 C4
Dan-y-Coed Rd
  CYN/LLD/PWYN CF23 .... 100 C3
Dan-y-Darren CAER CF83 ...... 33 H1
Dan-y-Deri CAER CF83 .... 46 A5
Dan-y-Felin LLTR/LLH CF72 ... 94 D2
Dan-y-Graig CAER CF83 .... 47 F2
Danygraig CAER CF83 .... 50 C3
Dan y Graig CWM NP44 .... 98 C2
Danygraig Cl LLTR/LLH CF72 .. 20 B1
Danygraig Dr LLTR/LLH CF72 .. 94 D2
Dan y Graig Hts
  LLTR/LLH CF72 .... 94 D2
Dan y Graig Rd
  ABRC/NBR/RIS NP11 .... 37 E4
Danygraig St PPRD CF37 ...... 44 C5
Danylan Rd PPRD CF37 .... 44 B3
Dan y Mynydd CDFN CF14 ..... 85 F4
Dan-yr-Allt Cl PPRD CF37 .... 46 A4
Dan yr Ardd CAER CF83 .... 46 B5
Dan-yr-Heol
  CYN/LLD/PWYN CF23 .... 100 B4
Darby Rd CATH/RTH/SPL CF24.. 117 E5
Darent Cl NWPT NP20 .... 39 F5
Darent Rd NWPT NP20 .... 39 F5
Dartington Cl NWPTE NP19.... 57 E1
Darran Rd
  ABRC/NBR/RIS NP11 .... 36 D3
Darran St CATH/RTH/SPL CF24.. 5 G1
Darren Cl CAER CF83 .... 49 G4
  COWBR CF71 .... 122 A3
Darren Dr
  ABRC/NBR/RIS NP11 .... 22 D2
Dartington Dr
  CYN/LLD/PWYN CF23 .... 101 F1
Dart Rd NWPT NP20 .... 39 H5
Darwin Dr NWPT NP20 .... 40 B4
David Cl NWPT NP20 .... 76 D3
David Davies Rd BARRYE CF63. 139 H5
David St BARRYE CF63 .... 140 A1
  CCDF CF10 .... 3 H3
Davids Whf BARRYE CF63 ..... 3 H3
Davies Dr CAER CF83 .... 48 C3
Davies Pl CAE/CAN/FWR CF5 .. 118 A4
Davies Sq NWPT NP20 .... 9 F7
Daviot St CATH/RTH/SPL CF24.. 112 D4
Davis Cl PPOOL/BLNAV NP4 ... 14 B3
Davis's Ter CATH/RTH/SPL CF24. 5 H1
Davnic Cl BARRYE CF63 .... 139 H3

Davy La NWPT NP20 .... 40 B3
Dawan Cl BARRY/W CF62 ...... 138 C4
Dawson Cl NWPT NP20 .... 54 A5
Dean Cl CWM NP44 .... 24 C5
Deanery Gdns NWPT NP20 * .. 8 D2
Deans Cl CAE/CAN/FWR CF5 ... 111 F5
Deans Gdns CHEP NP16 .... 28 B5
Dean Hl CHEP NP16 .... 28 B4
Dean St NWPTE NP19 .... 57 E3
De-Bartt St CHEP NP16 ...... 65 G3
De Bawdip Rd
  CATH/RTH/SPL CF24 .... 113 H5
De Braose Cl
  CAE/CAN/FWR CF5 ...... 110 B2
De Burgh Pl GTN/RVSD CF11... 119 F3
De Burgh St GTN/RVSD CF11... 119 F3
De Clare Dr
  PENT/RAD/TFW CF15 .... 98 A5
De Croche Pl GTN/RVSD CF11.. 119 F3
Deemuir Rd
  CATH/RTH/SPL CF24 .... 121 E1
Deemuir Sg
  CATH/RTH/SPL CF24 * .. 121 E1
Deepdale Cl
  CYN/LLD/PWYN CF23 .... 112 D5
Deepfield Cl
  CAE/CAN/FWR CF5 ...... 116 C3
Deepweir CALD/MAG NP26 ..... 63 F4
Deepweir Gdns
  CALD/MAG NP26 .... 63 F4
Deepwood Cl
  CAE/CAN/FWR CF5 ...... 116 C3
Deere Cl CAE/CAN/FWR CF5 ... 117 E4
Deere Pl CAE/CAN/FWR CF5 ... 117 E4
Deere St CAE/CAN/FWR CF5 ... 117 E4
  CHV/BDAU CF38 .... 80 D4
Deganwy Cl CDFN CF14 .... 99 H1
De Havilland Rd
  CATH/RTH/SPL CF24 .... 121 F1
Dehewydd Isaf
  LLTR/LLH CF72 .... 81 E5
Dehewydd La CHV/BDAU CF38 . 81 E5
Delfryn LLTR/LLH CF72 .... 107 G1
Delius Cl NWPTE NP19 .... 58 B4
  RSTN NP10 .... 54 D3
The Dell CDFNE CF3 .... 102 C2
  CHV/BDAU CF38 .... 65 G4
Dell Vw CHEP NP16 .... 28 C4
Delphinium Rd RSTN NP10 .... 54 A2
Delta St GTN/RVSD CF11 ...... 118 D4
Denbigh Cl CHV/BDAU CF38 ... 65 G5
Denbigh Dr CAER CF83 .... 47 H5
Denbigh Dr CHEP NP16 .... 30 D5
  LLMJ CF61 .... 137 F5
Denbigh Rd NWPTE NP19...... 57 F1
  PNRTH/DP CF64 .... 133 G2
Denbigh St GTN/RVSD CF11 ... 118 D2
Denbigh Wsh GTN/RVSD CF11.. 139 F2
Denison Wy
  CAE/CAN/FWR CF5 ...... 116 C3
Denmark Dr CHEP NP16 .... 29 F5
Denny Vw CALD/MAG NP26 .... 63 F4
Dental Dr CDFN CF14 .... 112 A2
Denton Rd CAE/CAN/FWR CF5 . 118 B3
Dents Cl NWPTE NP19 .... 58 A1
Dents Hl NWPTE NP19 .... 58 A1
Denys Cl PNRTH/DP CF64 ..... 133 F2
Dering Dv NWPTE NP19 .... 78 A2
Dering Rd
  CYN/LLD/PWYN CF23 .... 102 A1
Derwen Ct
  CYN/LLD/PWYN CF23 * .. 100 D3
Derwen Cl
  CYN/LLD/PWYN CF23 .... 100 D2
  LLTR/LLH CF72 .... 107 F1
Derwent Cl CDFN CF14 .... 85 H5
Derwent St NWPTE NP19 ...... 58 A1
Derwyn Las CAER CF83 .... 49 F2
Despenser Av LLTR/LLH CF72.. 95 E3
Despenser Gdns
  GTN/RVSD CF11 .... 4 A6
Despenser Pl GTN/RVSD CF11.. 4 A6
Despenser Rd
  PNRTH/DP CF64 .... 141 E4
Despenser St GTN/RVSD CF11.. 4 A6
Dessmuir Rd
  CATH/RTH/SPL CF24 .... 121 E1
Devon Av BARRYE CF63 .... 139 F3
Devon Pl GTN/RVSD CF11 ..... 119 F5
  NWPT NP20 .... 6 A2
  PPOOL/BLNAV NP4 ...... 12 B4
Devon St GTN/RVSD CF11 ..... 119 F5
Dewberry Vw NWPTE NP19 .... 54 A1
Dew Crs CAE/CAN/FWR CF5 ... 117 H4
De Winton Ter CAER CF83 .... 33 G5
Dewi St PPRD CF37 .... 45 F1
Dewsland Park Rd
  NWPT NP20 .... 8 D5
Dewstow Cl CALD/MAG NP26 .. 62 C3
Dewstow Gdns
  CALD/MAG NP26 .... 62 C3
Dewstow Rd CALD/MAG NP26.. 62 B1
Dewstow St NWPTE NP19 ...... 58 C3
Diamond Cl CAER CF83 .... 48 C5
Diamond St
  CATH/RTH/SPL CF24 .... 5 K3
Diana La CATH/RTH/SPL CF24.. 112 A4
Diana St CATH/RTH/SPL CF24.. 112 A4
Dibdin Cl NWPTE NP19 .... 59 E4
Dickens Av CDFNE CF3 .... 102 A3
Dickens Dr NWPT NP20 .... 75 H2
Digby Cl CAE/CAN/FWR CF5 ... 110 C3
Digby St BARRYE CF63 .... 2 C5
Dimlands Rd LLMJ CF61 .... 136 A3
Dinas Cl GTN/RVSD CF11 ...... 6 B2
Dinas Path CALD/MAG NP26 ... 134 A4
Dinas Rd PNRTH/DP CF64 ..... 134 C2
Dinch Hl CALD/MAG NP26 ..... 60 C5
Dinch Hill La CALD/MAG NP26. 146 B2
Dingle La PNRTH/DP CF64 .... 134 C2
Dingle Rd PNRTH/DP CF64 .... 134 C2
Distillery Rd
  PPRD CF37 * 44 A2
Dobbins Rd BARRYE CF63 .... 140 B1
Dochdwy Rd PNRTH/DP CF64 .. 128 A5

Dock Rd BARRY/W CF62 .... 3 H6
Dock St PNRTH/DP CF64 ...... 134 B1
Docks Wy NWPT NP20 .... 76 B4
Dock View Rd BARRYE CF63 ... 3 H2
Dodington Pl PNRTH/DP CF37*. 45 F2
Doe Cl CYN/LLD/PWYN CF23 .. 113 C4
Dogfield St
  CATH/RTH/SPL CF24 .... 112 C4
Dogo St GTN/RVSD CF11 ...... 119 E1
Dol Fran CAER CF83 .... 49 G5
Dolgellau Av CHV/BDAU CF38 . 65 H3
Dolgoch Cl CDFNE CF3 .... 102 D5
Dol Gwaetheg PNRTH/DP CF64. 134 A4
Dolphin St NWPT NP20 .... 9 G6
Dolwen Rd CDFN CF14 .... 111 E3
Dol-y-Felin CAER CF83 .... 49 F2
Dol-y-Llan LLTR/LLH CF72 .... 95 E5
Dol y Pandy CAER CF83 ...... 49 F2
Dol y Paun CAER CF83 .... 68 B2
Dol-y-Eos CAER CF83 .... 49 F5
Dombey Cl CDFNE CF3 .... 86 A5
Dominions Ar CCDF CF10 ..... 4 D4
Dominion Wy
  CATH/RTH/SPL CF24 .... 113 G5
Donald St CATH/RTH/SPL CF24. 112 D4
Don Cl NWPT NP20 .... 39 G5
Doniford Cl PNRTH/DP CF64 .. 141 F3
Donnington Rd
  CDFNE CF3 .... 140 C3
Doralit Cl CWM NP44 .... 24 B2
Doralit Vw CWM NP44 .... 24 B3
Dorchester Av
  CYN/LLD/PWYN CF23 .... 113 F3
Dorleigh Ct CWM NP44 .... 19 E3
Dorothy Av BARRY/W CF62 .... 139 E1
Dorothy Cl BARRY/W CF62 .... 139 E1
Dorothy St PPRD CF37 .... 45 E2
Dorset Cl NWPTE NP19 .... 78 A2
Dorset Crs NWPTE NP19 ...... 78 A2
Dorset St GTN/RVSD CF11 .... 6 A2
Douglas Cl CAE/CAN/FWR CF5. 110 C3
Dovedale Cl
  CYN/LLD/PWYN CF23 .... 112 D2
Dovey Cl BARRY/W CF62 ...... 138 C3
  CDFNE CF3 .... 102 C5
Dowlais Ar CCDF CF10 * 7 G4
Dowlais Rd
  CATH/RTH/SPL CF24 .... 7 K1
Dowland Cl NWPTE NP19 ...... 58 C4
Dowlands Wy PNRTH/DP CF64.. 134 A5
Downfield Cl PNRTH/DP CF64.. 128 A5
Downing St NWPTE NP19 ...... 77 H1
Downs Vw COWBR CF71 .... 123 F2
Downs View Cl COWBR CF71 .. 123 F2
Downton Ri CDFNE CF3 .... 114 B3
Downton Rd CDFNE CF3 .... 114 B3
Doyle Av CAE/CAN/FWR CF5 .. 110 C5
Drake Cl NWPTE NP19 .... 58 D3
Drake Wk CCDF CF10 * 7 H6
Drangway LLMJ CF61 .... 136 C4
Dranllwyn Cl CAER CF83 ..... 51 G2
Dranllwyn La CAER CF83 ..... 51 G2
Drawlings Cl CDFNE CF3 ..... 102 C2
Drinkwater Gdns NWPT NP20.. 76 A2
Drinkwater Vw NWPT NP20 ... 76 A2
Drinkwater Vw NWPT NP20 ... 76 A2
The Drive CAE/CAN/FWR CF5 . 117 C1
  LLTR/LLH CF72 .... 107 H2
  PNRTH/DP CF64 .... 133 G3
Drope Rd CAE/CAN/FWR CF5 .. 116 B4
Drope Ter CAE/CAN/FWR CF5 . 116 B4
Dros y Mor PNRTH/DP CF64 .. 134 D4
Dros-y-Morfa CDFNE CF3 ..... 114 C3
Drovers Ms NWPT NP20 .... 9 F6
Druids Vw
  PENT/RAD/TFW CF15 .... 97 C5
Druids Cl NWPTE NP19 .... 122 D3
Druidstone Rd CDFNE CF3 .... 102 D1
Drum Tower Vw CAER CF83 ... 68 A2
Drury Cl CDFN CF14 .... 85 H5
Drybrook Cl CDFNE CF3 ...... 102 C2
  CWM NP44 .... 20 A5
Dryburn Av CDFN CF14 .... 99 C5
Dryden Cl CDFNE CF3 .... 102 A3
Dryden Rd PNRTH/DP CF64 .... 134 B2
Dryden Ter BARRY/W CF62 .... 139 F1
Dryla PNRTH/DP CF64 .... 133 E4
Drysgol Rd
  PENT/RAD/TFW CF15 .... 97 G4
Duckpool Rd NWPTE NP19 .... 9 J1
Dudley Cl BARRY/W CF62 ..... 138 C3
Dudley Pl BARRY/W CF62 ..... 2 C2
Dudley St BARRY/W CF62 ..... 2 C2
  NWPTE NP19 .... 9 K4
Duffryn Av
  CYN/LLD/PWYN CF23 .... 100 C5
Duffryn Cl
  CYN/LLD/PWYN CF23 .... 100 B4
  RSTN NP10 .... 74 D1
Duffryn Dr RSTN NP10 .... 75 H5
Duffryn Rd
  ABRC/NBR/RIS NP11 .... 35 F3
  CYN/LLD/PWYN CF23 .... 100 D3
Duffryn Wy RSTN NP10 .... 91 H1
Dugdale Wk GTN/RVSD CF11 *. 119 E5
Duke St CCDF CF10 .... 4 C5
  PPRD CF37 .... 65 G1
Dulverton Av CDFNE CF3 ..... 96 B3
Dulverton Dr PNRTH/DP CF64. 141 F4
Dulwich Gdns
  CATH/RTH/SPL CF24 .... 118 C1
Dumballs Rd CCDF CF10 ...... 6 E3
Dumfries Pl CCDF CF10 ...... 4 E3
Dummer Cl CDFNE CF3 .... 103 E2
Dunbar Cl
  CYN/LLD/PWYN CF23 .... 101 H1
Duncan Cl CDFNE CF3 .... 102 C4
Dungarvan Dr
  CYN/LLD/PWYN CF23 .... 101 G1
Dunkery Cl CDFNE CF3 .... 102 A4
Dunleavy Dr GTN/RVSD CF11.. 128 A3
Dunlin Ct BARRYE CF63 ...... 117 E5
Dunnet Gdns
  PPOOL/BLNAV NP4 ...... 17 H2
Dunn Sq NWPT NP20 * 9 F7
Dunraven Cl PNRTH/DP CF64 .. 133 G3

Dunraven Ct CAER CF83 ...... 47 H4
Dunraven Crs LLTR/LLH CF72.. 94 B3
Dunraven Dr RSTN NP10 ...... 91 G2
Dunraven Rd CWM NP44 ...... 26 C1
  GTN/RVSD CF11 .... 119 E4
Dunraven St BARRY/W CF62 .. 2 A4
Dunsmuir Rd
  CATH/RTH/SPL CF24 .... 121 E2
Dunstable Rd NWPTE NP19 ... 58 D4
Dunster Dr PNRTH/DP CF64 ... 141 F4
Dunster Rd CDFNE CF3 .... 102 D4
Durand Rd CALD/MAG NP26 ... 62 D4
Durell St LLMJ CF61 .... 136 C3
Durham La NWPTE NP19 * 57 E2
Durham Rd NWPTE NP19 ...... 57 F2
Durleigh Cl CDFNE CF3 ...... 102 D3
Durlston Cl CDFN CF14 ...... 110 D2
Duxford Cl CAE/CAN/FWR CF5. 118 A2
Dyfan Rd BARRYE CF63 .... 117 G1
Dyfed Dr CAER CF83 .... 48 C4
Dyffryn Cl CAE/CAN/FWR CF5.. 65 H1
Dyffryn Crs LLTR/LLH CF72 ... 124 A2
Dyffryn Gdns PPRD CF37 ..... 65 H1
Dyffryn Pl LLTR/LLH CF72 .... 124 A3
  RSTN NP10 .... 91 F5
Dyffryn Rd PPRD CF37 .... 138 D2
Dyfnallt Rd BARRYE CF63 .... 139 G1
Dyfrig Cl CAE/CAN/FWR CF5 .. 118 A2
Dyfrig Rd CAE/CAN/FWR CF5 . 118 A2
Dyfrig St BARRY/W CF62 ..... 3 J6
  GTN/RVSD CF11 .... 118 D1
Dylan Av CHV/BDAU CF38 ..... 80 B5
Dylan Cl BARRY/W CF62 ...... 138 D3
Dylan Crs BARRYE CF63 ...... 139 H2
Dylan Dr CAER CF83 .... 48 D4
Dylan Pl CATH/RTH/SPL CF24. 5 G1
Dynea Cl PPRD CF37 .... 46 A4
Dynea Rd PPRD CF37 .... 46 A4
Dynevor Rd
  CYN/LLD/PWYN CF23 .... 113 F2
Dyserth Rd PNRTH/DP CF64 .. 134 B3

E

Eagle La CALD/MAG NP26 ..... 63 E4
Eagle La COWBR CF71 .... 122 C3
Eagle Rd BARRY/W CF62 ...... 137 G3
Eagleswell Rd LLMJ CF61 .... 137 E3
Earl Crs BARRYE CF63 .... 3 F6
Earle Pl CAE/CAN/FWR CF5 ... 119 E3
Earl La GTN/RVSD CF11 ...... 6 B5
Earl Rd PNRTH/DP CF64 ...... 133 G3
Earls Court Pl
  CYN/LLD/PWYN CF23 .... 113 F4
Earl's Court Rd
  CYN/LLD/PWYN CF23 .... 113 F3
Earl St GTN/RVSD CF11 ...... 6 B6
Earlswood Rd CDFN CF14 .... 85 H5
East Av CAER CF83 .... 48 C5
  PPOOL/BLNAV NP4 ...... 17 E4
East Bank Rd NWPTE NP19 ... 77 F4
East Bay Cl CCDF CF10 ...... 5 H3
Eastbrook Cl
  PNRTH/DP CF64 .... 133 F2
East Dock Rd NWPT NP20 .... 9 J7
Eastern Av CDFN CF14 .... 112 A2
  CYN/LLD/PWYN CF23 .... 113 G1
Eastern Cl CDFNE CF3 .... 102 C2
Eastfield Ct LLTR/LLH CF72 .. 5 G3
Eastfield Dr
  CLN/RNWPTE NP18 ...... 41 H2
Eastfield Rd
  CLN/RNWPTE NP18 ...... 41 H2
Eastfield Wy
  CLN/RNWPTE NP18 ...... 41 H2
Eastgate COWBR CF71 .... 122 D3
East Grove CCDF CF10 .... 5 G3
East Grove Rd NWPTE NP19 .. 58 A4
East Lynne Gdns
  CLN/RNWPTE NP18 ...... 42 B3
East Market St NWPT NP20 .. 9 G6
Eastmoor Rd NWPTE NP19 .... 78 B1
East Moors Rd
  CCDF CF10 .... 5 H7
East Rd CWM NP44 .... 26 A3
East Roedin CWM NP44 ...... 25 F3
  LLMJ CF61 .... 136 C3
East Tyndall St CDFF CF10 .. 5 H2
East Usk Rd NWPTE NP19 .... 9 F1
East Vw CAER CF83 .... 69 E2
  PPOOL/BLNAV NP4 ...... 14 B4
East View Ter
  BARRY/W CF62 * 2 C5
East Wk BARRY/W CF62 .... 139 E3
East Way Rd NWPT NP20 ..... 77 E4
Ebbw Rd CALD/MAG NP26 ..... 62 D2
Ebbw St NWPTE NP19 .... 58 A3
Ebbw Valley Wk
  ABRC/NBR/RIS NP11 .... 22 C2
Ebenezer Dr RSTN NP10 ...... 55 E5
Ebenezer St PPRD CF37 ...... 65 F5
Ebenezer Ter NWPT NP20 .... 9 F5
Eckley Rd PNRTH/DP CF64 .... 141 E4
Eclipse St
  CATH/RTH/SPL CF24 .... 5 H4
Eddystone Cl
  GTN/RVSD CF11 * 119 F5
Edgehill CWM NP44 .... 26 C2
Edgehill Av CDFN CF14 ...... 99 F2
Edinburgh Cl CWM NP44 ..... 11 G3
Edington Av CDFN CF14 ...... 112 B3
Edmonton Dr CWM NP44 ...... 24 D3
Edison Rdg NWPT NP20 .... 40 B3
Edith Rd PNRTH/DP CF64 ..... 133 F3
Edlogan Wy CWM NP44 .... 20 A4
Edmond Cl CHEP NP16 .... 29 F4

Edmond's Ct
  CATH/RTH/SPL CF24 .... 112 D4
Edmund Pl BARRYE CF63 * ... 140 B3
Edney Vw RSTN NP10 .... 76 A5
Edward Clarke Cl
  CAE/CAN/FWR CF5 ...... 110 C3
Edward German Crs
  NWPTE NP19 .... 58 D4
Edwardian Wy LLTR/LLH CF72. 107 H1
Edward Nicholl Ct
  CYN/LLD/PWYN CF23 .... 113 F3
Edward St
  ABRC/NBR/RIS NP11 .... 23 F3
  BARRYE CF63 .... 139 H2
  PPOOL/BLNAV NP4 ...... 17 E3
Edward Ter CAER CF83 .... 47 F1
Edward VII Av NWPT NP20 ... 56 A5
Edward VII Crs NWPT NP20 .. 56 A4
Edward VII La NWPT NP20 ... 56 A4
Edwin St NWPT NP20 .... 56 D2
Egerton St CAE/CAN/FWR CF5. 118 D2
Egham St CAE/CAN/FWR CF5 . 118 D2
Eglwysilan Rd PPRD CF37 .... 45 H2
Egremont Rd
  CYN/LLD/PWYN CF23 .... 112 D2
Egypt St PPRD CF37 .... 45 F4
Eider Cl CDFNE CF3 .... 102 D2
Eifion Cl BARRYE CF63 ...... 139 G1
Eisteddfod Wk NWPTE NP19 .. 58 D3
Eithinen Ber BARRYE CF63 ... 131 H5
Elaine Cl CDFN CF14 .... 85 H5
Elan Cl BARRY/W CF62 .... 138 C3
  NWPT NP20 .... 39 H5
Elan Rd CDFN CF14 .... 100 B2
Elan Wy CALD/MAG NP26 ..... 63 E2
Elderberry Rd
  CAE/CAN/FWR CF5 ...... 110 B3 (?)
Elder Cl CLN/RNWPTE NP18 .. 41 G4
Elder Wood Cl
  CYN/LLD/PWYN CF23 .... 113 G2
Eleanor Pl CCDF CF10 .... 6 E7
Eleven St PNRTH/DP CF64 .... 140 C3
Elfed Av PNRTH/DP CF64 ..... 134 A3
Elfed Gn CAE/CAN/FWR CF5 .. 118 A3
Elfed Wy BARRYE CF63 .... 139 H2
Elford Rd CAE/CAN/FWR CF5 . 117 F3
Elgar Av NWPTE NP19 .... 58 C4
Elgar Cir NWPTE NP19 .... 58 C4
Elgar Cl NWPTE NP19 .... 58 C3
Elgar Crs CDFNE CF3 .... 102 C3
Elgar Rd CAE/CAN/FWR CF5 .. 134 B5
Elizabeth Av BARRY/W CF62 .. 131 F5
Elizabethan Ct
  PNRTH/DP CF64 .... 128 A5
Elled Rd PPOOL/BLNAV NP4 .. 14 A2
Ellen St CCDF CF10 .... 5 F6
Ellesmere Ct CDFNE CF3 ..... 102 C4
The Ellipse PPRD CF37 ...... 5 H1
Ellwood Cl CDFNE CF3 .... 103 E4
Elm Cl CALD/MAG NP26 .... 60 D4
Elm Cl CHEP NP16 .... 29 E2
  PPOOL/BLNAV NP4 ...... 14 D2
Elm Dr ABRC/NBR/RIS NP11 .. 37 F4
Elmfield Cl CDFNE CF3 ...... 103 E4
Elm Gv CAER CF83 .... 140 A1
Elmgrove CAER CF83 .... 46 A5
Elm Gv NWPT NP20 .... 40 C4
Elm Grove La PNRTH/DP CF64. 133 F3
Elm Grove Pl PNRTH/DP CF64. 133 F3
Elmgrove Rd CDFN CF14 ...... 110 C1
Elm Grove Rd PNRTH/DP CF64. 133 F3
Elmhurst Cl
  PPOOL/BLNAV NP4 ...... 14 B1
Elm Pk CALD/MAG NP26 .... 62 C2
  CHEP NP16 .... 29 E2
Elms Hl CALD/MAG NP26 ..... 61 E5
Elms Pk LLTR/LLH CF72 ...... 107 H2
The Elms CALD/MAG NP26 .... 61 E2
Elm St CATH/RTH/SPL CF24 .. 5 H2
Elm St CCDF CF10 .... 65 H2
Elm Street La
  CATH/RTH/SPL CF24 .... 5 H1
Elworthy Cl PNRTH/DP CF64 .. 141 F4
Ely Rd CAE/CAN/FWR CF5 ..... 111 E5
Elysia St NWPTE NP19 .... 57 E2
Ely Valley Rd LLTR/LLH CF72. 94 C2
Emanuel Ct CAER CF83 .... 68 B3
Emblem Cl CAE/CAN/FWR CF5 . 117 H4
Emerald St
  CATH/RTH/SPL CF24 .... 5 J3
Emerson Dr
  CAE/CAN/FWR CF5 ...... 125 H1
Emlyn Dr CAER CF83 .... 48 D5
Emlyn Rd PPOOL/BLNAV NP4 .. 12 A2
Emlyn Sq NWPT NP20 .... 9 F7
Emlyn Ter
  PPOOL/BLNAV NP4 * 12 A2
Enbourne Dr
  CYN/LLD/PWYN CF23 .... 101 H1
Energlyn Cl CAER CF83 ...... 48 C5
Enfield Dr BARRY/W CF62 .... 138 C2
Ennerdale Cl
  CYN/LLD/PWYN CF23 .... 112 D3
Ennerdale Ct NWPTE NP19 ... 57 G1
Enterprise Wy NWPT NP20 ... 9 G7
Enville Cl NWPT NP20 .... 55 H5
Enville Rd NWPT NP20 .... 55 H5
Eppynt Cl
  ABRC/NBR/RIS NP11 .... 37 H4
Epsom Cl CDFNE CF3 .... 103 E2
Epstein Cl CAE/CAN/FWR CF5. 110 B3
Eric Coates Cl NWPTE NP19 .. 58 D4
Eridge Rd PNRTH/DP CF64 .... 133 G3
Erw Fach CHV/BDAU CF38 .... 81 E1
Erw Las CDFN CF14 .... 95 E2
Erw-r-Delyn Cl
  PNRTH/DP CF64 .... 133 H2
Erw Wen CDFN CF14 .... 99 E2
Eschol Cl NWPTE NP19 .... 78 A1
Esperanto Wy NWPTE NP19 .. 77 F3
Essex St NWPTE NP19 .... 9 J4
Essich St CATH/RTH/SPL CF24. 113 G4
Estate Rd PPOOL/BLNAV NP4 . 14 A2

Estuary Rd NWPTE NP19 ..... 78 C3
Estuary Vw CALD/MAG NP26 ..... 63 F4
Ethel St CAER CF83 ..... 118 C2
Eton Ct CDFN CF14 ..... 99 H4
Eton Pl CAE/CAN/FWR CF5 ..... 119 E3
Eton Rd NWPTE NP19 ..... 9 H5
Eton St BARRY/-/W CF62 ..... 3 J4
Eugene Cl CDFN CF14 ..... 103 F2
Eurgan Cl LLMJ CF61 ..... 136 C4
Eurwg Crs CDFN CF14 ..... 102 C2
Evansfield Rd CDFN CF14 ..... 110 D2
Evans Sq PPRD CF37 ..... 45 F1
Evans St BARRY/-/W CF62 ..... 3 G1
  NWPT NP20 ..... 56 D5
Evelyn St BARRY/-/W CF62 ..... 139 G4
Evenlode Av PNRTH/DP CF64 ..... 134 B4
Evenwood Cl
  CYN/LLD/PWYN CF23 ..... 101 F1
Everard St BARRYE CF63 ..... 139 H3
Everard Wy
  CYN/LLD/PWYN CF23 ..... 112 D1
Everest Av CDFN CF14 ..... 100 A1
Everest Wk CDFN CF14 ..... 100 A1
Everswell Av
  CAE/CAN/FWR CF5 ..... 117 G1
Everswell Rd
  CAE/CAN/FWR CF5 ..... 117 G1
Evesham Cl NWPT NP20 ..... 56 B2
Eveswell La NWPTE NP19 ..... 57 G4
Eveswell St NWPTE NP19 ..... 57 G4
Ewbank Cl BARRYE CF63 ..... 140 A1
Ewenny Cl BARRYE CF63 ..... 139 G1
Ewenny Rd CDFN CF14 ..... 100 B5
Excalibur Dr CDFN CF14 ..... 85 G5
Excelsior Cl NWPT NP20 ..... 9 J6
Excelsior Rd CDFN CF14 ..... 111 H4
Exchange Rd
  ABRC/NBR/RIS NP11 ..... 37 E3
The Exchange CCDF CF10 * 7 F5
Exemouth Pl CHEP NP16 ..... 28 C4
Exe Rd NWPT NP20 ..... 39 G3
Exeter Cl CDFN CF14 ..... 18 D5
Exeter Pl PPOOL/BLNAV NP4 ..... 12 C4
Exeter Rd NWPTE NP19 ..... 9 J2
Exeter St NWPTE NP19 ..... 9 H2
Exford Crs CDFNE CF3 ..... 101 H5
Eyre St CATH/RTH/SPL CF24 ..... 120 D2

F

Faber Wy GTN/RVSD CF11 ..... 119 E5
Factory La PPOOL/BLNAV NP4 ..... 12 C4
  PPRD CF37 ..... 44 C3
Factory Rd COWBR CF71 ..... 122 B5
  NWPT NP20 ..... 8 D1
Fairacre Cl CDFN CF14 ..... 99 E2
Fairbrook Cl CDFN CF14 ..... 99 G4
Fairfax Rd CDFN CF14 ..... 99 G4
  NWPTE NP19 ..... 57 H5
Fairfield PPOOL/BLNAV NP4 * 14 A3
Fairfield Av
  CAE/CAN/FWR CF5 ..... 118 B2
Fairfield Cl CAE/CAN/FWR CF5 ..... 118 A1
  CALD/MAG NP26 ..... 62 C3
  CLN/RNWPTE NP18 ..... 41 G3
  LLMJ CF61 ..... 136 C3
  PPRD CF37 ..... 65 H5
Fairfield Crs LLMJ CF61 ..... 136 D3
Fairfield La PPRD CF37 ..... 65 H3
Fairfield Ri LLMJ CF61 ..... 136 D3
Fairfield Rd CHEP NP16 ..... 30 C1
  CLN/RNWPTE NP18 ..... 41 G3
  PNRTH/DP CF64 ..... 134 B2
Fairfields PPOOL/BLNAV NP4 * 14 A1
Fairford St BARRYE CF63 ..... 139 H4
Fairhaven Cl CDFNE CF3 ..... 103 F2
Fairhill CWM NP44 ..... 10 B5
Fairhill Dr CHV/BDAU CF38 ..... 81 H1
Fairland Cl LLTR/LLH CF72 ..... 79 J2
Fairleigh Ct GTN/RVSD CF11 ..... 111 H5
Fairleigh Rd GTN/RVSD CF11 ..... 111 H5
Fairmeadow
  PENT/RAD/TFW CF15 ..... 96 B3
Fairmound Pl CHV/BDAU CF38 ..... 81 H1
Fairoak Av NWPTE NP19 ..... 9 J1
Fairoak Ct
  CYN/LLD/PWYN CF23 ..... 112 D3
Fairoak Gv RSTN NP10 ..... 74 C2
Fairoak La CWM NP44 ..... 20 B4
Fairoak Ms
  CATH/RTH/SPL CF24 ..... 112 C3
  NWPTE NP19 * 9 K1
Fairoak Rd
  CATH/RTH/SPL CF24 ..... 112 C4
  CYN/LLD/PWYN CF23 ..... 112 D3
Fairoaks PNRTH/DP CF64 ..... 133 F3
Fairoak Ter NWPTE NP19 ..... 9 K1
Fairthorn Cl CDFN CF14 ..... 85 H4
Fair Vw NWPT NP20 ..... 30 B1
Fairview CHV/BDAU CF38 ..... 80 C3
Fairview Av
  ABRC/NBR/RIS NP11 ..... 37 F4
Fairview Cl CDFNE CF3 ..... 103 F2
Fair View Cl LLTR/LLH CF72 ..... 107 F1
Fairview Ct
  CYN/LLD/PWYN CF23 ..... 101 E3
Fairwater Av
  CAE/CAN/FWR CF5 ..... 118 A1
Fairwater Cl CDFNE CF3 ..... 89 F2
  CWM NP44 ..... 25 E1
Fairwater Gn
  CAE/CAN/FWR CF5 * 117 G1
Fairwater Gv East
  CAE/CAN/FWR CF5 ..... 110 D5
Fairwater Gv West
  CAE/CAN/FWR CF5 ..... 110 D5
Fairwater Rd
  CAE/CAN/FWR CF5 ..... 110 C5
Fairwater Wy CWM NP44 ..... 25 E2
Fairway Cl RSTN NP10 ..... 54 D2
Fairway Dr CAER CF83 ..... 48 C3
Fairways Crs
  CYN/LLD/PWYN CF23 ..... 117 F1
Fairways Vw
  LLTR/LLH CF72 ..... 94 B2
The Fairway
  CYN/LLD/PWYN CF23 ..... 100 D3

Fairwood Cl
  CAE/CAN/FWR CF5 ..... 110 C4
Fairwood Rd
  CAE/CAN/FWR CF5 ..... 110 C4
Falcon Cl CALD/MAG NP26 ..... 63 E4
Falcon Gv PNRTH/DP CF64 ..... 142 C2
Falcon Rd BARRYE CF63 ..... 140 B2
Falconwood Dr
  CAE/CAN/FWR CF5 ..... 116 C4
Falfield Cl CDFN CF14 ..... 86 B5
Fallowfield Dr NWPTE NP19 ..... 78 B1
Fanheulog LLTR/LLH CF72 ..... 94 C3
Fanny St CATH/RTH/SPL CF24 ..... 112 C5
Faraday Cl NWPT NP20 ..... 40 A4
Fardre Cs CHV/BDAU CF38 ..... 65 F5
Fardre Crs CHV/BDAU CF38 ..... 81 G1
Farlays CWM NP44 ..... 24 D2
Farlow Wk CWM NP44 ..... 25 F1
Farm Cl CAER CF83 ..... 47 F2
Farm Dr CYN/LLD/PWYN CF23 ..... 112 D1
Farmhouse Wy
  CAE/CAN/FWR CF5 ..... 117 E5
  NWPTE NP19 * 57 F2
Farmleigh CDFNE CF3 ..... 114 B1
Farm Rd CAER CF83 ..... 69 F1
  PPOOL/BLNAV NP4 ..... 12 A2
Farmville CWM NP44 ..... 14 C5
Farmville
  CATH/RTH/SPL CF24 ..... 120 D2
Farmwood Cl NWPTE NP19 ..... 58 C4
Farnaby Cl NWPTE NP19 ..... 58 C4
Farriers Ga RSTN NP10 ..... 75 E2
The Farthings
  CYN/LLD/PWYN CF23 ..... 101 G1
Faulkner Rd NWPT NP20 ..... 56 A4
Feeder Rw
  ABRC/NBR/RIS NP11 ..... 23 F4
Feering St NWPTE NP19 ..... 9 J4
Felbridge Cl CCDF CF10 ..... 7 G1
Felbrigg Crs
  CYN/LLD/PWYN CF23 ..... 101 F1
Felin Fach CDFN CF14 ..... 111 E2
Felin Wen CDFN CF14 ..... 99 F3
Felsted Cl
  CYN/LLD/PWYN CF23 ..... 101 G1
Fennel Cl CDFNE CF3 ..... 103 F2
  PNRTH/DP CF64 ..... 134 A1
Fenner Brockway Cl
  NWPTE NP19 * 58 C2
Fenviolet Cl CCDF CF10 ..... 105 G4
Ferndale St GTN/RVSD CF11 ..... 6 B3
Ferney Cross CALD/MAG NP26 ..... 62 C3
Fernlea ABRC/NBR/RIS NP11 ..... 37 E3
Fernleigh Rd CALD/MAG NP26 ..... 62 C4
Fern Pl CAE/CAN/FWR CF5 ..... 110 B5
Fern Ri NWPT NP20 ..... 40 C5
Fernside NWPTE NP19 ..... 78 A1
Fern St CAE/CAN/FWR CF5 ..... 118 C2
Ferntree Dr CDFNE CF3 ..... 102 D3
Fernwood Ct CYN/LLD/PWYN CF23 ..... 113 F3
Ferrier Av CAE/CAN/FWR CF5 ..... 110 B3
Ferry Rd GTN/RVSD CF11 ..... 6 A6
Ferry Wy CHEP NP16 ..... 31 F5
Fescue Pl CAE/CAN/FWR CF5 ..... 116 D3
Festiniog Rd CDFN CF14 ..... 111 E3
Festival Crs
  PPOOL/BLNAV NP4 ..... 17 H1
Fford Cefn-yr-Hendy
  LLTR/LLH CF72 ..... 107 H1
Ffordd Bodlyn
  CYN/LLD/PWYN CF23 ..... 112 D2
Ffordd Camlas RSTN NP10 ..... 55 F4
Ffordd Celyn CDFN CF14 ..... 111 F1
Ffordd Cwellyn
  CYN/LLD/PWYN CF23 ..... 112 D2
Ffordd Cweli Yn
  CYN/LLD/PWYN CF23 * 113 E2
Ffordd Cwm Cidi
  BARRY/-/W CF62 ..... 138 B4
Ffordd Deg CAER CF83 ..... 69 E3
Ffordd Erw CAER CF83 ..... 68 B4
Ffordd Eynon Evans
  CAER CF83 ..... 48 A3
Ffordd Ffagan CDFNE CF3 ..... 103 F2
Ffordd Garthonne CCDF CF10 ..... 7 G3
Ffordd Gerdinan
  CHV/BDAU CF38 ..... 65 H5
Ffordd Glas-y-Dorlan
  CHV/BDAU CF38 ..... 80 C5
Ffordd Gwern
  CHV/BDAU CF38 ..... 80 C5
Ffordd Gwynno
  CHV/BDAU CF38 ..... 80 C5
Ffordd Hylgen LLTR/LLH CF72 ..... 106 B3
Ffordd Las CAER CF83 ..... 47 F1
  PENT/RAD/TFW CF15 ..... 97 F4
Ffordd Morgannwg
  CDFN CF14 ..... 98 A4
Ffordd Pengam
  CATH/RTH/SPL CF24 ..... 114 A5
Ffordd Penrhos CAER CF83 ..... 68 A1
Ffordd Talygarn
  LLTR/LLH CF72 ..... 107 E1
Ffordd Traws Cwm
  CAER CF83 ..... 68 B3
Ffordd Trecastell
  LLTR/LLH CF72 ..... 106 A2
Ffordd Treforgan
  PENT/RAD/TFW CF15 ..... 97 F2
Ffordd Tryweryn PPRD CF37 ..... 45 G1
Ffordd Ty Unnos CDFN CF14 ..... 99 G4
Fford-y-Barcer
  CAE/CAN/FWR CF5 ..... 116 C3
Ffordd-y-Berllan
  PENT/RAD/TFW CF15 ..... 97 F3
Ffordd y Bryniau
  PENT/RAD/TFW CF15 ..... 82 C3
Ffordd-y-Capel
  CHV/BDAU CF38 ..... 81 G3
Ffordd-y-Gollen
  CHV/BDAU CF38 ..... 65 G5
Ffordd y Milenivm
  BARRYE CF63 ..... 3 H3
  BARRY/-/W CF62 ..... 3 H3
Ffordd yr Afon
  PENT/RAD/TFW CF15 ..... 83 F4

Fford Garthorne CCDF CF10 ..... 7 F3
Fford Traws Cwn CAER CF83 ..... 68 A3
Fford-yr-Ywen
  CHV/BDAU CF38 ..... 65 H5
Fforest Gld NWPTE NP19 ..... 57 C3
Fforest Rd LLTR/LLH CF72 ..... 106 A4
Fforest Vw BARRY/-/W CF62 ..... 138 B5
Ffos-y-Fran RSTN NP10 ..... 74 C2
Ffos y Fran Cl RSTN NP10 ..... 74 C2
Ffos-yr-Hebog CAER CF83 * 33 H1
Ffrwd Wy PNRTH/DP CF64 ..... 142 C2
Ffrwd Ter CAER CF83 ..... 33 G4
Ffwrwm Rd CAER CF83 ..... 57 F2
Ffynnonbwla Rd PPRD CF37 ..... 46 D5
Fidlas Av CDFN CF14 ..... 100 B3
Fidlas Rd CDFN CF14 ..... 100 A2
Fieldfare Dr CDFNE CF3 ..... 103 F4
Fielding Cl CDFNE CF3 ..... 102 A4
Fields Av CWM NP44 ..... 19 G2
Fields Park Av NWPT NP20 ..... 56 A4
Fields Park La NWPT NP20 ..... 56 A4
Fields Park Crs NWPT NP20 ..... 8 A3
Fields Park Gdns NWPT NP20 ..... 56 A4
Fields Park Rd
  GTN/RVSD CF11 ..... 111 G5
  NWPT NP20 ..... 8 A3
Fields Park Ter
  ABRC/NBR/RIS NP11 ..... 36 A1
Fields Rd ABRC/NBR/RIS NP11 ..... 36 A1
  CWM NP44 ..... 25 H3
  NWPT NP20 ..... 8 A3
Field Ter PENT/RAD/TFW CF15 ..... 96 B1
Field Vw CWM NP44 ..... 20 B3
Fieldview Cl PNRTH/DP CF64 ..... 134 A1
Field Wy CDFN CF14 ..... 99 H4
Fifth Av NWPTE NP19 ..... 77 H5
Fifth St NWPTE NP19 ..... 77 H5
Finchley Rd
  CAE/CAN/FWR CF5 ..... 117 H1
Firbank Av NWPTE NP19 ..... 57 H3
Firbank Crs NWPTE NP19 ..... 57 H3
Firbanks Wy LLTR/LLH CF72 ..... 94 B2
Firs Av CAE/CAN/FWR CF5 ..... 109 H5
First Av CAER CF83 ..... 68 B1
Firstbrook Cl
  CYN/LLD/PWYN CF23 ..... 113 C4
The Firs NWPT NP20 ..... 40 D4
  PPOOL/BLNAV NP4 * 12 D2
First St NWPTE NP19 ..... 77 H4
Firtree Cl CALD/MAG NP26 ..... 110 A5
  CLN/RNWPTE NP18 ..... 41 F4
Firwood Cl CDFN CF14 ..... 110 D1
Fisher Cl NWPT NP20 ..... 59 E2
Fisher Hill Wy
  PENT/RAD/TFW CF15 ..... 98 A5
Fisherman's Wk CHEP NP16 ..... 30 D2
Fishguard Cl CDFN CF14 ..... 100 A4
Fishguard Rd CDFN CF14 ..... 100 A3
Fishpond Rd CDFNE CF3 ..... 102 A4
Fitzalan Ct
  CATH/RTH/SPL CF24 * 5 F4
Fitzalan Pl
  CATH/RTH/SPL CF24 ..... 5 F4
Fitzalan Rd
  CATH/RTH/SPL CF24 ..... 5 F4
Fitzhamon Av LLMJ CF61 ..... 136 C4
Fitzhamon Emb
  GTN/RVSD CF11 ..... 4 B6
Fitzhamon La GTN/RVSD CF11 ..... 4 B6
Fitzosborn Cl CHEP NP16 ..... 28 B5
Fitzwalter Rd
  CALD/MAG NP26 ..... 62 D4
Fitzwilliam Cl LLTR/LLH CF72 ..... 95 F3
Five Locks Cl CWM NP44 ..... 19 G1
Five Locks Rd CWM NP44 ..... 19 H1
Five Oaks La CWM NP44 ..... 20 B3
Flanders Meadow LLMJ CF61 ..... 136 C4
Flanders Rd LLMJ CF61 ..... 136 C4
Flavius Cl CLN/RNWPTE NP18 ..... 41 G3
Flaxland Av CDFN CF14 ..... 112 A2
Fleet Wy GTN/RVSD CF11 ..... 128 A1
Fleetwood Cl NWPTE NP19 ..... 57 F5
Fleming Cl NWPT NP20 ..... 40 B4
Fleming Wk CDFNE CF3 ..... 81 E2
Flindo Crs GTN/RVSD CF11 ..... 111 G5
Flint Av LLMJ CF61 ..... 137 E2
Flint Cl CWM NP44 ..... 19 G1
Flint Cl CLN/RNWPTE NP18 ..... 41 F4
Flint St CDFN CF14 ..... 112 A4
Flora St CATH/RTH/SPL CF24 ..... 112 C5
Florence Av BARRY/-/W CF62 ..... 139 E1
Florence Gv CDFN CF14 ..... 68 D2
Florence Pl
  PPOOL/BLNAV NP4 ..... 17 E3
Florence St
  CATH/RTH/SPL CF24 ..... 120 D1
Florentia St
  CATH/RTH/SPL CF24 ..... 112 C4
Foel View Cl CHV/BDAU CF38 ..... 80 C5
Folly La PPOOL/BLNAV NP4 ..... 13 H5
Folly Rd PPOOL/BLNAV NP4 ..... 14 D3
Folly Vw PPOOL/BLNAV NP4 ..... 14 D3
Fonmon Crs
  CAE/CAN/FWR CF5 ..... 117 G3
Fonthill Pl GTN/RVSD CF11 ..... 119 E5
Fontigary Rd CDFNE CF3 ..... 114 C2
Fontygary Rd BARRY/-/W CF62 ..... 144 A3
Ford Pl PPRD CF37 ..... 44 B5
Ford St NWPT NP20 ..... 8 C3
Fordwell CAE/CAN/FWR CF5 ..... 111 E4
Foreland Rd CDFN CF14 ..... 98 D5
Forest Cl CWM NP44 ..... 25 E5
Forest Ci CDFNE CF3 ..... 121 E5
Forest Cl CWM NP44 ..... 25 E5
  NWPTE NP19 ..... 57 G3
Forest Farm Rd CDFN CF14 ..... 98 A5
Forest Gv PPRD CF37 ..... 44 B3
Forest Hills Dr LLTR/LLH CF72 ..... 94 B3
Forest Oak Cl
  CATH/RTH/SPL CF24 ..... 100 D1
Forest Rd CHV/BDAU CF38 ..... 80 B4
  PPRD CF37 ..... 44 B3
Forest Vw CAE/CAN/FWR CF5 ..... 117 F1
  CWM NP44 ..... 24 B3
  LLTR/LLH CF72 ..... 94 D3
Forest Wk LLTR/LLH CF72 ..... 94 B3

Forge Cl CLN/RNWPTE NP18 ..... 42 A3
Forge Hammer Rw
  PPOOL/BLNAV NP4 * 14 A2
Forge La RSTN NP10 ..... 75 E2
Forge Pl RSTN NP10 ..... 75 E1
Forge Pl CAE/CAN/FWR CF5 ..... 117 E4
Forge Rd CAER CF83 ..... 57 F2
  RSTN NP10 ..... 75 E3
Forge Rw CALD/MAG NP26 ..... 63 G4
Forgeside CWM NP44 ..... 19 H1
Forrest Rd CAE/CAN/FWR CF5 ..... 118 C2
  PNRTH/DP CF64 ..... 134 C5
Forrest St GTN/RVSD CF11 ..... 6 B5
Forsythia Cl
  CYN/LLD/PWYN CF23 ..... 101 E3
Forsythia Dr
  CYN/LLD/PWYN CF23 ..... 101 E3
Fortran Rd CDFNE CF3 ..... 103 C2
Fort Rd PNRTH/DP CF64 ..... 142 B3
Fort St CATH/RTH/SPL CF24 ..... 120 D1
Fort Vw RSTN NP10 ..... 74 D1
Fosse Cl NWPTE NP19 ..... 78 B2
Fosse Rd NWPTE NP19 ..... 78 B2
Fountain La CDFNE CF3 ..... 103 C2
Fountain Rd
  PPOOL/BLNAV NP4 ..... 15 E5
Four Acre LLMJ CF61 ..... 136 D2
Fountain Wy CHEP NP16 ..... 30 D3
Four Elms Rd
  CATH/RTH/SPL CF24 ..... 5 J2
Fourth St NWPTE NP19 ..... 77 H4
Fowler St CAE/CAN/FWR CF5 ..... 14 A2
Foxberry Cl
  CYN/LLD/PWYN CF23 ..... 102 A1
Foxglove Cl
  CAE/CAN/FWR CF5 ..... 117 E4
Foxglove Ri PNRTH/DP CF64 ..... 133 H1
Fox Russell Cl CDFN CF14 ..... 111 E2
Fox St LLTR/LLH CF72 * 5 K1
Foxwood Cl RSTN NP10 ..... 74 D1
Frampton La LLMJ CF61 ..... 136 D2
Francis Dr NWPT NP20 ..... 9 F7
Francis Rd BARRY/-/W CF62 ..... 131 C5
Francis St
  ABRC/NBR/RIS NP11 ..... 37 F5
  CAER CF83 ..... 47 E2
  NWPT NP20 ..... 9 F7
  PPRD CF37 ..... 44 C3
Franklen Rd CDFN CF14 ..... 111 G2
Franklen St CDFN CF14 ..... 111 G2
Frank Rd CAE/CAN/FWR CF5 ..... 117 F2
Frank St NWPT NP20 ..... 8 B6
Fred Edwards Cl NWPTE NP19 ..... 59 E4
Frederick Ms NWPT NP20 * 8 D3
Frederick St NWPT NP20 * 8 C6
Freehold Land Rd
  PPOOL/BLNAV NP4 ..... 12 C5
Fremington Pl CDFNE CF3 ..... 102 B5
Freshmoor Rd
  CATH/RTH/SPL CF24 ..... 120 D4
Freshwater Rd NWPTE NP19 ..... 78 C3
Frewer Av CAE/CAN/FWR CF5 ..... 110 B4
Friars Ct NWPT NP20 ..... 8 D5
Friars Fid NWPT NP20 ..... 26 C2
Friars Gdn CWM NP44 ..... 26 C2
Friars La NWPT NP20 ..... 8 E4
Friars Rd BARRY/-/W CF62 ..... 3 F7
  NWPT NP20 ..... 8 C6
Friary NWPT NP20 * 8 D6
Frigate Rd CCDF CF10 ..... 7 K5
Frobisher Rd NWPTE NP19 ..... 78 A1
Fron Ter PPRD CF37 ..... 45 F2
Fryatt St BARRYE CF63 ..... 3 H2
Fryth Wd CHEP NP16 ..... 28 C5
Fulmar Cl CDFNE CF3 ..... 103 E2
  PNRTH/DP CF64 ..... 142 C2
Furnace St PNRTH/DP CF64 ..... 140 C3
Furness Cl CAE/CAN/FWR CF5 ..... 116 D4
Fuschia Cl RSTN NP10 ..... 54 A3

G

Gabalfa Av CDFN CF14 ..... 111 E3
Gabalfa Rd CDFN CF14 ..... 111 E3
The Gables CHEP NP16 * 28 D3
  PNRTH/DP CF64 * 133 F4
Gadlys Rd East
  BARRY/-/W CF62 ..... 2 D1
Gadlys Rd West
  BARRY/-/W CF62 ..... 2 D2
Gaen St BARRY/-/W CF62 ..... 2 B2
Gaer Park Av NWPT NP20 ..... 75 H2
Gaer Park Dr NWPT NP20 ..... 75 H2
Gaer Park Hl NWPT NP20 ..... 75 H1
Gaer Park La NWPT NP20 ..... 75 H1
Gaer Park Pde NWPT NP20 ..... 75 H1
Gaer Park Rd NWPT NP20 ..... 75 H1
Gaer Rd NWPT NP20 ..... 76 B2
Gaer St NWPT NP20 ..... 76 A3
Gaer V NWPT NP20 ..... 76 A3
Gaerwen Cl CDFN CF14 ..... 99 G2
Gainsborough Cl CWM NP44 ..... 26 B3
Gainsborough Dr
  NWPTE NP19 ..... 57 H1
Gainsborough Rd
  PNRTH/DP CF64 ..... 134 B1
Galahad Cl CDFN CF14 ..... 99 F1
Galdames Pl
  CATH/RTH/SPL CF24 ..... 7 K1
Gallanuir Rd
  CATH/RTH/SPL CF24 ..... 121 E1
Galleon Wy CCDF CF10 ..... 7 H3
Galston St
  CATH/RTH/SPL CF24 ..... 5 J4
Garden City Wy CHEP NP16 ..... 28 C4
Garden Cl CAER CF83 ..... 33 H4
Gardenia Cl
  CYN/LLD/PWYN CF23 ..... 101 E3
The Gardens CALD/MAG NP26 ..... 60 B2
Garden St CAER CF83 ..... 33 H4
Garden Suburbs
  ABRC/NBR/RIS NP11 ..... 23 F5
Caresfield St
  CATH/RTH/SPL CF24 ..... 5 H5
Gareth Cl CDFN CF14 ..... 85 G5
Garrick Dr CDFN CF14 ..... 85 H4
Garth Cl CAER CF83 ..... 70 C1
  PENT/RAD/TFW CF15 ..... 97 F2
  PPOOL/BLNAV NP4 ..... 13 E5
  RSTN NP10 ..... 74 D1
Garth Est CAER CF83 ..... 46 D2
Garth Hl CAER CF83 ..... 70 C1
Garth Lwyd CAER CF83 ..... 68 C3
Garth Olwg
  PENT/RAD/TFW CF15 ..... 83 E2
Garth Pl CDFN CF14 ..... 111 H3
Garth Rd CWM NP44 ..... 25 G3
Garth St PENT/RAD/TFW CF15 ..... 83 E2
The Garth CAER CF83 ..... 47 E2
Garth Vw CAER CF83 ..... 49 G2
  CHV/BDAU CF38 ..... 80 B4
  PENT/RAD/TFW CF15 ..... 67 F4
Garvey Cl CHEP NP16 ..... 30 D3
Garw Rw CWM NP44 ..... 20 C3
The Garw CWM NP44 ..... 20 C3
Garw Wood Dr CWM NP44 ..... 20 B2
Garwy Cl CWM NP44 ..... 20 C3
Gas Rd PPRD CF37 ..... 44 D3
Gatehom Cl BARRY/-/W CF62 ..... 139 F1
Gateside Cl
  CYN/LLD/PWYN CF23 ..... 87 H5
The Gateway CDFN CF14 ..... 112 A2
Gaudi Wk RSTN NP10 ..... 54 D5
Gaulden Gv
  CYN/LLD/PWYN CF23 ..... 101 F2
Gawain Cl CDFN CF14 ..... 85 G5
Gelli Av ABRC/NBR/RIS NP11 ..... 37 F5
Gelli Cl ABRC/NBR/RIS NP11 ..... 37 F4
Gelli Crs ABRC/NBR/RIS NP11 ..... 37 F4
Gelli Dawel CAER CF83 ..... 48 C5
Gellidawel Rd PPRD CF37 ..... 65 G1
Gelli Deg CAER CF83 ..... 48 C4
Gelideg Rd PPRD CF37 ..... 44 B4
Gelli Fawr Ct CWM NP44 ..... 24 C3
Gelligaer Gdns
  CATH/RTH/SPL CF24 ..... 112 B4
Gelligaer La
  CATH/RTH/SPL CF24 ..... 112 B4
Gelligaer St
  CATH/RTH/SPL CF24 ..... 112 B4
Gelli Rhwg Rd
  PPOOL/BLNAV NP4 ..... 12 B1
Gelli Rd LLTR/LLH CF72 ..... 106 A3
Gelli-Unig Rd
  ABRC/NBR/RIS NP11 ..... 23 F5
Gelliwastad Gv PPRD CF37 ..... 44 D3
Gelliwion Rd PPRD CF37 ..... 44 A5
Gelliwion Wd PPRD CF37 ..... 44 B4
Gelli'r Felin CAER CF83 ..... 48 C4
Gelynis Ter North
  PENT/RAD/TFW CF15 ..... 97 G2
Gelynog Ct CHV/BDAU CF38 ..... 80 A2
Gelyn-y-Cler BARRYE CF63 ..... 131 H5
General Rees Sq CWM NP44 * 19 H5
George Cl
  CYN/LLD/PWYN CF23 ..... 85 E4
George Lansbury Dr
  NWPTE NP19 ..... 58 C2
Georges Rw PNRTH/DP CF64 ..... 133 G2
George St
  ABRC/NBR/RIS NP11 ..... 35 G2
  BARRYE CF63 ..... 3 K1
  CWM NP44 ..... 19 H5
  LLTR/LLH CF72 ..... 95 E2
  NWPT NP20 ..... 9 F6
  PPOOL/BLNAV NP4 ..... 14 A1
George Street Br
  NWPTE NP19 ..... 9 H5
Georgian Cl LLMJ CF61 ..... 137 E2
Georgian Wy CDFN CF14 ..... 100 A2
  LLTR/LLH CF72 ..... 107 H1
Geraint Cl CDFN CF14 ..... 85 G5
Geraints Cl COWBR CF71 ..... 122 B4
Geraint's Wy COWBR CF71 ..... 122 B3
Gerbera Dr RSTN NP10 ..... 54 A2
Gerddi Cy Telin CDFN CF14 ..... 98 C5
Gerddi Taf CDFN CF14 ..... 110 C2
Gernant CDFN CF14 ..... 99 F3
Gery-y-Llan CAE/CAN/FWR CF5 ..... 124 A2
Gibbet's Hl COWBR CF71 ..... 122 B3
Gibbons Cl NWPTE NP19 ..... 58 A4
Gibbonsdown Cl BARRYE CF63 ..... 139 G1
Gibbonsdown Ri
  BARRYE CF63 ..... 139 G2
Gibbs Rd NWPTE NP19 ..... 58 A4
Gibraltar Wy CHEP NP16 ..... 31 F3
Gibson Cl CDFN CF14 ..... 100 A4
Gifford Cl CWM NP44 ..... 10 C5
Gilbert Cl NWPTE NP19 ..... 58 C5
Gilbert La BARRYE CF63 ..... 132 A5
Gilbert Pl CDFN CF14 ..... 111 G3
Gilbert St BARRYE CF63 ..... 139 G3
Gileston Rd CLN/RNWPTE NP18 ..... 41 G3
Gileston Rd GTN/RVSD CF11 ..... 119 E1
Gillian Rd CAE/CAN/FWR CF5 ..... 100 C4
Gilwern Crs CDFN CF14 ..... 99 H1
Gilwern Farm Cl
  CLN/RNWPTE NP18 ..... 27 G4
Gilwern Pl CDFN CF14 ..... 99 H1
  CWM NP44 ..... 19 G3
Glade Cl CWM NP44 ..... 24 D3
Gladeside Cl CDFN CF14 * 85 H4
The Glades PNRTH/DP CF64 ..... 134 D3
Gladstone Br BARRY/-/W CF62 ..... 3 F3
Gladstone Pl
  PPOOL/BLNAV NP4 ..... 17 E5
Gladstone St
  ABRC/NBR/RIS NP11 ..... 36 A2
Gladys St CATH/RTH/SPL CF24 ..... 112 C5
Glamorgan Cl LLMJ CF61 ..... 137 E2
Glamorgan St BARRY/-/W CF62 ..... 2 A4
  CAE/CAN/FWR CF5 ..... 118 D2

Glamorgan Street Ms
  CAE/CAN/FWR CF5 .... 118 D2
Glandovey Gv *CDFNE* CF5 .... 102 D4
Glandwr Pl *CDFN* CF14 .... 111 F1
Glan Ely Cl *CAE/CAN/FWR* CF5 .. 117 F3
Glanfa Dafydd *BARRY/E* CF63 ...... 3 J3
Glan Ffrwd *CAER* CF83 .... 48 A3
Glanmor Crs *NWPT* NP20 .... 58 A4
Glanmore Crs *BARRY/I/W* CF62 .. 2 D1
Glannor Park Av
  NWPTE NP19 .... 58 A3
Glanmuir Rd
  CATH/RTH/SPL CF24 .... 114 A5
Glannant St
  PPOOL/BLNAV NP4 .... 34 B3
Glan Rhyd *CAER* CF83 .... 48 C5
Glanrhyd *CDFN* CF14 .... 99 F3
Glan Rhyd *CWM* NP44 .... 24 D3
Glan Rhymni
  CATH/RTH/SPL CF24 .... 114 A4
Glantorvaen Rd
  PPOOL/BLNAV NP4 .... 14 C4
Glanwern Av *NWPTE* NP19 .... 58 B3
Glanwern Crs *NWPTE* NP19 ...... 58 B4
Glanwern Gv *NWPTE* NP19 .... 58 B4
Glanwern Rd *NWPTE* NP19 .... 58 B4
Glanwern Ri *NWPTE* NP19 .... 58 B4
Glan-y-Ffordd
  PENT/RAD/TFW CF15 .... 83 F1
Glan-y-Mor *BARRY/I/W* CF62 * .. 5 G1
Glanymor *LLMJ* CF61 .... 137 F3
Glan-y-Mor Rd *CDFNE* CF5 ...... 102 D5
Glan y Nant *CDFN* CF14 .... 99 F3
Glan-y-Nant Cl *CWM* NP44 ...... 25 C2
Glan-y-Nant Ter *CDFN* CF14 ...... 99 E5
Glas Canol *CDFN* CF14 .... 111 F2
Glascoed Rd
  PPOOL/BLNAV NP4 .... 17 H1
Glas Efail *CDFN* CF14 .... 99 G3
Glas Ifor *CDFN* CF14 .... 99 F5
Glasllwch Crs *NWPT* NP20 .... 55 F4
Glasllwch La *NWPT* NP20 .... 55 F1
Glasllwch Vw *NWPT* NP20 .... 55 F4
Glaslyn Cl *BARRY/I/W* CF62 ...... 138 C4
Glaslyn Ct *CWM* NP44 .... 20 A3
Glas Av *CATH/RTH/SPL* CF24 ...... 120 D5
Glastonbury Cl *NWPT* NP20 ...... 56 D3
Glastonbury Rd
  PNRTH/DP CF64 .... 141 F3
Glastonbury Ter *CDFNE* CF3 ...... 102 A4
Glas y Llwyn *BARRY/E* CF63 ...... 132 A5
Glas-y-Pant *CDFN* CF14 .... 98 C4
Glebe Pl *CDFN* CF14 .... 100 A2
Glebe St *BARRY* CF63 .... 139 G2
  CAER CF83 .... 49 H3
  NWPTE NP19 .... 9 J2
  PNRTH/DP CF64 .... 134 C2
Glen Affric Cl *BARRY/I/W* CF62 * .. 138 D3
Glenbrook Cl *BARRY* CF63 .... 140 B1
Glenbrook Dr *BARRY* CF63 .... 140 B1
Glencoe St *BARRY* CF63 .... 139 C5
Glencourt *PPOOL/BLNAV* NP4 .. 17 E4
Glendale Av *CDFN* CF14 .... 99 H1
Glengarriff Ct
  PPOOL/BLNAV NP4 .... 17 F1
Glen Mavis Wy
  BARRY/I/W CF62 .... 138 D3
Glenmount Wy *CDFN* CF14 .... 85 C5
Glenrise Cl *CDFNE* CF3 .... 103 G2
Glenroy St
  CATH/RTH/SPL CF24 .... 112 D5
Glenside *CWM* NP44 .... 19 G2
Glenside
  CYN/LLD/PWYN CF23 .... 113 E3
Glen-Usk Vw
  CLN/RNWPTE NP18 .... 41 H2
Glen Vw *CDFN* CF14 .... 100 A4
  CWM NP44 .... 10 C3
  PPOOL/BLNAV NP4 * 12 C3
Glen View Rd
  NWPTE NP19 .... 13 E5
Glenview Ter *CAER* CF83 .... 31 G4
Glenwood
  CYN/LLD/PWYN CF23 .... 101 G4
Glossop Rd
  CATH/RTH/SPL CF24 .... 5 H3
Gloster Pl *NWPTE* NP19 * 9 H1
Gloster's Pde
  PPOOL/BLNAV NP4 .... 17 H2
Gloster St *NWPTE* NP19 .... 9 H1
Glos y Sgubor
  PPOOL/BLNAV NP4 .... 13 E5
Gloucester Cl *BARRY/I/W* CF62 .. 139 F3
  CWM NP44 .... 20 C5
Gloucester Rd *CHEP* NP16 .... 29 E2
Gloucestershire Wy
  CHEP NP16 .... 28 C4
Gloucester St *GTN/RVSD* CF11 .. 119 A6
Glyn Bedw *CAER* CF83 .... 33 H2
Glynbridge Cl *BARRY/I/W* CF62 .. 131 F5
Glyn Coed Rd
  CYN/LLD/PWYN CF23 .... 101 F4
Glyn Collen *CAER* CF83 .... 33 H2
Glyn Derwen *CAER* CF83 .... 48 D5
Glynderw *CAER* CF83 .... 33 H3
Glyn-Dwr *PPRD* CF37 .... 65 G1
Glyndwr Rd *BARRY/I/W* CF62 .. 117 F2
  CAE/CAN/FWR CF5 .... 20 A4
  PNRTH/DP CF64 .... 134 A3
Glyn Eiddew *CAER* CF83 .... 33 H2
Glyn Eirw *CYN/LLD/PWYN* CF23 * .. 101 F2
Glyn Llwyfen *CAER* CF83 .... 33 H2
Glynne St *GTN/RVSD* CF11 ...... 119 E2
Glynrhondda St
  CATH/RTH/SPL CF24 .... 4 D2
Glyn Rhosyn
  CYN/LLD/PWYN CF23 .... 101 E2
Glyn Rhymni *CDFNE* CF3 .... 114 C3
Glyn Simon Cl
  CAE/CAN/FWR CF5 .... 110 C2
Glynstell Cl *GTN/RVSD* CF11 .. 127 H1
Glyntaff Rd *PPRD* CF37 .... 45 G4
Glyntirion *CWM* NP44 .... 20 A4
Glyn-y-Gog *BARRY/I/W* CF62 .. 131 E5
Godfrey Rd *CWM* NP44 .... 19 G3
  NWPT NP20 .... 8 B2
Godwin Cl *CAE/CAN/FWR* CF5 .. 110 B2

Golate *CCDF* CF10 .... 4 C6
Goldcliff Ct *CWM* NP44 .... 20 A5
Goldcrest Dr
  CLN/RNWPTE NP18 .... 42 A4
Golden Mile Vw *NWPT* NP20 .... 75 F1
Goldfinch Cl *CALD/MAG* NP26 .. 62 D4
Goldsland Pl *BARRY/I/W* CF62 .. 2 B1
Goldsmith Cl *CDFNE* CF3 .... 102 A4
  NWPTE NP19 .... 75 H3
Golf Rd *PPOOL/BLNAV* NP4 ...... 15 H5
Gold Tops *NWPT* NP20 .... 8 C2
Golf Rd *PPOOL/BLNAV* NP4 ...... 15 H5
Golwg y Coed *CAER* CF83 .... 48 A4
Golwg yr Eglwys *CAER* CF85 .... 48 D1
Golygafar Eglwys *PPRD* CF37 .. 44 B5
Golynos *PPOOL/BLNAV* NP4 * .. 12 A2
Golynos Pl
  PPOOL/BLNAV NP4 * 12 A2
Goodrich Av *CAER* CF85 .... 69 F2
Goodrich Crs *NWPT* NP20 .... 56 C2
Goodrich Gv *RSTN* NP10 .... 91 H2
Goodrich La *NWPT* NP20 .... 56 C2
Goodrich St *CAER* CF83 .... 69 F2
Goodwick Cl *BARRY/I/W* CF62 .. 139 F1
Goodwood *CAE/CAN/FWR* CF3 .. 114 C2
Goodwood Cl
  CAE/CAN/FWR CF5 .... 116 C4
Goossens Cl *NWPTE* NP19 .... 59 E3
Gordon Rd
  CATH/RTH/SPL CF24 .... 4 E2
Gordon St *NWPTE* NP19 .... 9 J5
Gore St *NWPTE* NP19 .... 57 E2
Gorsedd Gardens Rd
  CCDF CF10 .... 4 D3
Gorse Pl *CAE/CAN/FWR* CF5 .... 110 A5
Goscombe Dr *PNRTH/DP* CF64 .. 134 B1
Gough Rd *CAE/CAN/FWR* CF5 .. 117 F3
Gould Cl *CDFNE* CF3 .... 102 D3
Govilion Pl *CWM* NP44 .... 20 A5
Gowan Ct *CDFN* CF44 .... 85 G4
Gower Gn *CWM* NP44 .... 20 B2
Gower St *CATH/RTH/SPL* CF24 .. 112 C4
Goya Cl *NWPT* NP20 .... 57 H2
Gradon Cl *BARRY* CF63 .... 140 A3
Grafton Cl
  CYN/LLD/PWYN CF23 .... 113 F2
Grafton Dr *LLTR/LLH* CF72 ...... 95 F3
Grafton La *NWPTE* NP19 .... 9 F2
Grafton Rd *NWPTE* NP19 .... 9 F2
Grafton Ter *CDFN* CF14 .... 99 F4
Graham Bell Cl *NWPT* NP20 .... 40 A2

Graham Ct *CAER* CF83 .... 113 G4
Grahamstown Gv *CHEP* NP16 .. 29 E4
Grahamstown Rd *CHEP* NP16 .. 29 E4
Graham St *NWPT* NP20 .... 8 C5
Graig Wk *GTN/RVSD* CF11 .... 119 E3
Graig Cl *RSTN* NP10 .... 74 D1
Graig Fach *PPRD* CF37 .... 45 C5
Graig Hir *PENT/RAD/TFW* CF15 .. 97 C4
Graig Llwyn Rd *CDFN* CF14 .... 86 D3
  CDFN CF14 .... 87 G3
Graig Lwyd
  PENT/RAD/TFW CF15 .... 97 G3
Graig Park Av *NWPT* NP20 ...... 40 B4
Graig Park Cir *NWPT* NP20 ...... 40 B5
Graig Park Gn *NWPT* NP20 ...... 40 C5
Graig Park Hl *NWPT* NP20 ...... 40 C5
Graig Park Pde *NWPT* NP20 .... 40 B5
Graig Park Vls *NWPT* NP20 ...... 40 B5
Graig Rd *CAER* CF83 .... 70 B5
  CDFN CF14 .... 86 B2
  CWM NP44 .... 18 D5
Graig St *PPRD* CF37 .... 44 C4
Graig Ter *PPRD* CF37 .... 44 D4
Graig Vw *ABRC/NBR/RIS* NP11.. 37 E4
  CAER CF83 .... 52 A2
  CDFN CF14 .... 86 B4
Graigwen Crs *CAER* CF83 .... 47 G2
Graigwen Parc *PPRD* CF37 ...... 44 C3
Graigwen Pl *PPRD* CF37 .... 44 C3
Graigwen Rd *PPRD* CF37 .... 44 C2
Graig Wood Cl *NWPT* NP20 .... 40 C5
Graig-yr-Helfa Rd *PPRD* CF37 .. 45 E1
Graigyrhesg Rd *PPRD* CF37 .... 45 E1
Graig yr Wylan *CAER* CF83 ...... 68 B1
Grand Av *CAE/CAN/FWR* CF5 .. 116 D4
Grange Cl *CAE/CAN/FWR* CF5 .. 125 G4
Grange Ct *CAER* CF83 .... 48 C5
Grange St
  PPOOL/BLNAV NP4 * 14 A1
Grange Gdns *GTN/RVSD* CF11 .. 4 B4
  LLMJ CF61 .... 136 D2
Grange La *CWM* NP44 .... 19 H4
Grangemoor Ct
  GTN/RVSD CF11 .... 128 A4
Grange Pl *GTN/RVSD* CF11 ...... 6 C4
Grange Rd *CALD/MAG* NP26 .... 60 C2
  CWM NP44 .... 26 A1
The Grange
  CAE/CAN/FWR CF5 .... 111 E5
  CDFNE CF3 .... 104 A2
  CHV/BDAU CF38 .... 80 D4
  PNRTH/DP CF64 .... 134 B3
Grangetown Link
  GTN/RVSD CF11 .... 127 G1
Grangewood Cl
  CYN/LLD/PWYN CF23 .... 102 A1
Grantham Cl
  CAE/CAN/FWR CF5 .... 110 C3
Grant's Cl
  PENT/RAD/TFW CF15 .... 97 H2
Grant's Fld *CAE/CAN/FWR* CF5 .. 124 C1
Granville Av
  CAE/CAN/FWR CF5 .... 118 B1
Granville La *RSTN* NP10 .... 55 F5
Granville St *NWPT* NP20 .... 9 G5
Grasmere Av
  CYN/LLD/PWYN CF23 .... 112 C2

Grasmere Wy *CHEP* NP16 .... 31 E3
Grassmere Cl *PNRTH/DP* CF64 .. 128 A5
The Graylands *CDFN* CF14 ...... 99 F4
Gray La *GTN/RVSD* CF11 .... 119 E2
Grays Gdns *CAER* CF85 .... 50 D2
Gray St *GTN/RVSD* CF11 .... 119 E2
Grays Wk *COWBR* CF71 .... 122 D3
Great Burnet Cl *CDFNE* CF3 .... 103 G4
Great House Mdw *LLMJ* CF61 .. 136 C2
Great Oaks Pk *RSTN* NP10 ...... 54 C2
Great Western La *CCDF* CF10 .. 4 D6
Greave Cl *CAE/CAN/FWR* CF5 .. 125 G4
Greek Church St *CCDF* CF10 * .. 6 E1
Greenacre Dr *CAER* CF83 .... 49 G3
Greenacre Gdns *CAER* CF83 .... 101 H1
Greenacres *BARRY* CF63 .... 140 B1
Green Av *CALD/MAG* NP26 ...... 62 D5
Greenbanks Dr
  BARRY/I/W CF62 .... 138 D3
Greenbay Rd
  CATH/RTH/SPL CF24 .... 121 F2
Green Cl *CALD/MAG* NP26 ...... 62 A4
Greenclose Rd *CDFN* CF14 ...... 111 C1
Greencourt *CWM* NP44 .... 10 A5
Greencroft Av
  CAE/CAN/FWR CF5 .... 118 A2
Greene Cl *NWPTE* NP19 .... 59 E4
Green Farm Cl
  CAE/CAN/FWR CF5 .... 116 D4
Green Farm Rd
  CAE/CAN/FWR CF5 .... 116 D4
Greenfield *CALD/MAG* NP26 .... 62 D3
Greenfield Av *CDFN* CF14 ...... 99 F5
  CLN/RNWPTE NP18 .... 41 G3
  PNRTH/DP CF64 .... 133 E3
Greenfield Cl *CWM* NP44 .... 19 G1
Greenfield Rd *CDFN* CF14 ...... 99 F5
Greenfield Wy *COWBR* CF71 .... 122 B4
Greenforge Wy *CWM* NP44 ...... 19 F5
Greenhaven Ri
  PNRTH/DP CF64 .... 128 A5
Greenhill Rd *CWM* NP44 .... 19 G4
  PPOOL/BLNAV NP4 .... 17 E3
Greenland Crs
  CAE/CAN/FWR CF5 .... 110 A5
Greenland Rd
  PPOOL/BLNAV NP4 .... 14 B1
Greenlands Rd *LLTR/LLH* CF72 .. 95 F2
Green La *BARRY* CF63 .... 140 A1
  CALD/MAG NP26 .... 62 D3
  LLMJ CF61 .... 136 A2
  RSTN NP10 .... 91 G3
Green Lawns *BARRY/I/W* CF62 .. 139 G2
Greenlawns
  CYN/LLD/PWYN CF23 .... 113 F3
Greenmeadow *CAER* CF83 ...... 51 E4
Greenmeadow Av
  CYN/LLD/PWYN CF23 .... 113 F2
Greenmeadow Cl *CWM* NP44 .. 25 G1
  PNRTH/DP CF64 .... 133 G2
Greenmeadow Ct
  LLTR/LLH CF72 .... 95 F3
Greenmeadow Dr
  ABRC/NBR/RIS NP11 .... 36 C2
  PENT/RAD/TFW CF15 .... 98 A1
Greenmeadow Rd
  ABRC/NBR/RIS NP11 .... 34 C3
  NWPTE NP19 .... 78 B1
Green Mdw *CDFNE* CF3 .... 20 D5
Greenmeadow Wy *CWM* NP44 .. 19 F5
Green Moor La
  CALD/MAG NP26 .... 60 A3
Greenock Rd *CDFNE* CF3 .... 102 C4
Green Pk *LLTR/LLH* CF72 .... 94 D5
Green Pn *PENT/RAD/TFW* CF15 .. 97 G5
Green Rw *CAER* CF85 .... 51 G3
Green St *CHEP* NP16 .... 28 C5
  CWM NP44 .... 10 C5
The Green *GTN/RVSD* CF11 .... 127 F2
  PENT/RAD/TFW CF15 .... 97 H5
Greenway Cl *CAER* CF83 .... 49 F3
Greenway Rd *BARRY* CF63 ...... 140 B1
Greenway Av *CDFNE* CF3 .... 114 C2
Greenway Dr *PNRTH/DP* CF64 .. 127 G4
Greenway Dr *BARRY* CF63 ...... 140 B1
Greenway Dr
  PPOOL/BLNAV NP4 .... 16 D2
Greenway Rd *CDFNE* CF3 .... 114 C2
The Greenways
  CALD/MAG NP26 .... 60 B3
Greenwich Rd
  CAE/CAN/FWR CF5 .... 118 C1
  NWPT NP20 .... 76 B3
Greenwillows *CWM* NP44 .... 26 A3
Greenwood Av *CWM* NP44 ...... 19 G3
Greenwood Cl
  CYN/LLD/PWYN CF23 .... 87 H5
Greenwood Ct *CAER* CF83 ...... 69 F1
Green Wood Dr
  CHV/BDAU CF38 .... 80 C3
Greenwood Dr *CWM* NP44 ...... 24 B3
Greenwood La
  CAE/CAN/FWR CF5 .... 116 D1
Greenwood Rd
  CAE/CAN/FWR CF5 .... 110 D4
  PPOOL/BLNAV NP4 .... 12 C2
Greenwood St *BARRY* CF63 ...... 3 G2
Grenadier Dr
  CLN/RNWPTE NP18 .... 59 H1
Grenville Rd
  CYN/LLD/PWYN CF23 .... 113 F5
Grenville Ter
  CALD/MAG NP26 .... 62 A4
Gresford Cl *CDFNE* CF3 .... 102 A4
Greyfriars Rd *CCDF* CF10 .... 4 D4
Greyfriars Rd *CCDF* CF10 .... 4 D4
Grey Hill Vw *CALD/MAG* NP26 .. 63 G3
Grey's Dr *LLMJ* CF61 .... 137 E3
Greys Rd *PPOOL/BLNAV* NP4 .. 16 C1
Grey Waters *CWM* NP44 .... 20 B5
Griffin Cl *BARRY/I/W* CF62 ...... 138 C1
Griffin St *NWPT* NP20 .... 9 G5
The Griffith *RSTN* NP10 .... 74 D2
Griffiths Wy
  PPOOL/BLNAV NP4 .... 12 B2
Grimson Cl *PNRTH/DP* CF64 .. 141 F4

Grisedale Cl
  CYN/LLD/PWYN CF23 .... 112 D3
Groes Cl *RSTN* NP10 .... 54 D2
Groes Lon *CDFN* CF14 .... 99 E3
Groeswen Dr *CAER* CF83 .... 48 A5
Groeswen Rd *CAER* CF83 .... 48 A5
  PENT/RAD/TFW CF15 .... 97 G5
Gron Ffordd *CDFN* CF14 .... 99 E1
Grongaer Ter *PPRD* CF37 .... 44 C4
Grosmont Pl *CWM* NP44 .... 20 B2
Grosmont Rd
  PPOOL/BLNAV NP4 .... 17 H1
Grosmont Wy *RSTN* NP10 .... 91 G2
Grosvenor Pl
  NWPTE NP19 .... 17 E5
Grosvenor St
  CAE/CAN/FWR CF5 .... 118 C3
Grouse St *CATH/RTH/SPL* CF24 .. 5 H1
Grove Crs *PPOOL/BLNAV* NP4 .. 14 B1
Grove Est *PPOOL/BLNAV* NP4 * .. 11 H1
Grove Gdns *CALD/MAG* NP26 * .. 63 E3
Groveland Rd *CDFN* CF14 ...... 100 B3
Grovenor Rd *RSTN* NP10 .... 74 C1
Grove Pk *CWM* NP44 .... 19 H2
Grove Park Av *CWM* NP44 ...... 19 H2
Grove Park Dr *NWPT* NP20 .... 40 C4
Grove Pl *CDFN* CF14 .... 99 C3
  PNRTH/DP CF64 .... 134 C2
  PPOOL/BLNAV NP4 .... 17 E3
Grove Place La
  PNRTH/DP CF64 .... 134 C2
Grove Rd *ABRC/NBR/RIS* NP11.. 37 E5
Grover St *CDFN* CF37 .... 44 C4
Groves Rd *NWPT* NP20 .... 55 F5
Grove St *CAER* CF83 .... 33 G5
Grove Ter *PNRTH/DP* CF64 ...... 134 C2
The Grove *BARRY/I/W* CF62 ...... 2 B6
  CALD/MAG NP26 .... 63 E3
  CDFNE CF3 .... 114 B2
  NWPT NP20 * 8 E6
Cruffyd Dr *CAER* CF83 .... 48 D4
Guenever Cl *CDFN* CF14 .... 85 F5
Guest Rd *CATH/RTH/SPL* CF24 .. 120 D4
Guildford Crs *CCDF* CF10 .... 5 F5
Guildford Cl *CCDF* CF10 .... 5 F5
Guildhall Pl *CCDF* CF10 .... 5 F6
Guthrie St *BARRY* CF63 .... 139 C4
Guy's Rd *BARRY* CF63 .... 139 E4
Gwaelod y Foel
  CHV/BDAU CF38 .... 81 E2
Gwaelod-y-Garth Rd
  PPRD CF37 .... 66 B2
Gwalch y Penwaig
  BARRY/I/W CF62 .... 3 G7
Gwalia Gv *PPRD* CF37 .... 65 G1
Gwalin y Cwrt *CAER* CF83 ...... 68 A3
Gwaun Cl *CDFN* CF14 .... 110 C1
Gwaun-Hyfryd *CAER* CF83 ...... 49 G5
Gwaunmiskin Rd
  CHV/BDAU CF38 .... 80 A3
Gwaun Newydd *CAER* CF83 .... 49 G5
Gwaun Rd *PPRD* CF37 .... 45 G4
Gwaun-Ruperra Rd
  LLTR/LLH CF72 .... 95 E1
Gwbert Cl *CDFNE* CF3 .... 102 D5
Gwendoline Rd
  ABRC/NBR/RIS NP11 .... 37 E5
Gwendoline St
  CATH/RTH/SPL CF24 .... 5 K5
Gwenfo Dr *CAE/CAN/FWR* CF5 .. 125 G4
Gwenllian St *CAE/CAN/FWR* CF5 .. 140 A3
Gwennol y Craig
  BARRY/I/W CF62 .... 3 H7
Gwennol y Graig
  BARRY/I/W CF62 .... 147 F3
Gwennol y Mor
  BARRY/I/W CF62 .... 3 G7
Gwennyth St
  CATH/RTH/SPL CF24 .... 112 C4
Gwentlands Cl *CHEP* NP16 ...... 28 C5
Gwent Rd *CAE/CAN/FWR* CF5 .. 117 E4
  PPRD CF37 .... 66 C3
Gwent Sq *CWM* NP44 .... 19 H4
Gwilym Rd *BARRY* CF63 .... 139 C1
Gwilym St *PPRD* CF37 .... 65 C3
Gwladys Pl
  CLN/RNWPTE NP18 .... 41 H3
Gwy Ct *CHEP* NP16 .... 28 D3
Gwyddon Rd
  ABRC/NBR/RIS NP11 .... 23 E1
Gwynant Crs
  CYN/LLD/PWYN CF23 .... 100 C5
Gwyn Crs *PPOOL/BLNAV* NP4 .. 16 C3
Gwyn Dr *CAER* CF83 .... 49 G5
Gwyndy Rd *CALD/MAG* NP26 .. 60 D5
Gwynllyw *CWM* NP44 .... 19 F3
Gwyn St *PPRD* CF37 .... 65 F2
Gypsy La *PENT/RAD/TFW* CF15.. 67 H3

H

Habershon St
  CATH/RTH/SPL CF24 .... 120 D2
Hackerford Rd
  CYN/LLD/PWYN CF23 .... 100 D2
Haden St *PPOOL/BLNAV* NP4 .. 14 B4
Hadfield Cl *GTN/RVSD* CF11 .... 127 G1
Hadfield Rd *GTN/RVSD* CF11 .. 127 H1
Hadrian Cl *CLN/RNWPTE* NP18.. 41 H3
Hafan-Werdd *CAER* CF83 .... 49 G4
Hafod Cl *CLN/RNWPTE* NP18.... 41 H2
Hafod Ct Rd *CDFN* CF14 .... 85 F5
Hafod Gdns
  CLN/RNWPTE NP18 * 27 G5
Hafod La *PPRD* CF37 .... 44 A2
Hafod Ms
  CLN/RNWPTE NP18 * 27 G5
Hafod Rd *PPRD* CF37 .... 44 A2
Hafod St *GTN/RVSD* CF11 .... 6 B1
Hafon Ms *CLN/RNWPTE* NP18 .. 27 G5
Hafren Ct *GTN/RVSD* CF11 ...... 119 E1

Hafren Rd *BARRY/I/W* CF62 ...... 3 F1
  CWM NP44 .... 18 D4
Haig Pl *CAE/CAN/FWR* CF5 .... 116 D5
Haines Cl *CAER* CF83 .... 68 B3
Hairbro' Rd *NWPT* NP20 .... 57 F1
Haldane Cl *CAER* CF83 .... 69 C1
Haldane Pl *NWPT* NP20 .... 40 B4
Hale Wd *CHEP* NP16 .... 28 A4
Half Acre Ct *CAER* CF83 .... 49 E5
Halifax Cl *CATH/RTH/SPL* CF24.. 121 F1
Halle Cl *NWPT* NP20 .... 59 F4
Halley Ct *BARRY/I/W* CF62 ...... 144 C3
Halliard Ct *CCDF* CF10 .... 7 G3
Hall's Road Ter
  ABRC/NBR/RIS NP11 .... 23 F5
Halsbury Rd
  CAE/CAN/FWR CF5 .... 118 C1
Halstead St *NWPTE* NP19 .... 9 K4
Halton Cl *PNRTH/DP* CF64 ...... 142 C1
Hamadryad Rd *CCDF* CF10 ...... 6 D6
Hamilton Ct *PNRTH/DP* CF64 * .. 119 F2
  NWPTE NP19 .... 57 F5
Ham La East *LLMJ* CF61 .... 136 D4
Ham La South *LLMJ* CF61 ...... 136 D4
Hammond Dr *NWPTE* NP19 .... 57 C5
Hammond Wy
  CYN/LLD/PWYN CF23 .... 113 G4
Hampden Cl *NWPTE* NP19 ...... 77 H1
Hampden Rd *NWPTE* NP19 .... 77 H1
Hampshire Av *NWPTE* NP19 .... 78 A2
Hampshire Cl *NWPTE* NP19 .... 78 A2
Hampshire Crs *NWPTE* NP19 .. 78 A2
Hampton Court Rd
  CYN/LLD/PWYN CF23 .... 113 G3
Hampton Crs East
  CYN/LLD/PWYN CF23 .... 101 E1
Hampton Crs West
  CYN/LLD/PWYN CF23 .... 100 D1
Hampton Rd *CDFN* CF14 .... 111 H1
Hanbury Cl *CDFNE* CF3 .... 98 B5
Hanbury Rd *NWPTE* NP18 ...... 42 B5
  CWM NP44 .... 19 H4
Hanbury Gdns
  PPOOL/BLNAV NP4 .... 14 A2
Hanbury Rd
  PPOOL/BLNAV NP4 .... 14 C4
Handel Cl *NWPTE* NP19 .... 59 E4
  PNRTH/DP CF64 .... 134 B5
Hand Farm Rd
  PPOOL/BLNAV NP4 .... 15 F5
Handley Rd
  CATH/RTH/SPL CF24 .... 121 F1
Handsworth St *NWPTE* NP19 .. 57 C5
Hanfield Pk *CWM* NP44 .... 20 B4
Hannah Cl *CDFN* CF14 .... 100 A4
Hannah St *BARRY* CF63 .... 139 C3
  CCDF CF10 .... 7 F5
Hanover Cl *CDFN* CF16 .... 28 B3
Hanover Ct *CDFN* CF14 .... 29 E4
Hanover St *BARRY/I/W* CF62 .. 139 F4
  CAE/CAN/FWR CF5 .... 118 D3
Hansom Pl *GTN/RVSD* CF11 * .. 119 F5
Harbour Dr *CCDF* CF10 .... 7 F5
Harbour Rd *BARRY/I/W* CF62 .. 2 B4
Harbour View Rd
  BARRY/I/W CF62 .... 134 C1
Harding Av *NWPT* NP20 .... 40 B3
Harding Cl *LLMJ* CF61 .... 137 F3
Hardwick Av *CHEP* NP16 .... 28 C4
Hardwicke Ct
  CATH/RTH/SPL CF24 .... 111 E5
Hardwick Hl *CHEP* NP16 .... 28 B5
Hardy Cl *BARRY/I/W* CF62 ...... 99 H5
  NWPT NP20 .... 75 H3
Hardy Pl *CATH/RTH/SPL* CF24 .. 5 G2
Harefield Cl
  CYN/LLD/PWYN CF23 .... 102 A1
Harford Cl *CDFN* CF14 .... 98 B5
Hargreaves Dr *NWPT* NP20 .... 40 B3
Harlech Cl *CWM* NP44 .... 20 A2
  PNRTH/DP CF64 .... 133 G3
Harlech Ct *CAER* CF83 .... 48 A5
Harlech Crs *CAE/CAN/FWR* CF5 .. 133 G3
  RSTN NP10 .... 74 B1
Harlech Gdns *BARRY/I/W* CF62 .. 139 F1
Harlech Rd *CDFNE* CF3 .... 114 C2
Harlequin Ct
  CATH/RTH/SPL CF24 .... 113 G5
  NWPT NP20 .... 56 C5
Harlequin Dr *NWPT* NP20 ...... 56 C5
Harold St *CATH/RTH/SPL* CF24.. 120 D1
  CWM NP44 .... 19 H3
Harper's Rd
  PPOOL/BLNAV NP4 .... 12 C2
Harpur St *CCDF* CF10 .... 6 C1
Harriet Ct *CAE/CAN/FWR* CF5 .. 112 C5
  PNRTH/DP CF64 .... 134 B1
Harris Cl *CDFN* CF14 .... 114 D1
Harrismith Rd
  CYN/LLD/PWYN CF23 .... 113 E4
Harrison Dr *CDFNE* CF3 .... 103 E5
Harrogate Rd *NWPTE* NP19 .... 57 F1
Harrowby La *CCDF* CF10 .... 6 E6
Harrowby St *CCDF* CF10 .... 7 F6
Harrow Cl *CLN/RNWPTE* NP18 .. 41 G2
Harrow Rd *NWPTE* NP19 .... 9 H2
Hart Gdns *NWPT* NP20 .... 9 F2
Hartland Rd *CDFNE* CF3 .... 101 H5
Hartley Pl *GTN/RVSD* CF11 ...... 119 E5
Hart Pl *CATH/RTH/SPL* CF24 .... 114 A5
Hartridge Farm Rd
  CDFNE CF3 .... 58 D5
Hartshorn Ct *CAER* CF83 .... 49 E5
Harvey Cl *NWPT* NP20 .... 40 B4
Harvey St *BARRY* CF63 .... 139 H3
Hastings Av *PNRTH/DP* CF64 .. 134 A2
Hastings Cl *PNRTH/DP* CF64 .. 134 A2
Hastings Pl *CDFNE* CF3 .... 102 C2
Hastings Pl *PNRTH/DP* CF64 .. 134 A2
Hathaway St *NWPTE* NP19 ...... 57 C5
Hatherleigh *NWPTE* NP19 .... 58 A4
Hatherleigh Rd *CDFNE* CF3 .... 114 A1
Haul Fryn *CDFN* CF14 .... 98 C2
Havannah St *CCDF* CF10 .... 7 F5
Havard Cl *BARRY/I/W* CF62 .... 144 C5
Havard St *BARRY* CF63 .... 47 E2
Havard Rd *CAER* CF83 .... 68 B2
Havelock Pl *GTN/RVSD* CF11 .. 119 E5
Havelock St *CCDF* CF10 .... 4 C6

NWPT NP20 .... 8 D4
Havenwood Dr CDFN CF14 .... 85 G4
Haverford Wy
 CAE/CAN/FWR CF5 .... 117 G4
Hawarden Gn CWM NP44 .... 26 C1
Hawarden Rd NWPTE NP19 .... 57 H5
Hawfinch Cl
 CAE/LLD/PWYN CF23 .... 101 E5
Hawke Cl NWPTE NP19 .... 58 D2
Hawker Cl
 CATH/RTH/SPL CF24 .... 121 F1
Hawkes Rdg CWM NP44 .... 24 C1
Hawkins Crs NWPTE NP19 .... 58 D2
Hawks Moor Cl RSTN NP10 .... 55 E3
Hawksworth Gv NWPTE NP19 .... 55 E3
Hawkwood Cl
 CAE/CAN/FWR CF5 .... 109 H4
Hawse La RSTN NP10 .... 105 F1
Hawthorn Av PNRTH/DP CF64 ...... 134 A3
Hawthorn Cl CALD/MAC NP26 .... 60 C2
 CHEP NP16 .... 30 C3
 PNRTH/DP CF64 .... 133 F4
Hawthorn Crs PPRD CF37 .... 46 A5
Hawthorne Av NWPTE NP19 .... 58 A5
Hawthorne Fosse
 NWPTE NP19 .... 58 A5
Hawthorne Sq NWPTE NP19 .... 57 H5
Hawthorn Rd CDFN CF14 .... 110 D2
 LLTR/LLH CF72 .... 106 A3
 PPOOL/BLNAV NP4 .... 16 D4
 PPRD CF37 .... 46 A5
Hawthorn Rd East CDFN CF14 .... 110 D2
Hawthorn Rd West
 CDFN CF14 .... 110 D2
The Hawthorns
 CLN/RNWPTE NP18 .... 42 B3
 CWM NP44 * 19 E2
 CYN/LLD/PWYN CF23 .... 101 F4
Hayes Bridge Rd CCDF CF10 .... 4 D6
Hayes La BARRYE CF63 .... 140 B5
Hayes Rd BARRYE CF63 .... 140 B5
 PNRTH/DP CF64 .... 140 C5
The Hayes CCDF CF10 .... 4 D6
Hayling Cl NWPTE NP19 .... 57 G2
Haynes Ct NWPT NP20 .... 77 E2
Hazel Av CALD/MAC NP26 .... 62 A2
Hazel Cl PPOOL/BLNAV NP4 .... 17 H1
Hazeldene Av
 CATH/RTH/SPL CF24 .... 112 C3
Hazel Gv CAER CF83 .... 49 F5
 PNRTH/DP CF64 .... 133 F4
Hazelhurst Ct CDFN CF14 .... 110 D2
Hazelhurst Rd CDFN CF14 .... 110 D2
Hazell Dr RSTN NP10 .... 91 E1
Hazel Rd PNRTH/DP CF64 .... 134 A4
Hazel Tree Cl
 PENT/RAD/TFW CF15 .... 97 G4
Hazel Wk CLN/RNWPTE NP18 .... 41 G4
 CWM NP44 .... 20 B2
Hazelwood Dr CDFNE CF3 .... 102 D3
Hazledene Cl BARRYE CF63 .... 139 G2
Hazlitt Cl CDFNE CF3 .... 102 A2
 NWPT NP20 .... 75 H3
The Headland CHEP NP16 .... 31 E3
Hearte Cl BARRY/W CF62 .... 144 C2
Heath Av PNRTH/DP CF64 .... 133 H4
Heathbrook CDFN CF14 .... 100 B5
Heathcliffe Cl CDFN CF14 .... 102 C2
Heath Cl NWPTE NP19 .... 78 B2
Heather Av CAE/CAN/FWR CF5 ... 118 A2
Heather Cl CHEP NP16 .... 30 D2
Heather Ct CWM NP44 .... 24 C2
Heather Rd NWPTE NP19 .... 57 F2
The Heathers BARRY/W CF62 ...... 138 D4
Heathfield Dr BARRY/W CF62 ...... 139 E2
Heathfield Pl CDFN CF14 .... 112 A3
Heathfield Rd CDFN CF14 .... 112 A3
Heath Mdl Rd CDFN CF14 .... 100 B5
Heath Md CDFN CF14 .... 112 C1
Heath Park Av CDFN CF14 .... 100 A5
Heath Park Crs CDFN CF14 .... 112 C1
Heath Park Dr CDFN CF14 .... 100 B5
Heath Park La CDFN CF14 .... 111 H2
Heath Park Wy CDFN CF14 .... 112 A3
Heath St GTN/RVSD CF11 .... 119 F3
Heathway CDFN CF14 .... 99 H5
Heathwood Gv CDFN CF14 .... 112 C1
Heathwood Rd CDFN CF14 .... 111 H1
Hebbles La BARRYE CF63 .... 139 H2
Hector Cl CATH/RTH/SPL CF24 ... 121 G1
Heddfaen N
 CYN/LLD/PWYN CF23 .... 101 G1
Heddfaen S
 CYN/LLD/PWYN CF23 .... 101 F3
Hedel Rd GTN/RVSD CF11 .... 118 B2
Heidenheim Wy NWPT NP20 .... 56 D1
Helen Pl CATH/RTH/SPL CF24 .... 5 K2
Helen St CATH/RTH/SPL CF24 .... 5 K2
Helford Sq NWPT NP20 .... 39 G4
Hellas Dr BARRY/W CF62 .... 138 C3
Hemingway Rd CCDF CF10 .... 7 G4
Hendre CAER CF83 .... 48 C3
Hendre Cl CAE/CAN/FWR CF5 ...... 111 E5
Hendre Ct CWM NP44 .... 24 C3
Hendredenny Dr CAER CF83 .... 47 H5
Hendre Farm Dr NWPTE NP19 .... 58 D4
Hendre Farm Gdns
 NWPTE NP19 .... 58 D4
Hendre Gdns
 CAE/CAN/FWR CF5 .... 111 E5
Hendre Rd CAER CF83 .... 46 D2
 CDFNE CF3 .... 102 D5
Hendrick Dr CHEP NP16 .... 29 E4
Hendy St
 CYN/LLD/PWYN CF23 .... 112 D4
Henfron CAER CF83 .... 48 B3
Hengoed Cl
 CAE/CAN/FWR CF5 .... 117 F4
Henke Ct CCDF CF10 .... 7 C2
Henllys La CWM NP44 .... 24 C4
Henllys
 CYN/LLD/PWYN CF23 .... 100 C4
Henllys Village Rd CWM NP44 ...... 24 C3
Henllys Wy CWM NP44 .... 24 C4
Henry Morgan Cl RSTN NP10 .... 92 A1
Henry St BARRYE CF63 .... 140 B3
 CCDF CF10 .... 7 F5
 PPRD CF37 .... 28 B2

Henry Wood Cl NWPTE NP19 .... 58 B5
Hensol Cl CWM NP44 .... 20 B5
 RSTN NP10 .... 55 E3
Hensol Rd LLTR/LLH CF72 .... 107 G2
Henson St NWPTE NP19 .... 58 B5
Henwysg Cl PPRD CF37 .... 44 A2
Heol Aer CDFN CF14 .... 99 F2
Heol Amlwch CDFN CF14 .... 111 F2
Heol Aneurin CAER CF83 .... 48 A4
Heol Ap Pryce
 CHV/BDAU CF38 .... 80 B4
Heol Aradur
 CAE/CAN/FWR CF5 .... 110 B2
Heol Barri CAER CF83 .... 48 C4
Heol Berllan CAER CF83 .... 48 C4
Heol Berry
 PENT/RAD/TFW CF15 .... 83 E4
Heol Beulah
 PPOOL/BLNAV NP4 .... 15 G5
Heol Beuno
 PPOOL/BLNAV NP4 .... 15 G5
Heol Billingsley
 PENT/RAD/TFW CF15 .... 83 F4
Heol Blakemore CDFN CF14 .... 110 D1
Heol Booker CDFN CF14 .... 98 B5
Heol Briwnant CDFN CF14 .... 99 E1
Heol Broadland
 BARRY/W CF62 .... 3 F3
Heol Bro Wen CAER CF83 .... 49 E4
Heol Brynglas CDFN CF14 .... 98 D2
Heol Bryn Glas
 CHV/BDAU CF38 .... 81 E3
Heol Bryn Heulog
 CHV/BDAU CF38 .... 81 E2
Heol Brynhyfryd
 CHV/BDAU CF38 .... 80 C3
Heol Brynmor John
 CHV/BDAU CF38 .... 80 C3
Heol Cae Bach CAER CF83 .... 49 E1
Heol Cae Celynnen CAER CF83 ..... 49 E4
Heol Cae Fan Heulog
 CAER CF83 .... 49 E4
Heol Cae Gwyn CAER CF83 * 68 B3
Heol Cae Maen CAER CF83 .... 49 F4
Heol Caerhys CDFN CF14 .... 99 F4
Heol Caerlan CHV/BDAU CF38 ...... 80 A4
Heol Camddwr
 CYN/LLD/PWYN CF23 .... 102 A1
Heol Carnau
 CAE/CAN/FWR CF5 .... 117 G5
Heol Carne CDFN CF14 .... 99 F1
Heol Cattwg CDFN CF14 .... 111 F2
Heol Cawrdaf CHV/BDAU CF38 ..... 80 B4
Heol Cefn On CDFN CF14 .... 86 B4
Heol Cefn-yr Hendy
 LLTR/LLH CF72 .... 107 G1
Heol Ceiniog BARRYE CF63 .... 3 G2
Heol Celyn CHV/BDAU CF38 .... 81 G1
Heol Celynnen CAER CF83 .... 106 B3
Heol Chappell CDFN CF14 .... 98 C5
Heol Cliffrydd BARRYE CF63 .... 3 J3
Heol Clwyddau
 CHV/BDAU CF38 .... 80 B5
Heol Clyd CAER CF83 .... 48 A4
Heol Coed Cae CDFN CF14 .... 111 F1
Heol Collen CAE/CAN/FWR CF5 .. 125 C1
Heol Coroniad
 CHV/BDAU CF38 .... 80 B3
Heol Creigiau CHV/BDAU CF38 ..... 81 E5
Heol Crochendy
 PENT/RAD/TFW CF15 .... 66 D3
 PPRD CF37 .... 66 D3
Heol Cwarrel CAER CF83 .... 48 A2
Heol Cwm Ifor CAER CF83 .... 48 A3
Heol Danyrodyn
 PENT/RAD/TFW CF15 .... 96 B1
Heol Dderwen
 CHV/BDAU CF38 .... 65 H5
Heol Ddeusant
 CHV/BDAU CF38 .... 80 A4
Heol Deg CHV/BDAU CF38 .... 81 G1
Heol Deinio
 PPOOL/BLNAV NP4 .... 15 G5
Heol Dennant
 CAE/CAN/FWR CF5 .... 110 C5
Heol Derlwyn CDFN CF14 .... 99 E2
Heol Derwen
 PPOOL/BLNAV NP4 .... 15 G5
Heol Deva CAE/CAN/FWR CF5 .... 117 F5
Heol Dewi Sant
 BARRY/W CF62 .... 2 D1
 CDFN CF14 .... 99 G4
Heol Dolwen CDFN CF14 .... 111 G1
Heol Don CDFN CF14 .... 98 C5
Heol Dowlais CHV/BDAU CF38 ...... 81 E5
Heol Draenen Wen
 CAE/CAN/FWR CF5 .... 125 G1
Heol Dyfed CDFN CF14 .... 99 G5
 CHV/BDAU CF38 .... 80 A5
Heol Dyfodwg LLTR/LLH CF72 ...... 95 E1
Heol Dyhewydd
 CHV/BDAU CF38 .... 80 C3
Heol Ebwy CAE/CAN/FWR CF5 ... 117 G4
Heol Edwards
 PENT/RAD/TFW CF15 .... 67 F4
Heol Eglwys
 CAE/CAN/FWR CF5 .... 117 H4
Heol Erwin CDFN CF14 .... 99 F1
Heol Erw-y-Rhos CAER CF83 * 48 B3
Heol Eryr Mor BARRY/W CF62 .... 3 H7
Heol Esgyn
 CYN/LLD/PWYN CF23 .... 100 B4
Heol Fach CAER CF83 .... 48 B5
 PENT/RAD/TFW CF15 .... 67 F4
Heol Faenor CHV/BDAU CF38 .... 80 A5
Heol Fair CAE/CAN/FWR CF5 ...... 111 E4
Heol Fawr CAER CF83 .... 48 A3
Heol Fer CAER CF83 .... 48 B5
Heol Ffrwd Philip
 CHV/BDAU CF38 .... 81 G5
Heol Ffynnon Wen
 CDFN CF14 .... 99 E1
Heol Fioled BARRYE CF63 .... 131 H5
Heol Gabriel CDFN CF14 .... 111 F1
Heol Gam
 PENT/RAD/TFW CF15 .... 96 A1
Heol Ganol CAER CF83 .... 68 C1
Heol Gelynog CHV/BDAU CF38 ...... 80 B4
Heol Glandulais
 CYN/LLD/PWYN CF23 .... 101 G1
Heol Glan Elai LLTR/LLH CF72 .... 107 E2

Heol Glan-yr-Afon
 ABRC/NBR/RIS NP11 .... 34 D3
Heol Glaslyn CALD/MAC NP26 ...... 63 E1
 CYN/LLD/PWYN CF23 .... 102 A1
Heol Cledyr CAER CF83 .... 68 B3
Heol Glyn CAER CF83 .... 48 C4
Heol Goch
 PENT/RAD/TFW CF15 .... 96 C1
Heol Graig Wen CAER CF83 .... 48 B3
Heol Groeswen PPRD CF37 .... 66 C1
Heol Gwaun Rhos CAER CF83 .... 49 E4
Heol Gwendoline
 BARRY/W CF62 .... 3 F5
Heol Gwent CDFN CF14 .... 99 G5
Heol Gwerthyd BARRYE CF63 ..... 131 G5
Heol Gwilym
 CAE/CAN/FWR CF5 .... 110 B4
Heol Gwrgan CDFN CF14 .... 99 G4
 CHV/BDAU CF38 .... 80 A4
Heol Gwyndaf CDFN CF14 .... 100 A3
Heol Gwynedd CDFN CF14 .... 99 G5
Heol Gwynno LLTR/LLH CF72 .... 95 E1
Heol Gyfinir BARRY/W CF62 .... 3 H7
Heol Harlech
 CAE/CAN/FWR CF5 .... 111 E5
Heol Hendre CDFN CF14 .... 99 F2
Heol Hendy LLTR/LLH CF72 .... 107 G1
Heol Hensol CHV/BDAU CF38 .... 66 C1
Heol Hir CDFN CF14 .... 85 H5
Heol Homfray
 CAE/CAN/FWR CF5 .... 116 D5
Heol Ida CHV/BDAU CF38 .... 99 E5
Heol Iestyn CDFN CF14 .... 99 E5
Heol Illtyd LLTR/LLH CF72 .... 95 E1
Heol Isaf CDFN CF14 .... 80 C5
 PENT/RAD/TFW CF15 .... 97 G3
 PPOOL/BLNAV NP4 .... 15 G5
Heol Isaf Hendy
 LLTR/LLH CF72 .... 107 G1
Heol Iscoed CDFN CF14 .... 99 F2
 CHV/BDAU CF38 .... 81 F5
Heol Johnson LLTR/LLH CF72 .... 94 B5
Heol Las CAER CF83 .... 48 A4
 CDFNE CF3 .... 103 H3
 LLTR/LLH CF72 .... 94 B5
Heol Leubren BARRY/W CF62 ...... 131 G5
Heol Lewis CAER CF83 .... 49 G4
 CDFN CF14 .... 99 F1
Heol Llangam CDFN CF14 .... 99 E2
Heol Llanishen Fach
 CDFN CF14 .... 99 E2
Heol Llinos CDFN CF14 .... 85 H5
Heol Lodwig CHV/BDAU CF38 .... 81 F2
Heol Mabon CDFN CF14 .... 99 E2
Heol Madoc CDFN CF14 .... 111 G1
 PPOOL/BLNAV NP4 .... 15 G5
Heol Maerdy CAER CF83 .... 49 G5
Heol Maes Elwrg CDFNE CF3 ...... 103 F4
Heol Mathew CDFN CF14 .... 98 C5
Heol Merlin CDFN CF14 .... 100 A3
Heol Miles LLTR/LLH CF72 .... 94 C3
Heol Miskin LLTR/LLH CF72 .... 94 C3
Heol Muston
 CHV/BDAU CF38 .... 81 G1
Heol Mwyndy CHV/BDAU CF38 .... 80 A4
Heol Mynydd CAER CF83 .... 81 G1
Heol Mynydd Bychan
 CDFN CF14 .... 99 G4
Heol Nant CHV/BDAU CF38 .... 81 G1
Heol Nant Castan CDFN CF14 .... 99 E1
Heol Nest CDFN CF14 .... 99 E5
Heol Newydd CDFN CF14 .... 114 D1
Heol Padarn
 PPOOL/BLNAV NP4 .... 15 G5
Heol Pantycelyn
 BARRY/W CF62 .... 2 D1
 CHV/BDAU CF38 .... 98 C3
Heol Pantyderi
 CAE/CAN/FWR CF5 .... 117 F4
Heol Pant y Rhyn CHV/BDAU CF38 98 C3
Heol Pardoe
 PENT/RAD/TFW CF15 .... 67 E3
Heol Pearetree
 CAE/CAN/FWR CF5 .... 145 E4
Heol Pencarreg CDFN CF14 .... 111 F3
Heol Penlan CDFN CF14 .... 98 C3
Heol Penllwyn
 PENT/RAD/TFW CF15 .... 96 A1
Heol Penmaen LLTR/LLH CF72 ...... 95 E2
Heol Pennar
 CAE/CAN/FWR CF5 .... 117 G4
Heol Penyfai CHV/BDAU CF38 ...... 84 B2
Heol Penyfai CDFN CF14 .... 111 G1
Heol Pen-y-Parc
 PENT/RAD/TFW CF15 .... 67 E3
Heol Peredur CDFN CF14 .... 95 E2
Heol Pilipala BARRY/W CF62 .... 144 D4
Heol Pontprennau
 CYN/LLD/PWYN CF23 .... 101 H1
 CYN/LLD/PWYN CF23 .... 101 H1
Heol Powis CDFN CF14 .... 99 G5
Heol Poyston
 CAE/CAN/FWR CF5 .... 117 F5
Heol Pwllypant CAER CF83 .... 48 C3
Heol Pwllyplaca CDFNE CF3 .... 103 G4
Heol Rhayader CDFN CF14 .... 110 C1
Heol Rhos CAER CF83 .... 68 A1
Heol Rhosyn CHV/BDAU CF38 .... 80 A4
Heol St y Nyll
 CAE/CAN/FWR CF5 .... 108 B3
Heol Salem CHV/BDAU CF38 .... 81 G1
Heol Seddon
 CAE/CAN/FWR CF5 .... 110 B3
Heol Seward CHV/BDAU CF38 ...... 80 A4
Heol Sirhwi BARRY/W CF62 .... 138 C3
Heol Solva CAE/CAN/FWR CF5 ... 117 H4
Heol Sticil-y-Beddau
 CHV/BDAU CF38 .... 80 A4
Heol Stradling CDFN CF14 .... 99 E5
Heol Syr Lewis
 PENT/RAD/TFW CF15 .... 97 G2
Heol Teifi CALD/MAC NP26 .... 63 E2
Heol Teilo GTN/RVSD CF11 .... 118 C3
Heol Tirbach CAER CF83 .... 48 A3

Heol Tir Coch CHV/BDAU CF38 ..... 81 F5
Heol Tir Gibbon CAER CF83 .... 95 E1
Heol Tir Ton
 ABRC/NBR/RIS NP11 .... 34 C3
Heol Towy CALD/MAC NP26 .... 63 E1
Heol Trecastell CAER CF83 .... 68 C2
Heol Tredwen CCDF CF10 .... 6 E5
Heol Treferig CHV/BDAU CF38 ...... 80 B4
Heol Trefgarne
 CAE/CAN/FWR CF5 .... 117 F5
Heol Tre Forys
 PNRTH/DP CF64 .... 134 A5
Heol Trelai CAE/CAN/FWR CF5 ... 117 E5
Heol Trenewydd
 CAE/CAN/FWR CF5 .... 117 F5
Heol Trostre CDFNE CF3 .... 103 E5
Heol Ty Crwn CAER CF83 .... 49 E4
Heol Tyddyn CAER CF83 .... 68 A3
Heol Ty Ffynnon
 CYN/LLD/PWYN CF23 .... 101 G1
Heol Ty-Gwyn CAER CF83 .... 33 H3
Heol Ty Maen PPRD CF37 .... 66 C2
Heol Ty Merchant CAER CF83 .... 49 E4
Heol Ty-n-y-Cae CDFN CF14 .... 99 E3
Heol Ty'n y Coed CDFN CF14 .... 99 F2
Heol Uchaf CDFN CF14 .... 99 E1
Heol Undeb CHV/BDAU CF38 .... 80 A4
Heol Urban CAE/CAN/FWR CF5 .. 110 C3
Heol Waun PPOOL/BLNAV NP4 .... 12 B5
Heol Waun Fawr CAER CF83 .... 49 E4
Heol Waun Waelod
 CAER CF83 .... 48 B3
Heol Waun y Nant CDFN CF14 .... 111 F2
Heol Wen CDFN CF14 .... 99 E1
Heol Wernlas CDFN CF14 .... 111 G1
Heol y Barcud CDFN CF14 .... 85 H3
 CHV/BDAU CF38 .... 80 B3
Heol-y-Beiliau LLTR/LLH CF72 ...... 95 E2
Heol-y-Berllan
 CAE/CAN/FWR CF5 .... 117 F4
Heol-y-Berth CAER CF83 .... 68 B4
Heol y Brenin PNRTH/DP CF64 .... 134 A4
Heol-y-Bryn CDFN CF14 .... 99 F5
 LLTR/LLH CF72 .... 107 G1
Heol-y-Cadno CDFN CF14 .... 85 G4
Heol y Carnau CAER CF83 .... 85 H4
Heol-y-Carw CDFN CF14 .... 85 H4
Heol-y-Castell
 CAE/CAN/FWR CF5 .... 117 F5
Heol-y-Cawl PNRTH/DP CF64 ...... 133 E3
Heol y Clun CHV/BDAU CF38 .... 80 A4
Heol-y-Coed CDFN CF14 .... 98 D2
 LLTR/LLH CF72 .... 94 C5
Heol-y-Cwm CAER CF83 .... 67 F4
Heol y Cyttir CAER CF83 .... 97 E3
Heol-y-Dderwen
 PENT/RAD/TFW CF15 .... 67 F4
Heol-y-Ddol CAER CF83 .... 49 E4
Heol-y-Deri CDFN CF14 .... 99 E5
 PPRD CF37 .... 44 B2
Heol-y-Dreflan CAER CF83 .... 49 E4
Heoly Dryw BARRY/W CF62 .... 144 D3
Heol-y-Fedwen
 CHV/BDAU CF38 .... 65 H5
Heol-y-Felin
 CAE/CAN/FWR CF5 .... 117 G4
 CAER CF83 .... 68 C1
 CDFN CF14 .... 99 F2
 PENT/RAD/TFW CF15 .... 67 E1
Heol-y-Fforest
 PENT/RAD/TFW CF15 .... 84 A4
Heol-y-Ffynnon
 PENT/RAD/TFW CF15 .... 81 F4
Heol-y-Foel CHV/BDAU CF38 .... 81 E2
Heol-y-Forlan CDFN CF14 .... 98 D2
Heol y Frenhines
 PNRTH/DP CF64 .... 133 E4
Heol-y-Gaer
 CAE/CAN/FWR CF5 .... 117 F4
Heol-y-Gamlas
 PENT/RAD/TFW CF15 .... 66 D3
 CAER CF83 .... 66 C5
Heol y Garth CAER CF83 .... 70 C1
Heol-y-Goedwig
 CHV/BDAU CF38 .... 81 F2
Heol-y-Gogledd CAER CF83 .... 48 B3
Heol-y-Gors CAER CF83 .... 49 E4
 CDFN CF14 .... 111 H1
 PENT/RAD/TFW CF15 .... 67 G4
Heol y Graig LLTR/LLH CF72 .... 94 D3
Heol y Gyfraith LLTR/LLH CF72 .... 94 D3
Heol-y-Maes CHV/BDAU CF38 ...... 81 E5
Heol-y-Nant BARRYE CF63 .... 139 G2
 CAER CF83 .... 68 C1
 CDFN CF14 .... 99 E4
 CDFN CF14 .... 83 G4
Heol Ynys Ddu CAER CF83 .... 68 B3
Heol-y-Parc CAER CF83 .... 68 C1
 CDFN CF14 .... 99 E1
 CHV/BDAU CF38 .... 81 E5
 PENT/RAD/TFW CF15 .... 96 A4
Heol-y-Pavin
 CAE/CAN/FWR CF5 .... 111 E4
Heol y Pentir BARRY/W CF62 ...... 144 C3
Heol y Pentre
 PENT/RAD/TFW CF15 .... 96 B1
Heol y Pia CAER CF83 .... 68 B1
Heol y Pwca CWM NP44 .... 19 F2
Heol y Pwll
 PENT/RAD/TFW CF15 .... 67 E4
Heol-yr-Efail CDFN CF14 .... 99 G3
Heol y Rhosog CDFNE CF3 .... 114 D3
Heol-yr-Odyn
 CAE/CAN/FWR CF5 .... 117 E5
Heol-yr-Onen CAER CF83 .... 68 C1
Heol yr Onnen LLTR/LLH CF72 .... 106 D3
Heol-yr-Ynys
 PENT/RAD/TFW CF15 .... 83 G5
Heol-yr-Ysbyty CAER CF83 .... 48 B3

Heol yr Ysgol CAER CF83 .... 50 A3
Heol-y-Sarn LLTR/LLH CF72 .... 95 E1
Heol Ysgawen LLTR/LLH CF72 .... 106 B3
Heol Ysgubor CAER CF83 .... 88 B4
Heol-y-Waun CDFN CF14 .... 111 F2
Heol-y-Wern CAER CF83 .... 49 E4
 CDFN CF14 .... 99 E4
Herbert Av
 ABRC/NBR/RIS NP11 .... 53 H1
Herbert Ct CDFNE CF3 .... 104 B2
Herbert Dr CAER CF83 * 48 C4
Herbert March Cl
 CAE/CAN/FWR CF5 .... 110 B2
Herbert Rd CALD/MAC NP26 .... 62 D2
 NWPTE NP19 .... 57 E3
Herbert's Cl
 PPOOL/BLNAV NP4 .... 12 B1
Herbert's Rd
 PPOOL/BLNAV NP4 .... 10 B5
Herbert St CCDF CF10 .... 4 E7
 CDFN CF14 .... 112 A4
 NWPT NP20 .... 8 E6
Herbert Ter PNRTH/DP CF64 ...... 134 C2
Hereford St GTN/RVSD CF11 ...... 119 F4
 NWPTE NP19 .... 9 H1
Heritage Cl NWPT NP44 .... 26 C4
Heritage Dr BARRY/W CF62 .... 138 D4
Heritage Pk CDFNE CF3 .... 103 E2
Hermon Hl
 PENT/RAD/TFW CF15 .... 97 H1
Heron Rd CALD/MAC NP26 .... 61 H1
Heronston Cl CALD/MAC NP26 .... 114 C2
Herons Wy CAER CF83 .... 68 B3
Heron Wy RSTN NP10 .... 76 A5
Herrick Pl CAER CF83 .... 51 E2
Hertford Pl NWPTE NP19 .... 57 G3
Hewell St GTN/RVSD CF11 .... 119 H4
 PNRTH/DP CF64 .... 134 B1
Hibiscus Ct CHV/BDAU CF38 .... 80 D5
Hickman Rd PNRTH/DP CF64 ...... 134 C2
Hickory Ct
 CATH/RTH/SPL CF24 .... 5 J5
High Bank
 CYN/LLD/PWYN CF23 .... 88 A5
High Banks NWPTE NP19 .... 57 F1
High Beech La CHEP NP16 .... 30 B1
Highbridge Cl PNRTH/DP CF64 .. 141 G5
Highbury Pl
 CAE/CAN/FWR CF5 .... 117 E4
Highbury Rd
 CAE/CAN/FWR CF5 .... 117 F5
High Cl CWM NP44 .... 20 A2
Highcroft Rd NWPT NP20 .... 56 B5
High Cross Dr RSTN NP10 .... 55 E4
High Cross La RSTN NP10 .... 55 F5
Highcross Rd RSTN NP10 .... 55 E5
Highdale Rd LLTR/LLH CF72 .... 95 F3
Highfield Cl
 ABRC/NBR/RIS NP11 .... 37 E4
 BARRY/W CF62 .... 2 B4
 CHV/BDAU CF38 * 81 H1
 CLN/RNWPTE NP18 .... 41 G2
 NWPT NP20 .... 26 C5
 PNRTH/DP CF64 .... 133 C2
Highfield Gdns RSTN NP10 .... 74 C1
Highfield La RSTN NP10 .... 74 C1
Highfield Rd BARRY/W CF62 .... 138 D2
 CDFN CF14 .... 112 A4
 CLN/RNWPTE NP18 .... 41 G3
 NWPT NP20 .... 75 H1
 RSTN NP10 .... 74 D1
Highfields CAE/CAN/FWR CF5 .... 110 D3
Highfield Wy
 PNRTH/DP CF64 .... 141 G2
Highland Gv CWM NP44 .... 19 H2
Highlands CDFNE CF3 .... 114 A3
Highlight La BARRY/W CF62 .... 138 B1
High Meadow LLMJ CF61 .... 115 F4
Highmead Rd
 CAE/CAN/FWR CF5 .... 117 G3
High St Arcade Chambers
 CCDF CF10 * 4 C5
High St ABRC/NBR/RIS NP11 .... 34 B1
 ABRC/NBR/RIS NP11 .... 36 B1
 BARRY/W CF62 .... 2 D3
 CAE/CAN/FWR CF5 .... 111 F5
 CAER CF83 .... 48 B3
 CCDF CF10 .... 4 C5
 CHEP NP16 .... 28 C4
 CHV/BDAU CF38 .... 80 C3
 CLN/RNWPTE NP18 .... 42 A4
 COWBR CF71 .... 122 C3
 LLDC CF36 .... 136 C2
 LLTR/LLH CF72 .... 95 E2
 LLTR/LLH CF72 .... 106 D2
 NWPT NP20 .... 8 E2
 PNRTH/DP CF64 .... 134 C1
 PPOOL/BLNAV NP4 .... 12 B1
 PPOOL/BLNAV NP4 .... 14 D4
 PPOOL/BLNAV NP4 .... 17 E2
 PPRD CF37 .... 44 C4
High Street Ar CCDF CF10 .... 4 C5
High Trees
 ABRC/NBR/RIS NP11 .... 37 G4
High Vw CHEP NP16 .... 28 C4
Highview Rd PNRTH/DP CF64 ..... 134 B1
Highwalls Av PNRTH/DP CF64 .... 132 D3
Highwalls End
 PNRTH/DP CF64 .... 133 E3
Highwalls Rd PNRTH/DP CF64 ... 133 E3
The Highway CWM NP44 .... 20 C4
 PPOOL/BLNAV NP4 .... 17 F1
The High Wy
 PPOOL/BLNAV NP4 .... 17 G1
Hilda St BARRY/W CF62 .... 2 E2
 PPRD CF37 .... 28 B2
Hiles Rd CAE/CAN/FWR CF5 .... 117 E5
Hilla Rd NWPT NP20 .... 8 A4
Hillary Cl CDFN CF14 .... 100 A4
Hillary Ri ABRC/NBR/RIS NP11 .... 23 H4
 BARRYE CF63 .... 139 H3
Hillcot Cl CDFN CF14 .... 86 B5
Hill Crest CLN/RNWPTE NP18 ...... 41 G2
Hillcrest PPOOL/BLNAV NP4 .... 9 C4
 PPOOL/BLNAV NP4 .... 17 H1
Hillcrest Cl CDFN CF14 .... 86 A4

Hillcrest Rd
PPOOL/BLNAV NP4 .... 15 F5
Hill Dr *CHV/BDAU* CF38 .... 81 E3
Hillfort Cl *CAE/CAN/FWR* CF5 ... 117 C5
Hill Gv *PPOOL/BLNAV* NP4 * 14 B3
Hillrise *CYN/LLD/PWYN* CF23 .. 100 D5
Hillside *CAER* CF83 .... 69 E3
Hillside Av *CAER* CF83 .... 46 D2
Hillside Cl *CHV/BDAU* CF38 .... 80 D4
CWM NP44 .... 19 G3
Hillside Crs *RSTN* NP10 .... 55 E5
Hillside Dr *PPOOL/BLNAV* NP4 .. 14 C5
Hill Side Rd *PPOOL/BLNAV* NP4 .. 16 D1
Hillside Ter *CAER* CF83 .... 49 H3
Hillside Vw *PPRD* CF37 .... 44 C2
Hill-Snook Rd
CAE/CAN/FWR CF5 .... 117 F3
Hill's St *CCDF* CF10 .... 4 D5
Hill St *ABRC/NBR/RIS* NP11 ..... 37 F5
BARRYE CF63 .... 139 H3
CWM NP44 .... 25 H2
NWPT NP20 .... 8 E5
PPOOL/BLNAV NP4 .... 14 A2
Hilltop *CDFN* CF14 .... 102 C4
Hilltop Cl *CHEP* NP16 .... 28 B5
Hilltop Crs *PPRD* CF37 .... 45 G1
Hilltop Gn *CWM* NP44 .... 19 F5
Hill Top Rd *CWM* NP44 .... 25 G1
Hill Vw *CHV/BDAU* CF38 .... 80 B4
Hillview Crs *NWPTE* NP19 .... 78 A1
Hilton Pl *CDFN* CF14 .... 110 D2
Hinchsliff Av *BARRYI/W* CF62 .. 138 D1
Hind Cl *CATH/RTH/SPL* CF24 .... 121 G1
Hinton St *CATH/RTH/SPL* CF24 .. 120 D3
Hirst Crs *CAE/CAN/FWR* CF5 .... 116 B4
Hirwain St
CATH/RTH/SPL CF24 .... 112 B5
Hitchen Hollow *CHEP* NP16 ..... 31 F3
Hillside Dr *COWBR* CF71 .... 122 D4
Hobart Cl *NWPT* NP20 .... 55 H5
Hodges Rw *CCDF* CF10 .... 7 F5
Hodges Sq *CCDF* CF10 .... 7 F5
Hogarth Cl *CWM* NP44 .... 26 A3
NWPTE NP19 .... 57 C2
Holbein Rd *NWPTE* NP19 .... 57 H2
Holden Rd *GTN/RVSD* CF11 ..... 127 H1
Holdings La
CAE/CAN/FWR CF5 .... 96 A5
Holgate Cl *CAE/CAN/FWR* CF5 .. 116 B1
Holland Cl *RSTN* NP10 .... 54 D2
The Hollies *LLTR/LLH* CF72 .... 107 E2
RSTN NP10 * 73 H4
Hollington Dr
CYN/LLD/PWYN CF23 .... 101 H1
Hollins Cl *CHEP* NP16 .... 28 D3
Hollyash Av *NWPT* NP20 .... 40 B4
Hollybush Cl *CHV/BDAU* CF38 ... 81 H1
CWM NP44 .... 25 C2
NWPT NP20 .... 40 B4
Hollybush Hts
CYN/LLD/PWYN CF23 .... 101 E4
Hollybush Ri
CYN/LLD/PWYN CF23 .... 101 E4
Hollybush Rd
CYN/LLD/PWYN CF23 .... 101 E4
Hollybush Ter *CHV/BDAU* CF38 . 81 H1
PPOOL/BLNAV NP4 * 14 A2
Hollybush Vw *CWM* NP44 .... 25 G3
Hollybush Wk *RSTN* NP10 .... 55 E1
Hollybush Wy *CWM* NP44 .... 25 C3
Holly Cl *CHEP* NP16 .... 30 C2
Hollycroft Cl
CAE/CAN/FWR CF5 .... 117 H2
Holly Gv *CDFN* CF14 .... 86 B3
Hollylodge Cl *CWM* NP44 .... 20 C2
Holly Lodge Gdns *CWM* NP44 ... 20 C3
Holly Lodge Gn *CWM* NP44 * 20 C2
Holly Lodge Rd *CWM* NP44 ...... 20 B2
Hollyoake Ter
PPOOL/BLNAV NP4 * 12 C5
Holly Rd *ABRC/NBR/RIS* NP11 ... 37 F4
CAE/CAN/FWR CF5 .... 116 C4
Hollyrood Cl *BARRYI/W* CF62 ... 138 C1
Holly St *PPRD* CF37 .... 65 H2
Holly Ter *CDFN* CF14 * 111 E3
Holmesdale St
GTN/RVSD CF11 .... 6 B6
Holmside *CDFN* CF14 .... 86 B4
Holmside *BARRYE* CF63 .... 138 B5
Holmsdale Pl *PNRTH/DP* CF64 .. 134 C5
Holmsview Cl *CDFN* CF3 .... 114 C1
Holmwood *CHV/BDAU* CF38 ..... 80 B4
Holmwood Cl
CYN/LLD/PWYN CF23 .... 113 E1
Holst Cl *NWPTE* NP19 .... 59 F3
Holton Reach *BARRYE* CF63 ..... 3 H3
Holton Rd *BARRYE* CF63 .... 3 G1
Holybush Est *CAER* CF83 .... 98 B5
Holyhead Cl *CAER* CF83 .... 48 B5
Holyheck Cl *RSTN* NP10 .... 54 B5
Holyrell Rd *CHV/BDAU* CF38 .... 65 H5
Home Farm Cl
CLN/RNWPTE NP18 .... 41 G4
Home Farm Crs
CLN/RNWPTE NP18 .... 41 G4
Home Farm Gr
CLN/RNWPTE NP18 .... 41 G4
Homelands Rd *CDFN* CF14 .... 99 F5
Honddu Cl *CALD/MAG* NP26 ..... 62 D2
Honeysuckle Cl
CAE/CAN/FWR CF5 .... 110 A5
Honiton Rd *CDFN* CF3 .... 102 B3
Hood Rd *BARRYI/W* CF62 .... 2 D4
Hopefield *NWPT* NP20 .... 55 E2
Hopewell Cl *CHEP* NP16 .... 31 E3
The Hop Gdn *CHEP* NP16 .... 30 D2
Hopkinstown Rd *PPRD* CF37 ..... 44 D2
Hopkins Wk *NWPTE* NP19 .... 59 E4
Hopyard Meadow
CAER CF83 .... 122 B3
Horace Ter *CAER* CF83 .... 48 C1
Horle Cl *GTN/RVSD* CF11 .... 6 A7
Hornbeam Cl
CLN/RNWPTE NP18 .... 41 F4
Hornbeam Wk *RSTN* NP10 .... 74 C1
Hornchurch Cl
CAE/CAN/FWR CF5 .... 110 C3

Horrocks Cl *NWPT* NP20 .... 40 B2
Horton Wy *PNRTH/DP* CF64 ..... 140 C3
Horwood Cl
CATH/RTH/SPL CF24 .... 120 D1
Hoskins St *NWPT* NP20 .... 56 D2
Hospital Rd
PPOOL/BLNAV NP4 .... 14 A1
PPRD CF37 .... 45 F3
Hotham Cl
CYN/LLD/PWYN CF23 * 101 H1
Housman Cl *CDFNE* CF3 .... 102 A2
Hove Av *NWPTE* NP19 .... 57 H3
Howard Cl *NWPTE* NP19 .... 58 D3
Howard Dr *NWPTE* NP19 .... 57 H2
Howard Dr *CAER* CF83 .... 48 D4
Howard Gdns
CATH/RTH/SPL CF24 .... 5 G4
Howardian Cl
CYN/LLD/PWYN CF23 * 113 G4
Howard Pl
CATH/RTH/SPL CF24 .... 5 G3
Howard St
CATH/RTH/SPL CF24 .... 5 K5
Howard Ter
CATH/RTH/SPL CF24 .... 5 G4
Howe Cir *NWPTE* NP19 .... 58 D2
Howell Rd *CAE/CAN/FWR* CF5 .. 116 B3
Howell's Crs
CAE/CAN/FWR CF5 .... 111 F5
Hubert Rd *NWPTE* NP19 .... 57 F2
Hughes Crs *CHEP* NP16 .... 28 C5
Hughs Cl *CAE/CAN/FWR* CF5 ... 110 C2
Hugon Cl
CYN/LLD/PWYN CF23 .... 113 G4
Hugon Dr
CYN/LLD/PWYN CF23 .... 113 G4
Humber Cl *NWPT* NP20 .... 39 H5
Humber Rd *NWPT* NP20 .... 39 G5
Hunt Cl *CDFN* CF14 .... 100 A1
Hunter Cl *RSTN* NP10 .... 54 B5
Hunters Rdg *CALD/MAG* NP26 .. 60 D3
Hunter St *BARRYE* CF63 .... 139 H5
CYN/LLD/PWYN CF23 .... 112 D1
Huntfield Rd *CHEP* NP16 .... 28 A4
Huntingdon Cl *CWM* NP44 .... 18 D5
Huntingdon Dr
CYN/LLD/PWYN CF23 .... 101 G1
Huntly Rd *BARRYE* CF63 .... 139 H3
Huntsmead Cl *CDFN* CF14 .... 85 H4
Hurford Crs *PPRD* CF37 .... 44 C3
Hurford Pl
CYN/LLD/PWYN CF23 .... 100 D2
Hurford St *PPRD* CF37 .... 44 B4
Hurst St *CCDF* CF10 .... 6 E5
Huron Crs
CYN/LLD/PWYN CF23 .... 112 D1
Huxley Gn *NWPT* NP20 .... 40 B4
Hydrangea Cl
CYN/LLD/PWYN CF23 .... 101 E3
RSTN NP10 .... 75 E1
Hynam Pl *PPOOL/BLNAV* NP4 ... 12 C2
Hyssop Cl
CYN/LLD/PWYN CF23 .... 101 E2

I

Idencroft Cl
CYN/LLD/PWYN CF23 .... 101 H1
Iestynian Av *GTN/RVSD* CF11 ... 119 E1
Ifor Hael Rd *RSTN* NP10 .... 54 C3
Ifor Jones Ct
CYN/LLD/PWYN CF23 .... 100 D5
Ifton Av *CALD/MAG* NP26 .... 62 A4
Ifton La *CALD/MAG* NP26 .... 62 A3
Ifton Pl *NWPTE* NP19 .... 77 H1
Ifton Rd *CALD/MAG* NP26 .... 62 A4
Ifton Ter *CALD/MAG* NP26 .... 62 A4
NWPTE NP19 .... 77 H1
Ilan Av *PPRD* CF37 .... 65 G1
Ilan Rd *CAER* CF83 .... 47 E2
Ilchester Rd *CDFNE* CF3 .... 102 B4
Ilex Cl *CDFN* CF14 .... 100 A2
Ilfracombe Crs *CDFNE* CF3 ...... 102 B5
Illtyd Av *LLDW* LLH* CF61 .... 136 D4
Illtyd Rd *CAE/CAN/FWR* CF5 .... 117 E2
Illtyd St *PPRD* CF37 .... 44 C5
Ilminster St *BARRYE* CF63 ...... 139 H5
Ilton Rd *CYN/LLD/PWYN* CF23 .. 113 F4
Imperial Buildings Rw
CAE/CAN/FWR CF5 .... 111 E5
Imperial Wy *RSTN* NP10 .... 91 G1
Inchmarnock St
CATH/RTH/SPL CF24 .... 5 J5
Incline La *CWM* NP44 .... 24 C2
Incline Rd *PPOOL/BLNAV* NP4 ... 12 C3
Inglefield Av *CDFN* CF14 .... 112 B3
Inner Loop Rd *CHEP* NP16 .... 31 F1
Insole Cl *CAE/CAN/FWR* CF5 .... 110 D5
Insole Gdns
CAE/CAN/FWR CF5 .... 111 E5
Insole Gv East
CAE/CAN/FWR CF5 .... 110 D5
Insole Gv West
CAE/CAN/FWR CF5 .... 110 D5
Insole Pl *CAE/CAN/FWR* CF5 .... 118 B1
Instow Pl *CDFNE* CF3 .... 102 C4
Inverness Pl
CATH/RTH/SPL CF24 .... 112 D4
Iolo Pl *BARRYE* CF63 .... 139 H2
Ipswich Rd
CYN/LLD/PWYN CF23 .... 113 H4
Ireland Cl *CDFNE* CF3 .... 103 F5
Ireton Cl *CYN/LLD/PWYN* CF23 . 100 H1
Iron Bridge Rd
CYN/LLD/PWYN CF23 .... 54 A3
Iron Bridge Rd
CYN/LLD/PWYN CF23 .... 97 H2
Iron St *CATH/RTH/SPL* CF24 ..... 5 J4
Irving Pl *BARRYE* CF63 .... 139 E4
Isaf St *ABRC/NBR/RIS* NP11 .... 37 G5
Isca Cl *CWM* NP44 .... 24 B5
Isca Rd *CLN/RNWPTE* NP18 ..... 42 B1
Island Rd *BARRYI/W* CF62 .... 2 C3
Islwyn Rd *CAER* CF83 .... 48 C5
Islwyn Rd
ABRC/NBR/RIS NP11 .... 35 G3
Islwyn St *ABRC/NBR/RIS* NP11 .. 34 C1

Islwyn Wy *BARRYE* CF63 .... 139 G2
Is-y-Coed *CAE/CAN/FWR* CF5 .. 125 F5
Itchen Cl *NWPT* NP20 .... 39 G5
Itchen Rd *NWPT* NP20 .... 39 G3
Ivor Pk *LLTR/LLH* CF72 .... 107 E2
Ivor St *ABRC/NBR/RIS* NP11 .... 23 F4
Ivydale *CDFN* CF14 .... 86 B4
Ivy Dene Cl *PPOOL/BLNAV* NP4 .. 14 B1
Ivy Rd *NWPT* NP20 .... 8 A4
Ivy St *CAE/CAN/FWR* CF5 .... 118 C2
PNRTH/DP CF64 .... 134 C2

J

Jackson Cl *BARRYI* CF62 .... 144 C2
Jackson Ct *NWPTE* NP19 .... 9 K1
Jackson Pl *NWPTE* NP19 .... 9 K1
Jackson Rd *CAE/CAN/FWR* CF5 . 117 E3
Jade Cl *CDFN* CF14 .... 86 B3
Jamaica Dr *RSTN* NP10 .... 75 H5
Jamaica Gdns *RSTN* NP10 .... 75 H5
James Pl *PPRD* CF37 .... 44 B5
James St *BARRYE* CF63 .... 140 B5
CAER CF85 .... 33 G5
CAER CF83 .... 50 B2
CCDF CF10 .... 7 F5
NWPT NP20 .... 74 C2
PPOOL/BLNAV NP4 .... 14 C2
PPRD CF37 .... 45 F5
Jane Cl *CYN/LLD/PWYN* CF23 .. 102 A1
Jane Cl *RSTN* NP10 .... 92 A2
Janet St *CATH/RTH/SPL* CF24 ... 5 K4
Japonica Cl *NWPT* NP20 .... 40 C3
Jasmine Cl *RSTN* NP10 .... 54 A2
Jasmine Dr *CDFNE* CF3 .... 103 F3
Jasper Cl *CAE/CAN/FWR* CF5 ... 110 C3
Jaycroft Cl
CYN/LLD/PWYN CF23 * 102 A1
Jeans Cl *NWPT* NP20 .... 40 B3
Jeddo St *NWPT* NP20 .... 76 D2
Jeddo St *NWPT* NP20 .... 76 D2
Jeffcott Pl *PNRTH/DP* CF64 * ... 128 C5
Jeffrey St *NWPTE* NP19 .... 9 J3
Jellicoe Cl *NWPTE* NP19 .... 59 E2
Jellicoe Gdns
CYN/LLD/PWYN CF23 .... 100 B5
Jenkins St *NWPTE* NP19 .... 77 C1
Jenkins Wy *CDFNE* CF3 .... 103 E5
Jenner Rd *BARRYI/W* CF62 .... 2 C2
Jenner St *BARRYE* CF63 .... 140 A3
Jenner Wk *CHV/BDAU* CF38 ..... 81 F1
Jerry's La *CAER* CF83 .... 49 C2
Jerusalem Cl
PPOOL/BLNAV NP4 .... 17 H2
Jerusalem La
PPOOL/BLNAV NP4 .... 17 H2
Jesmond Dene
PENT/RAD/TFW CF15 .... 83 G3
Jessop Cl *RSTN* NP10 .... 55 E3
Jessop Rd *RSTN* NP10 .... 55 E3
Jestyn Cl *CAE/CAN/FWR* CF5 ... 116 C4
Jevan Cl *CAE/CAN/FWR* CF5 .... 110 B2
Jewell La *NWPT* NP20 * 56 C1
Jewel St *BARRYE* CF63 .... 3 K1
Jim Driscoll Wy
GTN/RVSD CF11 .... 6 C6
Jindabyne Ct *CDFNE* CF3 .... 89 E5
John Baker Cl *CWM* NP44 .... 26 A3
John Batchelor Wy
PNRTH/DP CF64 .... 128 C5
John Bull Cl *NWPTE* NP19 .... 58 D3
John Fielding Gdns
CWM NP44 .... 26 C4
John Fields Wk *NWPTE* NP19 ... 58 C5
John Frost Sq *NWPT* NP20 .... 8 E4
John Ireland Cl *NWPTE* NP19 .. 58 C4
John Morgan Cl
CAE/CAN/FWR CF5 .... 110 C2
John Pl *PPRD* CF37 .... 65 F1
Johns La *CDFN* CF14 .... 111 E3
Johnston Cl *RSTN* NP10 .... 54 D2
Johnston Rd *CDFN* CF14 .... 99 H5
John St *ABRC/NBR/RIS* NP11 ... 23 F3
ABRC/NBR/RIS NP11 .... 34 A1
BARRYE CF63 .... 140 B3
NWPT NP20 .... 9 G6
PNRTH/DP CF64 .... 134 D1
PPOOL/BLNAV NP4 .... 14 C4
PPRD CF37 .... 65 F1
Jolyons Ct *CALD/MAG* NP26 .... 63 E3
Jones Pl *NWPT* NP20 .... 56 B2
Jones St *NWPT* NP20 .... 8 D4
Jonquil Cl *CDFNE* CF3 .... 103 F3
Joseph Parry Cl
PNRTH/DP CF64 .... 128 A5
Joyce Cl *NWPT* NP20 .... 40 B3
Jubilee Gdns *BARRYE* CF63 .... 140 B1
CDFN CF14 .... 99 H4
Jubilee La *PNRTH/DP* CF64 ..... 134 D2
Jubilee Pl *PPOOL/BLNAV* NP4 ... 12 C2
Jubilee St *GTN/RVSD* CF11 ...... 119 F4
Jubilee Wy *CALD/MAG* NP26 .... 62 D2
Judkin Ct *CCDF* CF10 .... 6 E5
Jule Rd *CWM* NP44 .... 25 E2
Julius Cl *CLN/RNWPTE* NP18 .... 41 G3
Junction Rd *NWPTE* NP19 .... 9 H1
Junction Ter
PENT/RAD/TFW CF15 .... 98 A5
Juniper Crs *CWM* NP44 .... 24 D3
Justin Cl *CYN/LLD/PWYN* CF23 . 113 E1

K

Kames Pl *CATH/RTH/SPL* CF24 .. 5 H5
Kane Cl *CDFN* CF14 .... 100 A3
Kathleen St *BARRYI/W* CF62 ..... 2 B3
Keats Cl *CWM* NP44 .... 25 G1

NWPT NP20 .... 75 H2
Keats Rd *CALD/MAG* NP26 .... 62 C3
Keats Wy *BARRYI/W* CF62 .... 139 E1
Keene Av *RSTN* NP10 .... 75 F1
Keene St *NWPTE* NP19 .... 57 G5
Keen Rd *CATH/RTH/SPL* CF24 ... 5 J6
Keir Hardie Rd *NWPTE* NP19 .... 57 H2
Kelston Cl *CDFN* CF14 .... 98 C5
Kelston Pl *CDFN* CF14 .... 98 C5
Kelston Rd *CDFN* CF14 .... 98 C5
Kelvedon St *NWPTE* NP19 .... 9 J5
Kelvin Rd
CYN/LLD/PWYN CF23 .... 112 D4
Kember Cl *PNRTH/DP* CF64 ...... 133 F4
Kemeys Fawr Cl
PPOOL/BLNAV NP4 .... 16 D4
Kemeys Rd *BARRYI/W* CF62 ..... 144 C3
Kemm Cl *PENT/RAD/TFW* CF15 .. 15 J1
Kemys Pl *CDFN* CF14 .... 111 G2
Kemys St *PPOOL/BLNAV* NP4 ... 17 E3
Kenfig Pl *CWM* NP44 .... 20 B5
Kenfig Rd *CDFN* CF14 .... 111 G2
Kenilworth Ct
CAE/CAN/FWR CF5 .... 118 A1
Kenilworth Rd *BARRYE* CF63 .... 139 H2
NWPTE NP19 .... 57 H5
Kenley Cl *CAE/CAN/FWR* CF5 ... 110 C3
Kenmare Ms
CYN/LLD/PWYN CF23 .... 87 G5
Kenmuir Rd
CYN/LLD/PWYN CF23 .... 121 E1
Kennedy Cl *CHV/BDAU* CF38 .... 80 B3
Kennedy Ri *BARRYI/W* CF62 ..... 2 A7
Kennerleigh Rd *CDFNE* CF3 ..... 114 A1
Kennington Cl *CDFN* CF14 ...... 110 A1
Kensington Av
CAE/CAN/FWR CF5 .... 118 B2
Kensington Gv *NWPTE* NP19 ... 57 G4
Kensington Pk
CALD/MAG NP26 .... 60 A3
Kensington Rd *NWPTE* NP19 ... 57 G4
Kenson Cl *BARRYI/W* CF62 .... 144 A3
Kent Cl *RSTN* NP10 .... 54 D2
Kent Gn *BARRYI/W* CF62 .... 139 E3
Kent St *GTN/RVSD* CF11 .... 6 B5
Kenwood Rd
CAE/CAN/FWR CF5 .... 117 G3
Kenyon Rd
CATH/RTH/SPL CF24 .... 121 F1
Keppoch St
CATH/RTH/SPL CF24 .... 113 E5
Kerrigan Cl *CAE/CAN/FWR* CF5 . 110 A4
Kerrycroy St
CATH/RTH/SPL CF24 .... 5 J5
Kestell Dr *GTN/RVSD* CF11 ...... 128 C3
Kestrel Cl *CALD/MAG* NP26 ..... 62 D4
Kestrel Cl *CDFN* CF3 .... 101 E3
Kestrel Wy *PNRTH/DP* CF64 ..... 142 C1
RSTN NP10 .... 75 H5
Keswick Av
CYN/LLD/PWYN CF23 .... 112 C2
Keteringham Cl
PNRTH/DP CF64 .... 141 E4
Kewstoke Av *CDFNE* CF3 .... 102 A5
Kewstoke Pl *CDFNE* CF3 .... 102 A5
Keyes Av
CYN/LLD/PWYN CF23 .... 100 B5
Keynsham Av *NWPT* NP20 .... 8 E6
Keynsham Rd *CDFN* CF14 .... 111 G2
Keyston Rd
CAE/CAN/FWR CF5 .... 110 B3
Kidwelly Cl *RSTN* NP10 .... 91 H2
Kidwelly Ct *CAER* CF85 .... 48 A5
Kidwelly Rd *CWM* NP44 .... 26 B1
Kier Hardie Crs *NWPTE* NP19 ... 58 C5
Kilcattan St
CATH/RTH/SPL CF24 .... 5 J5
Kilgetty Cl *CAE/CAN/FWR* CF5 . 117 F4
Kiln Wy *CALD/MAG* NP26 .... 60 D3
Kimberley Rd
CYN/LLD/PWYN CF23 .... 113 F4
Kimberley Ter *CDFN* CF14 .... 100 A2
Kincraig St
CATH/RTH/SPL CF24 .... 5 J3
King Alfreds Rd *CHEP* NP16 ..... 29 E5
Kingarth St
CATH/RTH/SPL CF24 .... 5 J5
King Edward Av *CAER* CF85 ..... 69 E2
King Edward VII Av
CCDF CF10 .... 4 B2
Kingfisher Cl *CALD/MAG* NP26 .. 63 E4
Kingfisher St *CDFNE* CF3 .... 103 E3
King George V Dr East
CDFN CF14 .... 112 B1
King George V Dr North
CDFN CF14 .... 100 A5
King George V Dr West
CDFN CF14 .... 99 H5
King Harold's Vw
CALD/MAG NP26 .... 63 H3
King La *NWPT* NP20 .... 9 F6
Kings Acre *NWPT* NP20 .... 56 A4
King's Av
PENT/RAD/TFW CF15 .... 97 H5
Kings Cl *CAER* CF83 .... 47 F2
Kings Cl *PNRTH/DP* CF64 .... 133 E4
Kingsland Crs *BARRYE* CF63 .... 3 J1
Kingsland Rd
CDFN CF14 .... 118 C2
CDFN CF14 .... 110 D1
Kingsland Ter *PPRD* CF37 .... 44 D3
Kingsley Cl *PNRTH/DP* CF64 .... 141 F4
Kingsley Ct *PNRTH/DP* CF64 .... 137 G5
Kingsmark La *CHEP* NP16 .... 28 A3
Kingsmill Ter *NWPT* NP20 .... 8 E2
King's Pde *NWPT* NP20 .... 77 E2
Kings Ride *PNRTH/DP* CF64 ..... 137 G5
King's Rd *GTN/RVSD* CF11 .... 119 E2
PENT/RAD/TFW CF15 .... 97 H5
Kingston Rd *GTN/RVSD* CF11 ... 119 E3
NWPTE NP19 .... 9 J3
King St *ABRC/NBR/RIS* NP11 .... 34 A1
CAER CF83 .... 47 F2
NWPT NP20 .... 8 E5
PENT/RAD/TFW CF15 .... 83 H4
PNRTH/DP CF64 .... 134 C1

PPOOL/BLNAV NP4 .... 14 B3
PPRD CF37 .... 45 F5
Kingsway *CCDF* CF10 .... 4 C4
NWPT NP20 .... 8 E3
Kingsway Fforrdd y Brenin
CCDF CF10 .... 4 C4
Kingswood Coed-y-Brenin
.... 44 B4
King Wood Cl
CYN/LLD/PWYN CF23 .... 113 G2
Kinnock Ct *CWM* NP44 .... 20 B2
Kinsale Cl
CYN/LLD/PWYN CF23 .... 87 H5
Kipling Cl *CDFNE* CF3 .... 102 A3
Kipling Rd *PNRTH/DP* CF64 ..... 134 B1
Kipling Hl *NWPT* NP20 .... 75 H2
Kipling Rd *CALD/MAG* NP26 .... 62 C3
Kirby La *NWPT* NP20 .... 8 E7
Kirkby Ct *CCDF* CF10 .... 7 G1
Kirkhouse St *PPRD* CF37 .... 44 C4
Kirkwall Ct
CATH/RTH/SPL CF24 .... 121 E1
Kirriach *CALD/MAG* NP26 .... 62 B3
Kirton Cl *CAE/CAN/FWR* CF5 .... 110 C4
Kitchener Rd *GTN/RVSD* CF11 ... 119 E3
Kitty Hawk Dr *NWPTE* NP19 .... 77 H1
Knap Car Ter *BARRYI/W* CF62 .. 146 B2
Knight Cl *NWPT* NP20 .... 9 F7
Knights Wk *CAER* CF83 .... 68 A2
Knightswell Cl
CAE/CAN/FWR CF5 .... 125 C1
Knightswell Rd
CAE/CAN/FWR CF5 .... 116 D5
Knole Cl *CYN/LLD/PWYN* CF23 . 101 H1
Knowbury Av *PNRTH/DP* CF64 .. 142 D1
Knox Rd *CATH/RTH/SPL* CF24 ... 5 F4
Kyle Av *CDFN* CF14 .... 99 F5
Kyle Crs *CDFN* CF14 .... 99 F5
Kymin Rd *PNRTH/DP* CF64 ...... 134 D2
Kymin Ter *PNRTH/DP* CF64 ...... 134 D2
Kyveilog St *GTN/RVSD* CF11 ..... 119 E1

L

Laburnam Wy
PNRTH/DP CF64 .... 134 A3
Laburnham Bush Cots
NWPTE NP19 .... 78 A1
Laburnum Av *NWPTE* NP19 ..... 58 A5
Laburnum Cl *BARRYI/W* CF62 .. 139 G2
Laburnum Dr *CALD/MAG* NP26 . 60 D2
RSTN NP10 .... 54 A2
Laburnum Dr *CWM* NP44 .... 24 D3
PPOOL/BLNAV NP4 .... 15 H5
Laburnum Pl
CYN/LLD/PWYN CF23 .... 110 B5
Laburnum Ter *PPRD* CF37 .... 65 H2
Laburnum Wy *CHEP* NP16 .... 30 C1
Lady Margaret Ct
CHEP NP16 .... 30 D3
Ladyhill Rd *NWPTE* NP19 .... 58 B5
Lady Margaret Cl
CATH/RTH/SPL CF24 .... 5 J5
Lady Mary Rd
CYN/LLD/PWYN CF23 .... 112 D3
Ladysmith Rd
CYN/LLD/PWYN CF23 .... 113 F4
Ladywell *CWM* NP44 .... 19 H3
Lake Hill Dr *COWBR* CF71 .... 122 D4
Lake Rd *NWPTE* NP19 .... 78 B3
Lake Rd East
CYN/LLD/PWYN CF23 .... 112 D2
Lake Rd North
CYN/LLD/PWYN CF23 .... 100 B5
Lake Rd West
CYN/LLD/PWYN CF23 .... 112 C1
Lakeside *BARRYI/W* CF62 .... 2 A7
Lakeside Cl *CWM* NP44 .... 26 B5
Lakeside Dr
CYN/LLD/PWYN CF23 .... 112 D1
RSTN NP10 .... 91 F1
Lake Vw *CWM* NP44 .... 26 B5
Lake View Cl
CYN/LLD/PWYN CF23 .... 112 D1
Lakin Dr *BARRYI/W* CF62 .... 138 C1
Laleston Cl *BARRYE* CF63 .... 139 G3
CAE/CAN/FWR CF5 .... 117 F4
Lamb Cl *NWPT* NP20 .... 75 H3
Lambert Cl
CATH/RTH/SPL CF24 .... 5 K6
Lamberton Wy
CATH/RTH/SPL CF24 .... 5 K6
Lambert St *NWPT* NP20 .... 56 C3
Lamb La *CLN/RNWPTE* NP18 .... 27 F4
Lambourne Crs *CDFN* CF14 ..... 99 H3
NWPT NP20 .... 39 G4
Lambourne Wy *NWPT* NP20 ..... 39 G4
Lamby Wy
CATH/RTH/SPL CF24 .... 114 B5
Lamby Way Workshops
.... 114 C3
Lancaster Dr *CHV/BDAU* CF38 .. 81 E3
Lancaster Rd
PPOOL/BLNAV NP4 .... 17 G3
Lancaster Wy *CHEP* NP16 .... 28 B4
Lancing Av *GTN/RVSD* CF11 ..... 119 E3
Lan Cl *PPRD* CF37 .... 44 C2
Landau Cl *CALD/MAG* NP26 ..... 60 D3
Landraw Rd *PPRD* CF37 .... 44 A3
Landseer Cl *NWPTE* NP19 .... 57 H2
Landwade Cl
CAE/CAN/FWR CF5 .... 117 F1
Lanelay Cl *LLTR/LLH* CF72 ...... 94 B3
Lanelay Crs *PPRD* CF37 .... 44 B3
Lanelay Pk *LLTR/LLH* CF72 ...... 94 B3
Lanelay Rd *LLTR/LLH* CF72 ...... 94 B3
Lanelay Ter *PPRD* CF37 .... 44 B3
The Lanes *LLMJ* CF61 .... 136 C4
The Lane *CAE/CAN/FWR* CF5 ... 124 D1
Langdale Cl
CYN/LLD/PWYN CF23 .... 113 C2
Langdale Wy *GTN/RVSD* CF11 .. 119 E3
Langland Rd *CDFNE* CF3 .... 114 C2
Langlands Rd *BARRYE* CF63 .... 140 A1
Langland Wy *NWPTE* NP19 ...... 77 H3

Langley Cl *CALD/MAC* NP26 — 60 C3
Langport Av *CYN/LLD/PWYN* CF5 — 102 C4
Langstone Ct *CWM* NP44 * — 25 F2
Langstone Court Rd
 CLN/RNWPTE NP18 — 59 H1
Langstone La
 CLN/RNWPTE NP18 — 59 G4
Lanhydrock Cl *CDFNE* CF3 — 103 E4
Lanpark Rd *PPRD* CF37 — 44 D1
Lansbury Cl *CAER* CF83 — 48 C4
Lansdale Dr *CHV/BDAU* CF38 — 81 H1
Lansdowne
 PPOOL/BLNAV NP4 — 17 E5
Lansdowne Av *CDFN* CF14 — 99 F4
Lansdowne Av East
 GTN/RVSD CF11 — 118 C3
Lansdowne Av West
 GTN/RVSD CF11 — 118 C3
Lansdowne Gdns *CWM* NP44 — 40 B1
Lansdowne Rd
 CAE/CAN/FWR CF5 — 118 C2
 CLN/RNWPTE NP18 — 42 A4
 PENT/RAD/TFW CF15 — 76 D2
Lanwern Rd *PPRD* CF37 — 44 C4
Lanwood Rd *PPRD* CF37 — 44 C2
Lapwing Av *CALD/MAC* NP26 — 63 E4
Lapwing Cl *PNRTH/DP* CF64 — 142 C2
Larch Cl *PPOOL/BLNAV* NP4 — 7 G3
Larch Ct *PENT/RAD/TFW* CF15 — 98 A1
Larch Dr *LLTR/LLH* CF72 — 95 G2
Larch Gv *CDFN* CF14 — 86 C4
 NWPT NP20 — 40 C3
Larchwood *CAE/CAN/FWR* CF5 — 125 F5
Larkfield Av *CHEP* NP16 — 28 B5
Larkfield Cl
 CLN/RNWPTE NP18 — 41 G3
Larkfield Ct *CHEP* NP16 — 28 B5
Larkfield Pk *CHEP* NP16 — 28 B5
Larkhill Cl *CHEP* NP16 — 28 B5
Larkwood Av *PNRTH/DP* CF64 — 134 C4
Lascelles Dr
 CYN/LLD/PWYN CF23 — 102 A1
Lasgarn La *PPOOL/BLNAV* NP4 — 13 F5
Lasgarn Pl *PPOOL/BLNAV* NP4 — 12 D4
Lasgarn Vw
 PPOOL/BLNAV NP4 — 10 B5
Latch Sq *NWPT* NP20 — 9 F7
Latteys Cl *CDFN* CF14 — 99 G5
Laugharne Av *CDFNE* CF3 — 103 E4
Laugharne Ct *BARRY/-W* CF62 — 139 F2
Laugharne Rd *CDFNE* CF3 — 114 C2
Launcelot Crs *CDFN* CF14 — 85 G5
Laundry Rd *PPRD* CF37 — 44 C3
Laura St *BARRYE* CF63 — 140 B5
 PPRD CF37 — 45 E4
Laureate Cl *CDFNE* CF3 — 102 A3
Laurel Av *PPRD* CF37 — 46 A5
Laurel Cl *CALD/MAC* NP26 — 60 D2
Laurel Ct *CAE/CAN/FWR* CF5 — 110 B5
 CAER CF83 — 49 H5
Laurel Crs *NWPT* NP20 — 27 G4
Laurel Dr *RSTN* NP10 — 75 E1
Laurel Rd *RSTN* NP10 — 74 C1
The Laurels *CDFN* CF14 — 86 B4
Lauriston Cl
 CAE/CAN/FWR CF5 — 126 A1
Lauriston Pk
 CAE/CAN/FWR CF5 — 126 A1
Lavender Gv
Lavender Wy *RSTN* NP10 — 54 A2
Lavernock Rd
 PNRTH/DP CF64 — 141 H4
Lavery Cl *NWPTE* NP19 — 57 H2
Lawn Ter *PPRD* CF37 — 45 F5
Lawrence Hill Av *NWPTE* NP19 — 58 A4
Lawrence St *CAER* CF83 — 69 E1
Lawrenny Av *GTN/RVSD* CF11 — 118 C4
Laybourne Cl *CWM* NP44 — 19 H3
Laytonia Av *CDFN* CF14 — 86 A4
Leach Rd *NWPT* NP20 — 39 F3
Lea Cl *CALD/MAC* NP26 — 60 C2
 NWPT NP20 — 39 G4
Leacroft Pl
 CYN/LLD/PWYN CF23 — 101 F1
Leadon Cl *CWM* NP44 — 18 D4
Lead St *CATH/RTH/SPL* CF24 — 5 J3
Leamington Rd *CDFN* CF14 — 99 E4
The Leas *CWM* NP44 — 19 F3
Leckwith Av *GTN/RVSD* CF11 — 118 C3
Leckwith Cl *GTN/RVSD* CF11 — 118 C3
Leckwith Pl *GTN/RVSD* CF11 — 119 E3
Leckwith Rd *GTN/RVSD* CF11 — 127 F1
 PNRTH/DP CF64 — 127 F3
Ledbrooke Cl *CWM* NP44 — 25 F2
Lee Cl *CYN/LLD/PWYN* CF23 — 119 H1
 PNRTH/DP CF64 — 133 F2
Lee Ct *CDFN* CF14 — 99 F1
Lee St *PPRD* CF37 — 44 C3
Lee Wy *NWPTE* NP19 — 78 B3
Leeway Ct *NWPTE* NP19 — 78 B3
Leicester Dr *CWM* NP44 — 18 D5
Leicester Rd *NWPTE* NP19 — 57 F3
Leigh Cl *LLMJ* CF61 — 137 E3
Leigh Rd *PPOOL/BLNAV* NP4 — 14 C2
Lennard St *NWPTE* NP19 — 9 J4
Lennox Gn *BARRYE* CF63 * — 140 B3
Leoline Cl *COWBR* CF71 — 122 B3
Leon Av
 PENT/RAD/TFW CF15 — 83 F4
Le Pouliguen Wy *LLMJ* CF61 — 136 C3
Letterston Rd *CDFNE* CF3 — 102 C5
Letton Rd *CCDF* CF10 — 2 C7
Lettons Wy *CATH/RTH/SPL* CF24 — 133 E2
Letty St *CATH/RTH/SPL* CF24 — 112 C5
Leven Cl *CYN/LLD/PWYN* CF23 — 100 C5
Lewis Cl *NWPT* NP20 — 9 H1
 PPOOL/BLNAV NP4 — 12 B1
Lewis Dr *CDFNE* CF3 — 48 C4
Lewis Rd *CATH/RTH/SPL* CF24 — 5 K6
 PNRTH/DP CF64 — 127 G4
Lewis St *BARRY/-W* CF62 — 138 D1
 CAER CF83 — 51 H2
 CHV/BDAU CF38 * — 81 G2
 GTN/RVSD CF11 — 119 F3
 LLTR/LLH CF72 — 94 C5
 PPOOL/BLNAV NP4 — 12 C3
 PPRD CF37 — 44 D2
Lewis Ter *PPRD* CF37 — 44 D2
Lewis Wy *CHEP* NP16 — 30 D3

Leydene Cl
 ABRC/NBR/RIS NP11 — 37 E3
Leyshon St *PPRD* CF37 — 44 D3
Libeneth Rd *NWPTE* NP19 — 58 A5
Library Rd *PPRD* CF37 — 44 D3
Library St *CAE/CAN/FWR* CF5 — 119 E2
Liddel Cl *CYN/LLD/PWYN* CF23 — 102 A1
Lidmore Rd *BARRY/-W* CF62 — 138 C4
Lighthouse Rd *RSTN* NP10 — 75 H4
Lilac Cl *CAER* CF83 — 48 C4
Lilac Dr *CHV/BDAU* CF38 — 80 D4
Lilac Gv *NWPT* NP10 — 54 A2
Lilburne Cl
 CYN/LLD/PWYN CF23 — 101 H1
Lilleshall St *NWPTE* NP19 — 9 K5
Lily St *CATH/RTH/SPL* CF24 — 5 G1
Lily Wy *RSTN* NP10 — 54 B5
Limeburne St *NWPTE* NP19 — 57 G5
Limebourne Ct *CDFN* CF14 — 111 E2
Lime Cl *NWPT* NP20 — 76 D2
Lime Crs *NWPTE* NP19 — 58 A5
Lime Gv *CAE/CAN/FWR* CF5 — 109 H4
Limekiln Rd
 PPOOL/BLNAV NP4 — 12 D5
Limeslade Cl
 CAE/CAN/FWR CF5 — 118 A1
The Limes *CALD/MAC* NP26 — 65 H2
Lime St *PPRD* CF37 — 44 D3
Limetree Cl *CHV/BDAU* CF38 — 81 H3
Limewood Cl *CDFNE* CF3 — 102 D3
Lincoln Cl *NWPT* NP20 — 57 G5
Lincoln Ct *CLN/RNWPTE* NP18 — 41 H5
 CYN/LLD/PWYN CF23 — 101 E5
Lincoln St *CAE/CAN/FWR* CF5 — 118 C2
Lindbergh Cl *NWPTE* NP19 — 77 H1
Linden Av
 CYN/LLD/PWYN CF23 — 113 E4
Linden Cl *CHEP* NP16 — 29 F4
Linden Gv *CAER* CF83 — 49 E4
 CDFNE CF3 — 114 B1
Linden Rd *NWPTE* NP19 — 57 H4
Lingholm Cl *CDFNE* CF5 — 103 E3
Link Rd *PPOOL/BLNAV* NP4 — 17 G1
The Links *PPOOL/BLNAV* NP4 — 14 C1
Linley Cl *NWPTE* NP19 — 59 F3
Linnet Cl *CYN/LLD/PWYN* CF23 — 81 H4
Linnet Rd *CALD/MAC* NP26 — 62 D4
Lionel Rd *CAE/CAN/FWR* CF5 — 118 C2
Lionel Ter *PPRD* CF37 — 65 G2
Liscombe St *NWPTE* NP19 — 57 H5
Liscum Wy *BARRY/-W* CF62 — 138 C2
Lisnagarvey Ct *CDFN* CF14 — 86 C2
Lister Cl *CHV/BDAU* CF38 — 81 E1
Lister Gn *NWPT* NP20 — 40 B4
Lisvane Rd *CDFN* CF14 — 100 C1
Lisvane Dr
 CATH/RTH/SPL CF24 — 112 B4
Liswerry Cl *CWM* NP44 — 26 C1
Liswerry Dr *CWM* NP44 — 26 B1
Liswerry Park Dr
 NWPT NP19 — 58 B5
Liswerry Rd *NWPTE* NP19 — 58 A5
Little Brynhill La
 BARRY/-W CF62 — 138 D1
Littlecroft Av
 CAE/CAN/FWR CF5 — 118 A2
Littledene *CWM* NP44 — 18 D5
Little Dock St *PNRTH/DP* CF64 — 134 B1
Little Frederick St *CCDF* CF10 — 4 E5
Little Mill *CDFN* CF14 — 112 A1
Little Moors Hl *BARRYE* — 140 A3
Little Oaks Vw *RSTN* NP10 — 54 E5
Little Orch *CAE/CAN/FWR* CF5 — 110 D4
 PNRTH/DP CF64 — 133 G4
Littleton St *GTN/RVSD* CF11 — 119 E3
Livale Cl *NWPT* NP20 — 39 H4
Livale Rd *NWPT* NP20 — 39 H4
Liverpool St *NWPT* NP20 — 9 J1
Livingstone Pl *NWPTE* NP19 — 9 G1
Llanarth St
 ABRC/NBR/RIS NP11 — 35 E3
 CAER CF83 — 52 A3
 NWPT NP20 — 8 E4
Llandaff Cha
 CAE/CAN/FWR CF5 — 110 C4
Llandaff Gn *CWM* NP44 — 19 H4
Llandaff Pl *CAE/CAN/FWR* CF5 — 118 C1
Llandaff Rd *GTN/RVSD* CF11 — 118 D1
Llandaff St *NWPT* NP20 — 8 B7
Llandegefedd Wy
 PPOOL/BLNAV NP4 — 17 G2
Llandegfedd Cl *CDFN* CF14 * — 86 A4
 RSTN NP10 — 54 A4
Llandegveth Cl *CWM* NP44 — 20 C3
Llandennis Av
 CYN/LLD/PWYN CF23 — 100 C4
Llandennis Ct
 CYN/LLD/PWYN CF23 — 100 B4
Llandennis Gn
 CYN/LLD/PWYN CF23 — 100 B4
Llandennis Rd
 CYN/LLD/PWYN CF23 — 100 B4
Llanderfel Ct *CWM* NP44 — 18 D4
Llandetty Rd
 CAE/CAN/FWR CF5 — 117 H1
Llandilo Cl *PNRTH/DP* CF64 — 133 G3
Llandinam Crs *CDFN* CF14 — 111 H4
Llandinam Rd *BARRY/-W* CF62 — 3 F1
Llandogo Rd *CDFNE* CF3 — 103 E3
Llandough Hl
 PNRTH/DP CF64 — 127 H4
Llandough St
 CATH/RTH/SPL CF24 — 4 D1
Llandovery Cl
 CAE/CAN/FWR CF5 — 117 H4
Llandowlais St *CWM* NP44 — 25 H2

Llandow Rd
 CAE/CAN/FWR CF5 — 117 G4
Llandraw Woods *PPRD* CF37 — 44 B4
Llandudno Rd *CDFNE* CF3 — 114 C1
Llandyfrig Cl
 PNRTH/DP CF64 * — 133 G3
Llanedeyrn Cl
 CYN/LLD/PWYN CF23 — 113 F2
Llanedeyrn Dr
 CYN/LLD/PWYN CF23 — 101 F5
Llanedeyrn Rd
 CYN/LLD/PWYN CF23 — 113 F3
Llanerch Goed
 CHV/BDAU CF38 — 81 E1
Llanewrwg Wy *CDFNE* CF3 — 102 D3
Llanfabon Dr *CAER* CF83 — 49 H3
Llanfair Rd *GTN/RVSD* CF11 — 118 D1
Llanfair Ct *CAER* CF83 — 49 H4
Llanfrechfa Wy *CWM* NP44 — 26 A1
Llangattock Rd
 CAE/CAN/FWR CF5 — 117 H1
Llangefni Pl *CDFN* CF14 — 99 H1
Llangorse Dr *RSTN* NP10 — 55 E3
Llangorse Rd *CWM* NP44 — 26 B1
 CYN/LLD/PWYN CF23 — 100 D3
Llangranog Pl *CDFN* CF14 — 99 G1
Llangranog Rd *CDFN* CF14 — 99 G1
Llangwm Pl *CDFN* CF14 — 99 H1
Llangwm Rd *CDFNE* CF3 — 114 C1
Llangyndir Rd
 CAE/CAN/FWR CF5 — 117 H1
Llanharry Rd *LLTR/LLH* CF72 — 106 A2
Llanhonddu
 PPOOL/BLNAV NP4 * — 12 C5
Llanidloes Rd *CDFN* CF14 — 111 F3
Llanina Gv *CDFNE* CF3 — 102 D5
Llanishen Ct *CDFN* CF14 — 100 A2
Llanishen St *CDFN* CF14 — 112 B3
Llanmaes Rd *LLMJ* CF61 — 136 D2
Llanmaes St *GTN/RVSD* CF11 — 4 B7
Llanmead Gdns
 BARRY/-W CF62 — 144 A2
Llanmihangel Rd *COWBR* CF71 — 122 B1
Llanmorlais Rd *CDFN* CF14 — 111 G4
Llanover Cl *CWM* NP44 — 26 A1
Llanover Ct *NWPT* NP20 — 40 B5
Llanover Rd
 CAE/CAN/FWR CF5 — 116 C5
 PPOOL/BLNAV NP4 — 10 C3
 PPRD CF37 * — 45 E3
Llanover St *BARRYE* CF63 — 139 F4
 PPRD CF37 — 45 E3
Llanquian Cl *CWM* NP44 — 20 C2
Llanquian Rd *COWBR* CF71 — 123 F2
Llanrumney Av *CDFNE* CF3 — 114 B1
Llansannor Dr *CCDF* CF10 — 7 F1
Llanstephan Rd *CDFNE* CF3 — 114 C2
Llantarnam Dr
 PENT/RAD/TFW CF15 — 97 G5
Llantarnam Gdns *CWM* NP44 — 26 A1
Llantarnam Park Wy
 CWM NP44 — 26 A4
Llantarnam Rd *CDFNE* CF3 — 111 H3
 CWM NP44 — 26 A1
Llanthewy Cl *CWM* NP44 — 20 C2
Llanthewy Rd *NWPT* NP20 — 8 A4
Llanthony Cl *CALD/MAG* NP26 — 63 E2
Llantrisant Ri
 CATH/RTH/SPL CF24 — 112 B5
Llantrisant Rd
 CHV/BDAU CF38 — 80 A4
 LLTR/LLH CF72 — 107 F1
 PENT/RAD/TFW CF15 — 109 G1
 PPRD CF37 — 64 B3
Llantrisant St
 CATH/RTH/SPL CF24 — 112 B5
Llantwit Rd *BARRY/-W* CF62 — 137 G4
 PPRD CF37 — 65 G3
Llantwit St *BARRYE* CF63 — 3 J1
 CDFN CF14 — 4 E2
Llanvair Rd *NWPTE* NP19 — 9 G1
Llanwern Rd
 CAE/CAN/FWR CF5 — 117 H4
 NWPTE NP19 — 58 D2
Llanwern St *NWPTE* NP19 — 9 J3
Llanwonno Cl *PPRD* CF37 — 44 B2
Llanwonno Rd *PPRD* CF37 — 44 B1
Llan-yr-Avon Sq *CWM* NP44 — 26 B1
Llan-yr-Avon Wy *CWM* NP44 — 26 B1
Llety'r Eos *BARRY/-W* CF62 — 144 D4
Llewelen Goch
 CAE/CAN/FWR CF5 — 96 D5
Llewellin St *NWPTE* NP19 — 57 H4
Llewellyn Av
 CAE/CAN/FWR CF5 — 117 G2
Llewellyn Dr *CAER* CF83 — 48 C5
Llewellyn Gn *CWM* NP44 — 19 H4
Llewellyn St *NWPTE* NP19 — 9 K5
 PPRD CF37 * — 44 B3
Lloyd Av *BARRY/-W* CF62 — 139 E3
Lloyd George Av *CCDF* CF10 — 118 A1
Lloyd Pl *CDFNE* CF3 — 103 F4
Lloyd St *NWPTE* NP19 — 77 H1
Llwyn Coed *CDFN* CF14 — 98 C1
Llwyd y Berth *CAER* CF83 * — 68 B2
Llwyn Bryn Melyn
 PENT/RAD/TFW CF15 — 97 F4
Llwyn Castan
 CYN/LLD/PWYN CF23 — 101 F3
Llwyn Celyn *CWM* NP44 — 25 C2
Llwyncrwn Rd
 CHV/BDAU CF38 — 80 A4
Llwyn David *BARRY/-W* CF62 — 2 E3
Llwyn Deri Cl *RSTN* NP10 — 74 B2
Llwyn Eithin Rd *NWPT* NP20 — 8 A3
Llwynderw Rd *CDFNE* CF3 — 111 H2
Llwyn Drysgol
 PENT/RAD/TFW CF15 — 97 F4
Llwyn Eithin *CAER* CF83 — 49 G4
Llwynfedw Gdns *CDFN* CF14 — 86 B4
Llwynfedw Rd *CDFN* CF14 — 86 B4
Llwynfen Rd *LLTR/LLH* CF72 — 107 F1
Llwyn On *CLN/RNWPTE* NP18 — 42 C2
Llwyn Mallt
 PENT/RAD/TFW CF15 — 98 A2
Llwynon
 ABRC/NBR/RIS NP11 * — 37 F4
Llwyn On *CLN/RNWPTE* NP18 — 27 H5

Llwyn-On Cl CF83 — 48 C5
Llwyn Onn *CDFN* CF14 — 98 C2
 CWM NP44 — 20 C4
 LLTR/LLH CF72 — 94 B5
Llwyn-On St *CAER* CF83 — 44 D3
Llwyn Passat *PNRTH/DP* CF64 — 134 C1
Llwyn Rhosyn *CDFN* CF14 — 99 F2
Llwyn y Gog *BARRY/-W* CF62 — 144 D4
Llwyn-y-Grant Pl
 CYN/LLD/PWYN CF23 — 113 F3
Llwyn-y-Grant Rd
 CYN/LLD/PWYN CF23 — 113 F3
Llwyn-y-Grant Ter
 CYN/LLD/PWYN CF23 — 113 F3
Llwyn y Pia Rd *CDFN* CF14 — 86 C4
Llyn Berwyn Cl *RSTN* NP10 — 55 E3
Llyn Celyn Cl *RSTN* NP10 — 55 E2
Llyn Cl *CYN/LLD/PWYN* CF23 — 100 C5
Llyn Pandy *CAER* CF83 — 49 H3
Llys Cambria *CAER* CF83 — 48 C1
Llys Catwg *LLTR/LLH* CF72 — 94 D3
Llys Coed Derw
 CHV/BDAU CF38 — 81 E2
Llys Corwg *PPRD* CF37 — 46 A4
Llys Derwen *LLTR/LLH* CF72 — 95 E3
Llys Fach *CHV/BDAU* CF38 — 81 G2
Llys Garth *CHV/BDAU* CF38 — 81 E1
Llys Gwent *BARRYE* CF63 — 140 A1
Llys Hafn
 PENT/RAD/TFW CF15 — 83 F4
Llys Llywelyn *CHV/BDAU* CF38 — 81 E2
Llys Nant y Aber *CAER* CF83 — 68 C1
Llys Pum Cyfair *CDFN* CF14 — 111 C3
Llys Tal-y-Bont Rd *CDFN* CF14 — 111 H4
Llys Tripp
 PENT/RAD/TFW CF15 — 83 F4
Llys Ty Gwyn *PPRD* CF37 — 45 F2
Llyswen *CAER* CF83 — 51 C2
Llyswen Rd
 CYN/LLD/PWYN CF23 — 100 C3
Llys-y-Celyn *CAER* CF83 * — 49 F4
Llys-y-Fedwen *CAER* CF83 * — 49 F5
Llys y Fran *CHV/BDAU* CF38 — 81 F3
Llywelyn Rd *CWM* NP44 — 19 H5
Lochaber St
 CATH/RTH/SPL CF24 — 113 E4
Locke Gv *CDFNE* CF3 — 103 F5
Locke St *NWPT* NP20 — 8 D2
Locks Rd *CCDF* CF10 — 7 H7
Lock-Up La *PPOOL/BLNAV* NP4 — 12 C4
Lodden Cl *NWPT* NP20 — 39 H4
Lodge Av *CLN/RNWPTE* NP18 — 41 G3
Lodge Cl *CDFN* CF14 — 86 B3
Lodge La *CLN/RNWPTE* NP18 — 41 G3
Lodge Rd *CLN/RNWPTE* NP18 — 41 H5
The Lodges *NWPTE* NP19 * — 9 K5
Lodge Wy *CALD/MAC* NP26 — 63 G3
Lodge Wd *PPOOL/BLNAV* NP4 — 15 E5
Lodwick Ri *CDFNE* CF3 — 103 F5
Loftus St *CAE/CAN/FWR* CF5 — 118 C2
Lombard St *BARRY/-W* CF62 — 3 G1
Lomond Crs
 CYN/LLD/PWYN CF23 — 100 D5
Loncae Porth *CDFN* CF14 — 99 F1
Lon Cefn Mably
 BARRY/-W CF62 — 144 B2
Lon Cwrt Ynyston
 GTN/RVSD CF11 — 127 G1
London St *NWPTE* NP19 — 9 J2
Lon Elai *LLTR/LLH* CF72 — 94 C5
Lon Fach *CAER* CF83 — 68 C2
 CDFN CF14 — 99 E3
Lon Fawr *CAER* CF83 — 68 C2
Lon Fferm Felin
 BARRY/-W CF62 — 2 A2
Longacre Cl *BARRYE* CF63 — 140 B1
 LLTR/LLH CF72 — 95 F3
Lon Ganol *CDFN* CF14 — 99 E3
Longbridge
 CLN/RNWPTE NP18 — 27 G5
Longcroft Rd *CALD/MAG* NP26 — 62 D3
Longcross St
 CATH/RTH/SPL CF24 — 5 H3
Longditch Rd *NWPTE* NP19 — 78 D3
Longfellow Cl
 CALD/MAC NP26 — 62 C3
Longfellow Ct
 CALD/MAC NP26 — 62 C4
Longfellow Rd
 CALD/MAC NP26 — 62 C3
Long Hollow *CWM* NP44 — 24 A2
Long House Ct *CDFNE* CF3 — 114 A4
Longhouse Gv *CWM* NP44 — 24 C3
Longleat Cl *CDFN* CF14 — 86 C5
Longmeadow Ct *NWPTE* NP19 — 78 B1
Long Meadow Dr
 BARRY/-W CF62 — 139 F2
Longmeadow Dr
 PNRTH/DP CF64 — 133 F4
Longreach Cl
 CAE/CAN/FWR CF5 — 116 C4
Longships Rd *CCDF* CF10 — 129 F3
Longspears Av *CDFN* CF14 — 112 A2
Longtown Gv *RSTN* NP10 — 91 H2
Longueil Cl *CCDF* CF10 — 7 G2
Longwood Dr *CDFN* CF14 — 97 H3
Lon Hafren *CAER* CF83 — 68 C3
Lon Helyg *CWM* NP44 — 24 C4
Lon Isa *CDFN* CF14 — 99 E3
Lon Isaf *CAER* CF83 — 68 C3
Lon Lindys *BARRY/-W* CF62 — 144 D4
Lon Madoc *CDFN* CF14 — 111 G1
Lon Nant *CWM* NP44 — 20 A2
Lon Owain *CAE/CAN/FWR* CF5 — 117 E5
Lon Penllyn *CDFN* CF14 — 99 E4
Lon Robin Goch *CAER* CF83 — 68 B1
Lonsdale Rd
 CYN/LLD/PWYN CF23 — 113 G2
Lon Ty'n-y-Cae *CDFN* CF14 — 99 E3
Lon Ucha *CDFN* CF14 — 99 E3
Lon Uchaf *CAER* CF83 — 68 C2
Lon-Werddi Cl

Lon y Cadno *CHV/BDAU* CF38 — 81 F3
Lon-y-Castell
 CAE/CAN/FWR CF5 — 117 F5
Lon-y-Celyn *CDFN* CF14 — 98 C4
Lon-y-Dail *CDFN* CF14 — 99 E3
Lon-y-Dderwen *CDFN* CF14 — 99 E2
Lon-y-Deri *CAER* CF83 — 68 C2
Lon-y-Ffin *CAE/CAN/FWR* CF5 — 116 D3
Lon y Fran *CAER* CF83 — 68 B1
Lon-y-Fro
 PENT/RAD/TFW CF15 — 96 B2
Lon-y-Garwa *CAER* CF83 — 68 C4
Lon y Goch
 PENT/RAD/TFW CF15 — 96 B4
Lon-y-Gors *CAER* CF83 — 68 B2
Lon-y-Groes *CDFN* CF14 — 111 H1
Lon-y-Llyn *CAER* CF83 — 68 C2
Lon-y-Mynydd *CDFN* CF14 — 99 F3
Lon y Nant *CDFN* CF14 — 99 F3
Lon-y-Parc *CDFN* CF14 — 99 E4
Lon-yr-Afon *CAER* CF83 — 33 H4
Lon-yr-Awel *LLTR/LLH* CF72 — 94 D5
Lon-yr-Efail
 CAE/CAN/FWR CF5 — 117 E5
Lon-y-Rhedyn *CAER* CF83 — 69 E3
Lon-y-Rhyd *CDFN* CF14 — 99 E3
Lon yr Odyn *CAER* CF83 — 49 F5
Lon y Ysgol *CAER* CF83 — 49 G3
Lon-ysgubor *CDFN* CF14 — 98 D2
Lon y Tresglen *CAER* CF83 — 68 B1
Lon-y-Twyn *CAER* CF83 — 69 E2
Lon-y-Waun *CAER* CF83 — 68 B2
Lon-y-Wern *CAER* CF83 — 68 C1
Lon-y-Winci *CDFN* CF14 — 98 D2
Loop Rd *CHEP* NP16 — 31 F1
Lord Eldon Dr *CHEP* NP16 — 30 D3
Lord St *NWPTE* NP19 — 9 H1
 PNRTH/DP CF64 — 134 D1
Lothian Crs
 CYN/LLD/PWYN CF23 — 113 F2
Loudoun Sq *CCDF* CF10 — 6 E3
Louisa Pl *CCDF* CF10 — 7 F5
Louis La
 CYN/LLD/PWYN CF23 — 101 F2
Love La *COWBR* CF71 — 122 C4
Lowdon Ter *BARRY/-W* CF62 — 3 F1
Lower Acre
 CAE/CAN/FWR CF5 — 117 E5
Lower Bridge St
 PPOOL/BLNAV NP4 — 14 C4
Lower Brynhyfryd Ter
 CAER — 32 A3
Lower Cathedral Rd
 GTN/RVSD CF11 — 119 F3
Lower Church St *CHEP* NP16 — 28 D3
Lowerdale Dr *LLTR/LLH* CF72 — 95 F3
Lower Dock St *NWPT* NP20 — 9 F5
Lower Farm Ct
 BARRY/-W CF62 — 144 C2
Lower Glyn-Gwyn St
 CAER CF83 — 50 B3
Lower Harper's Rd
 PPOOL/BLNAV NP4 — 14 A1
Lower Leigh Rd
 PPOOL/BLNAV NP4 — 14 A1
Lower Morel St *BARRYE* CF63 — 3 K1
Lower Park Gdns
 PPOOL/BLNAV NP4 — 14 C4
Lower Park Ter
 PPOOL/BLNAV NP4 — 14 C4
Lower Pyke St *BARRYE* CF63 — 3 K1
Lower Stoney Rd
 ABRC/NBR/RIS NP11 — 37 G5
Lowfield Dr *CDFNE* CF3 — 85 G5
Lowland Dr *CHV/BDAU* CF38 * — 81 H1
Lowlands Crs *CWM* NP44 — 19 H2
Lowlands Rd *CWM* NP44 — 19 H2
Lowndes Cl *RSTN* NP10 — 74 C1
Lowther Rd
 CATH/RTH/SPL CF24 — 4 E1
Lucas La *CAER* CF83 — 65 G3
Lucas St *CATH/RTH/SPL* CF24 — 112 C5
 NWPT NP20 — 8 D1
Lucerne Dr *CDFN* CF14 — 85 G4
Lucknow St *GTN/RVSD* CF11 — 119 F5
Ludlow Cl *CWM* NP44 — 26 C2
 GTN/RVSD CF11 — 6 C5
 NWPTE NP19 — 57 G5
Ludlow La *PNRTH/DP* CF64 — 134 C3
Ludlow St *CAER* CF83 — 68 D2
 GTN/RVSD CF11 — 6 B5
 PNRTH/DP CF64 — 134 C2
Lulworth Rd
 CLN/RNWPTE NP18 — 42 B5
Lundy Cl *BARRY/-W* CF62 — 99 H2
Lundy Dr *NWPTE* NP19 — 57 G3
Lupin Cl *RSTN* NP10 — 54 B3
Lydford Cl *CDFNE* CF3 — 99 E4
Lydstep Crs *CDFN* CF14 — 99 H2
Lydstep Cres *BARRY/-W* CF62 — 139 F2
Lydwood Cl *CAER* CF83 — 51 H2
Lynch Blosse Cl
 CAE/CAN/FWR CF5 — 110 C3
Lyncroft Cl *CDFNE* CF3 — 102 C2
Lyncroft Gv *CDFNE* CF3 — 102 C2
Lyndhurst St *GTN/RVSD* CF11 — 119 E3
Lyne Rd *ABRC/NBR/RIS* NP11 — 37 F3
 NWPT NP20 — 56 D2
Lynmouth Crs *CDFNE* CF3 — 114 A2
Lynton Cl *CDFNE* CF3 — 114 A2
 PNRTH/DP CF64 — 141 F4
Lynton Ct *CCDF* CF10 — 6 E4
Lynton Ter *CDFNE* CF3 — 114 A1
Lyon Cl *GTN/RVSD* CF11 — 102 A5
Lyric Wy *CDFN* CF14 — 85 H5
Lysander Ct
 CATH/RTH/SPL CF24 — 121 F1

M

Maberly Ct *CDFN* CF14 — 100 B3
Macaulay Av *CDFNE* CF3 — 102 A3

Macaulay Gdns *NWPT* NP20.... 75 H3
Macdonald Cl
  CAE/CAN/FWR CF5 .... 116 D4
Macdonald Pl
  CAE/CAN/FWR CF5 .... 116 D4
Macdonald Rd
  CAE/CAN/FWR CF5 .... 116 D4
Machen Cl
  ABRC/NBR/RIS NP11 .... 37 G5
  CDFNE CF3 .... 103 E3
Machen Pl *GTN/RVSD* CF11 .... 119 F3
Machen St
  ABRC/NBR/RIS NP11 .... 37 G4
  GTN/RVSD CF11 * 119 F5
  PNRTH/DP CF64 .... 134 B2
Machine Meadow
  PPOOL/BLNAV NP4 .... 14 A1
Mackintosh Pl
  CATH/RTH/SPL CF24.... 112 D4
Mackintosh Rd *PPRD* CF37 .... 45 E3
Madoc Cl *PNRTH/DP* CF64 .... 133 G3
Madocke Rd *CHEP* NP16 .... 29 E5
Madoc Pl
  CYN/LLD/PWYN CF23.... 121 E2
Madoc St *PPRD* CF37 .... 44 D4
Maelfa *CYN/LLD/PWYN* CF23 .. 113 G1
Maelog Cl *LLTR/LLH* CF72 .... 94 C5
Maelog Rd *CDFN* CF14 .... 112 A4
Maelog Rd *CDFN* CF14 .... 111 H3
Maendy Av *NWPT* NP20.... 19 F2
Maendy Rd *COWBR* CF71.... 123 F1
Maendy Wy *NWPT* NP20.... 19 F3
Maendy Wood Ri *CWM* NP44.... 19 F3
Maerdy Cl *NWPT* NP20.... 76 A5
Maerdy La *CDFN* CF14.... 86 D5
Maes Briallu *CAER* CF83 .... 49 G5
Maes Brith y Garn
  CYN/LLD/PWYN CF23.... 101 H3
Maes-Cefn-Mabley
  LLTR/LLH CF72 .... 95 E1
Maesderwen Crs
  PPOOL/BLNAV NP4 .... 14 D5
Maesderwen Ri
  PPOOL/BLNAV NP4 * 14 D5
Maesderwen Rd
  PPOOL/BLNAV NP4 .... 14 D5
Maes Ganol *PPRD* CF37.... 46 B5
Maes Glas *BARRY/W* CF62 .... 2 A1
  CAER CF83 .... 69 F2
  CDFN CF14 .... 111 E2
Maesglas Av *NWPT* NP20.... 76 A3
Maesglas Cl *NWPT* NP20.... 76 A4
Maesglas Crs *NWPT* NP20.... 76 A4
Maesglas Gv *NWPT* NP20.... 76 A4
Maesglas Rd *NWPT* NP20.... 76 A4
Maesglas St *NWPT* NP20.... 76 A4
Maes Gwyn *CAER* CF83 .... 69 E2
Maesgwyn *CWM* NP44 .... 19 G2
Maes Hir *CAER* CF83 .... 48 C4
Maes Lindys *BARRY/W* CF62 .. 144 D4
Maes Lloi *COWBR* CF71.... 123 F2
Maes Maelwg *CHV/BDAU* CF38.. 80 A4
Maes Slowes Leyes
  BARRY/W CF62 .... 144 D3
Maesteg Crs *CHV/BDAU* CF38.. 81 H1
Maesteg Gdns
  CHV/BDAU CF38.... 81 H1
Maesteg Gv *CHV/BDAU* CF38.. 81 H1
Maes Trane *CHV/BDAU* CF38.. 80 B4
Maes Uchaf *PPRD* CF37 .... 46 B5
Maes Watford *CAER* CF83 .... 68 C4
Maes y Briallu
  PENT/RAD/TFW CF15.... 97 F3
Maes y Bryn
  CYN/LLD/PWYN CF23.... 101 H2
Maes-y-Bryn Rd *CDFN* CF14.... 87 H5
Maes-y-Celyn
  PPOOL/BLNAV NP4 .... 14 D5
Maes-y-Coed *BARRY/W* CF62.. 146 B2
Maes-y-Coed Rd *CDFN* CF14 .. 99 H4
Maesycoed Rd *PPRD* CF37 .... 44 C3
Maes-y-Crochan *CDFN* CF3.... 103 G3
Maes y Crofft
  PENT/RAD/TFW CF15.... 97 F3
Maes-y-Cwm St
  BARRY/W CF62 .... 139 F4
Maes-y-Deri *CDFN* CF14 .... 99 E5
  PPRD CF37 .... 44 B2
Maes y Draenog
  PENT/RAD/TFW CF15.... 97 F3
Maes-y Drudwen *CAER* CF83 .. 68 B2
Maes-y-Felin *CAER* CF83 .... 69 E1
  CDFN CF14 .... 99 E4
Maes-y-Fioled
  PENT/RAD/TFW CF15.... 97 F3
Maes y Grug *CHV/BDAU* CF38.. 81 F1
Maes y Gwenyn
  BARRY/W CF62 .... 145 E3
Maes y Hedydd
  CYN/LLD/PWYN CF23.... 87 G5
Maes y Odyn
  PENT/RAD/TFW CF15.... 97 F3
Maes y Pandy *CAER* CF83 .... 49 F2
Maes y Parc *CDFN* CF14 * 99 E4
Maes yr Annedd
  CAE/CAN/FWR CF5 .... 118 C1
Maes yr Awel
  PENT/RAD/TFW CF15.... 97 G4
  PPRD CF37 .... 46 B5
Maes yr Haf *CDFN* CF14 .... 98 C2
Maes-y-Rhedyn
  LLTR/LLH CF72 .... 94 C3
Maes-y-Rhiw Ct *CWM* NP44.... 18 D5
Maes yr Orchis
  PENT/RAD/TFW CF15.... 97 F3
Maes-y-Sarn
  PENT/RAD/TFW CF15.... 96 A1
Maes y Siglen *CAER* CF83 .... 68 B1
Maes y Wennol
  CYN/LLD/PWYN CF23.... 87 G5
  LLTR/LLH CF72 .... 95 E5
Mafeking Rd
  CYN/LLD/PWYN CF23.... 113 E4
Magellan Cl *BARRY/W* CF62.... 139 G1
Maghausel Cl *CALD/MAG* NP26.. 60 C3
Magna Porta Gdns *CWM* NP44.. 26 C5
Magnolia Cl *CHEP* NP16 .... 30 D2
Magnolia Ct
  CYN/LLD/PWYN CF23.... 101 E3
  NWPT NP20.... 40 C3

Magnolia Wy *CHV/BDAU* CF38.. 80 D4
Magor St *NWPT* NP19.... 77 G1
Magpie Rd *BARRY/W* CF62.... 137 G3
Magreton Pl *CCDF* CF10.... 7 F2
Maillard's Hvn
  PNRTH/DP CF64.... 134 C5
Main Av *PPRD* CF37 .... 66 C2
Maindee Pde *NWPT* NP19.... 9 J1
Maindee Rd
  ABRC/NBR/RIS NP11 .... 34 B1
Maindee Ter *CWM* NP44.... 19 G3
Maindy Ms
  CATH/RTH/SPL CF24.... 112 C5
Maindy Rd
  CATH/RTH/SPL CF24.... 112 B4
Maindy Rd
  CATH/RTH/SPL CF24.... 64 C1
Main Rd *CALD/MAG* NP26.... 60 C3
  CALD/MAG NP26.... 63 H5
  CHV/BDAU CF38.... 81 G2
  LLTR/LLH CF72 .... 95 F3
  PENT/RAD/TFW CF15.... 83 E4
Main St *BARRY* CF63 .... 139 H2
Maitland Pl *CYN/RVSD* CF11 .. 119 F4
Maitland St *CDFN* CF14 .... 112 A3
Major Cl *CWM* NP44.... 24 C1
Major Rd *CAE/CAN/FWR* CF5.. 116 B3
Malcolm Sargent Cl
  NWPTE NP19 .... 58 C5
Maldwyn St *GTN/RVSD* CF11 .. 119 E1
Malefant St
  CATH/RTH/SPL CF24.... 112 C4
Mallard Av *CALD/MAG* NP26.. 62 D4
Mallard Cl *CDFNE* CF3.... 102 D5
Mallards Reach *CHEP* NP16 .. 31 G4
Mallard Wy *PNRTH/DP* CF64 .. 142 C2
  RSTN NP10.... 91 H1
Malmesbury Cl *NWPT* NP20.... 56 D3
Malmesmead Rd *CDFNE* CF3.. 102 B3
Malpas Cl *CDFNE* CF3.... 102 D2
Malpas La *NWPT* NP20.... 56 C1
Malpas Rd *NWPT* NP20.... 56 B1
Malpas St *CWM* NP44.... 25 H1
Malthouse Av
  CYN/LLD/PWYN CF23.... 87 H5
Malthouse La
  PPOOL/BLNAV NP4 .... 14 B3
Malthouse Rd
  CLN/RNWPTE NP18 .... 41 C1
  CWM NP44.... 40 B1
The Maltings
  CYN/LLD/PWYN CF23.... 101 G1
Malus Av *CHV/BDAU* CF38.... 80 D5
Malvern Cl
  ABRC/NBR/RIS NP11 .... 38 A5
  NWPTE NP19 .... 57 G1
Malvern Dr *BARRY/W* CF62.... 99 G3
Malvern Rd *NWPTE* NP19.... 9 H3
Malvern Ter
  ABRC/NBR/RIS NP11 .... 37 F5
Mandeville Pl
  GTN/RVSD CF11 * 119 F3
Mandeville St *GTN/RVSD* CF11.. 119 F3
Manitoba Ct
  CYN/LLD/PWYN CF23.... 100 D5
Manley Rd *NWPT* NP20.... 8 A4
Manod Cl *CHV/BDAU* CF14.... 111 E3
Manorbier Cl *CHV/BDAU* CF62.. 139 F1
Manorbier Crs *CDFNE* CF3.... 114 C1
Manorbier Dr *CWM* NP44.... 26 B1
  CHV/BDAU CF38.... 80 B5
Manor Cha *CALD/MAG* NP26.. 60 C3
Manor Cl *CDFN* CF14.... 99 E5
Manor Ct *CHV/BDAU* CF38.... 81 H3
Manor Hl *LLTR/LLH* CF72 .... 107 H1
Manor Pk *LLMJ* CF61.... 136 D4
  RSTN NP10.... 92 A1
Manor Rd
  ABRC/NBR/RIS NP11 .... 37 G5
  PPOOL/BLNAV NP4 .... 14 B3
Manor Sq *LLMJ* CF61.... 136 D5
Manor St *CDFN* CF14.... 112 A3
The Manor *CWM* NP44.... 40 B1
Manor Wy
  ABRC/NBR/RIS NP11 .... 37 G5
  CALD/MAG NP26.... 63 H3
  CDFN CF14.... 99 F5
  PPOOL/BLNAV NP4 .... 12 C3
Manor Wd *CHEP* NP16 .... 28 A4
  CHEP NP16 * 28 A4
Mansell Av *CAE/CAN/FWR* CF5.. 116 C4
Mansel St *BARRY/W* CF62 .... 117 H1
Mansfield St *GTN/RVSD* CF11.. 119 F3
Manston Cl *CAE/CAN/FWR* CF5.. 110 C4
Maple Av *ABRC/NBR/RIS* NP11.. 30 C3
  CHEP NP16.... 30 C3
Maple Cl *BARRY/W* CF62 .... 139 G2
  CALD/MAG NP26.... 62 D2
Maple Gdns
  NWPT NP20.... 53 H1
Maple Rd *CAE/CAN/FWR* CF5.. 109 H4
  PNRTH/DP CF64.... 134 A3
Maple Rd South
  PPOOL/BLNAV NP4 .... 16 D4
Maple St *PPRD* CF37 .... 65 H2
Maple Tree Cl
  PENT/RAD/TFW CF15.... 97 F4
Maplewood Av *CDFN* CF14.... 110 D2
Marayat Wk *NWPT* NP20.... 75 H3
Marchwood Ct *CDFNE* CF3 * .. 102 B5
Marconi Av *PNRTH/DP* CF64.... 128 B5
Marconi Cl *NWPT* NP20.... 41 E4
Marcross Rd
  CAE/CAN/FWR CF5 .... 116 C4
Mardy Cl *CAER* CF83 .... 69 F1
Mardy Crs *CAER* CF83.... 69 F2
Mardy Rd *CDFN* CF14.... 114 C3
Mardy St *GTN/RVSD* CF11.... 4 A7
Margam Rd *CDFN* CF14 .... 111 H3
Margaret Av *CALD/MAG* NP26.. 60 C3
Margaret Av *BARRY/W* CF62 .. 145 F5
  NWPTE NP19 .... 57 E2
Margaret St *PPRD* CF37.... 45 E3
Margretts Wy
  NWPT NP20.... 62 D2
Marguerites Wy
  CAE/CAN/FWR CF5 .... 116 D3

Maria St *CCDF* CF10.... 6 E1
Marigold Cl *RSTN* NP10.... 54 A3
Marine Dr *BARRY/W* CF62.... 146 A2
Marine Pde *PNRTH/DP* CF64.... 134 D4
Mariner's Hts *PNRTH/DP* CF64.. 134 D1
Mariners Reach *CHEP* NP16.... 31 E3
Mariners Wy *BARRY/W* CF62.. 144 B5
Mariner Wy *NWPTE* NP19.... 77 F5
Marion Cl *CDFN* CF14.... 100 B1
Marion Pl *NWPT* NP20.... 76 D2
Marion St *CATH/RTH/SPL* CF24. 120 D2
  NWPT NP20.... 76 D2
Marionville Gdns
  CAE/CAN/FWR CF5.... 110 C5
Maritime St *PPRD* CF37 .... 44 C4
Maritime Ter *PPRD* CF37.... 44 C4
Market Ar *NWPT* NP20 * 8 E2
Market Pl
  ABRC/NBR/RIS NP11 .... 23 E1
  CAER CF83 .... 119 E2
Market Rd *CAE/CAN/FWR* CF5.. 118 D2
  CAER CF83 .... 2 C4
  NWPT NP20.... 69 E2
  PENT/RAD/TFW CF15.... 97 H1
  PPRD CF37 .... 44 D3
Mark St *GTN/RVSD* CF11 .... 4 A5
Marlborough D
  BARRY CF63 .... 140 A2
  CHV/BDAU CF38.... 81 E4
Marlborough Rd *CWM* NP44.... 19 F5
  CATH/RTH/SPL CF24.... 113 E4
Marl Ct *CWM* NP44.... 19 E5
Marle Cl *CYN/LLD/PWYN* CF23.. 101 G2
Marloes Cl *BARRY/W* CF62.... 139 F2
Marloes Rd *CAE/CAN/FWR* CF5.. 116 C4
Marlowe Gdns *NWPT* NP20.... 75 H3
Marne St *ABRC/NBR/RIS* NP11.. 3 J6
Marquis Cl *BARRY/W* CF62.... 139 F1
Marshfield Rd *CDFN* CF3.... 89 H4
Marshfield St *NWPTE* NP19.... 77 G1
Marsh Rd *CHEP* NP16 .... 30 D2
Marston Ct *NWPT* NP20.... 56 B2
Marten Rd *CHEP* NP16 .... 30 C1
Martindale Rd
  PPOOL/BLNAV NP4 .... 17 E3
Martin Rd *CATH/RTH/SPL* CF24. 121 F4
The Martins *CHEP* NP16.... 29 E3
Mary Ann St *CCDF* CF10 .... 4 E5
Maryland
  ABRC/NBR/RIS NP11 .... 37 F5
Maryport Rd
  CYN/LLD/PWYN CF23.... 112 D3
Marysfield Cl *CDFNE* CF3.... 104 B2
Mary St *CAER* CF83 .... 46 D5
  CDFN CF14.... 110 D3
Masefield Rd *CALD/MAG* NP26.. 62 C4
  PNRTH/DP CF64.... 134 A2
Masefield V *NWPT* NP20.... 75 H2
Masefield Wy *PPRD* CF37.... 46 A3
Maxton Pth *CWM* NP44.... 39 H1
Mathern Rd *CHEP* NP16 .... 30 A3
Mathern Wy *CHEP* NP16.... 30 C1
Mathias Cl
  CYN/LLD/PWYN CF23.... 113 G4
Matthew Rd *BARRY/W* CF62.... 144 A2
Matthew St *CDFN* CF14.... 111 C2
Matthysens Wy *CDFNE* CF3.... 105 F5
Maugham Cl *NWPT* NP20.... 76 A3
Maughan Ter *PNRTH/DP* CF64.. 134 D1
Maureen Av
  CAE/CAN/FWR CF5 .... 117 C2
Mavis Cl *CDFN* CF14.... 99 C4
Mawsons Md
  CAE/CAN FWR CF5.... 124 A2
Maxwell Cl *CAE* CF83.... 69 F1
Maxwell Rd *CDFNE* CF3.... 114 B1
Mayfair Dr *CWM* NP44.... 85 H4
Mayfield Av
  CAE/CAN/FWR CF5.... 118 B2
Mayfield Pl *LLTR/LLH* CF72 .... 94 C2
Mayfield Rd *PPRD* CF37.... 44 C2
Mayflower Av *CDFN* CF14.... 99 G1
Mayflower Wy
  CAE/CAN/FWR CF5.... 144 B2
McCale Av *CAE/CAN/FWR* CF5.. 116 D4
McQuade Pl *BARRY/W* CF62 .. 3 F6
Meadow Brook *CAER* CF83.... 81 C2
Meadowbrook Av *CWM* NP44.. 19 G2
Meadow Cl
  ABRC/NBR/RIS NP11 .... 36 C2
  CYN/LLD/PWYN CF23.... 101 E2
  PPOOL/BLNAV NP4 .... 17 E5
Meadow Ct
  CLN/RNWPTE NP18 .... 59 H1
Meadow Crs
  ABRC/NBR/RIS NP11 .... 53 C1
  CAER CF83 .... 69 E2
  CHV/BDAU CF38.... 81 H1
Meadow Cft *BARRY/W* CF62 .. 144 D2
Meadowcroft *CALD/MAG* NP26.. 62 A4
Meadowgate Cl *CDFN* CF14.... 98 C3
Meadow Hl *CHV/BDAU* CF38.... 81 E2
Meadowland Dr *RSTN* NP10.... 53 H2
Meadow La *CHEP* NP16 * 28 C3
  CWM NP44.... 20 C3
  PNRTH/DP CF64.... 134 B5
Meadowlark Cl *CDFNE* CF3.... 102 D3
Meadow Ri *CALD/MAG* NP26.. 60 C3
Meadowside *PNRTH/DP* CF64.. 133 H5
Meadow Rd *NWPTE* NP19.... 78 B1
The Meadows
  ABRC/NBR/RIS NP11 .... 36 A3
  CALD/MAG NP26.... 104 A1
  LLTR/LLH CF72 .... 107 E1
Meadow St *GTN/RVSD* CF11.... 118 D1
Meadow Sweet Dr *CDFNE* CF3.. 105 F4
The Meadow *CALD/MAG* NP26.. 60 B3

Meadow V *BARRYE* CF63.... 140 A1
Meadow Vw *BARRYE* CF63.... 140 B1
Meadow View Ct
  PNRTH/DP CF64.... 141 E4
Meadow Wk *CHEP* NP16.... 28 B4
Meadow Wy *CAER* CF83.... 68 A5
Meads Cl *NWPTE* NP19.... 78 B2
Meads Ct *CHEP* NP16 * 30 C1
Meadvale Rd *CDFNE* CF3.... 102 C5
Medart Pl
  ABRC/NBR/RIS NP11 .... 36 B2
Medart St
  ABRC/NBR/RIS NP11 .... 36 C2
Medlock Cl *NWPT* NP20.... 39 G3
Medlock Crs *NWPT* NP20.... 39 G3
Medway Cl *NWPT* NP20.... 39 G3
Medway Rd *NWPT* NP20.... 39 F4
Meggitt Rd *BARRY/W* CF62 .. 139 E1
Meirion Cl *BARRY* CF63.... 139 H1
Meirion Pl
  CATH/RTH/SPL CF24.... 121 E2
Meirwen Dr
  CAE/CAN/FWR CF5.... 125 C1
Melbourne Ct *CWM* NP44.... 19 G5
Melbourne Rd *CDFN* CF14.... 100 A2
Melfort Gdns *NWPT* NP20.... 75 G1
Melfort Rd *NWPT* NP20.... 76 A1
Meliden La *CYN/LLD/PWYN*.... 134 B3
Meliden Rd *PNRTH/DP* CF64.. 134 B3
Melin Dwr *RSTN* NP10.... 91 F2
Melin Gwian *CAER* CF83.... 68 C1
Melin St *ABRC/NBR/RIS* NP11.. 34 C3
Mellon St *NWPT* NP20.... 9 F5
Melrose Av
  CYN/LLD/PWYN CF23.... 113 E4
Melrose Cl *CDFNE* CF3.... 105 E2
Melrose St *BARRYE* CF63.... 139 H3
Melville Cl *BARRY/W* CF62.... 102 D2
Melville Ter *CAER* CF83 .... 49 G5
Melyn y Gors *BARRYE* CF63.... 132 A5
Menai Cl *CYN/LLD/PWYN*.... 65 F5
Menai Wy *CDFNE* CF3.... 102 C4
Mendalgief Rd *NWPT* NP20.... 76 C2
Mendip Cl
  ABRC/NBR/RIS NP11 .... 38 A5
  NWPTE NP19 .... 58 B3
Mendip Rd *CDFNE* CF3.... 101 H5
Meon Cl *NWPT* NP20.... 40 A4
Merchant's Hl
  PPOOL/BLNAV NP4 .... 14 B2
Merches Pl *GTN/RVSD* CF11 .. 6 B1
Mercian Wy *CHEP* NP16.... 29 E5
Mercia Rd
  CATH/RTH/SPL CF24.... 121 E2
Meredith Rd
  CATH/RTH/SPL CF24.... 121 E2
Merevale *PNRTH/DP* CF64.... 132 D3
Merganser Ct *BARRYE* CF63.... 3 H1
Merianeth Pl *BARRY/W* CF62 .. 139 F2
Merlin Cl *CALD/MAG* NP26.... 61 H2
  PNRTH/DP CF64.... 142 C1
Merlin Crs *NWPTE* NP19.... 57 G2
Merlin Pl *CAE/CAN/FWR* CF5.. 116 A2
Mermaid Qy *CCDF* CF10.... 7 G6
Merret Ct *CATH/RTH/SPL* CF24.. 121 F1
Merriots Pl *NWPTE* NP19.... 9 J2
Merthyr Dyfan Rd
  BARRY/W CF62 .... 139 F1
Merthyr Rd *CDFN* CF14.... 98 D5
  PENT/RAD/TFW CF15.... 97 H1
  PPRD CF37 .... 45 E2
Merthyr St *BARRYE* CF63.... 3 H1
  CATH/RTH/SPL CF24.... 112 B5
Mervyn Rd
  CATH/RTH/SPL CF24.... 121 E2
  CDFN CF14.... 111 F1
Mervyn St *PPRD* CF37.... 45 E2
Mervyn Ter
  PPOOL/BLNAV NP4 * 14 B3
Mescoed Rd *RSTN* NP10.... 55 E1
Metal St *CATH/RTH/SPL* CF24.... 5 J3
Meteor St *CATH/RTH/SPL* CF24.. 68 A5
Methodist La *LLMJ* CF61.... 136 C3
Methuen Rd *NWPT* NP19.... 9 H3
The Mews *LLTR/LLH* CF72 .... 95 E2
  NWPT NP20 * 8 A6
Meyrick Cl *NWPT* NP20.... 25 E3
Meyricks *CWM* NP44.... 39 F4
Michael Ct *PPOOL/BLNAV* NP4.. 14 B3
Michaelston Rd
  CAE/CAN/FWR CF5.... 116 C2
Michael Wy
  PPOOL/BLNAV NP4 .... 14 B3
Middlegate Ct *NWPT* NP20.... 122 D5
Middlegate Wk *COWBR* CF71.. 122 D5
Middle St *CHEP* NP16.... 30 D2
  PPRD CF37 .... 45 E2
Middle Wy *CHEP* NP16.... 30 D2
Milburn Cl *BARRY/W* CF62.... 144 B3
Mildred Cl *CHV/BDAU* CF38.... 80 B3
Mildred St *CHV/BDAU* CF38.... 80 B2
Miles Ct *PENT/RAD/TFW* CF15.. 83 F4
Milestone Cl *CDFN* CF14.... 99 C4
Milford Cl *CHV/BDAU* CF38.... 65 G5
Millbrook Cl *PNRTH/DP* CF64.. 133 F2
Millbrook Pk *PNRTH/DP* CF64.. 86 B4
Millbrook Rd *PNRTH/DP* CF64.. 133 F2
Mill Cl *CAER* CF83 .... 48 C5
  CDFN CF14.... 100 B1
  PNRTH/DP CF64.... 133 F2
Mill Common *CALD/MAG* NP26.. 60 C3
Millfield *CDFN* CF14.... 100 B1
  LLTR/LLH CF72 .... 107 H1
Millfield Cl *CDFN* CF14.... 100 B1
Millfield Dr *COWBR* CF71.... 122 D3
Millgate *CDFN* CF14.... 100 B2
Mill Heath *NWPT* NP20.... 39 H3

Millheath Dr *CDFN* CF14.... 86 B5
Millicent St *CCDF* CF10.... 4 E6
Mill La *CAE/CAN/FWR* CF5.... 111 F5
  CALD/MAG NP26.... 63 E4
  CCDF CF10.... 4 D7
  CDFNE CF3.... 102 B2
  CHEP NP16.... 26 B1
Mill Lay La *LLMJ* CF61.... 136 C5
Mill Pde *NWPT* NP20.... 77 E2
Mill Pk *COWBR* CF71.... 122 C4
Mill Race *LLTR/LLH* CF72.... 117 H2
Mill Race Rd *CDFNE* CF3.... 86 B4
Millrace CF *CDFN* CF14.... 86 B5
Mill Reen *CALD/MAG* NP26.... 60 C3
Mill St *CAE/CAN/FWR* CF5.... 117 H2
  CAER CF83 .... 68 D1
  CDFN CF14.... 86 B5
  PENT/RAD/TFW CF15.... 97 H1
  PNRTH/DP CF64.... 133 E5
  PPOOL/BLNAV NP4 .... 14 A2
Mills Cl *BARRY/W* CF62.... 144 C3
Millward Cl
  ABRC/NBR/RIS NP11 .... 34 B2
  CLN/RNWPTE NP18 .... 53 C1
  NWPT NP20.... 42 B4
  PPRD CF37 .... 8 D2
Millwood Cl *CDFN* CF14.... 86 B5
Millwood Ri *BARRY/W* CF62.... 2 A2
Milman St *NWPT* NP20.... 76 D3
Milner St *NWPTE* NP19.... 77 G1
Milton Cl *CHV/BDAU* CF38.... 80 B4
  LLMJ CF61.... 137 F4
Milton Hl *CLN/RNWPTE* NP18.. 59 G4
Milton Pl *CAE/CAN/FWR* CF5.. 110 C5
Milton Rd *BARRY/W* CF62.... 139 E1
  NWPTE NP19 .... 57 C4
Milton St *CATH/RTH/SPL* CF24.. 5 C2
Milverton Rd *CDFNE* CF3.... 102 B3
Milward Rd *BARRYE* CF63.... 139 H3
Minafon *CDFN* CF14.... 99 E1
Minehead Av *PNRTH/DP* CF64.. 141 E4
Minehead Rd *CDFNE* CF3.... 102 B4
Minister St
  CATH/RTH/SPL CF24.... 112 B5
Minnett's La *CALD/MAG* NP26.. 61 H1
Minore Cl *CDFNE* CF3.... 112 C5
Minsmere Cl *CDFNE* CF3.... 105 F5
Minster Cl *BARRYE* CF63.... 139 H1
Minster Rd
  CATH/RTH/SPL CF24.... 113 C5
Min-y-Coed
  PENT/RAD/TFW CF15.... 97 G3
Min-y-Nor *BARRY/W* CF62.... 146 B2
Min-y-Nant *CDFN* CF14.... 99 E3
Min yr Afon *CAER* CF83.... 51 H2
Miskin Cl *CALD/MAG* NP26.... 80 B4
Miskin Crs *LLTR/LLH* CF72 .... 107 H1
Miskin Gn *CWM* NP44.... 25 E3
Miskin St *BARRY/W* CF62 .... 2 B5
  CATH/RTH/SPL CF24.... 4 C1
Mitchell Cl *CDFNE* CF3.... 103 F5
  CWM NP44.... 24 C1
Miterdale Cl
  CYN/LLD/PWYN CF23.... 112 D2
Mithras Wy
  CAE/CAN/FWR CF5.... 41 H2
Mitre Pl *CAE/CAN/FWR* CF5.. 111 E4
Moel Fryn *CAER* CF83.... 48 A3
Moira Pl *CATH/RTH/SPL* CF24.. 5 G4
Moira St *CATH/RTH/SPL* CF24.. 5 G4
Moira Ter *CATH/RTH/SPL* CF24.. 5 G4
Moir Ct *CAER* CF83.... 48 C4
Mole Cl *NWPT* NP20.... 39 F4
Mona Cl *CWM* NP44.... 20 A3
Mona Pl *CATH/RTH/SPL* CF24.. 5 K6
Monet Crs *NWPTE* NP19.... 57 H2
Monk's Ditch
  CLN/RNWPTE NP18 .... 78 C5
Monkstone Cl
  PNRTH/DP CF64.... 134 A5
Monkstone Ct *CDFNE* CF3.... 102 B5
Monkton Cl
  CAE/CAN/FWR CF5.... 117 E1
Monmouth Cl *CHV/BDAU* CF38.. 81 G5
  PPOOL/BLNAV NP4 .... 17 C5
Monmouth Dr *NWPTE* NP19.. 48 A5
Monmouth Vw *CAER* CF83.... 33 H5
Monmouth Wy
  BARRY/W CF62 .... 139 F3
Monnow Ct *NWPT* NP20.... 39 F4
Monnow Wy *NWPT* NP20.... 39 F4
Mons Cl *NWPT* NP20.... 56 B3
Montgomery Rd
  CAER CF83 .... 2 D2
  NWPT NP20.... 40 B2
Montgomery St
  CATH/RTH/SPL CF24.... 113 E4
Monthermer Rd
  CATH/RTH/SPL CF24.... 112 C4
Montreal Cl *NWPT* NP20.... 75 G1
Montresor Ct *CWM* NP44.... 26 C4
Moorby Ct *CCDF* CF10.... 7 F1
Moordale Rd *GTN/RVSD* CF11.. 6 B1
Moore Cl *CAE/CAN/FWR* CF5.. 117 E3
Moore Rd *CAE/CAN/FWR* CF5.. 117 E3
The Moorings *NWPTE* NP19.... 9 F4
  PNRTH/DP CF64.... 134 C1
Moorland Av *NWPTE* NP19.... 9 G2
Moorland Crs *CHV/BDAU* CF38.. 80 B3
Moorland Hts *PPRD* CF37.... 45 F3
Moorland Pk *NWPTE* NP19.... 78 B1
Moorland Rd
  CATH/RTH/SPL CF24.... 120 D2
Moorlands Vw
  CALD/MAG NP26.... 63 F4
The Moorings
  PPOOL/BLNAV NP4 .... 15 E5
Moors La
  CATH/RTH/SPL CF24 * 5 K6
Moor St *CHEP* NP16.... 28 C4
Mopla Rd *CHEP* NP16.... 28 D2

Morden La *NWPTE* NP19 57 F2
Morden Rd *NWPTE* NP19 57 F2
Morel Ct *GTN/RVSD* CF11 128 B3
Morel St *BARRYE* CF63 139 G3
Morfa Crs *CDFNE* CF3 102 D5
Morfa La *CAE/CAN/FWR* CF5 125 G5
LLMJ CF61 136 B1
Morgan Ar *CCDF* CF10 4 D6
Morgan St *BARRYE* CF63 139 H4
CAER CF83 48 D5
CCDF CF10 5 F6
NWPTE NP19 57 E3
PPRD CF37 44 D3
Morgan Wy *RSTN* NP10 92 A1
Morgraig Av *RSTN* NP10 91 H2
Moriah Hl
ABRC/NBR/RIS NP11 37 F4
Morien Crs *PPRD* CF37 65 G1
Morlais Ct *CAER* CF83 48 A5
Morlais St *BARRYE* CF63 140 A3
CYN/LLD/PWYN CF23 112 D4
Morley Cl *NWPTE* NP19 58 C4
Morningside Wk
BARRYI/W CF62 131 F5
Morris Av *CDFN* CF14 99 G1
Morris Finer Cl
CAE/CAN/FWR CF5 117 H3
Morris St *NWPTE* NP19 9 H4
Mortimer Rd *GTN/RVSD* CF11 119 E1
Morton Wy *NWPT* NP20 75 H2
Moss Rd *CWM* NP44 19 E5
Mostyn Rd *CAE/CAN/FWR* CF5 116 D4
Mound Rd *PPRD* CF37 44 B4
Mountain La
PPOOL/BLNAV NP4 16 D2
Mountain Rd
ABRC/NBR/RIS NP11 37 G2
CAER CF83 49 G1
CAER CF83 69 E2
CWM NP44 19 E1
PENT/RAD/TFW CF15 96 A1
PPOOL/BLNAV NP4 16 C3
RSTN NP10 54 D1
Mountain Vw *CAER* CF83 48 D3
CAER CF83 51 G2
Mountbatten Cl
CYN/LLD/PWYN CF23 100 B5
NWPTE NP19 59 E2
Mountbatten Rd
BARRYI/W CF62 131 G5
Mountford Cl *RSTN* NP10 54 D2
Mountjoy Av *PNRTH/DP* CF64 134 A2
Mountjoy Cl *PNRTH/DP* CF64 134 B2
Mountjoy Crs *PNRTH/DP* CF64 134 A3
Mountjoy La *PNRTH/DP* CF64 134 A3
Mountjoy Pl *NWPT* NP20 9 F6
PNRTH/DP CF64 134 A2
Mountjoy Rd *NWPT* NP20 9 F6
Mountjoy St *NWPT* NP20 9 F6
Mounton Cl *CHEP* NP16 28 B5
Mounton Dr *CHEP* NP16 28 B5
Mounton Rd *CHEP* NP16 28 A5
Mount Pleasant *BARRYE* CF63 139 H3
CHEP NP16 28 C4
NWPT NP20 * 40 B3
PPOOL/BLNAV NP4 * 12 C3
Mount Pleasant Av
CDFNE CF3 102 B4
Mount Pleasant Cl *CWM* NP44 19 G3
Mount Pleasant La
CDFNE CF3 102 B4
Mount Pleasant Rd
ABRC/NBR/RIS NP11 37 F4
CWM NP44 19 G3
Mount Pleasant Ter
ABRC/NBR/RIS NP11 23 F5
Mount Rd
ABRC/NBR/RIS NP11 37 F4
PNRTH/DP CF64 133 E3
PPOOL/BLNAV NP4 14 D1
Mount St Denys *CDFN* CF14 * 86 C3
Mountside
ABRC/NBR/RIS NP11 38 A5
Mount Stuart Sq *CCDF* CF10 7 F5
The Mount
CAE/CAN/FWR CF5 * 118 D1
PNRTH/DP CF64 133 E3
PPOOL/BLNAV NP4 * 14 A3
Mount Wy *CHEP* NP16 28 B3
Moxon Rd *NWPT* NP20 40 B5
Moxon St *BARRYE* CF63 140 A3
Moyle Gv *CLN/RNWPTE* NP18 27 G5
Moy Rd *CATH/RTH/SPL* CF24 112 D5
PENT/RAD/TFW CF15 83 F3
Muirton Rd
CATH/RTH/SPL CF24 121 E2
Mulberry Cl *CHV/BDAU* CF38 80 D5
RSTN NP10 54 B2
Mulberry Dr *CDFN* CF14 87 H4
Mulcaster Av *NWPTE* NP19 78 A2
Mullins Av *CDFNE* CF3 102 C5
Mundy Pl *CATH/RTH/SPL* CF24 112 C5
Munnings Dr *NWPTE* NP19 57 H2
Munro Pl *BARRYI/W* CF62 139 E3
Murch Crs *PNRTH/DP* CF64 133 G3
Murch Rd *PNRTH/DP* CF64 133 F3
Mur Gwyn *CDFN* CF14 99 F2
Murlande Wy *BARRYI/W* CF62 145 E2
Murrayfield Rd *CDFN* CF14 99 G5
Murray Wk *GTN/RVSD* CF11 119 E3
Murrel Cl *CAE/CAN/FWR* CF5 125 G1
Murrells Cl *CHV/BDAU* CF38 80 D4
Museum Av *CCDF* CF10 4 C2
Museum Ct
PPOOL/BLNAV NP4 17 E3
Museum Pl *CCDF* CF10 4 D2
Mylo-Griffiths Cl
CAE/CAN/FWR CF5 110 C2
Mynachdy Rd *CDFN* CF14 111 G3
Mynydd Maen Rd *CWM* NP44 19 F2
Mynydd Vw
PPOOL/BLNAV NP4 16 C1
Myra Hess Cl *NWPTE* NP19 59 E3
Myrtle Cl *PNRTH/DP* CF64 134 A3
RSTN NP10 75 E1
Myrtle Cots
CLN/RNWPTE NP18 42 B4
Myrtle Dr *RSTN* NP10 55 E5
Myrtle Gv *BARRYE* CF63 140 A2
NWPTE NP19 58 A4
Myrtle Pl *CHEP* NP16 28 D3
The Myrtles *CHEP* NP16 29 E2

N

Nailsea Ct *PNRTH/DP* CF64 141 F4
Nantcarn Rd
ABRC/NBR/RIS NP11 23 F3
Nant Celyn Cl *CWM* NP44 19 F2
Nant Coch Dr *NWPT* NP20 55 H5
Nant Coch Ri *NWPT* NP20 55 H5
Nant Ddu *CAER* CF83 68 D2
Nant Dyfed *CHV/BDAU* CF38 80 A5
Nant-Fawr Cl
CYN/LLD/PWYN CF23 100 C4
Nant-Fawr Crs
CYN/LLD/PWYN CF23 100 C4
Nant-Fawr Rd
CYN/LLD/PWYN CF23 100 C4
Nantgarw Rd *CAER* CF83 68 A3
Nant Isaf *CAE/CAN/FWR* CF5 125 G4
Nant Talwg Wy
BARRYI/W CF62 138 B4
Nant Walla *CDFN* CF14 99 F2
Nant y Coed *PPRD* CF37 44 A2
Nant-y-Dall Av *PPRD* CF37 65 G3
Nant y Dowlais
CAE/CAN/FWR CF5 116 B4
Nant-y-Drope
CAE/CAN/FWR CF5 116 C4
Nant y Fedw *CDFN* CF14 111 G1
Nant y Felin *CHV/BDAU* CF38 81 F5
Nant y Garn
ABRC/NBR/RIS NP11 36 D2
Nant y Garth
PENT/RAD/TFW CF15 * 83 E4
Nant y Gwladys
CAE/CAN/FWR CF5 96 C5
Nant y Hwyad *CAER* CF83 * 68 B1
Nant-y-Milwr Cl *CWM* NP44 24 C4
Nanty-Moor Cl *RSTN* NP10 90 D1
Nant y Pepra
CAE/CAN/FWR CF5 * 116 C4
Nant y Plac
CAE/CAN/FWR CF5 * 116 C4
Nant yr Arthur
CAE/CAN/FWR CF5 * 116 C4
Nant-yr-Ely
CAE/CAN/FWR CF5 * 116 B4
Nant y Rhos
CAE/CAN/FWR CF5 116 C4
Nant y Wedal *CDFN* CF14 112 C3
Napier St *CAER* CF83 51 G2
Narberth Ct *BARRYI/W* CF62 * 139 F2
CAER CF83 47 H5
Narberth Crs *CWM* NP44 26 C1
Narberth Rd
CAE/CAN/FWR CF5 117 G4
Narbeth Cl *RSTN* NP10 91 H2
Narcissus Gv *RSTN* NP10 54 B3
Nash Cl *RSTN* NP10 55 E3
Nash Dr *NWPTE* NP19 78 A2
Nash Gv *NWPTE* NP19 78 A1
Nash Md *NWPTE* NP19 78 B4
Nash Rd *CLN/RNWPTE* NP18 78 B4
NWPTE NP19 78 A3
Nasturtium Wy
CYN/LLD/PWYN CF23 101 E1
Navigation Rd
ABRC/NBR/RIS NP11 37 E3
Navigation St *CAER* CF83 50 B3
Neale St *BARRYI/W* CF62 139 E3
Neath Ct *CWM* NP44 18 D4
Neath St
CATH/RTH/SPL CF24 * 120 D3
Neddern Ct *CALD/MAG* NP26 * 62 D2
Neddern Wy *CALD/MAG* NP26 62 D2
Neerings *CWM* NP44 24 D1
Neilson Cl *CATH/RTH/SPL* CF24 5 J5
Nelson Dr *NWPTE* NP19 58 D3
Nelson Rd *BARRYI/W* CF62 139 G1
Nelson St *CHEP* NP16 28 C4
Nesta Rd *CAE/CAN/FWR* CF5 118 C2
Neston Rd *NWPTE* NP19 58 C3
Netherwent Vw
CALD/MAG NP26 60 B2
Nettlefold Rd
CATH/RTH/SPL CF24 7 K2
Neuadda Cl *RSTN* NP10 74 C2
Neville Pk *RSTN* NP10 105 H1
Neville Pl *GTN/RVSD* CF11 4 A6
Neville St *GTN/RVSD* CF11 119 F3
PPOOL/BLNAV NP4 12 B1
Nevin Crs *CDFNE* CF3 114 C1
Newborough Av *CDFN* CF14 99 H2
Newbridge Ct *PPRD* CF37 45 E2
Newbridge Rd *LLTR/LLH* CF72 95 F1
Newby Ct *CCDF* CF10 7 F1
New Chapel Ct *CWM* NP44 * 25 G2
Newent Rd *CDFNE* CF3 103 E4
Newfoundland Rd *CDFN* CF14 112 A3
Newgale Cl *BARRYI/W* CF62 139 F1
Newgale Pl *CAE/CAN/FWR* CF5 117 G4
Newgale Rw *CWM* NP44 20 A5
New George St *CCDF* CF10 7 G6
Newlands Ct *CDFN* CF14 100 B1
Newlands St *BARRYI/W* CF62 139 F4
Newman Cl *NWPTE* NP19 59 E4
Newman Rd
PPOOL/BLNAV NP4 14 B1
New Mill Cnr *LLTR/LLH* CF72 107 H2
Newmill Gdns *LLTR/LLH* CF72 95 E5
Newminster Rd
CYN/LLD/PWYN CF23 113 G5
New Park Crs *PPRD* CF37 * 45 F5
New Park Rd
ABRC/NBR/RIS NP11 36 C3
New Park Ter *PPRD* CF37 45 F5
New Pastures *NWPT* NP20 76 B2
Newport Ar *NWPT* NP20 8 D3
Newport Br *NWPT* NP20 8 E2
Newport Rd
ABRC/NBR/RIS NP11 23 E3
ABRC/NBR/RIS NP11 53 G1
CAER CF83 49 H3
CALD/MAG NP26 60 B3
CATH/RTH/SPL CF24 5 G3
CDFNE CF3 102 B5
CDFNE CF3 114 A3
CHEP NP16 28 B5
CWM NP44 20 C2
CWM NP44 40 B1
CYN/LLD/PWYN CF23 113 H4
PPOOL/BLNAV NP4 17 G4
Newport Road La
CATH/RTH/SPL CF24 5 G4
Newport St *GTN/RVSD* CF11 6 B4
New Quay Rd *NWPTE* NP19 77 F4
New Rd *ABRC/NBR/RIS* NP11 34 C2
CALD/MAG NP26 62 C3
CDFNE CF3 114 A3
CLN/RNWPTE NP18 42 B5
PPOOL/BLNAV NP4 12 B1
PPOOL/BLNAV NP4 17 F2
New Rw *CAER* CF83 51 G3
New Ruperra St *NWPT* NP20 * 9 F5
New St *CAER* CF83 48 C3
CWM NP44 19 H3
NWPT NP20 77 E2
New Ter *PPOOL/BLNAV* NP4 * 14 A2
Newton Rd *CDFNE* CF3 115 E2
GTN/RVSD CF11 119 E4
Newton St *BARRYE* CF63 139 H3
Newton Wy *NWPT* NP20 40 A4
New Zealand Rd *CDFN* CF14 112 A4
Neyland Cl *CHV/BDAU* CF38 65 G5
Neyland Pl *CAE/CAN/FWR* CF5 117 G4
Niagara St *PPRD* CF37 45 E4
Nicholas Cl
PENT/RAD/TFW CF15 98 A5
Nicholas St *PPOOL/BLNAV* NP4 14 C4
Nicholson Webb Cl
CAE/CAN/FWR CF5 110 B2
Nidd Cl *NWPT* NP20 39 F5
Nightingale Cl
CALD/MAG NP26 63 E4
Nightingale Gdns
CHV/BDAU CF38 81 E1
Nightingale Pl
PNRTH/DP CF64 133 G4
Nile St *PPRD* CF37 45 E4
Nine Mile Point Rd
ABRC/NBR/RIS NP11 35 F3
Ninian Park Rd
GTN/RVSD CF11 119 E3
Ninian Rd
CYN/LLD/PWYN CF23 112 D3
Nolton Pl *CWM* NP44 25 F2
The Nook *PPOOL/BLNAV* NP4 * 12 B2
Nora St *CATH/RTH/SPL* CF24 5 K2
Norbury Av
CAE/CAN/FWR CF5 117 H1
Norbury Rd
CAE/CAN/FWR CF5 117 H1
Nordale Ri *BARRYE* CF63 140 A3
Nordale Rd *LLMJ* CF61 137 E3
Norfolk Ct
PENT/RAD/TFW CF15 * 97 G4
Norfolk Rd *NWPTE* NP19 57 G3
Norfolk St *CAE/CAN/FWR* CF5 118 C2
Norman Ct *CALD/MAG* NP26 62 D4
Normandy Wy *CHEP* NP16 28 B3
Norman Rd *CDFN* CF14 111 F1
Norman St
CATH/RTH/SPL CF24 112 D5
CLN/RNWPTE NP18 42 A4
Norman Wy *CALD/MAG* NP26 63 G4
Norrell Cl *GTN/RVSD* CF11 118 C3
Norris Cl *PNRTH/DP* CF64 133 H1
Norseman Cl *BARRYI/W* CF62 144 A2
Norse Wy *CHEP* NP16 29 F5
Northam Av *CDFNE* CF3 101 H5
North Church St *CCDF* CF10 6 E1
Northcliffe *PNRTH/DP* CF64 134 D1
Northcliffe Dr
PNRTH/DP CF64 134 D1
North Clive St *GTN/RVSD* CF11 119 F5
Northcote La
CATH/RTH/SPL CF24 5 F1
Northcote St
CATH/RTH/SPL CF24 5 F1
Northcote Ter *BARRYE* CF63 140 A3
North Edward St *CCDF* CF10 4 E5
Northern Av *CDFN* CF14 98 B2
CDFN CF14 111 G1
Northern Avenue Ash Gv
CDFN CF14 98 D4
Northfield Cl
CLN/RNWPTE NP18 41 G2
Northfield Rd
CLN/RNWPTE NP18 41 H2
Northlands *CDFNE* CF3 114 A3
North Luton Pl
CATH/RTH/SPL CF24 5 H5
North Morgan St
GTN/RVSD CF11 * 119 F3
North Park Rd
CATH/RTH/SPL CF24 120 D2
North Ri *CDFN* CF14 100 B1
North Rd
ABRC/NBR/RIS NP11 23 F4
CCDF CF10 4 C4
CDFN CF14 111 H2
COWBR CF71 122 C3
CWM NP44 20 B3
PNRTH/DP CF64 140 C3
PPOOL/BLNAV NP4 12 C4
North Side *CCDF* CF10 * 129 G2
North St *GTN/RVSD* CF11 6 A3
NWPT NP20 8 D3
PPRD CF37 45 E2
Northumberland Rd
NWPTE NP19 57 G3
Northumberland St
CAE/CAN/FWR CF5 118 D3
North Vw
PENT/RAD/TFW CF15 83 G3
PPOOL/BLNAV NP4 * 14 A1
North View Ter *CAER* CF83 69 E1
North Wk *BARRYI/W* CF62 138 D3
Norton Av *CDFN* CF14 111 H1
Norwich Rd
CYN/LLD/PWYN CF23 113 H4
Norwood *CDFN* CF14 86 A5
Norwood Crs *BARRYE* CF63 140 A2
Nottage Rd
CAE/CAN/FWR CF5 117 F4
Nottingham St
CAE/CAN/FWR CF5 118 C3
Novello Wk *NWPTE* NP19 58 D4
Nuns Crs *PPRD* CF37 44 C2
Nursery Ri *CAER* CF83 49 F2
Nurston Cl *BARRYI/W* CF62 144 A2
Nut Wk *LLMJ* CF61 136 D5
Nyth-y-Dryw *BARRYI/W* CF62 144 C3
Nyth-yr-Eos *BARRYI/W* CF62 145 E4

O

Oak Cl *CALD/MAG* NP26 60 C3
CHEP NP16 30 C2
LLTR/LLH CF72 94 D3
Oak Ct *PENT/RAD/TFW* CF15 84 A5
Oakdale Cl *CLN/RNWPTE* NP18 41 G4
Oakdene Cl
CYN/LLD/PWYN CF23 113 E1
Oakfield *CLN/RNWPTE* NP18 41 G3
Oakfield Av *CHEP* NP16 28 B3
Oakfield Crs *CHV/BDAU* CF38 81 H1
Oakfield Gdns *CAER* CF83 52 A2
NWPT NP20 8 A4
Oakfield Rd *BARRYI/W* CF62 138 C2
CWM NP44 26 A2
NWPT NP20 8 A4
Oakfields *CDFNE* CF3 104 A1
Oakfield St *CAER* CF83 33 H3
CATH/RTH/SPL CF24 5 H1
Oakford Cl
CYN/LLD/PWYN CF23 101 F1
Oaklands *CLN/RNWPTE* NP18 27 F5
LLTR/LLH CF72 95 E5
Oaklands Cl *CDFNE* CF3 102 D3
Oaklands Pk *CALD/MAG* NP26 63 H3
Oaklands Park Dr *RSTN* NP10 74 B1
Oaklands Rd *NWPTE* NP19 57 G4
PPOOL/BLNAV NP4 16 D5
Oaklands Vw *CWM* NP44 18 D5
Oak La *CAER* CF83 52 A3
Oakleafe Dr
CYN/LLD/PWYN CF23 101 F2
Oakleigh Ct *CWM* NP44 24 C3
Oakley Cl *CALD/MAG* NP26 62 C2
Oakley Pl *GTN/RVSD* CF11 6 B5
Oakley St *NWPTE* NP19 77 G1
Oakley Wy *CALD/MAG* NP26 62 C2
Oakmeadow Dr *CDFNE* CF3 103 E4
Oakridge *CDFN* CF14 85 H5
Oakridge West *CDFN* CF14 86 A5
Oak Rd *RSTN* NP10 54 C3
Oaks Cl *NWPT* NP20 76 B2
Oaks Ct *PPOOL/BLNAV* NP4 12 C4
Oaksford *CWM* NP44 24 D1
Oaks Rd *PPOOL/BLNAV* NP4 12 C4
The Oaks *CAER* CF83 52 A3
CDFN CF14 86 C4
CHV/BDAU CF38 81 E2
CWM NP44 20 C3
Oak St *CWM* NP44 25 H1
NWPTE NP19 57 E1
PPRD CF37 65 H2
Oak Ter *ABRC/NBR/RIS* NP11 36 B1
Oak Tree Cl
PENT/RAD/TFW CF15 97 F4
PPOOL/BLNAV NP4 15 G5
Oak Tree Dr *RSTN* NP10 54 A2
Oakway *CAE/CAN/FWR* CF5 117 F1
Oak Wood Av
CYN/LLD/PWYN CF23 113 G3
Oakwood Cl *PNRTH/DP* CF64 128 A5
Oakwood St *PPRD* CF37 65 F2
Oban St *BARRYE* CF63 139 H3
Ocean Wy
CATH/RTH/SPL CF24 5 J7
CCDF CF10 121 E5
Ochr y Coed *CDFN* CF14 86 A4
Octavivs Cl *RSTN* NP10 91 H2
Odet Ct *CDFN* CF14 98 B3
O'Donnell Rd *BARRYE* CF63 139 G2
Odyn's Fee *BARRYI/W* CF62 144 A2
Offas Cl *CHEP* NP16 29 E5
Offa's Dyke Pth *CHEP* NP16 28 D2
Offway *CWM* NP44 25 F3
Ogmore Ct *CAER* CF83 47 H5
Ogmore Crs *NWPT* NP20 39 F5
Ogmore Pl *BARRYE* CF63 139 G1
CWM NP44 26 C1
Ogmore Rd
CAE/CAN/FWR CF5 117 F4
Ogwen Dr
CYN/LLD/PWYN CF23 100 C4
Okehampton Av *CDFNE* CF3 102 B2
Old Barn *NWPTE* NP19 57 G1
Old Barn Ct *CALD/MAG* NP26 61 E3
Old Barry Rd *PNRTH/DP* CF64 128 A5
Oldbridge Ct *CWM* NP44 18 D3
Old Bulwark Rd *CHEP* NP16 28 C5
Oldbury Rd *CWM* NP44 25 H1
Old Cardiff Rd *NWPT* NP20 76 A3
Old Castle Cl *RSTN* NP10 91 H2
Old Chepstow Rd
CLN/RNWPTE NP18 59 H1
Old Church Rd *CDFN* CF14 98 D5
Old Clipper Rd *CCDF* CF10 129 G1
Old Coach Rd *CHEP* NP16 31 G4
Old Estate Yd
PPOOL/BLNAV NP4 * 15 E5
Old Farm Ms *PNRTH/DP* CF64 133 E3
Old Field Rd
PENT/RAD/TFW CF15 98 B2
Old Furnace Rd *CAER* CF83 48 B5
Old Hall Cl *RSTN* NP10 76 A5
Old Hl *CDFNE* CF3 102 C4
CLN/RNWPTE NP18 58 B1
Old Hill Crs *CLN/RNWPTE* NP18 58 C2
Old Hill Rd *CLN/RNWPTE* NP18 58 C2
Old La *PPOOL/BLNAV* NP4 12 C3
Old Langstone Court Rd
CLN/RNWPTE NP18 59 G1
Old Malthouse
PNRTH/DP CF64 * 133 E4
Old Market *CAE/CAN/FWR* CF5 125 G5
Old Mill Dr *CAE/CAN/FWR* CF5 96 D5
Oldmill Rd *BARRYE* CF63 140 A3
Old Mill Rd *CDFN* CF14 86 B5
Old Nantgarw Rd
PENT/RAD/TFW CF15 67 F4
Old Newport Rd *CDFNE* CF3 103 E2
Old Oak Cl *CHEP* NP16 30 D2
Old Park Ter *PPRD* CF37 45 F5
Old Port Rd
CAE/CAN/FWR CF5 125 F2
Old Rd *PPOOL/BLNAV* NP4 12 C4
Old Roman Rd
CLN/RNWPTE NP18 43 H4
Old School Rd
CAE/CAN/FWR CF5 117 H3
Old Station Yd *CAER* CF83 49 G2
Old Stone La *CALD/MAG* NP26 60 D3
Old Town Dock *NWPT* NP20 77 F2
Old Vicarage Cl *CDFN* CF14 100 A2
Old Village Rd *BARRYI/W* CF62 2 A5
O'Leary Dr *GTN/RVSD* CF11 128 B3
Oliphant Cir *NWPT* NP20 40 A3
Oliver Rd *NWPTE* NP19 57 H5
Oliver St *PPRD* CF37 44 B3
Ollivant Cl *CAE/CAN/FWR* CF5 110 B2
Olway Cl *CWM* NP44 26 B2
Ombersley La *NWPT* NP20 56 A5
Ombersley Rd *NWPT* NP20 56 A5
O'Neal Av *NWPTE* NP19 77 H4
Ontario Wy
CYN/LLD/PWYN CF23 100 C5
Open Hearth Cl
PPOOL/BLNAV NP4 17 E3
Orange Gv *CAE/CAN/FWR* CF5 110 A4
Orangery Wk *RSTN* NP10 76 A5
Orbit St *CATH/RTH/SPL* CF24 5 H3
Orchard Av *CHEP* NP16 30 C2
Orchard Castle *CDFN* CF14 85 G5
Orchard Cl *CAE/CAN/FWR* CF5 125 F4
CALD/MAG NP26 62 D4
CDFNE CF3 104 A2
LLMJ CF61 137 G4
PPOOL/BLNAV NP4 13 E5
RSTN NP10 74 C1
Orchard Ct *CDFN* CF14 86 A3
NWPTE NP19 57 E2
Orchard Crs *PNRTH/DP* CF64 133 F3
Orchard Dr *BARRYI/W* CF62 139 F3
CDFN CF14 98 D5
LLMJ CF61 136 D5
Orchard Farm Cl *CHEP* NP16 29 F5
Orchard Gdns
CALD/MAG NP26 63 H3
CHEP NP16 28 D3
Orchard Gv
PENT/RAD/TFW CF15 * 97 G2
Orchard La *CWM* NP44 19 H3
NWPTE NP19 57 F2
Orchard Ldg *LLMJ* CF61 137 F3
Orchard Ms *NWPTE* NP19 57 E2
Orchard Pk *CDFNE* CF3 102 C3
Orchard Park Cl *CDFNE* CF3 102 D3
Orchard Pl *CWM* NP44 25 G1
GTN/RVSD CF11 119 E2
Orchard Ri *PNRTH/DP* CF64 134 A2
Orchard Rd
CLN/RNWPTE NP18 41 H2
Orchard St *NWPTE* NP19 57 E2
The Orchard
CLN/RNWPTE NP18 27 G5
COWBR CF71 123 F2
Orchid Cl *CDFNE* CF3 103 G4
Orchid Ct *CWM* NP44 24 D2
Orchid Dr *CALD/MAG* NP26 63 F4
Ordell St *CATH/RTH/SPL* CF24 5 K4
Oregano Cl *CDFNE* CF3 103 F2
Oriel Rd *NWPTE* NP19 9 J3
Ormerod Rd *CHEP* NP16 29 F5
Ormonde Cl
CYN/LLD/PWYN CF23 113 G2
Osborne Cl *NWPTE* NP19 9 K2
Osborne Rd
PPOOL/BLNAV NP4 14 A2
Osborne Sq *GTN/RVSD* CF11 119 F5
Osprey Cl *CDFNE* CF3 102 D2
PNRTH/DP CF64 142 C2
Osprey Ct *BARRYE* CF63 3 H2
Osprey Dr *CALD/MAG* NP26 63 E4
Oswald Rd *NWPT* NP20 76 D2
Oswestry Cl *CDFNE* CF3 114 C2
Othery Pl *CDFNE* CF3 102 B2
Otter Cl *NWPT* NP20 39 F4
Outfall La *RSTN* NP10 105 G2
Ovington Ter
CAE/CAN/FWR CF5 118 C1
Owain Cl *CYN/LLD/PWYN* CF23 112 D1
PNRTH/DP CF64 134 A3
Owen Cl *CLN/RNWPTE* NP18 41 H2
Owendale Ter
PPOOL/BLNAV NP4 12 C5
Owens Cl *BARRYI/W* CF62 139 E4
Owen St *PPRD* CF37 65 H3
Oxford Ar *CCDF* CF10 4 D5
Oxford Cl *CLN/RNWPTE* NP18 41 G2
Oxford La *CATH/RTH/SPL* CF24 5 G3
Oxford St *BARRYI/W* CF62 2 A4
CATH/RTH/SPL CF24 5 G2
CHEP NP16 28 C4
NWPTE NP19 9 K3
PENT/RAD/TFW CF15 66 D4
PPOOL/BLNAV NP4 17 E2
PPRD CF37 65 F1
Oxtens *CWM* NP44 25 E3
Oxwich Cl *CAE/CAN/FWR* CF5 117 H1
Oxwich Gv *RSTN* NP10 91 G2
Oxwich Rd *NWPTE* NP19 77 G3
Oyster Bend
PNRTH/DP CF64 141 F5
Oystermouth Wy *RSTN* NP10 91 H2

P

Pace Cl *CAE/CAN/FWR* CF5 110 B3
Pace Rd *CWM* NP44 25 E2
Pacific Rd
CATH/RTH/SPL CF24 121 E4
Padarn Cl
CYN/LLD/PWYN CF23 100 C5
Paddock Cl *CWM* NP44 19 G3
Paddock Pl *BARRYE* CF63 139 H2

Paddock Ri CWM NP44 .... 26 C2
Paddocks Crs LLTR/LLH CF72 .... 106 D2
The Paddocks
 CALD/MAG NP26 .... 61 E3
 CHV/BDAU CF38 .... 81 E1
 CLN/RNWPTE NP18 .... 41 G3
 CWM NP44 .... 26 C1
 PNRTH/DP CF64 .... 134 C5
The Paddocks CDFN CF14 .... 86 B1
 CHEP NP16 .... 30 B1
 COWBR CF71 .... 123 E4
 CYN/LLD/PWYN CF23 .... 113 E3
Page Dr CATH/RTH/SPL CF24 .... 114 A4
Paget La GTN/RVSD CF11 .... 6 A5
Paget Pl PNRTH/DP CF64 .... 134 D1
Paget Rd BARRY/W CF62 .... 3 F7
Paget St GTN/RVSD CF11 .... 6 A5
Paget Ter PNRTH/DP CF64 .... 134 D1
Palace Av CAE/CAN/FWR CF5 .... 111 F5
Palace Ct
 CYN/LLD/PWYN CF23 * 100 C4
Palace Rd CAE/CAN/FWR CF5 .... 111 F5
Palalwyf Av LLTR/LLH CF72 .... 107 F1
Pallot Wy CDFN CF14 * 95 E2
Palm Cl PPOOL/BLNAV NP4 .... 15 H5
Palmers Dr CAE/CAN/FWR CF5 .... 116 D1
Palmerston Rd BARRYE CF63 .... 140 B2
Palmer St BARRYE CF63 .... 140 B2
Palm Sq NWPT NP19 .... 57 H5
Palmyra Pl NWPT NP20 .... 4 A4
Pandy CWM NP44 .... 19 F5
Pandy La CAER CF83 .... 51 H2
Pandy-Mawr Rd CAER CF83 .... 49 F1
Pandy Vw
 ABRC/NBR/RIS NP11 .... 36 B1
Pantbach
 PENT/RAD/TFW CF15 .... 96 B2
Pantbach Av CDFN CF14 .... 111 H1
Pantbach Pl CDFN CF14 .... 111 H1
Pant-Bach Rd CDFN CF14 .... 111 H1
Panteg PENT/RAD/TFW CF15 .... 96 B2
Panteg Cl CAE/CAN/FWR CF5 .... 116 C5
Panteg Wy PPOOL/BLNAV NP4 .... 17 F1
Pant Glas CAER CF83 .... 23 G5
 CYN/LLD/PWYN CF23 .... 101 H5
Pantglas PENT/RAD/TFW CF15 .... 96 B2
Pant Glas Ct NWPT NP20 .... 74 C2
Pant Gwyn Cl CWM NP44 .... 24 C2
Pantgwynlais
 PENT/RAD/TFW CF15 .... 97 H1
Pant Llygodfa CAER CF83 .... 68 A3
Pantmawr Rd CDFN CF14 .... 98 C3
Pant Rd NWPT NP20 .... 56 C1
Pant Tawel La
 PENT/RAD/TFW CF15 .... 97 E4
Pantycelyn Dr CAER CF83 * 48 C4
Pantycelyn Rd
 PNRTH/DP CF64 .... 127 H5
Pant y Dderwen
 LLTR/LLH CF72 .... 94 B4
Pant-y-Deri Cl
 CAE/CAN/FWR CF5 * 117 F4
Pantygraigwen Rd
 PPRD CF37 .... 44 C1
Pant-y-Rheol Cl CWM NP44 .... 24 C4
Paper Mill Rd GTN/RVSD CF11 .... 118 B2
Parade PPRD CF37 .... 45 E2
The Parade BARRY/W CF62 .... 2 B7
 CATH/RTH/SPL CF24 .... 5 H1
 CDFN CF14 .... 110 D1
 CHV/BDAU CF38 .... 81 F2
 PNRTH/DP CF64 .... 133 G3
Parc Av CDFN CF14 .... 49 F4
 CWM NP44 .... 19 G4
Parc Cots CAER CF83 .... 32 A4
Parc Nant Celyn
 CHV/BDAU CF38 .... 81 H3
Parc Pontypandy CAER CF83 .... 49 F4
Parc St Catwg
 PENT/RAD/TFW CF15 .... 96 B2
Parc Ty Glas CDFN CF14 .... 99 H3
Parc-y-Brain Rd RSTN NP10 .... 55 E1
Parc-y-Bryn CHV/BDAU CF38 .... 81 E3
Parc-y-Felin St CAER CF83 .... 48 D5
Parc-Y-Nant
 PENT/RAD/TFW CF15 .... 67 F5
Pardoe Crs BARRY/W CF62 .... 139 E3
Pardoe-Thomas Cl
 NWPT NP20 * 9 F7
Parfitt St NWPT NP19 .... 78 A1
Parfitt Ter CWM NP44 .... 19 H2
Parish Rd CHV/BDAU CF38 .... 80 B5
Park Av BARRY/W CF62 .... 2 B6
 CAER CF83 .... 98 C4
 CDFN CF14 .... 98 C4
 NWPT NP20 .... 75 H3
 RSTN NP10 .... 54 C3
Park Cl CWM NP44 .... 24 C3
 NWPT NP20 .... 75 H3
 PPRD CF37 .... 65 E1
Park Ct CALD/MAG NP26 .... 61 E3
Park Crs BARRY/W CF62 .... 2 B5
 CDFN CF14 .... 98 C4
 LLTR/LLH CF72 .... 107 E1
 NWPT NP20 .... 75 H3
Parkdale Vw LLTR/LLH CF72 .... 95 F3
Park Dr NWPT NP20 .... 76 A3
Park End CLN/RNWPTE NP18 .... 43 H5
Park End Ct
 CYN/LLD/PWYN CF23 .... 100 B4
Park End La
 CYN/LLD/PWYN CF23 .... 100 B4
Parker Cl CAE/CAN/FWR CF5 .... 117 E4
Parker Rd CAE/CAN/FWR CF5 .... 117 E4
Parkers Rw
 CALD/MAG NP26 .... 12 C3
Parke's La PPOOL/BLNAV NP4 .... 14 A5
Parkfield Pl CATH/RTH/SPL CF24 .... 112 A4
 NWPT NP20 .... 8 A3
Park Gdns PPOOL/BLNAV NP4 .... 14 A5
Park Gv CCDF CF10 .... 4 D2
Parklands Cl RSTN NP10 .... 75 F1
Parkland Wk BARRY/W CF62 .... 2 B5
Park La CAER CF83 .... 68 D2
 CCDF CF10 .... 4 D2
 CDFN CF14 .... 98 C4
 PENT/RAD/TFW CF15 .... 83 E5

Parklawn Cl CWM NP44 .... 19 H2
Park Pl ABRC/NBR/RIS NP11 .... 37 F5
 CCDF CF10 .... 4 D1
Park Prospect PPRD CF37 .... 44 D2
Park Rd ABRC/NBR/RIS NP11 .... 37 F5
 BARRY/W CF62 .... 2 A5
 CALD/MAG NP26 .... 62 C2
 CDFN CF14 .... 98 C4
 PENT/RAD/TFW CF15 .... 108 D1
 PNRTH/DP CF64 .... 133 E2
 PPOOL/BLNAV NP4 .... 14 C3
Parkside CWM NP44 * 25 H1
 PPOOL/BLNAV NP4 .... 14 C3
Park Side La PPRD CF37 * 44 D3
Park Sq NWPT NP20 * 4 C4
Parkstone Av CDFNE CF3 .... 102 D2
Park St ABRC/NBR/RIS NP11 .... 36 B1
 CCDF CF10 .... 4 C4
 PPOOL/BLNAV NP4 .... 14 C3
 PPRD CF37 .... 45 E2
The Park PPOOL/BLNAV NP4 * 15 F5
Park Vw ABRC/NBR/RIS NP11 .... 36 A1
 CHEP NP16 .... 19 H2
 CWM NP44 .... 19 H2
 LLTR/LLH CF72 .... 95 E2
 PPOOL/BLNAV NP4 * 14 A1
 RSTN NP10 .... 75 E2
Park View Ct CDFN CF14 .... 98 D4
Park View Gdns RSTN NP10 .... 75 F1
Parkwall Rd
 CYN/LLD/PWYN CF23 .... 87 G5
Parkway CDFNE CF3 .... 114 D3
Park Wood Cl
 CLN/RNWPTE NP18 .... 41 F3
Parkwood Dr RSTN NP10 .... 75 E2
Parracombe Cl CDFNE CF3 .... 102 B3
Parracombe Crs CDFNE CF3 .... 102 A3
Parret Cl NWPT NP20 .... 40 A4
Parret Rd NWPT NP20 .... 40 A4
Parry Dr NWPT NP19 .... 58 B4
Parry St CAE/CAN/FWR CF5 .... 118 D2
Partridge La
 CATH/RTH/SPL CF24 .... 5 H1
Partridge Rd BARRY/W CF62 .... 137 H3
 CATH/RTH/SPL CF24 .... 5 H1
Pascal Cl CDFN CF14 .... 105 G2
Pasteur Gv CHV/BDAU CF38 .... 81 F1
The Pastures PNRTH/DP CF62 .... 139 E2
Patchway Crs CDFNE CF3 .... 114 A1
Patmore Cl
 PENT/RAD/TFW CF15 * 83 E3
Patreane Wy
 CAE/CAN/FWR CF5 .... 116 C5
Patterdale Cl
 CYN/LLD/PWYN CF23 .... 112 D3
Patti Cl NWPT NP19 .... 59 E3
Pavaland Cl CDFNE CF3 .... 103 E4
Pavilion Rd CHEP NP16 .... 31 F5
Paxton Wk RSTN NP10 .... 54 D2
Pearce Cl CDFNE CF3 .... 103 F4
Pearce Ct BARRYE CF63 .... 139 C1
Pearl Cl CATH/RTH/SPL CF24 .... 5 K4
Pearl St CATH/RTH/SPL CF24 .... 5 K3
Pearson St
 CATH/RTH/SPL CF24 .... 5 F1
Pear Tree Cl
 CLN/RNWPTE NP18 .... 41 F4
Pear Tree La NWPTE NP19 .... 78 A1
Peckham Cl
 CAE/CAN/FWR CF5 .... 110 B2
Pedlar Erw Rd CDFN CF14 .... 99 G5
Pellett St CCDF CF10 .... 5 F6
Pembroke Dr
 PNRTH/DP CF64 .... 134 B1
Pembroke Ct CAER CF83 .... 67 H1
 CHV/BDAU CF38 .... 65 C5
 PNRTH/DP CF64 .... 133 G3
Pembroke Gv NWPTE NP19 .... 77 H2
Pembroke Pl CWM NP44 .... 19 G4
 LLMJ CF61 .... 137 E3
Pembroke Rd
 CAE/CAN/FWR CF5 .... 118 C2
 CHEP NP16 .... 30 C2
Pembroke Ter
 PNRTH/DP CF64 .... 134 D1
Pembrook Ms
 CAE/CAN/FWR CF5 .... 118 C2
Penally Rd CAE/CAN/FWR CF5 .... 117 H5
Penarth Head La
 PNRTH/DP CF64 .... 134 D2
Penarth Portway
 PNRTH/DP CF64 .... 134 C1
Penarth Rd CCDF CF10 .... 4 D7
 GTN/RVSD CF11 .... 127 H2
 PNRTH/DP CF64 .... 127 H4
Penbedw CWM NP44 .... 19 G2
Penbryn Coch LLTR/LLH CF72 .... 106 A3
Pen Bryn Hendy
 LLTR/LLH CF72 .... 107 G1
Penbury Ct
 PENT/RAD/TFW CF15 * 97 G2
Pencader Rd
 CAE/CAN/FWR CF5 .... 117 H2
Pencarn Av RSTN NP10 .... 91 F1
Pencarn La RSTN NP10 .... 91 F1
Pencarn Wy RSTN NP10 .... 91 F1
Pencerrig St CAER CF83 .... 33 G5
Pencisely Crs
 CAE/CAN/FWR CF5 .... 118 B1
Pencisely Ri
 CAE/CAN/FWR CF5 .... 118 B1
Pencisely Rd
 CAE/CAN/FWR CF5 .... 118 B1
Pencisely Av
 CAE/CAN/FWR CF5 .... 118 B1
Penclawdd CAER CF83 * 49 G4
Pencoed Av PPRD CF37 .... 49 G4
Pencoed Pl CWM NP44 .... 20 A2
Pencoedtre Rd BARRYE CF63 .... 131 G4
Penda Rd CWM NP44 .... 20 A2
Pendine Cl BARRY/W CF62 .... 139 F1
Pendine Rd
 CAE/CAN/FWR CF5 .... 117 H3
Pendoylan Cl BARRYE CF63 .... 139 H1

Pendoylan Ct
 CAE/CAN/FWR CF5 .... 117 H2
Pendragon Cl CDFN CF14 .... 85 C5
Pendraw Pl
 CYN/LLD/PWYN CF23 .... 100 C4
Pendwyallt Rd CDFN CF14 .... 98 B3
Pendyris St GTN/RVSD CF11 .... 4 B7
Penedre CAE/CAN/FWR CF5 .... 111 E4
Penffordd
 PENT/RAD/TFW CF15 .... 96 B2
Pengam Rd
 CATH/RTH/SPL CF24 .... 113 H5
Pengwern Rd
 CAE/CAN/FWR CF5 .... 117 H2
Pen Hendy LLTR/LLH CF72 .... 107 G1
Penheol Ely Rd PPRD CF37 .... 45 G2
Penhevad St GTN/RVSD CF11 .... 6 A7
Penhill Cl CAE/CAN/FWR CF5 .... 118 D1
Penhill Rd GTN/RVSD CF11 .... 118 D1
Penkin Cl NWPTE NP19 .... 58 C5
Penkin Hl NWPTE NP19 .... 58 C5
Penlan Ri PNRTH/DP CF64 .... 127 H5
Penlan Rd PNRTH/DP CF64 .... 127 H4
Pen Lasgan CDFNE CF3 .... 103 E4
Penline Cl CDFN CF14 .... 98 D5
Penline Rd CDFN CF14 .... 98 D5
Penline St
 CATH/RTH/SPL CF24 .... 5 F2
Penllwyn La CAER CF83 .... 51 E2
Penllwyn St
 ABRC/NBR/RIS NP11 .... 34 B2
Penllyn Av NWPT NP20 .... 56 A5
Penllyn La CWM NP44 .... 19 H2
Penllyn Rd CAE/CAN/FWR CF5 .... 119 E3
Penmaes
 PENT/RAD/TFW CF15 .... 96 B2
Penmaes Rd CWM NP44 .... 18 C5
Penmark Gn
 CAE/CAN/FWR CF5 .... 116 D3
Penmark Rd
 CAE/CAN/FWR CF5 .... 116 D4
Penmoel La CHEP NP16 .... 29 E1
Pennant Crs
 CYN/LLD/PWYN CF23 .... 100 D4
Pennard Cl RSTN NP10 .... 91 H2
Pennard Pl CDFN CF14 .... 111 H2
Pennine Cl
 ABRC/NBR/RIS NP11 .... 38 A4
 CDFN CF14 .... 99 H3
Pennsylvania
 CYN/LLD/PWYN CF23 .... 113 F1
Penny Crs NWPT NP20 .... 40 A3
Pennyfarthing La
 CALD/MAG NP26 .... 60 C3
Pennycross Cl CDFNE CF3 .... 103 F2
Pennyroyal La CAER CF83 .... 51 H1
Penrhiw Rd
 ABRC/NBR/RIS NP11 .... 37 F4
 PPRD CF37 .... 44 C5
Penrhos Crs CDFNE CF3 .... 97 F5
Penrhos Dr CDFNE CF3 .... 114 C1
Penrhos Dr
 CLN/RNWPTE NP18 .... 42 B2
Penrhyn Cl CDFNE CF3 .... 102 D5
Penrice Gn CWM NP44 .... 24 C4
Pensarn Rd CDFNE CF3 .... 102 D5
Pensarn Wy CWM NP44 .... 24 C3
Pensidan Vw RSTN NP10 .... 74 C2
Penterry Pk CWM NP44 .... 28 B4
Pentir y De BARRY/W CF62 .... 145 E3
Pentland Cl
 ABRC/NBR/RIS NP11 .... 38 A5
 CDFN CF14 .... 99 G3
Pentonville NWPT NP20 .... 8 D2
Pentrebach Rd PPRD CF37 .... 45 F4
Pentrebane Rd
 CAE/CAN/FWR CF5 .... 110 A4
Pentrebane St CAER CF83 .... 68 D2
 GTN/RVSD CF11 .... 6 A4
Pentre Cl CWM NP44 .... 25 E3
Pentre Gdns GTN/RVSD CF11 .... 6 A4
Pentre La CWM NP44 .... 39 G2
Pentre-Poeth Cl RSTN NP10 .... 74 B2
Pentre-Poeth Rd RSTN NP10 .... 74 A3
Pentre St GTN/RVSD CF11 .... 6 A4
Pentre Tai Rd RSTN NP10 .... 54 B4
Pentwyn CAER CF83 .... 48 B3
 PENT/RAD/TFW CF15 .... 97 F4
Pentwyn Dr
 CYN/LLD/PWYN CF23 .... 101 F4
Pentwynmawr Rd
 CYN/LLD/PWYN CF23 .... 50 C5
Pen-Twyn Hts
 PPOOL/BLNAV NP4 .... 12 C4
Pentwyn Isaf CAER CF83 .... 48 C5
Pentwyn Isaf Rd CAER CF83 .... 48 C5
Pen-Twyn La NWPT NP20 .... 39 H5
Pentwyn Link Rd CDFNE CF3 .... 88 A5
Pentwyn Rd
 CYN/LLD/PWYN CF23 .... 101 E1
 CYN/LLD/PWYN CF23 .... 114 B2
Pentwyn Ter CDFNE CF3 .... 104 B2
Pentyrch St
 CATH/RTH/SPL CF24 .... 112 B5
Penuel La PPRD CF37 .... 44 D3
Penuel Rd
 PENT/RAD/TFW CF15 .... 96 A2
Pen-y-Bryn BARRY/W CF62 .... 146 B2
 CAER CF83 .... 48 A3
Pen-y-Bryn Cl NWPT NP20 .... 39 H4
Pen-y-Bryn Pl CDFN CF14 .... 112 A3
Pen-y-Bryn Rd CDFN CF14 .... 112 A3
 CYN/LLD/PWYN CF23 .... 100 D3
Pen-y-Bryn Wy CDFN CF14 .... 112 A3
Pen-y-Cae CAER CF83 .... 49 G4
Penycae Rw
 PPOOL/BLNAV NP4 * 12 C4
Pen-y-Cefn CDFN CF14 .... 85 C5
Penycoedcae Rd PPRD CF37 .... 80 A1
Pen-y-Darren La PPRD CF37 .... 44 D2
Penydarren Dr CDFN CF14 .... 98 B5
Pen-y-Dre CAER CF83 .... 48 B5
 CDFN CF14 .... 99 E4
Penyfford CAER CF83 .... 48 B5
Penygarn Rd
 CAE/CAN/FWR CF5 .... 117 G2
 PPOOL/BLNAV NP4 .... 14 C2
Penygraig CDFN CF14 .... 99 E1

Pen-y-Graig Ter
 PPOOL/BLNAV NP4 .... 14 C5
Pen-y-Groes CAER CF83 .... 48 B5
Pen-y-Groes Av CDFN CF14 .... 99 G2
Pen y Groes Gv RSTN NP10 .... 74 B2
Pen-y-Groes Rd CDFN CF14 .... 99 F3
Penylan Cl PPOOL/BLNAV NP4 .... 17 H1
 RSTN NP10 .... 74 D1
Penylan Court CWM NP44 * 27 E3
Penylan Ct
 CYN/LLD/PWYN CF23 .... 113 E2
Penylan Ov
 CYN/LLD/PWYN CF23 .... 113 E2
Pen-y-Lan Rd
 CATH/RTH/SPL CF24 .... 113 E4
 COWBR CF71 .... 125 G2
Penylan Rd NWPTE NP19 .... 57 H4
 PPOOL/BLNAV NP4 .... 10 B5
 PPRD CF37 .... 44 D1
 RSTN NP10 .... 90 A1
Pen-y-Lan Ter
 CATH/RTH/SPL CF24 .... 113 F3
Penylan Wy CWM NP44 .... 24 D3
Pen-y-Llan La
 PPOOL/BLNAV NP4 .... 15 H2
Penyparc CWM NP44 .... 19 G2
Pen-y-Peel Rd
 CAE/CAN/FWR CF5 .... 118 C2
Pen-yr-Allt CAER CF83 .... 68 C4
Pen-yr-Eglwys
 CHV/BDAU CF38 .... 81 E2
Penyrheol Rd
 PPOOL/BLNAV NP4 .... 16 C2
Pen-y-Turnpike Rd
 PNRTH/DP CF64 .... 133 F1
Pen-y-Wain La
 CATH/RTH/SPL CF24 .... 112 D4
Pen-y-Wain Pl
 CATH/RTH/SPL CF24 .... 112 D4
Pen-y-Wain Rd
 CATH/RTH/SPL CF24 .... 112 D4
Penywain St
 PPOOL/BLNAV NP4 .... 14 A3
Pen-y-Waun CHV/BDAU CF38 .... 81 F5
Pen-y-Waun
 PENT/RAD/TFW CF15 .... 96 A1
Pen-y-Waun Rd CWM NP44 * 25 G1
Pen-y-Waun Rd CWM NP44 .... 25 F1
Peppermint Dr
 CYN/LLD/PWYN CF23 .... 101 E1
Pepys Gv NWPT NP20 .... 75 H2
Percival Cl CDFN CF14 .... 85 C5
Perclose PNRTH/DP CF64 .... 133 F3
Percy Smith Rd LLMJ CF61 .... 137 F3
Peregrine Ct CALD/MAG NP26 .... 60 D3
Perrots Cl CAE/CAN/FWR CF5 .... 110 C5
Perry Ct CWM NP44 .... 18 D4
Persondy La
 CAE/CAN/FWR CF5 .... 116 C3
Perthy Cl CWM NP44 .... 25 E3
Peterswell Rd BARRY/W CF62 .... 2 B1
Petherton Pl CDFNE CF3 .... 102 B4
Pethybridge Rd
 CAE/CAN/FWR CF5 .... 117 E2
Petrel Cl PNRTH/DP CF64 .... 142 C2
Pettingale Rd CWM NP44 .... 20 C2
Petunia Wk RSTN NP10 .... 54 A2
Philip Cl CAE/CAN/FWR CF5 .... 99 G4
Philip St GTN/RVSD CF11 .... 119 E3
Philip St NWPTE NP19 .... 9 K3
Phillip St ABRC/NBR/RIS NP11 .... 37 E4
 NWPTE NP19 .... 9 K3
 PPRD CF37 .... 44 C5
The Philog CDFN CF14 .... 111 G1
Phoenix Rd CWM NP44 .... 31 E5
Phoenix Wy CDFNE CF3 .... 99 G5
Phyllis St BARRY/W CF62 .... 3 F6
The Piazza GTN/RVSD CF11 .... 6 C6
Piccadilly COWBR CF71 .... 122 B5
Pickwick Ct CDFN CF14 .... 85 C5
Picton Ct LLMJ CF61 .... 136 C2
Picton Pl GTN/RVSD CF11 .... 119 E3
Picton Rd BARRY/W CF62 .... 144 C2
 NWPTE NP19 .... 12 B5
Piercefield Av CHEP NP16 .... 28 A3
Piercefield Pl
 CATH/RTH/SPL CF24 .... 5 H2
Pierhead St CCDF CF10 .... 5 H5
Pierhead Vw PNRTH/DP CF64 .... 128 B5
Piermont Dr CHEP NP16 .... 29 E2
Pilgrim Cl
 PENT/RAD/TFW CF15 .... 97 G5
Pillmawr Cir NWPT NP20 .... 40 C4
Pillmawr Rd NWPT NP20 .... 40 C4
Pill Rw CALD/MAG NP26 .... 63 F3
Pill St CALD/MAG NP26 .... 63 G5
The Pill CALD/MAG NP26 .... 63 F3
Pilton Ct CDFN CF14 .... 111 H3
Pilton V NWPT NP20 .... 40 C3
Pine Cl CYN/LLD/PWYN CF23 .... 112 B2
Pine Ct CHV/BDAU CF38 .... 80 D5
Pine Gdns PPOOL/BLNAV NP4 .... 14 A4
Pine Gv RSTN NP10 .... 76 A4
Pinehurst Rd
 CAE/CAN/FWR CF5 .... 110 A5
The Pines CAER CF83 .... 50 D4
 CDFN CF14 .... 98 D5
Pine Tree Cl
 PENT/RAD/TFW CF15 .... 97 F3
Pine Tree Rd
 PPOOL/BLNAV NP4 .... 17 G1

Pinewood Av PPRD CF37 .... 46 A4
Pinewood Cl NWPT NP20 .... 40 C4
 PNRTH/DP CF64 .... 128 A5
Pinewood Dr
 CYN/LLD/PWYN CF23 .... 113 G2
Pinewood Hl LLTR/LLH CF72 .... 94 B3
Pinnell Pl NWPT NP20 * 9 F7
Pioden For BARRY/W CF62 .... 147 F3
Piper Ct CAE/CAN/FWR CF5 .... 111 E4
Pipkin Cl CYN/LLD/PWYN CF23 .... 101 G1
Pisgah Cl PPOOL/BLNAV NP4 .... 12 A2
Pisgah Cl PPOOL/BLNAV NP4 .... 12 B2
Pisgah Rd PPOOL/BLNAV NP4 .... 12 B2
Pitman La GTN/RVSD CF11 .... 119 F2
Pitman St GTN/RVSD CF11 .... 119 F2
Pitmedden Cl CDFNE CF3 .... 103 E3
Plane Cl PPRD CF37 .... 65 H2
Plane Tree Cl
 CLN/RNWPTE NP18 .... 41 G4
Planet St CATH/RTH/SPL CF24 .... 5 H4
Plantagenet St
 GTN/RVSD CF11 .... 4 A6
The Plantation CDFN NP44 .... 20 C4
 CALD/MAG NP26 .... 60 C3
Plas Bryn Gomer CWM NP44 .... 33 G5
Plas Cae Llwyd CAER CF83 .... 33 G5
Plas Carmel PPRD CF37 * 44 C2
Plas Cleddau BARRY/W CF62 .... 138 C4
Plas Craig CWM NP44 .... 20 A4
Plas Derwen CWM NP44 .... 26 A3
Plas Derwen CWM NP44 .... 20 B4
Plas Essyllt PNRTH/DP CF64 .... 133 E3
Plas Gwyn CDFN CF14 .... 68 C3
Plas Islwyn CWM NP44 .... 19 H4
Plas-Mawr Rd
 CAE/CAN/FWR CF5 .... 110 A4
Plas Nant CAER CF83 .... 47 F2
Plasnewydd Pl
 CATH/RTH/SPL CF24 .... 113 E5
Plasnewydd Rd
 CATH/RTH/SPL CF24 .... 5 G1
Plasnewydd Sq
 CATH/RTH/SPL CF24 .... 112 D5
Plas Pamir PNRTH/DP CF64 .... 128 B5
Plas St Andresse
 PNRTH/DP CF64 .... 134 D1
Plas St Pol De Leon
 PNRTH/DP CF64 .... 134 C1
Plassey Sq PNRTH/DP CF64 .... 134 C1
Plassey St PNRTH/DP CF64 .... 134 C1
Plas Taliesin PNRTH/DP CF64 .... 128 D5
Plas Treoda CDFN CF14 .... 111 F1
Plas Trosnant CWM NP44 .... 19 H3
Plasturton Av GTN/RVSD CF11 .... 119 G2
Plasturton Gdns
 GTN/RVSD CF11 .... 119 G2
Plasturton Pl GTN/RVSD CF11 .... 119 G2
Plas Twyn CWM NP44 .... 20 A3
Plas Ty-Coch CWM NP44 .... 20 A3
Plas Windsor CCDF CF10 * 4 E5
Plas y Biswail CDFNE CF3 * 103 E3
Plas-y-Coed
 CYN/LLD/PWYN CF23 * 112 D2
Plas y Delyn CDFN CF14 .... 86 C4
Plas-y-Llan CDFN CF14 .... 98 D5
Plas-y-Mynach
 PENT/RAD/TFW CF15 .... 110 A1
Playford Crs NWPTE NP19 .... 59 E3
Pleasant Ct
 PPOOL/BLNAV NP4 .... 12 D4
Pleasant Pl CAER CF83 .... 48 B4
Pleasant Vw BARRY/W CF62 .... 138 D1
 CHV/BDAU CF38 .... 80 B4
 PPOOL/BLNAV NP4 * 12 C3
 PPRD CF37 .... 45 E2
Plover Cl NWPTE NP19 .... 78 D3
Plover Crs CALD/MAG NP26 .... 63 E4
Plover Wy PNRTH/DP CF64 .... 142 C1
Plum Tree La
 CALD/MAG NP26 * 62 D4
Plymouth Dr
 PENT/RAD/TFW CF15 .... 97 H5
Plymouth Rd BARRY/W CF62 .... 3 F6
 PNRTH/DP CF64 .... 134 C5
Plymouth St CCDF CF10 .... 44 B2
Plymouth Wood Cl
 CAE/CAN/FWR CF5 .... 117 G2
Plymouth Wood Crs
 CAE/CAN/FWR CF5 .... 117 F2
Plymouth Wood Rd
 CAE/CAN/FWR CF5 .... 117 G2
Plym Wk NWPT NP20 .... 39 H4
Poets Cl PPRD CF37 .... 65 H1
Poets Field Rd
 BARRY/W CF62 .... 139 E1
Pollard Cl CLN/RNWPTE NP18 .... 41 F4
Pomeroy St CCDF CF10 .... 6 E6
Pommergelli Rd CDFN CF14 .... 119 E1
Pontalun Cl BARRYE CF63 .... 119 E1
Pontcanna Pl GTN/RVSD CF11 .... 119 G1
Pontcanna St GTN/RVSD CF11 .... 119 G1
Pontfaen
 CYN/LLD/PWYN CF23 .... 101 E2
Pont Faen Rd NWPTE NP19 .... 78 B1
Ponthir Rd
 CLN/RNWPTE NP18 .... 42 A2
Ponthydyrun Rd CWM NP44 .... 20 A1
Pontilas Cl
 CAE/CAN/FWR CF5 .... 116 C5
Pontshonnorton Rd
 PPRD CF37 .... 45 F1
Pont-y-Felin Av
 PPOOL/BLNAV NP4 .... 17 G3
Pont-y-Felin La
 PPOOL/BLNAV NP4 .... 17 G3
Pont-y-Felin Rd
 PPOOL/BLNAV NP4 .... 17 G3
Pontygwindy Rd CAER CF83 .... 48 B3
Pontymason Cl RSTN NP10 .... 54 B2
Pontymason La RSTN NP10 .... 54 B2
Pontypandy La CAER CF83 .... 48 D3
Pontypridd Rd
 BARRY/W CF62 .... 2 A1
Pontypridd St BARRYE CF63 .... 139 E4
Pool La NWPTE NP19 * 57 F3
Poplar Av PPOOL/BLNAV NP4 .... 15 H5
Poplar Cl CAE/CAN/FWR CF5 .... 110 A4

CALD/MAG NP26 .... 62 A3
Poplar Cl BARRY/-W CF62 ...... 139 G2
Poplar Rd CAE/CAN/FWR CF5 ... 110 A5
CAER CF83 .... 69 F4
CWM NP44 .... 20 B3
NWPTE NP19 .... 58 A4
PPRD CF37 .... 65 H2
The Poplars LLTR/LLH CF72 ..... 106 A3
Poppyfield Cl CDFNE CF3 ...... 102 D4
Poppy Pl RSTN NP10 .... 54 A2
Porfa Ballas BARRY/-W CF62 .... 145 E4
Porlock Dr PNRTH/DP CF64 ..... 141 F4
Porlock Rd CDFNE CF3 .... 102 C3
Porset Cl CAER CF83 .... 69 E1
Porset Dr CAER CF83 .... 69 E1
Portfield Crs CDFN CF14 .... 100 A3
Porthamal Gdns CDFN CF14 .... 99 F4
Porthamal Rd CDFN CF14 ...... 99 F4
Porthcawl Rd
CAE/CAN/FWR CF5 .... 117 F4
Porthkerry Pl CDFN CF14 ...... 111 H3
Porthkerry Rd
BARRY/-W CF62 .... 2 C3
Porth Mawr Rd CWM NP44 ..... 19 H4
Porth-y-Castell
BARRY/-W CF62 .... 146 B2
Porth-y-Green Cl COWBR CF71.. 122 C4
Portland Cl PNRTH/DP CF64 .... 134 D4
Portland Pl CDFN CF14 .... 77 E2
Portland St NWPT NP20 .... 77 F2
Port Madoc St CDFN CF14 ...... 102 D5
Portmanmoor Rd
CATH/RTH/SPL CF24 .... 120 D2
Portmanmoor Road La
CATH/RTH/SPL CF24 .... 120 D2
Port Ms BARRY/-W CF62 .... 131 F4
Portreeve Cl LLTR/LLH CF72 .... 95 E3
Port Rd BARRY/-W CF62 .... 138 C4
BARRY/-W CF62 .... 184 B1
NWPT NP20 .... 76 C3
Port Rd East BARRY/-W CF62 .. 138 D1
Port Rd West BARRY/-W CF62 .. 138 A4
Portwall Rd CHEP NP16 .... 28 C4
Potters Cft CHEP NP16 .... 31 F5
Potters Pde NWPT NP20 * 77 E2
Potter St NWPT NP20 .... 77 E2
Pottery Rd CDFN CF14 .... 77 E2
Pottery Ter NWPT NP20 .... 76 D2
Pound La RSTN NP10 .... 90 B2
Pound La CAE/CAN/FWR CF5 .. 125 F5
Powderham Dr
GTN/RVSD CF11 .... 119 E4
Powell Duffryn Wy
BARRY/-W CF62 .... 2 D3
Powell's Pl NWPT NP20 .... 9 G5
Power St NWPT NP20 .... 56 C5
Powis Cl RSTN NP10 .... 91 G2
Powis Vw BARRY CF63 .... 140 A2
Powys Cl PNRTH/DP CF64 .... 133 F2
Powys Dr PNRTH/DP CF64 ...... 133 F2
Powys Gdns PNRTH/DP CF64 .. 133 F2
PPRD CF37 .... 65 G1
Powys Rd PNRTH/DP CF64 ...... 134 B4
PPRD CF37 .... 66 C5
The Precinct
CHV/BDAU CF38 * 81 H1
Prendergast Pl
CAE/CAN/FWR CF5 .... 117 G5
Prescell Cl
ABRC/NBR/RIS NP11 .... 37 H4
Prescoch La
PPOOL/BLNAV NP4 .... 16 C2
Prestatyn Rd CDFNE CF3 .... 102 C3
Presteign Av CHV/BDAU CF38 .. 81 G1
Preston Av NWPT NP20 .... 56 A5
Preston Cl CHEP NP16 .... 30 D3
Preswylfa St
CAE/CAN/FWR CF5 .... 118 C2
Price Av BARRY CF63 .... 139 H2
Price Cl NWPT NP20 .... 76 A2
PPOOL/BLNAV NP4 .... 14 C1
Priestley Cl NWPT NP20 .... 76 A2
Priest Rd CATH/RTH/SPL CF24 .. 5 K1
Primrose Cl CDFNE CF3 .... 114 B3
COWBR CF71 .... 123 E4
Primrose Ct CWM NP44 .... 24 C2
Primrose Hl COWBR CF71 ...... 123 E4
Primrose Wy RSTN NP10 .... 54 A2
Prince Leopold St
CATH/RTH/SPL CF24 .... 5 J4
Prince of Wales Dr
CAE/CAN/FWR CF5 .... 96 D5
Princes Av CAER CF83 .... 69 E3
CATH/RTH/SPL CF24 .... 5 J4
Princes Ct
CATH/RTH/SPL CF24 .... 5 F3
Princes Ri CAER CF83 * 45 E5
Princess St BARRY CF63 .... 2 D3
CATH/RTH/SPL CF24 .... 5 H2
Prince St NWPT NP19 .... 9 H1
PPOOL/BLNAV NP4 .... 14 B3
Priory Cl CALD/MAG NP26 ...... 62 D2
CHEP NP16 .... 28 B3
CLN/RNWPTE NP18 .... 41 F4
PPRD CF37 .... 44 C1
Priory Crs ABRC/NBR/RIS NP11 .. 23 E3
Priory Ct CLN/RNWPTE NP18 .. 59 G1
Priory Dr BARRY CF63 .... 139 H1
Priory Gdns BARRY CF63 .... 139 H1
CLN/RNWPTE NP18 .... 43 G5
Priory Gv CLN/RNWPTE NP18 .. 59 F1
Priory St ABRC/NBR/RIS NP11 .. 37 F5
Priory Wy CLN/RNWPTE NP18 .. 43 G5
Pritchard Cl
CAE/CAN/FWR CF5 .... 110 C3
Probert Pl NWPTE NP19 .... 9 J2
Proctor Cl BARRY/-W CF62 ..... 138 C4
Promenade BARRY/-W CF62 ... 147 E3
The Promenade
PPOOL/BLNAV NP4 .... 12 B4
Prospect Crs CALD/MAG NP26 .. 63 E3
Prospect Dr
CAE/CAN/FWR CF5 .... 110 C5
Prospect Pl CWM NP44 .... 25 H1
PPOOL/BLNAV NP4 .... 17 G2
Prospect St NWPT NP20 .... 56 D5
Pugsley St NWPT NP20 .... 56 D3

Pum Erw Rd CDFN CF14 .... 99 G5
Pump St NWPT NP20 .... 8 D5
Purbeck St CAE/CAN/FWR CF5 .. 118 D2
Purcell Rd CDFNE CF3 .... 102 C3
PNRTH/DP CF64 .... 134 B5
Purcell Sq NWPTE NP19 .... 58 B4
Purdey Cl BARRY/-W CF62 ...... 138 C2
Pwllgwaun Rd PPRD CF37 ...... 44 C3
Pwllhelig
CAE/CAN/FWR CF5 .... 98 A2
Pwll Mawr Av CDFNE CF3 .... 115 E3
Pwllmawr Ct CDFNE CF3 .... 114 C3
Pwllmelin La
CAE/CAN/FWR CF5 .... 110 D5
Pwllmelin Rd
CAE/CAN/FWR CF5 .... 110 B4
Pye Cnr RSTN NP10 .... 75 F1
Pyle Rd CAE/CAN/FWR CF5 .... 117 F4
Pytchley Cl LLTR/LLH CF72 ..... 95 F3

Q

Quail Ct CATH/RTH/SPL CF24 .. 5 H1
Quantock Cl
ABRC/NBR/RIS NP11 .... 37 H5
Quantock Dr NWPTE NP19 ..... 58 B3
Quarella St BARRY CF63 .... 139 H5
Quarry Cl CAE/CAN/FWR CF5 .. 110 A5
Quarry Crs CAE/CAN/FWR CF5 .. 117 F1
Quarry Dl CDFNE CF3 .... 114 B3
Quarry Rd CAE/CAN/FWR CF5 .. 60 C2
Quarry Rd PPRD CF37 .... 44 B3
Quarry St
PENT/RAD/TFW CF15 .... 67 E4
Quay St CCDF CF10 .... 4 C5
Quebec Cl NWPT NP20 .... 8 D5
Queen Anne Sq CCDF CF10 .... 4 B1
Queen Ar CCDF CF10 * 4 D4
Queensbury Rd
CYN/LLD/PWYN CF23 .... 113 G2
Queen's Cft NWPT NP20 .... 56 C3
Queen's Cft NWPT NP20 .... 56 C3
Queen Cl CAE/CAN/FWR CF5 .. 125 C1
CHV/BDAU CF38 .... 81 E4
Queens Gdns CALD/MAG NP26 .. 60 B3
Queen's Hl NWPT NP20 .... 8 D1
Queen's Hill Crs NWPT NP20 ... 8 C1
Queen's Rd CHEP NP16 .... 30 C1
PNRTH/DP CF64 .... 134 D1
Queens Rd South CCDF CF10 .. 129 F4
Queen St BARRY/-W CF62 .... 2 C5
CCDF CF10 .... 4 D4
NWPT NP20 .... 8 E6
PENT/RAD/TFW CF15 .... 97 H1
PPRD CF37 .... 45 F5
Queensway NWPT NP20 .... 8 D3
PENT/RAD/TFW CF15 .... 83 G3
Queensway NWPT NP20 .... 8 D3
Queenswood
CYN/LLD/PWYN CF23 .... 113 G2
Queen Wood Cl
CYN/LLD/PWYN CF23 .... 113 E2
Quentin St CDFN CF14 .... 112 A3
Quilter Cl NWPTE NP19 .... 58 C5

R

Rachel Cl CAE/CAN/FWR CF5 .. 110 B2
Rachel Sq RSTN NP10 .... 91 H1
Radnor Cl CHV/BDAU CF38 ..... 65 G5
Radnor Rd CAE/CAN/FWR CF5 .. 118 C2
LLMJ CF61 .... 137 F3
NWPTE NP19 .... 57 F3
Radnor Wy CWM NP44 .... 19 H5
Radyr Court Cl
CAE/CAN/FWR CF5 * 110 D3
Radyr Court Ri
CAE/CAN/FWR CF5 * 110 D3
Radyr Court Rd
CAE/CAN/FWR CF5 .... 110 B3
Radyr Farm Rd
PENT/RAD/TFW CF15 .... 110 A1
Radyr Pl CDFN CF14 .... 111 H3
Radyr Rd CDFN CF14 .... 110 D3
Raglan Cl CDFNE CF3 .... 103 F3
PPOOL/BLNAV NP4 .... 15 E5
Raglan Ct CAER CF83 * 48 A5
CWM NP44 .... 20 A2
NWPT NP20 .... 9 F7
Raglande Ct LLMJ CF61 .... 136 C4
Raglan St ABRC/NBR/RIS NP11 .. 36 D3
Raglan Wy CHEP NP16 .... 30 D2
Ragnall Cl CDFN CF14 .... 85 H4
Railway Crs
CATH/RTH/SPL CF24 .... 5 J4
Railway St
ABRC/NBR/RIS NP11 .... 37 G4
CAER CF83 .... 5 K4
CDFN CF14 .... 112 A4
CLN/RNWPTE NP18 .... 42 A3
NWPT NP20 .... 8 E3
Railway Ter CAER CF83 .... 69 F5
GTN/RVSD CF11 .... 119 E3
LLTR/LLH CF72 .... 94 C4
PENT/RAD/TFW CF15 .... 97 H1
PNRTH/DP CF64 .... 134 D2
PPOOL/BLNAV NP4 .... 17 E5
Railway Vw CALD/MAG NP26 .. 63 F4
Raisdale Gdns
PNRTH/DP CF64 .... 134 D4
Raisdale Rd PNRTH/DP CF64 .. 134 C4
Raldan Cl BARRY CF63 .... 133 G5
Raleigh Wk CCDF CF10 * 5 F7
Rambler Cl CDFN CF14 .... 85 H4
Ramping Rd
ABRC/NBR/RIS NP11 .... 23 F5
The Ramp CALD/MAG NP26 .... 61 E4
Ramsey Rd BARRY/-W CF62 ... 139 F1
Ramsey Wk NWPTE NP19 .... 57 G2

Ramsons Wy
CAE/CAN/FWR CF5 .... 116 D3
Rankine Cl NWPT NP20 .... 40 A4
Rannoch Dr
CYN/LLD/PWYN CF23 .... 100 D5
Raphael Cl NWPTE NP19 .... 57 H2
Ravensbrook
CWM NP44 .... 19 E5
Ravenscourt CWM NP44 .... 19 E5
Ravenshoe Rd BARRYE CF63 .. 140 B2
Ravenswood Ct
ABRC/NBR/RIS NP11 .... 36 D3
Raven Wk
CATH/RTH/SPL CF24 .... 22 B3
Raven Wy PNRTH/DP CF64 ..... 142 C2
Rawden Ms GTN/RVSD CF11 .. 119 F5
Rawden Pl GTN/RVSD CF11 .... 119 F5
Readers La BARRY/-W CF62 .... 144 C5
Readers Wy BARRY/-W CF62 .. 144 C5
Reardon Smith Ct
CAE/CAN/FWR CF5 .... 110 B5
Rectory Cl CAE/CAN/FWR CF5 .. 110 A3
CAER CF83 .... 68 D3
Rectory Ct LLMJ CF61 .... 137 E1
Rectory Gdns CAER CF83 * 49 H2
CAER CF83 .... 51 H2
CALD/MAG NP26 .... 61 E4
Rectory Rd BARRYE CF63 .... 139 H3
CAE/CAN/FWR CF5 .... 118 D2
CAER CF83 .... 49 H2
PNRTH/DP CF64 .... 134 D2
Rectory Road La
PNRTH/DP CF64 .... 134 D2
Redberth Cl BARRY/-W CF62 .. 139 F2
Red Brink Ct
CAE/CAN/FWR CF5 * 117 F2
Redbrink Crs BARRY/-W CF62 .. 3 H7
Redbrook Av CAER CF83 .... 50 B3
Redbrook Ct CAER CF83 .... 50 B3
Redbrook Rd NWPT NP20 ...... 55 H4
Redbrook Wy CWM NP44 .... 19 H5
Redcliffe Av
CAE/CAN/FWR CF5 .... 118 B2
The Reddings CHEP NP16 ...... 30 D2
Rede Rd CWM NP44 .... 25 E2
Red House Cl
CAE/CAN/FWR CF5 .... 117 F2
Red House Crs
CAE/CAN/FWR CF5 .... 117 F3
Red House Pl
CAE/CAN/FWR CF5 .... 117 G2
Red House Rd
CAE/CAN/FWR CF5 .... 117 F2
Redlands Av PNRTH/DP CF64 .. 133 H2
Redlands Rd PNRTH/DP CF64 .. 134 A2
The Redlands NWPTE NP19 .... 58 B5
Redland St NWPT NP20 .... 56 D4
Redlaver St GTN/RVSD CF11 .. 6 A3
Redmeadow Crs
CALD/MAG NP26 .... 63 F4
Redvers St NWPTE NP19 .... 57 G5
Redwick Cl NWPT NP20 .... 55 H4
Redwick Rd CALD/MAG NP26 .. 60 B3
Redwood Cl CDFNE CF3 .... 102 D5
CWM NP44 .... 30 C2
CLN/RNWPTE NP18 .... 41 F4
LLMJ CF61 .... 137 F4
Redwood Ct CDFN CF14 .... 100 A2
Redwood Dr CHV/BDAU CF38 .. 80 D4
Reene Ct NWPTE NP19 .... 57 H2
Rees Cl NWPT NP20 .... 40 B3
Rees Rd NWPT NP20 .... 40 B3
Regency Cl LLMJ CF61 .... 136 D2
Regent Gdns CDFN CF14 .... 98 D2
Regents Ga CDFNE CF3 .... 103 E5
Regent's Ga PNRTH/DP CF64 .. 134 A4
Regina Ter CAE/CAN/FWR CF5 .. 98 C2
Reigate Cl CDFN CF14 .... 85 H4
Relf Rd CDFNE CF3 .... 114 C1
Rembrandt Wy NWPTE NP19 .. 57 G2
Rennie St GTN/RVSD CF11 ..... 119 F3
Renoir Rd NWPTE NP19 .... 57 H2
Reservoir Ct RSTN NP10 .... 75 H1
Restways Cl
CAE/CAN/FWR CF5 .... 110 A3
The Retreat CALD/MAG NP26 .. 62 D4
CYN/LLD/PWYN CF23 .... 113 G2
Reynolds Cl NWPT NP20 .... 57 G2
Rheidol Cl CDFN CF14 .... 100 B2
Rheidol Dr BARRY/-W CF62 .... 138 D3
Rhigos Gdns
CATH/RTH/SPL CF24 .... 112 B4
Rhine Cl CDFNE CF3 .... 98 D2
Rhiw Fach CAER CF83 .... 48 B4
Rhiw Felin PPRD CF37 .... 65 H1
Rhiwias CDFN CF14 .... 85 E5
Rhiw Melin CWM NP44 .... 19 E2
Rhiw'r Ddar
PENT/RAD/TFW CF15 .... 83 F2
Rhiwsaeson Rd
LLTR/LLH CF72 .... 95 H3
Rhodfa Felin BARRY/-W CF62 .. 2 A2
Rhodfa Marics LLTR/LLH CF72 .. 94 C1
Rhodfa Mor BARRY/-W CF62 ... 145 E4
Rhodfar Orsaf
CHV/BDAU CF38 .... 81 G2
Rhodfa Sweldon
BARRY/-W CF62 .... 3 F3
Rhododendron Ct
CYN/LLD/PWYN CF23 .... 101 E3
Rhodri Pl CWM NP44 .... 26 C1
Rhondda Rd PPRD CF37 .... 44 C3
Rhoose Rd BARRY/-W CF62 .... 144 D5
Rhos Ddu PNRTH/DP CF64 .... 134 A4
Rhos Helyg CAER CF83 .... 49 G5
Rhos Llan CDFN CF14 .... 99 F3
Rhossily Av CDFNE CF3 .... 114 C1
Rhos St CAER CF83 .... 48 D4
Rhuddlan Cl RSTN NP10 .... 74 B1
Rhuddlan Ct CAER CF83 .... 47 H4
Rhuddlan Wy PNRTH/DP CF64 .. 133 G2
Rhydlafar Dr CDFN CF14 .... 111 H1
Rhyd-y-Gwern Cl CAER CF83 .. 49 G4
Rhyd y Gwern Isaf CAER CF83 .. 51 H2
Rhyd y Nant LLTR/LLH CF72 .. 107 F1
Rhyd-y-Penau Cl
CYN/LLD/PWYN CF23 .... 100 B4

Rhyd-y-Penau Rd CDFN CF14 .. 100 B4
Rhygoes St
CATH/RTH/SPL CF24 .... 112 B4
Rhyl Rd CDFNE CF3 .... 114 C1
Rhymney Crs CWM NP44 .... 18 D5
Rhymney River Bridge Rd
CYN/LLD/PWYN CF23 .... 113 H4
Rhymney St
CATH/RTH/SPL CF24 .... 4 E1
Rhymney Ter CAER CF83 .... 68 D2
CATH/RTH/SPL CF24 .... 112 C5
Rhymney Valley
Ridgeway Footpath
ABRC/NBR/RIS NP11 .... 35 H4
CAER CF83 .... 85 F1
PENT/RAD/TFW CF15 .... 47 E4
Rhyswg Rd
ABRC/NBR/RIS NP11 .... 23 E1
Rialto Ct CAE/CAN/FWR CF5 .. 99 E5
Richard Lewis Cl
CAE/CAN/FWR CF5 .... 110 C3
Richards Pl
CATH/RTH/SPL CF24 .... 5 K1
Richards St
CATH/RTH/SPL CF24 .... 112 C5
Richards Ter
CATH/RTH/SPL CF24 .... 5 K1
Richard St BARRY/-W CF62 ..... 3 H1
Richmond Cl CAER CF83 .... 48 C5
Richmond Crs
CATH/RTH/SPL CF24 .... 5 F2
PNRTH/DP CF64 .... 134 D2
Richmond Rd
CATH/RTH/SPL CF24 .... 5 F2
CWM NP44 .... 19 H3
NWPTE NP19 .... 57 F2
PPOOL/BLNAV NP4 .... 17 E5
Richs Rd CDFN CF14 .... 111 H1
Ridgeway CAER CF83 .... 48 C5
CDFN CF14 .... 86 B4
NWPT NP20 .... 55 H5
PPOOL/BLNAV NP4 .... 14 D1
Ridgeway Cl NWPT NP20 .... 55 H5
Ridgeway Cr NWPT NP20 .... 55 H5
Ridgeway Crs NWPT NP20 ..... 55 H5
Ridgeway Hl NWPT NP20 .... 56 A4
Ridgeway Vw NWPT NP20 ...... 56 A4
Ridgeway Pl
PPRD CF37 .... 44 C2
Ridgeway Pk Rd
NWPT NP20 .... 55 H4
Ridgeway Pl CHV/BDAU CF38 .. 81 H1
Ridgeway Reach NWPT NP20 .. 56 A4
Ridgeway Ri NWPT NP20 .... 56 A4
Ridgeway Rd CDFNE CF3 .... 101 H5
Ridgeway Vw NWPT NP20 ...... 56 A4
Ridgeway Vls NWPT NP20 ...... 56 A4
Ridgeway Vw NWPT NP20 ...... 56 A4
The Ridings CHV/BDAU CF38 .. 81 H1
Rifleman St
ABRC/NBR/RIS NP11 .... 37 E3
Ringland Cir NWPTE NP19 ...... 58 C5
Ringland Wy NWPTE NP19 ..... 58 C5
Ringwood Av NWPTE NP19 .... 58 C5
Ringwood Hl NWPTE NP19 .... 58 C5
Ringwood Pl NWPTE NP19 ..... 58 C4
Risca Cl CDFNE CF3 .... 103 E3
Risca Rd ABRC/NBR/RIS NP11 .. 54 A1
RSTN NP10 .... 54 A1
The Rise CDFN CF14 .... 100 B1
CHV/BDAU CF38 .... 65 G5
NWPT NP20 .... 19 F3
PPRD CF37 .... 66 B1
River Gld
PENT/RAD/TFW CF15 .... 83 E3
Rivermead Wy RSTN NP10 ..... 54 A2
River Rw PPOOL/BLNAV NP4 .. 14 A1
Riversdale CAE/CAN/FWR CF5 .. 110 C5
Rivers Edge LLTR/LLH CF72 ... 107 E1
Riverside PPOOL/BLNAV NP4 .. 14 A1
Riverside Pl BARRYE CF63 ...... 140 B3
Riverside St
PENT/RAD/TFW CF15 .... 83 E2
Riverside Ter
CAE/CAN/FWR CF5 .... 118 A2
CAER CF83 .... 51 G3
River St PPRD CF37 .... 45 F5
River Vw CDFN CF14 .... 111 E3
CWM NP44 .... 28 C4
River View Ct
CAE/CAN/FWR CF5 .... 110 D3
River Wk COWBR CF71 .... 122 C4
River Wy PNRTH/DP CF64 ...... 136 C3
LLMJ CF61 .... 128 B5
Roath Court Pl
CATH/RTH/SPL CF24 .... 113 F5
Roath Court Rd
CATH/RTH/SPL CF24 .... 113 F5
Roath Dock Rd CCDF CF10 .... 120 D5
Robbins La NWPT NP20 .... 9 F5
Robert Cl NWPT NP20 .... 76 D2
Roberts Cl RSTN NP10 .... 54 D2
Robertson Wy NWPT NP20 .... 40 D3
Robert St BARRYE CF63 .... 139 H4
CAE/CAN/FWR CF5 .... 118 A2
CATH/RTH/SPL CF24 .... 112 C4
Robin Cl CYN/LLD/PWYN CF23 .. 101 E3
Robin Hl PNRTH/DP CF64 ...... 133 F4
Robins La BARRYE CF63 .... 139 H3
Robinswood Cl
PNRTH/DP CF64 .... 134 C4
Robinswood Crs
PNRTH/DP CF64 .... 134 C4
Roche Crs CAE/CAN/FWR CF5 .. 110 A4
Rochester Rd NWPTE NP19 .... 57 G4
Rockdale CALD/MAG NP26 .... 61 E3
Rockfield Gv CALD/MAG NP26 .. 61 E3
Rockfield Ri CALD/MAG NP26 .. 61 E3
Rockfield St NWPTE NP19 ...... 57 F2
Rockfield Vw CALD/MAG NP26 .. 61 E2
Rockfield Wy CALD/MAG NP26 .. 61 E2
Rockfield Crs CALD/MAG NP26 .. 61 E3
Rockhill Rd PPOOL/BLNAV NP4 .. 15 H4
Rock Villa Cl
PPOOL/BLNAV NP4 .... 10 B5
Rock Villa La CHEP NP16 .... 28 D3
Rockwood Rd CHEP NP16 ...... 28 C5

PENT/RAD/TFW CF15 .... 83 G3
Roding Cl NWPT NP20 .... 39 G5
Rodney Rd NWPTE NP19 .... 9 F2
Rogersmoor Cl
PNRTH/DP CF64 .... 134 C4
Rogerstone Cl CDFNE CF3 ...... 103 E3
Rogiate Rd CALD/MAG NP26 .. 62 B3
Roland Dr CAER CF83 .... 68 B3
Roland St CCDF CF10 .... 5 F7
Rolls Cl CWM NP44 .... 24 D1
Rolls St CAE/CAN/FWR CF5 .... 119 E3
Rolls Wk RSTN NP10 .... 54 D1
Roman Cl CAE/CAN/FWR CF5 .. 117 G5
Roman Gates
CLN/RNWPTE NP18 .... 42 B4
Roman Reach
CLN/RNWPTE NP18 .... 41 F4
Roman Wy
CLN/RNWPTE NP18 .... 41 H3
Romilly Crs GTN/RVSD CF11 .. 119 E2
Romilly Park Rd
BARRY/-W CF62 .... 2 A5
Romilly Pl CAE/CAN/FWR CF5 .. 118 D2
Romilly Rd BARRY/-W CF62 .... 2 C4
CAE/CAN/FWR CF5 .... 144 C2
Romilly Rd West
CAE/CAN/FWR CF5 .... 118 C1
Romney Cl NWPTE NP19 .... 57 H2
Ronald Pl CAE/CAN/FWR CF5 .. 117 G2
Ronald Rd NWPTE NP19 .... 57 F3
Rook Cl BARRY/-W CF62 .... 137 G4
Rookery Wd
PNRTH/DP CF64 .... 141 E4
Rookwood Av
CAE/CAN/FWR CF5 .... 110 D4
Rookwood Cl
CAE/CAN/FWR CF5 .... 110 D4
Rookwood St
GTN/RVSD CF11 .... 119 F5
Roper Cl CAE/CAN/FWR CF5 .. 110 B3
Rosamund Cl RSTN NP10 .... 92 A2
The Rosary CHEP NP16 .... 28 B3
Rosebery Pl PNRTH/DP CF64 .. 141 E4
Rosebery St
PPOOL/BLNAV NP4 .... 17 E2
Rose Ct CWM NP44 .... 24 C1
Rosecroft Dr
CLN/RNWPTE NP18 .... 59 H1
Rosedale Cl
CAE/CAN/FWR CF5 .... 110 A5
The Rosegarden NWPTE NP20 .. 56 A4
Rosemary La
PPOOL/BLNAV NP4 .... 14 C4
Rosemary St CCDF CF10 .... 5 F6
Rosemead CWM NP44 .... 18 C5
Rosemont Av
ABRC/NBR/RIS NP11 .... 37 F4
Rosemount Pl CDFN CF14 ...... 111 H2
Rosendale Ct NWPTE NP19 .... 57 G4
Rose St CATH/RTH/SPL CF24 .. 5 G1
NWPTE NP19 .... 8 D1
Rose Wk RSTN NP10 .... 54 A2
Rosewood Cl CDFN CF14 .... 86 B4
Ross Cl PPRD CF37 .... 64 C1
Rosser St PPOOL/BLNAV NP4 .. 14 A3
PPRD CF37 .... 44 C4
Rosset Cl CDFNE CF3 .... 102 D4
Rossetti Cl CAE/CAN/FWR CF5 .. 57 H2
Ross La NWPT NP20 .... 56 C2
Rosslyn Rd NWPTE NP19 .... 57 E4
Ross St NWPT NP20 .... 56 C1
Rother Cl NWPT NP20 .... 39 G5
Rothesay Rd NWPTE NP19 ..... 57 G4
Rougemont Gv CHEP NP16 .... 30 D3
Roundel Cl CDFN CF14 .... 86 A3
Round Wd
CYN/LLD/PWYN CF23 .... 101 F5
Round Wood Cl
CYN/LLD/PWYN CF23 .... 113 G2
Routs Vw CLN/RNWPTE NP18 .. 59 G4
Rover Wy CATH/RTH/SPL CF24 .. 113 H5
CCDF CF10 .... 129 H1
Rowan Cl CALD/MAG NP26 * .. 60 D2
PNRTH/DP CF64 .... 134 C5
PPRD CF37 .... 64 C1
Rowan Crs PPOOL/BLNAV NP4 .. 16 D3
Rowan Dr CHEP NP16 .... 30 D2
Rowan Rd
ABRC/NBR/RIS NP11 .... 37 G4
Rowan Tree La LLTR/LLH CF72 .. 95 E5
Rowan Wy CDFN CF14 .... 86 C4
NWPT NP20 .... 40 C3
Rowen Gdns CHV/BDAU CF38 .. 81 F3
Roxburgh Garden Ct
PNRTH/DP CF64 * 134 D3
Roxby Ct CCDF CF10 .... 7 F1
Royal Ar CCDF CF10 * 4 D6
Royal Cl CDFNE CF3 .... 134 C1
Royal Cl CAER CF83 .... 52 A3
Royal Oak Cl CAER CF83 .... 52 A3
Royal Oak Dr
CLN/RNWPTE NP18 .... 58 D2
Royal Oak Hl
CLN/RNWPTE NP18 .... 58 C2
Royal Stuart La CCDF CF10 .... 7 F5
Royde Cl CAE/CAN/FWR CF5 .. 116 B4
Royston Crs NWPTE NP19 ...... 58 A5
Rubens Cl NWPTE NP19 .... 57 G2
Ruby St CATH/RTH/SPL CF24 .. 5 J3
Rudry Cl CAER CF83 .... 49 H4
Rudry Rd CAER CF83 .... 49 G4
CAER CF83 .... 86 D4
Rudry St GTN/RVSD CF11 ...... 119 F5
PNRTH/DP CF64 .... 134 B2
Ruffet's Cl CHEP NP16 .... 28 B4
Rugby Rd NWPTE NP19 .... 9 H3
Runcorn Cl BARRYE CF63 ...... 140 B2
Runway Rd
CATH/RTH/SPL CF24 .... 121 F1
Ruperra Cl CDFNE CF3 .... 102 C1
RSTN NP10 .... 75 E1
Ruperra La NWPT NP20 .... 9 F6
Ruperra St LLTR/LLH CF72 ..... 94 C5
NWPT NP20 .... 9 F6
Rupert Brooke Dr NWPT NP20 .. 76 A2
Rushbrook Cl CDFN CF14 .... 110 C1

Ruskin Av RSTN NP10.....54 D2
Ruskin Cl CDFNE CF3.....102 A3
CWM NP44.....24 C1
Ruskin Ri NWPT NP20.....75 H2
Russell Cl PPOOL/BLNAV NP4.....17 H1
RSTN NP10.....74 C1
Russell Dr NWPT NP20.....75 H2
Russell St CATH/RTH/SPL CF24.....5 H3
CWM NP44.....19 H3
Russet Cl CLN/RNWPTE NP18 *.....59 E1
Rutherford Hl NWPT NP20.....40 B3
Ruthin Gdns
CATH/RTH/SPL CF24.....4 D1
Ruthin Wy CHV/BDAU CF38.....65 G5
Ruth Rd PPOOL/BLNAV NP4.....15 F5
Rutland Pl NWPT NP20.....8 E7
Rutland St GTN/RVSD CF11.....119 F2
Ryder St GTN/RVSD CF11.....119 F2

S

Sable Cl CDFN CF14.....86 B3
Sachville Av CDFN CF14.....112 A3
Saffron Ct CWM NP44.....24 C2
Saffron Dr CDFNE CF3.....103 F2
St Agatha Rd CDFN CF14.....112 A1
St Agnes Rd CDFN CF14.....111 H1
St Aidan Crs CDFN CF14.....111 H1
St Alban Av CDFN CF14.....111 H1
St Ambrose Cl
PNRTH/DP CF64.....133 E4
St Ambrose Rd CDFN CF14.....112 A1
St Andrew's Av CHEP NP16.....28 C5
St Andrews Cl
CHV/BDAU CF38 *.....81 E4
CWM NP44.....20 A1
St Andrew's Cl PPRD CF37.....64 C1
St Andrew's La CCDF CF10.....4 E3
St Andrew's Pl CCDF CF10.....4 E3
St Andrew's Wy
BARRY/I/W CF62.....139 E3
PNRTH/DP CF64.....132 A2
St Angela Rd CDFN CF14.....112 A1
St Anne's Av PNRTH/DP CF64.....134 B4
St Anne's Cl CWM NP44.....19 H5
RSTN NP10.....55 E5
St Annes Ct LLTR/LLH CF72.....106 D3
St Annes Crs CALD/MAC NP26.....61 E3
St Anne's Crs NWPTE NP19.....57 F2
St Annes Dr CHV/BDAU CF38.....81 E4
St Annes Gdns CAER CF83.....47 F3
St Anns Ct BARRY/I/W CF62 *.....139 C1
St Ann St CHEP NP16.....28 D3
St Anthony Rd CDFN CF14.....112 A1
St Anthony's Ct
PPOOL/BLNAV NP4.....16 D3
St Arvans Crs CDFNE CF3.....103 E3
St Arvans Rd CWM NP44.....24 C1
St Asaph Cl CDFN CF14.....99 H4
St Asaph's Wy CAER CF83.....68 D3
St Athan Rd COWBR CF71.....122 D5
St Athan's Ct CAER CF83.....68 C1
St Augustine's Crs
PNRTH/DP CF64.....134 D1
St Augustine's Pl
PNRTH/DP CF64.....134 D1
St Augustine's Rd
PNRTH/DP CF64.....134 D1
St Baruch Cl PNRTH/DP CF64.....133 E4
St Baruchs Ct BARRY/I/W CF62.....3 G6
St Basil's Crs RSTN NP10.....74 D1
St Benedict Cl
PPOOL/BLNAV NP4 *.....16 D3
St Benedict Crs CDFN CF14.....112 A1
St Bleddian Cl COWBR CF71.....122 B5
St Brannocks Cl
BARRY/I/W CF62.....138 C4
St Bride's Cl CALD/MAC NP26.....60 B2
St Brides Cl CWM NP44.....26 B1
St Brides Gdns NWPT NP20.....8 C5
St Brides Gdns NWPT NP20.....76 A4
St Brides Mnr CHV/BDAU CF38.....81 E5
St Bride's Rd
CAE/CAN/FWR CF5.....108 B5
CALD/MAC NP26.....60 B1
St Bride's Wy BARRY/I/W CF63.....139 G1
St Brigid Rd CDFN CF14.....99 H4
St Brioc Rd CDFN CF14.....99 H5
St Cadoc Rd CDFN CF14.....99 H5
St Cadoc's Av PNRTH/DP CF64.....133 G3
St Cadoc's Cl
CLN/RNWPTE NP18.....41 H3
St Cadoc's Ri BARRY/I/W CF63 *.....140 B5
St Cadoc's Rd
PPOOL/BLNAV NP4.....14 D2
St Catherine's Cl CAER CF83 *.....49 G3
St Catherine's Ct
ABRC/NBR/RIS NP11.....36 A2
BARRY/I/W CF62.....139 F1
St Catherines Ms
GTN/RVSD CF11 *.....119 E1
St Catherines Pk
CATH/RTH/SPL CF24.....114 A5
St Cenydd Cl CAER CF83.....48 B5
St Cenydd Rd CAER CF83.....68 B1
CDFN CF14.....100 A4
St Christopher's Cl CAER CF83.....48 C5
St Christopher's Dr CAER CF83.....68 C2
St Clears Cl CAER CF83.....68 D2
St Curig's Cl BARRY/I/W CF62.....144 C3
St Cyres Cl PNRTH/DP CF64.....134 A3
St Cyres Rd PNRTH/DP CF64.....134 A3
St David Av PNRTH/DP CF64.....133 F2
St David's Av CHV/BDAU CF38.....81 F2
LLMJ CF61.....136 D4
St David's Cl CHEP NP16.....28 E3
St Davids Crs
CAE/CAN/FWR CF5.....117 G3
NWPT NP20.....76 A3
St David's Crs PNRTH/DP CF64.....133 F1
St David's Dr CAER CF83.....50 C3
St David's Hts LLTR/LLH CF72.....94 D5

St Davids Link CCDF CF10.....4 E5
St David's Pl LLTR/LLH CF72 *.....95 F1
St David's Rd CWM NP44.....111 E1
St David's Rd CWM NP44.....20 A5
St David's Rd CWM NP44.....20 A5
St David's Rd LLTR/LLH CF72.....107 H2
St David's Wy CAER CF83.....68 C3
St Denis Rd CDFN CF14.....100 A5
St Dials Rd CWM NP44.....19 E5
St Dogmael's Av CDFN CF14.....100 A3
St Dominics Retreat
PPOOL/BLNAV NP4.....14 B4
St Donats Cl CDFN CF14.....133 F3
St Donat's Ct CAER CF83.....68 C2
St Donats Pl CWM NP44 *.....19 H3
St Donats Rd GTN/RVSD CF11.....119 E4
St Dubricius Gdns
CALD/MAC NP26.....61 E3
St Dyfrig Cl PNRTH/DP CF64.....133 F4
St Dyfrig Rd PNRTH/DP CF64.....134 A4
St Edeyrns Cl
CYN/LLD/PWYN CF23.....101 E4
St Edeyrns Rd
CYN/LLD/PWYN CF23.....100 D4
St Edward St NWPT NP20.....8 C5
St Edwen Gdns CDFN CF14.....99 H5
St Ewens Rd CHEP NP16.....30 C1
St Fagans Av BARRY/I/W CF62.....139 E3
St Fagans Cl
CAE/CAN/FWR CF5.....117 H1
St Fagans Dr
CAE/CAN/FWR CF5.....109 C5
St Fagans Ri
CAE/CAN/FWR CF5.....110 A5
St Fagans Rd
CAE/CAN/FWR CF5.....117 F1
St Fagans St CAER CF83.....68 D2
St Fagan's St GTN/RVSD CF11.....6 A5
St Francis Rd CDFN CF14.....98 D5
St Garmon Rd
PNRTH/DP CF64.....134 A4
St George Rd CHEP NP16.....28 C5
St George's Crs NWPTE NP19.....57 H2
St Georges Ct CDFN CF14.....111 H2
St Georges Wy CHEP NP16.....31 F3
St Gildas Rd CDFN CF14.....99 H5
St Govan's Cl BARRY/I/W CF62.....139 F1
St Gwynno Cl
PNRTH/DP CF64 *.....133 F3
St Helen's Ct CAER CF83.....68 C2
St Helen's Rd CDFN CF14.....111 H1
St Hilda's Rd
PPOOL/BLNAV NP4.....17 E3
St Ilan's Wy CAER CF83.....68 D3
St Illtyd Cl PNRTH/DP CF64 *.....133 F3
St Illtyd Rd CWM NP44.....19 H3
St Ina Rd CDFN CF14.....99 H5
St Isan Rd CDFN CF14.....99 H5
St James Cl CAER CF83.....49 H4
St James Ct PNRTH/DP CF64.....134 A4
St James Crs BARRY/I/W CF62.....138 B4
St James' Rd
PPOOL/BLNAV NP4.....14 C4
St John's Cl COWBR CF71.....122 D4
St Johns Ct PPOOL/BLNAV NP4.....14 A3
St John's Crs
CAE/CAN/FWR CF5.....119 E5
CDFN CF14.....98 D4
RSTN NP10.....54 C3
St John's Gdns CHEP NP16.....28 A3
St John's Pl BARRY/I/W CF62.....144 A2
CDFN CF14.....98 D4
St Johns Rd NWPTE NP19.....77 C1
St John St CCDF CF10.....4 C5
St Joseph Pl CWM NP44.....26 C4
St Josephs Cl CALD/MAC NP26.....60 B2
St Josephs Ct CDFN CF14.....112 A3
St Julian Cl PNRTH/DP CF64.....140 A2
St Julian's Av NWPTE NP19.....57 F2
St Julian's Ct CAER CF83.....68 C2
St Julians Ct NWPTE NP19.....57 F2
St Julians St NWPTE NP19.....57 F2
St Julian St NWPT NP20.....8 C5
St Kingsmark Av CHEP NP16.....28 A5
St Lawrence La CHEP NP16.....28 A5
St Lawrence Pk CHEP NP16.....28 A4
St Lawrence Rd CHEP NP16.....28 A5
St Luke's Av PNRTH/DP CF64.....134 A4
PPRD CF37.....65 H3
St Luke's Rd
PPOOL/BLNAV NP4.....14 A1
St Lythan Cl PNRTH/DP CF64 *.....133 E4
St Lythan's Rd BARRY/I/W CF62.....138 C4
St Lythans Rd
CAE/CAN/FWR CF5.....125 F3
St Malo Rd CDFN CF14.....99 H4
St Margarets Cl CAER CF83.....50 A3
St Margaret's Crs
CATH/RTH/SPL CF24.....113 F5
St Margaret's Pk
CATH/RTH/SPL CF24.....117 H2
St Margaret's Rd CDFN CF14.....98 D4
St Margaret's Rd CAER CF83.....68 C2
CDFN CF14.....98 D5
St Mark's Crs NWPT NP20.....8 B5
St Mark's Gdns CDFN CF14 *.....112 A2
St Mark's Rd CDFN CF14.....134 B4
St Martin's Cl
PNRTH/DP CF64.....134 A4
St Martin's Crs CDFN CF14.....68 D3
St Martins Crs CDFN CF14.....100 A3
St Mary's Av BARRY/I/W CF63.....3 J1
St Mary's Cl
CAE/CAN/FWR CF5 *.....117 G5
St Mary's Cl
PPOOL/BLNAV NP4.....16 D2
St Marys Ct CAE/CAN/FWR CF5.....126 A1
NWPT NP20.....8 D4
St Mary's Pl CALD/MAC NP26.....63 H3
St Mary's Rd CDFN CF14.....98 D4
CWM NP44 *.....20 B5
St Marys Rd CAER CF83.....49 G3
St Mary St
ABRC/NBR/RIS NP11.....36 D3
CCDF CF10.....4 D6

CHEP NP16.....28 C4
NWPT NP20.....8 C4
PPOOL/BLNAV NP4.....16 D2
St Mary's Well Bay Rd
PNRTH/DP CF64.....142 A5
St Matthew's Rd
PPOOL/BLNAV NP4.....14 D5
St Maur Gdns CHEP NP16.....28 A5
St Mellons Cl CALD/MAC NP26.....60 D3
St Mellons Ct CAER CF83.....68 A3
St Mellons Rd CDFN CF14.....87 E4
St Mellons Rd CDFNE CF3.....103 H5
CYN/LLD/PWYN CF23.....87 G5
St Michael Gv CWM NP44.....26 C4
St Michael's Av PPRD CF37.....45 E5
St Michaels Cl CHV/BDAU CF38.....80 A4
St Michael's Cl
PENT/RAD/TFW CF15 *.....97 H1
St Michaels Gdns
BARRY/I/W CF62 *.....139 E1
St Michaels Ms NWPT NP20.....77 E2
St Michael's Rd
CAE/CAN/FWR CF5.....118 B1
St Michael St NWPT NP20.....77 E2
St Nicholas Cl BARRY/I/W CF62.....2 B5
St Nicholas Ct BARRY/I/W CF62.....2 B5
CAER CF83.....68 C2
CYN/LLD/PWYN CF23.....101 F2
St Nicholas' Rd
BARRY/I/W CF62.....2 B4
St Oswalds Cl
PPOOL/BLNAV NP4.....17 E4
St Oswald's Rd BARRYE CF63.....140 A2
St Paul's Av BARRY/I/W CF62.....2 E2
St Pauls Cl PNRTH/DP CF64.....133 E4
St Peters Ct CWM NP44.....25 F3
St Peter's Rd PNRTH/DP CF64.....134 A4
St Peter's St
CATH/RTH/SPL CF24.....5 F2
St Pierre Cl CDFNE CF3.....103 F2
St Quentins Cl COWBR CF71.....122 C4
St Quentins Hl COWBR CF71.....122 A4
St Siors Meade
BARRY/I/W CF62.....144 B2
St Stephens Ct
CALD/MAC NP26.....61 E3
St Stephen's Rd NWPT NP20.....77 E2
St Tanwg Rd CDFN CF14.....99 H5
St Tecla Rd CHEP NP16.....30 C1
St Teilo Av BARRY/I/W CF62.....139 E3
St Teilo Rd PNRTH/DP CF64 *.....133 F4
St Teilo Ct CALD/MAC NP26.....61 E3
St Teilo's Wy CAER CF83.....68 C3
St Tewdric Rd CHEP NP16.....28 C5
St Thomas Cl CDFN CF14.....99 F5
St Vincent Rd NWPTE NP19.....9 F2
St Winifreds Cl
PNRTH/DP CF64 *.....133 E4
St Woolos Pl NWPT NP20.....8 C5
St Woolos Rd NWPT NP20.....8 D4
Salem La CALD/MAC NP26.....61 E3
Salisbury Av PNRTH/DP CF64.....134 B3
Salisbury Cl NWPT NP20.....56 D3
PNRTH/DP CF64.....134 B4
Salisbury Rd BARRY/I/W CF62.....2 B3
Salisbury St
ABRC/NBR/RIS NP11.....36 B2
Salmon Cl
CYN/LLD/PWYN CF23.....113 G4
Salop Pl PNRTH/DP CF64.....134 C1
Salop St CAER CF83.....69 E2
PNRTH/DP CF64.....134 C1
Salvia Cl PNRTH/DP CF64.....103 F3
Samson's Av
PPOOL/BLNAV NP4.....10 B5
Samson St LLMJ CF61.....136 C2
Samuels Crs CDFN CF14.....98 B5
Sanatorium Rd
GTN/RVSD CF11.....118 C3
Sanctuary Ct
CAE/CAN/FWR CF5.....125 G1
The Sanctuary
CAE/CAN/FWR CF5.....125 G1
Sandbrook Rd CDFNE CF3.....103 F4
Sanderling Dr CDFNE CF3.....103 E2
Sandon St
CATH/RTH/SPL CF24.....5 F5
Sandpiper Cl CDFNE CF3.....103 E2
Sandpiper Wy RSTN NP10.....91 H1
Sandringham Cl
CYN/LLD/PWYN CF23.....113 E4
Sandringham Rd
CATH/RTH/SPL CF24.....113 E4
Sandy La CALD/MAC NP26.....52 F2
RSTN NP10.....76 A4
Sandybrook Cl CWM NP44.....52 F2
Sansom St
CATH/RTH/SPL CF24.....5 H6
Sapele Dr CATH/RTH/SPL CF24.....5 J6
Sapphire St
CATH/RTH/SPL CF24.....5 J2
Sardis Rd PPRD CF37.....44 C4
Saron St PPRD CF37.....45 F5
Saundersfoot Cl
CAE/CAN/FWR CF5.....117 G5
Saunders Rd CCDF CF10.....4 C7
Saxon Pl CDFN CF14.....29 E5
Scarborough Rd NWPTE NP19.....57 E1
PPRD CF37.....45 F2
Scard St NWPT NP20.....8 A6
School Cl PPOOL/BLNAV NP4.....14 D4
School Crs PPOOL/BLNAV NP4.....17 E4
School Hl CHEP NP16.....28 C4
School La NWPT NP20.....8 E4
PENT/RAD/TFW CF15.....88 E3
PPOOL/BLNAV NP4.....12 C5
PPRD CF37.....46 A5
School Pk CALD/MAC NP26.....63 H3
School Rd LLTR/LLH CF72.....107 H2
School St CAER CF83.....48 C1
LLTR/LLH CF72.....94 C5
School Vw PPOOL/BLNAV NP4.....14 D5
Schooner Cir RSTN NP10.....92 A1

Schooner Wy CCDF CF10.....7 G3
Scotney Wy
CYN/LLD/PWYN CF23.....101 H1
Scott Cl NWPT NP20.....75 H3
Scott Ct CYN/LLD/PWYN CF23.....113 D2
Scott Rd CCDF CF10.....4 C6
Seaback Rd PNRTH/DP CF64 *.....134 D3
Seabank PNRTH/DP CF64 *.....134 D3
Seager Dr GTN/RVSD CF11.....128 B3
Sealawns BARRY/I/W CF62.....146 C3
Sea Point BARRY/I/W CF62.....146 A3
Seasons Cl CALD/MAC NP26.....60 B3
Seaton's Pl PPRD CF37.....45 E5
Seaview Pl LLMJ CF61.....136 C3
Sea View Ter BARRYE CF63.....140 B4
Seaview Ter
CATH/RTH/SPL CF24.....125 E3
CALD/MAC NP26 *.....62 A4
Seawall Rd
CATH/RTH/SPL CF24.....121 E3
Second Av CAER CF83.....68 B1
Second St NWPTE NP19.....77 H4
Sedbury Cha CHEP NP16.....29 E2
Sedbury La CHEP NP16.....29 E3
Sedgemoor Ct NWPT NP20.....56 D3
Sedgemoor Rd CDFNE CF3.....102 B3
Sefton Cl
PENT/RAD/TFW CF15 *.....97 G4
Selby Cl CWM NP44.....26 C3
Senghennydd Pl
CATH/RTH/SPL CF24.....4 E2
Senghennydd Rd
CATH/RTH/SPL CF24.....4 E2
Senni Cl BARRY/I/W CF62.....138 C3
Serpentine Rd NWPT NP20.....8 B2
Sevenoaks Rd
CAE/CAN/FWR CF5.....117 E4
Sevenoaks St GTN/RVSD CF11.....6 B6
Seven Stiles Av NWPT NP20.....78 C2
Severn Av BARRY/I/W CF62.....138 B3
CHEP NP16.....29 E3
Severn Cl ABRC/NBR/RIS NP11.....37 G5
Severn Gv GTN/RVSD CF11.....119 E1
Severn Rd CDFN CF14.....119 E1
Severn Rd GTN/RVSD CF11.....119 E1
Severn Ter NWPT NP20.....8 B2
Severn Vw CALD/MAC NP26.....62 C3
Seymour St
CATH/RTH/SPL CF24.....120 D2
Seys Cl COWBR CF71.....122 B3
Sgubor Goch LLTR/LLH CF72 *.....94 C5
Shaftesbury Cl NWPTE NP19.....85 H4
Shaftesbury St NWPT NP20.....56 D3
Shaftesbury Wk NWPT NP20 *.....56 D3
Shakespeare Av
PNRTH/DP CF64.....134 A2
Shakespeare Cl
CATH/RTH/SPL CF24.....62 C3
Shakespeare Ct
CATH/RTH/SPL CF24.....5 G2
Shakespeare Crs NWPT NP20.....56 D3
Shakespeare Dr
CATH/RTH/SPL CF24.....62 C4
LLMJ CF61.....137 E4
Shakespeare Ri PPRD CF37.....65 H1
Shakespeare Rd
BARRY/I/W CF62.....139 F1
NWPT NP20.....25 F1
Shakespeare St
CATH/RTH/SPL CF24.....5 G2
Shamrock Rd
CAE/CAN/FWR CF5.....110 A5
Shannon Rd NWPT NP20.....40 A4
Sharpe Cl
CYN/LLD/PWYN CF23.....113 G4
Sharps Wy CHEP NP16.....30 D2
Shaw Cl CDFNE CF3.....102 A3
Shaw Gv NWPT NP20.....56 D3
Shea Gdns NWPTE NP19.....9 F3
Shearman Pl GTN/RVSD CF11.....128 B3
Shears Rd CAE/CAN/FWR CF5.....116 A1
Shearwater Cl
PNRTH/DP CF64.....142 C2
Sheerwater Cl CDFNE CF3.....103 D3
Shelburn Cl GTN/RVSD CF11.....119 F4
Shelley Cl CALD/MAC NP26.....62 C3
Shelley Crs BARRY/I/W CF62.....139 E1
PNRTH/DP CF64.....134 A2
Shelley Rd NWPTE NP19.....25 F1
Shelley Wk CATH/RTH/SPL CF24.....57 G4
Shelley Wk
CATH/RTH/SPL CF24.....5 G2
PPRD CF37.....65 H1
Sheppard St PPRD CF37.....44 B3
Sherborne Av
CYN/LLD/PWYN CF23.....100 D3
Sherbourne Av
BARRY/I/W CF62.....139 E1
Sherbourne Rd
CATH/RTH/SPL CF24.....17 E4
Sheridan Cl CDFNE CF3.....102 A3
NWPT NP20.....75 H2
Sherwsbury Cl NWPT NP20.....56 D3
Shetland Cl NWPTE NP19.....57 G2
Shetland Wk NWPTE NP19.....57 G2
Shields Cl
CYN/LLD/PWYN CF23 *.....102 A1
Ship La CCDF CF10.....7 G5
The Shires CDFNE CF3.....104 A1
Shirley Rd
CATH/RTH/SPL CF24.....112 C3
Shop Rd PPOOL/BLNAV NP4.....10 C3
Showle Acre BARRY/I/W CF62.....144 B2
Sickert Cl NWPT NP20.....57 H3
Silley's Cl CHEP NP16.....28 D2
Siloam Hl CAER CF83.....69 F4
Silure Wy
CLN/RNWPTE NP18.....59 C1
Silurian Pl CCDF CF10.....7 G5
Silver Birch Cl CDFN CF14.....111 G2
CLN/RNWPTE NP18.....41 H4
Silver Fir Sq RSTN NP10.....75 E1
Silverstone Cl CDFNE CF3.....102 C3
Silver St ABRC/NBR/RIS NP11.....36 A2
Silverton Dr LLTR/LLH CF72.....95 F3
Simpson Cl NWPT NP20.....40 B3
Sims Sq NWPTE NP19.....58 C4

Sinclair Dr
CYN/LLD/PWYN CF23.....113 G4
Sindercombe Cl
CYN/LLD/PWYN CF23.....101 G1
Singleton Rd
CATH/RTH/SPL CF24.....120 D3
Sir Alfred Owen Wy
CAER CF83.....48 D3
Sir Charles Crs RSTN NP10.....91 H2
Sir Charles Sq RSTN NP10.....92 A1
Sir Howys La NWPT.....19 E4
Sirhowy Valley Wk
ABRC/NBR/RIS NP11.....52 D1
NWPT NP20.....75 G2
Sir Ivor Pl PNRTH/DP CF64.....133 G4
Sir Stafford Cl CAER CF83.....49 F4
Sixth St NWPTE NP19.....78 A5
Skaithmuir Rd
CATH/RTH/SPL CF24.....121 E1
Skelmuir Rd
CATH/RTH/SPL CF24.....121 E1
Skenfrith Ms RSTN NP10.....91 H2
Skibereen Cl
CYN/LLD/PWYN CF23.....101 H1
Skinner La NWPT NP20.....8 E3
Skinner Rw NWPTE NP19 *.....58 B5
Skinner St NWPT NP20.....8 D3
Skomer Rd BARRY/I/W CF62.....139 F1
Slade Cl PNRTH/DP CF64.....141 E3
Slade Rd BARRY/I/W CF62.....139 F2
Slade St NWPT NP20.....57 G5
The Slipway PNRTH/DP CF64.....134 C1
Sloper Rd GTN/RVSD CF11.....119 E4
Smallbrook Cl CWM NP44.....26 B1
Small Meadow Ct CAER CF83.....49 E5
Smeaton Cl BARRY/I/W CF62.....144 A3
Smeaton St GTN/RVSD CF11.....119 F3
Smithies Av PNRTH/DP CF64.....141 F5
Snail Creep Ter
PPOOL/BLNAV NP4.....10 C4
Snatchwood Rd
PPOOL/BLNAV NP4.....12 C5
Snatchwood Ter
PPOOL/BLNAV NP4.....12 C5
Sneyd St GTN/RVSD CF11.....119 E1
Sniphill Br CHEP NP16.....29 G2
Snipe St CATH/RTH/SPL CF24.....5 H1
Snowden Rd
CAE/CAN/FWR CF5.....117 E4
Snowdon Cl
ABRC/NBR/RIS NP11.....37 G4
Snowdon Ct CDFN CF14.....20 B5
Snowdrop La RSTN NP10.....53 H2
Soane Cl RSTN NP10.....54 D2
Soar Cl CWM NP44.....20 C2
Soarel Ct CDFNE CF3.....103 E5
Soberton Av CDFN CF14.....112 A3
Soho St NWPTE NP19.....9 K3
Solent Rd BARRYE CF63.....140 A4
Solva Av CDFN CF14.....100 B2
Solva Cl BARRY/I/W CF62.....139 F2
Somerset Ct CDFNE CF3.....102 B3
Somerset Rd BARRY/I/W CF62.....2 A4
CWM NP44.....20 A4
NWPT NP20.....57 F2
Somerset Rd East
BARRY/I/W CF62.....139 F3
Somerset Vw PNRTH/DP CF64.....119 F4
Somerset Wy PNRTH/DP CF64.....141 F5
Somerset Wy CHEP NP16.....30 D2
Somerton Crs NWPTE NP19.....58 A4
Somerton La NWPTE NP19.....57 H5
Somerton Pk NWPTE NP19.....57 H5
Somerton Rd NWPTE NP19.....58 A4
Somerton Rd NWPTE NP19.....57 H5
Sophia Cl GTN/RVSD CF11.....119 F1
Sophia Wk GTN/RVSD CF11.....119 F1
Sorrel Dr NWPT NP20.....8 B1
South Av PPOOL/BLNAV NP4.....16 D4
Southbrook Vw
CALD/MAC NP26.....63 G4
South Clive St GTN/RVSD CF11.....26 C2
South Ct CWM NP44.....26 C2
Southcourt Rd
CYN/LLD/PWYN CF23.....113 F3
South Dr LLTR/LLH CF72.....95 F2
Southern St CAER CF83.....69 E2
Southern Wy
CYN/LLD/PWYN CF23.....113 H2
Southesk PPOOL/BLNAV NP4.....2 B6
Southey St BARRY/I/W CF62.....139 E4
CATH/RTH/SPL CF24.....5 H2
Southgate Av LLTR/LLH CF72.....95 F2
South Gld
PENT/RAD/TFW CF15.....83 F4
Southglade PNRTH/DP CF64.....141 F5
South Gv CALD/MAC NP26.....62 A3
South Lake Dr RSTN NP10.....91 G2
South Loudoun Pl CCDF CF10.....7 F3
South Luton Pl
CATH/RTH/SPL CF24.....5 H5
South Market St NWPT NP20.....9 G6
South Morgan Pl
GTN/RVSD CF11.....119 E1
South Pandy Ct CAER CF83.....48 D4
South Park Rd
CATH/RTH/SPL CF24.....121 E5
Southra PNRTH/DP CF64.....133 E4
South Rd CDFN CF14.....100 B2
South Rd CWM NP44.....26 A3
PNRTH/DP CF64.....141 E4
South St PPOOL/BLNAV NP4.....17 F2
PPRD CF37.....45 E3
South Vw BARRY/I/W CF62.....144 C3
South View Dr CDFNE CF3.....102 B5
Southville Rd NWPT NP20.....56 A5
South Wk BARRY/I/W CF62.....139 E3
Southway PPOOL/BLNAV NP4.....15 H1
Sovereign Gdns
LLTR/LLH CF72.....107 H1
Spartan Cl
CLN/RNWPTE NP18.....59 H1
Speedwell Dr BARRY/I/W CF62.....144 B3
Speke St NWPTE NP19.....9 J2
Spencer David Wy CDFNE CF3.....103 E5
Spencer Dr PNRTH/DP CF64.....127 H4

Spencer La *PPRD* CF37 .... 65 H3
Spencer Rd *NWPT* NP20 .... 8 B4
Spencers Rw
  CAE/CAN/FWR CF5 ...... 111 E4
Spencer St
  CATH/RTH/SPL CF24 ..... 112 C4
Spinney Cl *CAE/CAN/FWR* CF5 .. 117 F2
The Spinney *CDFN* CF14 .... 86 C4
NWPT NP20 .... 40 C4
Spires Wk *BARRYE* CF63 .... 139 H1
Spitzkop *LLMJ* CF61 .... 136 C3
Splott Rd *CATH/RTH/SPL* CF24 .. 120 D2
Spooner Ct *RSTN* NP10 .... 91 E1
Springfield
  CAE/CAN/FWR CF5 .... 125 G5
NP44 .... 20 B2
RSTN NP10 .... 74 A1
Springfield Dr *NWPTE* NP19 ..... 58 C3
Springfield Gdns
  PENT/RAD/TFW CF15 ..... 97 G2
Springfield La *RSTN* NP10 .... 74 A1
Springfield Pl *GTN/RVSD* CF11 .. 119 E2
Springfield Ri *BARRYE* CF63 ..... 139 G2
Springfield Rd
  ABRC/NBR/RIS NP11 ...... 53 G1
RSTN NP10 .... 16 D4
RSTN NP10 .... 74 A1
Springfields *CDFNE* CF3 .... 90 A5
Springfield Ter
  PPOOL/BLNAV NP4 .... 17 G2
PPRD CF37 .... 65 C1
Spring Gardens Pl *NWPT* NP20 .. 76 C2
Spring Gardens Ter
  CATH/RTH/SPL CF24 ...... 120 D1
Spring Gardens Ter
  CATH/RTH/SPL CF24 ...... 120 D1
Spring Gv *CDFN* CF14 .... 86 A5
CWM NP44 .... 18 D5
Springhurst Cl *CDFN* CF14 ...... 98 C3
Spring La *NWPT* NP20 .... 9 B6
Spring Meadow Rd
  CDFNE CF3 .... 114 C3
Spring St *BARRYE* CF63 .... 140 A3
NWPT NP20 .... 56 C2
Spring Ter *PPOOL/BLNAV* NP4 ... 16 D3
Springvale *CWM* NP44 .... 19 F4
Springvale Wy *CWM* NP44 .... 19 F4
Springwood
  CYN/LLD/PWYN CF23 ...... 101 E5
Spruce Cl *CATH/RTH/SPL* CF24 .. 5 J3
Spytty La *NWPTE* NP19 .... 77 H2
Spytty Rd *NWPT* NP20 .... 77 F2
The Square *CAER* CF83 .... 47 E2
Squires Cl *RSTN* NP10 .... 55 E3
Squires Ct *CHV/BDAU* CF38 ...... 80 B5
Squires Ga *RSTN* NP10 .... 54 D5
Stacey Rd
  CATH/RTH/SPL CF24 .... 5 K1
  PNRTH/DP CF64 .... 133 E3
Stadium Cl *GTN/RVSD* CF11 ..... 128 A2
Stafford Rd *CALD/MAG* NP26 ... 62 D4
  GTN/RVSD CF11 .... 119 F4
  NWPTE NP19 .... 16 D2
  PPOOL/BLNAV NP4 .... 16 D2
Stag La *LLMJ* CF61 .... 136 C5
Staines St *CAE/CAN/FWR* CF5 .. 118 C1
Stallcourt Av
  CYN/LLD/PWYN CF23 ...... 113 F5
  LLMJ CF61 .... 136 C4
Stallcourt Cl *COWBR* CF71 ...... 122 B4
  CYN/LLD/PWYN CF23 ...... 113 G4
Stamford Ct *NWPT* NP20 .... 55 G4
Standard St *CAER* CF83 .... 50 B3
Stanford Rd *NWPT* NP19 .... 58 C5
Stanier Ct *CATH/RTH/SPL* CF24 . 5 K4
Stanley Rd *CAER* CF83 .... 48 C4
  NWPTE NP19 .... 19 H5
Stanley Rd *NWPT* NP20 .... 8 D2
  PPOOL/BLNAV NP4 .... 12 B1
Stanley St
  ABRC/NBR/RIS NP11 ...... 34 B2
Stanton Wy *PNRTH/DP* CF64 ... 142 C1
Stanway Rd *CAE/CAN/FWR* CF5 . 117 E2
Stanway Rd
  CAE/CAN/FWR CF5 .... 117 E3
Stanwell Crs *PNRTH/DP* CF64 ... 134 D1
Stanwell Rd *PNRTH/DP* CF64 .... 134 B5
Starbuck St *CAER* CF83 .... 29 H2
Star La *CAE/CAN/FWR* CF5 ...... 98 A4
  PPOOL/BLNAV NP4 .... 14 B2
Starling Rd *BARRYE/W* CF62 .... 137 G3
Star St *CATH/RTH/SPL* CF24 ..... 5 J3
Station Ap Ll *LLTR/LLH* CF72 .... 94 B5
  PNRTH/DP CF64 .... 134 C3
  RSTN NP10 .... 75 E1
Station Approach Rd
  BARRYI/W CF62 .... 3 F7
Station Av
  ABRC/NBR/RIS NP11 ...... 34 A1
Station Cl *CALD/MAG* NP26 ..... 62 C4
Station Farm *CWM* NP44 .... 20 A3
Station Pl
  ABRC/NBR/RIS NP11 ...... 37 E4
Station Rd
  ABRC/NBR/RIS NP11 ...... 37 E5
  BARRYI/W CF62 .... 144 C5
  CAER CF83 .... 33 G5
  CALD/MAG NP26 .... 62 C4
  CDFN CF14 .... 100 A2
  CHEP NP16 .... 28 D4
  CHV/BDAU CF38 .... 81 G2
  CLN/RNWPTE NP18 .... 27 F5
  CLN/RNWPTE NP18 .... 59 G5
  CWM NP44 .... 9 J5
  LLMJ CF61 .... 136 C3
  PENT/RAD/TFW CF15 .... 97 H5
  PNRTH/DP CF64 .... 133 E3
  PNRTH/DP CF64 .... 134 A1
  PPOOL/BLNAV NP4 .... 17 E2
Station Rd East
  CAE/CAN/FWR CF5 .... 125 G4
Station Rd West
  CAE/CAN/FWR CF5 * 125 G5
Station St *BARRYE* CF63 .... 3 J1
  CAER CF83 .... 51 H2
Station Ter *CAE/CAN/FWR* CF5 . 118 A2

  CAER CF83 .... 48 B4
  CCDF CF10 .... 5 F4
  LLTR/LLH CF72 .... 106 B2
  PNRTH/DP CF64 .... 134 C3
St Clements Cl
  CYN/LLD/PWYN CF23 ..... 101 F2
Steepfield *CWM* NP44 .... 20 B2
Steeps St *CHEP* NP16 .... 28 D4
  PNRTH/DP CF64 .... 134 C1
Steer Cres *NWPTE* NP19 .... 58 C3
Stella Cl *CDFN* CF14 .... 86 A4
Stella Maris Ct
  PENT/RAD/TFW CF15 ..... 97 G5
Stelvio Park Av *NWPT* NP20 ..... 76 A1
Stelvio Park Cl *NWPT* NP20 ..... 76 A1
Stelvio Park Crs *NWPT* NP20 ... 76 A1
Stelvio Park Dr *NWPT* NP20 ..... 76 A1
Stelvio Park Gdns *NWPT* NP20 . 76 A1
Stelvio Park Rd *NWPT* NP20 ..... 76 A1
Stelvio Park Vw *NWPT* NP20 .... 76 A1
Stenhousemuir Pl
  CATH/RTH/SPL CF24 ..... 121 E1
Stepaside *CHEP* NP16 .... 30 A4
Stephenson St
  GTN/RVSD CF11 .... 119 F3
  NWPTE NP19 .... 77 E3
Sterling Cl
  CATH/RTH/SPL CF24 ..... 121 C1
  NWPTE NP19 .... 58 D4
Sterndale Bennett Rd
  NWPTE NP19 .... 59 E3
Steveley *CWM* NP44 .... 15 H4
Stevenson Cl *RSTN* NP10 .... 54 D3
Stevenson Ct *RSTN* NP10 .... 54 D3
Stiels *CWM* NP44 .... 144 C3
Stirling Rd *BARRYI/W* CF62 ...... 138 C2
  CAE/CAN/FWR CF5 .... 116 D4
St Michaels Ct
  CYN/LLD/PWYN CF23 ..... 101 H1
Stockland St *CAER* CF83 * 68 D2
  GTN/RVSD CF11 .... 6 A4
Stockton Cl *NWPTE* NP19 .... 41 F5
Stockton Rd *NWPTE* NP19 .... 57 E1
Stockwave Cl
  CLN/RNWPTE NP18 .... 43 G5
Stockwood Vw 59 G1
Stokes Ct *CLN/RNWPTE* NP18 .. 27 G5
Stokes Cl *CLN/RNWPTE* NP18 ... 27 G5
Stonebridge Pk *CWM* NP44 ...... 20 A3
Stonechat Cl *CDFNE* CF3 * 103 F4
The Stone Yd
  GTN/RVSD CF11 * 119 E3
Stony Rd *PPOOL/BLNAV* NP4 .... 12 C2
Storrar Rd
  CATH/RTH/SPL CF24 ..... 114 A5
Stour Ct *CWM* NP44 .... 18 D4
Stow Hl *NWPT* NP20 .... 8 B5
Stow Park Av *NWPT* NP20 .... 8 A6
Stow Park Cir *NWPT* NP20 .... 8 A6
Stow Park Crs *NWPT* NP20 .... 8 A5
Stow Park Dr *NWPT* NP20 .... 8 B6
Stow Park Gdns *NWPT* NP20 ..... 8 A5
Stradling Cl *BARRYI/W* CF62 ..... 2 C4
  COWBR CF71 .... 122 B3
  PNRTH/DP CF64 .... 141 E4
Stradling Pl *LLMJ* CF61 .... 136 D4
Stradmore Cl
  PENT/RAD/TFW CF15 ..... 83 E2
Strathnairn St
  CATH/RTH/SPL CF24 ..... 112 D5
Strathy Rd *CDFNE* CF3 .... 103 D5
Striguil Rd *CHEP* NP16 .... 30 C2
Strongbow Rd *CHEP* NP16 .... 30 C2
Stryd Silurian *LLTR/LLH* CF72 .. 106 B3
Stuart Av *CHEP* NP16 .... 28 B3
  GTN/RVSD CF11 .... 127 H3
Stuart Cl *CHEP* NP16 .... 28 B3
Stuart Pl *CCDF* CF10 .... 7 G6
  CHEP NP16 .... 28 B3
  LLTR/LLH CF72 .... 107 E1
Sturminster Rd
  CYN/LLD/PWYN CF23 ..... 113 G5
Stuttgater Strasse *CCDF* CF10 .. 4 D5
Subway Rd *BARRYE* CF63 .... 3 J5
Sudbrook Rd *CALD/MAG* NP26 . 63 H4
Sudbury Wk *NWPT* NP20 .... 56 D2
Sudcroft St *CAE/CAN/FWR* CF5 . 118 D4
Suflex Est
  ABRC/NBR/RIS NP11 * 53 G1
Sullivan Cir *NWPT* NP20 .... 58 C5
Sullivan Cl *CDFNE* CF3 .... 102 C5
  PNRTH/DP CF64 .... 134 B5
Sully Moors Rd
  PNRTH/DP CF64 .... 140 D3
Sully Pl *PNRTH/DP* CF64 .... 134 C4
Sully Rd *PNRTH/DP* CF64 .... 141 G3
Sully Ter *PNRTH/DP* CF64 .... 134 C4
Sully Vw *BARRYE* CF63 .... 140 D2
Summerau Ct
  CAE/CAN/FWR CF5 .... 118 D1
Summerfield Av *CDFN* CF14 .... 112 B3
Summerfield Dr
  LLTR/LLH CF72 .... 95 F5
Summerfield La *CAER* CF83 ..... 50 D5
Summerfield Pl *CDFN* CF14 .... 99 G5
Summerhill Av *NWPTE* NP19 .... 57 F3
Summerhouse La *CHEP* NP16 ... 30 D5
Summerland Cl
  PNRTH/DP CF64 .... 127 H5
Summerland Crs
  PNRTH/DP CF64 .... 127 H5
Summerwood Cl
  CAE/CAN/FWR CF5 .... 109 H5
Sumner Cl *CAE/CAN/FWR* CF5 .. 110 C3
Sunbean Cl *NWPTE* NP19 .... 9 J5
Sundew Cl
  CAE/CAN/FWR CF5 .... 110 A3
Sunea Crs *PPOOL/BLNAV* NP4 .. 15 F4
Sunglade *CAER* CF83 .... 50 D5
Sunningdale Cl
  CYN/LLD/PWYN CF23 ..... 112 D1
Sunnybank *RSTN* NP10 .... 74 C2
Sunnybank Cl *CDFN* CF14 ...... 111 H1
Sunnybank Rd
  PPOOL/BLNAV NP4 .... 16 D2
Sunny Bank Ter *CAER* CF83 ..... 51 G2

Sunnycroft Cl 133 F3
Sunnycroft La
  PNRTH/DP CF64 .... 133 F3
Sunnycroft Ri
  PNRTH/DP CF64 .... 133 F4
Surrey Pl *CATH/RTH/SPL* CF24 .. 125 C4
Suran-y-Gog *BARRYE* CF63 ..... 131 H5
Surrey Pl *NWPTE* NP19 .... 57 F2
Surrey St *CAE/CAN/FWR* CF5 * . 118 C1
Sussex Cl *NWPTE* NP19 .... 77 H2
Sussex St *GTN/RVSD* CF11 .... 6 A1
Sutherland Crs *NWPTE* NP19 .... 57 E1
Sutton Rd *NWPTE* NP19 .... 57 E1
Swallow Dr *CALD/MAG* NP26 ... 63 E4
Swallowhurst Cl
  CAE/CAN/FWR CF5 .... 116 C4
Swallow Wy *RSTN* NP10 .... 75 H4
Swanage Cl *CDFNE* CF3 .... 103 F3
Swanbridge Gv
  PNRTH/DP CF64 .... 141 G5
Swanbridge Rd
  PNRTH/DP CF64 .... 141 G5
Swan Cl *CALD/MAG* NP26 .... 63 E4
Swansea St
  CATH/RTH/SPL CF24 * 120 C3
Swan Sq *PPOOL/BLNAV* NP4 ..... 12 C1
Swan St *LLTR/LLH* CF72 .... 95 E2
Sward Cl *RSTN* NP10 .... 54 D5
Sweldon Cl *CAE/CAN/FWR* CF5 . 117 E5
Swift Cl *CDFNE* CF3 .... 102 A4
Swinburne Cl *NWPTE* NP19 ...... 59 E3
Swinton St
  CATH/RTH/SPL CF24 ..... 120 D2
Swn-y-Mor *BARRYI/W* CF62 ..... 144 C5
Swn-y-Nant *CHV/BDAU* CF38 ... 81 F1
Sycamore Av
  CALD/MAG NP26 * 62 C2
  CHEP NP16 .... 30 C2
  NWPTE NP19 .... 19 F1
Sycamore Cl *LLTR/LLH* CF72 ... 107 H1
  PNRTH/DP CF64 .... 133 F4
Sycamore Ct *CWM* NP44 .... 24 C3
Sycamore Crs
  ABRC/NBR/RIS NP11 ...... 37 G5
Sycamore Rd *LLTR/LLH* CF72 ... 94 B1
  PPOOL/BLNAV NP4 .... 16 D4
Sycamore Rd South
  PPOOL/BLNAV NP4 .... 14 B4
The Sycamores
  PPOOL/BLNAV NP4 .... 14 B4
Sycamore St
  CAE/CAN/FWR CF5 * 83 F3
  PPRD CF37 .... 65 H2
Sycamore Ter
  CALD/MAG NP26 .... 62 C3
Sycamore Tree Cl
  RSTN NP10 .... 97 F4
Sylvan Cl *CAE/CAN/FWR* CF5 ... 110 C3
  NWPT NP20 .... 40 C3
Symondscliff Wy
  CALD/MAG NP26 .... 63 G4
Syndicate Ter
  ABRC/NBR/RIS NP11 ...... 34 B2
Syn Park Cl *CDFNE* CF3 .... 103 E3
Syr David's Av
  CAE/CAN/FWR CF5 .... 118 C1
Syr David's Ct
  CAE/CAN/FWR CF5 .... 118 C1
System St
  CATH/RTH/SPL CF24 .... 5 H3

T

Tabor St *PENT/RAD/TFW* CF15 .. 83 F3
Taff Cl *BARRYI/W* CF62 .... 138 C3
Taff Ct *CWM* NP44 .... 18 D5
Taff Emb *GTN/RVSD* CF11 .... 6 C5
Taff Fall Rd *PPRD* CF37 .... 66 C2
Taffs Mead Emb
  GTN/RVSD CF11 .... 4 B7
Taffs Mead Rd *PPRD* CF37 ...... 66 A2
Taff St *PENT/RAD/TFW* CF15 .... 97 H1
  PPRD CF37 .... 44 D3
Taff Ter *GTN/RVSD* CF11 .... 97 H5
Taff Trail *CDFN* CF14 .... 110 D3
Taff Wy *BARRYI/W* CF62 .... 138 D2
Tafwys Wk *CAER* CF83 .... 5 G2
Tai Duffryn
  PENT/RAD/TFW CF15 ..... 67 F5
Tair Erw Rd *CDFN* CF14 .... 111 H1
Tair Gwaun *PNRTH/DP* CF64 ... 134 A5
Talbot Cl *LLTR/LLH* CF72 .... 94 D5
Talbot Gn *LLTR/LLH* CF72 .... 94 D3
Talbot La *NWPT* NP20 .... 8 E4
Talbot Rd *LLTR/LLH* CF72 .... 94 D5
Talbot St *GTN/RVSD* CF11 ...... 119 F2
Talfan Cl *PPOOL/BLNAV* NP4 ... 25 H1
Taigarth Cl *CWM* NP44 .... 25 H1
Taliesin Cl *RSTN* NP10 .... 75 H1
Taliesin Dr *RSTN* NP10 .... 75 H1
Tallard's Pl *CHEP* NP16 .... 29 E4
Tallis Cl *NWPTE* NP19 .... 58 D2
Talworth St
  CATH/RTH/SPL CF24 .... 5 G2
Tal-y-Bryn *PNRTH/DP* CF64 .... 134 A4
Talygarn Cl *COWBR* CF71 ...... 122 D4
Talygarn Dr *LLTR/LLH* CF72 ... 106 D3
Talygarn St *CDFN* CF14 .... 112 B3
Tamar Cl *NWPT* NP20 .... 39 H4
Tanglewood Cl *NWPTE* NP19 ... 86 B5
Tangmere Dr
  CAE/CAN/FWR CF5 .... 110 B3
Tan House Dr
  CLN/RNWPTE NP18 .... 42 B4
Tank Farm Wy 140 C3
Tansy Cl *CDFN* CF14 .... 85 F4
Tanybryn *ABRC/NBR/RIS* NP11 . 53 H1

Tan-y-Bryn *CAER* CF83 .... 32 A5
  CHV/BDAU CF38 .... 80 B3
Tan-y-Fron *BARRYI/W* CF62 .... 146 B1
Tapley Cl *CAE/CAN/FWR* CF5 ... 117 F5
Tarragon Wy
  CYN/LLD/PWYN CF23 ..... 101 F1
Tarrws Cl *CAE/CAN/FWR* CF5 .. 125 C4
Tarwick Dr *CDFNE* CF3 .... 102 D4
Tasker Dr *CDFN* CF14 .... 99 G3
Tatem Dr *CAE/CAN/FWR* CF5 ... 117 E1
Tatton Dr *NWPTE* NP19 .... 78 C4
Taunton Av *CDFNE* CF3 .... 102 B5
Taunton Crs *CDFNE* CF3 .... 102 B5
Tavistock St
  CATH/RTH/SPL CF24 ..... 112 D5
Taylor St *ABRC/NBR/RIS* NP11 .. 37 E3
Taymuir Rd
  CATH/RTH/SPL CF24 ..... 113 H5
Teal Cl *CALD/MAG* NP26 .... 60 D3
Tealham Dr *CDFNE* CF3 .... 103 F3
Teal St *CATH/RTH/SPL* CF24 ...... 5 H2
Teasel Av *PNRTH/DP* CF64 ...... 134 A1
Tedder Cl *CDFN* CF14 .... 100 A3
Tees Cl *NWPT* NP20 .... 40 A4
Tegfan *CAER* CF83 .... 48 B5
  LLTR/LLH CF72 .... 107 E2
Tegfan Cl *GTN/RVSD* CF11 .... 99 H2
Tegfan Ct *CWM* NP44 .... 24 C3
Teifi Dr *BARRYI/W* CF62 .... 138 C4
Teifi Pl *CAE/CAN/FWR* CF5 ..... 117 G5
Teilo St *GTN/RVSD* CF11 .... 119 E1
Telekkebir Rd *PPRD* CF37 .... 44 B2
Telford St *GTN/RVSD* CF11 ..... 119 F3
  NWPTE NP19 .... 19 F3
Telor-y-Coed *CAER* CF83 .... 33 H1
Temperance Pl *PPRD* CF37 ...... 44 D3
Tempest Dr *CHEP* NP16 .... 28 B4
Temple St *NWPT* NP20 .... 76 D2
Templeton Av *CDFN* CF14 ...... 99 G1
Templeton Cl *CDFN* CF14 .... 99 H1
Tenby St *CATH/RTH/SPL* CF24 .. 20 B5
Tenby Ct *CAER* CF83 .... 48 A5
Tenison Rd *PPOOL/BLNAV* NP4 . 14 D1
Tennyson Av
  CLN/RNWPTE NP18 .... 59 F5
Tennyson Cl *CALD/MAG* NP26 .. 62 C3
Tennyson Rd *BARRYI/W* CF62 . 139 E1
  CALD/MAG NP26 .... 62 C3
  NWPTE NP19 .... 57 G4
Tennyson Wy *LLMJ* CF61 .... 137 E4
Tensing Cl *CDFN* CF14 .... 100 A1
Tensing Ter *BARRYE* CF63 ...... 139 H3
Tern Cl *CDFNE* CF3 .... 103 E2
Tern Ct *CWM* NP44 .... 18 D3
Terra Nova Wy
  PNRTH/DP CF64 .... 128 B5
Tetbury Cl *NWPT* NP20 .... 56 D2
Tewdric Ct *CWM* NP44 .... 20 C3
Tewdrig Cl *LLMJ* CF61 .... 136 C4
Tewkesbury Pl
  CATH/RTH/SPL CF24 ..... 112 C3
Tewkesbury St
  CATH/RTH/SPL CF24 ..... 112 C4
Tewkesbury Wk *NWPT* NP20 * . 56 D3
Teynes *CWM* NP44 .... 24 C3
Thackeray Crs *CDFNE* CF3 ..... 102 A3
Thames Cl *NWPT* NP20 .... 39 H5
Tharsis Cl *CATH/RTH/SPL* CF24 . 5 C5
Thaw Cl *BARRYI/W* CF62 .... 144 A2
Theobald Rd
  CAE/CAN/FWR CF5 .... 118 D3
Theodora St
  CATH/RTH/SPL CF24 ..... 120 D1
Thesiger Ct
  CATH/RTH/SPL CF24 ..... 112 C5
Thesiger St
  CATH/RTH/SPL CF24 ..... 112 C5
Third Av *CAER* CF83 .... 68 B1
Third St *NWPTE* NP19 .... 77 H4
Thirlmere Pl *NWPTE* NP19 * 57 G1
Thistle Cl *BARRYI/W* CF62 ..... 138 D3
Thistle Ct *CWM* NP44 .... 24 C1
Thistle Wy
  ABRC/NBR/RIS NP11 ...... 37 G4
  CAE/CAN/FWR CF5 .... 117 E5
Thomas St *CAER* CF83 .... 50 B3
  CHEP NP16 .... 28 C4
  GTN/RVSD CF11 .... 6 A3
  NWPT NP20 * 8 E2
  PPRD CF37 .... 44 D3
Thomasville *CAER* CF83 .... 48 B5
Thompson Av
  CAE/CAN/FWR CF5 .... 118 B3
  NWPTE NP19 .... 78 A1
Thompson Cl *NWPTE* NP19 ..... 78 A1
Thompson Pl
  CAE/CAN/FWR CF5 .... 118 B3
Thompson St *BARRYE* CF63 ..... 3 H1
  PPRD CF37 * 44 B3
Thorley Cl
  CYN/LLD/PWYN CF23 ..... 112 D1
Thornaby Ct *CCDF* CF10 .... 7 F1
Thornbury Cl *CDFN* CF14 .... 99 F5
Thorne Wy *CAE/CAN/FWR* CF5 116 C5
Thorn Gv *PNRTH/DP* CF64 ..... 142 C1
Thornhill Cl *BARRYE* CF63 ...... 139 H4
Thornhill Gdns *RSTN* NP10 ..... 54 B2
Thornhill Rd *CDFN* CF14 .... 99 F3
  NWPT NP44 .... 19 E1
Thornhill St
  CAE/CAN/FWR CF5 .... 118 D1
Thorn Tree Dr *CHEP* NP16 ...... 30 D2
Thornwell Rd *CHEP* NP16 .... 30 C2
Thornwood Cl *CDFN* CF14 ...... 85 H4
Three Arches Av *CDFN* CF14 .. 100 D2
Three Oaks Cl *CAER* CF83 ...... 48 D2
Threipland Dr *CDFN* CF14 .... 99 H3
Thrush Cl *CDFNE* CF3 .... 103 F4
Thurston Rd *PPRD* CF37 .... 45 E2
Thurston St
  CAE/CAN/FWR CF5 .... 118 D3
Tidal Sidings
  CATH/RTH/SPL CF24 ..... 120 D4

Tide Fields Rd
  CATH/RTH/SPL CF24 ..... 121 F3
Tidenham Rd
  CAE/CAN/FWR CF5 .... 117 G4
Till Gv *CLN/RNWPTE* NP18 ...... 41 G3
Tillsland *CWM* NP44 .... 25 F3
Timbers Sq
  CATH/RTH/SPL CF24 ..... 113 F5
Timothy Rees Cl
  CDFN CF14 .... 110 B2
Tin St *CATH/RTH/SPL* CF24 ...... 5 J4
Tintagel Cl *CDFN* CF14 .... 85 G5
Tintern Cl *CWM* NP44 .... 19 G3
Tintern St *CAE/CAN/FWR* CF5 . 118 D2
Tippett Cl *NWPTE* NP19 .... 59 E3
Tir Coed *CAER* CF83 .... 48 B4
Tir Deri *CDFNE* CF3 .... 103 F4
Tir Meibion La *LLTR/LLH* CF72 . 95 E2
Tir-y-Coed *CHV/BDAU* CF38 .... 81 H4
Tir-y-Cwm La
  ABRC/NBR/RIS NP11 ...... 36 D5
Tir-y-Cwm Rd
  ABRC/NBR/RIS NP11 ...... 37 E5
Titan Rd *CATH/RTH/SPL* CF24 .... 5 K7
Tiverton Dr *CDFNE* CF3 .... 114 A1
Toftingall Av *CDFN* CF14 .... 99 G5
Toghill Dr
  PENT/RAD/TFW CF15 ..... 83 G4
Toll *NWPT* NP20 .... 77 E3
Tollgate Cl *CAER* CF83 .... 49 G4
  GTN/RVSD CF11 .... 127 H2
Tolpath *CWM* NP44 .... 24 D2
Tom Mann Cl *NWPTE* NP19 ..... 58 D2
Tonegwynlais Gv *CWM* NP44 ... 39 G4
Tone Rd *NWPT* NP20 .... 39 G4
Ton Rd *CWM* NP44 .... 25 E1
Tonteg Cl *CHV/BDAU* CF38 ..... 66 A2
The Ton *CDFNE* CF3 .... 103 F5
Ton-y Felin *PPRD* CF37 .... 65 H1
Ton-y-Felin Rd *CAER* CF83 ...... 69 E1
Ton-yr-Ywen Av *CDFN* CF14 .... 99 H5
Topaz St *CATH/RTH/SPL* CF24 .. 5 K5
Torbay Ter *BARRYI/W* CF62 .... 12 B1
Tordoff Wy *BARRYI/W* CF62 ... 139 E3
Toronto Cl *NWPT* NP20 .... 75 G1
Torridge Rd *NWPT* NP20 .... 39 H4
Torrens Dr
  CYN/LLD/PWYN CF23 ..... 112 D1
Torrington Rd *CDFNE* CF3 ...... 102 B3
Tor Vw *CAER* CF83 .... 49 F2
Tower Hl *PNRTH/DP* CF64 ...... 134 D3
Tower St *PPRD* CF37 .... 65 H1
Tower Wy *PNRTH/DP* CF64 ..... 134 D3
Town Hall Sq *COWBR* CF71 .... 122 D3
Town Mill Rd *COWBR* CF71 .... 122 C4
Town Reach *NWPT* NP20 .... 8 D4
Town Rd *CDFNE* CF3 .... 18 D3
Towyn Wy *CHV/BDAU* CF38 .... 65 H5
Towy Rd *CDFN* CF14 .... 100 B3
Trade La *CCDF* CF10 .... 6 C2
Trade St *CCDF* CF10 .... 6 C1
Trafalgar Rd
  CATH/RTH/SPL CF24 ..... 113 F5
Trafalgar Ter
  ABRC/NBR/RIS NP11 ...... 53 F1
Traherne Dr
  CAE/CAN/FWR CF5 .... 116 C4
Tram La *CWM* NP44 .... 26 D4
Tramore Wy
  CYN/LLD/PWYN CF23 ..... 101 H1
Tram Rd *CLN/RNWPTE* NP18 ... 44 D4
Tramroad *NWPT* NP20 .... 19 E2
Tramway Cl *CWM* NP44 .... 24 D4
Trannon Ct *CWM* NP44 .... 19 E4
Tranquil Pl *CWM* NP44 .... 25 H2
Trap Well *CAER* CF83 .... 49 G4
Traston Av *NWPTE* NP19 .... 78 A3
Traston Cl *NWPTE* NP19 .... 78 A3
Traston La *NWPTE* NP19 .... 78 A3
Traston Rd *NWPTE* NP19 .... 79 H3
Trawsmawr La *NWPT* NP20 ..... 39 H3
Trebanog Cl *CDFNE* CF3 .... 102 D4
Trebanog Crs *CDFNE* CF3 ...... 102 D4
Tre-Beferad *LLMJ* CF61 .... 137 F4
Treberth St *NWPTE* NP19 .... 58 D3
Treberth Vw *NWPTE* NP19 ...... 58 C3
Treborth Rd *CDFNE* CF3 .... 102 D5
Trecastle Av *CDFN* CF14 .... 99 H1
Trecenydd Rd *CDFNE* CF3 ...... 103 E5
Tredegar Dr *CALD/MAG* NP26 .. 61 E3
Tredegar House Dr
  RSTN NP10 .... 75 G5
Tredegar Park Vw *RSTN* NP10 .. 55 F5
Tredegar St
  ABRC/NBR/RIS NP11 ...... 36 A2
  CCDF CF10 .... 4 E6
  NWPT NP20 .... 9 F6
Tredegar Ter
  ABRC/NBR/RIS NP11 ...... 36 A2
Tredelerch Rd *CDFNE* CF3 ..... 114 D1
Tredogan Rd *BARRYI/W* CF62 . 145 E1
Tree Tops *CALD/MAG* NP26 ..... 61 E4
Treetops Cl
  CAE/CAN/FWR CF5 .... 109 H4
Trefaser Crs *CDFNE* CF3 .... 102 D4
Tregare St *NWPTE* NP19 .... 9 G1
Tregaron Rd
  CAE/CAN/FWR CF5 .... 117 E3
Tregwilym St *RSTN* NP10 .... 54 D5
Tregwilym Rd *RSTN* NP10 .... 54 C4
Tregwilym Wk *RSTN* NP10 ...... 54 D5
Treharne Rd *BARRYE* CF63 ..... 139 G2
Treharris St
  CATH/RTH/SPL CF24 .... 5 G1
Tre-Herbert Rd *CWM* NP44 ..... 20 C1
Treherbert St
  CATH/RTH/SPL CF24 ..... 112 B5
Trelawney Av *CDFNE* CF3 ...... 114 B2
Trelech Cl *CWM* NP44 .... 26 A1
Trelewis Cl *BARRYI/W* CF62 ... 144 D3
Trem Maggol *BARRYE* CF63 .... 146 B2
Trem Twynbarlwm
  CWM NP44 .... 25 G2
Trem y Castell *CAER* CF83 ...... 68 A3
Trem y Coed *BARRYE* CF63 .... 131 H5
Trem-y-Don *BARRYI/W* CF62 .. 146 B2
  BARRYI/W CF62 .... 146 B2
Trem-y-Garth *LLTR/LLH* CF72 .. 106 B3

Trenchard Dr *CDFN* CF14.....100 A3
Trent Rd *NWPT* NP20.....39 G4
Treorky St
  CATH/RTH/SPL NP11.....112 B5
Treseder Wy
  CAE/CAN/FWR CF5.....117 H3
Tresigin Rd *CDFNE* CF5.....102 D4
Tresilian Ct *LLMJ* CF61.....136 C4
Tresillian Ter *CCDF* CF10.....6 D1
Tresillian Wy *CCDF* CF10.....6 D1
Trevelyan Ct *CAER* CF83.....69 F1
  LLMJ CF61.....136 C4
Treverbick St *CTN/RVSD* CF11.....119 F3
Trewithick Cl *NWPT* NP20.....40 A3
Trewartha Cl *CHV/BDAU* CF14 *.....99 E5
The Triangle *BARRY/W* CF62.....3 H6
Tribute Av
  ABRC/NBR/RIS NP11.....23 F3
Trident Ct
  CATH/RTH/SPL CF24 *.....5 H7
Tridwr Rd *CAER* CF83.....47 E2
Trinity La *CLN/RNWPTE* NP18.....41 G3
Trinity Pl *NWPT* NP20.....77 E2
Trinity Rd *CWM* NP44.....19 G3
Trinity St *BARRYI/W* CF62.....2 D2
  CCDF CF10.....4 D5
Trinity Vw *CLN/RNWPTE* NP18.....41 F3
Triscombe Dr
  CAE/CAN/FWR CF5.....110 C4
Tristram Cl *CDFN* CF14.....85 G5
Troddi Cl *CALD/MAG* NP26.....62 D2
Troed-y-Bryn *CAER* CF83.....48 B4
Troed-y-Garth
  PENT/RAD/TFW CF15.....96 A1
Troed y Rhiw *CDFN* CF14.....100 D4
Troed-y-Rhiw Rd
  ABRC/NBR/RIS NP11.....35 F2
Trosnant St
  PPOOL/BLNAV NP4.....19 E5
Trostrey *CWM* NP44.....25 F3
Trostrey Cl *PPOOL/BLNAV* NP4.....17 H1
Trostrey St *NWPTE* NP19.....57 E3
Trotman Dickenson Pl
  CDFN CF14.....112 A4
Trowbridge Gn *CDFNE* CF3.....102 D4
Trowbridge Rd *CDFNE* CF3.....102 C5
Trussel Rd *CWM* NP44.....19 H4
Tudor Cl *CAE/CAN/FWR* CF5.....117 G1
  PNRTH/DP CF64.....134 C5
Tudor Crs *RSTN* NP10.....60 D3
Tudor Ct *CALD/MAG* NP26.....61 E3
Tudor Dr *CHEP* NP16.....28 A4
Tudor La *GTN/RVSD* CF11.....4 A7
Tudor Ms *LLTR/LLH* CF72.....107 H1
Tudor Pl *LLMJ* CF61.....136 D4
Tudor Rd *CWM* NP44.....19 H5
  NWPTE NP20.....57 E3
Tudor St *GTN/RVSD* CF11.....119 F5
  PPRD CF37.....65 H3
Tudor Wy *CHV/BDAU* CF38.....81 E4
Tudor Woods *CWM* NP44.....26 C1
Tulloch St *CATH/RTH/SPL* CF24.....119 F4
Tunmel Cl
  CYN/LLD/PWYN CF23.....100 D5
Tump La *CALD/MAG* NP26.....60 D3
Tunnel Ter *NWPT* NP20.....8 C4
Turberville Pl
  CTN/RVSD CF11 *.....119 E2
Turberville Rd *CWM* NP44.....19 H4
Turkey St *LLMJ* CF61.....136 C2
Turner Rd *CAE/CAN/FWR* CF5.....118 C2
Turner St *NWPTE* NP19.....57 E3
Turnham Gn
  CYN/LLD/PWYN CF23.....113 G3
Turnpike Cl *CHEP* NP16.....28 A3
  PNRTH/DP CF64.....133 F2
Turnpike End *CHEP* NP16.....15 F4
Turnpike Rd *CHEP* NP16.....9 F3
Turnpike Rd *CWM* NP44.....26 C2
The Turnstiles *NWPT* NP20.....56 D2
Tuscan Ct *PNRTH/DP* CF64.....127 H4
Tutshill Gdns *CHEP* NP16.....19 F2
Tweedsmuir Rd
  CATH/RTH/SPL CF24.....121 'E1
Tweedy La *NWPTE* NP19.....57 G4
Twissell's Rd
  PPOOL/BLNAV NP4.....14 B4
Twm Barlwm Cl
  ABRC/NBR/RIS NP11.....37 H4
Twmbarlwm Ri *CWM* NP44.....24 B2
Twm Barlwm Vw *CWM* NP44.....26 C1
Twmpath Gdns
  PPOOL/BLNAV NP4.....14 B4
Two Locks Rd *CWM* NP44.....25 G2
Twmpath Rd
  PPOOL/BLNAV NP4.....14 B4
Twyncarn Rd
  ABRC/NBR/RIS NP11.....23 E4
Twyngwyn *PNRTH/DP* CF64.....132 D5
Twyn Oaks *CLN/RNWPTE* NP18.....42 B5
The Twyn *CAER* CF83.....69 F2
Twyn-y-Fedwen *CDFN* CF14.....111 H1
Twyn-y-Fedwen Rd
  CDFN CF14.....111 H1
Ty Box Cl *CWM* NP44.....19 G3
Ty Box Rd *CWM* NP44.....19 G3
Ty-Canol La *CAER* CF83.....50 B3
Ty-Canol Rw *CWM* NP44.....20 D1
Ty-Canol Wy *CWM* NP44.....19 H3
Ty-Cefn Rd *CAE/CAN/FWR* CF5.....117 G2
Ty Cerrig *CYN/LLD/PWYN* CF23.....101 F2
Ty-Coch La *RSTN* NP10.....74 C2
Ty-Coch Rd *CAE/CAN/FWR* CF5.....117 F2
Ty Coch Wy *CWM* NP44.....19 G2
Ty-Coed *CWM* NP44.....19 E3
Ty Draw *CHV/BDAU* CF38.....81 F2
Tydfil Pl *CYN/LLD/PWYN* CF23.....112 D3
Tydfil Rd *CAER* CF83.....50 B3
Tydfil St *BARRYE* CF63.....139 H3
Tydies *CWM* NP44.....25 E5
Ty Draw *CHV/BDAU* CF38.....81 F1
Ty-Draw Pl
  CYN/LLD/PWYN CF23.....113 E4
Ty-Draw Rd
  CYN/LLD/PWYN CF23.....112 D3
Tydu Vw *RSTN* NP10.....55 E4
Tyfica Crs *PPRD* CF37.....44 D3

Tyfica Rd *PPRD* CF37.....44 D3
Ty-Fry Av *CDFNE* CF3.....114 B2
Ty-Fry Gdns *CDFNE* CF3.....114 B1
Ty-Fry Rd *CDFNE* CF3.....114 B2
Ty-Glas Av *CDFN* CF14.....99 H2
Ty-Glas Rd *CDFN* CF14.....99 G2
Ty-Gwyn Av
  CYN/LLD/PWYN CF23.....113 E3
Ty-Gwyn Crs
  CYN/LLD/PWYN CF23.....113 E2
Ty Gwyn Rd *CWM* NP44.....24 D1
Ty-Gwyn Rd
  CYN/LLD/PWYN CF23.....113 E3
  CDFN CF14.....99 F3
Tygwern Rd *CHV/BDAU* CF38.....81 F3
Ty Gwyn Wy *CWM* NP44.....18 D5
Ty-Isaf *CAER* CF83.....48 A4
Ty-Isaf Crs
  ABRC/NBR/RIS NP11.....53 G1
Ty-Isaf Park Av
  ABRC/NBR/RIS NP11 *.....53 H1
Ty-Isaf Park Cir
  ABRC/NBR/RIS NP11 *.....53 H1
Ty-Isaf Park Crs
  ABRC/NBR/RIS NP11 *.....53 G1
Ty-Isaf Park Rd
  ABRC/NBR/RIS NP11.....53 G1
Ty Glas *CAER* CF83.....68 C4
Tyla Gwyn
  PENT/RAD/TFW CF15.....67 E5
Tyla La *CDFNE* CF3.....89 F4
Tyla Rhosyr *COWBR* CF71.....122 B3
Tyle Teg *CDFN* CF14.....98 C2
Tyle Garw *LLTR/LLH* CF72.....106 B2
Tyle House Cl *LLMJ* CF61.....137 E1
Tyle'r Hendy *LLTR/LLH* CF72.....107 G1
Tyler St *CATH/RTH/SPL* CF24.....120 C1
Tylers Wy *CHEP* NP16.....29 F4
Ty-Mawr Av *CDFNE* CF3.....114 A5
Ty-Mawr Cl *CDFNE* CF3.....114 A3
Ty Mawr La *CDFNE* CF3.....104 B2
Ty Mawr Parc *PPRD* CF37.....44 A2
Ty Mawr Rd *CDFN* CF14.....100 C1
  CDFNE CF3.....114 A5
Tymawr Rd *PPRD* CF37.....44 A2
Ty Mynydd *CWM* NP44.....19 H3
Tymynydd Cl
  PENT/RAD/TFW CF15.....97 G3
Ty Nant *CAER* CF83.....48 B5
Tynant *CDFN* CF14.....111 F1
Ty Nant Ct
  PENT/RAD/TFW CF15.....97 G1
Tynant Rd *CTN/RVSD* CF11.....119 F5
Ty-Nant Rd
  PENT/RAD/TFW CF15.....97 G1
Tyndall St *CCDF* CF10.....5 F7
Tyneside Rd *CCDF* CF10.....7 H7
Ty Newydd *CDFN* CF14.....111 E1
Tynewydd Av *CWM* NP44.....111 F1
Tynewydd Dr *CDFNE* CF3.....89 H4
Tynewydd Farm Cl
  CWM NP44.....19 H2
Tynewydd North Cl
  CWM NP44.....19 H2
Ty-Newydd Rd
  BARRYI/W CF62.....139 F3
  CWM NP44.....19 H2
Tynewydd South Cl
  CWM NP44.....19 H2
Ty'N-y-Cae Gv *CDFN* CF14.....99 F4
Ty'N-y-Coed Pl
  CATH/RTH/SPL CF24.....112 D4
Ty'N-y-Graig Rd *CAER* CF83.....33 G5
Ty'N-y Parc *CAER* CF83.....47 E1
Ty'N-y-Parc Rd *CDFN* CF14.....99 E5
Ty'N-y-Pwll Rd *CDFN* CF14.....98 D5
Tyn y Waun Rd *CAER* CF83.....51 H2
Tynywern Ter *CAER* CF83.....50 B2
Ty Parc Cl *CAE/CAN/FWR* CF5.....125 G4
Ty-Pica Dr *CAE/CAN/FWR* CF5.....125 G4
Ty Pucca Cl *CAER* CF83.....51 H3
Ty Pwca Pl *CWM* NP44.....19 F2
Ty Pwca Rd *CWM* NP44.....19 F2
Ty Rhiw *PENT/RAD/TFW* CF15.....83 G3
Tyr-Rosser-Gwyn
  PPOOL/BLNAV NP4.....12 B1
Tyr'r Person *CHV/BDAU* CF38.....81 F1
Tyrwhitt Crs
  CYN/LLD/PWYN CF23.....100 B5
Tyr Winch Rd *CDFNE* CF3.....103 G2
Tyr-y-Sarn Rd *CDFNE* CF3.....114 B2
Ty-to-Maen Cl *CDFNE* CF3.....102 D2
Ty Trappa *CWM* NP44.....19 F2
Ty Trappa Pl *CWM* NP44.....19 F2
Ty Twyn *CHV/BDAU* CF38.....81 F2
Ty-Uchaf *PNRTH/DP* CF64.....134 A4
Ty-Wern Av *CDFN* CF14.....99 F4
Ty-Wern Rd *CDFN* CF14.....99 F4

U

Ullswater Av
  CYN/LLD/PWYN CF23.....112 C2
Underhill Dr *CHV/BDAU* CF38.....81 H1
Underwood *CAER* CF83.....69 E3
Underwood Ter *CAER* CF83.....47 G2
Union St *PPOOL/BLNAV* NP4.....14 D5
Universal St *GTN/RVSD* CF11.....6 A6
University Pl
  CATH/RTH/SPL CF24.....120 D2
Uphill Cl *PNRTH/DP* CF64.....141 F3
Upland Dr *PPOOL/BLNAV* NP4.....102 B1
Upland Pr *PPOOL/BLNAV* NP4.....14 C3
Uplands Crs *PNRTH/DP* CF64.....135 E1
Uplands Rd *CDFNE* CF3.....114 A3
The Uplands
  PENT/RAD/TFW CF15 *.....97 H4
  RSTN NP10.....77 E5
Upper Bridge St
  PPOOL/BLNAV NP4.....14 B4

Upper Brynhyfryd Ter
  PPRD CF37.....32 A3
Upper Church St *CHEP* NP16.....28 C3
Uppercliff Cl *PNRTH/DP* CF64.....134 D1
Uppercliff Dr *PNRTH/DP* CF64.....135 E1
Upper Clifton St
  CATH/RTH/SPL CF24.....5 J2
Upper Cosmeston Farm
  PNRTH/DP CF64.....142 C2
Upper Cwmbran Rd
  CWM NP44.....19 E2
Upper Dock St *NWPT* NP20.....8 E2
Upper Francis St *CAER* CF83.....50 C4
Upper Glyn Gwyn St
  CAER CF83.....50 B3
Upper Kincraig St
  CATH/RTH/SPL CF24.....113 E5
Upper Meadow
  CAE/CAN/FWR CF5.....117 E5
Upper Nelson St *CHEP* NP16.....28 C4
Upper Park Ter
  PPOOL/BLNAV NP4.....14 C4
Upper Power St *NWPT* NP20.....56 C3
Upper Tennyson Rd
  NWPTE NP20.....57 G4
Upper Tribute Av
  ABRC/NBR/RIS NP11.....23 F3
Upper Trosnant St
  PPOOL/BLNAV NP4.....14 C4
Upper Vaughan St *PPRD* CF37.....44 C3
Upton La *NWPT* NP20.....56 A5
Upton Pl *CHV/BDAU* CF38.....80 C4
Upton Rd *NWPT* NP20.....56 A5
Usk Cl *CALD/MAG* NP26.....63 E1
Usk St *CWM* NP44.....19 E4
Uskley Ct *CDFNE* CF3.....102 D4
Usk Rd *CDFN* CF14.....100 B2
  CLN/RNWPTE NP18.....42 A3
  PPOOL/BLNAV NP4.....15 E5
Usk St *NWPTE* NP19.....57 E3
Usk Vale Cl
  CLN/RNWPTE NP18 *.....42 A3
Usk Vale Ct *PPOOL/BLNAV* NP4.....15 F4
Usk Vale Dr
  CLN/RNWPTE NP18.....42 A3
Usk Valley Wk
  CLN/RNWPTE NP18.....42 C5
Usk Wy *BARRY1/W* CF62.....138 C3
  NWPT NP20.....9 G4

V

Vachell Ct *LLMJ* CF61.....137 E3
Vachell Rd *CAE/CAN/FWR* CF5.....117 F3
Vaendre Cl *CDFNE* CF3.....103 F1
Vaendre Ct *CDFNE* CF3.....103 E2
Vaendre La *CDFNE* CF3.....103 F2
Vaindre Cl *CDFNE* CF3.....103 F2
Vaindre Dr *CDFNE* CF3.....103 G2
Valarian Cl *CDFNE* CF3.....103 G4
Vale Ct *COWBR* CF71.....123 E4
Vale Gdns *PNRTH/DP* CF64.....133 F3
Valentine Cl *LLMJ* CF61.....136 C4
Valentine Ct *PNRTH/DP* CF64.....30 D3
Valentine Rd
  PPOOL/BLNAV NP4.....12 D5
Vale Rd *CTH/RTH/SPL* CF24.....120 D1
Vale St *BARRYI/W* CF62.....37 F4
Vale Vw *ABRC/NBR/RIS* NP11.....37 F4
Vale View Ct *PNRTH/DP* CF64.....127 H5
Vale View Crs *PNRTH/DP* CF64.....127 H5
Valley Vw *CDFNE* CF3.....115 E1
Vanbrugh Cl *RSTN* NP10.....55 E3
Vanbrugh Gdns *NWPT* NP20.....75 H3
Vancouver Dr *NWPT* NP20.....75 G1
Van Dyke Cl *NWPT* NP20.....57 G2
Vanfield Cl *CAER* CF83.....69 F2
Vanguard Wy
  CATH/RTH/SPL CF24.....7 K1
Van Rd *CAER* CF83.....69 E2
Van St *GTN/RVSD* CF11.....119 F5
Varteg Rd *PPOOL/BLNAV* NP4.....10 B5
Vaughan Av
  CAE/CAN/FWR CF5.....110 D5
Vaughan Williams Dr
  NWPTE NP20.....58 B4
Vauxhall La *CHEP* NP16.....28 A4
Vauxhall Rd *CHEP* NP16.....28 A4
Veindre Cl *CDFNE* CF3.....103 F1
Velindre Rd *CDFN* CF14.....98 B5
Vellacott Cl *CCDF* CF10.....7 F1
Ventnor Pl *CDFN* CF14.....111 H3
Ventnor Rd *CWM* NP44.....25 H1
Venwood Cl
  CAE/CAN/FWR CF5.....125 G5
Verallo Dr *GTN/RVSD* CF11.....118 C4
Verbena Cl *CDFNE* CF3.....103 F2
Vere St *BARRYE* CF63.....140 A3
Verland Cl *CAE/CAN/FWR* CF5.....111 E5
The Verlands *COWBR* CF71.....122 B3
Verlon Cl *BARRYE* CF63.....140 C2
Vermeer Crs *NWPTE* NP19.....57 H2
Veronica Ct *RSTN* NP10 *.....77 E5
Vervain Cl *CAE/CAN/FWR* CF5.....116 D3
Viaduct Cl *RSTN* NP10.....75 E1
Viaduct Rd *BARRYE* CF63.....139 H5
  PENT/RAD/TFW CF15.....83 F4
  PPRD CF37.....44 D4
Viaduct Wy *RSTN* NP10.....75 E1
Vibernum Ri *CHV/BDAU* CF38.....80 D5
Vicarage Cl *PNRTH/DP* CF64.....75 E2
Vicarage Ct *CDFNE* CF3.....90 A5
Vicarage Gdns *CDFNE* CF3.....90 A5
  RSTN NP10 *.....54 B3
Vicarage Hl *NWPT* NP20.....8 D5
Vicarage La
  CYN/LLD/PWYN CF23.....12 C2
Victoria Av *CAE/CAN/FWR* CF5.....118 C2
  NWPTE NP19.....9 K2
  PNRTH/DP CF64.....134 C3

Victoria Ct *NWPTE* NP19.....9 K2
Victoria Rd *NWPT* NP20.....9 H2
Victoria La *NWPTE* NP19.....57 G3
Victoria Ms *CDFN* CF14.....112 A3
  LLTR/LLH CF72.....94 B5
Victoria Park Rd *BARRYE* CF63.....139 H2
Victoria Park Rd East
  CAE/CAN/FWR CF5.....118 C2
Victoria Pl *NWPT* NP20.....8 E5
Victoria Park Rd West
  CAE/CAN/FWR CF5.....118 B3
Victoria Rd *BARRYI/W* CF62.....2 C2
  CHEP NP16.....30 D2
  NWPT NP20.....8 E5
  PNRTH/DP CF64.....134 C2
  PPOOL/BLNAV NP4.....14 D5
Victoria Sq *PNRTH/DP* CF64.....134 C3
  CWM NP44.....25 H1
Victoria St *CATH/RTH/SPL* CF24.....33 H3
Victoria Wy *CALD/MAG* NP26.....60 D3
Viking Pl *CCDF* CF10.....129 H1
Village Wy
  PENT/RAD/TFW CF15.....98 B2
Vincent Ct *BARRYE* CF63.....140 A1
Vincent Rd *CAE/CAN/FWR* CF5.....117 H2
Vine Cots *CHEP* NP16.....9 J1
Vinegar Hl *CALD/MAG* NP26.....60 D3
Vine Pl *NWPTE* NP19.....9 J1
Violet Pl *CDFN* CF14.....142 C2
Violet Row *CTN/RVSD* CF11.....112 D5
Violet Wk *RSTN* NP10.....52 D3
Virgil St *GTN/RVSD* CF11.....119 F5
Virgil St *GTN/RVSD* CF11.....119 F5
Virginia Cl *CAER* CF83.....49 E5
Viscount Evan Dr *RSTN* NP10.....76 A5
Vishwell Rd
  CAE/CAN/FWR CF5.....118 C1
  CAE/CAN/FWR CF5.....131 C1
Vista Ri *CAE/CAN/FWR* CF5.....111 H2
Vivian Rd *NWPTE* NP19.....9 K4
Voss Park Cl *LLMJ* CF61.....137 E3
Voss Park Dr *LLMJ* CF61.....137 E3

W

Wagtail Rd *BARRYI/W* CF62.....137 H3
Wainfelin Av
  PPOOL/BLNAV NP4.....14 B3
Wainfelin Rd
  PPOOL/BLNAV NP4.....14 B2
Wakehurst Pl *CDFNE* CF3.....103 E3
Wakelin Cl *CHV/BDAU* CF38.....81 F2
Walden Grange Cl
  NWPTE NP19.....58 A4
Walford Davies Dr
  NWPTE NP19.....58 B4
Walford Pl *GTN/RVSD* CF11.....119 E3
Walford St *NWPT* NP20.....56 C2
Walker Rd *BARRYI/W* CF62.....139 E3
  CATH/RTH/SPL CF24.....120 D3
Walk Farm Dr *CDFNE* CF3.....89 H3
The Walk *CATH/RTH/SPL* CF24.....5 H4
  PPOOL/BLNAV NP4.....17 G1
Wallis St *NWPT* NP20 *.....77 E2
Wallwern Wd *CHEP* NP16.....28 A3
Walmer Rd *NWPTE* NP19.....57 H3
Walnut Cl *LLTR/LLH* CF72.....95 E5
Walnut Dr *CLN/RNWPTE* NP18.....41 F4
Walnut Tree Cl
  PENT/RAD/TFW CF15.....97 H1
Walpole Cl *CDFNE* CF3.....102 B2
Walsall St *NWPTE* NP19.....9 K4
Walston Cl *CAE/CAN/FWR* CF5.....125 G4
Walston Rd
  CAE/CAN/FWR CF5.....125 F4
Walters Rd *PPRD* CF37.....58 B5
Walton Cl *NWPT* NP20 *.....58 D5
Walton Pl *GTN/RVSD* CF11.....119 E3
Walwyn Pl *CDFNE* CF3.....103 E5
Wanderers Crs
  CAE/CAN/FWR CF5.....116 D4
Wansford Av *CDFNE* CF3.....102 A1
Ward Rd *CAER* CF83.....68 B3
Warlock Cl *NWPTE* NP19.....59 E4
Warren Ct *PPRD* CF37.....65 G2
Warren La *CAER* CF83.....69 G1
Warren Rd *CAER* CF83.....69 G1
Warren Slade *CHEP* NP16.....30 D2
Warwick Cl *CHEP* NP16.....30 B1
Warwick La *NWPTE* NP19.....57 H4
Warwick Pl *GTN/RVSD* CF11.....57 H5
Warwick Rd *NWPTE* NP19.....57 H5
Warwick St *GTN/RVSD* CF11.....6 A2
Warwick Wy *BARRYI/W* CF62.....139 F3
Wasdale Cl
  CYN/LLD/PWYN CF23.....113 G2
Washford Av *CDFNE* CF3.....102 B3
Watchet Cl *CDFNE* CF3.....102 A1
Watch House Pde
  NWPT NP20 *.....77 E3
Water Avens Cl *CDFNE* CF3.....103 G4
Waterfall Ms *LLMJ* CF61.....136 D5
Waterford Cl *GTN/RVSD* CF11.....119 F4
Waterhall Rd
  CAE/CAN/FWR CF5.....118 A1
Waterhouse Dr
  GTN/RVSD CF11.....119 E5
Waterloo Cl
  CYN/LLD/PWYN CF23.....113 G3
Waterloo Gdns
  CYN/LLD/PWYN CF23.....113 G3
Waterloo Pl *CAER* CF83.....51 E4
Waterloo Rd *CAER* CF83.....51 E4
  PPOOL/BLNAV NP4.....12 B3
Waterloo Terrace Rd
  CAER CF83.....51 E4

Waterquarter *CCDF* CF10.....7 H3
Waterside Cl *RSTN* NP10.....54 D2
Waterside Rd West
  RSTN.....54 D3
Waters La *NWPT* NP20.....8 D3
Waterston Rd *CDFN* CF14.....111 F3
Waters Wy *CHEP* NP16.....28 C5
Waterworks La
  PPOOL/BLNAV NP4.....12 D2
Watery La *COWBR* CF71.....123 G1
Watford Cl *CAER* CF83.....68 C3
Watford Ri *CAER* CF83.....68 C3
Watford Rd *CAER* CF83.....68 C3
  CATH/RTH/SPL CF24.....113 G5
Watkins La *NWPT* NP20 *.....56 A5
Watkins Sq *CDFN* CF14.....99 G3
Watson Rd *CDFN* CF14.....111 E3
Watson St *BARRYE* CF63.....139 G4
Watts Cl *RSTN* NP10.....55 E3
Waun Dyfal *CDFN* CF14.....99 G3
Waun Erw *CAER* CF83.....49 E4
Waun Fach
  CYN/LLD/PWYN CF23.....101 F3
Waunfach Flats *CAER* CF83.....48 D5
Waunfach St *CAER* CF83.....48 D5
Waunfain *CAER* CF83.....48 D5
Waunarlwydd Park Rd
  ABRC/NBR/RIS NP11.....36 B2
Waunfawr Rd
  ABRC/NBR/RIS NP11.....36 B2
Waun-Fawr Rd *CAER* CF83.....99 F4
Waunfawr Ter
  ABRC/NBR/RIS NP11.....36 B2
Waun Ganol *PNRTH/DP* CF64.....134 A5
Waun Ganol St *CAER* CF83.....48 D5
Waun-Gron Rd
  CAE/CAN/FWR CF5.....118 A1
Waun Hir *CHV/BDAU* CF38.....81 G5
Waun Hywel Rd *CWM* NP44.....19 F2
Waun Rd *CWM* NP44.....25 F2
Waunreoda Rd *CAER* CF83.....111 G2
Waunwaelod Wy *CAER* CF83.....49 E5
Waun Wern Pk
  PPOOL/BLNAV NP4.....14 B5
Waun-y-Groes Av *CDFN* CF14.....99 F5
Waun-y-Groes Rd *CDFN* CF14.....99 F5
Wavell Cl *CDFN* CF14.....100 A4
Wavell Dr *NWPT* NP20.....58 D4
Waveney Cl *NWPT* NP20.....40 A4
Waverley Cl *PNRTH/DP* CF64.....128 A5
Waverley Sq *CCDF* CF10.....6 E6
Waycock Rd *BARRYI/W* CF62.....138 A2
Wayfield Crs *CWM* NP44.....19 H5
Wayne St *CAER* CF83.....50 C4
Weare Cl *NWPT* NP20.....39 F4
Webley Cl *CLN/RNWPTE* NP18 *.....41 H2
Webley Gdns
  CLN/RNWPTE NP18.....41 H2
Wedgewood Ct *CAER* CF83.....69 F1
Wedmore Rd *GTN/RVSD* CF11.....119 F4
Wednesbury St *NWPTE* NP19.....9 K5
Weekes Cl *CDFNE* CF3.....102 C3
Welby Rd *CAE/CAN/FWR* CF5.....118 C1
Weldon Cl *CWM* NP44.....20 C3
Welford St *BARRYI/W* CF62.....2 C5
Welland Crs *NWPT* NP20.....39 F4
Welland Crs *NWPT* NP20.....39 F4
Well Cl *CHEP* NP16.....30 D3
Wellfield *CHV/BDAU* CF38.....80 C4
Wellfield Ct *CDFNE* CF38.....104 A2
  CDFNE CF38.....65 F5
Wellfield La
  PPOOL/BLNAV NP4.....16 D5
Wellfield Pl
  CATH/RTH/SPL CF24.....113 E5
Wellfield Rd
  CATH/RTH/SPL CF24.....113 E5
  CDFNE CF3.....104 A2
Wellington Dr *CWM* NP44.....18 D5
Wellington Rd *NWPT* NP20.....58 G1
  PPOOL/BLNAV NP4.....12 D3
Wellington St *GTN/RVSD* CF11.....119 F3
  PENT/RAD/TFW CF15.....97 H1
Wellright Rd
  CAE/CAN/FWR CF5.....117 C1
Wells Cl *NWPT* NP20.....75 H3
Wellspring Ter
  ABRC/NBR/RIS NP11.....37 F5
Wells St *GTN/RVSD* CF11.....119 E3
  BARRYI/W CF62.....2 A7
Wellwood
  CYN/LLD/PWYN CF23.....113 G2
Well Wood Cl
  CYN/LLD/PWYN CF23.....113 G3
Welsh St *CHEP* NP16.....28 C3
Welwyn Rd *CDFN* CF14.....99 F5
Wembley Gn
  CAE/CAN/FWR CF5.....118 C3
Wenallt Ct *CDFN* CF14.....118 C4
Wenallt Rd *CAER* CF83.....84 D5
  CDFN CF14.....84 D5
Wentloog Av *CDFNE* CF3.....114 D2
Wentloog Cl *CDFNE* CF3.....114 B2
Wentloog Corporate Pk
  CDFNE CF3 *.....115 G2
Wentloog Ri *CDFNE* CF3.....89 H4
Wentloog Rd *CDFNE* CF3.....114 B2
Wentsland Crs
  PPOOL/BLNAV NP4.....14 A4
Wentsland Rd
  PPOOL/BLNAV NP4.....14 A4
Wentwood Rd *CWM* NP44.....19 F2
Wentwood Vw
  CLN/RNWPTE NP18.....41 H4
Wentwood Vw
  CALD/MAG NP26.....62 D1
Wentworth Cl *CDFNE* CF3.....103 F2
  RSTN NP10.....74 C1
Wentworth La *CDFNE* CF3.....103 G2
Wenvoe Ter *BARRYI/W* CF62.....2 B5
Werfa St *CYN/LLD/PWYN* CF23.....112 D4
Wern Fawr La *CDFNE* CF3.....102 D2
Wern Gethin La *CDFNE* CF3.....103 E2
Wern Goch East
  CYN/LLD/PWYN CF23.....101 F4

Werngoch Rd
 CYN/LLD/PWYN CF23........ 100 D4
Wern Goch Wy
 CYN/LLD/PWYN CF23........ 101 E4
Wern Goch West
 CYN/LLD/PWYN CF23........ 101 E4
Wern Hl PPOOL/BLNAV NP4 .... 14 B4
Wern Migna
 CAE/CAN/FWR CF5 .... 96 D5
Wern Rd PPOOL/BLNAV NP4 .... 54 C3
Wern School Cl
 PPOOL/BLNAV NP4 .... 17 E4
Wern Ter RSTN NP10 .... 54 C2
Wesley Av BARRYI/W CF62 .... 144 B2
Wesley Cl CWM NP44 .... 25 C1
Wesley Ct PNRTH/DP CF64 .... 133 E5
Wesley Hl CAER CF83 .... 51 F2
Wesley La CCDF CF10 .... 4 E5
Wesley Pl ABRC/NBR/RIS NP11.. 37 E5
Wesley Rd CAER CF83 .... 68 A3
Wesley St CWM NP44 .... 25 C1
 LLMJ CF61 .... 136 C3
Wessex Pl BARRYI/W CF62 .... 2 B7
Wessex St CAE/CAN/FWR CF5 .. 118 C2
West Acre LLMJ CF61 .... 137 E1
West Av CAER CF83 .... 68 B1
 PPOOL/BLNAV NP4 .... 16 D4
West Bank CWM NP44 .... 25 E3
Westbourne Ct CDFNE CF3 .... 114 C3
Westbourne Crs CDFNE CF3 .... 110 C1
Westbourne Rd CDFN CF14 .... 110 D1
 PNRTH/DP CF64 .... 134 C5
Westbury Cl BARRYE CF63 .... 139 G2
Westbury Ter
 CAE/CAN/FWR CF5 .... 118 C1
West Cl CCDF CF10 .... 7 F4
West Ct PNRTH/DP CF64 * 134 C2
West End CALD/MAG NP26 .... 60 B4
West End Gdns
 CALD/MAG NP26 .... 60 D4
Western Av
 CAE/CAN/FWR CF5 .... 118 A1
 CHEP NP16 .... 30 C2
 NWPT NP20 .... 55 F5
Western Av North CDFN CF14 111 C4
Western Dr CDFN CF14 .... 111 C4
Western Ter
 ABRC/NBR/RIS NP11 .... 34 B2
 ABRC/NBR/RIS NP11 .... 8 B2
Western Valley Rd RSTN NP10.. 75 E1
Westfield CALD/MAG NP26 .... 62 C3
 CDFN CF14 .... 99 F5
 NWPT NP20 .... 40 B4
Westfield Cl
 CLN/RNWPTE NP18 .... 41 G3
Westfield Ct LLTR/LLH CF72 .... 95 F3
Westfield Dr NWPT NP20 .... 40 B4
 PNRTH/DP CF64 .... 134 A4
Westfield Rd CDFN CF14 .... 111 C1
 CLN/RNWPTE NP18 .... 41 G3
 NWPT NP20 .... 8 A3
Westfield Wy NWPT NP20 .... 40 B4
Westgate COWBR CF71 .... 122 B3
Westgate Ct
 CLN/RNWPTE NP18 .... 42 A4
Westgate St CCDF CF10 .... 4 B5
West Gv CAE/CAN/FWR CF5 .. 125 F1
West Gv CATH/RTH/SPL CF24.. 5 H5
Westhill Dr LLTR/LLH CF72 .... 95 F3
West Hill Rd
 PPOOL/BLNAV NP4 .... 14 B1
West St LLMJ CF61 .... 136 C3
Westland Cl
 CATH/RTH/SPL CF24.. 121 F1
West Lee GTN/RVSD CF11 * 119 F2
West Luton Pl
 CATH/RTH/SPL CF24.. 5 H5
West Market St NWPT NP20 .... 9 F6
Westminster Crs
 CYN/LLD/PWYN CF23 .... 100 D3
Westminster Dr
 CYN/LLD/PWYN CF23 .... 100 D1
 PNRTH/DP CF64 .... 78 B1
Westmoor Cl NWPT NP19 .... 78 B1
Westmoreland St
 CAE/CAN/FWR CF5 .... 118 C3
West Mount Crs
 CHV/BDAU CF38 .... 81 H1
West Nash Rd
 CLN/RNWPTE NP18 .... 93 G3
Weston Av PNRTH/DP CF64 ... 141 F5
Westonbirt Cl CDFNE CF3 .... 25 E3
Weston Ct CHV/BDAU CF38 .... 81 C2
Weston Rd CDFNE CF3 .... 102 A5
Weston St BARRYE CF63 * 139 H3
West Orchard Crs
 CAE/CAN/FWR CF5 .... 118 B1
West Park La NWPT NP20 .... 56 A5
West Park Rd NWPT NP20 .... 56 A5
Westra PNRTH/DP CF64 .... 132 C4
Westray Cl NWPTE NP19 .... 57 G2
West Ri CWM NP44 .... 100 B2
West Rd CDFN CF14 .... 110 D2
West Roedin CWM NP44 .... 25 E3
West St LLMJ CF61 .... 136 B3
 NWPT NP20 .... 8 D3
 PPRD CF37 .... 45 E2
West Ter PNRTH/DP CF64 .... 134 C2
Westville Rd
 CYN/LLD/PWYN CF23 .... 113 E4
 NWPT NP20 .... 56 A5
Westville Wk
 CYN/LLD/PWYN CF23 .... 113 E4
West Wk BARRYI/W CF62 .... 138 C3
Westward Ri BARRYI/W CF62.. 146 A1
Westway CALD/MAG NP26 .... 62 A4
West Way Rd NWPT NP20 .... 56 A5
West Wharf Rd CCDF CF64.. 134 C5
Wexford Ct
 CYN/LLD/PWYN CF23 .... 87 H5
Wharfedale Rd
 CYN/LLD/PWYN CF23 .... 101 G2
Wharf La NWPTE NP19 .... 9 K3
Wharton Cl BARRYI/W CF62.. 144 A3
Wharton St CCDF CF10 .... 4 D6

The Wheate Cl
 BARRYI/W CF62 .... 144 C2
Wheatley Rd
 CAE/CAN/FWR CF5 .... 117 F4
Wheatsheaf Ct
 CALD/MAG NP26 .... 60 C3
Wheeler St NWPT NP20 .... 56 D2
Whinberry Wy
 CAE/CAN/FWR CF5 .... 116 D3
Whinchat Cl CDFNE CF3 * 103 F3
Whistler Cl NWPTE NP19 * 57 C2
Whitaker Rd
 CATH/RTH/SPL CF24.. 114 A5
Whitby Pl NWPTE NP19 .... 9 H1
Whitchurch Pl
 CATH/RTH/SPL CF24.. 112 C4
Whitchurch Rd CATH/RTH.. 112 A3
Whitcliffe Dr PNRTH/DP CF64 .. 142 D1
Whiteacre Cl CDFNE CF3 .... 86 A5
White Ash Gld
 CLN/RNWPTE NP18 .... 41 G4
White Av RSTN NP10 .... 91 H2
White Barn Rd CDFN CF14 .... 99 G2
Whitebrook Wy CWM NP44 .. 25 H1
Whitechapel Wk
 CALD/MAG NP26 .... 60 D2
White Cross La CAER CF83 .... 48 A5
Whitefield Rd CDFN CF14 .... 111 E3
Whitehall Cl
 CAE/CAN/FWR CF5 .... 125 F4
Whitehall Gdns
 CALD/MAG NP26 .... 61 E4
White Hall La CWM NP44 .... 26 C1
Whitehall Pde CDFNE CF3 .... 114 B2
Whitehall Pl CDFNE CF3 .... 114 A2
Whitehart La
 CLN/RNWPTE NP18 .... 42 B5
White Hart Dr CAER CF83 .... 51 F2
Whitehart La
 CLN/RNWPTE NP18 .... 42 B5
White House BARRYI/W CF62 .. 146 C3
White House Rd CWM NP44 .. 20 B3
White Oaks Dr CDFNE CF3 .... 102 D2
Whiterock Av PPRD CF37 * 44 C2
Whiterock Ct PPRD CF37 * 44 C2
Whiterock Dr PPRD CF37 .... 44 C2
Whitesands Rd CWM NP44 .... 99 G1
White St CAER CF83 .... 69 E2
Whitethorn Wy CDFNE CF3 .. 102 B2
Whitewall CALD/MAG NP26 .. 60 C4
Whiteways LLMJ CF61 .... 137 E2
Whitewell Dr LLMJ CF61 .... 136 C4
Whitewell Rd BARRYI/W CF62 .. 139 E2
Whitland Cl
 CAE/CAN/FWR CF5 .... 110 B4
Whitland Crs
 CAE/CAN/FWR CF5 .... 110 B4
Whitmuir Rd
 CATH/RTH/SPL CF24.. 121 E1
Whitstone Rd NWPTE NP19 .. 58 A3
Whittan Cl BARRYI/W CF62 .. 144 A2
Whittle Rd GTN/RVSD CF11 .. 118 D5
Whitworth Sq CDFNE CF14 .. 98 B3
Wicken Cl CDFNE CF3 * 103 F3
Wicklow Cl
 CYN/LLD/PWYN CF23 .... 101 H1
Wick Rd LLMJ CF61 .... 136 B2
Widecombe Dr CDFNE CF3 .. 114 A2
Wiesenthal Cl
 CALD/MAG NP26 .... 63 E2
Wigmore Cl CDFNE CF14 .... 85 H5
Wilcrick Pl CWM NP44 .... 20 A3
Wild Gardens Rd
 CYN/LLD/PWYN CF23 .... 100 B5
Wilfred St BARRYE CF63 .... 139 H4
Wilkinson Cl
 CATH/RTH/SPL CF24.. 5 J5
Willenhall St NWPTE NP19 .... 9 J5
William Belcher Dr CDFNE.. 103 F5
William Brown Cl CWM NP44 .. 26 B4
William Lovett Gdns
 NWPT NP20 .... 8 C4
William Morris Dr
 NWPTE NP19 .... 58 C3
William Nicholls Dr
 NWPT NP20 .... 102 D2
Williams Cl NWPT NP20 .... 9 F7
 PPRD CF37 .... 66 B1
Williams Crs BARRYI/W CF62.. 139 E4
William St
 ABRC/NBR/RIS NP11 .... 34 C3
 CAER CF83 .... 47 F2
 CAER CF83 .... 50 B2
 GTN/RVSD CF11 .... 119 E1
Willins CWM NP44 .... 25 E3
Williton Rd CDFNE CF3 .... 85 H5
Willowbrook Gdns CDFNE .. 103 E2
Willowbrook Dr CDFNE CF3 .. 102 D5
Willowbrook Gdns CDFNE .. 103 E2
Willow Cl CALD/MAG NP26 .... 62 D2
 CHV/BDAU CF38 .... 80 A5
 NWPTE NP19 .... 78 A2
 PNRTH/DP CF64 .... 134 A3
Willow Ct CATH/RTH/SPL CF24.. 5 H2
Willowdale Rd
 CAE/CAN/FWR CF5 .... 109 H5
Willowdene Wy CDFNE CF3 .. 103 F2
The Willowford PPRD CF37 .... 66 D4
Willow Gv CDFNE CF3 .... 103 F2
Willow Herb Cl CDFNE CF3 .. 103 G4
Willowmere PNRTH/DP CF64 .. 127 H4
Willow Rd LLTR/LLH CF72 .... 106 A3
Willows Av
 CATH/RTH/SPL CF24.. 121 G2
Willows Crs BARRYE CF63 .... 139 G2
The Willows CALD/MAG NP26 .. 60 C3
 CWM NP44 .... 8 D3
Willow St PPRD CF37 .... 65 H2
Willow Tree Cl
 PENT/RAD/TFW CF15 .... 97 E4
Willow Wk RSTN NP10 .... 54 D2
Wilson Pl CAE/CAN/FWR CF5 .. 117 F4
Wilson Rd CAE/CAN/FWR CF5 .. 117 E2
 NWPTE NP19 .... 57 H2
Wilson St CATH/RTH/SPL CF24.. 120 D1
 NWPT NP20 .... 77 E2
Wimborne Crs
 PNRTH/DP CF64 .... 141 F4
Wimborne Ri CWM NP44 .... 19 F3

Wimborne Rd BARRYE CF63 .. 140 A5
Wimborne Cl LLMJ CF61 .... 136 B3
Winchester Av
 CYN/LLD/PWYN CF23 .... 113 F3
Winchester Cl BARRYI/W CF62.. 138 D4
 NWPT NP20 .... 76 B3
Windermere Av
 CYN/LLD/PWYN CF23 .... 112 C2
Windermere Sq
 NWPTE NP19 * 57 F1
Windflower Cl CDFNE 103 F3
Windhover Cl CDFNE CF3 .... 103 F4
Windlass Ct CCDF CF10 .... 7 G2
Windmill Cl CDFNE CF14 * 85 H5
 LLMJ CF61 .... 136 C2
Windmill La CALD/MAG NP26.. 61 H1
 COWBR CF71 .... 122 C4
 LLMJ CF61 .... 136 D2
Windmill Sq NWPT NP20 .... 9 F6
Windrush Cl NWPT NP20 .... 39 H4
Windsor Av
 PENT/RAD/TFW CF15 .... 97 G4
Windsor Clive Dr
 CAE/CAN/FWR CF5 .... 96 D5
Windsor Cl CALD/MAG NP26.. 60 B3
 PENT/RAD/TFW CF15 .... 97 G4
Windsor Ct LLTR/LLH CF72 .... 107 F1
Windsor Esp PNRTH/DP CF64 *.. 134 D3
Windsor Crs
 PENT/RAD/TFW CF15 .... 97 H5
Windsor Dr CALD/MAG NP26.. 60 B3
 LLTR/LLH CF72 .... 107 H1
Windsor Esp CCDF CF10 .... 6 E7
Windsor Gdns
 CALD/MAG NP26 .... 60 B3
 CHV/BDAU CF38 .... 80 B2
Windsor Gn
 CAE/CAN/FWR CF5 .... 117 H2
Windsor Gv
 PENT/RAD/TFW CF15 .... 97 G4
Windsor La CCDF CF10 .... 4 E4
Windsor Ms
 CALD/MAG NP26 .... 62 D4
Windsor Pk CALD/MAG NP26.. 60 B3
Windsor Pl CAER CF83 .... 47 E2
 CCDF CF10 .... 4 E3
 PNRTH/DP CF64 .... 134 C2
Windsor Qy CYN/RVSD CF11 .. 128 C3
Windsor Rd BARRYI/W CF62 .. 2 C4
 CWM NP44 .... 25 E1
 NWPTE NP19 .... 57 H2
 PENT/RAD/TFW CF15 .... 97 G5
 PNRTH/DP CF64 .... 134 B1
 PPOOL/BLNAV NP4 .... 17 E2
 PPRD CF37 .... 45 F5
Windsor St CAER CF83 .... 69 E2
Windsor Ter CCDF CF10 .... 7 H1
 NWPT NP20 .... 8 C4
 PNRTH/DP CF64 .... 134 D2
Windsor Terrace La
 PNRTH/DP CF64 .... 134 D2
Windway Av
 CAE/CAN/FWR CF5 .... 118 B2
Windway Rd
 CAE/CAN/FWR CF5 .... 118 A1
Windyridge PNRTH/DP CF64.. 133 G4
Wine St LLMJ CF61 .... 136 C3
Wingate Dr CDFN CF14 .... 100 A4
Wingate St NWPT NP20 .... 8 A5
Wingfield Av
 CHV/BDAU CF38 * 80 A3
Wingfield Cl PPRD CF37 .... 38 E1
Wingfield Crs CAER CF83 .... 33 H1
Wingfield Rd CDFN CF14 .... 110 D1
Winifred Av BARRYI/W CF62 .. 139 E1
Winnipeg Dr
 CYN/LLD/PWYN CF23 .... 100 D5
Winsford Rd PNRTH/DP CF64.. 141 G4
Winston Av
 CAE/CAN/FWR CF5 .... 125 G1
Winstone Av
 CAE/CAN/FWR CF5 * 125 G1
Winton Ms
 PPOOL/BLNAV NP4 .... 14 B1
Winston Rd BARRYI/W CF62 .. 139 E1
Wintour Cl CHEP NP16 .... 28 B3
Wirewood Cl CHEP NP16 .... 28 D2
Wirewood Crs CHEP NP16.. 29 E2
Wisley Pl CYN/LLD/PWYN CF23.. 101 F1
Wistaria Cl NWPT NP20 .... 40 C3
Witham St NWPTE NP19 .... 9 J4
Withycombe Rd CDFNE CF3 .. 102 B2
Withy Wk CALD/MAG NP26 .. 60 B3
Witla Court Rd CDFNE CF3 .. 102 B5
Wolfe Cl BARRYE CF63 .... 140 A2
Wolffe Cl COWBR CF71 .... 122 C4
Wolfs Castle Av CDFN CF14 .. 99 H1
Wolseley Cl NWPT NP20 .... 76 D3
Wolseley St NWPT NP20 .... 76 D3
Womanby St CCDF CF10 .... 4 C5
Woodbine Gdns
 CALD/MAG NP26 .... 60 C3
Wood Cl CDFN CF14 .... 99 G2
 CWM NP44 .... 26 C2
 RSTN NP10 .... 54 D2
Woodcock St
 CATH/RTH/SPL CF24.. 5 H1
Wood Crs RSTN NP10 .... 54 D2
Woodfield Av
 PENT/RAD/TFW CF15 .... 110 A1
Woodfield Cl CDFNE CF3 .... 104 B2
Woodfield Rd LLTR/LLH CF72.. 94 B3
 PPOOL/BLNAV NP4 .... 17 G1
Woodford Cl
 CAE/CAN/FWR CF5 .... 110 C4
Woodham Pk CDFNE CF3.. 138 D3
Woodham Rd BARRYE CF63.. 139 H5
Woodland Crs
 CYN/LLD/PWYN CF23 .... 113 E1
Woodland Dr PNRTH/DP CF64.. 134 C2
 RSTN NP10 .... 74 C1
Woodland Park Rd
 NWPTE NP19 .... 57 G3
Woodland Pl
 PNRTH/DP CF64 .... 5 G2
 PNRTH/DP CF64 .... 134 C2
 PPRD CF37 * 64 C1

Woodland Rd CDFN CF14 .... 110 C1
 CHV/BDAU CF38 .... 80 B4
 CWM NP44 .... 40 B2
 NWPTE NP19 .... 57 C3
Woodlands
 CHV/BDAU CF38 .... 80 C3
Woodlands Cl COWBR CF71 .. 122 B3
Woodlands Ct
 BARRYI/W CF62 .... 139 E4
Woodlands Dr NWPT NP20 ... 40 B2
Woodlands Park Dr
 CAE/CAN/FWR CF5 .... 117 F5
Woodlands Rd
 BARRYI/W CF62 .... 139 E4
The Woodlands CDFN CF14 .. 86 C5
 PPOOL/BLNAV NP4 .... 14 D3
Woodland St CWM NP44 .... 19 F5
Woodland Ter CAER CF83 .... 47 E2
 PPRD CF37 .... 44 C4
Woodland Vw
 CALD/MAG NP26 .... 62 A4
 CHV/BDAU CF38 .... 81 E2
 CYN/LLD/PWYN CF23 .... 113 E3
Woodlawn Wy CDFN CF14.. 85 H4
Wood Pth CWM NP44 * 20 B2
Woodpecker Sq
 BARRYI/W CF62 .... 137 H3
Woodruff Wy CDFN CF14 .... 85 G4
Woods Gelliwion PPRD CF37.. 44 B4
Woodside Ct CDFN CF14 .... 100 B1
Woodside Rd CWM NP44 .... 19 H4
 PPOOL/BLNAV NP4 .... 13 E5
Woodside Wk
 ABRC/NBR/RIS NP11 .... 35 F3
Woodside Wy CWM NP44 .... 19 F4
Woodstock Cl
 BARRYI/W CF62 .... 138 D4
 CALD/MAG NP26 * 62 D4
Woodstock Ms
 CALD/MAG NP26 .... 62 D4
Woodstock Wy
 CALD/MAG NP26 .... 62 D4
Wood St GTN/RVSD CF11 .... 4 B7
 PNRTH/DP CF64 .... 134 C2
Woodsy Cl
 CYN/LLD/PWYN CF23 .... 87 H4
Woodvale Av
 CYN/LLD/PWYN CF23 .... 100 D3
Wood View Crs
 ABRC/NBR/RIS NP11 .... 37 F4
Wood View Rd
 ABRC/NBR/RIS NP11 .... 37 F4
Woodville Ct
 CATH/RTH/SPL CF24 * 112 C5
Woodville Rd
 CATH/RTH/SPL CF24 .... 112 C5
 NWPT NP20 .... 56 A5
Woodward Av
 ABRC/NBR/RIS NP11 .... 36 A2
Woolacombe Av CDFNE CF3.. 102 B5
Woolaston Av
 CYN/LLD/PWYN CF23 .... 100 D3
Woolmer Cl
 CAE/CAN/FWR CF5 .... 110 B3
Woolpitch CWM NP44 .... 19 E5
Woolpitch Wd CHEP NP16 .... 28 A4
Woosnam Cl
 CYN/LLD/PWYN CF23 .... 113 G4
Worcester Crs NWPTE NP19 .. 57 G1
Worcester St
 GTN/RVSD CF11 .... 6 A5
Wordsworth Av
 CATH/RTH/SPL CF24 .... 5 H2
 PNRTH/DP CF64 .... 134 B2
Wordsworth Cl
 CALD/MAG NP26 .... 62 C4
 CWM NP44 .... 25 C1
 LLMJ CF61 .... 137 E3
Wordsworth Gdns PPRD CF37.. 65 H1
Wordsworth Rd NWPTE NP19.. 57 G4
Working St CCDF CF10 .... 4 D5
Worle Pl CDFNE CF3 .... 102 A5
Worle Pl CDFNE CF3 .... 102 A5
Wren Cl CDFNE CF3 .... 103 F4
Wren Rd BARRYI/W CF62 .... 137 H3
Wrexham Ct CDFNE CF3 .... 102 D5
Wright Cl NWPTE NP19 .... 78 A1
Wroughton Pl
 CAE/CAN/FWR CF5 .... 117 H1
Wyebank Av CHEP NP16 .... 29 E3
Wyebank Crs CHEP NP16 .... 29 E4
Wyebank Pl CHEP NP16 .... 29 E4
Wyebank Ri CHEP NP16 .... 29 E4
Wyebank Ri CHEP NP16 .... 29 E4
Wyebank Rd CHEP NP16 .... 29 E4
Wyebank Vw CHEP NP16 .... 29 E4
Wyebank Wy CHEP NP16 .... 29 E4
Wye Cl BARRYI/W CF62 .... 138 C3
Wye Ct CWM NP44 .... 19 E4
Wye Crs CHEP NP16 .... 28 C5
 NWPT NP20 .... 39 H4
Wye Valley Link Rd
 CHEP NP16 .... 30 B1
Wye Valley Wk CHEP NP16 .. 28 D1
Wyeverne Rd
 CATH/RTH/SPL CF24.. 4 D1
 NWPTE NP19 .... 57 H4
Wyfan Pl CDFN CF14 .... 111 H3
Wyncliffe Rd
 CYN/LLD/PWYN CF23 .... 101 H2
Wyndham Ar CCDF CF10 .... 4 D6
Wyndham Crs GTN/RVSD CF11.. 119 E2
Wyndham Pl GTN/RVSD CF11.. 119 E2
Wyndham Rd GTN/RVSD CF11.. 119 E2
Wyndham St BARRYE CF63 .. 139 F4
 CAER CF83 .... 51 E2
 GTN/RVSD CF11 .... 119 F3
 NWPT NP20 .... 8 E1
 PENT/RAD/TFW CF15 .... 97 H1
Wyndham Ter
 ABRC/NBR/RIS NP11 .... 37 G5
 CDFN CF14 .... 100 B3
Wynd St BARRYE CF63 .... 139 H3
Wynnstay Cl GTN/RVSD CF11.. 119 F3
Wyon Cl CAE/CAN/FWR CF5.. 110 B2
Wyvern Rd CHEP NP16 .... 31 F5

Wyverne Rd
 CATH/RTH/SPL CF24 .... 4 D1

Y

Yarrow Cl CAE/CAN/FWR CF5.. 116 D3
Y Cligant CAER CF83 .... 48 B3
Y Deri CHV/BDAU CF38 .... 80 D4
Y Dolydd CAER CF83 .... 68 C3
Yeo Cl NWPT NP20 .... 39 G5
Yeo Rd NWPT NP20 .... 39 H5
The Yetts CHEP NP16 .... 29 F5
Yewberry Cl NWPT NP20 .... 40 C3
Yewberry La NWPT NP20 .... 40 B3
Yew St PENT/RAD/TFW CF15.. 83 F3
Yewtree Cl CAE/CAN/FWR CF5.. 110 A5
Yew Tree Cl CALD/MAG NP26.. 60 D4
Yew Tree Ct BARRYI/W CF62.. 2 B5
Yew Tree La
 CLN/RNWPTE NP18 .... 42 A3
Yew Tree Rd CALD/MAG NP26.. 62 B4
Yew Tree Ter CWM NP44 .... 25 C1
Y Felin Ffrwd CAER CF83 .... 48 B1
Y Goedwig CDFN CF14 .... 98 D2
Y Groes CDFN CF14 .... 99 E2
Ynysangharad Rd PPRD CF37.. 45 E3
Ynysbryn Cl LLTR/LLH CF72.. 94 D2
Ynys Ci PPRD CF37 .... 45 E2
Ynyscorrwg Rd PPRD CF37.. 46 A5
Ynysddu LLTR/LLH CF72 .... 94 B5
Ynys-Cyfeilion Rd
 PPRD CF37 * 44 D2
Ynys La CWM NP44 .... 20 B3
Ynyslyn Rd PPRD CF37 .... 65 G2
Ynys Ter PPRD CF37 .... 65 G2
Ynys y Coed
 CLN/RNWPTE NP18 .... 111 E5
Yorath Rd CDFN CF14 .... 99 E5
York Cl CWM NP44 .... 18 D5
York Ct PENT/RAD/TFW CF15 *.. 97 G4
York Pl BARRYI/W CF62 .... 2 C4
 CTN/RVSD CF11 .... 6 A6
 NWPT NP20 .... 8 C5
York Rd NWPTE NP19 .... 57 F2
York St CCDF CF10 .... 118 D2
Youghal Cl
 CYN/LLD/PWYN CF23 .... 87 H5
Yr Allt LLTR/LLH CF72 .... 95 E2
Yr Graig LLTR/LLH CF72 .... 94 D2
Y Rhodfa BARRYE CF63 .... 3 H3
 BARRYI/W CF62 .... 3 C3
Ysgol Pl CWM NP44 .... 19 F2
Ysgubor Fach CAER CF83 .... 51 C2
Ystrad Cl CDFNE CF3 .... 103 F3
Ystrad St GTN/RVSD CF11 .... 6 C4

Z

Zinc St CATH/RTH/SPL CF24 .... 5 K4

Aber ⇌
CAER CF83 .... 68 C1
Abersychan Clinic
PPOOL/BLNAV NP4 .... 12 C4
Abersychan
Comprehensive School
PPOOL/BLNAV NP4 .... 12 C3
Abersychan Industrial Estate
PPOOL/BLNAV NP4 .... 12 D4
Acorn Camping &
Caravan Site
LLMJ CF61 .... 136 D5
Adamsdown Primary School
CATH/RTH/SPL CF24 .... 5 J4
Albany Industrial Estate
NWPT NP20 .... 56 D1
Albany Primary School
CATH/RTH/SPL CF24 .... 113 E5
Albany Trading Estate
NWPT NP20 .... 56 D2
Albert Primary School
PNRTH/DP CF64 .... 134 D1
Alexandra Industrial Estate
CDFNE CF3 .... 114 D2
Allensbank Primary School
CDFN CF14 .... 112 B3
All Saints CW J & I School
PENT/RAD/TFW CF15 .... 138 C4
All Saints CW Primary School
CYN/LLD/PWYN CF23 .... 113 F2
Alway Primary School
NWPTE NP19 .... 58 B5
The Amphitheatre
CLN/RNWPTE NP18 .... 42 A5
Anchor Industrial Estate
CCDF CF10 .... 6 C1
Archbishop Rowan Williams
Primary School
CALD/MAC NP26 .... 63 H3
ARD Business Park
PPOOL/BLNAV NP4 .... 17 F1
Art & Aesthetics Department
(University of Wales
Institute of Cardiff)
CATH/RTH/SPL CF24 .... 5 G4
Ashgrove School
PNRTH/DP CF64 .... 133 H3
Atlantic Trading Estate
BARRYE CF63 .... 140 A5
Atlantic Wharf Leisure Village
CCDF CF10 .... 7 G4
Avalon Leisure Complex
PNRTH/DP CF64 .... 141 H5
The Avenue Industrial Park
CYN/LLD/PWYN CF23 .... 101 H2
Avondale Industrial Estate
CWM NP44 .... 20 A2
Baden Powell Primary School
CATH/RTH/SPL CF24 .... 121 E2
Baltic House
CCDF CF10 .... 7 F5
Barry ⇌
BARRYI/W CF62 .... 2 D5
Barry Castle (Ruins)
BARRYI/W CF62 .... 2 A5
Barry Cemetery
BARRYI/W CF62 .... 139 E2
Barry College of
Further Education
BARRYI/W CF62 .... 138 D3
Barry Dock ⇌
BARRYE CF63 .... 139 G3
Barry Hospital
BARRYI/W CF62 .... 138 D2
Barry Island ⇌
BARRYI/W CF62 .... 3 F7
Barry Island Heritage
Railway Centre
BARRYI/W CF62 .... 3 G6
Barry Island J & I School
BARRYI/W CF62 .... 2 E6
Barry Island Pleasure Park
BARRYI/W CF62 .... 3 F7
Barry Island
Primary School
BARRYI/W CF62 .... 3 G5
Barry Leisure Centre
BARRYE CF63 .... 3 H2
Barry RFC
BARRYI/W CF62 .... 131 F5
Barry Sports Club
BARRYI/W CF62 .... 138 D2
Barry Town Association FC
BARRYE CF63 .... 139 G3
Bartlett Street
Industrial Estate
CAER CF83 .... 69 G2
Bassaleg
Comprehensive School
RSTN NP10 .... 74 D2
BBC Cymru Wales
CAE/CAN/FWR CF5 .... 110 D4
Beachley Army Barracks
CHEP NP16 .... 31 F4
The Bear Hotel
COWBR CF71 .... 122 C3
Beddau RFC
CHV/BDAU CF38 .... 80 A3
Bedwas High School
CAER CF83 .... 49 H3
Bedwas House
Industrial Estate
CAER CF83 .... 49 F3
Bedwas Infant School
CAER CF83 .... 49 G3
Bedwas Junior School
CAER CF83 .... 49 G3
Bedwas RFC
CAER CF83 .... 49 H3
Beeches Industrial Estate
LLTR/LLH CF72 .... 94 B4
Bettws High School &
Leisure Centre
NWPT NP20 .... 39 H5
Bettws RFC
NWPT NP20 .... 39 H5
Bettws Shopping Centre
NWPT NP20 .... 39 G4
Birchgrove ⇌
CDFN CF14 .... 99 G4

Birchgrove Primary School
CDFN CF14 .... 111 H1
Birds Industrial Estate
ABRC/NBR/RIS NP11 .... 53 F1
Bishop Childs CW J & I School
CDFNE CF3 .... 103 E2
Bishop of Llandaff CW
High School
CAE/CAN/FWR CF5 .... 110 D4
Black Fraiers Priory
CCDF CF10 .... 4 B4
Blenheim Square
Shopping Centre
CWM NP44 .... 19 F5
Boxer Trading Estate
CLN/RNWPTE NP18 .... 41 H2
Brickyard Business Park
CWM NP44 .... 19 H5
Brookfield Primary School
CWM NP44 .... 19 H5
Bryn Celynnog
Comprehensive School
CHV/BDAU CF38 .... 80 A3
Bryn Celyn Primary School
CYN/LLD/PWYN CF23 .... 101 G3
Bryn Deri Primary School
PENT/RAD/TFW CF15 .... 97 F3
Brynglas Primary School
NWPT NP20 .... 40 C5
Bryn Hafod Primary School
CDFNE CF3 .... 102 A3
Bryn Hafren
Comprehensive School
BARRYI/W CF62 .... 131 G5
Brynhill Golf Club
BARRYI/W CF62 .... 138 D1
Bulwark Industrial Estate
CHEP NP16 .... 30 C1
Bute Town History &
Arts Centre
CCDF CF10 .... 7 G4
Cadoxton ⇌
BARRYE CF63 .... 140 A3
Cadoxton Clinic
BARRYE CF63 .... 139 H2
Cadoxton Primary School
BARRYE CF63 .... 139 H2
Caerau Infant School
CAE/CAN/FWR CF5 .... 117 F5
Caerleon ⇌
CLN/RNWPTE NP18 .... 41 H4
Caerleon
Comprehensive School
CLN/RNWPTE NP18 .... 41 H4
Caerleon Endowed J &
I School
CLN/RNWPTE NP18 .... 42 A4
Caerleon Golf Club
CLN/RNWPTE NP18 .... 42 A5
Caerleon Lodge Hill
Infant School
CLN/RNWPTE NP18 .... 41 G3
Caerleon Lodge Hill
Junior School
CLN/RNWPTE NP18 .... 41 G3
Caerleon Roman Baths
CLN/RNWPTE NP18 .... 42 B4
Caerphilly ⇌
CAER CF83 .... 69 E2
Caerphilly Business Park
CAER CF83 .... 69 F2
Caerphilly Castle
CAER CF83 .... 69 E1
Caerphilly County Court
CAER CF83 .... 68 D2
Caerphilly District
Miners Hospital
CAER CF83 .... 68 C3
Caerphilly Golf Club
CAER CF83 .... 69 E3
Caerphilly Recreation Centre
CAER CF83 .... 49 F5
Caerphilly RFC
CAER CF83 .... 69 E3
Caldicot ⇌
CALD/MAC NP26 .... 62 C4
Caldicot Castle &
Country Park
CALD/MAC NP26 .... 63 F2
Caldicot Castle Museum
CALD/MAC NP26 .... 63 F3
Caldicot Community Clinic
CALD/MAC NP26 .... 62 D3
Caldicot Community College
CALD/MAC NP26 .... 62 C3
Caldicot Leisure Centre
CALD/MAC NP26 .... 63 E3
Caldicot St Marys
Junior School
CALD/MAC NP26 .... 63 E2
Caldicot School
CALD/MAC NP26 .... 63 E3
Cambrian Centre
NWPT NP20 .... 8 D3
Cambrian Industrial Estate
East Side
LLTR/LLH CF72 .... 94 B5
Cambrian Industrial Estate
West Side
LLTR/LLH CF72 .... 94 A4
Campanile Hotel
CYN/LLD/PWYN CF23 .... 101 H2
Candwr Brook Medical Centre
CLN/RNWPTE NP18 .... 27 H5
Cantonian High School
CAE/CAN/FWR CF5 .... 110 C5
Canton Rugby Club
GTN/RVSD CF11 .... 118 D4
Capital Business Park
CDFNE CF3 .... 114 D3
Capitol Shopping Centre
CCDF CF10 .... 4 E4
The Cardiff Academy
CATH/RTH/SPL CF24 .... 5 G3
Cardiff Athletic Stadium
GTN/RVSD CF11 .... 118 D4
Cardiff Bay ⇌
CCDF CF10 .... 7 F4

Cardiff Bay Barrage
CCDF CF10 .... 129 E4
Cardiff Bay Barrage
Visitor Centre
PNRTH/DP CF64 .... 135 E1
Cardiff Bay Business Centre
CCDF CF10 .... 5 K7
Cardiff Bay Retail Park
GTN/RVSD CF11 .... 6 A7
Cardiff Bay Visitor Centre
CCDF CF10 .... 7 H6
Cardiff Business Park
CDFN CF14 .... 99 H3
Cardiff Business School
(Cardiff University)
CATH/RTH/SPL CF24 .... 112 B1
Cardiff Business
Technology Centre
CATH/RTH/SPL CF24 .... 4 C1
Cardiff Castle
CCDF CF10 .... 4 C4
Cardiff Central ⇌
CCDF CF10 .... 4 C7
Cardiff Centre of Excellence
CYN/LLD/PWYN CF23 .... 100 D3
Cardiff City FC
(Ninian Park)
GTN/RVSD CF11 .... 118 D4
Cardiff County Library
CCDF CF10 .... 4 D6
Cardiff Gate Business Park
CYN/LLD/PWYN CF23 .... 87 H5
Cardiff Gate Retail Park
CYN/LLD/PWYN CF23 .... 88 A5
Cardiff Golf Club
CYN/LLD/PWYN CF23 .... 101 E3
Cardiff High School
CYN/LLD/PWYN CF23 .... 100 C4
The Cardiff High School Old
Boys FC
CDFN CF14 .... 98 B4
Cardiff Industrial Estate
CDFN CF14 .... 99 H3
Cardiff Industrial Park
CDFN CF14 .... 99 G3
Cardiff Institute for the Blind
CATH/RTH/SPL CF24 .... 5 G2
Cardiff International Airport
BARRYI/W CF62 .... 144 D1
Cardiff International Arena
CCDF CF10 .... 4 E6
Cardiff International
Sports Village
GTN/RVSD CF11 .... 128 C4
Cardiff Lawn Tennis Club
CCDF CF10 .... 4 B3
Cardiff RFC (Cardiff
Arms Park)
GTN/RVSD CF11 .... 4 B5
Cardiff Road Business Park
BARRYE CF63 .... 140 A3
Cardiff Royal Infirmary
CATH/RTH/SPL CF24 .... 5 H3
Cardiff Superbowl
CYN/LLD/PWYN CF23 .... 113 H4
Cardiff Tertiary College
CATH/RTH/SPL CF24 .... 5 G2
Cardiff University
CATH/RTH/SPL CF24 .... 4 C1
CCDF CF10 .... 4 D1
CYN/LLD/PWYN CF23 .... 113 E2
GTN/RVSD CF11 .... 128 A1
Cardiff University
(Department of Music)
CCDF CF10 .... 4 B1
Cardiff Wales Airport
Business Park
BARRYI/W CF62 .... 144 C2
Cardinal Newman
Catholic School
PPRD CF37 .... 46 A4
Castell Coch
PENT/RAD/TFW CF15 .... 83 H5
Castell Heights Golf Club
CAER CF83 .... 84 B2
Castle Bingo
NWPT NP20 .... 8 G5
Castle Court Shopping Centre
CAER CF83 .... 69 E1
Castle View Hotel
CHEP NP16 .... 28 C3
Cathays ⇌
CATH/RTH/SPL CF24 .... 4 D1
Cathays Cemetery
CDFN CF14 .... 112 C3
Cathays High School
CDFN CF14 .... 112 A4
Cathedral of St Woolos
NWPT NP20 .... 8 D5
The Cathedral School
CDFN CF14 .... 111 F5
Cefn Onn Primary School
CDFN CF14 .... 99 H1
Cefn Wood J & I School
RSTN NP10 .... 54 D4
The Celtic Manor Resort
CLN/RNWPTE NP18 .... 43 E5
Cemetery Park
CATH/RTH/SPL CF24 .... 5 G4
Central Bus Station
CCDF CF10 .... 4 C7
Central Library
NWPT NP20 .... 8 E4
Centre Trading Estate
CCDF CF10 .... 5 F7
Chapel Farm Industrial
Estate
ABRC/NBR/RIS NP11 .... 36 B2
Chapter Arts Centre
GTN/RVSD CF11 .... 119 E2
Charles Street Community
Learning Centre
NWPT NP20 .... 8 E4
Cheesemans Industrial
Estate
CALD/MAC NP26 .... 62 A3
Chepstow ⇌
CHEP NP16 .... 28 D4
Chepstow Athletic Club
CHEP NP16 .... 30 C1

Chepstow Business Park
CHEP NP16 .... 28 C5
Chepstow Castle
CHEP NP16 .... 28 C3
Chepstow Cemetery
CHEP NP16 .... 30 B1
Chepstow
Community Hospital
CHEP NP16 .... 28 B4
Chepstow
Comprehensive School
CHEP NP16 .... 28 B2
Chepstow Leisure Centre
CHEP NP16 .... 28 B3
Chepstow Museum
CHEP NP16 .... 28 C3
Chepstow Racecourse
CHEP NP16 .... 28 A1
Chepstow Town FC
CHEP NP16 .... 28 B5
Christchurch Cemetery
NWPTE NP19 .... 58 B2
Christ the King RC
Primary School
CDFN CF14 .... 100 A1
Cineworld
CDFN CF14 .... 4 E6
NWPTE NP19 .... 78 C2
City Cinema
NWPT NP20 .... 9 F4
Civil Service Sports Club
CYN/LLD/PWYN CF23 .... 118 B3
Cleppa Park Industrial Estate
RSTN NP10 .... 75 F5
Clydesmuir
Industrial Estate
CATH/RTH/SPL CF24 .... 120 D1
Clytha Primary School
NWPT NP20 .... 8 A4
Coedcae Lane
Industrial Estate
LLTR/LLH CF72 .... 94 A4
Coed Eva J & I School
CWM NP44 .... 25 E2
Coed Glas Primary School
CDFN CF14 .... 100 A2
Coedpenmaen
Primary School
PPRD CF37 .... 45 E2
Coed-y-Brain J & I School
CAER CF83 .... 48 C1
Coed-y-Lan Comprehensive
Lower School
PPRD CF37 .... 44 D2
Coed-y-Lan Primary School
PPRD CF37 .... 44 D2
Cogan ⇌
PNRTH/DP CF64 .... 128 A5
Cogan Primary School
PNRTH/DP CF64 .... 134 A1
Colcot Health Clinic
BARRYI/W CF62 .... 138 D2
Colcot Primary School
BARRYI/W CF62 .... 131 E5
Coleg Glan Hafren
CDFNE CF3 .... 115 E1
Coleg Gwent
ABRC/NBR/RIS NP11 .... 36 B2
NWPTE NP19 .... 78 B2
PPOOL/BLNAV NP4 .... 14 B5
Coleg Morgannwg
PPRD CF37 .... 65 G2
Congress Theatre
CWM NP44 .... 19 H5
Copthorne Hotel
CAE/CAN/FWR CF5 .... 125 F1
Coryton ⇌
CDFN CF14 .... 98 C4
Coryton Primary School
CDFN CF14 .... 98 B3
Cosmeston Lakes Country
Park & Medieval Village
PNRTH/DP CF64 .... 142 B2
The Council of Museums
in Wales
CATH/RTH/SPL CF24 .... 112 C5
Court Road Industrial Estate
CWM NP44 .... 26 B2
The Court School
CWM NP44 .... 100 B1
Cowbridge
Community College
BARRYI/W CF62 .... 138 D2
Cowbridge
Comprehensive School
COWBR CF71 .... 123 E3
Craig-y-Parc School
PENT/RAD/TFW CF15 .... 96 A4
Crawford Trading Estate
NWPTE NP19 .... 57 E2
Crindau J & I School
NWPT NP20 .... 8 C1
Croesceiliog North Road
Infant School
CWM NP44 .... 20 B2
Croesyceiliog School
CWM NP44 .... 20 B4
Crosskeys ⇌
ABRC/NBR/RIS NP11 .... 36 B2
Cross Keys RFC
ABRC/NBR/RIS NP11 .... 36 A2
Crossways Retail Park
CAER CF83 .... 49 F3
Crownbridge Special School
PPOOL/BLNAV NP4 .... 17 E4
Cwmaber Infant School
CAER CF83 .... 47 F1
Cwmaber Junior School
CAER CF83 .... 47 F1
Cwmbran ⇌
CWM NP44 .... 19 G4
Cwmbran Cemetery
CWM NP44 .... 26 A2
Cwmbran Retail Park
CWM NP44 .... 19 G4
Cwmbran RFC
CWM NP44 .... 19 H3
Cwmbran Stadium
Sports Centre
CWM NP44 .... 25 H2

Cwmbran Town Sports Club
CWM NP44 .... 19 H5
Cwmcarn Forest Drive &
Visitor Centre
ABRC/NBR/RIS NP11 .... 23 G3
Cwmcarn High School
ABRC/NBR/RIS NP11 .... 23 E2
Cwmcarn Primary School
ABRC/NBR/RIS NP11 .... 23 E4
Cwmcarn United RFC
ABRC/NBR/RIS NP11 .... 23 D2
Cwm Colhuw Nature Reserve
LLMJ CF61 .... 136 B5
Cwmfelinfach Clinic
ABRC/NBR/RIS NP11 .... 34 C2
Cwmfelinfach Primary School
ABRC/NBR/RIS NP11 .... 34 B2
Cwm Glas Infant School
CAER CF83 .... 33 H3
Cwm Ifor Primary School
CAER CF83 .... 48 A4
Cwrt Rawlin Primary School
CAER CF83 .... 68 B2
Cwrt-yr-Ala Junior School
CAE/CAN/FWR CF5 .... 117 E4
Danescourt ⇌
CAE/CAN/FWR CF5 .... 110 D3
Danescourt J & I School
CAE/CAN/FWR CF5 .... 110 C3
David Lloyd Leisure Centre
CYN/LLD/PWYN CF23 .... 113 G3
The Dell Primary School
CHEP NP16 .... 28 C3
Dewi Sant Hospital
PPRD CF37 .... 44 D4
Dewstow Golf Club
CALD/MAC NP26 .... 62 B1
Diamond Sports Ground
CDFN CF14 .... 110 C1
Dinas Powys ⇌
PNRTH/DP CF64 .... 133 E4
Dinas Powys Athletic
Club (RFC)
PNRTH/DP CF64 .... 132 D3
Dinas Powys Golf Club
PNRTH/DP CF64 .... 132 D2
Dinas Powys Infant School
PNRTH/DP CF64 .... 133 F2
Dingle Road ⇌
PNRTH/DP CF64 .... 134 C2
Dolman Theatre
NWPT NP20 .... 9 F5
Dominion Way
Industrial Estate
CATH/RTH/SPL CF24 .... 113 G5
Dr William Price
Business Centre
PPRD CF37 .... 65 F1
Duffryn High School
RSTN NP10 .... 92 A1
Duffryn J & I School
RSTN NP10 .... 75 H5
The Duffryn
RSTN NP10 .... 91 E2
Durand Primary School
CALD/MAC NP26 .... 63 E4
Durham Road J & I Schools
NWPTE NP19 .... 57 E2
Dyffryn Gardens
CAE/CAN/FWR CF5 .... 130 B1
Eaglesville Primary School
LLMJ CF61 .... 137 E5
Eastbrook ⇌
PNRTH/DP CF64 .... 133 G2
Eastern Leisure Centre
CDFNE CF3 .... 114 B1
East Moors Business Park
CATH/RTH/SPL CF24 .... 7 J1
East Moors Industrial Estate
CATH/RTH/SPL CF24 .... 5 J6
Edwin Industrial Estate
NWPT NP20 .... 56 C2
Egerton Grey Country
House Hotel
BARRYI/W CF62 .... 145 G1
Eglwys Newydd
J & I School
CDFN CF14 .... 99 E5
Eglwys Wen J & I School
CDFN CF14 .... 111 E1
Ely Bridge Industrial Estate
CAE/CAN/FWR CF5 .... 117 H1
Ely Hospital
CAE/CAN/FWR CF5 .... 117 H3
Ely Valley Industrial Estate
LLTR/LLH CF72 .... 107 G1
Enterprise Park
Industrial Estate
NWPT NP20 .... 9 G7
Eurocast Trading Estate
CDFN CF14 .... 98 A4
Evenlode J & I School
PNRTH/DP CF64 .... 134 C4
Eveswell Primary School
NWPTE NP19 .... 57 G4
Evtol Industrial Estate
NWPT NP20 .... 9 G7
Evtol Trading Estate
NWPT NP20 .... 77 E2
Excelsior Industrial Estate
CDFN CF14 .... 111 G3
Exchange Building
CCDF CF10 .... 7 F5
Express by Holiday Inn
RSTN NP10 .... 75 F5
Fairfield Industrial Estate
PENT/RAD/TFW CF15 .... 83 F5
Fairfield Primary School
PNRTH/DP CF64 .... 134 B1
Fairwater ⇌
CAE/CAN/FWR CF5 .... 110 D5
Fairwater High School &
Leisure Centre
CWM NP44 .... 24 D1
Fairwater J & I School
CWM NP44 .... 25 F1
Fairwater Leisure Centre
CAE/CAN/FWR CF5 .... 110 A3
Fairwater Primary School
CAE/CAN/FWR CF5 .... 117 G1

Felnex Industrial Estate
  PPRD CF37 ....77 F4
Ffynnon-Taf Primary School
  PENT/RAD/TFW CF15 ....83 E3
Fields Park Pontllanfraith AFC
  ABRC/NBR/RIS NP11 ....34 C3
Fitzalan High School
  GTN/RVSD CF11 ....118 C3
Forest Farm Industrial Estate
  CDFN CF14 ....97 H3
Forge Hammer
  Industrial Estate
  CWM NP44 ....19 G4
Gabalfa Primary School
  CDFN CF14 ....111 F3
Gaer Infant School
  NWPT NP20 ....76 A1
Gaer Medical Centre
  NWPT NP20 ....75 H1
Garndiffaith J & I School
  PPOOL/BLNAV NP4 ....12 B1
Garndiffaith RFC
  PPOOL/BLNAV NP4 ....12 C1
Garnteg Primary School
  PPOOL/BLNAV NP4 ....12 C1
Garth Industrial Estate
  PENT/RAD/TFW CF15 ....83 F5
Gelli-Hirion Industrial Estate
  PPRD CF37 ....46 B5
George Street Primary School
  PPOOL/BLNAV NP4 ....14 B3
Gladstone Primary School
  BARRI/W CF62 ....139 E4
  CATH/RTH/SPL CF24 ....112 C4
Glamorgan CCC
  (SWALEC Stadium)
  GTN/RVSD CF11 ....119 F1
Glamorgan Centre of
  Art Design
  PPRD CF37 ....45 C5
Glamorganshire Golf Club
  PNRTH/DP CF64 ....142 C1
Glamorgan Vale Retail Park
  LLTR/LLH CF72 ....95 E3
Glamorgan Wanderers RFC
  CAE/CAN/FWR CF5 ....116 D4
Glan Hafren College
  CATH/RTH/SPL CF24 ....5 F3
Glan Taf Infant School
  PPRD CF37 ....65 C1
Glan-y-Llyn Industrial Estate
  PENT/RAD/TFW CF15 ....83 F2
Glan yr Afon Primary School
  CDFN CF14 ....101 H5
Glasllwch Primary School
  NWPT NP20 ....55 G5
Glebelands Stadium
  NWPTE NP19 ....57 E1
Glyncoed J & I School
  CYN/LLD/PWYN CF23 ....101 F3
Glyn Derw High School
  CAE/CAN/FWR CF5 ....118 A4
Graddfa Industrial Estate
  CAER CF83 ....33 G4
Graig y Rhacca
  Primary School
  CAER CF83 ....50 D2
The Grange Clinic
  NWPT NP20 ....40 B4
Grange Industrial Estate
  NWPT NP20 ....26 A1
Grangetown ≷
  GTN/RVSD CF11 ....128 A1
Grangetown Primary School
  GTN/RVSD CF11 ....6 B4
Greenhill Special School
  CDFN CF14 ....98 D2
Green Lane Junior School
  CALD/MAG NP26 ....62 C3
Green Lawn Junior School
  PPOOL/BLNAV NP4 ....17 C1
Greenmeadow
  Community Farm
  CWM NP44 ....19 F5
Greenmeadow Golf &
  Country Club
  CWM NP44 ....20 D1
Greenmeadow
  Primary School
  CWM NP44 ....18 C5
Greenway Primary School
  CDFNE CF3 ....114 C1
Griffithstown Infant School
  PPOOL/BLNAV NP4 ....17 F4
Griffithstown Primary School
  PPOOL/BLNAV NP4 ....17 E3
Guardian Industrial Estate
  CATH/RTH/SPL CF24 ....121 E1
Gwaelod y Garth
  Industrial Estate
  PENT/RAD/TFW CF15 ....83 F5
Gwaelod y Garth
  Primary School
  PENT/RAD/TFW CF15 ....83 E3
Gwauncelyn Primary School
  CHV/BDAU CF38 ....81 C1
Gwaunmeisgyn
  Infant School
  CHV/BDAU CF38 ....80 B4
Gwaunmeisgyn
  Primary School
  CHV/BDAU CF38 ....80 B4
Gwent Primary School
  CAE/CAN/FWR CF5 ....125 G5
Gwent Tertiary College
  PPOOL/BLNAV NP4 ....14 A4
Harlech Retail Park
  NWPT NP20 ....76 B2
Harrowby Business Centre
  CCDF CF10 ....6 E6
Hartridge High School
  CLN/RNWPTE NP18 ....58 D5
Hawthorn High School
  PPRD CF37 ....66 A1
Hawthorn Infant School
  CDFN CF14 ....110 D2
Hawthorn Junior School
  CDFN CF14 ....110 D2
Hawthorn Leisure Centre
  PPRD CF37 ....65 H3

Hawthorn Primary School
  PPRD CF37 ....65 H3
Heath High Level ≷
  CDFN CF14 ....100 B5
Heath Low Level ≷
  CDFN CF14 ....100 A5
Heath Sports Centre
  CDFN CF14 ....112 B1
Hendredenny Park J &
  I School
  CAER CF83 ....48 A5
Henllys J & I School
  CWM NP44 ....24 C2
Heol-y-celyn Primary School
  CDFN CF14 ....65 H2
Heol y Rhosog Business Park
  CDFNE CF3 ....114 D3
Herbert Thompson
  Primary School
  CAE/CAN/FWR CF5 ....117 G2
High Cross Primary School
  RSTN NP10 ....55 F4
High Street J & I School
  BARRI/W CF62 ....2 E2
HM Prison
  CCDF CF10 ....5 F5
Holland House Hotel
  CATH/RTH/SPL CF24 ....5 G4
The Hollies School
  CYN/LLD/PWYN CF23 ....101 G2
Hollybush J & I School
  CWM NP44 ....25 F2
Hollywood Bowl
  NWPT NP20 ....7 H4
Holm View Leisure Centre
  BARRI/W CF62 ....139 F1
Holton Road School
  BARRE CF63 ....139 G4
Holy Family RC
  Primary School
  CAE/CAN/FWR CF5 ....109 H5
Hopkinstown CC
  PPRD CF37 ....44 A3
Hoskin Industrial Estate
  CCDF CF10 ....7 F4
Hotel Ibis
  CCDF CF10 ....5 F5
  CYN/LLD/PWYN CF23 ....88 A3
Howells School
  CAE/CAN/FWR CF5 ....118 C1
Hywel Dda Junior School
  CAE/CAN/FWR CF5 ....117 E4
Ifton Industrial Park
  CALD/MAG NP26 ....62 B3
Innkeeper's Lodge
  CDFN CF14 ....99 E4
Jacks Pill Industrial Estate
  NWPT NP20 ....9 H5
Jenner Park Athletic Stadium
  BARRI/W CF62 ....139 G3
Jenner Park Primary School
  BARRE CF63 ....139 G3
John Frost Centre
  NWPT NP20 ....8 E4
Jubilee Trading Estate
  CATH/RTH/SPL CF24 ....5 K5
Kings Monkton School
  CATH/RTH/SPL CF24 ....5 F3
Kingsway Centre
  NWPT NP20 ....9 F4
Kitchener Primary School
  GTN/RVSD CF11 ....119 E3
Lakeside Primary School
  CYN/LLD/PWYN CF23 ....100 D5
Lamby Industrial Park
  CDFNE CF3 ....114 C4
Lanelay Road
  Industrial Estate
  LLTR/LLH CF72 ....94 B4
Langstone Business Village
  CLN/RNWPTE NP18 ....59 F1
Lansdowne Primary School
  CAE/CAN/FWR CF5 ....118 C2
The Laurels Business Park
  CDFNE CF3 ....114 D3
Leeway Industrial Estate
  NWPTE NP19 ....78 B4
Lightship 2000
  CCDF CF10 ....7 H6
The Links Business Park
  CDFNE CF3 ....103 G2
Lisvane & Thornhill ≷
  CDFN CF14 ....86 A4
Liswerry Junior School
  NWPTE NP19 ....78 A1
Liswerry Leisure Centre
  NWPTE NP19 ....78 B3
Living Well Health &
  Leisure Centre
  CDFN CF14 ....99 H3
Llanbradach ≷
  CAER CF83 ....33 G5
Llandaf ≷
  CDFN CF14 ....110 D1
Llandaff Cathedral
  CAE/CAN/FWR CF5 ....111 F4
Llandaff City CW
  Primary School
  CAE/CAN/FWR CF5 ....111 E5
Llandaff RFC
  CAE/CAN/FWR CF5 ....111 G5
Llandough Hospital
  PNRTH/DP CF64 ....127 H5
Llandough Primary School
  PNRTH/DP CF64 ....127 H4
Llandough Trading Estate
  GTN/RVSD CF11 ....127 H3
Llanedeyrn Health Centre
  CYN/LLD/PWYN CF23 ....101 F5
Llanedeyrn High School
  CYN/LLD/PWYN CF23 ....113 C1
Llanedeyrn Primary School
  CYN/LLD/PWYN CF23 ....113 C1
Llanfrechfa Grange Hospital
  CWM NP44 ....26 D1
Llanilltud Faerdref
  Primary School
  CHV/BDAU CF38 ....81 C1
Llanilltud Fawr J & I School
  LLMJ CF61 ....136 D4

Llanilltud Leisure Centre
  LLMJ CF61 ....136 D3
Llanilltud Major
  Comprehensive School
  LLMJ CF61 ....136 D4
Llanishen ≷
  CDFN CF14 ....100 D1
Llanishen Fach J & I School
  CDFN CF14 ....99 F1
Llanishen Golf Club
  CDFN CF14 ....86 A2
Llanishen Health Centre
  CDFN CF14 ....100 A1
Llanishen High School
  CDFN CF14 ....100 A1
Llanishen Leisure Centre
  CDFN CF14 ....99 H2
Llanrumney Clinic
  CDFNE CF3 ....102 A5
Llanrumney High School
  CDFNE CF3 ....101 H4
Llantarnam Comprehensive
  School & Leisure Centre
  CWM NP44 ....26 B4
Llantarnam Industrial Park
  CWM NP44 ....26 A4
Llantrisant Castle
  LLTR/LLH CF72 ....95 E2
Llantrisant Leisure Centre
  LLTR/LLH CF72 ....95 E2
Llantrisant & Pontyclun
  Golf Club
  LLTR/LLH CF72 ....94 C2
Llantrisant Primary School
  LLTR/LLH CF72 ....94 D1
Llantrisant RFC
  LLTR/LLH CF72 ....95 E3
Llantwit Fardre RFC
  CHV/BDAU CF38 ....81 F2
Llantwit Fardre Sports Centre
  CHV/BDAU CF38 ....81 G1
Llantwit Major ≷
  LLMJ CF61 ....136 D3
Llantwit Major Cemetery
  LLMJ CF61 ....137 E4
Llanwern Golf Club
  CLN/RNWPTE NP18 ....59 F5
Llanyrafon Primary School
  CWM NP44 ....26 B1
Lisiwerry
  Comprehensive School
  NWPTE NP19 ....78 B3
Liwyn-Crwn Primary School
  CHV/BDAU CF38 ....80 A4
Llysfaen Primary School
  CDFN CF14 ....86 A4
Lord Chancellors Department
  PPOOL/BLNAV NP4 ....14 C3
Machen Primary School
  CAER CF83 ....51 G2
Machen RFC
  CAER CF83 ....52 A2
Mackintosh Sports Club
  CATH/RTH/SPL CF24 ....113 E5
Maendy J & I School
  CWM NP44 ....19 H4
Maendy Square Clinic
  CWM NP44 ....19 G3
Maesglas Industrial Estate
  NWPT NP20 ....76 C3
Maesglas J & I School
  NWPT NP20 ....76 B4
Maes Glas Retail Park
  NWPT NP20 ....76 C4
Maes-y-Bryn Primary School
  CHV/BDAU CF38 ....81 E3
Maes-y-Coed Primary School
  PPRD CF37 ....44 C4
Maes y Felin
  Chambered Tomb
  CAE/CAN/FWR CF5 ....130 C1
Magor Brewery
  CALD/MAG NP26 ....60 A2
Magor CW Primary School
  CALD/MAG NP26 ....60 C3
Magor Marsh Nature Reserve
  CALD/MAG NP26 ....60 C5
Magor Voluntary Aided
  Primary School
  CALD/MAG NP26 ....60 C4
Maindee Primary School
  NWPTE NP19 ....9 H3
Maindee Swimming Pool
  NWPTE NP19 ....9 H3
Maindy Pool & Cycle Track
  NWPT NP20 ....112 A4
Malpas Brook Health Centre
  NWPT NP20 ....56 B2
Malpas Court Primary School
  NWPT NP20 ....40 C4
Malpas CW Infant School
  NWPT NP20 ....40 C4
Malpas Medical Centre
  NWPT NP20 ....40 B3
Malpas Park J & I School
  NWPT NP20 ....40 B3
Manor Parc Country Hotel
  & Restaurant
  CDFN CF14 ....85 F4
Mansion House
  CATH/RTH/SPL CF24 ....5 F2
Maritime Industrial Estate
  PPRD CF37 ....44 B4
Marlborough Junior School
  CATH/RTH/SPL CF24 ....113 E5
Marriott Hotel
  CCDF CF10 ....4 D6
Marshfield School
  CDFNE CF3 ....89 H5
Mary Immaculate
  High School
  CAE/CAN/FWR CF5 ....116 D5
Meadowbank School
  CAE/CAN/FWR CF5 ....26 A3
Meadowlane Primary School
  CDFNE CF3 ....111 F3
Megabowl
  NWPTE NP19 ....78 C2
The Memorial Hall Theatre
  BARRI/W CF62 ....2 E2

Mendalgief Retail Park
  NWPT NP20 ....76 D3
Mermaid Quay Retail &
  Leisure Centre
  CCDF CF10 ....7 G6
Metro Mon Industrial Estate
  CWM NP44 ....20 A1
Michaelston
  Community School
  CAE/CAN/FWR CF5 ....116 C4
Millbank Primary School
  CDFN CF14 ....118 A2
Millbrook Junior School
  NWPT NP20 ....40 A4
Millennium Stadium
  CCDF CF10 ....4 B6
Mill Lane Industrial Estate
  NWPT NP20 ....28 D4
Milton J & I School
  NWPTE NP19 ....59 E3
Mitel Business Park
  CALD/MAG NP26 ....63 C3
Monnow J & I Schools
  NWPT NP20 ....39 G4
Moorland Primary School
  CATH/RTH/SPL CF24 ....121 E3
Mounton House School
  CHEP NP16 ....30 A1
Mounton Road Health Centre
  CHEP NP16 ....28 B4
Mount Pleasant
  RSTN NP10 ....54 D3
Mount Sorrel Hotel
  BARRI/W CF62 ....2 C3
Mountstuart Primary School
  CCDF CF10 ....7 F6
Murch Junior School
  PNRTH/DP CF64 ....133 F3
National Assembly for Wales
  CCDF CF10 ....7 H5
National Assembly Offices
  CCDF CF10 ....4 B1
National Indoor
  Athletics Centre
  CYN/LLD/PWYN CF23 ....113 F1
National Museum Cardiff
  CCDF CF10 ....4 D2
National Sports Centre
  for Wales
  GTN/RVSD CF11 ....119 F1
NCH Headlands School
  PNRTH/DP CF64 ....135 E1
New House Country Hotel
  CDFN CF14 ....85 E2
Newhouse Farm
  Industrial Estate
  CHEP NP16 ....30 C4
New Inn Medical Centre
  PPOOL/BLNAV NP4 ....17 H1
New Inn Primary School
  PPOOL/BLNAV NP4 ....17 G1
Newport ≷
  NWPT NP20 ....8 C3
Newport Bus Station
  NWPT NP20 ....8 E3
Newport Castle
  NWPTE NP19 ....8 E2
Newport Cattle Market
  NWPT NP20 ....9 G6
Newport City Live Arena
  NWPTE NP19 ....9 F2
Newport Golf Club
  RSTN NP10 ....54 C2
Newport Indoor
  Bowling Centre
  NWPTE NP19 ....57 E1
Newport Leisure Centre
  NWPT NP20 ....9 F3
Newport Lodge Hotel
  NWPT NP20 ....56 C1
Newport Museum &
  Art Gallery
  NWPT NP20 ....8 E4
Newport Retail Park
  NWPTE NP19 ....78 C2
Newport RFC
  (Rodney Parade)
  NWPTE NP19 ....9 G3
Newport Saracens RFC
  RSTN NP10 ....76 A4
Newport Stadium
  NWPTE NP19 ....9 F2
Newport Transporter Bridge
  NWPTE NP19 ....77 E3
Newport (Uskmouth)
  Sailing Club
  CLN/RNWPTE NP18 ....93 G2
New Theatre
  CCDF CF10 ....4 D4
Newtown Industrial Estate
  ABRC/NBR/RIS NP11 ....36 B3
  CHV/BDAU CF38 ....81 E3
Nine Mile Point
  Industrial Estate
  ABRC/NBR/RIS NP11 ....34 D3
Ninian Park ≷
  GTN/RVSD CF11 ....119 E4
Ninian Park Primary School
  GTN/RVSD CF11 ....119 F5
North Blackvein
  Industrial Estate
  ABRC/NBR/RIS NP11 ....35 H2
Norwegian Church Centre
  CCDF CF10 ....7 H7
Novotel
  CCDF CF10 ....5 F7
Oak Field
  BARRI/W CF62 ....139 F2
Oakfield Primary School
  CWM NP44 ....26 A3
Oasis Leisure Centre
  CWM NP44 ....20 A4
Odeon Cinema
  CCDF CF10 ....7 H4
Offas Mead CP School
  CHEP NP16 ....29 E4
Oldbury Business Centre
  CWM NP44 ....25 H1

Old Illtydian RFC
  CATH/RTH/SPL CF24 ....5 K3
The Old Post Office Hotel
  CAE/CAN/FWR CF5 ....116 C1
The Open University in Wales
  GTN/RVSD CF11 ....119 F2
Our Lady of the Angels RC
  Primary School
  CWM NP44 ....25 H1
Oxford House Industrial
  History Museum
  ABRC/NBR/RIS NP11 ....37 E4
Palmerstown J & I School
  BARRE CF63 ....140 B2
Palmerstown Trading Estate
  BARRE CF63 ....140 B2
Palmers Vale Business Centre
  BARRE CF63 ....140 A2
Palmers Vale Business Park
  BARRE CF63 ....140 A2
Panteg Cemetery
  PPOOL/BLNAV NP4 ....15 F4
Panteg Health Centre
  PPOOL/BLNAV NP4 ....17 E3
Panteg Industrial Estate
  PPOOL/BLNAV NP4 ....17 E2
Pant Glas Industrial Estate
  CAER CF83 ....50 A4
Paramount Angel Hotel
  CCDF CF10 ....4 B5
Parc Cefn Onn Country Park
  CDFN CF14 ....86 A2
Parc Golf Club
  RSTN NP10 ....91 E3
Parc Lewis Primary School
  PPRD CF37 ....45 F4
Parc Newydd
  Shopping Centre
  LLTR/LLH CF72 ....94 C3
Parc Ty Glas Industrial Estate
  CDFN CF14 ....99 H3
Parklands Industrial Estate
  CATH/RTH/SPL CF24 ....5 H6
Park Plaza Hotel
  CCDF CF10 ....4 D4
Park Road Industrial Estate
  CWM NP44 ....26 A4
Parkway Hotel
  CWM NP44 ....26 A4
Passport Office
  NWPT NP20 ....8 E3
Pavilion Industrial Estate
  CWM NP44 ....14 B2
Pembroke Primary School
  CHEP NP16 ....30 C1
Penarth ≷
  PNRTH/DP CF64 ....134 C3
Penarth Cemetery
  PNRTH/DP CF64 ....134 B5
Penarth Leisure Centre
  PNRTH/DP CF64 ....134 A1
Penarth RFC
  PNRTH/DP CF64 ....134 C4
Pentrebane Primary School
  CAE/CAN/FWR CF5 ....110 A4
Pentrepoeth Primary School
  RSTN NP10 ....74 C1
Pentwyn Health Centre
  CYN/LLD/PWYN CF23 ....101 G3
Pentwyn Leisure Centre
  CYN/LLD/PWYN CF23 ....101 G4
Pentwyn Shopping Precinct
  CYN/LLD/PWYN CF23 ....101 G3
Pentyrch Police Station
  PENT/RAD/TFW CF15 ....96 A2
Pentyrch Primary School
  PENT/RAD/TFW CF15 ....96 A2
Pen y Bryn Primary School
  CYN/LLD/PWYN CF23 ....102 C3
Penygarn Primary School
  PPOOL/BLNAV NP4 ....14 D2
Pen-y-Gawsi Primary School
  LLTR/LLH CF72 ....95 E3
Penyrheol Cemetery
  CAER CF83 ....48 B4
Peter Lea J & I School
  CAE/CAN/FWR CF5 ....110 B4
Peterstone Golf Club
  CDFNE CF3 ....104 D4
Pierhead Building
  CCDF CF10 ....7 H6
Pilkingtons RFC
  PPOOL/BLNAV NP4 ....17 F2
Pill Farm Industrial Estate
  CALD/MAG NP26 ....63 G4
Pilgwenlly Millennium Centre
  NWPT NP20 ....76 D2
Pilgwenlly Primary School
  NWPT NP20 ....76 D2
The Point Arts Centre
  CCDF CF10 ....7 G5
Polo Ground Industrial Estate
  PPOOL/BLNAV NP4 ....17 F1
Ponthir Church in
  Wales School
  CLN/RNWPTE NP18 ....27 F4
Pontnewydd Golf Club
  CWM NP44 ....19 F3
Pontnewydd J & I School
  CWM NP44 ....19 G3
Pontnewynydd
  Industrial Estate
  PPOOL/BLNAV NP4 ....14 A2
Pontnewynydd
  Primary School
  PPOOL/BLNAV NP4 ....12 D5
Pontyclun ≷
  LLTR/LLH CF72 ....107 F3
Pontyclun Primary School
  LLTR/LLH CF72 ....107 E1
Pontyfelin Industrial Estate
  PPOOL/BLNAV NP4 ....17 F2
Pontygwindy
  Industrial Estate
  CAER CF83 ....48 D4
Pontymister
  Industrial Estate
  ABRC/NBR/RIS NP11 ....53 F1
Pontymoile J & I School
  PPOOL/BLNAV NP4 ....14 C5

Pontypool Golf Club
  NWPT NP20................**13** F5
Pontypool Leisure &
  Ski Centre
  PPOOL/BLNAV NP4.......**14** D4
Pontypool & New Inn ⇌
  PPOOL/BLNAV NP4.......**15** C3
Pontypool RFC
  PPOOL/BLNAV NP4.......**14** C4
Pontypool United RFC
  PPOOL/BLNAV NP4.......**14** B3
Pontypridd ⇌
  PPRD CF37...................**44** D4
Pontypridd Athletic Club
  PPRD CF37...................**44** D3
Pontypridd Cemetery
  PPRD CF37...................**45** G5
Pontypridd College
  PPRD CF37...................**44** C3
Pontypridd College
  Advanced Technology
  Training Centre
  PENT/RAD/TFW CF15.....**67** E4
Pontypridd Crematorium
  PPRD CF37...................**45** G5
Pontypridd & District Hospital
  PPRD CF37...................**45** F3
Pontypridd Golf Club
  PPRD CF37...................**45** G2
Pontypridd Health Centre
  PPRD CF37...................**44** D3
Pontypridd RFC
  PPRD CF37...................**44** C4
Porthkerry Country Park
  BARRY/W CF62.............**138** B5
Portmanmoor Road
  Industrial Estate
  CATH/RTH/SPL CF24......**120** D3
Premier Inn
  CAE/CAN/FWR CF5.........**125** C4
  CAER CF83....................**49** F4
  CYN/LLD/PWYN CF23......**113** G3
Prince of Wales
  Industrial Estate
  ABRC/NBR/RIS NP11........**22** D1
Priority Business Park
  BARRYE CF63................**140** C2
  CCDF CF10....................**6** C2
Queens Arcade
  Shopping Centre
  CCDF CF10....................**4** D5
Queen's Dragoon
  Guards Museum
  CCDF CF10....................**4** C4
Queen Street ⇌
  CATH/RTH/SPL CF24........**5** F4
Queensway Meadows
  Industrial Estate
  NWPTE NP19..................**78** D3
Queens West
  Shopping Centre
  CCDF CF10....................**4** C4
Radnor Primary School
  CAE/CAN/FWR CF5........**118** D2
Radyr ⇌
  PENT/RAD/TFW CF15.......**98** A5
Radyr Comprehensive School
  PENT/RAD/TFW CF15......**110** B1
Radyr Golf Club
  PENT/RAD/TFW CF15.......**97** G5
Radyr J & I School
  PENT/RAD/TFW CF15.......**97** G4
Raglan Barracks
  NWPT NP20....................**56** B2
Reevesland Industrial Estate
  NWPTE NP19..................**77** H2
Rhiwbina ⇌
  CDFN CF14....................**99** E4
Rhiwbina Primary School
  CDFN CF14....................**99** E3
Rhws Primary School
  BARRY/W CF62.............**144** C3
Rhydri Primary School
  CAER CF83....................**71** E1
Rhydyfelin RFC
  PPRD CF37....................**65** G3
Rhydypennau Primary School
  CDFN CF14...................**100** B3
Richmond Clinic
  NWPTE NP19..................**57** F2
Ringland Health Centre
  NWPTE NP19..................**59** E3
Ringland Primary School
  NWPTE NP19..................**58** D4
Ringside Business Centre
  CDFNE CF3...................**114** C3
Risca Community
  Comprehensive School
  ABRC/NBR/RIS NP11.......**38** B5
Risca & Pontymister ⇌
  ABRC/NBR/RIS NP11.......**36** D2
Risca Primary School
  ABRC/NBR/RIS NP11.......**37** E5
Risca RFC
  ABRC/NBR/RIS NP11.......**37** E5
Riverbank School
  CAE/CAN/FWR CF5........**117** H3
The Riverfront Arts Centre
  NWPT NP20......................**9** F3
Riverside Industrial Park
  PPRD CF37....................**66** C3
Roath Park J & I School
  CATH/RTH/SPL CF24......**112** D4
Rogerstone ⇌
  RSTN NP10....................**54** C4
Rogerstone Primary School
  NWPT NP20....................**40** B4
Roman Legionary Museum
  CLN/RNWPTE NP18.........**42** A5
Romilly J & I School
  BARRY/W CF62................**2** C3
Rookwood Hospital
  CAE/CAN/FWR CF5........**111** E4
Rougemont Infant School
  NWPT NP20....................**55** G5
Rougemont Junior School
  NWPT NP20....................**40** B2
Rougemont Senior School
  NWPT NP20....................**40** B2

Royal Gwent Hospital
  NWPT NP20......................**8** D2
Royal Hamadryad Hospital
  CCDF CF10......................**6** D6
Royal Welsh College of Music
  & Drama
  CCDF CF10......................**4** D3
Rumney High School
  CDFNE CF3....................**102** B5
Rumney Junior School
  CDFNE CF3....................**114** B2
Rumney RFC
  CDFNE CF3....................**114** A1
St Albans RC
  Comprehensive School
  CDFNE CF3....................**14** C4
St Albans RC J & I School
  CDFNE CF3....................**14** B3
St Albans RC Primary School
  CATH/RTH/SPL CF24......**121** F1
St Almas School
  PNRTH/DP CF64............**134** C3
St Andrews J & I School
  NWPTE NP19..................**77** G1
St Andrews Major Golf Club
  BARRYE CF63................**132** B5
St Andrews Major
  Primary School
  PNRTH/DP CF64............**132** D3
St Annes Infants CW School
  CATH/RTH/SPL CF24........**5** H1
St Bernadettes RC
  Primary School
  CYN/LLD/PWYN CF23.....**101** G2
St Cadoc's Hospital
  CLN/RNWPTE NP18.........**41** H4
St Cadocs Primary School
  CDFNE CF3...................**102** A2
St Cenydd
  Comprehensive School
  CAER CF83......................**48** A5
St Cuthberts J & I School
  GTN/RVSD CF11...............**6** E5
St Cuthberts RC J & I School
  GTN/RVSD CF11...............**7** G2
St Cyres
  Comprehensive School
  PNRTH/DP CF64............**133** H2
St Davids Cathedral
  CCDF CF10......................**4** D5
St Davids Clinic
  NWPT NP20....................**76** C2
St Davids CW J & I School
  CYN/LLD/PWYN CF23.....**101** C3
St David's Hall
  CCDF CF10......................**4** D5
St David's Hospital
  GTN/RVSD CF11.............**119** F2
The St David's Hotel
  CCDF CF10......................**7** G7
St Davids RC J & I School
  CWM NP44......................**19** H2
St Davids RC Primary School
  NWPT NP20....................**75** H3
St David's Shopping Centre
  CCDF CF10......................**4** D4
St Dials Infants School
  CWM NP44......................**25** G1
St Fagans CW J & I School
  CAE/CAN/FWR CF5........**116** C4
St Fagans National
  History Museum
  CAE/CAN/FWR CF5........**116** C1
St Fagans Primary School
  CAE/CAN/FWR CF5........**116** C4
St Francis RC Primary School
  CAE/CAN/FWR CF5........**117** E3
St Gabriels RC J & I School
  NWPTE NP19..................**58** C3
St Helens Primary School
  CAER CF83....................**49** G5
St Helens RC Infant School
  BARRYE CF63................**139** F3
St Helens RC Junior School
  BARRY/W CF62.............**139** F3
St Ilan School
  CAER CF83....................**48** D5
St Illtyd Primary School
  LLMJ CF61.....................**136** C2
St Illtyds Catholic High School
  CDFNE CF3...................**102** C4
St John Lloyd RC
  Primary School
  CDFNE CF3...................**102** D5
St Johns College Limited
  CDFNE CF3...................**102** C2
St Johns-on-the-Hill School
  CHEP NP16......................**28** D2
St Josephs Catholic Primary &
  Infants School
  PNRTH/DP CF64............**133** H3
St Josephs Primary School
  CDFN CF14...................**112** A3
St Josephs Private Hospital
  CDFN CF14......................**40** C2
St Josephs RC High School
  RSTN NP10......................**75** G5
St Josephs RC Primary School
  NWPTE NP19....................**9** K1
St Julians
  Comprehensive School
  NWPTE NP19..................**57** G1
St Julians High School Old
  Boys (HSOB) RFC
  NWPTE NP19..................**57** E1
St Julians J & I School
  NWPTE NP19..................**57** H2
St Julians Medical Centre
  NWPTE NP19..................**57** F2
St Martins
  Comprehensive School
  CAER CF83......................**68** D5
St Marys Catholic
  Primary School
  GTN/RVSD CF11.............**119** E2
St Marys RC J & I School
  NWPT NP20......................**8** C1
St Marys RC Primary School
  CHEP NP16......................**28** C5

St Mary the Virgin CW
  J & I School
  CCDF CF10......................**6** D1
St Mellons Business Park
  CDFNE CF3....................**103** G2
St Mellons Church in Wales
  Primary School
  CDFNE CF3....................**102** C3
St Mellons Golf Club
  CDFNE CF3....................**103** C3
St Mellons Hotel
  CDFNE CF3....................**103** C1
St Michaels College
  CAE/CAN/FWR CF5........**111** E5
St Michaels Primary School
  PPRD CF37......................**65** F1
St Michaels RC J & I School
  NWPT NP20......................**76** D2
St Monicas CW
  Primary School
  CCDF CF10....................**112** B5
St Patricks RC J & I School
  CDFNE CF3......................**57** H5
St Patricks RC Primary School
  GTN/RVSD CF11................**6** A3
St Pauls Clinic
  NWPT NP20......................**8** E5
St Pauls Primary School
  GTN/RVSD CF11................**6** A5
St Peters RC Primary School
  CATH/RTH/SPL CF24........**5** H2
St Peters RFC
  CATH/RTH/SPL CF24........**5** J2
St Philip Evans RC
  Primary School
  CYN/LLD/PWYN CF23.....**101** F5
St Richard Gwyn RC
  High School
  CDFNE CF3....................**140** B1
St Telios Church in Wales
  High School
  CYN/LLD/PWYN CF23.....**113** F2
St Woolos Cemetery
  NWPT NP20......................**55** H5
St Woolos Hospital
  NWPT NP20......................**8** C6
St Woolos J & I School
  NWPT NP20......................**8** D4
Sandringham Hotel
  CCDF CF10......................**4** D6
Sandy Lane Infant School
  CALD/MAG NP26.............**62** C2
Scala Cinema
  PPOOL/BLNAV NP4..........**14** C3
Scene Cinema
  CWM NP44......................**19** H5
Seaview Industrial Estate
  CATH/RTH/SPL CF24......**120** D3
Sedbury Park
  CHEP NP16......................**29** G5
Sedbury Trading Estate
  CHEP NP16......................**29** F4
Senlan Industrial Estate
  CYN/LLD/PWYN CF23.....**114** A4
Severn Bridge
  Industrial Estate
  CALD/MAG NP26.............**63** G4
Severn Infant School
  GTN/RVSD CF11.............**119** E2
Severn Junior School
  GTN/RVSD CF11.............**119** E2
Severn Tunnel Junction ⇌
  CALD/MAG NP26.............**62** A4
Sherman Theatre
  CCDF CF10......................**4** D2
Showcase Cinema
  ROAD/NTFW CF15............**67** E4
Sirhowy Valley Country Park
  ABRC/NBR/RIS NP11........**35** G2
Skillion Business Centre
  NWPTE NP19..................**77** H5
Somerset Industrial Estate
  CWM NP44......................**20** A3
Somerton J & I School
  NWPTE NP19..................**58** A5
South Glamorgan Institute of
  Higher Education
  CAE/CAN/FWR CF5........**110** B5
South Pontypool
  Industrial Park
  PPOOL/BLNAV NP4..........**17** F1
South Wales Baptist College
  CATH/RTH/SPL CF24........**5** F2
Special Learning Centre
  PPOOL/BLNAV NP4..........**12** C3
Spencer Steelworks
  NWPTE NP19..................**79** G2
Splott Industrial Estate
  CATH/RTH/SPL CF24......**120** D3
Splott Swimming Pool
  CATH/RTH/SPL CF24......**121** E2
Springmeadow Business Park
  CDFNE CF3....................**114** C3
Springvale Industrial Estate
  CWM NP44......................**19** F4
Springwood CP School
  CYN/LLD/PWYN CF23.....**101** E5
Spytty Park Sports Complex
  NWPTE NP19..................**78** A3
Stacey Road Primary School
  CATH/RTH/SPL CF24........**5** K1
Stanwell School
  PNRTH/DP CF64............**134** B3
Star Leisure Centre
  CATH/RTH/SPL CF24......**120** C2
Star Trading Estate
  CLN/RNWPTE NP18.........**41** H1
Station Approach
  Industrial Estate
  PNRTH/DP CF64............**134** C2
Station Industrial Estate
  CHEP NP16......................**28** D4
Steel Wave
  NWPT NP20......................**8** E2
Stevenson Street
  Industrial Estate
  NWPTE NP19..................**77** G4
Stirling Road
  Shopping Precinct
  BARRY/W CF62.............**138** C2

Sudbrook CC
  CALD/MAG NP26.............**63** E4
Sully Primary School
  PNRTH/DP CF64............**141** E5
The Swift Business Centre
  CATH/RTH/SPL CF24........**5** J6
Tabouk Community School
  CCDF CF10......................**6** E1
Taff Business Centre
  PPRD CF37......................**66** B1
Taff-Ely Indoor Bowls Centre
  PPRD CF37......................**44** D3
Taffs Well ⇌
  PENT/RAD/TFW CF15.......**83** F4
Taffs Well Medical Centre
  PENT/RAD/TFW CF15.......**83** F5
Taff Vale Shopping Centre
  PPRD CF37......................**44** D3
Talbot Green Retail Park
  LLTR/LLH CF72................**94** D2
Talywain RFC
  PPOOL/BLNAV NP4..........**12** A1
Taymuir Green
  Industrial Estate
  CATH/RTH/SPL CF24......**113** H5
Techniquest
  CCDF CF10......................**7** F6
Templar Park
  Industrial Estate
  CATH/RTH/SPL CF24........**7** H1
Temple of Peace & Health
  CDFN CF14......................**4** B2
Theatre Royal
  CCDF CF10......................**3** F2
Thistle Hotel
  CCDF CF10......................**4** E4
Thornbury Park
  Shopping Centre
  RSTN NP10......................**54** D4
Thornhill Cemetery
  CDFN CF14......................**85** F5
Thornhill Crematorium
  CDFN CF14......................**85** F5
Thornhill Primary School
  CDFN CF14......................**85** H4
Thornwell Primary School
  CHEP NP16......................**30** D2
Tinkinswood
  (Standing Stones)
  CAE/CAN/FWR CF5........**124** A4
Tongwynlais Primary School
  PENT/RAD/TFW CF15.......**97** H1
Tonteg Hospital
  LLTR/LLH CF72................**45** H3
Ton-yr-Ywen Primary School
  CDFN CF14...................**100** A4
Tonysguboriau
  Primary School
  LLTR/LLH CF72................**94** C3
Torfaen Business Centre
  PPOOL/BLNAV NP4..........**17** F1
Torfaen Museum Trust
  PPOOL/BLNAV NP4..........**14** C3
Trallwng Infant School
  PPRD CF37......................**45** E2
Travelodge
  CALD/MAG NP26.............**60** B1
  CCDF CF10......................**3** G5
  CYN/LLD/PWYN CF23.....**101** C3
  LLTR/LLH CF72..............**108** A1
Traverner Trading Estate
  CLN/RNWPTE NP18.........**42** A4
Trecenydd Industrial Estate
  CAER CF83......................**68** C1
Tredegar House & Park
  RSTN NP10......................**75** G5
Tredegar Park Golf Club
  RSTN NP10......................**55** G2
Tredegarville J & I School
  CATH/RTH/SPL CF24........**5** G3
Treforest ⇌
  PPRD CF37......................**45** F5
Treforest Industrial Estate
  PENT/RAD/TFW CF15.......**66** B3
  PPRD CF37......................**66** B1
Tregwilym Industrial Estate
  RSTN NP10......................**54** D5
Trehopcyn Primary School
  PPRD CF37......................**44** B2
Trelai Primary School
  CAE/CAN/FWR CF5........**117** H3
Tremorfa Industrial Estate
  CATH/RTH/SPL CF24......**121** E4
Tresillian Way
  Industrial Estate
  CCDF CF10......................**6** D1
Trethomas Health Centre
  CAER CF83......................**50** B2
Trowbridge Health Centre
  CDFNE CF3....................**102** D5
Trowbridge Infant School
  CDFNE CF3....................**102** D5
Tutshill CE Primary School
  CHEP NP16......................**28** D1
The Twyn School
  CAER CF83......................**69** E2
Ty-Coch Industrial Estate
  CWM NP44......................**25** H3
Ty Glas ⇌
  CDFN CF14......................**99** G4
Ty Gwyn Education Centre
  LLTR/LLH CF72................**94** D3
Ty Gwyn School
  CYN/LLD/PWYN CF23.....**113** G2
Ty Isaf Infant School
  ABRC/NBR/RIS NP11........**37** G3
Tyndall Street
  Industrial Estate
  CCDF CF10......................**5** F6
Tyn-y-Wern Primary School
  RSTN NP10......................**53** A3
Ty Sign Primary School
  CAER CF83......................**38** A3
Ty Verlon Industrial Estate
  BARRYE CF63................**140** C2
Undy Primary School
  CALD/MAG NP26.............**60** D3

University College
  CCDF CF10......................**4** C1
University Hospital of Wales
  CDFN CF14...................**112** B2
University of Glamorgan
  PPRD CF37......................**65** F1
University of Wales
  CCDF CF10......................**4** B3
  NWPT NP20......................**8** D2
  NWPTE NP19....................**9** H1
University of Wales College
  of Cardiff
  CATH/RTH/SPL CF24........**5** F3
University of Wales
  Institute Cardiff
  CAE/CAN/FWR CF5........**111** E4
  CYN/LLD/PWYN CF23.....**113** G4
University of Wales Institute
  Cardiff Cyncoed Campus
  CYN/LLD/PWYN CF23.....**113** E1
University of Wales Institute
  Cardiff Llandaff Campus
  CAE/CAN/FWR CF5........**111** E4
University of Wales Institute
  Cardiff Outdoors
  Athletic Centre
  CYN/LLD/PWYN CF23.....**113** F1
University of Wales Institute
  Cardiff Tennis Centre
  CYN/LLD/PWYN CF23.....**113** E1
University of Wales (Medicine)
  CDFN CF14...................**112** B2
University of Wales Newport
  Caerleon Campus
  CLN/RNWPTE NP18.........**41** H3
Upper Boat Industrial Park
  PPRD CF37......................**66** B1
Usk Way Industrial Estate
  NWPT NP20......................**9** H7
Valegate Business Park
  CAE/CAN/FWR CF5........**125** F2
Valegate Retail Park
  CAE/CAN/FWR CF5........**125** E1
Velindre Hospital
  CDFN CF14......................**98** C5
Venosa Trading Estate
  CAER CF83......................**49** F5
Victoria Primary School
  PNRTH/DP CF64............**134** B3
  PPOOL/BLNAV NP4..........**12** C2
The Village Hotel &
  Leisure Club
  CDFN CF14......................**98** B3
Vue Cinema
  GTN/RVSD CF11................**4** B7
Wales Millennium Centre
  CCDF CF10......................**7** H5
Wales National Velodrome
  NWPTE NP19..................**78** A2
Waunfawr Business Park
  ABRC/NBR/RIS NP11........**36** B3
Waunfawr Primary School
  ABRC/NBR/RIS NP11........**36** B2
Waun-Gron Park ⇌
  CAE/CAN/FWR CF5........**118** A1
Wellspring Medical Centre
  ABRC/NBR/RIS NP11........**37** F5
Welsh Hawking Centre
  BARRY/W CF62.............**158** A2
Welsh Institute of Sport
  CDFN CF14...................**119** F1
Welsh National Cricket
  Centre
  GTN/RVSD CF11.............**119** F1
Welsh National Tennis Centre
  CATH/RTH/SPL CF24........**5** J7
Welsh National War Memorial
  CCDF CF10......................**4** C2
Welsh Regiment Museum
  CCDF CF10......................**4** C4
Wentloog Corporate
  Industrial Park
  CDFNE CF3....................**115** G1
Wern Industrial Estate
  RSTN NP10......................**54** D4
Westbourne School
  PNRTH/DP CF64............**134** C2
West End Infants School
  CALD/MAG NP26.............**62** C4
Western Business Centre
  CAE/CAN/FWR CF5........**118** A2
Western Cemetery
  CAE/CAN/FWR CF5........**116** D5
Western Industrial Estate
  CAER CF83......................**68** B3
  CLN/RNWPTE NP18.........**42** A2
Western Leisure Centre
  CAE/CAN/FWR CF5........**117** G4
Westfield Upper School
  NWPT NP20......................**76** A4
West Monmouth
  Comprehensive School
  PPOOL/BLNAV NP4..........**14** C3
West Point Industrial Estate
  GTN/RVSD CF11.............**127** H3
West Usk Lighthouse
  NWPT NP20......................**92** D5
Whitchurch ⇌
  CDFN CF14......................**98** D3
Whitchurch (Cardiff)
  Golf Club
  CDFN CF14......................**98** C3
Whitchurch High School
  CDFN CF14......................**98** D5
Whitchurch Hospital
  CDFN CF14......................**98** C4
Whitchurch RFC
  CDFN CF14......................**98** B5
Whiteheads Sports Club
  RSTN NP10......................**75** F1
Willowbrook J & I School
  CDFNE CF3....................**103** F4
Willows High School
  CATH/RTH/SPL CF24......**121** F2
Windsor Clive Infant School
  CAE/CAN/FWR CF5........**117** F3
Woodlands High School
  CAE/CAN/FWR CF5........**118** A3
Woodlands Primary School
  CWM NP44......................**19** E2

Wyclif Independent
Christian School
CAER CF85 ....**51** G2
Wyedean School
CHEP NP16 ....**29** E4
Y Bontfaen Primary School
COWBR CF71 ....**122** C4
Ynysddu RFC
ABRC/NBR/RIS NP11 ....**34** B1
Ynysddu School
ABRC/NBR/RIS NP11 ....**34** A1
Y Pant Comprehensive School
LLTR/LLH CF72 ....**94** D4
Ysgol Bro Eirwg
CDFNE CF3 ....**114** A1
Ysgol Erw'r Delyn
PNRTH/DP CF64 ....**133** H2
Ysgol Gyfun Bro Morgannwg
BARRY/W CF62 ....**138** D3

Ysgol Gyfun Cymraeg Glantaf
(University of Wales)
CAE/CAN/FWR CF5 ....**111** E3
Ysgol Gyfun Gwynllyw
PPOOL/BLNAV NP4 ....**14** C1
Ysgol Gyfun
Gymraeg Plasmawr
CAE/CAN/FWR CF5 ....**110** A4
Ysgol Gyfun Rhydfelen
PPRD CF37 ....**65** H2
Ysgol Gymraeg Casnewydd
CLN/RNWPTE NP18 ....**58** D5
Ysgol Gymraeg Cwmbran
CWM NP44 ....**25** H1
Ysgol Gymraeg
Cwm Gwyddon
ABRC/NBR/RIS NP11 ....**23** E1
Ysgol Gymraeg Evan James
PPRD CF37 ....**44** C3

Ysgol Gymraeg Gwaun y Nant
BARRY/W CF62 ....**139** F2
Ysgol Gymraeg Melin
Gruffydd Pri
CDFN CF14 ....**111** E1
Ysgol Gymraeg Pont
Sion Norton
PPRD CF37 ....**45** F1
Ysgol Gymraeg Pwll Coch
GTN/RVSD CF11 ....**118** C4
Ysgol Gynradd
Gymraeg Caerffili
CAER CF83 ....**48** D5
Ysgol Gynradd
Gymraeg Castellau
CHV/BDAU CF38 ....**80** A3
Ysgol Gynradd Gymraeg
Garth Olwg
CHV/BDAU CF38 ....**81** F1

Ysgol Gynradd
Gymraeg Llantrist
LLTR/LLH CF72 ....**94** D2
Ysgol Ifor Bach Senghenydd
CAER CF83 ....**32** A3
Ysgol Iolo Morganwg
COWBR CF71 ....**122** D4
Ysgol Maes Dyfan
BARRYE CF63 ....**139** G2
Ysgol Mynydd Bychan
CDFN CF14 ....**112** A4
Ysgol Pencae
CAE/CAN/FWR CF5 ....**110** D3
Ysgol Pen-y-Garth
PNRTH/DP CF64 ....**133** H2
Ysgol Saint Curig
BARRY/W CF62 ....**2** E1
Ysgol Sant Baruc
BARRY/W CF62 ....**2** E2

Ysgol Ty Coch
CHV/BDAU CF38 ....**66** A3
Ysgol y Berllan Deg
CYN/LLD/PWYN CF25 ....**113** G2
Ystrad Mynach College
CAER CF85 ....**69** E1

Acknowledgements

Schools address data provided by Education Direct.

Petrol station information supplied by Johnsons

Garden centre information provided by

Garden Centre Association ● Britains best garden centres

🌷 Wyevale Garden Centres

The statement on the front cover of this atlas is sourced, selected and quoted
from a reader comment and feedback form received in 2004

Speed camera locations

Speed camera locations provided in association with RoadPilot Ltd

RoadPilot

RoadPilot is the developer of one of the largest and most accurate databases of speed camera locations in the UK and Europe. It has provided the speed camera information in this atlas. RoadPilot is the UK's pioneer and market leader in GPS (Global Positioning System) road safety technologies.

microGo (pictured right) is RoadPilot's latest in-car speed camera location system. It improves road safety by alerting you to the location of accident black spots,

fixed and mobile camera sites. RoadPilot's microGo does not jam police lasers and is therefore completely legal.

RoadPilot's database of fixed camera locations has been compiled with the full co-operation of regional police forces and the Safety Camera Partnerships.

For more information on RoadPilot's GPS road safety products, please visit **www.roadpilot.com** or telephone 0870 240 1701

SPEED READING

ALARM MODE

GPS Antenna
microGo is directional, it only alerts you to cameras on your side of the road

Visual Countdown
To camera location

Your Speed
The speed you are travelling when approaching camera

Camera Types Located
Gatso, Specs, Truvelo, TSS/DSS, Traffipax, mobile camera sites, accident black spots, congestion charges, tolls

Voice Warnings
Only if you are exceeding the speed limit at the camera

Plug and Go
Easy to move from vehicle to vehicle

64 Colour Options
To match vehicle's illumination

Speed Limit at Camera
Screen turns red as additional visual alert

Single Button Operation
For easy access to speed display, camera warning, rescue me location, trip computer, congestion charge, max speed alarm, date and time

Discover Britain

With these fantastic atlases from the AA

To order these, or any other titles in our extensive range please visit:

www.theAA.com/bookshop

Also available in all good bookshops

Road Atlases

AA For the road ahead